Studies in Diversity Linguistics

Chief Editor: Martin Haspelmath

Consulting Editors: Fernando Zúñiga, Peter Arkadiev, Ruth Singer, Pilar Valenzuela

In this series:

1. Handschuh, Corinna. A typology of marked-S languages.

2. Rießler, Michael. Adjective attribution.

3. Klamer, Marian (ed.). The Alor-Pantar languages: History and typology.

4. Berghäll, Liisa. A grammar of Mauwake.

5. Wilbur, Joshua. A grammar of Pite Saami.

6. Dahl, Östen. Grammaticalization in the North: Noun phrase morphosyntax in Scandinavian vernaculars.

7. Schackow, Diana. A grammar of Yakkha.

8. Liljegren, Henrik. A grammar of Palula.

9. Shimelman, Aviva. A grammar of Yauyos Quechua.

ISSN: 2363-5568

A grammar of Mauwake

Liisa Berghäll

Liisa Berghäll. 2015. *A grammar of Mauwake* (Studies in Diversity Linguistics 4). Berlin: Language Science Press.

This title can be downloaded at:
http://langsci-press.org/catalog/book/67
© 2015, Liisa Berghäll
Published under the Creative Commons Attribution 4.0 Licence (CC BY 4.0):
http://creativecommons.org/licenses/by/4.0/
ISBN: 978-3-946234-27-2 (Digital)
    978-3-946234-28-9 (Hardcover)
    978-3-944675-54-1 (Softcover)
ISSN: 2363-5568

Cover and concept of design: Ulrike Harbort
Typesetting: Jessica Brown, Charles Lam, Constantin Freitag, Benedikt Singpiel, Sebastian Nordhoff, Felix Kopecky
Proofreading: Charlotte van Tongeren, Marsha Forbes-Barnett, Christian Döhler, Stephanie Natolo, Conor Pyle, Tamara Schmidt, Michelle Natolo, Tom Gardner, Charles Ko Ka Shing, Eitan Grossmann
Fonts: Linux Libertine, Arimo, DejaVu Sans Mono
Typesetting software: XƎLATEX

Language Science Press
Habelschwerdter Allee 45
14195 Berlin, Germany
langsci-press.org

Storage and cataloguing done by FU Berlin

Language Science Press has no responsibility for the persistence or accuracy of URLs for external or third-party Internet websites referred to in this publication, and does not guarantee that any content on such websites is, or will remain, accurate or appropriate. Information regarding prices, travel timetables and other factual information given in this work are correct at the time of first publication but Language Science Press does not guarantee the accuracy of such information thereafter.

Contents

Acknowledgements   xi

Abbreviations and symbols   xiii

1 Introduction   1
    1.1 Background   1
    1.2 Purpose and theoretical orientation of the study   1
       1.2.1 Purpose   1
       1.2.2 Theoretical considerations   2
       1.2.3 Audience   3
       1.2.4 On the data and examples   4
    1.3 The Mauwake people, their environment and culture   4
       1.3.1 Geography and administration   5
       1.3.2 On the history of the Mauwake people   5
       1.3.3 Demography   8
       1.3.4 Economy   10
       1.3.5 Cultural notes   10
       1.3.6 Mauwake kinship system   11
    1.4 The Mauwake language   13
       1.4.1 Genealogical affiliation and previous research   13
       1.4.2 Typological overview of morphological and syntactic features   16
          1.4.2.1 Mauwake as a Trans New Guinea language   16
          1.4.2.2 Mauwake as an sov language   19
       1.4.3 Dialects   21

2 Phonology: a brief overview   25
    2.1 Phonemes   25
       2.1.1 Consonants   25
       2.1.2 Vowels   32
       2.1.3 Suprasegmentals: stress and intonation   34
          2.1.3.1 Stress   34
          2.1.3.2 Intonation   34
       2.1.4 Orthographic symbols   38
    2.2 Syllables and phonotactics   39
       2.2.1 Syllable patterns   39
       2.2.2 Vowel sequences   39
       2.2.3 Consonant sequences   41

	2.3	Word	41
		2.3.1 Defining a phonological word in Mauwake	41
		2.3.2 Distribution of syllables in a word	43
		2.3.3 Morphophonology	44
		2.3.3.1 Elision of word-final vowel	44
		2.3.3.2 Reduplication	44
		2.3.3.2.1 Type 1	45
		2.3.3.2.2 Type 2: $v_1c_1v_1$ - $v_1c_1v_2c_2v(v_3)x$	45
		2.3.3.2.3 Type 3: $v_1v_1c_1$ - $v_1v_1c_1v_2x$	45
		2.3.3.2.4 Type 4: $c_1v_1v_2$ - $c_1v_1v_2x$	46
		2.3.3.2.5 Unusual reduplications	46
		2.3.3.3 Past tense and medial verb suffixes	47
		2.3.3.4 Inchoative suffix	50
		2.3.3.5 Completive aspect marker	50
		2.3.4 Loan words	50
3	**Morphology**		**53**
	3.1	Introduction	53
	3.2	Nouns	54
		3.2.1 General discussion	54
		3.2.2 Nouns and adjectives: one or two word classes?	55
		3.2.3 Common vs. proper nouns	60
		3.2.4 Alienable and inalienable possession	63
		3.2.5 Noun compounding	65
		3.2.6 Derived nouns	71
		3.2.6.1 Action nominals	72
		3.2.6.2 Noun reduplication	73
	3.3	Adjectives	74
	3.4	Quantifiers	81
		3.4.1 Numerals	82
		3.4.2 Non-numeral quantifiers	84
	3.5	Pronouns	87
		3.5.1 Introduction	87
		3.5.2 Free pronouns	90
		3.5.2.1 Unmarked pronouns	90
		3.5.2.2 Focal pronouns	94
		3.5.3 Accusative pronouns	95
		3.5.4 Genitive pronouns	100
		3.5.5 Dative pronouns	103
		3.5.6 Isolative pronouns	110
		3.5.7 Restrictive pronouns	111
		3.5.8 Reflexive-reciprocal pronouns	112
		3.5.9 Comitative pronouns	114

	3.5.10	Primary and secondary reference of personal pronouns	114
	3.5.11	Use of personal pronouns in text	115
3.6	Spatial deictics		116
	3.6.1	The basic spatial deixis in Mauwake	117
	3.6.2	Demonstratives	118
	3.6.3	Deictic locative adverbs	120
	3.6.4	Deictic manner adverbs	122
3.7	Question words and indefinites		123
	3.7.1	Question words	123
	3.7.2	Indefinites	127
3.8	Verbs		129
	3.8.1	General discussion	129
		3.8.1.1 Definition	129
		3.8.1.2 General characteristics of verbs in Mauwake	130
		3.8.1.3 Verb structure	131
	3.8.2	Verb derivatives	133
		3.8.2.1 Derivation vs. inflection	133
		3.8.2.2 Category-changing derivation: verb formation	134
		3.8.2.2.1 Zero verb formation	134
		3.8.2.2.2 Inchoative suffix	136
		3.8.2.3 Category-maintaining derivation: suffixes	138
		3.8.2.3.1 Causative suffix	138
		3.8.2.3.2 Distributive suffix	140
		3.8.2.3.3 Benefactive suffix	141
		3.8.2.4 Derivational prefixes	142
		3.8.2.4.1 Reduplication	142
		3.8.2.4.2 Bring-prefixes	144
	3.8.3	Verb inflection	144
		3.8.3.1 Beneficiary	145
		3.8.3.2 Counterfactual	146
		3.8.3.3 Mood	146
		3.8.3.3.1 Indicative	147
		3.8.3.3.2 Imperative	147
		3.8.3.4 Tense and person/number in final verbs	149
		3.8.3.5 Medial verb marking	151
		3.8.3.5.1 Same-subject marking	152
		3.8.3.5.2 Different-subject marking	153
		3.8.3.5.3 Tense and medial verbs	155
	3.8.4	Verb classes	156
		3.8.4.1 Conjugation classes	157
		3.8.4.2 Verb classes based on transitivity	157
		3.8.4.2.1 Intransitive verbs	158
		3.8.4.2.2 Transitive verbs	159

		3.8.4.2.3	Ambitransitive verbs	161
		3.8.4.2.4	Object cross-referencing verbs	162
	3.8.4.3	Valence changes		164
		3.8.4.3.1	Causatives	164
		3.8.4.3.2	Benefactive	167
		3.8.4.3.3	Decreasing semantic valence	167
	3.8.4.4	Semantically based verb classes		168
		3.8.4.4.1	Stative/existential verb *ik-*	168
		3.8.4.4.2	Position-taking verbs	171
		3.8.4.4.3	Location verbs	172
		3.8.4.4.4	Resultative verbs	172
		3.8.4.4.5	Directional verbs	173
		3.8.4.4.6	Utterance verbs	176
		3.8.4.4.7	Impersonal experience verbs	181
	3.8.4.5	Auxiliary verbs		182
3.8.5	Verbal clusters			183
	3.8.5.1	Verbal groups		184
		3.8.5.1.1	Main verb plus auxiliary: aspect	184
		3.8.5.1.1.1	Completive aspect	185
		3.8.5.1.1.2	Continuous aspect: progressive and habitual	186
		3.8.5.1.1.3	Stative aspect	188
		3.8.5.1.2	Serial verbs	189
	3.8.5.2	Adjunct plus verb constructions		194
		3.8.5.2.1	Nominal adjunct plus verb	194
		3.8.5.2.2	Adverbial adjunct plus verb	196

3.9 Adverbs 197
    3.9.1 Material adverbs 197
        3.9.1.1 Locative adverbs 198
        3.9.1.2 Temporal adverbs 199
        3.9.1.3 Manner adverbs 203
    3.9.2 Intensity adverbs 204
    3.9.3 Modal adverbs 206
    3.9.4 Free adverbs 206
3.10 Negators 208
3.11 Connectives 209
    3.11.1 Pragmatic connectives 210
    3.11.2 Semantic connectives 212
3.12 Postpositions and clitics 216
    3.12.1 Comitative clitic and postpositions 216
    3.12.2 Reason postposition *muuta (nain)* 219
    3.12.3 Comparison postposition *saarik* 219
    3.12.4 Locative clitic *-pa* 219

		3.12.5	Instrumental clitic -*iw* 221

		3.12.5	Instrumental clitic -*iw*	221
		3.12.6	Limiter -*iw*	222
		3.12.7	Topic and focus markers	222
			3.12.7.1 Topic markers	222
			3.12.7.2 Focus clitics	224
		3.12.8	Question marker	226
		3.12.9	Co-occurrence of the clitics	226
	3.13	Interjections		227
4	**Phrase level syntax**			**231**
	4.1	Noun phrase		231
		4.1.1	Basic noun phrase	231
		4.1.2	Coordinate noun phrase	237
		4.1.3	Comitative noun phrase	239
		4.1.4	Appositional noun phrase	240
	4.2	Adjective phrase		240
	4.3	Quantifier phrase		241
	4.4	Possessive phrase		242
	4.5	Verb phrase		242
	4.6	Adverbial phrases		243
		4.6.1	Locative phrases	243
		4.6.2	Temporal phrase	246
		4.6.3	Manner phrase	248
5	**Clause**			**251**
	5.1	Order of constituents		251
	5.2	Syntactic arguments		255
	5.3	Transitive clauses		259
		5.3.1	Monotransitive clauses	259
		5.3.2	Ditransitive clauses	260
			5.3.2.1 Inherent ditransitivity	261
			5.3.2.2 Derived ditransitivity	262
			5.3.2.3 Possessor raising	262
	5.4	Intransitive clauses		263
	5.5	Existential and possessive clauses		265
		5.5.1	Existential clauses	265
		5.5.2	Possessive clauses	266
	5.6	Verbless clauses		268
		5.6.1	Equative and classifying clauses	269
		5.6.2	Descriptive clauses	270
		5.6.3	Negated existential and possessive clauses	271
	5.7	Nominalized clauses		271
		5.7.1	Type 1: with a nominalized verb	272
		5.7.2	Type 2: with a finite verb	278

6 Functional domains — 281

- 6.1 Modality — 281
  - 6.1.1 Epistemic modality — 281
  - 6.1.2 Deontic modality — 283
- 6.2 Negation — 284
  - 6.2.1 Clausal negation — 284
  - 6.2.2 Constituent negation — 287
  - 6.2.3 Negative interjection — 290
  - 6.2.4 Other cases of negation — 290
- 6.3 Deixis — 293
  - 6.3.1 Person deixis — 294
  - 6.3.2 Locative deixis — 295
  - 6.3.3 Temporal deixis — 296
- 6.4 Quantification — 298
  - 6.4.1 Quantification in the noun phrase — 298
  - 6.4.2 Quantification devices in the verbs — 300
- 6.5 Comparison — 302
  - 6.5.1 Comparison of inequality: comparative constructions — 302
  - 6.5.2 Comparison of similarity: equative constructions — 304

7 Sentence types — 307

- 7.1 Statements — 307
- 7.2 Questions — 307
  - 7.2.1 Non-polar questions — 307
  - 7.2.2 Polar questions — 309
  - 7.2.3 Echo questions — 311
  - 7.2.4 Confirmation questions — 312
  - 7.2.5 Indirect questions — 312
  - 7.2.6 Rhetorical questions — 313
  - 7.2.7 Answers to questions — 314
- 7.3 Commands — 315

8 Clause combinations — 319

- 8.1 Coordination of clauses — 321
  - 8.1.1 Conjunction — 322
    - 8.1.1.1 Juxtaposition — 322
    - 8.1.1.2 Conjunction with coordinating connectives — 324
  - 8.1.2 Disjunction — 326
  - 8.1.3 Adversative coordination — 327
  - 8.1.4 Consecutive coordination — 328
  - 8.1.5 Causal coordination, "afterthought reason" — 331
  - 8.1.6 Apprehensive coordination — 332
- 8.2 Clause chaining — 333
  - 8.2.1 Chained clauses as coordinate clauses — 334

	8.2.2	Temporal relations in chained clauses 338
	8.2.3	Person reference in chained clauses 341
		8.2.3.1 Partitioning of the participant set 341
		8.2.3.2 Tracking a subject high in topicality 343
		8.2.3.3 Apparent mismatches of reference 346
		8.2.3.4 Medial clauses as a complementation strategy for perception verbs 348
		8.2.3.5 Tail-head linkage 349
8.3	Subordinate clauses: embedding and hypotaxis 352	
	8.3.1	Relative clauses 352
		8.3.1.1 The type and position of the relative clause 353
		8.3.1.2 The structure of the relative clause 355
		8.3.1.3 Relativizable noun phrase positions 358
		8.3.1.4 Non-restrictive relative clauses 360
	8.3.2	Complement clauses and other complementation strategies . . . 361
		8.3.2.1 Complements of utterance verbs 361
		8.3.2.1.1 Direct speech 362
		8.3.2.1.2 Indirect speech 363
		8.3.2.1.3 Desiderative clauses 366
		8.3.2.1.4 Purpose clauses 367
		8.3.2.1.5 Conative clauses: 'try' 369
		8.3.2.1.6 Complements of other utterance verbs 370
		8.3.2.2 Complements of perception verbs 372
		8.3.2.3 Complements of cognitive verbs 373
		8.3.2.4 Complement clauses as subjects 373
	8.3.3	Adverbial clauses 374
		8.3.3.1 Temporal clauses 374
		8.3.3.2 Locative clauses 375
	8.3.4	Adversative subordinate clause 375
	8.3.5	Conditional clauses 376
	8.3.6	Concessive clauses 380
	8.3.7	Coordination of subordinate clauses 381

9 Theme, topic, and focus   383

9.1 Theme 384
9.2 Topic 388
    9.2.1 Introducing a new topic 388
    9.2.2 Maintaining an established topic 390
    9.2.3 Re-activating an earlier topic 391
    9.2.4 Highlighted topic 393
9.3 Focus constructions 394
    9.3.1 Contrastive focus 395
    9.3.2 Neutral focus 398

Contents

        9.3.3   Other focusing devices 402

A List of main texts used   407

Appendix   407

B Texts   409
    B.1   World War 2 409
    B.2   Uncle Tup 428
    B.3   Catching a turtle 435
    B.4   Fishing customs 437
    B.5   Dog and snake 444
    B.6   Piglet 446
    B.7   Man's lover 450
    B.8   A flood story 452
    B.9   Copra work 456
    B.10 Garden work 458
    B.11 Girls' initiation customs 463
    B.12 Funeral customs 466
    B.13 Tidal wave 472

References   475

Index   486
    Name index 486
    Language index 489
    Subject index 490

Acknowledgements

There are several people without whom this description of Mauwake grammar would not have become a reality, and whom I want to thank from my heart.

My colleague for 25 years and a close friend since 1977, Kwan Poh San shared the joys and burdens of life and work with me during the whole of the Mauwake project. We learned the language together and analysed it together, and although I have written this grammar, she has also contributed significantly towards it. There are many sections where some of the analysis was done by her and some by myself, but since we worked together it is sometimes hard to distinguish who did which part. Her oral command of the language is better than mine, and I have benefitted from her insights and comments during the writing process.

The Mauwake people welcomed Kwan Poh San and myself to live with them in Moro village and the family of Leo Magidar adopted us as their daughters. The people built our house, and brought us food. They taught us their customs and shared their everyday lives with us for those over 20 years that we lived in Moro. Although we naturally had more contact with the people in Moro village, the inhabitants of the other Mauwake villages also showed their hospitality and friendship to us. For this I thank them all.

Several people helped us with language learning and analysis. Saror Aduna first became the main language teacher and later the co-translator for the whole time we were working with the Mauwake people. Others who gave us texts include Kalina Sarak, Balthasar Saakawa, Kululu Sarak, Albert Kiramaten, Alois Amdara, Charles Matuwina, John Meldia, Aduna, Kedem Saror, Bang, Kuumu, Komori, Darawin, and Muandilam. The New Testament checking committee members Balthasar Saakawa, Lukas Miime, Charles Matuwina, Lawrence Alinaw and Leo Nimbulel helped us to understand the language better during our long checking sessions.

The grammar was initially written as my PhD dissertation for the University of Helsinki. It was in the making for a very long time, and without the encouragement of Professor Fred Karlsson I would have given up many times. He believed in writing descriptive grammars even when it was not very fashionable, and gave me his unwavering support during the many years that the project lasted.

In my early years in Papua New Guinea, when I was not yet excited about grammar, Bob Litteral and Ger Reesink encouraged me to take up a study program. The numerous discussions with many SIL-PNG colleagues, Cynthia Farr, Larry Lovell, Robert Bugenhagen, Dorothy James, John Roberts, Carl Whitehead, Eileen Gasaway, René van den Berg, Catherine McGuckin and several others, helped me to gain a better understanding both of PNG languages and of linguistics. Betty Keneqa, the librarian in the SIL linguistic library, was always helpful in locating material and making photocopies. The instruction

Acknowledgements

received from the international linguistics consultants Thomas Payne and David Weber was inspiring and practical.

Others whose teaching, writings and/or personal interaction have shaped my thinking and writing include the late John Verhaar, Bernard Comrie, Talmy Givón, Malcolm Ross and Andrew Pawley, and many others.

The comments from the external readers of the dissertation, Malcolm Ross and Ger Reesink, helped me to clarify, modify and reorganize the text, and even re-analyze some of the data for the final version.

The financial assistance through scholarships from the Finnish Cultural Foundation, SIL International and SIL-PNG are gratefully acknowledged. My employer, the Finnish Evangelical Lutheran Mission, allowed some working time to be used for studies, and some of the writing was done as my work assignment.

I thank my husband Jouko for his love and encouragement, and for being there to remind me that there is a lot more to life besides language work.

My greatest thanks go to God, who in his Word gives life, and love, and hope.

Abbreviations and symbols

ACC	accusative	HN	head noun
ADD	additive connective	IMP	imperative
ADJ	adjective	INAL	inalienably possessed noun
ADV	adverb(ial)	INC	inceptive
ADVP	adverbial phrase	INCH	inchoative
ANTNP	antecedent noun phrase	INSTR	instrument
AP	adjective phrase	INTJ	interjection
APP	apposition(al)	ISOL	isolative
ASP	aspect	LIM	limiter
ASSOC	associative	LOC	locative
AUX	auxiliary	MAN	manner
BEN	benefactive	NEG	negation
BNFY1	beneficiary 1/2singular	NF	neutral focus
BNFY2	beneficiary non-1/2singular	NMZ	nominaliser
BP	bring-prefix	N	noun
CAUS	causative	NP	noun phrase
CC	complement clause	Np	non-past
CF	contrastive focus	NVP	non-verbal predicate
CL	clause	O	object
CNJ	connective	P,PL	plural
CNTF	counterfactual	P	phrase
COM	comitative	PA	past tense
CMPL	completive aspect	PAT	patient
CONT	continuous aspect	POSS	possessive
COORD	coordinate	PR	present tense
CTV	complement-taking verb	QM	question marker
DAT	dative	QP	quantifier phrase
DEM	demonstrative deictic	RC	relative clause
DISTR/A	distributive: "all"	RDP	reduplication
DISTR/PL	distributive: "many"	REC	recipient
D	dual	REFL	reflexive
DS	different subject following	RELNP	relative noun phrase
FC	focal (pronoun)	S	singular
FU	future tense	S	subject
GEN	genitive	SEQ	sequential action
HAB	habitual	SIM	simultaneous action

Abbreviations and symbols

SPEC	specifier	*	ungrammatical
SR	switch-reference	?	questionable
SS	same subject following	/ / or { }	phonemic transcription
TH	theme	[ ]	phonetic transcription
TNG	Trans-New Guinea	< >	grapheme
TP	topic	( )	variant; optional
T.P.	Tok Pisin	.	syllable break
UNM	unmarked (pronoun)	-	morpheme break
v,V	verb	=	clitic break
1	first person	Ø	zero morpheme
2	second person	'	primary stress
3	third person	"	secondary stress

1 Introduction

1.1 Background

"Mauwake used to be a big language. The neighbours knew it too, and it was used as a trade language in the area. But today it is not so important any more." This is what my colleague Kwan Poh San and I heard when we settled among the Mauwake people in the late 1970s to do linguistic and Bible translation work. Especially before the Second World War everybody, including the Mauwake speakers themselves, knew their neighbours' languages better than nowadays, but it may also be true that Mauwake did have a stronger position among the languages in the area. And it is certainly true that the language is fast losing ground to Tok Pisin (also called Melanesian Pidgin), the trade language *par excellence* in Papua New Guinea today. The process is so strong that Mauwake can be considered an endangered language.

1.2 Purpose and theoretical orientation of the study

1.2.1 Purpose

My aim is to give a synchronic description of grammatical structures and their functions in Mauwake. Occasionally some attention is given to diachronic aspects as well, when that is considered interesting or helpful for understanding the system at present (Evans & Dench 2006: 20).

This grammar covers mainly morphology and syntax, but a brief overview of phonology is also given, and some pragmatic features are discussed very briefly at the end. A short introduction to typological features and the basic clause structure is given in the introduction to familiarize especially those readers who are not reading the grammar from the beginning to the end with the language a little. The description proper of the morphology and clausal syntax is form-based (or analytic), starting with the structures of various units and describing their functions, as the basic structural features need to be understood first to get a good idea of the language (Mosel 2006: 59). But since functional domains increase in importance when one moves higher up in the unit hierarchy, this is reflected in the arrangement of the grammar: the syntax above the clause level starts from functions and describes different structures used for those functions. Another reason for this switch from a form-based to a function-based (synthetic) approach is the desire to make the grammar more useful for typologists (Cristofaro 2006 and Evans & Dench 2006: 15).[1]

---

[1] The form-based approach is also called *onomasiological* and the function-based approach *semasiological*.

1 Introduction

While documentation is the main purpose of this work, I have attempted to present enough of the analysis to show the reader reasons for certain choices,[2] even if I may not meet Dixon's (1997: 132) requirement of justifying all my choices "with a full train of argumentation".

This grammar does not include a vocabulary, as a Mauwake dictionary (Järvinen (=Berghäll), Kwan & Aduna 2001) is available electronically.

1.2.2 Theoretical considerations

In the analysis and writing I have been following the informal descriptive theory that was given the name Basic Linguistic Theory (BLT) by Dixon (1997) and elaborated by him (Dixon 2010a,b) and by Dryer (2006a,b), who also defends its status as a legitimate linguistic theory. BLT makes use of the cumulative knowledge acquired during decades, and centuries – even millennia – of grammatical studies, and in the writing of descriptive grammars (Dixon 2010a: 3). It is largely based on traditional grammar, but in contrast to traditional grammar it aims to describe the "essential nature" of each language rather than fitting the language into a pre-determined formal model.[3] Each language is seen "as a complete linguistic system" on its own (Dixon 2010a: 4). The theory has been modified over time, and is continually being modified, by developments in typological and formal linguistics (Evans & Dench 2006, Rice 2006a,b, Dixon 2010a: 3).

Even if BLT does not try to fit languages into any predetermined formal model, it may borrow formalisms from various models as far as they are appropriate and helpful for the description of a particular language (Dixon 1997: 128–135).[4] BLT is closely linked with language typology, "[setting] out a typological paradigm, by inductive generalization from reliable grammars" (Dixon 2010a: 205). Evans & Dench (2006: 6) note that grammars written in this framework tend to stand the test of time better than those following strict formal models. Formal theories have been and are useful in providing useful research questions – both bringing up completely new ones and deepening old ones – and in forcing the descriptions to be more rigorous. In Rice's (2006: 262) words, "[t]he theory informs and shapes, but does not control".

My own dislike of formalisms is certainly one reason why they are used so little in this grammar. A more important factor is my desire to make the grammar readable to as many people as possible regardless of their linguistic background. This is also reflected in the use of terminology. I have tried to use widely accepted and transparent terminology as much as possible, to avoid technical terms specific to some particular formalism, and to explain my terminology where necessary (cf. Cristofaro 2006).

For the description of Mauwake the following basic concepts familiar from traditional grammar are assumed as given:

---

[2] E.g. the status of adjectives as a separate word class and the question of serial verbs have received more discussion than some other topics.

[3] These models are often called "theories". For a comment on this, see Dixon (1997: 131). Dryer (2006a) prefers to call them theoretical frameworks. (Dryer 2006a: 211).

[4] Among others promoting the use of BLT, whether they use the name or not, are Noonan (2006: 354), Rice (2006a,b), Evans & Dench (2006), and Payne (1997; 2006).

- Word classes like noun, verb, pronoun, adverb (the status of adjective as a class of its own is discussed separately)
- Morphological cases like nominative, accusative, genitive and dative
- Syntactic roles of subject and object
- Semantic/case roles like agent, patient, recipient and beneficiary
- Phrases like noun phrase, adjective phrase and adverbial phrase
- Clause as a separate level from sentence

The concept of medial verbs, as against final/finite verbs, which is generally accepted in Papuan linguistics, is also presupposed.

Since frequency of occurrence is an important and interesting characteristic of grammatical usage, I initially planned to do a fair amount of quantification and frequency counting. But to do an adequate job would have required a much larger corpus, as well as better computer programs and knowledge of corpus linguistics, and much more time, than I had at my disposal. Even though actual percentages are seldom mentioned in the final product, I have occasionally included frequency statements based on whatever frequency counts I have made during the course of the work and on my personal experience with Mauwake.

To my knowledge there are no trained linguists among the Mauwake speakers, so the kind of cooperation between a native and a non-native speaker linguist, together with native speaker non-linguists, that Ameka (2006) advocates, was not possible. Even though I have aimed at checking the material as carefully as possible, there are bound to be mistakes both in the data and in the interpretation. It is necessary to heed Ameka's (ibid. 92) warning that "[o]ne of the most dangerous things about authoritative and influential foundation records ... is that their misanalyses which pertain to some theoretical or typological point are repeated over and over again in the literature. What is even worse is that the theories and generalizations are built on such mistakes".

1.2.3 Audience

One can anticipate the readership for a reference grammar of a previously undocumented and endangered language spoken by a couple of thousand speakers to consist mainly of linguists. I especially hope this grammar to be useful for those linguists who work on language typologies and typology-related questions. Naturally the material is also available for those interested in more formal models.

A grammar is expected to describe features that exist in a language, rather than those that do not exist. But for the benefit of typologists I have at times mentioned the non-existence of certain features that they might be looking for and wondering about, if there is no mention at all (Cristofaro 2006).

1 Introduction

Another readership I want to address are those people particularly in Papua New Guinea who are linguistically somewhat less trained, yet are vitally interested in language development and translation. If this grammar helps any of them to study and understand a language better, or encourages someone to write a grammar of yet another undocumented language, my work has been worthwhile.

It is unlikely that many outsiders would use this grammar to learn Mauwake. It may also be unrealistic to wish that many Mauwake speakers would become familiar with it. Yet it is my desire that it would help the Mauwake speakers in at least two ways: by preserving their language and giving them more pride in it as they realise that it does have a real grammar (Kadanya 2006: 255), and also by providing some help for those interested and involved in teaching vernacular literacy.

1.2.4 On the data and examples

The bulk of the text data used for this grammar were collected between 1979 and 1985, with some later additions. The basic data of 19 spoken and 7 written texts contain over 8300 words in all (200+ kb in plain text), edited by a native speaker. They consist mainly of narratives, including traditional stories (60%), but descriptive texts (15%), process descriptions (14%) and one long hortatory text (11%) are included as well, from different speakers and authors.[5] Many syntactic features were further checked against another set of texts about the same size.

When choosing examples, I have taken as many from text material as possible, especially when the examples consist of a clause or a sentence. Elicited examples were checked for correctness with native speakers.

In the examples the present orthography is used, but with morpheme breaks added. There is no gender distinction in Mauwake pronouns, so in the free translation the third person singular pronoun and verbal suffix are translated as either 'he' or 'she' whenever justified by either textual or cultural context, otherwise as '(s)he'.

Regarding the glosses, the reader will be wise to remember Mosel's (2006: 50) caution that the interlinear glossing is

> [not] an accurate form-meaning relationship ... The meaning of words and larger units of grammatical analysis does not equal the sum of the meanings of their component parts ... but results from the interaction of the meaning of the construction as such and the meanings of its parts. Thus interlinear glossing should only be seen as a tool to help the reader to understand the examples.

1.3 The Mauwake people, their environment and culture

The Mauwake language is spoken along the North coast of Madang province, about 120 km northwest of Madang town. The area comprises about 100 square kilometres, and there are 15 villages where Mauwake is the main language, seven of them along or near

---

[5] Appendix A provides a list of the texts used.

1.3 The Mauwake people, their environment and culture

the coast along a stretch of 15 km between the Kumil and Nemuru rivers, and up to 12 km inland from the coast.

1.3.1 Geography and administration

The Mauwake area is typical of the Madang North coast: coral reefs off the coast, white sand beaches,[6] a narrow belt of coastal plain, and hills about 200 to 400 feet in height. The soil is mostly coral limestone, with shallow alluvial soil. The lower hills close to the coast are covered by *kunai* grass (IMPERATA CYLINDRICA), the higher ones deeper inland by rainforest, some of which is garden regrowth (Haantjens et al. 1976: 22).

The climate is lowland tropical climate with temperatures varying between 20° and 32° centigrade. Humidity is high, especially during the wet season. The dry season is between May and October with average monthly rainfall of 40 mm, the wet season is between November and April and with average rainfall of 250 mm. The dry season is longer and drier in this area than in many other parts of the country apart from the Port Moresby area. However, during the last two decades there have been significant climate changes, and the weather patterns are less predictable than they used to be.

The North Coast Highway that was completed in 1973–1974 and sealed in 1999 passes close to all the coastal Mauwake villages. Almost all the inland villages are also accessible by a road of some kind.

The two main centres in the area are Ulingan, where there is a Roman Catholic mission station and community school, and Malala, where there is a high school and a community school, a sub-health centre sponsored by the high school, a reasonably well stocked store, and a market.

Administratively the Mauwake people belong to the Bogia sub-province and the Almami (derived from the language names Alam–Mauwake–Miani) local level government area.

There are four primary schools in the area, and one high school. In all of these schools there are students from more than one language area. The Roman Catholic Church was instrumental in getting the schools started, and is still administering the Malala High School. Nearly all of the children go to primary school, but the number of Mauwake students in the high school is not very high. Vernacular preschools were started in the whole Mauwake area in the early 1990s, but many of them have since changed into Tok Pisin preschools.

1.3.2 On the history of the Mauwake people

Until fairly recently, little was known about the pre-history of the Papuan-speaking people in Near Oceania (including New Guinea island, Bismarck Archipelago and the Solomon Islands), compared with the archaeological information available on the Austronesian-speaking people in the area. By the late 1990s it was established that human

---

[6] White and black sand beaches alternate on the coast, depending on the existence of coral reefs off the coast and on the closeness of the two of volcanic islands of Karkar and Manam.

1 Introduction

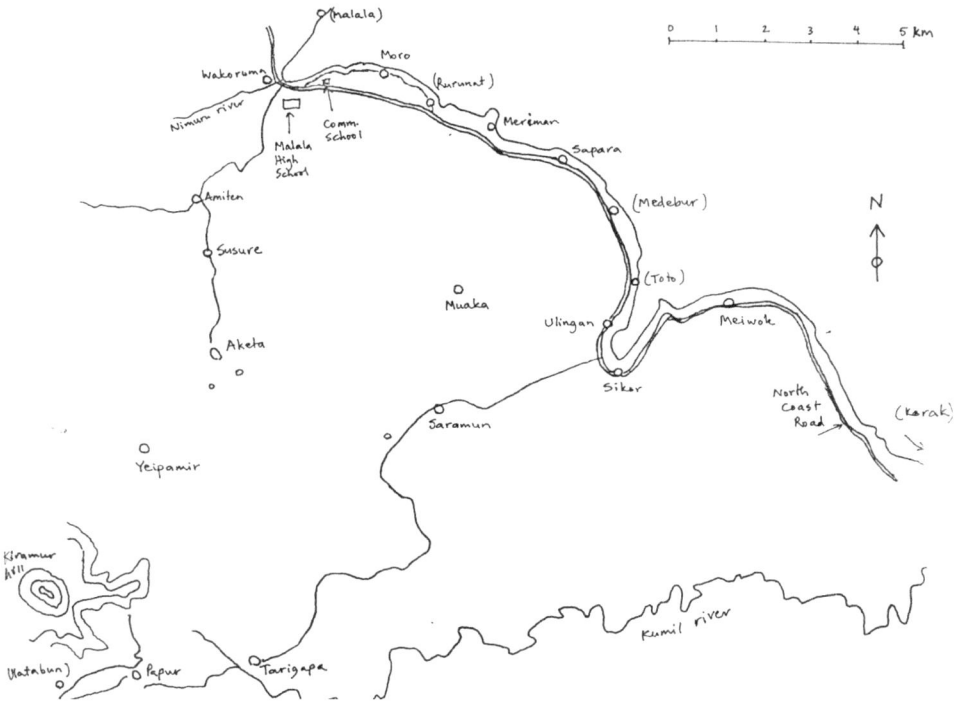

Figure 1.1: Mauwake language area (non-Mauwake speaking villages are in brackets)

occupation on the northern coast of New Guinea island dated back to at least 40 000 years. There are signs of semi-domestication of some tree crops from 20 000 to 10 000 years ago, and of agriculture from about 10 000 years ago, roughly the same time that the Highlands valleys became more habitable after the end of the Ice Age (Pawley 2005: xi–xvii).

From the great diversity of the languages around Cape Croisilles area across Karkar Island, Ross (1996: 27) hypothesizes that this probably is where the Croisilles linkage languages, including Mauwake (or its parent language), started spreading from.[7] He does not provide any dates for the migrations.

Besides some traditional myths we have not been able to obtain stories telling about life earlier than the first half of the 20th century. The majority of the Mauwake people agree that the language group has spread to the coast from inland, and they specify Aketa village as their place of origin. It is commonly believed that long ago the people of the Amiten village, now considered the "heart area" of the language by many speakers, spoke a different language, which has since disappeared. Figure 1.1 shows the map of Mauwake language area at present.

The hypothesis that the Mauwake people came from inland would at least partially explain the present language situation on the coast, where there are many languages

---

[7] See §1.4.1 for a description of the genealogical affiliation.

scattered in a small geographical area. If at some point in history the coast did not have permanent inhabitants to defend it from intruders, it would have been easy for people migrating from various directions and speaking different languages to settle there. One cultural trait that points towards an earlier home area inland is that among the Mauwake speakers fishing is not as important as it is for some other language groups. The coastal villagers mainly catch fish for their own needs, and only occasionally take it to the local market if they happen to have surplus. Gardening, rather than fishing, is the important activity for them.

Possibly the first mention of the larger area where the Mauwake people live is given by the German Hollrung (1888: 338), who mentions "the Tsimbin tribe", meaning the people of Simbine village,[8] speaking the Maiani language which borders the Mauwake language area. Höltker (1937: 964) calls Maiani and the related languages by the name "Móando languages" based on the word 'man' in those languages. He also mentions Mauwake as "Moro–Sapara–Ulingan" – picking names of three coastal villages – as a language deviating from the Móando languages (ibid.).

The written history of the Mauwake area itself began during the German colonial era (ca. 1884–1921) with the report of the killing of two Lutheran missionaries[9] and an officer of the Neu-Guinea-Compagnie,[10] as well as 14 accompanying native people, in Malala Bay in May 1891 (Tranel 1952: 454, Wagner & Reiner 1986: 106–109). After this the Lutheran church abandoned the plan to establish a mission station in the area, and founded one further southeast in the Bunabun area instead.

The Roman Catholic mission was then given the authority in 1891 to search the area between Ulingan and Bogia for suitable places for the mission (Duamba 1996: 8). The Ulingan-Sapara mission station was established in 1926, and a church big enough for a thousand people was built in Sapara village the same year (Brumm & Mihalic 1995: 21). A tsunami struck the coast in the morning of Christmas Eve, 1930, killing five people and destroying the new church and the priest's house.[11] The mission station was moved to the Ulingan village and a new church was built on top of a hill there (Davies 1999: 20–21). The Malala church was built in 1958 on land owned by the Moro villagers, and a high school started on the same compound in 1966 (Brumm & Mihalic 1995: 45). Both the high school and all the community schools in the area were established by the Catholic Church. Because of the many missionaries engaged in the work there the local people had a fair amount of contact with Westerners.

---

[8] Situated 8 km from Moro village, and 5 km from the closest Mauwake village.
[9] The Rhenish Mission had planned to start the work in the area for some time, but it was blocked by the Neu-Guinea-Compagnie. The reason for the killing of the two missionaries, Wilhelm Scheidt and Friedrich Bösch, was never found out, but it is likely that the local people associated them with the Compagnie and feared that they were in fact planters coming to start plantations in their area (Wagner & Reiner 1986: 106–107)
[10] The company had established a big coconut plantation further northwest on an island off Hatzfeldthafen in 1885. It developed quickly despite various problems, but had to be abandoned completely in 1891 because of the hostility of the inhabitants of the area. Within 20 years the site was again covered by rainforest (Tranel 1952: 450–51).
[11] Presumably the rest of the Sapara village was destroyed as well, as the church was probably the strongest building in the whole village.

1 Introduction

In the early years the priests were expected to learn the local language and to become familiar with the culture, especially religious beliefs (Brumm & Mihalic 1995: 25). The liturgy and some preaching were done in Mauwake too, and a few hymns and prayers were composed in it. But whatever written materials there may have been, they were all lost in the Second World War (Z'Graggen 1971: 3–4). And already in the 1930s Tok Pisin had started to replace the local languages as the official language for evangelization in the Catholic Church (Brumm & Mihalic 1995: 179). Especially in an area where five different languages are spoken along a 20 km stretch of the road, this is understandable.

The Second World War had a profound influence on the area. In December 1942 thousands of Japanese soldiers landed in Madang and Wewak (ibid. 37). From Wewak the troops marched down towards Madang, and some of them settled in Ulingan. They required the local men to help build bridges, and asked the people for food. The women and also many men from the coastal villages fled to inland villages and to the rainforest, because they were scared of the soldiers. They were suffering from a shortage of food, as they were not able to do their gardening in a normal way. The Japanese apparently did not commit cruelties, as was the case in some other areas, and the relationship between them and the local people was uneasy but not hostile. When the Allied forces started to bomb the Japanese-occupied areas, the people had to keep hiding even more and were not even able to cook, as they were afraid that the smoke from their cooking fires might attract the pilots' attention and cause the area to be bombed. A number of bombs were dropped in the Mauwake language area, and a few people died.

Before the war, the missionaries were almost the only outsiders that the local people met, but during the war they had contact especially with Japanese but also with Allied soldiers. After the war a number of young men went to work on plantations in different parts of the country or had other employment outside their home area, thus gaining knowledge of the wider world. The founding of Malala High School in 1966 and the completing of the North Coast Highway in the mid-70's further widened the people's horizons.

1.3.3 Demography

The inhabitants in the 15 Mauwake-speaking villages number about 4000; the number is based on the census figures in 2000. Not all of them speak the language, however, as most of the children now learn Tok Pisin as their first language.[12]

The Mauwake speakers are not a uniform group socially or politically. The basic political unit is a village made up of a few clans. There is usually a main village, with some hamlets attached to it. Recently there has been a tendency towards moving away from the main village and building small hamlets near the family's garden or coconut plot.

---

[12] Much of the contents of the sections §1.3.3–§1.3.6 is based on the Mauwake background study written by Kwan Poh San in 1988.

1.3 The Mauwake people, their environment and culture

A person's main responsibility is towards one's own family and clan. The basic unit is a nuclear family: parents and their children, either their own or adopted. The society is patrilineal: kinship is traced through, and the inheritance handed down from, the father. Adoption is widespread and always takes place within extended family, usually the husband's side of the family. Members of an extended family are expected to assist each other in various ways: providing food at feasts, helping to pay a debt, bride price or some other obligation, and looking after each other in general. The responsibilities towards one's clan are also strong but not quite as strong as to one's extended family. Traditionally the clans used to own all the land, but planting coconuts, and later cocoa, changed the situation. The use of garden land is still decided by the headmen (leaders) of each clan, but now there is rivalry even between members of the same clan about the existing coconut trees and about land where new coconut or cocoa trees can be planted.

Every clan has its own headman, and in earlier times the headman of the most prestigious clan also used to be the headman of the whole village. Decisions were based on consensus after discussions in the village meetings, but the final authority rested on the headmen.

After the establishment of the local level government system the authority of the headmen partly transferred to the local government member (*kaunsil*), to the magistrate and to the leader of the community work (*komiti*). The traditional authority structure has more or less broken down and since it has not been completely replaced by the new structure, this has given way to individualism and even disregard of any authority, especially among the young people. The Catholic Church is a somewhat cohesive force, but it has lost some of its authority with the social breakdown and also with the coming of other churches.

Each village has social ties with other, usually closely situated villages regardless of the language. Many of the Mauwake villages have close interaction with non-Mauwake-speaking villages. This has also resulted in extensive intermarrying between different language groups, which in the earlier times encouraged bilingualism or trilingualism, but which nowadays strengthens the use of Tok Pisin.

The six languages either bordering the Mauwake area, or inside it, are the Kaukombar[13] languages Maiani, Miani (Tani)[14] and Mala (Pay),[15] the Tibor language Mawak, the Korak-Waskia group language Amako (Korak), all of which are Trans New Guinea languages; the only Austronesian language is Beteka (Medebur), closely related to the Manam language. None of these languages is dominant compared with the others. The Mauwake speakers say that it used to be a prestigious language in the area, but I have not been able to confirm this with speakers of the other languages. Bi- and trilingualism used to be extensive in the whole area especially before the arrival of Tok Pisin.

---

[13] I am utilizing the grouping from Ross (2005) here. For a discussion on the classification of the Madang languages, see §1.4.1 below.

[14] The names without parentheses are what the speakers prefer to use for their languages, the ones in parentheses are those used in linguistic literature especially by Z'Graggen and those utilizing his data. Maiani and Miani are mentioned here as separate languages, but they can also be considered different dialects of one language.

[15] Mala has two distinct dialects, Mala and Alam. The latter is spoken in the two villages that have close contact with the Mauwake area.

1 Introduction

1.3.4 Economy

Subsistence farming is the main activity of the Mauwake people. They get most of their food and building materials from their own land. Traditionally the main staple was taro, supplemented with yam, sweet potato and cooking bananas; sago was used particularly when little other food was available. Especially on the coast yam and sweet potato have recently been replacing taro as the main staple, because there is not enough land for slash-and-burn gardening required by taro.

For a long time coconut has been the main cash crop, but with the falling copra prices the people have diversified into growing cocoa, coffee[16] and recently also vanilla. The cash crops are transported to Madang to sell. During the German colonial era tobacco was introduced in the area, and still in the 1930s Malala area was famous for its tobacco (Tranel 1952: 454). Nowadays the people mainly grow it for their own use, and sell any extra at the local market.

Hunting and fishing used to be important activities especially for men, but their significance has decreased. Wild pigs are getting scarce, and bandicoots are mainly hunted during the dry season. As the Mauwake people have probably come from further inland, fishing has not been as important for them as for some other groups on the coast. Both men and women do some fishing, but mainly for their own family's needs.

Any garden produce, fish or bandicoots not needed by the family may be sold at the Malala market, which is the biggest one between Madang and Bogia, or at the smaller Ulingan market.

The high school and a logging company provide employment for a few local men. In the area where logging is done landowners also get some royalties from it. Logging has caused controversy among the people.[17] Many of the more educated men, and some women, now in their 40s and 50s, have migrated into towns where they work as tradesmen, teachers, or in other occupations.

1.3.5 Cultural notes

In the traditional worldview the seen and the unseen are both important parts of the same universe. The unseen world consists of different kinds of spirits: clan spirits and other spirits in nature (*inasina*), spirits of the recently dead (*kukusa*) and spirits of those who have died a long time ago (*sawur*). The spirits need to be treated with respect so that they will not harm but rather help the people. Although the reliance on the spirits has decreased with the coming of Christianity, various rituals are still fairly widely practised to ensure the benevolence of the spirits, especially in connection with birth, death, sickness, hunting and gardening.

Sickness is normally attributed to one's bad relations with other people or disregard of the spirits, the work of a sorcerer, or in some cases to "natural causes". Death is still commonly believed to be caused by sorcery.

---

[16] Growing coffee was given up later, because it is very labour-intensive and the *robusta* coffee grown in the lowlands fetches a very low market price.

[17] The first logging company in the 1980s went bankrupt and the landowners received very little money for their timber. Even with subsequent logging the benefits for the local people have been rather modest.

Name taboos are a typical feature of the cultures in Oceania. It is forbidden to call one's in-laws by name, or call anyone else by name who has the same name as the in-laws. In the Mauwake culture both of the parents give a child the name of one of his or her own relatives, which the other parent naturally may not pronounce. In addition to these two names, a child also receives a Christian name at baptism, and may be given other names as well. Thus a person can have even five or six names, which are used by different people to call him or her. And when the person gets married, all those names are forbidden for the in-laws to use. They may use a kinship term or invent a nickname by which to address the person. In general, kinship terms are used widely both to address people and to refer to them.

Passing on the traditional culture and customs is hampered by the lessening use of the vernacular as well as the lack of interest especially among many young people. Grown-ups may deplore the situation, but there is little attempt to actively pass on the cultural heritage or to help the young generation to evaluate, appreciate and renew their own culture.

1.3.6 Mauwake kinship system

The kinship system of the Mauwake people is a slightly modified Iroquois system (Figure 1.2). Both gender (of the relative, and in some cases of ego) and generation are important, but also the distinction of parental siblings of the opposite sex. One's father's brother is also called *auwa* 'father' and his wife is *aite* 'mother'; likewise one's mother's sister is also 'mother' and her husband is 'father'. But mother's brother is called *yaaya* 'uncle', and his wife is *paapan* 'aunt'; father's sister is also 'aunt' and her husband is 'uncle'. The term 'father' is used for the following as well: one's own father's cross-cousins, one's father-in law and, for a female, elder sister's husband. Two generations up from self the grandparents are distinguished by gender: *kae* 'grandfather' and *kome* 'grandmother', but two generations down all the grandchildren are called *iimasip* 'grandchild'.

In one's own generation there are two sets of terms for brothers and sisters. Their use depends on whether relative age or gender is in focus: *paapa* 'older sibling' and *aamun* 'younger sibling' are used for siblings of either sex, whereas *yomokowa* 'brother' and *ekera* 'sister' are gender-bound terms. The latter are more commonly used by siblings of the opposite sex than by those of the same sex. All the parallel cousins are also considered one's siblings, whereas one's cross-cousins, the children of the 'uncles' and 'aunts', are called *yomar/emar* 'cousin', a term used for either sex.

One generation down from self, one's children include not only one's own sons (*muuka*) and daughters (*wiipa*), but also those of one's siblings of the same sex, *and* those of one's cross-cousins. For the sons and daughters of one's siblings of the opposite sex there is a single term, *eremena* 'nephew/niece'. Most of the terms for kin relations are inalienably possessed nouns (§3.2.4).

Mother's brother is a particularly important relative for performing rites of passage like initiation, marriage and funeral. When a person dies, his/her maternal uncle, together with the deceased person's male cross-cousins, is responsible for burying him/her

1 Introduction

and distributing his/her possessions.[18] These men are called *weria* men. *Weria* means 'planting stick', and the term is used as a metaphor for burial.[19] An uncle also has an important function as a mediator, if his nephew or niece has serious problems with his/her nuclear family. Although father's sister's husband is also called an 'uncle', he does not have a similar role to that of mother's brother.

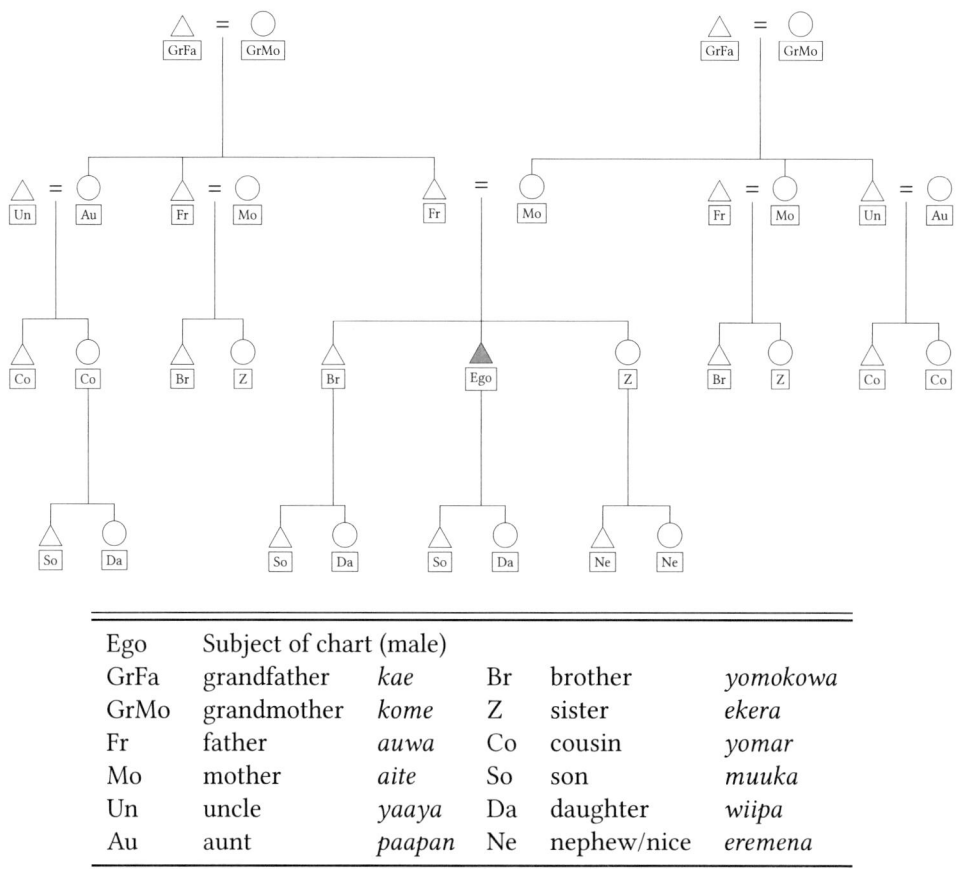

Ego	Subject of chart (male)		Br	brother	*yomokowa*
GrFa	grandfather	*kae*	Z	sister	*ekera*
GrMo	grandmother	*kome*	Co	cousin	*yomar*
Fr	father	*auwa*	So	son	*muuka*
Mo	mother	*aite*	Da	daughter	*wiipa*
Un	uncle	*yaaya*	Ne	nephew/nice	*eremena*
Au	aunt	*paapan*			

Figure 1.2: Mauwake kinship system chart

---

[18] For an older person whose uncles have already died, nephews (= sons of the siblings of opposite sex) take their place among these men.
[19] It is not unusual to have the same verb for 'burying' and 'planting' in Papuan languages, but in Mauwake they are different.

1.4 The Mauwake language

1.4.1 Genealogical affiliation and previous research

The name *Mauwake* means 'what?'[20] The Mauwake speakers themselves identify the language by this name, and the speakers of the related Kaukombaran languages use corresponding names to call their own languages. The people have a myth in which the spirit Turamun gives each group their land area, their main staple as well as their language, and the language name originates in this myth.

Before our taking residence in Moro village in 1978, there was only very sketchy research done on the Mauwake language, just enough to classify it.[21] The name Ulingan was taken from the main mission station in the area, although that is not how the speakers themselves call their language. Sometimes the alternative name Mawake is given in brackets in the earlier language lists.

Mauwake is a Papuan language. "Papuan" is just a cover term for a number of genetically unrelated language families, which are not Austronesian and are spoken in the New Guinea region (Figure 1.3).[22] The Papuan languages consist of several unrelated language families, the biggest of which is the Trans New Guinea (TNG) family.

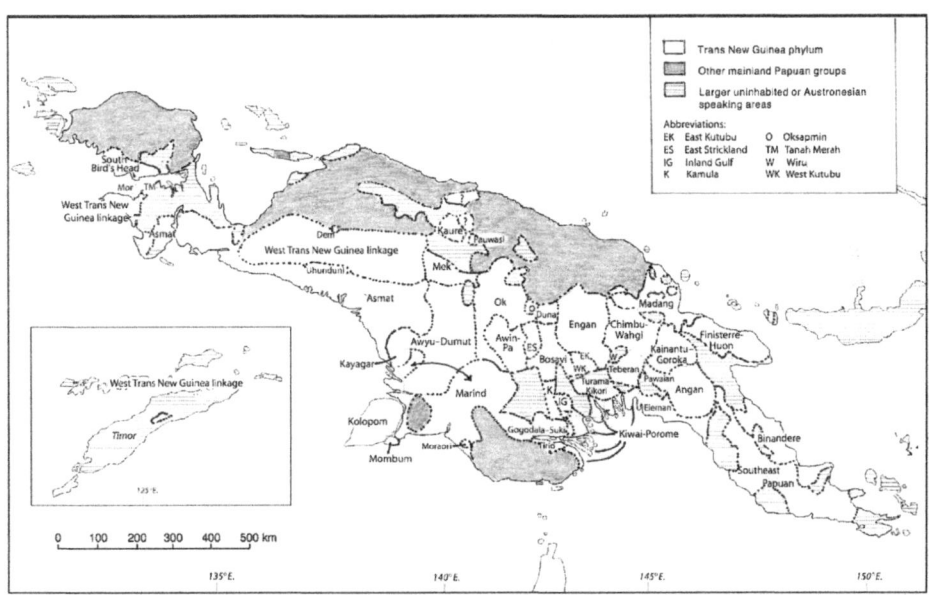

Figure 1.3: New Guinea island language map (Ross 2005: 34 Map 2)

---

[20] Actually it consists of the question word *mauwa* 'what' and the contrastive focus clitic *-ke*.

[21] Capell (1952), and following him Voegelin & Voegelin (1965), Greenberg (1971), then Z'Graggen (1971; 1975a) and Wurm, Laycock & Voorhoeve (1975); Wurm (1982).

[22] The name Papuan has been criticized (Capell 1969, Haiman 1979), but it is widely used instead of its alternative, non-Austronesian.

1 Introduction

The Trans New Guinea hypothesis was originally put forward by McElhanon & Voorhoeve (1970) to account for the similarities between the Finisterre-Huon languages on the one hand, and Central and South New Guinea Stock languages on the other. Later, Wurm, Laycock & Voorhoeve (1975) argued that a great number of additional languages belong to the phylum. Much of the work relied on lexico-statistical rather than more rigorous application of the standard comparative method, and because many of the claims are not well substantiated, the whole TNG hypothesis received a fair bit of criticism (Lang 1976, Haiman 1979, Foley 1986, Pawley 1995).

Most of the classificatory work done on the languages of Madang Province is based on groundbreaking research by Z'Graggen (1971; 1975a,b). According to Wurm, Laycock & Voorhoeve's (1975) classification following the language family tree model of lexico-statistics, Mauwake[23] belongs to the Madang-Adelbert Range sub-family, Adelbert Range superstock, Pihom stock, and Kumilan[24] language family together with two very small languages, Bepour and Moere (Figure 1.4).

For nearly two decades there was practically no comparative linguistics done on Papuan languages. But in the early 1990s more detailed research started on the Madang-Adelbert Range languages, now renamed the Madang group, and later on other TNG languages as well (Pawley 1998). As a result of that research Pawley (1995; 2001) and Ross (1995) came to the conclusion that the Trans New Guinea hypothesis is workable but needs modification. They also concluded that the Madang group definitely is part of the Trans New Guinea language family. According to their new classification Mauwake belongs to the Trans New Guinea family, the Madang group and the Croisilles linkage of languages. Ross (1996: 21–25) also discusses the relationships between the various languages within the Croisilles subgroup, using the term *Kumil* (Z'Graggen's *Kumilan*) for the family including Mauwake, and *Kaukombar* (Z'Graggen's *Kaukombaran*) for the four languages closest to the Kumil languages. He also does some regrouping within the families based on the pronoun forms in the languages. In the Kumil group he includes not only Mauwake, Bepour and Moere, but also the languages Musar and Bunabun (Figure 1.5).

Apart from Z'Graggen's survey no other linguistic study of any depth has been carried out on the Mauwake language except what has been done by Kwan Poh San and myself (Kwan 1980; 1983; 1988; 1989; 2002; Järvinen (=Berghäll) 1980; 1988b,a; 1989; 1990; 1991; Järvinen (=Berghäll), Kwan & Aduna 2001, and Berghäll (=Järvinen) 2006.) The grammatical work published on related languages includes the grammars of Usan by Reesink (1987), Tauya by MacDonald (1990) and Waskia by Ross & Paol (1978). Two grammars in manuscript form that were also used for reference are Maia grammar by Hardin (2002) and Bargam grammar by Hepner (2002). Both are available electronically and in the SIL-PNG library, Ukarumpa.

The ISO-639 code for Mauwake, based on Grimes (2000), is mhl, and the Glottolog code is mauw1238 (glottolog.org).

---

[23] In Z'Graggen's (1980) listing Mauwake has the code F2.
[24] Z'Graggen (1971) initially called the family Ubean, possibly based on the language names Ulingan and Bepour, but later (1975) changed the name into Kumilan based on the name of the Kumil river.

1.4 The Mauwake language

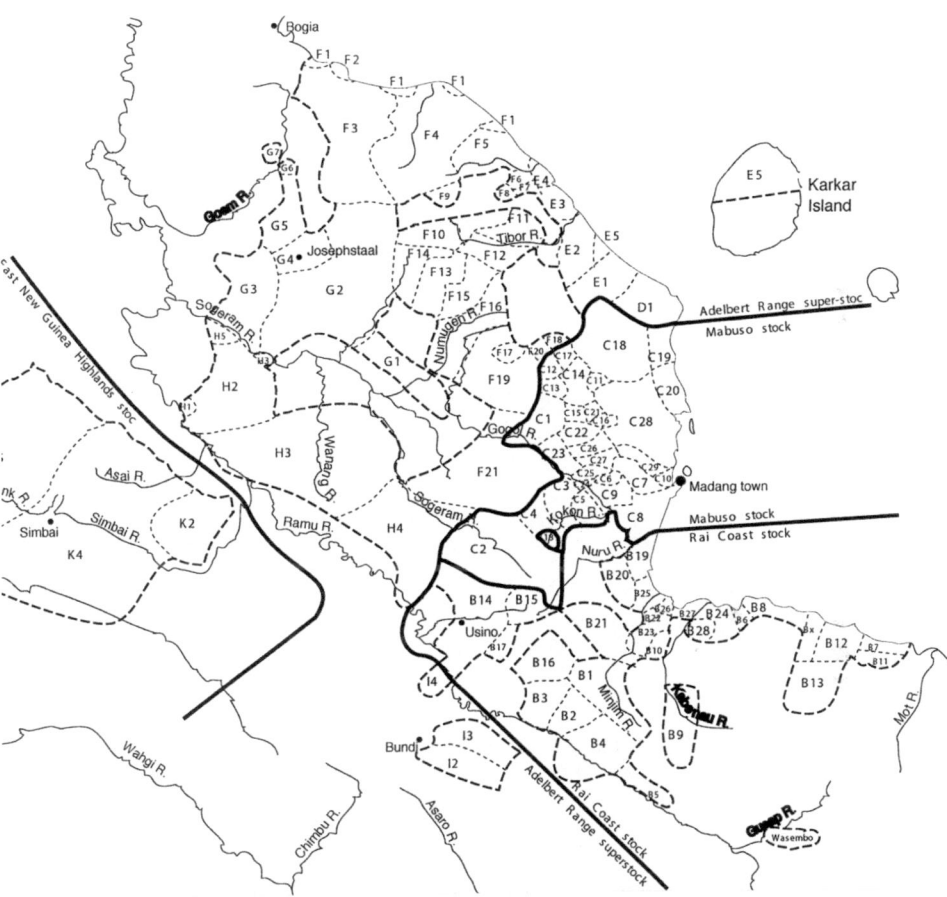

Figure 1.4: Wurm's grouping of Madang-Adelbert languages (Ross 1996: Map 3)

1 Introduction

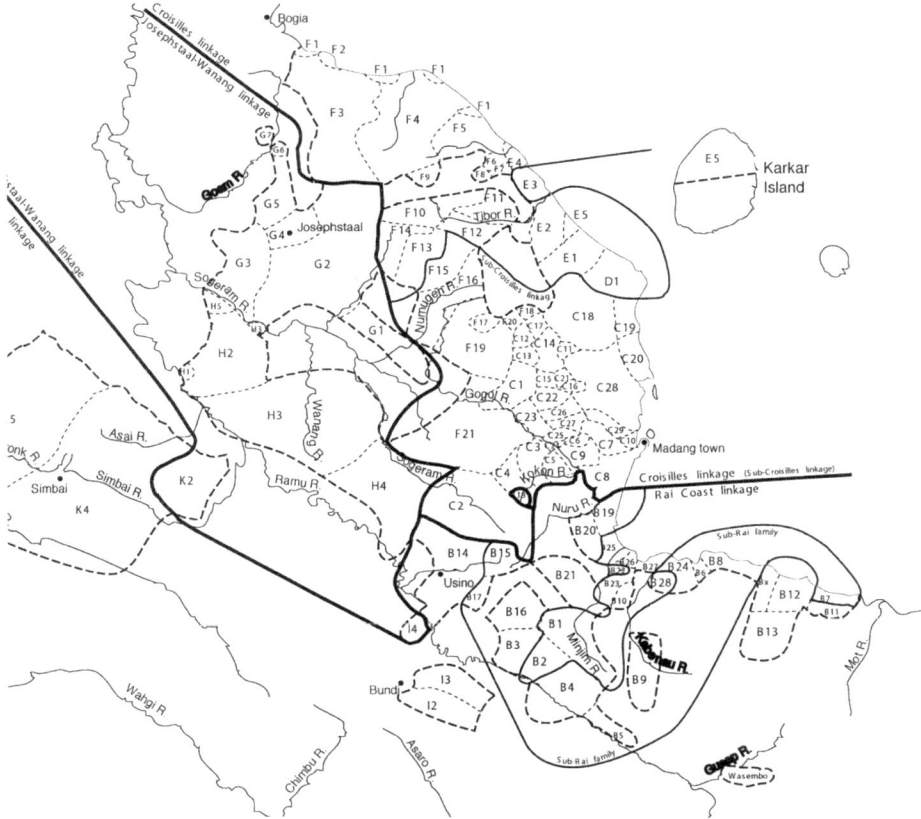

Figure 1.5: Ross' 1996 grouping of Madang-Adelbert languages (Ross 1996: Map 4)

1.4.2 Typological overview of morphological and syntactic features

In this section, morphological and syntactic characteristics of the Mauwake language are discussed in relation to the typology of Papuan/Trans New Guinea languages and to the universal word order[25] typology. To some extent these two overlap, as TNG languages typically are also SOV languages.

1.4.2.1 Mauwake as a Trans New Guinea language

Mauwake has many features typical of both Papuan languages in general and Trans New Guinea languages in particular.

The PHONOLOGY of the language is simple: there are five vowel and fourteen consonant phonemes, and only a few of them have more than one allophone. Morphology is quite transparent, so there is very little morphophonology.

---

[25] As Dixon (2010a: 72) notes, "word order" here should be called "the order of clausal constituents", as it is the ordering of constituents that the typology is based on rather than that of individual words.

1.4 The Mauwake language

The BASIC ORDER OF CLAUSAL CONSTITUENTS is verb-final. In neutral clauses with both subject and object the order is SOV (1), but it changes into OSV when the object is fronted (2) as a theme (§9.1). Adverbials are somewhat less constrained in their ordering. It is also very common to have a verb as the only element in a clause (3).

(1) [Ona   emeria nain=ke]$_S$ [maa]$_O$ wafur-a-k.
    3s.GEN woman that1=CF   thing   throw-PA-3s
    'His wife threw things.'

(2) [Wiipa   nain]$_O$ [eka=ke]$_S$ mu-o-k.
    daughter that1   water=CF   swallow-PA-3s
    'The daughter was swallowed by the water.'

(3) Uruf-a-m.
    see-PA-1s
    'I saw it.'

In COMPLEX SENTENCES, the subordinate clause usually precedes the main clause. Thus the reason/cause precedes the result/effect, in conditional sentences the protasis precedes the apodosis, and in intention/purpose sentences the intention precedes the expected result. When the reason follows the result, it is a very marked order.

Mauwake is clearly a nominative-accusative type language, rather than ergative-absolutive. The agent of a transitive verb (4) is marked in the same way as the actor of an intransitive verb (5), and most experiential verbs have the experiencer as a nominative subject (6).

(4) Yo   mauw-owa nia   asip-i-yem.
    1s.UNM work-NMZ 2p.ACC help-NP-PR.1s
    'I help you with work.'

(5) Yo   koka=pa   ik-e-m.
    1s.UNM jungle=LOC   be-PA-1s
    'I was in the jungle.'

(6) Yo   wuailal-i-yem   a.
    1s.UNM hunger-NP-PR.1s oh
    'Oh, I'm hungry.'

VERB MORPHOLOGY in Mauwake is extensive, even if not as extensive and complex as in some other Papuan languages. The morphology is agglutinative, and affixation is mostly very transparent. Suffixes are used for subject, tense and aspect, benefactive, distributive, causative and counterfactual marking. Prefixing is used very little, only for reduplication and to form verbs referring to bringing and taking. It is possible to have several derivational and inflectional affixes in one verb, as shown by the elicited example (7), but in actual usage this is rare.

1 Introduction

(7) Muuka wia   **arim-ow-omak-om-ek-a-k.**
     son   3p.ACC grow-CAUS-DISTR/PL-BEN-BNFY1.CNTF-PA-3s
     '(S)he would have brought up (many) sons for me.'

Mauwake has a clear three-tense system (§3.8.3.4). Even though the tense suffixes only distinguish between past and non-past, the distinction between present and future shows in the subject suffixes, which are different for these two tenses. Aspect marking is optional (§3.8.5.1.1). The auxiliary follows the main verb. There is no passive form in verbs.

A very typical feature in Papuan languages is a difference between final (§3.8.3.4) and medial verbs (§3.8.3.5). The former are finite verbs with full inflection for tense and subject number and person, and the most typical position for them is at the end of a declarative sentence. The medial verbs indicate whether the subject of a clause is the same as (8), or different from (9), that of the following clause. The same-subject forms also indicate whether the action of the second verb is simultaneous with that of the first verb, or sequential (8) in relation to it. Medial clauses (§8.2) are coordinate with, but also dependent on, the following clause. Because of the existence and extensive use of medial clauses, temporal subordinate clauses (§8.3.3.1) are used very little in Mauwake.[26]

(8) Owowa or-**op**,   wuailal-**ep**   akia   ik-e-k.
     village go-SS.SEQ be.hungry-SS.SEQ banana roast-PA-3s
     'He went to the village, was hungry and roasted bananas.'

(9) Mik-**amkun** me um-o-k, wiowa onaiya ikiw-em-ik-**eya**.   Olas=ke war-e-k.
     spear-1s/p.DS not die-PA-3s spear with go-SS.SIM-be-2/3s.DS Olas=CF kill-PA-3s
     'When I speared it, it didn't die, (but) as it was going with the spear Olas killed it.'

Medial verbs are also used in tail-head linkage (§8.2.3.5), another strategy common in Papuan languages. The last verb of a sentence is repeated in the first clause of the next sentence, but usually in medial form. In spoken Mauwake this recapitulation device is used to indicate actions that continue on the story line without a major break, but since the development of the written language the tail-head linkage is losing this function and is getting a new function as a marker of the climax in the story.

Another typical feature of many Papuan languages is the lack of a large inventory of verb stems (Foley 1986: 127). An extreme case is Kalam with its less than 100 verb stems; consequently, Kalam needs to use serial verb and adjunct plus verb constructions for most actions (Pawley 1987: 336–337). Mauwake has a reasonably large verb inventory, but in addition it uses both serial verbs (§3.8.5.1.2) and adjunct plus verb constructions (§3.8.5.2).

There is no inflection on NOUNS (§3.2) or ADJECTIVES (§3.3), nor are there gender/noun class distinctions. But Mauwake makes a distinction between alienably and inalienably

---

[26] Medial clauses in Papuan languages are often translated with temporal subordinate clauses in other languages, even if they are not subordinate in the original language.

possessed nouns (§3.2.4). Most kinship terms are inalienably possessed, but body parts are not.

The NOUN PHRASE (§4.1) most commonly consists of the head noun by itself, or with just one modifier. In a noun phrase a pluralizing (10) unmarked pronoun, a possessive noun phrase, a temporal phrase, or a qualifier noun phrase may precede the head noun; all the other modifiers follow it. A possessive preceding the head noun and an adjective following it (11) is quite common in Trans New Guinea languages (Reesink 1987: 19).

(10) wi   emeria teeria nain
     3p.UNM woman group that1

   'that group of women'

(11) yena   aamun   gelemuta kuisow
     1s.GEN 1s/p.younger.sibling small   one

   'my one younger brother' or 'one of my younger brothers'

Mauwake exhibits more variation in the PRONOUN forms (§3.5) than many other Papuan languages do. There is only singular and plural number, and no inclusive-exclusive distinction in the first person plural. But there are separate sets for unmarked, accusative, dative, genitive, isolative, reflexive-reciprocal and comitative pronouns. Mauwake is a typical Papuan language in that the subject pronoun may be left out; the third person subject pronoun is overt mainly when it is used for a re-activating an earlier topic (§9.2.3). But in imperative clauses a subject pronoun is very common, which is NOT usually mentioned as a typical feature of Papuan languages,[27] and is quite rare cross-linguistically.

1.4.2.2 Mauwake as an SOV language

Mauwake conforms very strongly to the typological patterns found to exist in the SOV, or hence, OV languages. The following discussion on various characteristics in Mauwake that correlate with the OV constituent order is based on Dryer (2007b).

Concerning the following sentence level features Mauwake shows itself a typical OV language. The interrogative marker -i always occurs sentence-finally in polar questions (12) (§7.2.2).

(12) Yo   emeria efar   uruf-a-man=i?
     1s.UNM woman 1s.DAT see-PA-2p=QM

   'Did you see my wife?'

In non-polar, or content questions (§7.2.1), the question word or phrase is in the same position that would be occupied by the non-interrogative word or phrase in a statement (13).

---

[27] To my knowledge this particular feature has not been studied much in Papuan languages.

(13) Ni   sira   **kamenap** on-a-man?
    2p.UNM custom what.like do-PA-2p
    'What did you do?'

In complex sentences (§8.3), the subordinate clause usually comes before the main clause (14).

(14) Mua imen-ap=**na** feeke wia   p-ekap-eka.
    man find-SS.SEQ=TP here.CF 3p.ACC BPX-come-IMP.2p
    'If you find the men, bring them here.'

Complement clauses (§8.3.2) behave like other subordinate clauses, preceding the main clause (15).

(15) **Mukuna kerer-e-k nain** i   me paayar-e-mik.
    fire   start-PA-3s that1 1p.UNM not understand-PA-1/3p
    'We didn't realise that a fire had started.'

The typical OV order for predicate-copula applies only partly in Mauwake, as a copular verb is not used for for the present tense. The OV order does show in the other tenses and the medial forms (16).

(16) O   somek mua(=pa) **ik-eya** ...
    3s.UNM song man-(LOC) be-2/3s.DS
    'When he was a teacher ...'

Clause and sentence level features that correlate with the OV order are as follows. The position of a complementizer or a subordinator is clause-final (17).

(17) Yo   emeria aaw-owa kookal-ek-a-m=**na** ...
    1s.UNM woman get-NMR like-CNTF-PA-1s=TP
    'If I had liked/wanted to get a wife ... '

Both manner adverbs, postpositional phrases, and non-argument noun phrases precede the verb (18).

(18) Fikera   nain **sira** **feenap** on-a-mik.
    kunai.grass that1 custom like.this do-PA-1/3p
    'This is what they did to the *kunai* grass.'

Typical OV features also manifest themselves in different phrases. In the VPs (or verbal groups, as they are called below in §3.8.5.1), the main verb precedes the auxiliary (19).

(19) Saa=iw   **ir-am-ika-i-mik**.
    sand=INST come-SS.SIM-be-NP-PR.1/3p
    'They are coming along the sand/beach.'

1.4 The Mauwake language

In basic noun phrases (§4.1.1) the genitive precedes the head noun (20):

(20) *yiena miiwa*
 1p.GEN land
 'our land'

Mauwake does not have articles. When the distal-1 deictic *nain* 'that' is used, there is often considerable semantic bleaching, and it seems to be becoming more like a definite article, but in many contexts it still clearly retains its deictic function.

Mauwake has postpositional phrases (PP), rather than prepositional phrases (21).

(21) *koor(a) kuenuma=pa*
 house underside=LOC
 'underneath the house'

An OV feature that shows on word level in Mauwake is that verbs have suffixes rather than prefixes (22).

(22) *Akia ik-**omak-e-mik**.*
 banana roast-DISTR/PL-PA-1/3p
 'We roasted many bananas.'

As there are no comparative forms for adjectives in Mauwake, one OV characteristic that does not apply in Mauwake is the standard of comparison and comparison marker preceding the adjective.

Case marking of transitive arguments with an affix is more common in OV than in VO languages. In Mauwake there are no case suffixes on either the subject or the object, but all human objects require an accusative pronoun (§3.5.3) to occur preceding the verb.

1.4.3 Dialects

The Mauwake speakers themselves do not identify clearly defined dialects, but they do refer to the speech differences between the inland villages and the coastal villages.[28] Some also separate the Ulingan group from the rest, and the Ulingan group people make a distinction between themselves and those further west along the coast.

The majority of the Mauwake speakers consider Aketa and Amiten as the centre of the language group. People in each village claim that their own way of speaking is the "true" way, but at the same time they credit Aketa as the place where the language originated. The Ulingan and Papur dialect groups do not admit the prestige of Aketa and Amiten quite as willingly.

---

[28] The data for this section is mainly taken from the Mauwake dialect survey report (Järvinen (=Berghäll) 1988a).

1 Introduction

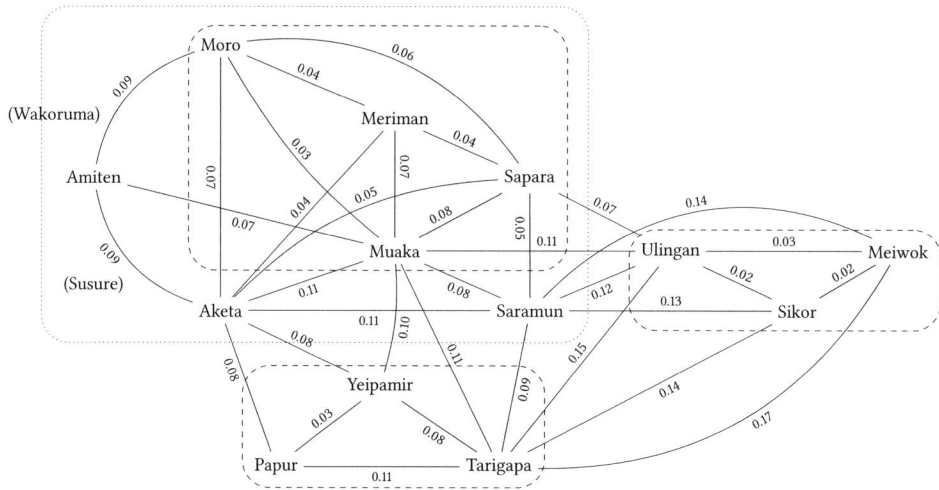

Figure 1.6: Mean degrees of pronunciation difference between some Mauwake villages

Comparing the Mauwake data[29] lexicostatistically would indicate that there are no distinct dialects in the language at all. The percentage of cognates between all the villages is 100. What variation an earlier survey seemed to show, turned out to be multiple cognates. But the phonostatistic method (Grimes & Agard 1959, modified as in Simons 1977: 177–178) yields some dialectal differences. There are pronunciation dissimilarities, on the basis of which the language area can be divided into three main dialect areas: Ulingan (Ulingan, Sikor and Meiwok), Papur (Papur, Tarikapa, Yeipamir) and Muaka (Muaka, Moro, Mereman, Sapara, Aketa, Amiten/Susure/Wakoruma,[30] and Saramun).

Of the 100 words in the list, 60% are pronounced identically in all the villages. Of the rest, a little over half (i.e. 21% of the whole data) are cases of non-phonemic variation, namely [w]~[β], and [j]~[ʒ]. The first one of these the speakers of the language do not even notice, the second one they notice to some extent. Figure 1.6 gives the mean degrees[31] of pronunciation differences between some of the Mauwake villages.

The Ulingan dialect is the most homogeneous, and also most clearly a separate group from the others. The mean degree of pronunciation differences between Ulingan and Sikor, and between Sikor and Meiwok is 0.02, which means that in a hundred-word list there are only two differences of one degree. The pronunciation difference between Tarikapa and Sikor or Meiwok is the biggest, 0.17 degrees. Table 1.1 gives the mean degrees of pronunciation differences between all the villages.

---

[29] The basic 100-word list by Ezard (1977: 55–59) was used with four semantically problematic words deleted and four other words added.

[30] Susure and Wakoruma were not included in this survey because of their closeness to Amiten both location- and dialect-wise.

[31] The mean degree of difference between two sounds was calculated by first counting hypothesized minimal steps from one to another, one minimal step given the value of one. These were added up and divided by the number of words in the data, i.e. 100.

1.4 The Mauwake language

Table 1.1: Mean degrees of pronunciation differences between Mauwake villages

Muaka												
.08	Saramun											
.11	.09	Tarikapa										
.10	.12	.11	Papur									
.10	.11	.08	.03	Yeipamir								
.07	.11	.07	.08	.08	Aketa							
.07	.07	.10	.08	.09	.09	Amiten						
.03	.07	.11	.08	.12	.07	.09	Moro					
.07	.08	.14	.10	.15	.06	.08	.04	Mereman				
.08	.05	.10	.11	.12	.05	.10	.06	.04	Sapara			
.11	.12	.15	.08	.10	.14	.13	.09	.11	.07	Ulingan		
.12	.13	.17	.08	.14	.13	.12	.08	.09	.09	.02	Sikor	
.15	.14	.17	.09	.14	.13	.16	.10	.09	.06	.03	.02	Meiwok

Indication of a dialect division similar to that mentioned above, especially setting the Muaka group apart from the others, was also provided by morphemes that were not in the 100-word list but which were checked during the survey, because they had been found to occur in a fairly clear pattern across the language area. These morphemes are given in Table 1.2.

Table 1.2: Extra words used in dialect comparison

inowa	*unowa*		'many'
urup(-iya)	*irip(-iya)*		'ascend'
ikiw(-iya)	*itiw(-iya)*		'go'
unan	*inuan*	*inon*	'yesterday'
-era	*-eya/-iya*		'2/3 p. medial verb suffix'

The isoglosses in Figure 1.7 show the distribution of the pronunciation of these morphemes in the various villages. The only case where the isoglosses would suggest a different dialect grouping from the one presented above is that of Saramun, which would seem to belong more closely to the Papur group than the Muaka group.

What complicates the dialect division is the fact that sometimes the same pronunciation, deviant from the more common way of pronouncing a word, can be found in villages far apart like Aketa and Meiwok (*imakuna* rather than *umakuna* 'neck'), or Papur, Moro and Mereman villages and the Ulingan group (*epia* rather than *ipia* 'rain'). Also, there is no clear pattern of pronunciation differences between villages; sometimes the

1 Introduction

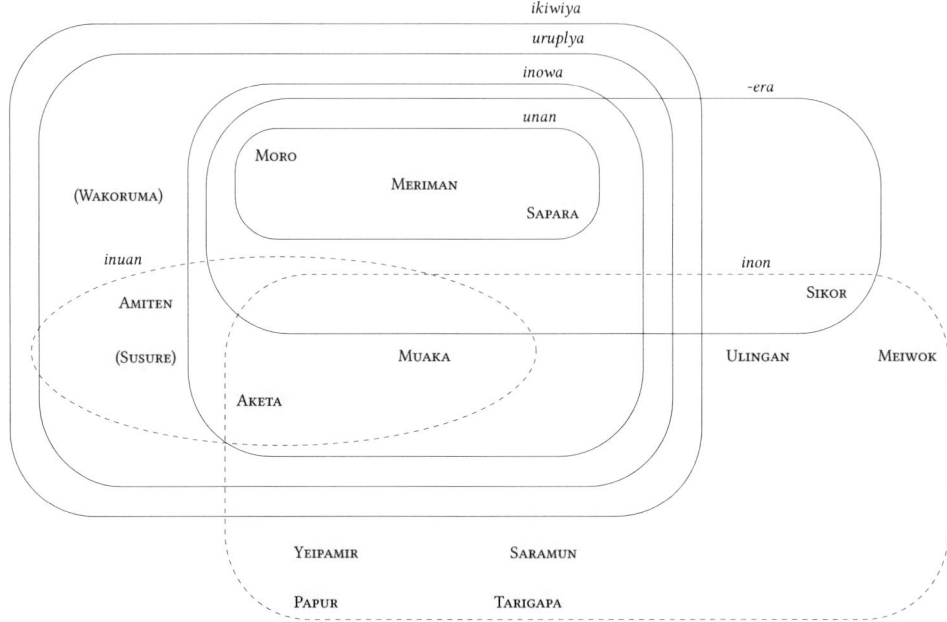

Figure 1.7: Distribution of some pronunciation differences

differences are opposite in the case of two vocabulary items. The word for 'many' in the Muaka dialect[32] is *inowa*, but the others pronounce it *unowa*, whereas the word for 'ascend/go up' in the Muaka dialect is *urupiya*, but in the other dialects it is *iripiya*. Likewise, the Ulingan group differs from the rest in the pronunciation of *omaiwia* 'tongue' (vs. *omaiwa* in others) and *awulak* 'sweet potato' (vs. *awuliak* in others), so the difference is almost exactly the reverse in the two cases.

No grammatical differences have been found to exist between the dialects. Neither are there social registers, nor special language for restricted uses like rituals.

---

[32] excluding Amiten/Susure/Wakoruma.

2 Phonology: a brief overview

2.1 Phonemes

The phonological system in Mauwake is quite regular and straightforward, even if not one of the very simplest found in Papuan languages (Foley 1986: 48–64). It has 14 consonants and 5 vowels in its phoneme inventory. Allophonic variation in Mauwake is very limited, and there is not much morphophonological complexity (§2.3.3) either. In the presentation of the phonology IPA standard phonetic symbols are used.

2.1.1 Consonants

The fourteen consonant phonemes in Mauwake are presented in Table 2.1. Z'Graggen (1971: 51) also lists the velar nasal /ŋ/ as a phoneme in Mauwake, but at least synchronically it is not part of the basic inventory. All the words in Mauwake that have the velar nasal are shared with a neighbouring language, so they are likely to be borrowings. For those words there is also a native synonym, although it may not be as frequently used. It is also possible that Mauwake has earlier had the velar nasal, as it is a very common areal feature in the Madang North Coast area (Z'Graggen 1971).

Table 2.1: Consonant phonemes

	Bilabial	Alveolar	Palatal	Velar
Plosive	p b	t d		k g
Nasal	m	n		
Fricative	ɸ	s		
Trill		r		
Lateral		l		
Approximant	w		j	

Most of the consonant phonemes in Mauwake have only one extrinsic allophone.

The voiceless PLOSIVES are unaspirated in all the word positions where they occur (1). They contrast as to bilabial, alveolar and velar points of articulation. Mauwake does not have the glottal stop typical of many Papuan languages.

(1) a. /paanek/ [ˈpaːnek] 'it crashed'
    b. /taanek/ [ˈtaːnek] 'it is full'

c. /kaanek(e)/ [ˈkaːnek(e)] 'where?'
d. /opa/ [oˈpa] 'hold!'
e. /otal/ [oˈtal] 'reef'
f. /oka/ [oˈka] 'hand drum'
g. /orop/ [oˈrop] 'descend.ss.SEQ'
h. /rotorot/ [roˈtorot] 'painted moray eel'
i. /orok/ [oˈrok] '(s)he descended'

The voiceless plosives occur word-initially, -medially and -finally (2).

(2) a. /pepek/ [peˈpek] 'enough'
b. /onap/ [oˈnap] 'do.ss.SEQ'
c. /teteke/ [teˈteke] 'take apart!'
d. /menat/ [meˈnat] 'tide'
e. /koka/ [koˈka] 'bush, jungle'
f. /onak/ [oˈnak] 'his/her mother'

The voiced plosives only occur word-initially or medially (3). Besides this distributional restriction, their frequency is also markedly lower than that of voiceless plosives. They are not utilized in the derivational or inflectional morphology, except in reduplication. There is voicing harmony affecting the plosives only: when the first two syllables begin with plosives, both of them are either voiced or voiceless.

(3) a. /bebeta/ [beˈbeta] 'thin'
b. /pepena/ [peˈpena] 'strange'
c. /duduwa/ [duˈduwa] 'blunt'
d. /tutupila/ [tuˈtupila] 'tadpole'
e. /googok/ [ˈgoːgok] 'trevally'
f. /kookalija/ [ˈkoːkalija] 'he/she likes'
g. /boga/ [boˈga] 'barren, empty (land)'
h. /poka/ [poˈka] 'sit down!'
i. /dabela/ [daˈbela] 'cold'
j. /tapaka/ [taˈpaka] 'cake'
k. /gubagel/ [guˈbagel] 'lizard sp.'
l. /kupakup/ [kuˈpakup] 'sago container'

The only exceptions to the voicing harmony are a few words starting with /k/, for instance (4):

(4) a. /kadilam/ [kaˈdilam] 'leech'
   b. /kibol/ [kiˈbol] 'stinging anemone'
   c. /kuben/ [kuˈben] 'prawn trap'

The two NASALS occur word-initially, medially and finally, and contrast as to bilabial and alveolar points of articulation (5).

(5) a. /manar/ [maˈnar] 'forehead decoration'
   b. /nanar/ [naˈnar] 'story'
   c. /moma/ [moˈma] 'taro'
   d. /mona/ [moˈna] 'fruit species'
   e. /onam/ [oˈnam] 'I did'
   f. /onan/ [oˈnan] 'you did'

The FRICATIVES contrast as to bilabial/labio-dental and alveolar points of articulation (6). They are both voiceless. The voiceless bilabial fricative /ɸ/ [ɸ] occurs word-initially and medially, the alveolar grooved fricative /s/ [s] occurs word-initially, -medially and -finally.

(6) a. /ɸariar-/ [ɸaˈriar-] 'abstain'
   b. /sariar-/ [saˈriar-] 'get well'
   c. /kosija/ [koˈsija] 'it comes out of mouth'
   d. /koɸija/ [koˈɸija] 'he hammers'
   e. /kawus/ [kaˈwus] 'smoke'

A possible reason for the restricted distribution of /ɸ/ is that it is a result of a sound change, which is discussed at the end of the consonant section.

The voiced alveolar TRILL /r/ [r] occurs in free variation with the voiced alveolar flap [ɾ] word-initially, -medially and -finally (7).

(7) a. /rowirow/ [roˈwirow] ~ [ɾoˈwiɾow] 'giant clam'
   b. /ewar/ [eˈvar] ~ [eˈvaɾ] 'west wind'

The voiced alveolar LATERAL /l/ [l] occurs word-initially, -medially and -finally (8).

(8) a. /lali/ [laˈli] 'small reef fish'
   b. /kaul/ [ˈkaul] 'hook'

In many Papuan languages [l] and [r] are allophones of the same phoneme, but in Mauwake they are separate phonemes, contrasting with each other (9):

(9) a. /liilin-/ [liːlin-] 'sting, smart (v.)'
 b. /riirin-/ [ˈriːrin] ~ [ˈriːɾin-] 'quarrel (v.)'
 c. /kalan-/ [kaˈlan-] 'have nausea'
 d. /karan-/ [kaˈran] ~ [kaˈɾan-] 'shake'
 e. /nanal/ [naˈnal] 'tree sp.'
 f. /nanar/ [naˈnar] 'story'

Yet in a few words the two fluctuate (10). This seems to be a dialectal difference.

(10) a. /eliwa/ [eˈliva] ~ [eˈriva] 'good'
 b. /saliwija/ [saˈlivija] ~ [saˈrivija] '(s)he heals/repairs'

There are two approximants, or SEMIVOWELS: [w] and [j]. They are interpreted as consonants when occurring in syllable onset or coda, and as vowels when forming part of the syllable nucleus.

The alveo-palatal semivowel /j/ [j] occurs word-initially and -medially. The voiced alveo-palatal grooved fricative [ʒ] is used instead of [j] in the inland (Papur) and Ulingan dialects (11).

(11) a. /jakiya/ [jaˈkija] ~ [ʒaˈkiʒa] '(s)he bathes'
 b. /jaisow/ [ˈjaisow] ~ [ˈʒaisow] 'I alone'

The bilabial semivowel /w/ has the following allophones (12):

- [w] the voiced bilabial semivowel occurs next to a rounded vowel, fluctuating with [v] when between a preceding unrounded and a following rounded vowel;
- [v] the voiced labio-dental frictionless continuant occurs elsewhere;
- [β] the voiced bilabial fricative occurs fluctuating with both [w] and [v] in the inland (Papur) dialect, very strongly in the village of Yeipamir.

(12) a. /wowosa/ [woˈwosa] ~ [βoˈβosa] 'bud'
 b. /now/ [now] ~ [noβ] 'stonefish'
 c. /kuwiwi/ [kuˈwiwi] ~ [kuˈβiβi] 'blue-lined surgeonfish'
 d. /iwoka/ [iˈwoka]~[iˈvoka]~[iˈβoka] 'yam'
 e. /iwera/ [iˈvera] ~ [iˈβera] 'coconut'
 f. /elew/ [eˈlev] ~ [eˈleβ][1] 'in-law'

The reasons for analyzing the semivowels as consonants are as follows:

---

[1] All these different optional allophonic variations of /w/ are not listed in the phonetic representations below, unless relevant to the discussion in the main text of the section. The same applies to the variation of /ɸ/, /r/ and /j/.

- There are no unambiguous 3-vowel sequences word-initially;
- Both the semivowels have a fricative allophone;
- There are no unambiguous glides starting with a mid vowel;
- The geminate non-high vowels only occur in initial syllables;
- If they were interpreted as vowels, the stress pattern of some words would not follow the otherwise exceptionless stress placement rule.

(13) a. /wiwisa/ [viˈvisa] ~ [βiˈβisa] 'murky'
b. /jaisow/ [ˈjaisow] ~ [ˈʒaisow] 'I alone'
c. /marew/ [maˈrev] ~ [maˈreβ] 'none'
d. /now/ [now] ~ [noβ] 'stonefish'
e. /jakijem/ [jaˈkijem] ~ [ʒaˈkiʒem] 'I bathe'
f. /uruwa/ [uˈruwa] ~ [uˈruβa] 'loincloth'

The following sets of examples show clear contrasts between the semivowel /w/ and the vowel /u/, and between the semivowel /j/ and the vowel /i/ (14):

(14) a. /wulinija/ [wuˈlinija] 'it shines'
b. /uusakija/ [ˈuːsakija] 'he/she roasts'
c. /wuunija/ [ˈwuːnija] '(wind) blows'
d. /uuwunija/ [ˈuːwunija] '(s)he talks'
e. /wuwusirap [wuˈwusirap] 'name of a month'
f. /lalu/ [laˈlu] 'parrotfish'
g. /diluw/ [diˈluw] ~ [diˈluβ] 'vine sp.'
h. /jena/ [jeˈna] ~ [ʒeˈna] 'my'
i. /jiena/ [jiˈena] ~ [ʒiˈena] 'our'
j. /iina/ [ˈiːna] 'mosquito'
k. /jiija/ [ˈjiːja] ~ [ˈʒiːʒa] '(s)he gives to me'

In a few words a semivowel is adjacent to a homorganic vowel, but such a contrast as above is not available, and the regular syllable patterns and the stress placement rule allow for two or more interpretations. Also, the pronunciation varies slightly from village to village and between individuals. In these cases the decision how to represent the word phonemically is somewhat arbitrary (15).

(15) a. /jaamun/ [ˈjaːmun] ~ [jɪˈamun] 'my/our younger sibling'
b. /jaaja/ [ˈjaːja] ~ [ˈjaija] 'my/our maternal uncle'
c. /waaja/ [ˈwaːja] ~ [ˈwaija] ~ [ˈwuaija] 'pig'
d. /wuija/ [ˈwuija] ~ [ˈwaija] ~ [ˈwuaija] '(s)he puts'

2 Phonology: a brief overview

The BILABIAL consonants contrast word-initially and -medially; those consonants that can occur word-finally contrast in this position too (16).

(16) a. /poka/ [poˈka] 'house post'
b. /boga/ [boˈga] 'empty, barren (land)'
c. /moma/ [moˈma] 'taro'
d. /ɸoma/ [ɸoˈma] 'ashes'
e. /womar/ [woˈmar] 'his cousin'
f. /epa/ [eˈpa] 'place'
g. /bebaura/ [beˈbaura] 'tree sp.'
h. /ema/ [eˈma] 'mountain'
i. /eɸa/ [eˈɸa] 'me'
j. /ewar/ [eˈvar] 'west wind'
k. /orop/ [oˈrop] 'descend.ss.SEQ'
l. /orom/ [oˈrom] 'I descended'
m. /arow/ [aˈrow] 'three'

The ALVEOLAR consonants contrast in word-initial and -medial positions, and those that can occur in word-final position contrast in that position as well (17).

(17) a. /tawowola/ [taˈwowola] 'rubbish'
b. /dabela/ [daˈbela] 'cold'
c. /nabena/ [naˈbena] 'carrying pole'
d. /sawur/ [saˈwur] 'spirit'
e. /raapa/ [ˈraːpa] 'bag'
f. /labuela/ [laˈbuela] 'pawpaw'
g. /otal/ [oˈtal] 'reef'
h. /odaweleka/ [oˈdaweleka] 'gill'
i. /onam/ [oˈnam] 'I did'
j. /osaiwa/ [oˈsaiva] 'bird of paradise'
k. /oraija/ [oˈraija] 'he/she descends'
l. /olal/ [oˈlal] 'fish species'
m. /menat/ [meˈnat] 'tide'
n. /konan/ [koˈnan] 'garfish'
o. /oras/ [oˈras] 'spinefoot (fish)'
p. /nanar/ [naˈnar] 'story'
q. /nanal/ [naˈnal] 'tree sp.'

2.1 Phonemes

The VELAR and ALVEO-PALATAL consonants contrast word-initially and -medially (18). Word-finally /j/ does not occur at all, and /g/ is extremely rare.[2]

(18) a. /kia/ [kɪˈa] 'white'
 b. /gia/ [gɪˈa] 'baby'
 c. /jia/ [jɪˈa] 'us'
 d. /magok/ [maˈgok] 'woven band'
 e. /makak/ [maˈkak] 'brown quail'
 f. /majona/ [maˈjona] 'brown-collared bush turkey'

Both the distributional restrictions of some consonant phonemes and some regular sound correspondences between Mauwake and the related Kaukombaran languages point to earlier sound changes. My tentative suggestion is that the voiced plosives /b/ and /g/[3] in Mauwake became devoiced at some earlier stage, and the present-day voiced plosives are a later development. In the Kaukombaran languages voiced plosives are much more frequent than in Mauwake, and there is a clear sound correspondence between many cognates.[4] Table 2.2 lists seven cognates in four languages. In the comparison the words are listed in phonetic form but without the brackets; the phonemic representation is basically the same.

Table 2.2: Sound correspondences in plosives

Mauwake	Miani	Maia	Pila	
paapa	baba	bab	mbab	'elder sibling'
pok-	bug-	buge-	buge-	'sit'
perek-	bereg-	bered-	buroaind-	'tear (v.)'
kemena	kema	goama	ŋgoama	'inside'
kukusa	gugun		gugut	'shadow, picture'

I suggest that /ɸ/ in Mauwake is a result of a sound change whereby /w/ in certain positions became devoiced and changed into a fricative. This can be seen in the sound correspondences in cognate words in related Kaukombaran languages Table 2.3.[5]

---

[2] There are only 4 occurrences of word-final /g/ in the lexicon of over 3600 words. Those may all be loans from neighbouring languages.
[3] There are too few words with /d/ and /t/ in the sample to make a meaningful comparison, and what data is available does not indicate that they participated in the change.
[4] The Kaukombaran data is from Loeweke & May (1982) and (Z'Graggen 1980).
[5] Note that within the Kaukombaran group there has also been change from /w/ into /b/. Another possibility is that /b/ has first changed into /w/ and further into /ɸ/ in Mauwake, but that seems less likely because there are numerous other words with /b/ which do not participate in this sound change.

31

2 Phonology: a brief overview

Table 2.3: Sound correspondences in bilabial continuants

Mauwake	Miani	Maia	Pila	
aɸila	abir	koawir	kuawir	'grease'
aɸura	ab	kab	kap	'lime'
iɸera	ibor	ibor	iwor	'sea'
uruɸ-	ruw-	uruw-		'see'
ɸar-	bar-	war-		'call'
uɸ-	uw-	ube-	waguwa-	'dance'

2.1.2 Vowels

There is variation in the Papuan languages from the 3-vowel systems in Ndu languages to an 8-vowel system in Vanimo. The basic and a very common one is a 5-vowel system (Foley 1986: 49–54), also the most common worldwide (Maddieson 1984: 126). It is employed by Mauwake as well, and the vowels are the ones that Maddieson (1984: 125) lists as the most common vowels universally (Table 2.4).

Table 2.4: Vowel phonemes

	Front	Central	Back
High	i		u
Mid	e		o
Low		a	

The five vowel phonemes are voiced and oral. They contrast as to front, central and back points of articulation. Front and back vowels also have a high vs. mid contrast. There is only one set of mid vowels in Mauwake, which are phonetically between the IPA higher and lower mid vowels. For the sake of simplicity, I have represented them with the IPA symbols for higher mid vowels, /e/ and /o/.[6] Both the front vowels are unrounded and the back vowels rounded.

The mid vowels could also be analyzed as non-high vowels together with the low central vowel /a/, thus simplifying the chart, since there are no front or back low vowels. That grouping is actually used in §2.3.3, where it simplifies the past tense suffix rule. But the distributional fact that there are no vowel glides beginning with either /e/ or /o/ justifies distinguishing them as a separate group of mid vowels.

---

[6] To distinguish the true mid vowels from higher mid vowels Maddieson (1984: 123) writes them with quote marks: "e" and "o".

2.1 Phonemes

The high vowels /i/ and /u/ have an open allophone, [ɪ] and [ʊ] respectively, following a word-initial consonant and preceding a central vowel /a/ (Rule 19). In other positions they have a more closed allophone [i] and [u] (20). The other vowels do not have allophonic variation.

(19)
V → V / __ V
+high +high +central
+close +open

(20) a. /ikina/ [iˈkina] 'smell'
b. /lali/ [laˈli] 'small fish'
c. /mia/ [mɪˈa] 'body'
d. /uruwa/ [uˈruwa] 'loincloth'
e. /lalu/ [laˈlu] 'parrotfish'
f. /mua/ [mʊˈa] 'man'

The vowels contrast word-initially, -medially and -finally (21):

(21) a. /aɸa/ [aˈɸa] 'flying fox'
b. /eɸa/ [eˈɸa] 'me'
c. /iɸa/ [iˈɸa] 'snake'
d. /oɸa/ [oˈɸa] 'colour'
e. /uɸa/ [uˈɸa] 'swing (n.)'
f. /marari/ [maˈrari] 'temporary (shelter)'
g. /maremuka/ [maˈremuka] 'corn (med.)'
h. /marija/ [maˈrija] '(s)he scrapes'
i. /maroka/ [maˈroka] 'prawn'
j. /saruwa/ [saˈruwa] 'tree sp.'
k. /popoka/ [poˈpoka] 'unripe fruit'
l. /ooke/ [ˈoːke] 'follow him!'
m. /loloki/ [loˈloki] 'plant sp.'
n. /papako/ [paˈpako] 'some'
o. /ooku/ [ˈoːku] 'let's (dual) follow him!'

Phonemic vowel length only occurs in word-initial syllables. Long vowels are interpreted as two vowels of the same quality for the following reasons:

- Other vowel sequences are common in Mauwake;
- The quality of the long and short vowel is the same;
- Economy of description: there are five vowels instead of ten.

Long and short vowels contrast with each other (22):

(22) a. /aasa/ [ˈaːsa] 'canoe'
 b. /asa/ [aˈsa] 'wild *galip* nut'
 c. /peela/ [ˈpeːla] 'rotten'
 d. /pela/ [peˈla] 'leaf'
 e. /kiira/ [ˈkiːra] 'side, shin'
 f. /kira/ [kiˈra] 'wild sugarcane'
 g. /ɸuura/ [ˈɸuːra] 'steep'
 h. /ɸura/ [ɸuˈra] 'knife'

2.1.3 Suprasegmentals: stress and intonation

Since Mauwake is not a tonal language, the only suprasegmentals discussed here are stress and intonation.

2.1.3.1 Stress

Stress is not phonemic in Mauwake, but three degrees of phonetic stress are discernible in a word. Primary stress is marked by greater intensity, higher fundamental frequency and often, but not always, by non-phonemic lengthening of the vowel. An unstressed syllable is considerably weaker, but the vowels still retain their essential quality. A syllable with a secondary stress is weaker than one with primary stress, but stronger than an unstressed syllable. Since stress is a defining factor on the word level, it is discussed further in §2.3.

Stress has a pragmatic function on clause and sentence level. The clausal stress manifests itself in slightly greater loudness and intensity than that of the ordinary word stress, and its default position is the verb or the non-verbal predicate. In a multi-clause sentence the final verb typically receives the strongest clausal stress; this may be called sentence stress if it needs to be distinguished from the clausal stress of the non-final clauses. The position of the clausal stress may be shifted to give added prominence to some element in the clause (§9.2.3). When this is done, the loudness and intensity of the stressed syllable are increased, and non-phonemic lengthening of the vowel may take place.

2.1.3.2 Intonation

The three grammatical units important from the point of view of intonation are a phrase, a (non-final) clause and a sentence. All final clauses are here treated as sentences.

Pitch variations in Mauwake are not very prominent, and in general the register is quite low compared e.g. with English. There is more register variation in the inland than on the coast.

The most common sentence intonation contour is falling. The first stressed syllable is the highest; after it the intonation falls very gradually until the word with the sentence stress, typically the final verb. There is a slight rise at the syllable with the sentence stress, and then a very sharp fall in the terminal contour. This same basic pattern occurs both in statements (23), commands (24), in non-polar questions (26) and certain polar questions (28). In the following examples, the word with the sentence stress is bolded.

(23) [jo mo'ma e'ni-m-i-jem]
I taro eat-NPS-PR.1s
'I (am) eat(ing) taro.'

In commands the intonation contour is very much the same as in a statement, but the pronunciation is phonetically more tense.

(24) [mo'ma e'**nim-eka**]
taro eat-IMP.2p
'Eat (PL) taro!'

In non-polar questions the sentence-final intonation is also falling. The stressed syllable of the question word carries the sentence stress if it is emphasized (25), but often there is only a slightly higher rise than there would be in other words in the same position, and the sentence stress is placed on the stressed syllable of the final verb (26), (27).

(25) ['muːka 'nain **mo'ram** o'mom-i-ja]
boy that1 why cry-Np-PR.3s
'*Why* is that boy crying?'

(26) [maː '**mauwa** e'nim-i-n]
thing what eat-Np-PR.2s
'What are you eating?'

(27) [mʊa '**naːrewe=ke** e'kap-o-k]
man who=CF come-PA-3s
'Who came?'

2 Phonology: a brief overview

The only instance where there can be any rising intonation sentence-finally is a polar question. It is only used when the speaker is uncertain whether the answer is going to be affirmative or negative (28). The rise is on the question clitic =*i*.

(28) ['auwa e'kap-o-k=i]
father come-PA-3s=QM
'Did father come?'

If the speaker strongly expects the answer to agree with the polarity of the question, the intonation is falling (29). Since polar questions are are also marked with a question marker =*i* sentence-finally, a separate intonation pattern is partly redundant.

(29) ['auwa e'kap-o-k=i]
father come-PA-3s=QM
'Did father come?' (Expecting "yes" as an answer.)

The intonation pattern in medial clauses, instead of falling at the end, is either level or slightly rising. The more expected the sequence, the more level the intonation is. In (30) the two clauses are part of an "expectancy chain", because coconuts are scraped only for preparing food. (In the following three examples, the medial and subordinate clauses are bolded rather than the verb of the finite clause.)

(30) [i'wera mu-'ep   maa 'uup-i-nen]
coconut scrape-SS.SEQ food cook-NP-FU.1s
'I will scrape a coconut and cook food.'

But (31) tells about an unexpected event, a person finding a turtle when he had just gone fishing; instead of catching it he might have either chosen to leave it or failed to catch it.

(31) [pon u'ruɸ-ap 'a:w-ep   p-e'kap-e-m]
turtle see-SS.SEQ take-SS.SEQ BPX-come-PA-1s
'I saw a turtle, caught it and brought it (here).'

The rising intonation is more common in subordinate clauses; in conditional clauses (32) it is particularly noticeable. As a rule, the more important the speaker considers the clause as a presupposition for the main clause, the more clearly there is an intonational rise clause-finally.

(32) [iˈɸa uˈruɸ-i-nen=na keˈker oˈp-i-nen]
    snake see-NP-FU.1s=TP fear hold-NPS-FU.1s
    'If I see a snake, I will be afraid.'

A phrase that is fronted as a left-dislocated theme (§9.1) also has a rising intonation at the end of the phrase. The phrase, bolded in (33), occurs at the beginning of the clause. The slash indicates a pause.

(33) [ˈjos=na / oˈwow maˈneka me iˈkiw-i-jem]
    1s.FC=TP village big   not go-NP-PR.1s
    'As for me, I don't go to town.'

In listing, the intonation rises very slightly at the final syllable of each non-final phrase listed, or is retained at the same level as the previous syllable(s) (34).

(34) [ma: uˈnowa seˈsenar-e-m/ oˈwora/ aˈɸura/ eˈpisowa/ aˈria moˈma]
    thing many buy-PA-1s   betelnut lime   tobacco   alright taro
    'I bought many things: betelnut, lime, tobacco and taro.'

A polite way of calling a person, of getting someone's attention, is to call the name or relationship term in such a way that the stressed syllable has a slight rise and a sharp fall in pitch, and following unstressed syllables, if any, have a low pitch (35).

(35) [eˈremena]
    nephew
    'Nephew!'

An impatient or exasperated call, or a call for someone distant, has a different pattern. The voice is louder, the pitch is retained relatively high and level, and the last syllable gets lengthened and, if unstressed, receives a stress almost as strong as that of the stressed syllable (36).

2 Phonology: a brief overview

(36) ['aiteeee]
　　 mother
　　 'Mother!'

Anger is typically expressed by shouting. The intonation stays fairly level, and the sentence is short and produced in a staccato manner.

Disgust or impatience is expressed by sentence-final interjection *yaa* [jaː], which retains a fairly level pitch and can be lengthened considerably (37). An impatient reaction to someone else's words or actions is expressed by sentence-initial interjection *se*, which has a very sharp falling intonation (38).

(37) [iˈkiw-eka jaaaa]
　　 go-IMP.2p INTJ
　　 'Go, for heaven's sake!'

(38) [se naːp ˈme ma-e]
　　 INTJ thus not say-IMP.2s
　　 'Goodness, don't say like that.'

2.1.4 Orthographic symbols

Table 2.5 shows the orthographic symbols for the phonemes. The semivowel /j/ is written as *y* due to the influence of Tok Pisin and English. Because the orthography represents the phoneme inventory so closely, it is the orthographic symbols that are used in the vernacular examples throughout this thesis after the phonology chapter.

Table 2.5: Orthographic symbols for Mauwake phonemes

Consonant phonemes	p	t	k	b	d	g	m	n	ɸ	s	l	r	w	j
Orthographic representation	p	t	k	b	d	g	m	n	f	s	l	r	w	y
Vowel phonemes	i	e	a	o	u									
Orthographic representation	i	e	a	o	u									

2.2 Syllables and phonotactics

2.2.1 Syllable patterns

The syllable in Mauwake consists of one or two vowels forming the nucleus, with optional onset and/or coda of one consonant, cv being by far the most frequent syllable structure.[7] The syllable patterns are given in Table 2.6.

Table 2.6: Syllable patterns

V	VC
CV	CVC
VV	VVC
CVV	CVVC

Any vowel can fill the simple nucleus slot of the syllable. The complex nucleus slot is filled either by a geminate vowel or a diphthong. Diphthongs can occur in non-initial syllables too, but geminate vowels cannot.

Any consonant can fill the onset slot, and all consonants except the voiced plosives, /ɸ/ and /j/ can fill the coda slot of a syllable. The distribution of the voiced plosives and /ɸ/ is also restricted in that they very seldom occur later than in the second syllable of a word and, except for /j/, do not appear in inflectional morphology. Table 2.7 shows the possible distribution of consonants in a syllable.

Table 2.7: Consonant distribution in a syllable

	c	v(v)	c		c	v(v)	c
p	+		+	n	+		+
t	+		+	ɸ	+		−
k	+		+	s	+		+
b	+		−	l	+		+
d	+		−	r	+		+
g	+		−	w	+		+
m	+		+	j	+		−

2.2.2 Vowel sequences

Table 2.8 shows the possible two-vowel sequences in Mauwake. The only possible sequences beginning with either of the two mid vowels are geminate vowels; no other

---

[7] Reesink (1987: 13) gives a short but good overview of syllable-final consonants in a number of TNG languages.

vowel sequences begin with a mid vowel. The other three vowels may combine with any vowel.

Table 2.8: Vowel sequences

ii		ai		ui
ie	ee	ae		ue
ia		aa		ua
io		ao	oo	uo
iu		au		uu

When the second vowel in a vowel sequence is articulatorily the same height or higher than the preceding vowel, the two form a diphthong, i.e., they are part of the same syllable (39).

(39) a. /kae/ [ˈkae] 'my/our grandfather'
      b. /kuina/ [ˈkui.na] 'woodborer'
      c. /aowa/ [ˈao.wa] 'to tie around waist'

When the second vowel is lower than the first, the two vowels form the nuclei of two separate syllables (40).

(40) a. /sier/ [sɪˈer] 'husking stick'
      b. /luaka/ [lʊˈa.ka] 'whitebait'
      c. /kia/ [kɪˈa] 'white'

The high back vowel /u/ is considered lower than the high front vowel /i/, as it behaves similarly to the non-high vowels when following /i/ (41).

(41) /niuk/ [nɪˈuk] 'let them give you'

In an open syllable, all the diphthongs allowed by the language are possible. In a closed syllable, /ao/ is the only diphthong that has not been found; but it is very infrequent in an open syllable too.

Sequences with three vowels are rare: /uau/ and /uai/ are the only ones I have found, and these only occur at morpheme breaks (marked with a hyphen in the examples), and there is a syllable break within the sequence as well (42).[8]

(42) a. /kua-i-jem/ [kʊˈai.jem] 'I build'
      b. /kua-uk/ [kʊˈauk] 'let them build'

---

[8] A syllable break does not need to coincide with a morpheme break; in the examples above it does not.

2.2.3 Consonant sequences

No consonant sequences occur word-initially or -finally. In words with three or more syllables there are some word-medial clusters, which I believe to have resulted from vowel elision. A vowel may be elided from a non-final syllable immediately following a stressed syllable, which is probably the least prominent syllable in the whole word.[9] It is mainly the high vowels that are dropped, since they are the least sonorant (43).

(43) a. /ikemika/ [iˈkemka] 'wound (nn)'
     b. /aakisa/ [ˈaːksa] 'now, today'
     c. /pisikulaw/ [piˈsiklaw] 'grasshopper sp.'

A non-high vowel can also be elided if the adjacent stressed syllable has an identical vowel (44):

(44) a. /kerekenam/ [keˈreknam] 'dollar bird'
     b. /toonowaw/ [ˈtoːnwaw] 'honey eater'

Occasionally vowel elision takes place in a later syllable than that immediately following the stressed syllable (45):

(45) a. /oɸaɸilika/ [oˈɸaɸilka] 'butterfly'
     b. /aakuniwikin/ [aːkuniwkin] 'talk.2/3p.DS'

In some of these words the original vowel can still be perceived in slow pronunciation, but in others it has disappeared. Consequently, phonemic vowel clusters are currently developing in Mauwake,[10] and the distribution of CVC syllables is being extended to include word-medial position as well, and that of VVC and CVVC to include initial position in two-syllable words that have earlier had three syllables (§2.3.2).

No clear rules have been found for the site of the vowel elision, but some tendencies are as follows. Nouns have more elision than verb stems. A vowel is dropped much more often between non-homorganic than homorganic consonants. The voiceless velar plosive /k/ is the most frequent phoneme on either side of the elided vowel.

2.3 Word

2.3.1 Defining a phonological word in Mauwake

A phonological word is defined on the basis of a primary stress. Words are composed of one or more syllables. The number of syllables seldom exceeds ten, but compound words

---

[9] According to Sommerstein (1977: 11) this is a common process in languages.
[10] The present orthography reflects this development in that consonant clusters are written especially 1) where the quality of the elided vowel cannot be established, and/or 2) when the elided form is in very frequent use.

2 Phonology: a brief overview

can be longer. A majority of the words have two or three syllables. Every word has one syllable with a primary stress, and usually one or more unstressed syllables.

In words of two or more syllables, the syllable containing the second vowel is stressed. Thus the first syllable is stressed if it contains a geminate vowel (46a) or a diphthong (46b). In all the other cases the second syllable is stressed (46c). When the stressed syllable is long, the stress falls equally on the whole vowel sequence (46d–e).

(46) a. /aasa/ [ˈaː.sa] 'canoe'
b. /kuija/ [ˈkui.ja] 'it bites'
c. /aɸura/ [a.ˈɸu.ra] 'lime'
d. /siowa/ [si.ˈo.wa] 'dog'
e. /isaimija/ [i.ˈsai.mi.ja] '(s)he heats (food)'

Both derivational and inflectional affixes may receive primary stress provided they are in a position where stress is normally placed (47):

(47) a. /aw-om-e/
[a.ˈwo.me]
weave-BEN-BNFY1.IMP.2s
'weave it for me'
b. /um-o-k/
[u.ˈmok]
die-PA-3s
'(s)he died'

Clitics, on the other hand, never receive stress placement. Grammatically they are words, but phonologically they attach to the preceding word. If the preceding word is monosyllabic and has a short vowel, it still takes the primary stress when a clitic is added. The unmarked pronouns are a case in point: they retain their stress when clitics are added. Some non-phonemic lengthening takes place in the vowel of the pronoun stem (48).

(48) a. /jo=ko/ [ˈjoˑ.ko] 'I (with neutral focus)'
b. /jos=ke/ [ˈjoˑs.ke] 'I (and not someone else)'

Compound words and some reduplicated words also have a secondary stress. In the second (and third) compound of a compound word, that syllable has a secondary stress which in a single word would receive primary stress (49).

(49) a. /soomare-jiawem-ikemik/ [ˈsoːmare-jɪˌawem-iˌkemik] 'we were walking around'
b. /suuw-orom-ikua/ [ˈsuːw-oˌrom-iˌkua] 'he is pushing it down'

In those words where a long initial syllable is reduplicated as a whole, the second syllable is also long and receives a secondary stress (50):

(50) a. /kui-kuisow/ ['kui."kui.sow] 'a few'
      b. /suu-suusia/ ['suː."suː.sia] 'thorny'

2.3.2 Distribution of syllables in a word

All syllable types except vc can form a monosyllabic word. In polysyllabic words, the occurrence of a certain syllable type is determined by both its position in the word and the stress.

Table 2.9 shows what syllable types occur in which positions in a word. A blank space indicates that the syllable type does not occur in that particular word position at all, and parentheses indicate a rare occurrence. Double parentheses indicate new positions for closed syllables formed as a result of vowel elision (see §2.2.3). "2nd" indicates the second non-final syllable, and "3rd-" stands for the third or later non-final syllable in a polysyllabic word.

Table 2.9: Distribution of syllable types

Syllable type	Stressed syllables			Unstressed syllables				The only syllable
	Initial	2nd	Final	Initial	2nd	3rd-	Final	
v		+	+	+		+	+	+
cv		+	+	+	+	+	+	+
vv	+	(+)	(+)			(+)	+	+
cvv	+	+	(+)			+		+
vc			+				+	
cvc		((+))	+	((+))	((+))	+		+
vvc	((+))		+				+	+
cvvc	((+))		+				+	+

Some distributional characteristics can be summarised as follows. The most frequent syllable type, cv, also has the widest distribution: a stressed initial syllable is the only position where it cannot occur, as an initial syllable with a single short vowel is always unstressed. The same reason accounts for the absence of v syllables in the same position. v syllables also never occur after a geminate vowel or diphthong, so they cannot occupy the second unstressed syllable position. A vv syllable in medial or final position is possible but very rare. The two previous statements may be combined to make the claim that there is some resistance towards vvv sequences in Mauwake. The syllables with a consonant coda only occur word finally, except where vowel elision has changed the syllable structure.

---

[10] '2nd' indicates the second non-final syllable, and '3rd-' stands for the third or later non-final syllable in a polysyllabic word.

2 Phonology: a brief overview

2.3.3 Morphophonology

There are not many morphophonological alternations in Mauwake. The most important is the rule system governing the vowel of the past tense suffix and the medial verb same-subject sequential action and simultaneous action suffixes (called the medial verb suffixes[11] in the discussion below). Others include the change in the verbaliser suffix and the form of the completive aspect marker.

2.3.3.1 Elision of word-final vowel

The phoneme /a/ has a very high frequency as the word-final phoneme, particularly in the nouns and adjectives. It accounts for approximately 85% of all the vowel-final words. In normal and fast speech this /a/ is often dropped from an unstressed word-final cv syllable, especially when followed by a word with an initial vowel. The elision rule is in (51) and examples in (52).

(51)   V   → ∅ / c __ # v
        +central
        −stress

(52) a. /koora unowa/ [ˈkoːr uˈnowa] 'many houses'
     b. /takira ɸaara/ [taˈkir ˈɸaːra] 'boys' house'
     c. /siiwa eliwa/ [ˈsiːw eˈliva] 'good/bright moon'
     d. /ikoka uura/ [iˈkok ˈuːra] 'later at night'

In some cases even a stressed /a/ is elided, and the stress moves to the following vowel in the utterance. This mainly happens with the accusative pronouns, which tend towards cliticization (53) (§3.5.3).

(53)   /me neɸa uruɸam/ [ˈme neɸ ˈuruɸam] 'I didn't see you'

In compound words the final /a/ is dropped from the first constituent even when the second begins with a consonant, except when the final syllable of the first constituent is stressed (54).

(54) a. /aara muuka/ [ˈaːr ˈmuːka] 'chick'
     b. /emera tapaka/ [eˈmer taˈpaka] 'sago cake'
     c. /mera soo/ [meˈra ˈsoː] 'fish trap'

2.3.3.2 Reduplication

There are various patterns of reduplication in Mauwake. With a few exceptions, reduplication takes place at the beginning of the word. The meaning involves plurality in

---

[11] There are also other medial verb suffixes, which are not affected by these morphophonological rules.

one way or another; with verbs it indicates repeated action and/or the object of the action ending up in several pieces. Occasionally with adjectives it also indicates enhanced quality (§3.3).

How a word is reduplicated can to some extent be predicted from the phonological shape of the word. Type 1 below is the most common, 2 and 3 are the only possible ones for the words with a short and a long initial vowel respectively. Reduplication process does not always respect syllable boundaries.

2.3.3.2.1 Type 1 Everything up to and including the first vowel of the stressed syllable is reduplicated. Even with the reduplication these words retain the normal stress pattern: the second syllable of the reduplicated form is stressed, because regardless of whether one or two syllables are reduplicated the first syllable in this type is always short. When two of syllables are reduplicated, the originally stressed syllable of the word root gets a secondary stress (55).

(55) a. /pu-puukija/ [pu.ˈpuː.ki.ja] 'cut into pieces'
      b. /pu-puija/ [pu.ˈpui.ja] 'break into pieces'
      c. /pere-perekija/ [pe.ˈre.pe.ˌre.ki.ja] 'tear into pieces'
      d. /kiri-kiripija/ [ki.ˈri.ki.ˌri.pi.ja] 'turn round & round, mix'
      e. /mane-maneka/ [ma.ˈne.ma.ˌne.ka] '(many) big (things)'

2.3.3.2.2 Type 2: $v_1c_1v_1 - v_1c_1v_2c_2v(v_3)x$ In the words of the second type, the reduplication repeats the initial vowel and consonant of the word root, adding another vowel of the same quality after the consonant. In these words the stress shifts from the second syllable of the root to the final vowel of the reduplicated element. Phonetically this vowel usually merges into one with the following vowel, which always has the same quality (56). Stresswise this creates an interesting pattern, where a syllable with a primary stress is followed by one with secondary stress. Types 3 and 4 also have this kind of stress pattern.

(56) a. /ele-eliwa/ [e.ˈle.ˌli.wa] '(many) good (things)'
      b. /ara-arow/ [a.ˈra.ˌrow] 'in threes'
      c. /oko-okaiwi/ [o.ˈko.ˌkai.wi] 'this side and that'

2.3.3.2.3 Type 3: $v_1v_1c_1 - v_1v_1c_1v_2x$ A very small group of words has this type of reduplication, where the initial geminate vowel and the following consonant are reduplicated. The result is a word where both the first and the second syllable have a complex nucleus, a word type not allowed in the simple non-reduplicated words. In these reduplicated words the first syllable receives primary stress and the second syllable secondary stress. The first syllable has a syllable pattern (vvc) which is not possible for the first syllable in a non-reduplicated polysyllabic word (57).

(57) a. /iiw-iiwa/ [ˈiːv.ˌiː.va] '(many) short (things)'
      b. /iin-iinan/ [ˈiːn.ˌiː.nan] '(the things) high up'

2.3.3.2.4 Type 4: $C_1V_1V_2 - C_1V_1V_2X$

In this type the long first syllable is repeated entirely, but nothing else. The two vowels in the initial syllable may be identical or different in quality (58). This is not a very common pattern.

(58) a. /kui-kuisow/ [ˈkui.ˈˈkui.sow] 'a few'

   b. /soo-soomarija/ [ˈsoː.ˈˈsoː.ma.ri.ja] 'amble, stroll'

2.3.3.2.5 Unusual reduplications

The word *gelemuta* 'small' has two unusual reduplicated forms, where the end of the word is changed: *gelemutitik* and *gelemutumut* '(many) small (things)'. Type 1 reduplication rule can also be applied to these already reduplicated forms, although not to the root (59).

(59) a. /gele-gelemutitik/ [ge.ˈle.ge.ˈˈle.mu.ti.tik] 'very small (pl.)'

   b. */gele-gelemuta/

The verb *wafuriya* 'throw' also has an irregular reduplicated form: only the second syllable is reduplicated (60).

(60) /waɸuɸurija/ [va.ˈɸu.ɸu.ri.ja] 'throw around'

The reduplication for the word *owowa* 'village' occurs at the beginning of the word, but it does not follow any of the patterns above (61). So far it is the only one of its kind found.

(61) /owow-owowa/ [o.ˈwo.wo.ˈˈwo.wa] '(many/all) villages'

Mauwake has a number of nouns of the following the pattern $C_1V_1C_2V_2\ C_1V_1C_2$, which looks like reduplication, but with the word-final vowel deleted. However, these words do not have any semantic relationship with a corresponding $C_1V_1C_2V_2$ word in cases where the latter may exist. Words of this type are not considered to have resulted from reduplication (62).

(62) a. /mulamul/ [muˈlamul] 'trevally'

   b. /jawejaw/ [jaˈvejav] 'hunting magic'

Similarly, words of the pattern $C_1V_1C_1V_1C_2V_2$ are not considered reduplicated forms (63). Firstly, there is no semantic relationship with a corresponding $C_1V_1C_2V_2$ word, even if the latter exists. Secondly, in Mauwake there is a very strong tendency to have the same vowel in the first two syllables of trisyllabic or longer words, whether the consonant is the same or not.

(63) a. /momora/ [moˈmo.ra] 'fool(ish)'

   b. /sisina/ [siˈsi.na] 'edge'

2.3.3.3 Past tense and medial verb suffixes

There are three past tense verb suffixes for second and third person singular forms, -*a*, -*e* and -*o*. Which one is chosen for which verb is determined mainly by the phonemes in the stem final syllable.[12]

The two basic allomorphs for the past tense suffix are {-a} and {-E}. /-o/ is a subgroup of the allomorph {-E}. The subgrouping is based on the fact that the -*a*/-*e* distinction runs through the whole past tense paradigms and occurs in the medial verb suffixes as well, whereas the -*e*/-*o* distinction only occurs in the second and third person past tense forms of some verbs. According to the rounding rule below (64), {-E} is realized as /-o/ when both following a [+ labial] phoneme (either a labial consonant or the high rounded vowel /u/) and preceding a non-labial consonant (65).

(64)   {E} > /o/ / X $_{LAB}$ __ C$_{NON-LAB}$

(65)   a. /aaw-o-k/ '(s)he got (it)' cf. /aaw-e-m/ 'I got (it)'
       b. /mu-o-n/ 'you swallowed' cf. /mu-e-m/ 'I swallowed'

The discussion below only mentions the past tense suffixes. The vowels in the the medial verb suffixes are the same but do not have the allophonic variation between /-e/ and /-o/.

The morphophonological rules governing the choice of past tense suffixes are listed in their order of relative strength, with regard to the number of cases in the data[13] as well as the number of exceptions.

(66)   RULE 1. With a stem-final high vowel /i/ or /u/, the past tense suffix is always {-E} (67).

(67)   a. /waki-e-k/ '(s)he fell down'
       b. /nepi-e-k/ '(s)he raised animals'
       c. /mu-o-k/ '(s)he swallowed'
       d. /karu-o-k/ '(s)he ran'

(68)   RULE 2. With a stem-final alveolar nasal /n/, the suffix is nearly always /-e/ (69).

(69)   a. /kekan-e-k/ 'it hardened'
       b. /peren-e-k/ 'it tore'
       c. /riirin-e-k/ '(s)he laughed'
       d. /solon-e-k/ 'it glided'
       e. /uuwun-e-k/ '(s)he chatted'

---

[12] Most of these rules were originally worked out by Kwan Poh San.
[13] The count included 273 verbs with the past tense suffix -*a*, 364 with the suffix -*e*.

2 Phonology: a brief overview

In the data there are 128 verb stems ending in /n/, and only 15 take the suffix {-a}. In some cases there is a conflict between rules 2 and 3 (below), and 13 of those exceptions follow Rule 3.

(70) RULE 3. When the stem final syllable has a low vowel, there is dissimilation between the vowels in the stem final syllable and the past tense suffix. For these morphophonological rules the mid vowels are also considered low, so that there is height distinction only between high and low vowels.

(71)
$$X \quad \underset{\substack{+\text{low}\\ \alpha\text{ central}}}{V} \quad (C) \quad + \quad \underset{\substack{+\text{low}\\ -\alpha\text{ central}}}{V}$$

The past tense suffix tends to be {-a}, when the last vowel in the stem is /e/ or /o/ (72).

(72) a. /aner-a-k/ '(s)he aimed at'
  b. /sirek-a-k/ 'it scratched'
  c. /imen-a-k/ '(s)he found'
  d. /on-a-k/ '(s)he did/made'
  e. /soop-a-k/ '(s)he buried'

In words with /a/ as the last vowel in the stem, the past tense suffix tends to be {-E} (73).[14]

(73) a. /serak-e-k/ '(s)he wiped'
  b. /war-e-k/ '(s)he killed it'
  c. /ma-e-k/ '(s)he said'
  d. /ekap-o-k/ '(s)he came'
  e. /aaw-o-k/ '(s)he got/took'

(74) RULE 4. When a high vowel is followed by a stem-final consonant /k/, /t/, /s/, /r/ or /l/, the past tense suffix is {-a}. This group of consonants includes nearly all of the non-labial consonant phonemes; /n/ is handled in Rule 2, the voiced stops never occur stem-finally and /j/ hardly ever does (75).

(75) a. /puuk-a-k/ '(s)he cut'
  b. /mik-a-k/ '(s)he speared'
  c. /itit-a-k/ '(s)he smashed'
  d. /anetir-a-k/ '(s)he tied'
  e. /ɸuur-a-k/ '(s)he blew'
  f. /aɸilil-a-k/ 'it was sweet'

---

[14] In the data there are 187 verbs that follow this rule and 19 that do not.

2.3 Word

With the rest of the verbs, i.e. total of about 25% of all the basic verbs, it is very difficult to find any rules governing the choice of the past tense suffix (76).

(76)   a. /tiim-a-k/ '(s)he touched'
      b. /aruɸ-a-k/ '(s)he hit'
      c. /oosip-o-k/ '(s)he sweated'
      d. /ɸiririm-o-k/ '(s)he squeezed'
      e. /uɸ-o-k/ '(s)he danced'
      f. /iw-o-k/ '(s)he gave him/her'

A few verbs apparently have dropped the past tense suffix altogether. Most of these have the stem ending in the vowel sequence /ua/ (77):

(77)   a. /kua-Ø-k/ 'he built'
      b. /wua-Ø-k/ '(s)he put'
      c. /piipua-Ø-k/ '(s)he left'

Another verb where the past tense suffix vowel seems to have disappeared is /oro-Ø-k/ '(s)he went down'. If the second vowel were to be taken as the suffix this verb would defy the basic rules, since the vowel /o/ is retained right through the past tense paradigm, and with the root vowel /o/ the suffix should be {-a}. Positing /oro-/ as the root solves the question why the present tense form is /ora-/: since /oi/ is not a permitted vowel sequence on Mauwake, the low back vowel /o/ has changed into the low central vowel /a/ when preceding the high front vowel /i/ of the present tense suffix.

The verbs in the Mauwake dictionary are marked as belonging to Class 1 or Class 2, the former taking {-a} and the latter {-ɛ} as the past tense suffix. This is because of the following reasons: 1) the rules are rather complicated, 2) there are a number of exceptions to the main rules, and 3) there are pairs of homophonous verb roots that take a different past tense suffix each (78).

(78)   a. /iw-a-k/ '(s)he went'
      b. /iw-o-k/ '(s)he gave him/her'
      c. /miim-a-k/ '(s)he heard'
      d. /miim-o-k/ '(s)he preceded'
      e. /op-a-k/ '(s)he held'
      f. /op-o-k/ 'it boiled'
      g. /keen-a-k/ 'it touched'
      h. /keen-e-k/ 'it was hot'

2.3.3.4 Inchoative suffix

The verbalizer for both adjectives and nouns is the inchoative suffix {-aʀ}, the root of the verb 'to become' (§3.8.2.2.2). In most environments it is realized as /-ar/, but becomes /-al/ when the last syllable of the root contains the lateral consonant /l/ (79). An illustrative example is the word *samora/damola* 'bad', which takes a different verbalizer depending on the root allomorph.

(79) a. /supuk-**ar**-e-k/ 'it got wet'
     b. /duduw-**ar**-e-k/ 'it became blunt'
     c. /samor-**ar**-e-k/ 'it broke/spoiled'
     d. /damol-**al**-e-k/ 'it broke/spoiled'
     e. /memel-**al**-e-k/ 'it became tame'
     f. /masi-**al**-e-k/ 'it became bitter'

In a few cases the inchoative suffix has the form /-al/ although there is no lateral consonant in the root. This might be expected, since there is some fluctuation between the liquids /l/ and /r/ in Mauwake: /eliwa/ ~ /eriwa/ 'good', /samora/ ~ /damola/ 'bad'.[15]

2.3.3.5 Completive aspect marker

The completive aspect marker (§3.8.5.1.1.1) has its origin in the verb for 'put', *wua-*,[16] but this connection has by now become opaque and the speakers consider it a morpheme on its own, *pu-* (80). The initial /p/ results from assimilation with the final /p/ of the same-subject sequential action medial verb form obligatorily preceding the completive morpheme.

(80) *en-ep*   *wu-a-k*   > *enep-pu-a-k*
     eat-ss.seq put-pa-3s > eat-ss.seq-cmpl-pa-3s
     '(s)he ate'

2.3.4 Loan words

When words are borrowed from other languages, they are usually made to conform to the Mauwake phonology, if they do not originally do so. Thus Tok Pisin *kikim* 'kick' becomes *kiikim-* in Mauwake; the word retains the original Tok Pisin word-initial stress, and the vowel in the first syllable becomes a geminate. The initial glottal fricative /h/ in the original becomes a lengthened vowel in Mauwake, e.g. Tok Pisin *handet* 'hundred' changes into *aandet* in Mauwake.

The only non-native phoneme regularly retained in the loan word is the velar nasal /ŋ/, particularly prominent in the neighbouring language, Mala, and also used in personal names (81):

---

[15] In Trans New Guinea, as well as other Papuan, languages it is also very common to have only one liquid, with /l/ and /r/ as allophones of the same phoneme (Wurm 1982: 55, Foley 1986: 55).

[16] The verb 'put' is commonly used as a completive aspect marker in Papuan languages (§3.8.5.1.1.1).

(81) /nadiŋ-ar-e-k/ '(s)he decorated him/herself'

Since consonant sequences are quite rare in Mauwake, loan words with consonant clusters tend to have vowels inserted between the consonants. With the ever-growing influence of Tok Pisin, vowel insertion is getting less common. A combination of a nasal plus a homorganic stop is always retained in a loan word (Table 2.10).

Table 2.10: Loanwords with a combination of nasal plus homorganic stop.

Tok Pisin	Mauwake	English
glas	*galas*	*glass*
trinde	*tirinde*	*Wednesday*
namba	*naamba*	*number*
handet	*aandet*	*hundred*

3 Morphology

3.1 Introduction

A grammatical word in Mauwake is defined on the basis of the following main criteria quoted from Dixon (2010b: 12–14):
A grammatical word

- has as its base one or more lexical roots to which morphological processes apply;
- has a conventionalized coherence and meaning.

When a grammatical word involves compounding or affixation, its component grammatical elements

- always occur together;
- generally occur in a fixed order

The following supplementary criteria also apply: a word only allows one inflectional affix of any one type (ibid. 15), and in derivation recursiveness is blocked except in the case of causatives (ibid. 16–17). Even here the recursion is more ostensible than real, as it does not add another argument into the clause (§3.8.2.3.1). Person/number suffixes act as word-final boundary markers in finite verbs (ibid. 17). Many words, especially those belonging to the major word classes, "may constitute a complete utterance" (ibid. 19) by themselves.

The boundaries of the grammatical and phonological words coincide, except in the case of clitics. Grammatically a clitic is a word but phonologically it is bound to the preceding word.

The classes of nouns, adjectives, personal pronouns, quantifiers, verbs and adverbials can be reasonably clearly defined both morpho-syntactically and semantically. The classes of question words and deictics include words with heterogeneous syntactic behaviour; question words have semantic and functional, and some morphological similarities as a group, whereas the category of deictics is based on strong morphological and semantic similarities. Connectives share the function of conjoining elements on the same level. As "functor words" postpositions and especially clitics are dependent on the preceding phrase. Interjections are different from all the other word classes in that they operate outside the normal syntax and often constitute a whole expression by themselves.

3 Morphology

Nouns are naturally the largest category, but verbs are morphologically the most complex and interesting word class.

Although the great majority of the words in Mauwake can be assigned to one of the categories above, there is some indeterminacy with regard to some words that seem to belong to two or more word classes and the meanings of which are clearly related.[1] They are not homonyms, since they are semantically related. Some transitive verbs have been derived by zero derivation from nouns and adjectives, and even from adverbs (§§3.8.2.2.1, 3.8.4.4.3). Nominalized verbs (§3.2.6.1) function as nouns or adjectives. At the end of (§3.2.2) there is a list of words that are originally nouns but have become adjectives as well. Some non-numeral quantifiers (§3.4.2) also function as intensity adverbs (§3.9.2). Besides these, there are individual words that function in more than one word class; these are mentioned where they occur.

3.2 Nouns

3.2.1 General discussion

Although the traditional semantic definition of the noun as the "name of a person, place or thing" is not valid as a basis for assigning members to the class, it still gives a good general description of the prototypical members of the class in Mauwake. In Frawley's (1992: 63) words, "when the traditional definition is reversed, the definition turns out to be true. Nouns are not always persons, places or things, but persons, places and things always turn out to be nouns."[2] Recognizing the semantic motivation of the class does not eliminate the need to define the class by its formal or functional properties.

No good morphological definition of nouns is possible in Mauwake, as there is no inflection for number (1), gender or class,[3] or case, in the noun itself. Especially the lack of plural marking is typical of the nouns in Trans-New Guinea languages (Wurm 1982: 36). The glosses in (1) indicate a singular/plural alternative in the nouns, but the singular form in the glosses of other examples is to be understood as neutral regarding number.

(1) siowa wiawi
     dog(s) father(s)
     'The dog's/dogs' owner(s)'

Nouns are usually monomorphemic, with the exception of a small group of inalienably possessed nouns (§3.2.4), nouns derived from verbs (§3.2.6.1), reduplicated nouns (§3.2.6.2) and compound nouns (§3.2.5). The division into COUNT and MASS nouns is not very noticeable. It is mainly shown in the choice between the quantifiers *unowa* 'many' and *maneka* 'big, much', and to some extent in verb agreement morphology (§3.4).

---

[1] In Austronesian languages it is common to have pre-categorial stems that may combine with affixation belonging to various word classes; only the whole word may be assigned to a particular word class.

[2] See also Sapir (1921: 117), Jespersen (1924: 60), Lyons (1977: 449) and Schachter (1985: 7).

[3] Gender or class systems are widespread in Papuan languages (Foley 1986: 77). Especially in the TNG languages a covert system is common (Wurm 1982: 58), where the noun class determines what existential verb is used with each noun.

The syntactic function provides the best criterion for defining a noun in Mauwake. Nouns function mainly as the head of a noun phrase, often the head being the only element in the NP.[4] They can also function as a qualifier or, more rarely, as a modifier in a NP. In (2), the NPs function as subject and object, and are manifested by just nouns.

(2) *Emeria=ke iwera fiirim-i-mik.*
woman=CF coconut gather-Np-PR.1/3p

'(The) women gather coconuts.'

Hopper & Thompson (1984: 710) also maintain that "from the discourse point of view, nouns function to introduce participants and 'props' and to deploy them."[5] This is true in Mauwake as well, but it is not used as a criterion for defining the nouns.

3.2.2 Nouns and adjectives: one or two word classes?

Since adjectives in Mauwake are phonologically, morphologically and syntactically very similar to nouns, the question must be asked whether the two form just one class of nominals or whether they belong to two separate word classes. In the following discussion they are treated on a semantic basis as if they were separate classes, i.e. certain words are called nouns and others adjectives, but a final conclusion as to their status is not drawn until the end of the section.

A PHONOLOGICALLY interesting feature common to nouns and adjectives is that the majority of both end in the vowel <a>.[6] Inside noun phrases this vowel, when unstressed, is usually elided preceding a vowel and often also preceding a consonant. In cases like (3), where there are two or more possible places for elision, the vowel most easily drops at the end of an adjective preceding an intensifier. Elision is also acceptable in two or more sites within one NP; this is shown in (3) and (4).

(3) *koora eliw(a) akena* also: *koor(a) eliw(a) akena*
house good very

'a very good house'

(4) *koor(a) kemena manek(a) akena nain*
house inside big very that1

'the very big room'

MORPHOLOGICALLY, nouns and adjectives resemble each other in that they lack inflection. There is no number, case, or gender marking in the adjectives, nor is there any inflection for comparison. (For comparison of adjectives, see §6.5.)

Both nouns (5) and adjectives (6) may be derived from verbs with the nominalizer suffix *-owa*.

---

[4] Sometimes an adjective, a quantifier or a genitive pronoun looks like a head of a NP, but those cases are elliptical, and the head noun is recoverable.
[5] Actually this is the function of a NP rather than a noun.
[6] In the other word classes words ending in <a> do occur but they are very infrequent.

3 Morphology

(5) mua **soop-owa** sira
man bury-NMZ custom
'the burial custom (lit: the custom of burying men)'

(6) Emi **kekan-owa** nain puuk-a-mik.
taboo be.strong-NMZ that1 cut-PA-1/3p
'They broke the strong taboo rule.'

Verbs can be derived from both adjectives and nouns by zero verb formation (7), (8) or by the inchoative verbalizer -ar (1). (See §3.8.2.2 for these processes and more examples.)

(7) Miiw-aasa samor-a-k.
land-canoe bad-PA-3s
'He broke/ruined the car.'

(8) Iwer(a) ififa palis-i-ya.
coconut dry pair.of.coconuts-NPS-PR.3s
'He is tying dry coconuts into pairs.'

(9) Miiw-aasa samor-ar-e-k.
land-canoe bad-INCH-PA-3s
'The car broke.'

A clear morphological DIFFERENCE between nouns and adjectives is that adverbs may be formed from some adjectives by deleting the word-final <a> (10), but they cannot be formed from nouns in the same way.

(10) samora > samor
'bad' 'badly'

SYNTACTICALLY, there are a few similarities between nouns and adjectives. Both can function as a modifier following the head noun in a NP, although adjectives (11) are much more common in this position. In Hopper & Thompson's (1985: 161) terms, it is nouns whose categorial status has been reduced, i.e. nouns that are not fully individuated in the discourse (12), that can function in this modifier position.

(11) aasa **awona** fain
canoe old this
'this old canoe'

(12) mua **sira** eliwa
man manner good
'a well-mannered man (=a good man)'

The intensifier akena 'real(ly), very' can also modify both adjectives (3) and nouns (13).

(13) *mua **akena***
    man real/true
    'a real man'

Complete or partial reduplication of adjectives is a common strategy for indicating plurality in Austronesian languages (Wurm 1982: 62), and it also occurs to some extent in many Papuan languages, including Mauwake. Reduplication is a more productive process in the adjectives (14), (15), but it is possible for a few nouns too (16), (17) (§3.2.6.2).

(14) *ifa   samo-samora*
    snake RDP-bad
    'bad snakes'

(15) *Maa   ele-eliwa sesek-a-mik.*
    thing/food RDP-good sell-PA-1/3p
    'They sold good foods (different kinds).'

(16) ***Owow-owowa** ikiw-e-mik.*
    RDP-village   go-PA-1/3p
    'They went to many villages.'

(17) ***sira-sira***
    custom-custom
    'many customs', 'different kinds'

The syntactic DIFFERENCES between nouns and adjectives are as follows. Adjectives do not function as head of a noun phrase. The cases where they would seem to do so are in fact cases of ellipsis, and the head noun must be recoverable from the context, either linguistic or extra-linguistic (18).

(18) *Ø awona nain p-ekap-e!*
    Ø old   that1 BPX-come-IMP.2s
    'Bring the old one!'

Only a noun may occur as a qualifier in a noun phrase, preceding the head noun (19). In some of these cases it is difficult to decide whether they are really NPs with a qualifier and a head noun, or compound nouns. But if the latter is the case, then the restriction applies that an adjective cannot be the first element in a compound noun.

(19) ***mera** eka*
    fish water
    'fish soup'

(20) *[[**mera eka**] en-owa] sira*
     fish water eat-NMZ custom
    'the custom of eating fish soup'

3 Morphology

An adjective cannot be the only element following a genitive pronoun, but a noun can. Even in elliptical expressions an adjective following a genitive pronoun is not very acceptable (21).

(21)　? *Yiena*　Ø ***awona*** *nain p-ekap-e!*
　　　　1p.GEN Ø old　　that1 BPX-come-IMP.2s
　　　　'Bring our old one(s)!'

An exception to this rule is the adjective *maneka* 'big' (22). The expression *yiena Maneka* 'our Lord' (literally: our Big one), is probably formed following Tok Pisin *Bikpela bilong yumi*.[7]

(22)　*wi*　　*Amerika **maneka**, unuma Magerka*
　　　　3p.UNM America big　　　name MacArthur
　　　　'the leader of the Americans, whose name was MacArthur'

Only an adjective functions as the head of an adjective phrase. In that position it may be modified by intensity adverbs (§3.9.2). Of these, *lawisiw* 'rather' does not modify nouns at all (23); *akena* 'very' and *pepek* 'enough' may modify nouns as well; *wenup* 'very' can do that too, but as a noun modifier it has a somewhat restricted use and a different meaning: 'many'.

(23)　*Mera nain **lawisiw** maneka akena.*
　　　　fish that1 rather　big　　very
　　　　'That fish is rather huge.'

What further obscures the area of nouns and adjectives is the fact that there are a number of words that sometimes function like nouns (24), sometimes like adjectives (25), and that also semantically could be like either.

(24)　***Pina***　*maneka kamenap?*
　　　　weight big　　what.like
　　　　'What is the weight like?', 'How big is the weight?'

(25)　*Maa　nain lawisiw **pina**.*
　　　　thing that1 rather　heavy
　　　　'The thing is rather heavy.'

The prototype view offers a plausible solution for the problem. Starting from the study of basic colour terms (Berlin & Kay 1969) it has been applied to other areas of semantics and also to linguistic categorization (e.g. Wierzbicka 1986; Taylor 1989 and Frawley 1992). The main idea that categories have more central, or focal, members as well as more

---

[7] Non-prototypical adjectives are discussed later in this section; 'big' is a prototypical adjective, so its use in a typically nominal position is an exception.

marginal members was also recognized by Crystal (1967) in his description of English word classes. The prototype approach allows for stability as well as flexibility (Taylor 1989: 53), both of which are needed in an attempt to describe a human language.

If prototypical linguistic categories are focal, or optimal, instances on a continuum (Seiler 1978: 321) and maximally distinct from one another (Hopper & Thompson 1984: 709), what are prototypical nouns like as opposed to prototypical adjectives? According to Wierzbicka (1986), a noun indicates CATEGORIZATION: most prototypical nouns identify a certain kind of person, thing or animal. Relative TEMPORAL STABILITY is for Givón what characterizes nouns, and the most prototypical nouns denote concrete, physical, compact entities (1984: 151). Instead of time stability, Frawley (1992: 66) claims it is relative ATEMPORALITY that makes an entity an entity. Adjectives, or property concepts, indicate DESCRIPTION, and they denote single properties unlike nouns which denote a cluster of properties (Wierzbicka 1986).

In Mauwake, a prototypical NOUN occurs as a head in a NP, as a pre-modifier or, less frequently, as a post-modifier in a NP, or as any element in a compound noun. It does not occur as the head in an AP. It can be modified by adjectives or genitive pronouns but not by the intensity adverbs *lawisiw* 'rather' and *wenup* 'very'. Prototypical ADJECTIVES occur as the head of an adjective phrase. They do not pre-modify nouns or function as the first element in a compound noun.

It turns out that in Mauwake the most prototypical nouns include names of concrete NON-human rather than human objects, when one would expect words referring to human beings to be nouns *par excellence* (see Taylor 1989: 192). Some human nouns may be used as post-modifiers in a NP: from the cluster of properties denoted by the noun one has been picked out, and the noun is used like an adjective (26), (27). The adjectival use of *mua* 'man' in (26) is particularly interesting, because the adjectives *morena* 'male' and *suwina* 'female' are used for animals.

(26) *labuel(a) mua*
 pawpaw man
 'male pawpaw'

(27) *donki takira*
 donkey young.person
 'young donkey'

The less prototypical status of human nouns also shows in words like *apura* 'widow' and *oosa* 'widower' which may occur by themselves as heads of a NP, but which are most typically used as post-modifiers of *emeria* 'woman' and *mua* 'man', respectively.[8] As age in human beings tends to be treated as a crucial determinant of KIND, even languages with large adjective classes often have special nouns for referring to old persons (Wierzbicka 1986: 368). In Mauwake, adjectives that indicate age in humans are non-prototypical, more noun-like than most adjectives: both *iperowa* 'middle-aged' (28) and *panewowa* 'old' are used as the head of a NP besides the typical adjectival use.

---

[8] Other words in this group are *muupera* 'visitor, guest' and especially *weria*, which as a human noun only occurs in the combination *mua weria*, 'uncle/ male cross cousin/ nephew'. The *mua weria*'s are responsible for burying a dead person and dispensing of his/her belongings (§1.3.6).

(28) ***Iperowa*** opora wiar miim-i-yen.
     middle-aged talk 3.DAT hear-Np-FU.1p
     'We will listen to the talk of the middle-aged (men).'

According to Dixon (1977: 56), if a language has adjectives at all, words expressing age, dimension, value and colour are likely to belong to the adjective class, however small the class. The most prototypical adjectives in Mauwake belong to these groups, with the exception of adjectives denoting human age. In the group of adjectives denoting either physical property or human propensity, some are ambiguous as to their basic category: *anima* is both 'blade' and 'sharp', and *pina* both 'weight, burden' and 'heavy'. Different groups of adjectives, as well as the use of adjectives, are discussed below in §3.3.

With the rules given above it is fairly straightforward to distinguish the nouns and adjectives in Mauwake. But a small group remains that seems to have a membership in both classes. Originally, they are are nouns that are now employed as adjectives as well. The claim is based on the fact that the noun category is the more basic and universally recognized, whereas the existence of the adjective category is disputed in some languages; in Mauwake the noun class is clearly established, large, and more easily definable. Also, there are at least two nouns in Mauwake that currently seem to be in the process of becoming regular adjectives: the meaning of the phrase stays the same with the pre-modifying noun and the post-modifying adjective (29)–(32).

(29) ***napum(a)*** *mua*
     sickness   man
     'a sick man'

(30) *mua* ***napuma***
     man sick
     'a sick man', also: 'human (lit: man's) sickness'

(31) ***wadol(a)*** *opora*
     lie/false talk
     'a lie'

(32) *opor(a)* ***wadola***
     talk   lie/false
     'a lie'

Table 3.1 gives a list of the most common of the words functioning both as nouns and as adjectives.

3.2.3 Common vs. proper nouns

There is very little difference between common and proper nouns in Mauwake, and it can be questioned whether the two should be grouped separately as is traditionally often

Table 3.1: Words functioning both as nouns and adjectives.

	TRANSLATION AS NOUN	TRANSLATION AS ADJ
anima	'blade, point, edge'	'sharp'
afila	'grease'	'greasy, sweet'
foma	'ashes'	'grey'
ikina	'smell'	'smelly'
irauwa	'hole'	'deep'
makena	'true'	'truth, essential nature'
napuma	'sickness, corpse'	'sick'
pina	'weight, burden, guilt'	'heavy'
siisia	'design, pattern'	'spotted, patterned'
tumina	'dirt'	'dirty'
wadola	'lie'	'false, fake'

done in language descriptions. Proper nouns are sometimes classified separately because they are said to be unable to have modifiers (Roberts 1987: 152), and in practice, they usually occur without any modifiers. This is related to the fact that they normally only have a referent, but no intension. In most of the cases where a proper noun is modified, "it lacks a unique reference and is being used as a common noun" (Van Valin & LaPolla 1997: 59):

(33)   *I mean the old and cranky Joe Smith, not the younger one.*

The most common type of a proper noun is a name of a PERSON. A proper noun may also become a true common noun, when one or more of the qualities of a person are used to characterise some other being (Jespersen 1924: 66). For example, the name of a well-known expatriate, Jooren, was borrowed by Mauwake speakers to mean 'a stingy shopkeeper' (that is, one who does not sell things on credit and does not give discount to relatives).

In Mauwake, proper names can be modified without difficulty, especially by the demonstrative *nain* 'that', but also by adjectives. In a culture where there are several namesakes, and surnames are rarely used, modifiers are occasionally needed to distinguish between people (34).

(34)   **Adek panewowa nain** *ma-i-yem.*
       Adek old   that1 say-Np-PR.1s
       'I am talking about the OLD Adek.'

But even proper names, that have a unique reference and do not need to be distinguished from any other referent can be modified (35):

(35) **Dabe fain** uuw-ow(a) mua=ke.
      Dabe this work-NMZ man=CF
      'Dabe here is a hard worker.'

In this case, the behaviour of proper names is similar to that of the personal pronouns, which also have unique reference, but can be modified nevertheless. Van Valin and LaPolla (ibid. 59–60) note that languages may vary in how freely they allow proper nouns and pronouns to take modifiers.

Name taboos influence the use of personal names in several ways. A person is given many different names: at least one from each parents' side (as in-laws may not mention each others' names), a baptismal name, and possibly others as well. These names are used by different people. Name taboos may be avoided by calling someone by a teknonym like 'Sarak's father', or by calling a wife by the husband's name when she is with the in-laws and the husband is not around. Nicknames, often referring to physical properties, are also very common: *buburia* 'bald', *mua kuuma* 'lame' (literally 'stick-man'). The term 'namesake' is very common and even used of people who have been named after different names of the same person. Two boys, Yoli and Wangali, were called namesakes of each other, as they were both named after the same ancestor.

Perhaps the most characteristic feature of personal names is DISCOURSE-PRAGMATIC: their token frequency is very low in texts. Especially the main participant, once (s)he has been mentioned by name – if (s)he ever is – (s)he is then usually referred to by other means: a NP, pronoun, or just person marking on the verb.

Besides the names of people, PLACE NAMES form another large group of proper names. In Mauwake, the proper name often modifies a generic noun: *Moro* (*owowa*) 'Moro (village), *Siburten* (*ema*) 'Siburten (mountain/hill)', *Nemuru* (*eka*) 'Nemuru (river)' (§4.1).

The place name is also used when the inhabitants are referred to. When reference is made to an individual or a select group, the place name is used as a qualifier in the noun phrase (36):

(36) **Amiten** mua oko   ekap-o-k.
      Amiten man other come-PA-3s
      'A man from Amiten came.'

When the whole group is referred to, a plural pronoun is added to the place name (37), (38):

(37) **I**   Moro=ke uf-e-mik.
      1p.UNM Moro=CF dance-PA-1/3p
      'We Moro people danced.'

(38) **(Wi)** **Lasen wia**   nokar-e-k.[9]
      3p.UNM Lasen 3p.ACC ask-PA-3s
      'He asked the Lasen people'

---

[9] The optional initial pronoun *wi* is part of the object here, not a subject pronoun.

3.2.4 Alienable and inalienable possession

The Austronesian languages in Melanesia tend to have very elaborate semantically based possessive systems that indicate the relationship between the "possessor" and the "possession": kin relation, body part, food, etc. Inalienable possession is indicated by affixation on the noun, alienable possession by a separate possessive pronoun. Because of this, the simpler inalienable possession marking – also evident in many TNG languages – could easily be attributed to influence from Austronesian languages. But Ross (1996: 28) claims it is likely that even Proto TNG had inalienable nouns before there was any contact with Austronesian languages.[10] In Mauwake the division into alienably and inalienably possessed nouns is along the lines of kinship terms (see §1.3.6 for a kinship chart). Most kin terms in Table 3.2 obligatorily indicate who the "possessor" is.

The possessive prefixes *y-*, *n-* and *w-* in the inalienably possessed nouns developed from the first, second, and third person pronouns. These prefixes are in the process of merging with the root. The terms (a-j) in Table 3.2 are somewhat more lexicalized than the ones in (k-t): the first person prefix is mostly lost, and in some cases there is suppletion in the stem. These are some of the socially most important and frequently used kinship terms. The frequent use probably accounts for the omission of the possession prefix in the first person: these terms are used more as terms of address, whereas the other kinship nouns are only needed as terms of reference. Also, there is a tendency to drop the first person prefix before the front vowel /e/ regardless of the closeness of the kinship relation.

The "possessors" are differentiated as first, second or third person but not as singular vs. plural. An unmarked (39) or a genitive pronoun (40) and (41) may be used to either make this number distinction or to emphasize the kin relationship, when the relationship is used as a term of reference rather than as a term of address.

(39) *Kuuten **wiawi** iperowa, **yo** **auwa** kapa=ke.*
Kuuten 3s/p.father firstborn 1s.UNM 1s/p.father lastborn=CF
'Kuuten's father was the firstborn, my father the lastborn.'[11]

(40) *Aakisa **yena auwa** kapa fain=ke yia uruf-i-ya.*
now 1s.GEN 1s/p.father lastborn this=CF 1p.ACC see-Np-PR.3s
'Now this lastborn of my "fathers" watches over us.'

(41) *Sa, a **nena nie=ke**, **nena nepua=ke**, **niawi=ke**.*
INTJ INTJ 2s.GEN 2s/p.uncle=CF 2s.GEN 2s/p.brother-in-law 2s/p.father
'(Don't you understand,) those are *your* uncle(-in-law), *your* brother-in-law and father(-in-law).'

When a neutral, "non-possessed", kinship term is needed, the first person form is used. This is interesting, as the third person singular is typically considered the neutral, or unmarked, form. The terms '(my) mother' and '(my) father' are also used as respectful

---

[10] On the time frames of TNG occupation and Austronesian migration, see e.g. Ross (2005: 39–41).
[11] Both of these fathers could be called *auwa* 'my/our father(s)' by the two men.

3 Morphology

Table 3.2: Inalienably possessed kinship nouns

	1s/p	2s/p	3s/p	possessor
a.	auwa	niawi	wiawi	'father'
b.	aite	niena	onak	'mother'
c.	paapa	neepe	weepe	'elder sibling'
d.	(y)aamun	niamun	wiamun	'younger sibling'
e.	yaaya	nie	wie	'uncle'
f.	paapan	noopan	woopan	'aunt'
g.	kae	neke	weke	'grandfather'
h.	kome	nokome	wokome	'grandmother'
i.	eremena	neremena	weremena	'nephew, niece'
j.	emar, yomar	nomar	womar	'(cross-)cousin'
k.	yomokowa	nomokowa	womokowa	'brother'[a]
l.	(y)ekera	nekera	wekera	'sister'
m.	(y)emi	nemi	wemi	'(man's) brother-in-law'
n.	epua	nepua	wepua	'(woman's) brother-in-law'[b]
o.	yomora	nomora	womora	'sister-in-law'
p.	yopariw	nopariw	wopariw	'husband's brother's wife'
q.	yamekua	namekua	wamekua	'daughter-in-law'[c]
r.	yar	nar	war	'son-in-law'
s.	yookati	nookati	wookati	'co-wife'[d]
t.	yomawa	nomawa	womawa	'namesake'

[a] Among siblings, age is more important than sex: *paapa* and *aamun* are used very frequently and for siblings of either gender. When the gender is in focus, *yomokowa* is used for 'my brother' and *ekera* for 'my sister' especially by siblings of the opposite sex.
[b] A woman calls her elder sister's husband *auwa* 'father', but the other brothers-in-law are *epua*.
[c] Some in-law relations are non-symmetrical: even though there are special terms for sons- and daughters-in-law, *auwa* '(my) father' and *aite* '(my) mother' are used for '(my) mother-in-law' and '(my) father-in-law'.
[d] This term dates back to the time when polygamy was practiced; it was used for the wives of the same man.

terms of address for almost any stranger regardless of age, or for anyone whose status in the kinship system is uncertain.[12]

Four alienably possessed nouns, namely those for 'man', 'woman', 'boy' and 'girl', have been taken into the kinship system for terms of some nuclear family members, as seen in Table 3.3.

Also the term *nembesir* 'ancestor (beyond grandparents)' or 'descendant (beyond grandchildren)' is an alienably possessed noun, possibly because relatives so far removed in time are considered less relevant. It is used both for males and females. But the term

---

[12] I have been addressed as "mother" by an old man who temporarily forgot what my status according to their kinship system was - I was actually his granddaughter!

Table 3.3: Alienably possessed nuclear kin terms

mua	'man, husband'
emeria	'woman, wife'
muuka	'boy, child, son'
wiipa	'girl, daughter'

for 'namesake', *yomawa*, is included in the inalienably possessed kinship terms, as a child is named after some relatives, and the namesake relation forms an additional bond between them.

3.2.5 Noun compounding

The distinction between compound nouns and noun phrases is a problematic area in many languages, including Mauwake. Both are formed by combining independent elements into larger units, and their form and meaning are largely based on the form and meaning of those elements (Anderson 1985b: 40). Phonological, morphological, syntactic as well as semantic criteria have been called upon to differentiate between compounds and phrases.

In many languages, "word accent" (Lyons 1968: 204), i.e. stress and/or pitch, helps to distinguish compounds. In Mandarin Chinese, contrastive stress can only fall on the "stress center" of a word, including compounds (Anderson 1985b: 41). In Finnish, the primary stress is on the first, and only on the first, syllable of even very long compound words like *kuluttajansuoja-asiamiesverkostokysymys* 'the question of consumer ombudsman network', but even in Finnish there are unclear cases like *valveillaolo* vs. *valveilla olo* 'being awake', of which native speakers find hard to decide whether they are one or two words. The varying writing convention reflects the ambiguity.

Linguists differ in their views about the importance of stress placement in interpreting English compounds. Bloomfield (1933: 228) and Anderson (1985b: 41) consider it criterial, and so do Quirk et al. (1989 [1985]: 1330), although more cautiously. Lees (1968: 120) takes it as one premise for his study of compounds while admitting that the case is not very well substantiated. Others, like Jespersen (1933: 31), Downing (1977) and Bauer (1983) do not consider a single primary stress essential for compounds. According to Bauer (1983: 105), Lyons's (1968: 20) criteria for judging "wordness" in English, i.e. positional mobility and uninterruptability (or internal stability) do not distinguish between single- and double-stressed compounds.

Morphology may place constraints on compounding. In English, the genitive is common in phrases but rare in compounds: *duck's egg* vs. DUCK-EGG (Anderson 1985b: 41).[13] In Finnish, the first part of a compound is often in the nominative or genitive case, whereas the other cases are infrequent in this position. In German, certain elements

---

[13] But note also women's lib(eration), a compound.

3 Morphology

may serve as morphological "glue" between the parts of a compound (ibid. 42).

The two criteria for wordness by Lyons (1968: 202) mentioned above are syntactic in nature: a word, hence also a compound, is moved as one unit, and cannot be interrupted by other words as a phrase often can. These criteria do not apply to all, and not only to compound words, but they are useful in trying to establish the difference between compounds and phrases in a given language. Bloomfield (1933: 232) adds another one: a member of a compound generally cannot serve as a constituent in a syntactic construction. One can say *a very black bird* but not * *a very blackbird*.

The semantic interpretation of phrases is generally quite compositional: the meaning of the whole can be deduced from the meanings of the words. Compounds are more heterogeneous in their interpretation: some are compositional, whereas others involve special interpretive principles not applicable to phrases. Also, compounds as words are subject to changes of meaning, so many compounds may have meanings that are only vaguely or metaphorically related to that which is predicted on the basis of the parts (Anderson 1985a:42). Knowledge of the pragmatics of the situation may be needed for the interpretation of many compound words (Bauer 1983:58). The more fully lexicalized the compounds are, the more the meaning of the whole may deviate from the meaning of the parts. The same compound word may also be fully lexicalized in a certain context, and still be open for other interpretations in other contexts (Andrew Pawley, p. c.).

While there are languages where it is easy to distinguish between compound nouns and noun phrases, in others there is an intermediate area between the two. Thus Downing (1977: 810) doubts that the dividing line is always well-defined, and Quirk et al. (1989 [1985]: 1569) suggest the concept of "partial compounding" to account for the formal and semantic gradience between compounds and phrases in English. Bringing a historical viewpoint to the question, citing developments in English both from phrase to compound and from compound to phrase, Jespersen (1924: 102) offers a very liberal view: "it is of no consequence whether we reckon [the] doubtful cases as one word or two words, for […] a word group (like a single word) may be either primary or an adjunct or a subjunct".

None of the criteria mentioned above can be easily applied in Mauwake. Semantically, there is a continuum between fully compositional noun phrases and fully lexicalized compounds. But Bloomfield (1933: 227) warns that the greater specialization in meaning in the compound words as against phrases should not be used as a criterion, as "we cannot gauge meanings accurately enough, and many a phrase is as specialized in meaning as any compound". This warning is all the more relevant when one studies a language not one's own.

The basic stress pattern of noun phrases and compounds is similar, as one of the modifiers usually receives the phrase stress rather than the head noun (42), (43). Likewise, in compound nouns the modifying formative receives the main stress and the main formative is only weakly stressed (44), (45): the "stress centre" (Anderson 1985b: 45) is on another element than the head.

(42) yo   ʹauwa   aasa¹
      1s.unm 1s/p.father canoe
      'my father's canoe'

(43) aas(a) ge'lemuta
 canoe small
 'a small canoe'

(44) 'miiw(a)-aasa[2]
 land-canoe
 'vehicle, car'

(45) enow(a) ge'lemuta[3]
 food/meal small
 'feast'

However, the head noun in a NP may receive the phrase stress if it is emphasized for contrast, clarification or some other reason, whereas the stress centre in a compound stays the same.

Since there is hardly any MORPHOLOGY in nouns and noun phrases, one would not expect to find much help here in distinguishing between compounds and phrases. But there is a minor factor that is relevant in this respect: a phrase containing a noun and an adjective can be pluralized by adjectival reduplication when the adjective allows reduplication (46), whereas a compound noun with a similar structure usually cannot (47), even if it is possible in some rare cases (48).

(46) maa gelemuti-tik
 thing small-RDP
 'small things'

(47) * enow(a) gelemuti-tik
 food/meal small-RDP
 'feasts'

(48) owow(a) mane-maneka
 village RDP-big
 'towns', 'big villages'

Uninterruptibility is more typical of compounds than phrases. The noun phrase *owow maneka* means 'a big village', as a compound it means 'a town/city'. As a phrase it is interruptible (49), as a compound it is not.

(49) owowa lawisiw maneka
 village rather big
 'a rather big village'

---

[1] In the examples (42)-(45) only the phrase stress is marked by ' preceding the stressed syllable.
[2] In Mauwake orthography, the parts of a compound word are usually written separately to help the new readers to identify the parts; *miiw-aasa* 'vehicle' is one of the exceptions.
[3] *Enow gelemuta* is not used with its literal meaning 'small meal'.

3 Morphology

Likewise, as a compound *kae sira* 'ancestral custom' (literally: 'grandfather's custom') is uninterruptible. When a genitive pronoun is inserted between the two parts, the meaning cannot be 'ancestral custom' (50):

(50) kae   ona   sira
      grandfather 3s.GEN   custom
      'grandfather's custom/habit'

In Mauwake, word combinations are treated as compounds if they (1) have a specialized meaning, (2) have a stress centre not affected by contrastive stress, and (3) tend to be uninterruptible. However, this distinction is very tentative in some cases. Some examples are provided where the same combination may be either a compound noun or a noun phrase.

Morphologically, there are four compound noun types in Mauwake: N+N, V_{NMZ} +V, N+V_{NMZ} and N+ADJ. Syntactically these correspond to a head noun with a nominal pre- or post-modifier in a NP, or a head noun with an adjective post-modifier in the NP. In most compound nouns the last noun is the head. But in generic-specific compounds, as well as the N+ADJ and N+V_{NMZ} compounds, the first part is the main element, and the scope of its meaning is restricted by the second part. In coordinate compounds the two parts are equally important.

On the basis of the semantic relations between the parts the N+N compounds can be divided into a few main groups. In the first one the relationship can be said to be characterized by ORIGIN understood very widely, e.g. in the sense of place of origin (51), source (50), or "possession" (52), (53).

(51) *piip(a)   mera*
      seaweed   fish
      'rainbow fish'

(52) *emeria   napuma*
      woman   sick(ness)
      'menstruation'

(53) *ibiamun sama*
      dove   ladder
      'cross-beam (in a roof)'

The compound noun (52) has the stress centre on the first part, but the noun phrase *emeria napuma*, with the phrase stress on *napuma*, may be used to mean either 'a sick woman', or more commonly 'a (dead) woman's body', a euphemistic expression.

The second relationship is a WHOLE-PART relationship: the first element states the whole, the second its part (54), (55).

(54) *mokok(a) oposia*
      eye   meat
      'pupil (of the eye)'

(55) ekek(a) muuna
      branch joint/projection
      'bud'

The third relationship is that of CONTAINER. As a compound *muuk(a) sia* (56) has the stress centre on the first word. In a noun phrase (57), however, the phrase stress may also be on the second item if it is emphasized, and a third person singular genitive pronoun may be added between the parts as well. Example (58) is an extended compound: *iinan aasa* is a "sky canoe", or vehicle, for flying in the sky, and *iinan aasa epa* a place for those vehicles.

(56) muuk(a) sia
      son   netbag
      'womb', 'pouch (of a marsupial)'

(57) muuk(a) sia
      son   netbag
      'a son's/child's netbag (used for carrying the baby)'

(58) iinan aasa epa
      sky   canoe place
      'airstrip, airport'

As was mentioned above, the GENERIC-SPECIFIC relationship is different in that the modifying part follows rather than precedes the main part (59)–(61). In this respect these compounds resemble phrases where the head noun has an adjective rather than a noun modifier. A particularly common word for the first part in these compounds is the maximally generic word in Mauwake, *maa* 'thing' (61).[14]

(59) mera nepa
      fish bird
      'eagle ray'

(60) oon(a) tiretira
      bone horizontal.cane (in roof structure)
      'rib'

(61) maa pela
      thing leaf
      '(edible) greens'

There are two compound types with nominalized verbs. When the nominalized verb follows the other noun, it behaves like an adjective and receives the phrase stress (62), (63).

---

[14] The scope of meaning for *maa* is like that of 'thing' in its widest sense in English.

(62) maa   en-owa
     thing/food eat-NMZ
     'food'

(63) emer(a) ik-owa
     sago   roast-NMZ
     'bread, roasted sago'

A compound type where the nominalized verb precedes the other noun is more common than the one above. When the second part is a human noun, it usually has to be the AGENT of the verb (64), but when the noun is non-human, it is harder to find a common denominator for the semantic relationships between the parts in different compounds. Quite often the meaning centers around function, purpose or "typical" action, place, time, etc. (65), (66).

(64) uuw-ow(a) mua
     work-NMZ man
     'worker'

(65) in-ow(a)   koora
     sleep-NMZ house
     'bedroom'

(66) om-ow(a) eka
     cry-NMZ water
     'tear'

This compound type particularly easily allows compounds with more than two roots (67)–(69):

(67) ikemik(a) kaik-ow(a) mua
     wound   tie-NMZ   man
     'doctor'

(68) emer(a) en-ow(a) mua
     sago   eat-NMZ   man
     'a Sepik man (lit: a sago eater)'[15]

(69) ama urup-ow(a) (epa/kame)
     sun rise-NMZ   place/side
     'east'

In the example (70) the main noun *epa/kame* can be dropped, and this happens in some other compounds as well:

---

[15] Sepik province is known for its main staple, sago starch.

(70) epir(a) suruk-ow(a) (tetelka)
plate wipe-NMZ finger
'forefinger'

The COORDINATE compounds are different from the other compounds in that neither of the parts modifies the other. The meaning of the whole is derived from the combined meaning of the two terms. Also, there is no stress centre: both parts of the compound are stressed equally. The number of these compounds is small (71), (72).

(71) emeria mua
woman man
'people'

(72) muuka wiipa
son daughter
'children'

The N+ADJ compounds are as hard to distinguish from phrases as some of the other groups mentioned above (73)–(75). Again the uninterruptibility and lexicalized meaning are the main criteria. If the adjective *sepa* 'black' is added between the two words in (73), the meaning changes into 'a small black man'.

(73) mua gelemuta
man small
'a little boy'

(74) mia yoowa
body/skin hot
'fever'

(75) maa samora
thing bad
'mosquito'

Compounding is a productive process in Mauwake, and it is the most common language-internal means used for adding new lexical items to the language.

3.2.6 Derived nouns

In this section I will discuss derivations where the END RESULT is a noun. There are only two of these: nouns made out of verbs, and noun reduplications.

3.2.6.1 Action nominals

The process of nominalizing verbs is a straightforward and fully productive process of adding the nominalizing suffix *-owa* to the verb stem. The nominalized verbs most commonly function as nouns (76)–(78), sometimes also as adjectives (79).[16]

(76) *uf-**owa***
 dance-NMZ
 '(the act of) dancing', '(traditional) dance'

(77) *irak-**owa***
 fight-NMZ
 'fighting', 'fight/war'

(78) *Fiirim-**owa**=pa opaimika aakun-e-mik.*
 gather-NMZ=LOC talk talk-PA-1/3p
 'In the meeting we talked.'

(79) *Amina puk-**owa** eliw(a) marewa=ke.*
 pot break-NMZ good none=CF
 'The pot is broken (and) not good' or: 'The broken pot is not good.'

Action nominals function like any regular nouns in Mauwake. They can be, for example, a head (80) or a qualifier (81) in a NP, and a first (82) or last element (83) in a compound noun.

(80) *Siowa **alu-owa** miim-ap ekap-o-k.*
 dog make.noise-NMZ hear-SS.SEQ come-PA-3s
 'He heard the dog's noise and came' or: 'The dog heard noise and came.'

(81) *Irak-owa kerer-owa epa weeser-em-ik-eya* ...[17]
 fight-NMZ appear-NMZ time finish-SS.SIM-be-2/3s.DS
 'As the time of the war was getting close...' (Lit: 'As the war-appearing time was coming to an end...')

(82) *Oram **niir-ow(a)** opora ma-e-m.*
 just laugh-NMZ talk say-PA-1s
 'I just said it as a joke.'

---

[16] In the Mauwake dictionary some of these nominalized forms have their own entry as if they were fully lexicalized as nouns, but this is to some extent a concession to other languages, where separate nouns may be required for the action nominals and more lexicalized deverbal nouns (for the distinction, see Ylikoski 2003: 193). In Mauwake it is often difficult to establish which of the nominalizations are lexicalized.

[17] *Kererowa* is both the head of *irakowa kererowa* and part of the qualifier phrase in *irakowa kererowa epa*.

(83) Kaul **wafur-owa** mera **aaw-owa** eliw.
 hook throw-NMZ fish get-NMZ all.right

 'As for throwing a hook, it is a good way of catching fish.' (Lit: 'Hook-throwing is all right for fish-catching.')

The following expressions form an interesting pair, as (84) is a NP with a nominalized verb as its head, and (85) is a compound noun with a nominalized verb as the first part.

(84) mua aakun-**owa**
 man talk-NMZ

 'talk(ing) of man/people', 'people's talk'

(85) aakun-**ow(a)** mua
 talk-NMZ man

 'a talker', 'a spokesman'

Action nominals keep their verb-like property of being able to take the same arguments and peripherals as the verb serving as the root of the noun. The result is a nominalized clause, which functions like a noun phrase. This is discussed further in §5.7 and §8.3.2.

Comrie & Thompson (2007: 334–342) list various kinds of other nominalization possibilities,[18] but in Mauwake the corresponding expressions are compound nouns or noun phrases consisting of the nominalized verb (or clause) plus another noun (86), (87), rather than simple nominalizations.

(86) ikemika kaik-**ow(a)** mua
 wound tie-NMZ man

 'doctor, nurse'

(87) maa eneka teek-**ow(a)** (maa)[19]
 thing tooth open-NMZ (thing)

 'can opener'

3.2.6.2 Noun reduplication

Reduplication of nouns to denote plurality is a very marginal process in Mauwake (88)–(90), whereas reduplication of verbs (§3.8.2.4.1) is much more frequent, and that of adjectives (§3.3) also more common. Usually the whole noun is reduplicated; final <a> is deleted in the reduplicated part of words that are longer than two syllables (90).

---

[18] Givón (1990: 500) calls all of these *lexical nominalizations*, and Ylikoski calls them *deverbal nouns* (2003: 193) to distinguish them from action nominals.

[19] *Maa eneka* is a compound referring to edible animals; the very generic noun *maa* 'thing' may be omitted from the end.

(88) Dabuel **poka-poka** nain=iw   biiris on-am-ik-e-mik.
     pawpaw RDP-trunk that1=INST bridge make-SS.SIM-be-PA-1/3p
     'They kept making the bridge with pawpaw trunks.'

(89) Waaya pa-ep   **kio-kiowa** naap uup-e-mik.
     pig   butcher-SS.SEQ RDP-piece   thus cook-PA-1/3p
     'We butchered the pig and cooked the pieces like that.'

(90) **Owow-owowa** ikiw-e-mik.
     RDP-village   go-PA-1/3p
     'We went to several villages.'

3.3 Adjectives

The existence of noun and verb as universal categories is generally acknowledged, but the status of adjectives is less clear. There is considerable variation among languages as to what belongs to the adjective class, and sometimes a question is posed whether the class exists at all. But when there is a class of adjectives, the following tendencies emerge: languages that have a small class of adjectives show a lot of similarity in what kinds of concepts they express through this class; and similarly, in languages where the adjective class is large the semantic content of the class is fairly constant (Dixon 1977: 20). Semantically it is somewhat of an in-between category sharing similarities with both nouns and verbs (Lyons 1977: 447). Nouns "connote the possession of a complex of qualities, and [adjectives] the possession of one single quality" (Jespersen 1924: 81; see also Wierzbicka 1986: 362). Nouns have reference, adjectives do not (Hakulinen & Karlsson 1979: 77). Instead of categorizing like nouns do, adjectives describe (Wierzbicka 1986: 357). They may also code transitory states, and in Givón's (1984: 52) time-stability scale they occupy the middle area between nouns and verbs.[20]

The morphological and syntactic coding of "property concepts" reflects their semantically ambivalent status: especially in languages which have either no adjectives or only a small adjective class, the concepts are usually expressed via verbs and/or nouns, sometimes by other means (Dixon 1977: 20).

The adjective class in Mauwake is a relatively small open class when compared with nouns and verbs. But compared with some other Papuan languages (Dixon 1977: 50–51) it is a fairly large class: the number of non-derived adjectives currently in the dictionary is about 80.[21] The morphological and syntactic similarities and differences between nouns and adjectives were discussed above in §3.2.2. Adjectives do not inflect at all.

A prototypical adjective functions as the head of an adjective phrase[22] (§4.2) (91), (92), and may be modified by different intensity adverbs (§3.9.2), including the pre-modifier *lawisiw* 'rather' (93) and various post-modifiers (94).

---

[20] But see Thompson's (1988) criticism on Givón's placing of adjectives on the time-stability scale.
[21] Usan also has a relatively large adjective inventory (Reesink 1987:63).
[22] Often the head is the sole constituent of the adjective phrase.

(91) *Nomokowa **maala** war-e-k.*
 tree long cut-PA-3s
 'He cut a tall tree.'

(92) *Waaya me **maneka**, muuka, **kia gelemuta**.*
 pig not big son white small
 'The pig was not big, it was a piglet, white (and) small.'

(93) *Malol **lawisiw yoowa**.*
 open.sea rather hard
 '(Fishing in the) open sea is rather hard.'

(94) *Koora nain **maneka wenup**.*
 house that1 big very
 'That house is very big.'

Only the adjectives in Table 3.4 have been found to be non-scalar. Of those, *enuma* is scalar when it has the meaning 'new' or 'green'.

Table 3.4: Non-scalar adjectives

morena	'male'
suwina	'female'
emi	'taboo(ed)'
enuma	'alive'

The typical adjectives in Mauwake are all non-derived, and among them are all those listed by Dixon (1977: 23) as the most common adjectives cross-linguistically: large, small, long, short, old, new, good, bad, black, white and red.

Of the various adjective groups mentioned by Dixon (1977), those of AGE Table 3.5 and value are quite small in Mauwake. Only two of the age adjectives are non-derived, the other two are derived:

Table 3.5: Adjectives denoting age

awona	'old'	*panewowa*	'old'
enuma	'new'	*iperowa*	'middle-aged, elder'

The adjective *awona* 'old' refers to the age of things, not people; when used of people, the meaning is 'previous' (95). Correspondingly, its antonym *enuma* 'new' refers to age of things or recency in humans (96). The adjective referring to age in people, *panewowa*

3 Morphology

'old'[23] does not have any adjective as an antonym; the noun *takira* 'youth' is used instead. *Panewowa* 'old' and *iperowa* 'middle-aged' do not only indicate age, but social status as well: it is the middle-aged men, rather than young or old, that have most power and make the important decisions in the community. *Iperowa* is also used for older siblings when the age of siblings is compared.

(95) *Emeria **panewowa** nain Kait emeria **awona**=ke.*
woman old that1 Kait woman old=CF
'The old woman is Kait's old (=previous) wife.'

(96) *Ona mua **enuma** iiriw pani-e-k.*
3s.GEN man new already grow.old-PA-3s
'Her new husband is (already) old.'

VALUE adjectives (97), (98) are listed in Table 3.6.

Table 3.6: Adjectives denoting value

eliwa	'good'	-	samora	'bad'
makena	'true'	-	wadola	'false'
emi	'taboo, forbidden'			

(97) *Inasin opaimika **eliwa** me yia maak-e-mik.*
spirit talk good not 1p.ACC tell-PA-1/3p
'They did not speak good Tok Pisin (lit: spirit talk) to us.'

(98) *Iiriw sira nain **emi** maneka wiar ik-ua.*
earlier custom that1 forbidden big 3.DAT be-PA.3s
'Earlier that custom was completely forbidden to them.'

The list of COLOUR adjectives (99)–(102) is also very limited; only the first three terms in Table 3.7 are purely colour terms, all the others have their origin elsewhere:

(99) *Aalbok mia **sepa** akena kerer-e-k.*
black.cuckoo.shrike body black very become-PA-3s
'The body of the black cuckoo-shrike became very black.'

(100) *Konima nain **sepa kia**.*
cloth that1 black white
'The cloth is black-and-white.'

---
[23] *Panewowa* is derived from the verb *pan-* 'grow old'.

Table 3.7: Adjectives denoting colour

sepa	'black'		
kia	'white'		
oka	'red', 'brown'		
enuma	'green'	<	'new'
ligam	'yellow'	<	'turmeric'
ekapina	'blue'	<	'shrub sp.' (used for blue dye)
foma	'grey'	<	'ashes'[a]

[a] cf. Berlin & Kay (1969: 4).

(101) *Mia afif(a) **oka**, **oka** gelemuta.*
body hair red, red small
'The feathers were red, (it was) red and small.'

(102) *Komora nain **kia** ne **maneka** wenup.*
cuscus that1 white ADD big very
'That cuscus is/was white/light-coloured and very big.'

In (101) the dimensional adjective for 'small' may follow directly after the colour adjective, whereas the adjective *maneka* 'big' needs a connective between the two adjectives in (102), because *maneka* is used as an intensifier when immediately following a colour term, and *kia maneka* would mean 'completely white'.

The darkness of a colour is expressed through the adjectives *sepa* 'black' and *kia* 'white' used as modifiers of the main colour adjective (103).

(103) *ifa **enuma** lawisiw sepa*
leaf new/green rather black
'a dark green leaf'

Among the adjectives denoting DIMENSION (104)–(106) there are a number of terms describing various kinds of thinness and thickness, as well as shortness (Table 3.8).

(104) *Epa dabela=pa mia suuw-owa **gawela** suuw-ap mia fulil-i-nan.*
place cold=LOC body push-NMZ thin push-ss.SEQ body feel.cold-Np-FU.2s
'When you wear thin clothes (mia suuwowa) in a cold place you will feel cold.'

(105) *Owor(a) ara **teena** nain ku-i-non.*
betelnut.palm trunk thin that1 break-Np-FU.3s
'The thin betelnut palm trunk will break.'

3 Morphology

Table 3.8: Adjectives denoting dimension

maneka	'large'	-	*gelemuta*	'small'
maala	'long'	-	*iiwa*	'short'
kuruma	'thick'	-	*gawela*	'thin'
fula(kia)	'fat'	-	*bebeta*	'slim, skinny'
teena	'thin'			
komosia	'small, short'			

(106) Epa dabel-al-eya mia suuw-owa **kuruma** wu-e.
place cold-INCH-2/3s.DS body push-NMZ thick put-IMP.2s
'When it gets cold, put thick clothes on.'

The group of adjectives denoting PHYSICAL PROPERTY (107), (108) is larger than any of the other groups and includes several antonym pairs. Table 3.9 lists just a sample of them.

Table 3.9: Adjectives denoting physical property

yoowa	'hot, hard'	-	*dabela*	'cold'
supuka	'wet'	-	*ififa*	'dry'
pina	'heavy'	-	*efefa*	'light'
kaken	'straight'	-	*meka*	'crooked'
melina	'clear'	-	*wiwisa*	'murky'
anima	'sharp'	-	*duduwa*	'blunt'
dubila	'slippery, smooth'			
itita	'soft'			
masia	'bitter (taste)'			
siina	'tight'			

(107) Iwera **ififa** ora-eya fiirim-i-mik.
coconut dry descend-2/3s.DS gather-Np-PR.1/3p
'When the dry coconuts drop we gather them'.

(108) ...epia foma lawisiw **yoowa** ik-ua.
fire(wood) ashes rather hot be-PA.3s
'... the ashes were rather hot.'

HUMAN PROPENSITY adjectives (Table 3.10) is the second largest group (109), (110).

3.3 Adjectives

Table 3.10: Adjectives denoting human propensity

lebuma	'lazy'	-	*topia*	'diligent'
asia	'wild'	-	*memela*	'tame'
lebuma	'lazy'			
momora	'foolish'			
popora	'quiet'			
yamunsia	'stingy'			

(109) *Takira=ke keker op-ap   popor(a) maneka ik-e-mik.*
boy=CF fear hold-SS.SEQ quiet big be-PA-1/3p
'The boys were afraid and very quiet.'

(110) *Mua **lebuma** nain emeria me wi-i-mik.*
man lazy that1 woman not give.them-Np-PR.1/3p
'We do not give wives to lazy men.'

Although Mauwake has a considerable inventory of adjectives for a Papuan language, in actual use they are rather infrequent.[24] Especially physical property and human propensity are frequently expressed through verbs which have been verbalized from adjectives. A true adjective is a more likely candidate to indicate a stable or essential quality of the head noun (110), whereas the verbalized form is used for more temporary characteristics (111)-(113).

(111) *Sama=pa or-owa   nain eliw, nain ikoka or-op   or-op*
stairs=LOC descend-NMZ that1 well that1 later descend-SS.SEQ descend-SS.SEQ
*or-op   **lebum(a)-ar-i-nan**, epasia akena.*
descend-SS.SEQ lazy-INCH-Np-FU.2s far very
'Descending on the stairs is all right, but later when you have gone down and down and down you will be lazy/tired, (as) it is very far.'

(112) *Moma **kasu(a)-ar-eya**   me enim-i-mik.*
taro hard-INCH-2/3s.DS not eat-Np-PR.1/3p
'We don't eat hard taro.' (Lit: 'When taro is hardened, we don't eat it.')

(113) ***Yamunsi(a)-ar-iwkin** me wia   nokar-e-m.*
stingy-INCH-2/3p.DS not 3p.ACC ask-PA-1s
'They were (being) stingy, (so) I didn't ask them.'

SPEED is expressed through adverbs or verbs rather than adjectives.

---
[24] Their frequency in the text material is about 1.5% of all the words.

3 Morphology

COMPARISON of adjectives is an area where there is very little differentiation in many Papuan languages, including Mauwake.[25] Intensifiers are used for this function, as well as the verb *nomak-* 'overcome, surpass' (114).

(114) *Poka fain maala, nain **nomak-e-k**, ne oko nain **maala akena**.*
stilt this long that1 surpass-PA-3s ADD other that1 long very
'This stilt is longer than that, and/but the other one is the longest (lit: very long).'

Two adjectives can also be compared by contrasting them (115):

(115) *Nomokow(a) kakawa fain **iiwa**, oko **maala** puuk-a-n.*
tree part this short other long cut-PA-2s
'You cut this plank shorter than the other one.' (Lit: 'You cut this plank short, the other long.')

Adjectives denoting size form a scale of three: *gelemuta* 'small', *manisiri* 'biggish', *maneka* 'big'. Usually, if three degrees of comparison are needed, it is possible to express them periphrastically, but that is seldom necessary. Comparison as a functional domain is discussed in §6.5.

Like nouns, adjectives can also be REDUPLICATED for plural (116) (§2.3.3.2). Reduplication of adjectives is not very common, but it is more frequent than that of nouns.

(116) *Maa eneka kes **mane-maneka** oram iw-e-mik.*
thing tooth case RDP-big just give.him-PA-1/3p
'They just gave him big cases of meat tins.'

The adjective *gelemuta* 'small' has several reduplicated forms: *gelemuti-tik, gelemutu-mut* (117), *gele-gelemuti-tik*.

(117) *Waaya **gelemutu-mut** pu-puuk-e.*
pig small-RDP RDP-cut-IMP.2s
'Cut the pig into small pieces.'

Occasionally reduplication can be used for an intensifying function as well. The noun modified by the reduplicated adjective in (118) is either singular or plural, in (119) it is definitely singular.

(118) *Biiris eliwa me on-a-mik, **damo-damola**=ko.*
bridge good not make-PA-1/3p RDP-bad=NF
'They didn't make a good bridge (but) very bad.' (or: '…good bridges but bad.')

(119) *…ifa=ke keraw-a-k, mamepaperuma **gele-gelemuti-tik** nain=ke.*
…snake=CF bite-PA-3s death.adder RDP-small-RDP that1=CF
'… a snake bit him, a very small death adder.'

---

[25] See Roberts (1987: 134–135); Reesink (1987: 68); Hardin (2002: 63–64). Haiman (1980: 268) reports only three or four true adjectives for Hua, and does not mention comparison.

NEW ADJECTIVES are derived from verbs with the nominalizing suffix *-owa* (120)–(122) (Table 3.11). This is not a very productive process.

Table 3.11: Adjectives derived from verbs

kekanowa	'strong'	<	*kekan-*	'be strong'
panewowa	'old'	<	*pan-*	'become old'
kainowa	'high (voice)'	<	*kain-*	'be high (voice)'
bolonowa	'slack'	<	*bolon-*	'be slack'

(120) No   mua samora, mua emin(a) **kekan-owa**   nefa   na-i-kuan.
2s.UNM man bad   man occiput be.strong-NMZ 2s.ACC say-Np-FU.3p
'They will call you a bad man, a pig-headed (lit: strong occiput) man.'

(121) *Someka aw-i-ya*   *nain iwakara* **kain-owa**   *maneka aw-i-ya.*
song   weave-Np-PR.3s that1 neck   be.high-NMZ big   weave-Np-PR.3s
'When (s)he sings, (s)he sings with a very high voice.'

(122) *Makera* **saawirin-owa** *kaik-a-m.*
cane   surround-NMZ tie-PA-1s
'I tied the cane round.'

Adjectives can be made into verbs by zero verb formation (§3.8.2.2.1) or by the inchoative verbaliser *-ar* (§3.8.2.2.2).

3.4 Quantifiers

Quantifiers are a small closed class of words. The group can be divided into numeral and non-numeral quantifiers. The reasons for treating them as a group of their own, separate from adjectives, are the following. Their position is after the adjectives in a NP.[26] Some of the numerals consist of a phrase or even a clause, but they still function as a single unit. And semantically quantifiers are quite different from adjectives.

A quantifier is the only obligatory element in a quantifier phrase (QP, §4.3). These are used as post-modifiers in a NP, where their position is between an adjective phrase (AP) and demonstrative (123), or by themselves as a non-verbal predicate (124).

(123) I   *koora maneka* **kuisow** *nain yiar*   *aw-o-k.*
1p.UNM house big   one   that1 1p.DAT burn-PA-3s
'That one big house of ours burned.'

---

[26] Actually it is the Quantifier Phrase that comes after the Adjective Phrase, but usually both the phrases consist of only one word, a quantifier in the former and an adjective in the latter.

3 Morphology

(124) *Mua iperowa* **arow muutiw.**
man middle-aged three only.

'There are/were only three middle-aged men.' (Lit: 'The middle-aged men (are/were) only three.')

The numerals, especially *erup* 'two', may be added to a pronoun to quantify it: the numeral occurs following a reflexive (or occasionally unmarked) form of the pronoun, but the resulting phrase functions like an unmarked pronoun (125).

(125) *Ne* **wiam erup** *pun epa neeke or-o-mik.*
ADD 3p.REFL two too place there.CF descend-PA-1/3p

'And the two of them too went down there.'

3.4.1 Numerals

The traditional counting system in Mauwake is quinary, i.e. based on five[27] (126) (Table 3.12), and counting is gestured using the fingers.[28]

Table 3.12: Vernacular numerals

kuisow	'one'
erup	'two'
arow	'three'
erepam	'four'
ikur / wapen inawiya	'five' / 'a hand sleeps'
(ikur) okai(wi)=pa kuisow	'six' (lit: '(five) one on/from the other side')
(ikur) okai(wi)=pa erup	'seven'
(ikur) okai(wi)=pa arow	'eight'
(ikur) okai(wi)=pa erepam	'nine'
iimeka kuisow / okaipa okaipa inek	'ten' / 'both sides sleep'

(126) *Uura ama* **ikur okai(wi)=pa** *arow naap in-e-mik.*
night sun five other.side=LOC three thus sleep-PA-1/3p

'In the evening we slept at around eight o'clock.'

Nowadays the borrowed Tok Pisin numerals have largely superseded the vernacular numerals, especially those indicating numbers ten and above (127). There are no terms for 'hundred', 'thousand' or bigger numbers in the vernacular system.

---

[27] In New Guinea languages, there are counting systems based on two, five ten and twenty, as well as systems that use different body parts as tallies. All of these systems are present in the Madang area languages as well (Lean 1991).

[28] To count, the fingers are bent down one by one, starting from the little finger of the right hand, and proceeding towards the thumb, then on to the little finger of the other hand, and so on.

(127) *Mokoma **ten arow** aaw-o-k.*
year ten three get-PA-3s
'He became 30 years old.'

Numerals can be modified with the intensity adverbs *kakeniw* 'correctly, exactly' (128), *akena* 'really, truly' (129), or *muutiw* 'only'.

(128) ***Erepam kaken=iw** mik-a-mik.*
four straight-ISOL spear-PA-1/3p
'We speared exactly four.'

(129) *Mua **arow akena** epa nain iimar-e-mik.*
man three truly place that stand.up-PA-1/3p
'Exactly three men stood at that place.'

When the number is somewhat uncertain and the disjunctive connective *e* 'or' and/or the question marker *-i* is used, either the smaller (130) or the bigger number (131) may be mentioned first.

(130) *Waaya maneka wiowa **erup=i e arow** naap mik-iwkin um-i-ya.*
pig big spear two=QM or three thus hit-2/3p.DS die-Np-PR.3s
'When a big pig is hit with two or three spears it dies.'

(131) *Mua wiam **ikur=i erepam** naap wia aaw-e-mik.*
man 3p.REFL five=QM four thus 3p.ACC get-PA-1/3p
'They took/got those four or five men.'

Repetition (132) or reduplication (133) of the numerals indicates manner: 'so and so many AT A TIME'. The reduplicated form of *kuisow* 'one', *kui-kuisow*, has two meanings: 'one by one' and 'a few'.

(132) *Naap **kuisow kuisow** aaw-ikiw-e-mik.*
thus one one get-go-PA-1/3p
'They kept getting them one at a time as they went.

(133) *Waaya merena **ere-erup** kaik-ap...*
pig leg RDP-two tie-SS.SEQ
'I tied the pig's legs two and two together and ...'

Money is counted using different nouns indicating certain amounts (Table 3.13).

(134) ***Kuuma kuisow ifa erup** naap yia sesenar-e-mik.*
stick[29] one leaf two thus 1p.ACC buy-PA-1/3p
'They paid to us (lit: bought us for) 14 kina.'

3 Morphology

Table 3.13: Currency terms

maamuma (< maa mumua)	'10 toea', also generic 'money', lit: 'seed'
fuluwa	'1 kina', lit: 'hole' (the coin has a hole)
ifa	'2 kina', lit: 'leaf'
ifa oka	'5 kina', lit: 'red leaf'
kuuma	'10 kina', lit: 'stick'

Mauwake has no separate words for ORDINAL numbers. To indicate numerical order, various structures are employed. In many cases the cardinal numbers can be used (135), (136).

(135) *Mua arow epa nain iimar-e-mik, yos=ke **erepam**.*
man three place that1 stand-PA-1/3p 1s.FC=CF four
'Three men were standing there, and I was the fourth.'

(136) *Koora tuun-e: **kuisow iki(w)-(e)p erepam**, ne oko nain ona   koora.*
house count-IMP.2s one   go-SS.SEQ four   ADD other that1 3s.GEN house
'His house is the fifth one' (Lit: 'Count the houses: one to four, and the other/next is his house.')

In the case of time units, cardinal numbers are combined with the verb *ikiw-* 'go' (137).

(137) ***Fofa okai(wi)=pa   arow ikiw-eya** ekap-i-non.*
day other.side=LOC three go-2/3s.DS come-Np-FU.3s
'He will come on the ninth day.' (Lit: 'When eight days have gone he will come').

Order can also be indicated through verbs like *murar-* and *ook-* 'follow' (138).

(138) *Wi   Ulingan=ke nomak-e-mik. Ne i   Moro **murar-e-mik**.*
3p.UNM Ulingan=CF win-PA-1/3p   ADD 1p.UNM Moro follow-PA-1/3p
'The Ulingan people/team won. And (we from) Moro came second.'

Numbers are NOT used when listing one's children. The terms *iperowa* 'firstborn', *ookap onarowa* 'following' (used repeatedly, if necessary) and *kapa* 'lastborn' are employed for that.

3.4.2 Non-numeral quantifiers

Some non-numeral quantifiers can only be used with either count or mass nouns, others with both (139)–(141) are shown in Table 3.14.

---

[29] A stick of tobacco, used for payment in the colonial days.

3.4 Quantifiers

Table 3.14: Quantifiers used with count and mass nouns

senam	'too much/too many'
unowiya	'all' (from: *unowa* 'many' plus comitative clitic =*iya*)
iiwawun	'all/altogether'

(139) *Moma **senam** en-e-mik.*
     taro too.much eat-PA-1/3p
     'We ate too much taro.'

(140) *Nomokowa **senam** war-e-man.*
     tree   too.many cut.PA-2p
     'You cut too many trees.'

(141) *Yagin eka=pa   **unow=iya** nan yaki-e-mik.*
     Yagin water=LOC many=COM there bathe-PA-1/3p
     'We all bathed there at Yagin together.'

The quantifiers in Table 3.15 are only used with COUNT nouns (142), (143). *Papako* is actually a plural indefinite 'other'(§3.7.2), but it has a secondary function as a quantifier.

Table 3.15: Quantifiers used only with count nouns

papako	'other/some/a few'
unowa	'many'
unow onaiya	'all' (from *unowa* plus *onaiya* 'together with')
wenup	'lots of'

(142) *Mua **unowa**, emeria **papako** um-e-mik.*
     man many   woman some   die-PA-1/3p
     'Many men and some women died.'

(143) *Ipia saana=pa   iina   **wenup**.*
     rain season=LOC mosquito lots.of
     'In the rainy season there are lots of mosquitoes.'

Both *wenup* (144) and *unowa* can be intensified with *akena* 'very'; *unowa* may also be intensified with *wenup* 'very' (145); or with *maneka* (lit: 'big') that gives it the meaning 'all' (146).

(144) *Siipepe kokora maroka **wenup akena** ika-i-ya.*
Siipepe riverbed prawn lots.of very be-Np-PR.3s

'There are lots of prawns in the Siipepe riverbed.'

(145) *Iinan aasa nepa saarik, **unow(a) akena/wenup**.*
sky canoe bird like many very

'The planes were like birds, very many.'

(146) *Emeria **unow(a) maneka** sosora bee-beela a-e-mik.*
woman many big grass.skirt RDP-rotten tie-PA-1/3p

'All the women put on rotten grass skirts.'

The quantifiers in Table 3.16 only occur with MASS nouns (147).

Table 3.16: Quantifiers used only with mass nouns

maneka	'a lot/much' (lit: 'big')
gelemuta	'little'
lawiliw	'somewhat/a little'

(147) *Eka yoowa=pa aaya **maneka/gelemuta** wu-e.*
water hot=LOC sugar big/little put-IMP.2s

'Put a lot of/a little sugar in the tea.'

The following non-numeral quantifiers also function as degree/intensity adverbs, modifying a verb: *lawiliw* (148), *senam* (149), *iiwawun* (150), and *wenup* (§3.9.2).

(148) *Yos=ke **lawiliw** asip-i-yem.*
1s=CF somewhat help-Np-PR.1s

'I am helping her somewhat/a little.'

(149) *Iperowa=ke **senam** kekan-e-mik.*
middle.aged=CF too.much be.strong-PA-1/3p

'The middle-aged men were very strong (in their opinion).'

(150) *Waaya mik-amkun **iiwawun** um-o-k.*
pig spear-1s/p.DS altogether die-PA-3s

'When I speared the pig it died completely.'

FRACTIONS are hard to express in Mauwake.[30] The noun *enakiwa* 'half' is sometimes also used for unspecified 'part', and *okaiwi* 'one/other side' can be used for 'half', when

---

[30] I have not seen fractions treated in grammars of Papuan languages, but know from discussions with colleagues that translating fractions is a major problem not only in Mauwake but in other Papuan languages as well.

a clearly bounded entity is divided in half (151). I have not found other terms indicating fractions. Longer expressions are needed for them e.g. 'divide into ten parts and take one part'.

(151) Yabuela **okaiwi** enak-e.
pawpaw one.side feed.me-IMP.2s
'Give me half of the pawpaw to eat.'

3.5 Pronouns

3.5.1 Introduction

Pronouns are a closed class of words. According to traditional grammar, pronouns can substitute for nouns, but actually they substitute for full noun phrases.

Pronouns in Mauwake only include personal pronouns.[31] Demonstratives, which are like pronouns in some respects, are discussed under deictics (§3.6.2). The indefinites, which are used as modifiers in a noun phrase, are closely related to question words and are treated in §3.7.2.

In principle all the pronouns in Mauwake are used for humans only. In legends also spirits can be referred to by these pronouns since they sometimes act like humans and can take human form. There is no third person singular pronoun for non-humans.

Wurm (1982) posited three typological sets of personal pronouns for Papuan languages, and mentioned Madang province as an area where set III is particularly widespread. The basic forms of Wurm's set III pronouns are shown in Table 3.17.

Table 3.17: Wurm's basic set III of TNG pronouns

	singular	plural
1	da~ta~ya	ki~ti
2	na	nik
3	nu[a]	(Wurm 1982: 40–42)

[a] The third person plural form is not included in Wurm's typology because of gaps in the material and greater variability than in the other person forms.

In all the three pronoun sets fronting of vowels often goes together with plurality (ibid. 78), the non-singular forms in Papuan languages being derived from the singular forms (Franklin 1979: 361).

With more data and after more rigorous and detailed work on the TNG pronouns, Ross (1995: 5) gives the following as reconstructions of Proto Madang and Proto Croisilles free pronouns (Table 3.18):

---

[31] Most of the material in this whole §3.5 has been published in my earlier paper (Järvinen (=Berghäll) 1991).

3 Morphology

Table 3.18: Proto Madang and Proto Croisilles free pronouns

	1s	2s	3s	1p	2p	3p
Proto Madang	*ya	*na	*ua/*nu	*i-	*ni-/*ta-	...
Proto Croisilles	*ya	*na/*ni	*ua/*nu	*i[ge]/*i[na]	*ni[ge]	*ua[ge]/*ua[na]

For different functions in the clause, Papuan languages often have one or two classes, or functional sets, of pronouns with or without prepositions or suffixes to mark the appropriate cases. Amele (Roberts 1987), Maia (Hardin 2002: 71), Hua (Haiman 1980: 215), Waskia (Ross & Paol 1978: 53) and Bargam (Hepner 2002: 29) have only one basic set each, to which postpositions or suffixes are added. Usan (Reesink 1987) and Siroi (Wells 1979) each have a nominative and a possessive set. Most Finisterre-Huon languages have different sets for regular and emphatic pronouns (McElhanon 1973).

Person is the more basic category than number in the pronoun systems of Papuan languages (Foley 1986: 69). As for number, it is most common just to have a two-way distinction between singular and plural, but dual forms are also quite widespread in TNG languages, and trial forms are found in some areas as well. An inclusive-exclusive distinction in the first person plural form is not common (Wurm 1982: 60) like it is in Austronesian languages, but according to Ross (2005: 56) it has probably been an areal feature for a long time, even before the Austronesians arrived.

Morphological resemblance between free pronouns and some verbal affixes, most commonly subject markers, is fairly widespread in Papuan languages (Franklin 1979). It is not unusual to find that verbal affixes, e.g. object markers, make fewer person/number distinctions than free pronouns (Foley 1986: 67).

In the following respects Mauwake manifests general typological features of TNG Madang pronouns. There is no gender or noun class system that would be indicated through concord and marking with nouns and/or pronouns. Also, the morphology is suffixal rather than prefixal. There is no inclusive-exclusive distinction. Possession is marked through suffixation on the personal pronouns (Wurm 1982: 40–42).

The basic unmarked pronouns in Mauwake reflect the Proto Croisilles forms rather closely, apart from the third person plural form *wi*, which Ross (1996: 23) mentions as an innovation *u-i- shared by the Kumil languages and the neighbouring Kaukombar languages. The ending -*fa* in the first and second person singular accusative pronouns is an innovation in the Kumil languages only.

Some features in the Mauwake pronoun system not typical of Papuan languages are the existence of dative pronouns and also their use as possessives, and the distinction between the unmarked pronouns and the focal pronouns.

3.5 Pronouns

The personal pronoun system in Mauwake is very regular, including the first, second and third persons both in singular and plural. Normally the plural form can also be used for dual; the dual number is only marked in one group, and there by adding a numeral rather than through affixation (§3.5.8). Since dual number does not occur in verb person marking either, apart from the first person imperative form, it is not very significant in the category of number. Spatial deixis is not marked in the personal pronoun system in Mauwake. The case is marked to some extent. Table 3.19 lists the personal pronouns in Mauwake.

Table 3.19: Personal pronouns

	Free					
	UNM	Focal	ACC	GEN	DAT	ISOLATIVE
1s	yo	yo-s	efa	y-ena	efa-r	ya-isow
2s	no	no-s	nefa	n-ena	nefa-r	na-isow
3s	(w)o	(w)o-s	Ø	o-na	wi-ar	wa-isow
1p	(y)i	(y)i-s	yia	yi-ena	yi-ar	(y)i-isow
2p	ni	ni-s	nia	ni-ena	ni-ar	ni-isow
3p	wi	wi-s	wia	wi-eña	wi-ar	wi-isow
	RESTRICTIVE			REFL		COMITATIVE
1s	yena-iw/yos-iw			y-ame		efa-m-iya
2s	nena-iw/nos-iw			n-ame		nefa-m-iya
3s	ona-iw/os-iw			w-ame		wama-iya
1p	yien-iw/is-iw			yi-am		yiam-iya
2p	nien-iw/nis-iw			ni-am		niam-iya
3p	wien-iw/wis-iw			wi-am		wiam-iya

Mauwake is a so-called pro-drop language, and a complete sentence can consist of a verb alone. The person of the subject is marked fully in the final verbs and partially in the medial verbs, so that besides the pragmatic clues there are also grammatical means for tracing the participants. But the pronouns are not completely optional: their use is rather strictly dictated by textual factors.

It is a fairly common feature in languages that pronouns can either modify a noun in a NP or replace a full NP, but cannot be the head of a NP taking modifiers (e.g. Hakulinen & Karlsson 1979; Saari 1985; Roberts 1987). In Mauwake the personal pronouns usually occur without modifiers, but they CAN be modified by a demonstrative, provided there is no collocational clash between the demonstrative and the personal pronoun (152), (153).

(152) **Ni   fain=ke ekap-eka!**
       2s.UNM this=CF come-IMP.2p
       'You here (or: This group of you), come!'

(153) O   **nain** fan me ik-ua.
     3s.UNM that1 here not be-PA.3s
     'He is not here.'

A pronoun copy after a full NP is hardly ever used in Mauwake for the subject. The rare example (154) is from a hortatory text and may show rhetoric style:

(154) *Maneka fain [wie* **wi**]   *eliw wiar op-i-kuan.*
     big   this uncle 3p.UNM well 3.DAT grab-NpFU.3p
     'These big ones the uncles may take from her.'

The example (155) is not a case of a genuine pronoun copy, since the genitive pronoun *wiena* adds the emphasizing meaning 'themselves':

(155) **Wi**   *iperowa*   **wi-ena** *ekap-e-mik.*
     3p.UNM middle.aged 3p-GEN come-PA-1/3p
     'The middle-aged (people) themselves came.'

For a pronoun copy of the genitive in a possessive NP, see §4.1.1.
Pronouns as deictic elements are discussed in §6.3.1.

3.5.2 Free pronouns

There are two sets of free pronouns: the unmarked pronouns, and the slightly longer focal pronouns.

3.5.2.1 Unmarked pronouns

Table 3.20: Unmarked pronouns.

	singular	plural
1	yo	(y)i
2	no	ni
3	(w)o	wi

The unmarked pronouns are as given in Table 3.20. The main use of the unmarked pronouns is as subjects. In narratives, only the person marking on the verb, rather than a pronoun, is used for an established, continuing subject/topic (§9.2.2). Especially third person unmarked pronouns marking the subject are quite rare in narrative texts (156), (157); first person pronouns are relatively much more common (158) (Järvinen (=Berghäll) 1991: 79–80).

(156) *Irak-owa=ke kerer-eya* **wi** *puk-omak-e-mik.*
fight-NMZ=CF appear-2/3p.DS 3p.UNM disperse-DISTR.PL-PA-1/3p
'When the fight started they (many) dispersed.'

(157) ***O*** *koora=pa naap ik-ok um-o-k.*
3s.UNM house=LOC thus be-SS die-PA-3s
'She was like that in the house and died.'

(158) *Bogia=pa nan wu-ap **i** kiiriw ekap-e-mik.*
Bogia=LOC there put-SS.SEQ 1p.UNM again come-PA-1/3p
'We buried his body (lit: put it) there in Bogia and came (back) again.'

However, with imperative verbs the subject pronoun is common (§3.5.11, §3.8.3.3.2, §7.3). In this Mauwake provides an interesting exception to a very strong cross-linguistic tendency of dropping subject pronouns in imperative clauses (Givón 1979: 80; Sadock & Zwicky 1985: 173–174). In this position the pronoun is usually unstressed (159), (160), unless it is contrasted with the subject of another clause coordinated with the imperative clause (161).

(159) "***No*** *me baurar-e," naap maak-e-k.*
2s.UNM not flee-IMP.2s thus tell-PA-3s
' "Don't run away," he told her.'

(160) ***I*** *or-u.*
1p.UNM descend-IMP.1d
'Let's go down.'

(161) ***No*** *feeke ik-e, yo Amerika wia akup-ikiw-i-yem.*
2s.UNM here.CF be-IMP.2s 1s.UNM America 3p.ACC search-go-Np-PR.1s
'You stay here, I will go searching the Americans.'

In an imperative clause the subject pronoun may also be used appositionally with a NP that has vocative function, to address a person (162).

(162) *Muuka, **no** aakisa emeria aaw-e!*
son 2s.UNM now woman take-IMP.2s
'Son, take a wife now!' (i.e. Son, it is time you got married.)

There are some cases where the imperative clauses tend not to have a subject pronoun. When the clause has a theme (§9.1) different from the subject (163), and especially when the theme is another pronoun (164), the imperative subject is blocked:

(163) *A, ifera$_{TH}$ feeke un-eka.*
ah salt.water here.CF draw/fetch-IMP.2p
'Ah, fetch the salt water (right) here.'

3 Morphology

(164) Yo_{TH, TP} momor   me yook-e.
       1s.UNM foolishly not follow.me-IMP.2s
       'Don't be foolish and follow me.' (Lit: 'Don't follow me foolishly.')

When an imperative final clause is preceded by a different-subject medial clause, it does not have a subject pronoun either (165):

(165) Nefa   war-iwkin   naap ma-e.
       2s.ACC shoot-2/3p.DS thus say-IMP.2s
       'When they shoot you, (then) say like that.'

A sentence-initial subject pronoun is quite common, when one or more same-subject medial clauses precede the imperative final clause and the scope of the imperative extends backwards over all the verbs (166):

(166) **Ni**   ikiw-ep   moma perek-eka!
       2p.UNM go-SS.SEQ taro pull.out-IMP.2p
       'Go and pull out (i.e. harvest) taro!'

The only example in the text data of a subject pronoun repeated in the final clause is a case where the medial clause is subordinated with the topic marker -na (167):

(167) **Ni**   uf-ep-na   **ni**   maadara   me iirar-eka...
       2p.UNM dance-SS.SEQ=TP 2s.UNM forehead.ornament not remove-IMP.2p
       'If/when you have danced, do not remove the forehead ornaments ...'

When the level of politeness is reduced, the subject pronoun is less common. Some acceptable reasons for this are urgency (168), or speech by an official that is expected to be brusque (169). Example (170) is from a situation where the behaviour of some men has been offensive to their wives, and when the men return home and give a blunt command, their wives react to this additional insult by repeating the command and then stating their own grievance and their revenge.

(168) Karu-eka, ikoka Yaapan ir-ami   ...
       run-IMP.2p later Japan   come-SS.SIM
       'Run, later the Japanese will come and ...'

(169) ...amia mua=ke ma-e-mik,   "Nainiw owowa ikiw-eka."
       bow   man=CF say-PA-1/3p again   village go-IMP.2p
       '...the policemen said, "Go back to the village." '

92

(170) *Ekap-emi   wia   maak-e-mik, "Maa iiw-eka."   "'Maa iiw-eka.'*
       come-ss.SIM 3p.ACC tell-PA-1/3p food dish.out-IMP.2p food dish.out-IMP.2p
       Nis=ke   sira   oko   on-ami…"
       2p.FC=CF custom other do-ss.SIM

       'They came and told them, "Dish out the food." " 'Dish out the food!' You acted offensively (lit: did another custom) and…" '

There is some tendency to have a pronominal form to occupy the sentence-initial theme position (§9.1), especially when the pronoun refers to the main participant of the sentence. In some cases this results in the restructuring of the sentence so that a medial clause appears in the middle of the finite clause, instead of coming before it as would be more normal. In (171) and (172) the medial clauses are enclosed in square brackets.

(171) *Yo   [eka   yoowa Magidar=ke kirip-ap   yi-eya]   en-e-m.*
       1s.UNM water hot   Magidar=CF mix-ss.SEQ give.me-2/3s.DS eat-PA-1s

       'Magidar made tea and gave it to me, and I drank it.'

(172) *No   [um-eya]   or-o-n.*
       2s.UNM die-2/3s.DS descend-PA-2s

       'After he died you went down.'

Sentence-initial unmarked pronouns are also used when they are not subjects but rather mark a pronoun with other than subject function as the theme. The first person pronoun in particular is placed in the theme position very frequently (173), (174), the second person less so and the third person least of all.

(173) *Yo   efa   uruf-e!*
       1s.UNM 1s.ACC look-IMP.2s

       'Look at me!'

(174) *I   yiena mua opora yia   asip-owa ekap-e-mik   nain*
       1p.UNM 1p.GEN man talk 1p.ACC help-NMZ come-PA-1/3p that1

       'Our men who have come to help us with the language …'

Especially in spoken language the unmarked pronouns may also be used, instead of genitive pronouns, to indicate possession. This is most commonly done with kinship terms (175) and body parts (176), sometimes with other nouns[32] too, referring to things closely associated with a person (177). This usage can be seen as a kind of widening of the range of inalienably possessed nouns beyond the kinship terms (§3.2.4) to other nouns that would be inalienably possessed in related languages or some other languages in the area.

---

[32] The following list covers most of them: *opora* 'talk, speech', *opaimika* 'mouth, speech', *unuma* 'name', *koora* 'house, home', *manina* 'garden', *siowa* 'dog' and *amina* 'saucepan'.

(175) **Yo** auwa nan ik-ua.
       1s.UNM 1s/p.father there be-PA.3s
       'My father is there.'

(176) Ikoka Yaapan=ke **ni** umakuna nia puuk-i-kuan.
       Later Japan=CF 2p.UNM neck 2p.ACC cut-Np-FU.3s
       'Later the Japanese will cut your necks.'

(177) Aria, **yo** opora muut nan-e-k.
       alright 1s.UNM talk only there-PA-3s
       'Alright, there is my talk.'

The third person plural unmarked pronoun is used to pluralize a noun phrase (178). It is also often used with a place name to refer to the inhabitants of the place collectively (179).

(178) **Wi** sawur nain=ke kuura puuk-a-mik.
       3p.UNM spirit that1=CF fly change.into-PA-3s
       'Those spirits changed into flies.'

(179) **Wi** Lasen=ke kuum-e-mik.
       3p.UNM Lasen=CF burn-PA-1/3p
       'The Lasen people burned it.' (Or: 'It was the Lasen people who burned it.')

The neutral focus marker -ko attaches itself to the unmarked pronoun rather than the focal pronoun (180). I do not know the reason for this.[33]

(180) Waaya en-e-man nain **yo=ko** me uruf-a-m.
       pig eat-PA-2p that1 1s.UNM=NF not see-PA-1s
       'I didn't (get to even) see the pig that you ate.'

The unmarked pronouns are used as the basic form for focal, genitive, reflexive-reciprocal and isolative pronouns.

3.5.2.2 Focal pronouns

The focal pronouns are similar to the unmarked pronouns but have final -s: *yos, nos, (w)os, (y)is, nis, wis*. These pronouns are never used for a neutral, non-focused subject. They are used in isolation and in lists (181), as well as with the topic marker *-na* (182), the contrastive focus marker *-ke* (183), the question marker *-i* (184) and the adverb *pun* 'also' (185). With the limiter *-iw* (186) the focal pronoun forms one of the two kinds of restrictive pronoun (§3.5.7).

---

[33] Kwan Poh San suggests as a possible reason that as the neutral focus does not give as strong an emphasis as the contrastive focus, it also attaches itself to a less emphasized form of the pronoun (p.c.).

(181) **Yos,** *yena emeria, ne Yoli gelemuta ...*
1s.FC 1s.GEN woman ADD Yoli little
'I, my wife and little Yoli ...'

(182) **Nos**=*na?*
2s.FC=TP
'What about you?'

(183) **Is**=*ke me kuum-e-mik.*
1p.FC=CF not burn-PA-1/3p
'WE didn't burn it.'

(184) **Yos**=*i?*
1sg.FC=QM
'I?'

(185) **Os** *pun opora kuisow naap=iw ma-e-k.*
3s.FC also talk one thus=LIM say-PA-3s
'HE also said the same thing.'

(186) *Anane* **nos**=*iw nefa maak-i-ya.*
always 2s.FC=LIM 2s.ACC tell-Np-PR.3s
'He always talks to you only.'

When the subject of an imperative clause is contrasted with some other possible subject, the focal pronoun with contrastive focus clitic is employed (187):

(187) **Nos**=*ke ikiw-e!*
2s.FC=CF go-IMP.2s
'YOU go (not someone else)!'

3.5.3 Accusative pronouns

The accusative pronouns may have been derived from the unmarked pronouns, but because at present there is little similarity between the singular forms of the two sets, the accusative pronouns are treated as a set of their own. Their main use is to mark the syntactic object of a clause, which is typically the semantic patient but with a few verbs may be a recipient (§5.2). The plural forms are also used for the beneficiary, as the beneficiary suffix -*a* in the verb (§3.8.3.1) does not distinguish between singular and plural. The accusative pronouns serve as a basis for some other pronoun forms with different functions as well. The form of the accusative pronouns is reflected very closely in the plural stems of the object cross-referencing verbs but not in the singular stems (§3.8.4.2.4). The accusative pronouns are listed in Table 3.21.

3 Morphology

Table 3.21: Accusative pronouns

	singular	plural
1	*efa*	*yia*
2	*nefa*	*nia*
3	Ø (zero)	*wia*

Only objects that are [+human] are marked with the pronoun. As there is no other case marking in NPs, except for oblique case marking like locative and instrument for [-human] NPs, the accusative pronouns provide some of this case marking, when the object is a [+human] NP. Much of the time there is no overt pronoun, as the third person singular form is zero.[34]

The position of the accusative pronouns in Mauwake is immediately preceding the verb. This is probably the main reason why Z'Graggen (1971) treats them as verbal prefixes. Likewise, Reesink (1987: 108) states that Usan has object prefixes, even if they have a rather loose status and can be detached from the verb. But I consider the object pronouns in Mauwake independent words, as they all have two syllables and follow the normal stress pattern of the language. They are, however, very closely bound to the verb, and it seems that a cliticization process is going on.[35]

The accusative pronouns are used for encoding semantic patient (188), or recipient (189), both of which are syntactic objects (§5.2, §5.3).

(188) *Irakowa=pa **wia** war-e-mik.*
      fight=LOC 3p.ACC kill-PA-1/3p
      'In the fight they killed them.'

(189) *Opora nain **efa** maak-e-k.*
      talk that 1s.ACC tell-PA-3s
      'He told me the story.'

The plural forms of the accusative pronouns are used together with the beneficiary form in the verb to disambiguate between the persons (190) (§3.8.3.1).

(190) *Aite maa **yia** p-or-om-a-k.*
      mother food 1p.ACC BPX-descend-BEN-BNFY2.PA-3s
      'Mother brought food down for us.'

---

[34] Zero pronoun for the third person singular is not exceptional cross-lingustically (Lyons 1968: 278; Foley 1986: 66; Givón 1976: 166), and in Papuan languages it is common especially for the object pronoun. All the 25 Northern Adelbert Range languages compared by Z'Graggen (1980: 9,160) have zero as object pronoun or object marking on the verb for the third person singular form.

[35] In Järvinen (=Berghäll) (1991) I discussed this question whether Mauwake pronouns are full words, clitics or affixes, at some length.

The only grammatical difference between the semantic roles of patient and beneficiary is shown in the verb, which can incorporate the benefactive suffix; and between patient and recipient there is no syntactic or morphological difference. The following hierarchy is followed: if there is a recipient not incorporated in the verb root,[36] the accusative pronoun refers to it (189), if there is no recipient but a plural beneficiary, the pronoun refers to the latter (190). And if there is neither recipient nor beneficiary, the accusative pronoun refers to the patient (188).[37]

Transitive verbs in Mauwake usually require an overt object, and verbs like 'teach', 'tell', 'ask', which can take two objects, require the presence of at least the human object, whether patient (191), or recipient (192). In (192) the pronoun *wia* '3p.ACC' may be definite or indefinite, hence the alternative free translations.

(191) **Nefa** nokar-i-yem.
2s.ACC ask-Np-PR.1s

'I'm asking you.'

(192) Inglis **wia** ofakow-i-ya.
English 3p.ACC teach-Np-PR.3s

'(S)he teaches them English.' (Or: '(S)he teaches English.')

In rare cases the human object may be left out (193):

(193) Oram nokar-i-yem.
just ask-Np-PR.1s

'I'm just asking.' (Asking nobody in particular, or for no particular reason.)

Transitive verbs with [+human] objects require pronouns even when the object is mentioned as a noun or a noun phrase (194), (195).

(194) Emeria **wia** amukar-e-k.
woman 3p.ACC scold-PA-3s

'He/she scolded the women.'

(195) Emeria **nia** amukar-e-k.
woman 2p.ACC scold-PA-3s

'He/she scolded (you) women.'

Since the third person singular form is zero, all the cases with [+human] object noun without overt object pronoun by default indicate the third person singular (196). Because there is no number or case distinction in the nouns for the arguments of the verb, without this indication by pronouns it would often be ambiguous whether the NP was subject or object, or whether the object was singular or plural.

---

[36] Verbs like 'give' and 'feed' incorporate the recipient object in the verb root itself (§3.8.4.2.4).
[37] Cf. a rather similar hierarchy for the distributive suffix in verbs (§3.8.2.3.2)

3 Morphology

(196) *Emeria amukar-e-k.*
woman scold-PA-3s

'He scolded his wife.'

In theory, the example (196) could also mean 'The woman scolded him/her' but in practice it does not. For when the subject is old/established information it is usually left out rather than marked by a NP, and when it is new information, it is marked by the contrastive focus marker *-ke*.[38]

It must be clearly indicated whether the speaker or addressee is included in the object (194), (195), (197).

(197) *Mua **yia** aaw-i-kuan.*
man 1p.ACC take-Np-FU.3p

'They will take (us) men.'

Reesink (1987: 52–53) mentions that Usan has object prefixes, but a free pronoun can also occupy the object position in the third person singular. This is not the case in Mauwake; in (198) the free pronoun *o* is a re-activated topic (§9.2.3). The negative clause (199) shows that the position of the free pronoun is not directly preceding the verb. The clauses (200), (201) have a similar structure with pronouns in non-third person marking a theme. When the pronoun is fronted as a theme (§9.1), it is this unmarked pronoun that is used in the theme position.

(198) *Wi teeria papako o Ø asip-a-mik...*
3p.UNM group other 3s.UNM Ø help-PA-1/3p

'Another group helped him...' (Or: 'He was helped by another group...')

(199) *O me Ø aaw-e-mik.*
3s.UNM not Ø take-PA-1/3p

'They did not take/choose him.' (Or: 'He was not taken by them.')

(200) *Yo me **efa** aaw-e-mik.*
1s.UNM not 1s.ACC take-PA-1/3p

'They didn't take/choose me.' (Or: 'I wasn't taken by them.')

(201) *Yo **efa** aaw-e-mik.*
1s.UNM 1s.ACC take-PA-1/3p

'They took/chose me.' (Or: 'I was taken by them.')

There is one instance where the free third person singular pronoun does occur after the negator and immediately preceding the verb, just like accusative pronouns. This is when there is constituent negation (§6.2.2.) on the object, which then also receives clausal

---

[38] To have the meaning 'He/she scolded a/the WOMAN', the noun would be followed by the non-numeral quantifier *oko* 'a, a certain' or the demonstrative *nain* 'that'.

stress (202) (§§2.1.3.1, 9.3.3). Here it is the negator that moves to precede the constituent it negates. The same process is also seen in (203) where the negator has moved in front of the whole object NP.

(202) *Me **o** uruf-a-m.*
not 3s.UNM see-PA-1s
'It wasn't him/her that I saw.'

(203) *Me **wi** owow mua **wia** arew-a-mik...*
not 3p.UNM village man 3p.ACC wait-PA-1/3p
'It wasn't the village people that we waited for...'

There are situations where it is impossible to determine whether the unmarked third person singular pronoun is marking a topic/subject or an object fronted as a theme (§9.1). The context would be needed to disambiguate between the slightly different meanings of (204), which do not come out well in the English translation. The first meaning is likely if the context mentions some other people seeing something; the second meaning is more probable elsewhere.

(204) ***O** me uruf-a-k.*
3s.UNM not see-PA-3s
'(S)he didn't see him/her/it.' (Or: '(S)he didn't see *him/her*.')

There are a few verbs in Mauwake that cross-reference the patient or recipient object in the verb root (§3.8.4.2.4). These verbs do not allow a separate accusative pronoun for the function that is already expressed by the verb root (205), (206), but it is possible to have a separate accusative pronoun for the patient when the verb cross-references the recipient rather than the patient (207).

(205) *Ipia=ke **yiar-eya** ekap-e-mik.*
rain=CF hit.us-2/3s.DS come-PA-1/3p
'The rain hit us and we/they came.'

(206) *Yomar, no uurika **yook-ap** urup-e.*
friend 2s.UNM tomorrow follow.me-SS.SEQ ascend-IMP.2s
'Friend, follow me up tomorrow.'

(207) *Iiriw **nefa** wi-e-mik.*
already 2s.ACC give.them-PA-1/3p
'We have already given you to them.'

When other verbs require both a [+human] recipient and a [+human] patient, it is encoded as a clause chain (208). The first verb then takes one of the arguments and the second the other.

(208) *Uuriw **wia** aaw-ep **nia** p-ekap-om-i-yen.*
morning 3p.ACC take-SS.SEQ 2p.ACC BPX-come-BEN-Np-FU.1p
'In the morning we will bring them (people) to you.'

3 Morphology

3.5.4 Genitive pronouns

Since possession can be expressed by means of three different kinds of personal pronouns in Mauwake, I call the function POSSESSIVE and the different grammatical forms GENITIVE, DATIVE and UNMARKED PRONOUN. All these forms have other functions besides possessive, as has already been shown for the unmarked pronoun.

Table 3.22: Genitive pronouns

	singular	plural
1	y-ena	yi-ena
2	n-ena	ni-ena
3	o-na	wi-ena

The genitive pronouns (Table 3.22) are derived from the unmarked pronouns by the ending *-ena*.[39] The main function of the genitive pronoun is to indicate the possessor in a NP, and the main strategy for expressing the possessor in a NP is to use either the genitive pronoun or a possessive noun phrase. Unlike most other modifiers of the noun, the genitive pronoun precedes the head noun. This is in accord with Givón's (1984: 202) implicational hierarchy of conformity to basic word order, as well as Dryer's (2007a:62) statement about word order correlations. In Mauwake only the nominal and genitive modifiers and noun complements, which are also at the top of Givón's 1984 hierarchy, precede the head noun in the NPs; all the other modifiers follow the head noun.

The genitive pronoun is used when the possessor is coreferential with the subject,[40] and its meaning is often close to English 'own' (209)–(211).

(209) *Sawur emeria nain=ke* **ona** *soma mua nain ifakim-o-k.*
spirit woman that1=CF 3S.GEN lover man that1 kill-PA-3S
'The spirit woman killed her (own) lover.'

(210) *Mua me wia imen-ap=na* **niena** *maa=ke ...*
man not 3P.ACC find-SS.SEQ=TP 2P.GEN thing=CF
'If you don't find the men, it's your (own) business ...'

(211) **Niena** *unuma maifa feeke siisim-eka.*
2P.GEN name paper here.CF write-IMP.2P
'Write your names on the paper here/ on this paper.'

In descriptive or equative clauses genitive pronouns can modify both the subject NP (212) and the non-verbal predicate NP (213), whereas the dative pronouns can modify neither.

---

[39] This ending is probably related to the specifier *-ena*.
[40] It does not have to be used when the possessive relationship is clear from the context; see (196) above.

(212) **Yena** koora maneka wenup.
1s.GEN house big very
'My house is very big.'

(213) Mua fain me **nena** niawi akena=ke.
man this not 2s.GEN 2s/p.father true=CF
'This man is not your real father.'

It is possible for a genitive pronoun to co-occur with a dative pronoun to modify the same noun which is not coreferential with the subject (214). (See §3.5.5 for a further discussion on the differences between genitive and dative possessives.)

(214) **Yena** koora **efar** aw-o-k.
1s.GEN house 1s.DAT burn-PA-3s
'My house burned.'

Even when the possessor is expressed by a noun or NP, the genitive pronoun is sometimes explicit, occurring either between the possessor and the possessed NP (215) or, quite frequently, preceding both (216).

(215) Om-em-ik-eya sawur emeria **ona** wiawi onak=ke
cry-SS.SIM-be-2/3s.DS spirit woman 3s.GEN 3s/p.father 3s/p.mother=CF
ekap-emi maak-e-mik...
come-SS.SIM tell-PA-1/3p
'While she was crying, the spirit woman's father and mother came and told her, ...'

(216) **Wiena** mia kia maa=iw on-a-mik.
3p.GEN skin white thing=INST do-PA-1/3p
'They did it with the Europeans' things.'

The reason for this addition of a pronoun may be the lack of case marking in nouns, which makes the processing of possessed NPs more difficult when there are modifying nouns in the NP. But it is also quite common for a possessive NP to occur without a genitive pronoun (217).

(217) Mua oko miira inawera=pa uruf-ap ma-i-mik, ...
man other face dream=LOC see-SS.SEQ say-Np-PR.1/3p
'When we see another man's face in a dream we say, ...'

The third person singular possessive pronoun provides an exception to the rule that the personal pronouns are only used for the humans. However, the cases where *ona* '3s.GEN' refers to a non-human possessor are few and seem to require the connotation 'own' (218).

3 Morphology

(218)   ...**ona** pia=pa   nan   karu-emi ...
         3s.GEN bamboo=LOC there run-SS.SIM
         '...it (molten copper) runs there in its pipe (lit:bamboo) and ...'

In those instances where the possessed NP in the predicative position lacks an overt head noun, three different strategies may be used. I have not observed any difference in meaning. The genitive pronoun may occur by itself, without a head noun, which can either be deleted completely (219) or substituted by *nain* 'that' (220), or the NP can be expressed by a possessive phrase (221) (§4.4). In all these instances the head noun occurs earlier in the same sentence, or occasionally in the preceding sentence.

(219)   *Ikiwosa* **yena**, *wapena* **yena**...
         head   1s.GEN, hand   1s.GEN
         'The head is mine (to eat), the hands are mine...'

(220)   *Fikera*   *pun* **wiena** *nain=ke.*
         kunai.grass too 3p.GEN that1=CF
         'The kunai grass is theirs, too.'

(221)   *Maa nain* **yo/yena**   *efarik*.
         thing that1 1s.UNM/1s.GEN 1s.DAT
         'That thing is mine.'

Like possessives in many other languages, the genitive pronoun may function as the subject of a nominalized clause (222) (§5.7). The unmarked pronoun is used in the same position too; I have not found any difference in their use.

(222)   **Yiena** *owow maneka ikiw-owa nain ma-i-yem.*
         1p.GEN village big   go-NMZ   that1 say-Np-PR.1s
         'I'm telling about our going to town.'

As ordinary main clause subjects the genitive pronouns are more emphatic than the unmarked pronouns.[41] The pronunciation reflects the emphasis too: these pronouns receive a stronger stress than the unmarked pronouns when used as a subject (223).

(223)   *Aasa enuma* **yena** *me suuw-i-yem.*
         canoe new   1s.GEN not push-Np-PR.1s
         'I don't take a new canoe down myself.'

The following example (224) has two identical genitive pronouns, the first one functioning as an emphatic subject pronoun and the second one as a possessive pronoun:

---

[41] Usan (Reesink 1987: 55), Siroi (Wells 1979: 20) and Maia (Hardin 2002: 73) also use the same pronoun forms for possessive and emphatic pronouns, whereas Waskia (Ross & Paol 1978) does not.

(224) **Yiena** iisow, **yiena** garanga muutiw aaw-ep   uup-ep   en-e-mik.
       1p.GEN 1p.ISOL 1p.GEN family   only   take-SS.SEQ cook-SS.SEQ eat-PA-1/3p

   'Only our family by ourselves (lit: we ourselves we only, our family only) took it, cooked and ate it.'

A genitive pronoun is also possible as the subject of a relative clause, when the subject is emphatic (225).

(225) Wi   teeria papako o   asip-a-mik, [**ona** eka   sesenar-ep
       3p.UNM group other   3s.UNM help-PA-1/3p 3s.GEN water buy-SS.SEQ
       wienak-e-k   nain]_RC.
       feed.them-PA-3s that1

   'Another group helped him, those for whom *he* had bought and given beer.'

When the limiting clitic -*iw* 'only' is added to the genitive pronoun, the result is a restrictive pronoun (226) (§3.5.7).

(226) Yo   me nia   maak-i-nen, **nien=iw**   ma-eka.
       1s.UNM not 2p.ACC tell-Np-FU.1s 2p.GEN=LIM say-IMP.2p

   'I will not tell you (what to do); discuss it on your own (among yourselves/as a group).'

3.5.5 Dative pronouns

The dative case is typically associated with the semantic function of goal. The pronouns called dative in Mauwake do sometimes function as goals, but mostly they have a locative or source function. So the term here is to be understood more as a [+human] LOCATIVE, which includes not only locative but goal and source as well. The dative pronouns have also grammaticalized as possessives to form possessive predicate construction (§5.5.2) and as attributive possessives to indicate that the possessor is non-coreferential with the subject.

The dative pronouns (Table 3.23) are formed by adding -r to the accusative pronouns, with the exception of third person singular, which is identical with the plural.[42]

The syntactic function of a dative pronoun may be clausal (a locative adverbial phrase §4.6.1), or NP-internal (a possessive modifier §4.1.1). Regardless of its function, the dative pronoun is always in immediately preverbal position.

The semantic function of a dative pronoun is related to the verb of the clause. With motion verbs it has goal function (227), (228):

(227) Pok-ap   ika-iwkin mua **wiar** ekap-e-mik.
       sit-SS.SEQ be-2/3p.DS man 3.DAT come-PA-1/3p

   'They were sitting and (their) husbands came to them.'

---

[42] For most Mauwake speakers the old singular form *wo-ar* has been replaced by the third person plural form, but it is still used in the Ulingan dialect group.

3 Morphology

Table 3.23: Dative pronouns

	singular	plural
1	efa-r	yia-r
2	nefa-r	nia-r
3	wia-r	wia-r

(228) Mia kokas-owa=ke **wiar** kerer-e-k.
skin itch-NMZ=CF 3.DAT appear/arrive-PA-3s

'Her skin started to itch.' (Lit: 'Skin itch appeared to her.')

With stative verbs the pronouns indicate location (229), (230). (Note that the free translation needs to use a comitative expression, since English does not have a [+human] locative expression equivalent to the Mauwake dative.)

(229) Feeke **wiar** ik-ok kiiriw mua wiar urup-e.
here.CF 3.DAT be-SS again man 3.DAT ascend-IMP.2s

'Having been here with him, go (back) to your husband again.'

(230) Wi sawur nain ir-ami fan **yiar** pok-a-mik.[43]
3p.UNM spirit that1 go.east-SS.SIM here 1p.DAT sit-PA-1/3p

'The spirits, going eastward, sat here with us.'

With verbs that indicate receiving something (take, get, buy, etc.) the dative has the semantic function of source (231)–(233).

(231) Yo emeria Lasen=pa **wiar** aaw-e-m.
1s.UNM woman Lasen=LOC 3.DAT get/take-PA-1s

'I got (my) wife from (the) Lasen (people).'

(232) Kuisow akena ika-eya yos=ke **wiar** sesenar-ep aaw-e-m.
one very be-2/3s.DS 1s.FC=CF 3.DAT buy-SS.SEQ get-PA-1s

'There was only one and (it was) I (who) bought it from them.'

(233) Mua oko=ke waaya nain mik-ap **nefar** aaw-i-non.
man other=CF pig that1 spear-SS.SEQ 2s.DAT get/take-Np-FU.3s

'Another man will spear the pig and take it from you.'

The "source" can also be more abstract. I have observed this use only with verbs indicating hearing or speaking (234).

---

[43] Although the most natural free translation is '…with us', comitative connotation should not be read into the Mauwake text; this is a locative.

(234) Naap **wiar** miim-a-m.
thus 3.DAT hear-PA-1s
'I heard thus about him/her/them.'

A locative phrase referring to a village or village area including its inhabitants is commonly used with a dative pronoun as well (235), otherwise it refers to just the location rather than the inhabitants. The pronoun may be used with towns or bigger areas as well, but the bigger the location, the less probable the pronoun is. In (236) the people ran away to the people in the Bogia area, whereas in (237) the people of Bogia town may not have been involved in the burial at all. In (238) the speaker was going to the Highlands, not in order to meet the Highlanders but to work in a location there.

(235) Lasen **wiar** ek-a-mik.
Lasen 3.DAT go.east-PA-1/3p
'We went to Lasen (=to the people of Lasen village).'

(236) Baurar-ep Bogia kame **wiar** ikiw-e-mik.
run.away-SS.SEQ Bogia area 3.DAT go-PA-1/3p
'They ran away to the Bogia area.'

(237) P-ikiw-ep Bogia=pa nan wu-a-mik.
BPX-go-SS.SEQ Bogia=LOC there put-PA-1/3p
'We/They took it (a body) and buried it in Bogia.'

(238) Uuriw iinan aasa aaw-ep Epa Dabela urup-e-mik.
morning sky canoe take-SS.SEQ place cold ascend-PA-1/3p
'In the morning we took an airplane and went up to the Highlands.'

Cross-linguistically a POSSESSIVE PREDICATE construction, a 'have' construction, has often been derived from a locative or a goal/dative construction, plus a verb of existence (Heine 1997: 50–61). In the possessive predicates in Mauwake the dative pronoun precedes the verb *ik-* 'be' (239) The possessive predicate construction is discussed in more detail in §5.5.2. .

(239) I sira naap **yiar** ik-ua.
1p.UNM custom thus 1p.DAT be-PA.3s
'We have a custom like that.' (Lit: 'A custom like that is to us.)'

The same dative pronoun has also grammaticalized as a possessive attribute in a noun phrase , but here it is the semantic function of [+HUMAN] SOURCE that is behind the development. Conceptually the structures 'X took Y from me' and 'X took my Y' are very close. In (240) *efar* can mean either 'my' or 'from me'.

(240) Nos=ke anane urema **efar** ikum-ar-i-n.
2s.FC=CF always bandicoot 1s.DAT illicitly-INCH-Np-PR.2s
'You always steal bandicoots from me / my bandicoots.'

3 Morphology

That it is difficult to distinguish between the roles of possessor and source is not unusual.[44] Heine (1997: 133) mentions that early in the grammaticalization process "these expressions can simultaneously be interpreted with reference to either their non-possessive source or to possession." In (241) and (242) the source interpretation is not possible. The example (242) describes a situation in future when the speaker will already be dead and his son is made to lose his inheritance.

(241) *A, yo aamun nan **efar** ik-ua.*
ah 1s.UNM younger.sibling there 1s.DAT be-PA.3s
'Ah, there is my younger brother.'

(242) *Ikoka yena yeepa muuka=ke yo muuka **efar** iirar-ep*
later 1s.GEN elder.sibling son=CF 1s.UNM son 1s.DAT remove-SS.SEQ
maak-i-non ...
tell-Np-FU.3s
'Later my elder brother's son will remove/displace/drive away my son and tell him, ...'

This grammaticalization probably started with the verbs denoting taking and getting, but it is only a short step from there to interpreting the dative as a possessor with other verbs as well, especially as it is likely that the dative pronoun was already earlier established in the possessive predicate structure (243)–(246).

(243) *Owowa **yiar** kuuf-owa ekap-e-mik.*
village 1p.DAT see-NMZ come-PA-1/3p
'They came to see our village.'

(244) *Auwa afura **wiar** akim-ap=ko uruf-e.*
1s/p.father lime 3.DAT try-SS.SEQ=NF see-IMP.2s
'Try father's lime and see (what it is like).'

(245) *Ikiwosa **wiar** pepekim-ep kaik-a-m.*
head 3.DAT measure-SS.SEQ tie-PA-1s
'I measured her head and tied it (a cane).'

(246) *No me emeria **nefar** maak-i-mik.*
2s.UNM not woman 2s.DAT tell-Np-PR.1/3p
'We are not telling/talking to your wife.'

Although the possessive is often associated with malefactive overtones as in (247) and (248), this is not part of its meaning (244), (245).

---

[44] Sometimes it is hard to distinguish even between a possessor and a goal. In the following sentence *efar* could also mean 'to my place/house', with the head noun deleted: *Yo me efar ekap-e!* [1s.UNM not 1s.DAT come-IMP.2s] 'Don't come to me!'

106

(247) *Buburia koora **wiar** aw-o-k.*
 bald house 3.DAT burn-PA-3s

 'The bald man's house burned (on him).'

(248) *Irak-emi amina **wiar** fo-fook-omak-e-mik.*
 fight-SS.SIM pot 3.DAT RDP-split-DISTR/PL-PA-1/3p

 'They_i fought and split their_j pots.'

But since Mauwake already had genitive pronouns to indicate possession, why did another possessive strategy develop? The answer may lie in the original source function of the dative pronoun. The referent of the participant with the source function is normally another than the referent of the clausal subject, and it is this feature of non-coreferentiality with the subject that became the distinctive feature for the new possessive.

The dative possessive construction is particularly useful for disambiguating between the subject and the possessor, if both of them are in third person. The following two pairs of examples, (249)–(250) and (251)–(252) show this clearly. The corresponding English sentences are ambiguous, whereas the Mauwake sentences are not:

(249) *Yena eremena=ke **ona** siowa aruf-eya kepura ku-o-k.*
 1s.GEN nephew=CF 3s.GEN dog hit-2/3s.DS leg break-PA-3s

 'My nephew_i hit his_i dog and its leg broke.'

(250) *Yena eremena=ke siowa **wiar** aruf-eya kepura ku-o-k.*
 1s.GEN nephew=CF dog 3.DAT hit-2/3s.DS leg break-PA-3s

 'My nephew_i hit his/her_j dog and its leg broke.'

(251) *Wis=ke wiawi maak-e-mik.*
 3p.FC=CF 3s/p.father tell-PA-1/3p

 '(It was) they_i (who) told their_i father.'

(252) *Wis=ke wiawi **wiar** maak-e-mik.*
 3p.FC=CF 3s/p.father 3.DAT tell-PA-1/3p

 '(It was) they_i (who) told their_j father.'

Currently the dative possessive has to be used when the possessor is non-coreferential with the subject or recipient of the clause (253)–(255).

(253) *Marasin nain=ke kema **wiar** iw-a-k.*
 medicine that1=CF liver 3.DAT go-PA-3s

 'The medicine went into his liver.'

(254) *Wiowa nain o wapena=pa **wiar** ku-o-k.*
 spear that1 3s.UNM hand=LOC 3.DAT break-PA-3s

 'The spear broke in his hand.'

3 Morphology

(255) Pina ... **nefar** kaken-ami welaw-i-kuan.
guilt ... 2s.DAT straighten-ss.SIM finish-Np-FU.3p

'They will straighten your(sg) ... guilt and finish it.'

It follows from the non-coreferentiality restriction that a possessed NP with the possessive pronoun in the dative cannot be the subject of a clause.

In the possessor function the dative pronoun does not co-occur with the accusative pronoun in the same clause (256). In the rare occasion where there would be rivalry for the position immediately preceding the verb, the accusative is chosen (257) rather than the dative (258).

(256) *Yena muuka erup **efar** wia aaw-o-k.
1s.GEN son two 1s.DAT 3p.ACC take-PA-3s

(257) Yena muuka erup **wia** aaw-o-k.
1s.GEN son two 3p.ACC take-PA-3s

'He took my two sons.'

(258) ?Yena muuka erup **efar** aaw-o-k.
1s.GEN son two 3.DAT take-PA-3s

But if the dative pronoun has the semantic role of goal, it may co-occur with an accusative pronoun; in this case it precedes the accusative pronoun (259).

(259) O **wiar nefa** sesek-i-yem.
3s.UNM 3.DAT 2s.ACC send-Np-PR.1s

'I am sending you to him.'

The use of the genitive possessive pronoun is much less restricted. Besides being employed where the possessor is coreferential with the subject (260) or recipient (261), it can also be used when a possessed NP is the subject or non-verbal predicate of a descriptive or equative clause (262).

(260) Eema=ke **ona** kolos Garamin iw-o-k.
Eema=CF 3s.GEN dress Garamin give.him/her-PA-3s

'Eema$_i$ gave her$_i$ dress to Garamin.'

(261) Eema=ke Garamin **ona** kolos iw-o-k.
Eema=CF Garamin 3s.GEN dress give.him/her-PA-3s

'Eema$_i$ gave Garamin$_j$ her$_j$ dress.'

(262) **Yena** koora maneka wenup.
1s.GEN house big very

'My house is very big.'

The genitive or unmarked pronoun may co-occur together with the dative pronoun referring to the same person, thus emphasizing the possessive function of the dative (263), (264).

(263) *Yo emeria **efar** uruf-a-man=i e wia?*
1s.UNM woman 1s.DAT see-PA-2p=QM or no
'Have you seen my wife or not?'

(264) ***Ona** koora=pa **wiar** wu-a-mik.*
3s.GEN house=LOC 3.DAT put-PA-1/3p
'They put it in his (own) house.'

Example (265) shows how the genitive and dative possessives, in DIFFERENT person forms, can modify the same noun. The dative pronoun can here be interpreted either as a possessive 'your (wives)' or as a source '(wives) from you'.

(265) *Emeria ikoka Yaapan **wiena niar** aaw-i-kuan.*
woman later Japanese 3p.GEN 2p.DAT take-Np-FU.3p
'Later the Japanese will take your wives as their own.'

In (266), where there are several possessive NPs, the two genitive pronouns both refer to the man who is identified in the preceding text. In the second clause the possessor is a modifier in the subject NP, so it has to be in the genitive. The subject in the third clause is the lover's spirit, and because only one dative possessive is possible in one clause, here it is naturally assigned to the man's wife whose things were thrown around, and the man is referred to by a genitive possessive. In this case the genitive possessive also underlines the fact that one of the women was the man's own wife. The clauses are separated by brackets.

(266) *[Ikiw-ep-ik-eya] [**ona** soma emeria nain kukusa nain=ke ekap-ep]*
go-SS.SEQ-be-2/3s.DS 3s.GEN lover woman that1 spirit that1=CF come-SS.SEQ
*[**ona** emeria nain maa **wiar** wafufur-eya] [naap maak-e-k,] ...*
3s.GEN woman that1 thing 3.DAT throw.around-2/3s.DS thus tell-PA-3s
'When he$_i$ was gone, his$_i$ lover-woman's$_j$ spirit came and threw around his$_i$ (own) wife's$_k$ things, and she$_k$ told her like this, ...'

Dative pronouns also have a longer form, with the suffix -*ik*: *efarik*, *nefarik* etc. The pronoun is a contracted form of the 'have' construction, with just the root left of the verb *ik*- 'be', which has been suffixed to the pronoun. In natural text the frequency of these pronouns is extremely low. They have to be used when the dative pronoun is clause final (267)-(268), as the regular dative pronoun only occurs pre-verbally. The longer form is often accompanied by either the genitive pronoun (267) or the unmarked pronoun (269), which suggests that it is more emphasized than the simple dative.

(267) Miiw ara   gelemuta nain **yiena yiarik**.
      land piece small   that1 1p.GEN 1p.DAT

'That small piece of ground is ours.'

(268) Wiawi=ke   amap-or-o-k=i,   weke   **wiarik**?
      3s/p.father=CF BPX-descend-PA-3s=QM 3s/p.grandfather 3.DAT

'Did her father take her down to her grandfather?'

The long dative with a "receive" type verb in the following example can be traced back to *niar ikeya* 'you had it, and...' (269).

(269) Yo   mesa   up-owa   fain **ni**   **niarik** aaw-ep   isak-e-m.
      1s.UNM winged.bean plant-NMZ this 2p.UNM 2p.DAT get-SS.SEQ plant-PA-1s

'I got these winged bean seeds from you and planted them.'

3.5.6 Isolative pronouns

The isolative pronoun forms (Table 3.24) are based on the unmarked pronouns. The ending *-isow,* which the numeral *kuisow* 'one' shares with these pronouns, may be an earlier morpheme possibly meaning 'alone'. The meaning of the isolative pronouns is roughly 'X alone' or 'by -self'. In the singular forms the vowel /o/ is replaced by /a/, since /oi/ is not a permissible vowel sequence in Mauwake.

Table 3.24: Isolative pronouns

	singular	plural
1	ya-isow	(y)i-isow
2	na-isow	ni-isow
3	wa-isow	wi-isow

When an isolative pronoun functions as a subject, which is NOT theme (§9.1), it is alone (270); but more commonly it is both theme and subject, and is preceded by the unmarked pronoun also showing the case marking overtly (271).

(270) Manina **waisow** mauw-ap   neeke   wu-a-k.
      garden 3s.ISOL work-SS.SEQ there.CF put-PA-3s

'He made his garden alone/by himself and left it there.'

(271) **No**   **naisow** or-op   kaul wafur-e.
      2s.UNM 2s.ISOL descend-SS.SEQ hook throw-IMP.2s

'Go down alone/by yourself and do fishing (lit: throw the hook).'

3.5 Pronouns

The example (272) has an accusative pronoun to show the case and an initial unmarked pronoun *yo* 'I' to mark the object as theme.

(272)   *Yo   yaisow me efa   keraw-a-k.*
        1s.UNM 1s.ISOL not 1s.ACC bite-PA-3s

        'It didn't bite only me.' (Or: 'It wasn't only me that it bit.')

When the isolative pronoun is preceded by the genitive/emphatic pronoun it is intensified (273).

(273)   *Aakisa mua iperowa   nain **ona**   **waisow** soor   owowa=pa   ika-i-ya.*
        now   man middle.aged that1 3s.GEN 3s.ISOL jungle village=LOC be-Np-PR.3s

        'Now that middle-aged man is staying all by himself in a jungle hamlet.'

In the plural the meaning is 'ONLY we/you/they (as a GROUP)' (274).

(274)   *Wi   feeke   ika-uk,   i   iisow   ikiw-i-yen.*
        3p.UNM here.CF be-IMP.3p 1p.UNM 1p.ISOL go-Np-FU.1p

        'Let them stay here, only we will go.'

When the first syllable of a plural isolative pronoun is reduplicated, the pronoun refers to INDIVIDUALS in the group (275).

(275)   ***Ii-iisow***   *pok-ap   opora siisim-ep   weeser-eya   unow=iya   aakun-e-mik.*
        RDP-1p.ISOL sit-SS.SEQ talk   write-SS.SEQ finish-2/3s.DS many=COM talk-PA-1/3p

        'We sat and wrote separately, and then talked together.'

Although the pronouns in (274) and (275) sound rather similar, there is a stress difference between them. In the former, *iisow* gets stronger stress than the unmarked pronoun *i*, in the latter the first syllable of the reduplicated word is stressed.

3.5.7 Restrictive pronouns

The restrictive pronouns are formed by adding the limiting clitic *-iw* 'only' either to a genitive pronoun or to a focal pronoun (§3.12.6). When it is added to a genitive pronoun it means 'on one's own' (276)–(278).

(276)   *No   **nena=iw**   ma-i-n=i?*
        2s.UNM 2s.GEN=LIM say-Np-PR.2s=QM

        'Do you say it on your own?' (i.e. 'Did you think of it yourself?')

(277)   *O=ko   me efa   maak-e-k, **yena=iw**   amis-ar-e-m.*
        3s.UNM=NF not 1s.ACC tell-PA-3s 1s.GEN=LIM knowledge-INCH-PA-1s

        'He/she didn't tell me, I learned it on my own.'

(278) **Yien=iw**   ikiw-ik-ua.
       1p.GEN=LIM go-be-PA.3s

       'Let's go on our own (as a group, or one by one).'

When the limiting clitic is added to the focal form of the free pronoun it adds the meaning of exclusiveness to the pronoun (279), (280).

(279) Anane **nos=iw**   nefa   maak-i-ya.
       always 2s.FC=LIM 2s.ACC tell-Np-PR.3s

       'He always talks to you only.'

(280) Wi   anane **is=iw**   yiam=iya   irak-i-mik.
       3p.UNM always 1p.FC=LIM 1p.REFL=COM fight-Np-PR.1/3p

       'They always fight with us only.'

3.5.8 Reflexive-reciprocal pronouns

The reflexive-reciprocal pronouns have the unmarked pronouns as their basis, but the derivative suffix is slightly different for singular and plural. They are shown in Table 3.25.

The singular forms are used as reflexives only (281), (282), the plural forms both as reflexives (283), (284) and as reciprocals (285), (286).

(281) Naap on-ap   **yame** amukar-e-m.
       thus do-ss.SEQ 1s.REFL scold-PA-1s

       'Having done so I scolded myself (i.e. was angry at myself).'

(282) Iinan   akena ikiw-ep   **wame** pipilim-ep   aakun-em-ika-i-non.
       on.top very go-ss.SEQ 3s.REFL hide-ss.SEQ speak-ss.SIM-be-Np-FU.3s

       'It (= a bird) will go very high up and hide itself and keep making its calls.'

(283) **Niam** tuun-ap   teeria erup wu-eka.
       2p.REFL count-ss.SEQ group two put-IMP.2p

       'Count yourselves and form two groups.'

Table 3.25: Reflexive-reciprocal pronouns

	singular	plural
1	y-ame[a]	yi-am
2	n-ame	ni-am
3	w-ame	wi-am

[a] In the coastal dialect the singular suffix is -ama.

(284) *Nainiw sande uura **yiam** fiirim-e-mik.*
again Sunday night 1p.REFL gather-PA-1/3p
'Again on Sunday night we gathered.'

(285) ***Wiam** fook-ap irak-e-mik.*
3p.REFL split-SS.SEQ fight-PA-1/3p
'They split from each other and fought.'

(286) *Sarir-ap ... **yiam** far-i-mik.*
surround-SS.SEQ ... 1p.REFL call-Np-PR.1/3p
'We surround (the fish) ... and call each other.'

In many contexts only the reflexive or the reciprocal interpretation is natural. But a potential ambiguity in some contexts is resolved by adding a genitive pronoun to mark the reflexive (287) and an unmarked or restrictive pronoun to mark the reciprocal pronoun (288).

(287) ***Niena niam** kookal-eka.*
2p.GEN 2p.REFL like-IMP.2p
'Like/love yourselves.'

(288) ***Ni/nieniw niam** kookal-eka.*
2p.UNM/2p.LIM 2p.REFL like-IMP.2p
'Like/love each other.'

The reflexives are not very frequent in Mauwake, because they seem to be fairly strongly connected with [+Control]. If one hurts oneself unintentionally, the cause(r) or instrument occupies the subject position instead of the person hurt. Thus, (289) is a semantically appropriate equivalent for the English clause 'I cut myself with a knife':

(289) *Fura=ke efa puuk-a-k.*
knife=CF 1s.ACC cut-PA-3s
'A knife cut me.'

But a reflexive pronoun is used especially in expressions involving body parts when one does something to oneself, and the instrument is not known or mentioned (290). In corresponding expressions English often uses possessive rather than reflexive pronouns.

(290) *Merena **yame** puuk-a-m.*
leg 1s.REFL cut-PA-1s
'I cut my leg.' (Or: 'I cut myself in the leg.')

The plural forms of the reflexive pronouns have another, quite different use: when they are followed by numerals, especially by 'two' or 'three', they function as dual/trial etc. forms for the personal pronouns. They are considered to be in the nominative case when not followed by other pronoun forms (291). Other cases need to be shown by appropriate additional pronouns (292).

3 Morphology

(291) **Yiam arow** nain miim-ap soran-e-mik.
1p.REFL three that1 hear-SS.SEQ be.startled-PA-1/3p
'The three of us heard that and were startled.'

(292) Amia mua=ke **wiam** erup nain **wia** nokar-e-k, ...
bow man=CF 3p.REFL two that1 3p.ACC ask-PA-3s
'The policeman asked those two ...'

3.5.9 Comitative pronouns

The comitative set of pronouns (Table 3.26) is a mixture as far as the basic forms are concerned. The first and second person singular forms have accusative pronouns, all the others have the reflexive pronouns as their roots. The ending is the comitative clitic -*iya* (§3.12.1), which can also be added to nouns and is one of several ways of expressing accompaniment in Mauwake. The first and second person singular forms have a transition consonant -*m*- preceding the comitative clitic.

Table 3.26: Comitative pronouns

	singular	plural
1	efa-m-iya	yiam-iya
2	nefa-m-iya	niam-iya
3	wama-iya	wiam-iya

(293) Lasen mua emeria **wiam=iya** me aakun-e-mik.
Lasen man woman 3p.REFL=COM not talk-PA-1/3p
'We didn't talk with the Lasen people.'

(294) Liisa Poh San ikos **yiam=iya** soomar-emi ...
Liisa Poh San with 1p.REFL=COM walk-SS.SIM
'Liisa and Poh San walked with us and ...'

3.5.10 Primary and secondary reference of personal pronouns

Typically pronouns refer to the persons the form indicates: first person singular to the speaker, second person singular to the addressee etc. Besides this primary, or default, reference some pronouns may also have a secondary reference, if the person and/or number of the referent(s) is different from that indicated by the pronoun.

In Mauwake both the first and second person singular forms as well as the third person plural marking on verbs can be used for non-specific, or generic, reference. They occur particularly in explanations of customs or general principles, and in examples.

The sentences are usually in the future tense and therefore hypothetical. In these texts the second person singular pronoun and the third person verb marking can alternate quite freely. Example (295) is from a text describing the adoption process in general, and example (296) was said to a person who does not even have a spirit name to call upon, nor does know how to spear pigs. Here the pronouns have acquired a non-deictic role: their correct interpretation does not depend on the non-linguistic context (Anderson & Keenan 1985: 260).

(295) *Yo   muuka kookal-ep **yena** samapora wia   maak-i-nen.*
      1s.UNM son   like-SS.SEQ 1s.GEN clan   3p.ACC tell-Np-FU.1s

   'When I like to have a son/child I will tell my clan.' (Or: 'When *one* wants a child he will tell his own clan.')

(296) ***No***   *waaya mik-ap   inasina unuma me unuf-i-nan=na   mua oko=ke*
      2s.UNM pig   spear-SS.SEQ spirit   name   not call-Np-FU.2s=TP man other=CF
      *nainiw mik-ap   **nefar** aaw-i-non.*
      again spear-SS.SEQ 2s.DAT take-Np-FU.3s

   'If you spear a pig and don't call your spirit name, another man will spear it again and take it from you.' (Or: 'If *one* spears a pig...')

When a maximally generic object is needed for a transitive verb, or when there is no overt object available, the first person plural accusative form is used (297), (298).

(297) *Ifa   nain=ke **yia**   keraw-i-ya.*
      snake that1=CF 1p.ACC bite-Np-PR.3s

   'That snake bites.'

(298) *Marasin fain **yia**   girin-i-ya.*
      medicine this 1p.ACC smart-Np-PR.3s

   'This medicine smarts.'

3.5.11 Use of personal pronouns in text

In Mauwake it is possible to leave the subject pronoun out, as the person and number of the subject are marked on the verb suffix. And this is not only possible but very common: approximately only 6% of all the clauses in narrative and descriptive texts have a pronominal subject, compared to about 30% of the clauses having a subject NP of any kind. As the other arguments are not marked on the verb, except for a two-way distinction for beneficiary (§3.8.3.1), other than subject pronouns need to be used for them if there is no full NP, and they are often employed even when there is a NP.

The frequency of subject pronouns depends on whether the person referred to is first, second or third, and on the type of text as well. The first person, both in singular and plural, is commonly referred to with a pronoun, instead of just a verb suffix. Second person pronouns are very frequent in hortatory texts and are used somewhat in conversations.

3 Morphology

Most narratives in the data have their main participants in third person, but pronouns are used to refer to them quite rarely.

A pronoun may be used for the second mention of a newly established topic (§9.2.2). In particular when an important participant has been introduced by a proper name, in the next sentence (s)he can be referred to by a personal pronoun (299).

(299) *Eema=ke waisow amis-ar-e-k. Os=ke uuriw urup-emi...*
Eema=CF 3s.ISOL knowledge-INCH-PA-3s 3s.FC=CF morning rise-SS.SIM

'Only Eema knew. She got up in the morning and ...'

When a participant has been established as the topic, (s)he is referred to with a verb suffix only, or with a NP if a better identification is needed. A pronoun is used mainly when the topic is re-activated after being inactive for a while (§9.2.3). The example (300) is from a text where a couple goes down to the husband's village and then returns to the wife's village. The wife's relatives, inactive as a topic for the span of five clauses, are re-assigned the topic status with the pronoun *wi* 'they'.

(300) *Or-op   ik-ok nainiw urup-e-mik.   Aria **wi** samapora maneka*
descend-SS.SEQ be-SS again ascend-PA-1/3p alright 3p.UNM floor   big
fook-ap   ...
split-SS.SEQ

'They (=the couple) went down and after a while they came up again. Alright they (=the wife's relatives) split (wood for) a big floor and ...'

In commands (§7.3) the subject pronouns are more frequent than in statements.[45] The pronoun here is not a vocative; that would be separated from the rest of the clause by a pause, whereas a subject is not. The example (301) is a fairly typical command in Mauwake. This is an unusual feature cross-linguistically, as languages tend to drop the subject pronoun in imperative clauses (Givón 1979: 80).[46]

(301) *Ni ikiw-eka!*
2p go-IMP.2p

'Go (2p)!'

3.6 Spatial deictics

This section brings together what are often called demonstrative pronouns and deictic locative adverbs. What is common to them is the spatial orientation based on the location

---

[45] As many as 39% of commands in the text material have a pronoun subject, as against 6% in statements.
[46] The relatively high frequency of subject pronouns in imperative clauses may not be a peculiarity of Mauwake only. The grammatical descriptions of Papuan languages often state that the subject pronoun is optional in these clauses, but give no information as to their actual frequency. Personal communication with other field linguists working on Papuan languages gives reason to suggest that an overt personal pronoun with the imperative may be more common than is generally assumed.

of the speaker, as well as morphological similarity. The whole deictic system, which also includes personal and temporal deixis, is discussed briefly in §6.3.

Deictics operate on the scale of proximity, making reference to something else on the basis of location (Halliday & Hasan 1976: 57–58). The relative proximity may be measured either from the speaker or from the speaker and addressee. Papuan languages manifest both these types as well as a combination of the two. Elevation and visibility may be additional parameters, so the demonstrative systems range from a simple and rather common two-term system to quite complicated ones (Foley 1986: 75–77). Two-way distinctions are found in Siroi (Wells 1979: 20) and Golin (Bunn 1974), three-way distinctions in Waskia (Ross & Paol 1978: 59), Bine (Saari 1985) and Korafe (Farr & Whitehead 1982: 65). Usan has four basic deictics, but derivations extend the system into an elaborate one (Reesink 1987: 76–81). Murane (1974: 38–39) reports 19 locatives in Daga that are also used as demonstrative pronouns.

3.6.1 The basic spatial deixis in Mauwake

The main factors dividing the deictic space in Mauwake are the relative proximity to the speaker, and visibility. There are four deictic roots, one of them proximal and three distal (Table 3.27).

Table 3.27: Deictic roots

fa-	'here' (close to speaker, visible)	proximal
na-	'there' (away from the speaker; generic)	distal-1
eef-	'here/there' (rather close, usually visible)	distal-2
een-	'there' (far away, usually not visible)	distal-3

The proximal deictic *fa-* indicates close proximity to the speaker: prototypically the referent marked with *fain* 'this' can be touched by the speaker, and *fan* 'here' indicates the speaker's location or close proximity to it. The distal-1 deictic *na-* indicates a distance that is out of touching distance to the speaker; the distance to the addressee is irrelevant. *Na-* is the most neutral and the least restricted of the three distal deictics, and its frequency is extremely high because of the various functions that the demonstrative *nain* has. On the other hand, the words formed with both the distal-2 root *eef-* and the distal-3 root *een-*, although available, are rarely used. They may be employed when the pragmatic situation meets the semantic specification for their occurrence, and they are needed when more than one far deictic is called for. Often the distance is a relative matter, and the speaker has a subjective choice between the different deictics.

The deictic roots suffixed with *-in*, marking given information, are used as demonstratives. When the roots are suffixed with *-an* 'locative', the words function as locative adverbs. The distribution of both these suffixes is very restricted: they are only attached to deictic or question word (§3.7.1) roots.

The deictic manner adverbs (§3.6.4) are also based on the same roots.

3.6.2 Demonstratives

The four demonstratives in Mauwake are formed by one of the deictic roots plus the suffix *-in* indicating given information.

In Mauwake the demonstratives are like the personal pronouns in that they can function as the sole head of a noun phrase. But they differ from the personal pronouns in that they do not have the case forms typical of the latter. In this respect the demonstratives are more like adjectives. Another feature that they share with adjectives is that they mainly function as modifiers in a NP. But unlike the adjectives, which only occur alone in complement position (unless the NP is elliptical), the demonstratives occur by themselves in several clause positions.

The numeral modifiers are positioned between an adjective and a demonstrative in a NP (302), but never between two adjectives (303).

(302) koora maneka arow **nain**
       house big   three that1
       'those three big houses'

(303) siowa sepa gelemuta erup
       dog   black small   two
       'two small black dogs'

There is a clear distinction in Mauwake between human and non-human reference, which shows in the choice of a pronoun vs. a demonstrative. A third person pronoun is not used for non-humans, whereas demonstratives in isolation[47] are normally only used for non-humans. The only exception in my data is example (304); *nain* 'that' would not be acceptable even here.

(304) No[48] **fain** me nena   niawi   akena=ke.
       2s.UNM this   not 2s.GEN 2s/p.father true=CF
       'This is not your true father.'

Apart from the proximal demonstrative *fain* 'this', the other demonstratives are not mutually exclusive. The distal-1 demonstrative *nain* 'that' is the least restricted of the three, and it is extremely frequent, whereas both *eefin* 'this/that' and *eenin* 'that' are very rarely used. In (305) the distances of the two mountains fit the specifications for *eefin* and *eenin*, and more than one distal demonstrative is needed for contrastive purposes:

(305) Ema   **eenin** fikera=ke   aw-o-k,   aria   **eefin** fikera=ke   me
       mountain that3   kunai.grass=CF burn-PA-3s, alright that2   kunai.grass=CF not
       aw-o-k.
       burn-PA-3s

       'The kunai grass on that mountain (far away, invisible) burned, but the grass on this/that one (somewhat closer) did not burn.'

---
[47] Demonstratives are common as *modifiers* of NPs referring to humans.
[48] *No* 'you' is an extra-clausal theme, not part of the subject.

3.6 Spatial deictics

There is no number distinction in demonstratives. When they modify a [+human] noun, plurality is shown in the person/number marking of the verb and optionally by an additional personal pronoun (306).

(306) *(Wi)* takira ***fain=ke*** niir-e-mik.
 3p.UNM boy this=CF play-PA-1/3p
 'It was these boys that played.'

With [-human] nouns, a quantifier in the NP may be used (307), or distributive suffix on the verb (308) to indicate plurality, or the number may be left unspecified (309).

(307) Mera ***arow nain*** aaw-e-m.
 fish three that1 get-PA-1s
 'I caught those three fish.'

(308) Mera ***nain*** aaw-***omak***-e-m.
 fish that1 get-DISTR.PL-PA-1s
 'I caught those (many) fish.'

(309) Amina ***fain*** p-ekap-e-mik.
 pot this BPX-come-PA-1/3p
 'We brought this pot / these pots.'

Besides the exophoric (text-external) deictic use described above, another common function for demonstratives cross-linguistically is endophoric, or text-internal anaphoric and cataphoric reference. The proximity in the case of demonstratives relates to the participants in the text, rather than the speech situation (Lyons 1968: 278).

Mauwake follows the typical pattern: the neutral distal demonstrative *nain* 'that' is anaphoric: it only refers to the text preceding it, as in (310), where the example sentence comes after the description of fishing with a fish trap. The proximal *fain* 'this' is cataphoric, referring to the text following it (311). The other two demonstratives, *eefin* and *eenin*, are not used for text-internal reference at all.

(310) ***Nain*** soo era=ke.
 that1 fish.trap way=CF
 'That is the way (to catch fish) with a fish trap.'

(311) Mua arow ***fain***: Kuuten, Dogimaw, aria Olas ...
 man three this: Kuten, Dogimaw, alright Olas
 'These three men: Kuuten, Dogimaw and Olas ...'

The demonstrative *nain* 'that' marks given/established information, and often has a similar function to a definite article (cf. Dryer 2007c:154). It has an important pragmatic function of marking topic continuity in Mauwake. A continuing [+human] topic, especially the main participant, is usually marked only by person/number inflection on the

3 Morphology

verb, whereas a minor participant or a [-human] established topic uses NPs modified by *nain*.

Still another function for the demonstrative *nain* 'that' is that of a nominalizer of otherwise finite verbal clauses (§5.7.2). A nominalized clause of this type may be a relative clause (312) (§8.3.1), a complement clause (313) (§8.3.2) or a temporal subordinate clause (314) (§8.3.3.1).[49]

(312) [Merena ifa   keraw-a-k **nain**]$_{RC}$ puuk-a-mik.
      leg   snake bite-PA-3s that1   cut-PA-1/3p

   'They cut the leg that the snake had bitten.'

(313) [Mukuna kerer-e-k **nain**]$_{CC}$ i   me paayar-e-mik.
      fire   start-PA-3s that1   1p.UNM not understand-PA-1/3p

   'We didn't know that a fire had started.'

(314) [Goron-ep ora-i-ya   **nain**,] maa muutitik iiwawun lalat-i-ya.
      fall-ss.SEQ descend-Np-PR.3s that1   thing all.kinds altogether sweep-Np-3s

   'When it goes down, it sweeps everything with it.'

The same demonstrative is also used as a strong adversative 'but' (315) (§8.1.3). In that function it is placed clause-initially rather than clause-finally.

(315) Wiawi   eliw   naak-e-k, **nain** me ikiw-o-k.
      3s/p.father all.right say-PA-3s that1 not go-PA-3s

   'He said yes (lit: all right) to his father, but didn't go.'

3.6.3 Deictic locative adverbs

The undebatable locative adverbs in Mauwake are all deictic (§3.9.1.1). For each of the four deictic roots there are two corresponding locative adverbs (Table 3.28). The first set contains the deictic root and the locative suffix -*an*. The homorganic vowels in the root and affix have merged into one. The second set is suffixed with the contrastive focus clitic -(*e*)*ke*. When the clitic is added, the deictic adverb is in focus, but not necessarily contrastive. The morphophonological change that has taken place in the root is unusual: the vowel /a/ has assimilated with the initial /e/ of the contrastive focus clitic.

The difference in the usage between the neutral and focused member of each pair is that the first is ONLY used with realis-type verb forms, i.e. past (316), (318) and present tense (320), whereas the second one is MAINLY used with future (317), imperative (319), and counterfactual (322), i.e. irrealis-type forms. Yet Mauwake does not differentiate between realis and irrealis in verbs, and a possible explanation here is that only locative adverbs that are in focus can make it into a future, imperative or counterfactual clause, whereas past or present clauses are less restrictive and use either focal or non-focal form.

---

[49] All these clauses have a function that is consistent with the core meaning of 'givenness' (Haiman 1978) or presupposition (Reesink 1987).

3.6 Spatial deictics

Table 3.28: Deictic locative adverbs

ADV	ADV + CF	
fa-an>fan	fa-eke>feeke	'here' (close to speaker, visible)
na-an>nan	na-eke>neeke	'there' (away from the speaker; generic)
eef-an	eef-eke	'here' (rather close, usually visible)
een-an	een-eke	'there' (far away, usually not visible)

(316) *Owowa=pa **fan** ik-emkun aasa maneka ekap-o-k.*
village=LOC here be-1s/p.DS canoe big come-PA-3s
'As I was here in the village the big ship came.'

(317) *Eliw **feeke** soop-i-yen.*
well here.CF bury-Np-FU.1p
'We can bury him HERE.'

(318) *Yo fura belemuta **eefan** piipu-a-m.*
1s.UNM knife small there2 leave-PA-1s
'I left the small knife (somewhere) here.'

(319) *Ni koora epa **eefeke** ku-eka.*
2p.UNM house place there2.CF build-IMP.2p
'Build a/the house OVER HERE in this place.'

(320) *Wi aakisa fain manina **eenan** on-i-mik.*
3p.UNM now this garden there3 make-Np-PR.1/3p
'Nowadays they make the garden(s) there (far away).'

(321) *Ni **eeneke** ikiw-ep momor naap niir-eka.*
2p there3.CF go-SS.SEQ foolish thus play-IMP.2p
'Go THERE (out of my sight) and play your foolish game.'

(322) ***Neeke** ik-ek-a-k=na iwer(a) ififa=ke ifakim-ek-a-k.*
there1.CF be-CNTF-PA-3s=TP coconut dry=CF kill-CNTF-PA-3s
'If he had been THERE a (falling) dry coconut would have killed him.'

(323) *Soo nainiw muf-owa pun naap, aana=pa **neeke** muf-i-mik.*
trap again pull-NMZ too thus rattan=LOC there1.CF pull-Np-PR.1/3p
'Pulling the trap again is also like that, we/they pull it THERE by the rattan.'

(324) *Malol=pa **neeke** nainiw suuw-urup-i-ya.*
open.sea there1.CF again push-ascend-Np-PR.3s
'THERE from the open sea it (= tsunami wave) again pushes up (to the coast).'

3 Morphology

In the following examples *neeke* and *feeke* are used with past (325) – (327) or present tense verbs (328) and indicate a temporary rather than permanent location, but this is probably secondary, or related, to the adverbs being focal: there is less need to focus on a permanent location than on a temporary one. Note that in these clauses it is possible to have two constituents with contrastive focus marking (325), (328).

(325) *Miiw(a) aasa fa-ow(a) mua=ke **neeke** wia aaw-o-k.*
land canoe drive-NMZ man=CF there1.CF 3p.ACC take-PA-3s
'THERE the truck driver picked them up.'

(326) *Or-op **neeke** ika-iwkin kokom-ar-e-k.*
descend-SS.SEQ there1.CF be-2/3p.DS dark-INCH-PA-3s
'When they had gone down and were THERE it became dark.'

(327) *Nainiw mukuna mamaiya **neeke** ikiw-o-k.*
again fire close there1.CF go-PA-3s
'Again he went THERE close to the fire.'

The following example is a comment from a man after he sees Japanese bombers in the sky:

(328) *Fa, Yaapan=ke **feeke** ik-e-mik!*
INTJ Japan=CF here.CF be-PA-1/3p
'Damn, the Japanese are HERE!'

3.6.4 Deictic manner adverbs

The four deictic manner adverbs are based on the deictic roots, but their derivation is less regular than that of either the demonstratives or the deictic locatives, due to the restriction that a geminate vowel is only possible in an initial syllable (Table 3.29). Again, the proximate (329) and especially the distal-1 adverbs (330) are common but the others are very infrequent.

Table 3.29: Deictic manner adverbs

feenap	'like this'	proximate
naap	'like that, thus'	distal-1
eefenap	'like that (further away)'	distal-2
eenap	'like that (far away)'	distal-3

(329) *Ikiw-e-mik=na **feenap** ma-em-ik-e-mik* ...
go-PA-1/3p=TP like.this say-SS.SIM-be-PA-1/3p
'They went and (unexpectedly) kept saying like this ...'

3.7 Question words and indefinites

(330) **Naap** maak-iwkin **naap** ik-ua.
thus tell-2/3.DS thus be-PA.3s

'They told him like that, and he was like that.'

In (331) there is a long temporal distance between the hearing and the recounting of the story, which is apparently reflected in the choice of the adverbial.

(331) Iiriw auwa-ke ma-iwkin **eefenap** miim-a-m.
earlier 1s/p.father=CF say-2/3p.DS thus2 hear-PA-1s

'The fathers spoke (about this) long ago and I heard it like that.'

In (332) there is both some temporal and a considerable locative distance between the original time and place of the quote and that of the rest of the example:

(332) "Mua nain opora=pa wu-ami ifakim-e," **eenap** efa maak-e-mik.
man that1 talk=LOC put-SS.SIM kill-IMP.2s thus3 1s.ACC tell-PA-1/3p

' "Accuse (lit: put to talk) that man and kill him," they told me like that.'

Location verbs (§3.8.4.4.3) are also based on the deictic roots, but directional verbs (§3.8.4.4.5), which also participate in the spatial deictic system in Mauwake, have different roots.

3.7 Question words and indefinites

Most of the indefinites in Mauwake are also question words, hence the treatment of both in the same subsection.

3.7.1 Question words

The question words are here grouped together because of their shared semantic features and their function and position in content questions, although on the basis of their syntactic function on clause level some are pronouns, others adjectives or adverbs.

The majority of the question words have an initial morpheme *ka-*, which indicates a question and is below in the derivations given the gloss 'what', although it is unrelated to the question word *mauwa* 'what'. The morphemes that make up the question words in Table 3.30 are given in parentheses when they can be reasonably clearly established.

Both the words translated with 'which', *kain* and *kaanin*, have the suffix *-in* marking givenness. They are both morphologically and semantically related to the demonstratives *fain* 'this' and *nain* 'that' (§3.6.2).

Kaan 'where' is formed by the question root *ka-* and the same locative affix *-an* that is used in the deictic locative adverbs *fan* 'here' and *nan* 'there' (333) (§3.6.3). The derivation with the contrastive focus marker *-(e)ke* is more frequently used than the non-focused form (334), possibly because the the other two most frequent question words, *mauwa* 'what' and *naarewe* 'who', so often take the contrastive focus clitic.

3 Morphology

(333) *Mua nain unuf-ami ma-i-kuan,   "Mua nain **kaan** ik-ua?"*
man that1 call-ss.SIM say-Np-FU.3p man   that1 where be-PA.3s

'They call the man's name and say, "Where is that man?" '

(334) *Oo Sarak, no   **kaan=eke** ik-ok kerer-e-n   a?*
INTJ Sarak 2s.UNM where=CF be-ss arrive-PA-2s INTJ

'Oh Sarak, where have you been (lit: where were you and arrived)?'

Kaanin 'which of two' also shares the locative morpheme *an-* with *kaan-* 'where' as well as *fan* 'here' and *nan* 'there', although in its present meaning it is not a locative question.

There is also a morphological relationship between *kamenap* 'how/ what…like?' and *kamin* 'how many/much?' and the deictic adverb *naap* 'thus', but synchronically their semantic relationship is opaque. *Kamenion* 'or what? / how is it?' has obviously developed from *kamin* 'how many/much?' and the modal clitic *-yon* 'perhaps' (§3.9.3), but again, the relationship is not transparent any more.

The question words, except for *kamenion* and *naap-i*, occupy the same syntactic position and clausal function (335), (337) as the corresponding non-interrogative element would have (336), (338).

(335) *Mua nain **iikamin** ekap-o-k?*
man that when   come-PA-3s

'When did that/the man come?'

Table 3.30: Question words

iikamin	'when?'[a]	(<*iir-kamin* 'time-how.much')
kaakew(e)	'of what place?'	
kaan	'where'	(<*ka-an* 'what=LOC')
kaaneke	'where?'	(<*ka-an-eke* 'what=LOC=CF')
kaanin	'which (of two)?'	(<*ka-an-in* 'what=LOC-GIVEN')
kain	'which?'	(<*ka-in* 'what-GIVEN')
kamin	'how many?', 'how much?'	
kamenap	'how?', 'what … like?'	(<*kamin-naap* 'how.much-thus')
mauwa	'what?'	
moram	'why?'	
naarew(e)	'who?'	
kamenion	'(or) what/how?'	(<*kamin-yon* 'how.much-perhaps')
naap-i	'like that?'	

[a] *Ama kamin* 'sun how much' is used when time measured by clock is inquired; *iikamin* is less specific.

3.7 Question words and indefinites

(336) *Mua nain **unan** ekap-o-k.*
man that yesterday come-PA-3s
'That/the man came yesterday.'

(337) *Maa **mauwa** en-e-n?*
thing/food what eat-PA-2s
'What did you eat?'

(338) *Maa **oposia** en-e-m.*
thing/food meat eat-PA-1s
'I ate meat.'

Neither number nor case is marked on the interrogative words themselves. If either marking is required, it is done through personal pronouns, but for [+human] NPs only (339), (340).

(339) *Mua **naarew** wia uruf-a-n?*
man who 3p.ACC see-PA-2s
'Whom (pl) did you see?'

(340) ***Naarew** wiar aaw-o-k?*
who 3.DAT get-PA-3s
'Who did he get it from?'

When an interrogative word is used as a subject, the contrastive focus marker *-ke* is added. This is natural since it is the question word that is the focal element in questions (341)–(343).

(341) ***Mauwa=ke** nefa aruf-a-k?*
what=CF 2s.ACC hit-PA-3s
'What hit you?'

(342) *Mua **kain=ke** nomak-e-k?*
man which=CF win-PA-3s
'Which man won?'

(343) *Masin **kaanin=ke** samor-ar-e-k?*
engine which.of.2=CF bad-INCH-PA-3s
'Which engine (of the two) broke?'

Naarew(e) 'who?' is only used for [+human] referents. When the contrastive focus maker *-ke* is suffixed to the question word, the last syllable is normally deleted. *Mauwa* 'what', on the other hand, is used almost solely for [-human] nouns. The only natural expression with *mauwa* referring to humans that I have encountered is of the type (344). When a person's name is inquired, either *naarewe* (345) or *kamenap* (350) is used rather than *mauwa*.

125

(344) *Emeria nain no/nena* **mauwa=ke?**
woman that 1s.UNM/1s.GEN what=CF
'What (relation) of yours is that woman?'

(345) *O unuma* **naare=ke?**
3s.UNM name who=CF
'What is his/her name?'

Kaanin 'which of two?' is specified for number (343), but *kain* 'which?' is not (346).

(346) *No* **kain** *kookal-i-n?*
2s.UNM which like-Np-PR.2s
'Which one (of two or many) do you like?'

The locative question word *kaan(eke)* 'where' is often used as a phrase by itself (333), (334). but it is also employed as a modifier of a locative noun phrase rather than *kain* or *kaanin* (347).

(347) [*Epa ara* **kaan=eke**]ₙₚ *ikiw-e-mik?*
place section where=CF go-PA-1/3p
'What/which area did they go to?'

Kamenap is a question word both for manner 'how?' (348) and for adjectives 'what ... like?'. In the latter sense it usually modifies the noun *sira* 'custom, kind' (349).

(348) *No* **kamenap** *ik-o-n?*
2s.UNM how be-PA-2s
'How are/were you?'

(349) *O koora* **sira** **kamenap** *ku-a-k?*
3s.UNM house custom/kind what.like build-PA-3s
'What kind of house did he build?'

It is also used with the noun *unuma* 'name' when the name of someone or something is inquired (350), (351):

(350) *O unuma* **kamenap?**
3s.UNM name what.like?
'What is his/her name?'

(351) *Nomokowa fain unuma* **kamenap?**
tree this name what.like
'What is the name of this tree?'

3.7 Question words and indefinites

In example (350) *kamenap* is interchangeable with *naare(we)-ke* 'who', but in (351) it is not interchangeable with *mauwa-ke* 'what'.

The interrogative *kamenion* forms a clause by itself and only occurs after the question clitic *-i* and/or the connective *e* 'or' (352).

(352) Maa en-owa=ko p-ekap-e-mik=i **kamenion**?
thing eat-NMZ=NF BPX-come-PA-1/3p=QM or.what
'Did they bring food, or what (happened)?'

The question word *naap-i* 'like that?' is different from the other question words. It is formed by adding the question marker *-i* to the demonstrative *naap* 'thus, like that', and it occurs by itself or sentence-finally after a statement, which often follows another question. It is mainly used in argumentation (353), (354).

(353) Siiwa arow ikiw-eya maa en-owa perek-i-mik. **Naap=i?**
moon three go-2/3s.DS thing eat-NMZ harvest-Np-1/3p thus=QM
'After three months we'll harvest the food, right?'

(354) Feenap eliw ma-i-yen=i? Sira nain eliw marew, **naap=i?**
like.this well say-Np-FU.1p=QM custom that1 good none thus=QM
'Should we say that that custom is not good – is that what you are saying?'

Question sentences are discussed in §7.2, which has more examples as well.

3.7.2 Indefinites

Indefinites are sometimes classified as pronouns, although they often are not very pronoun-like; sometimes they are grouped together with quantifiers (Hakulinen & Karlsson 1979: 81). By definition they lack definiteness which is typical of other pronouns (Quirk et al. 1989 [1985]: 376). Also their status as NP substitutes is questionable.

In Mauwake, the indefinites behave syntactically very much like quantifiers (355), (356). The position of the indefinites in the NP is after the adjective phrase and immediately preceding the demonstrative. They rarely co-occur with a quantifier phrase, but if they do, they follow the QP.

The number of indefinites in Mauwake is very small. The last four in Table 3.31 are actually question words (§3.7.1) that also function as indefinites.

(355) Iiriw muuka **oko** wiawi onak urera maa uup-e-mik.
long.ago boy other 3s/p.father 3s/p.mother evening food cook-PA-1/3p
'Long ago, a certain boy's father and mother cooked food.'

(356) Ne wia, **papako=ke** ma-e-mik, ...
ADD no, some/other=CF say-PA-1/3p
'But no, some/others said, ...'

3 Morphology

Table 3.31: Indefinites

oko	'a certain, (an)other'
papako	'some, other'
naarew(e)	'whoever, someone, one'
mauwa	'whatever, something'
kain	'whichever'
kaanin	'whichever (of two)'

The indefinite *oko* 'a certain, (an)other' also has the meaning 'otherwise' when it introduces an apprehensive clause (357) (§8.1.6).

(357) *Gurun-owa epasia=pa miim-am-ika-i-kuan,* **oko** *mua papako maa*
rumble-NMZ far=LOC hear-SS.SIM-be-Np-FU.3p other man some thing/food
ik-em-ik-owa nain kawus wiar uruf-i-kuan.
roast-SS.SIM-be-NMZ that1 smoke 3.DAT see-Np-FU.3p

'They (villagers) keep listening to the rumble from far away, otherwise/lest they (pilots) see the smoke from some men's/people's food-roasting fire.'

Those question words (§3.7.1) that may function as indefinites behave similarly to question words as NP constituents, but on the sentence level there are differences between them. The interrogatives occur either in a simple interrogative sentence or occasionally in a medial clause (358). The indefinites can occur in a medial clause (359), but they are more common in subordinate clauses, especially relative clauses (360).

(358) **Naarew** *wia far-ep ekap-o-n?*
who 3p.ACC call-SS.SEQ come-PA-2s

'Who did you call, and then came?'[50]

(359) *Masin* **kaanin**=*ke samor-ar-eya oko fain=ke asip-i-non.*
engine which.of.2=CF bad-INCH-2/3s.DS other this=CF help-Np-FU.3s

'Whichever engine breaks down, this other one will help/substitute.'[51]

(360) *Prais aaw-ep* [*uf-owa* **kain**=*ke nomak-e-k nain*]$_{RC}$ *wi-e-mik.*
prize take-SS.SEQ dance-NMZ which=CF win-PA-3s that1 give.them-PA-1/3p

'They took the prize and, whichever dance won, they gave it (the prize) to them (the dancers).'

The indefinite *mauwa* 'what' is also used as a generic substitute for any [-human] NP that is left unmentioned because the name of the particular thing is not known or is temporarily forgotten, like *whatchamacallit* in English (361).

---

[50] A more natural translation into English would be 'Who did you call before you came?', but it would hide the fact that medial clauses are coordinate.

[51] With question intonation it would mean: 'Which engine$_i$ will this other one$_j$ help, if it$_i$ breaks down?'

(361) *Mua nain **mauwa** nain akim-a-k=na weetak, **mauwa** nain me or-o-k.*
man that1 what that1 try-PA-3s=TP no, what that1 not descend-PA-3s
'The man tried the thing (press button), but the thing (lift) didn't go down.'

The locative question word *kaaneke* is also used as an indefinite locative adverb (362).

(362) *No **kaaneke** ikiw-i-nan=na, yos pun nook-i-nen.*
2s.UNM where.CF go-Np-FU.2s=TP 1s.FC too follow.you-Np-FU.1s
'Wherever you go, I will follow you.'

3.8 Verbs

3.8.1 General discussion

3.8.1.1 Definition

The verb category can be defined morphologically, syntactically, semantically and pragmatically. Of these, the first criterion is the most critical in Mauwake and covers the whole class; the others are less definitive, but help define a PROTOTYPICAL verb.

According to the MORPHOLOGICAL, or structural, criterion, a verb is a word that can be inflected for tense as well as the person and number of the subject. The derivational suffix categories of verbalizer, distributive and benefactive are not as useful in defining the class of verbs, as these can be used in the nominalized forms of verbs as well. Anderson (1985a: 190) also adds aspect and mood into inherent verbal inflections, but in Mauwake aspect is coded syntactically (§3.8.5.1.1), and modal categories either morphologically, syntactically or lexically.

SYNTACTICALLY a verb functions as the nucleus of a predication independently or as part of a verbal cluster (§3.8.5). Since single verbs and verbal clusters have such similar functions, the latter are described in the morphology chapter immediately after the verbs, and not in the chapter on phrase. Also, the term VERB is often used below as a generic term to cover both a single verb and a verbal cluster, unless specifically the verbal cluster is meant. The verb is the last element in a pragmatically neutral clause.

The verbal predicate is the only obligatory element in an intransitive clause. A transitive clause does require an object, but even it can often consist of a verb only, as the third person singular accusative pronoun, used for object, is zero (363). The directional verbs (§3.8.4.4.5) often co-occur with a goal, but when it is left implied the verb can be the only element (364). In a verbless clause the predicate is a noun, adjective, possessive pronoun or adverb.

(363) ***Aaw-e-m.***
get-PA-1s
'I got it.'

3 *Morphology*

(364) **Urup-e-mik**.
       go/come.up-PA-1/3p
       'We went/came up.'

The predicate verb selects the arguments in a predication. This argument selection can be used as an important basis for the division into different verb classes (§3.8.4).

SEMANTICALLY, according to Givón (1984: 64), a prototypical verb encodes "less time-stable experiences, primarily transitory states, events and actions". In Mauwake this lack of time-stability feature shows in the strong tendency to use inchoative verbs (365) (§3.8.2.2.2) instead of adjectives to describe non-permanent states.

(365) **supuk-ar-e-k** vs. **supuka** 'wet'
       wet-INCH-PA-3s
       '(it) is wet' (lit: 'has become wet')

But it is also possible to express less prototypical, time-stable states and events with verbs. In Frawley's (1992: 66) words, "verbs … require temporal fixing", when compared with the "relative atemporality" of an entity. So the RELATIVE TEMPORALITY is the main defining factor for verbs, regardless of the time-stability.

Hopper & Thompson (1984: 726) add a DISCOURSE perspective to the definition of verbs by suggesting that "verbs which do not report discourse events fail to show the range of oppositions characteristic of those which do", and are therefore less prototypical. According to them, categoriality is only weakly associated with the root forms, and the discourse use determines how clearly the verbhood manifests itself (ibid. 747). Theirs is an important viewpoint for the study of language in general and of those languages in particular that have plenty of root forms that can be used for different word classes. But for Mauwake I assume the existence of rather discrete categories of noun and verb, which the root forms belong to, rather than just having "a propensity or predisposition to become N's or V's" (ibid. 747). The number of roots that can be used across categories without special derivational suffixes is small.

3.8.1.2 General characteristics of verbs in Mauwake

Mauwake is a strongly verb-oriented language, and often a verb is the only element in the clause. In running text, there are roughly three words per clause, so approximately one word in three is a verb, as most of the clauses are verbal clauses.

The verb morphology is agglutinative; this shows mainly in the structure of the verbs. Suffixing is the basic strategy, but a few prefixes are used as well. Reduplication is of the prefixing type, with few exceptions.

Although the verb morphology in Mauwake is quite extensive, for a Papuan language it is not very complex, and the patterns are quite transparent. The verb morphology marks features of the event itself: tense, mood, sequentiality vs. simultaneity of actions, but also features related to the participants in the clause: subject, beneficiary, and distributive indicating the number of S, O or REC. Aspect is expressed through verbal groups (§3.8.5.1.1).

3.8 Verbs

To enlarge its verb inventory, Mauwake uses serial verbs (§3.8.5.1.2) or adjunct[52] plus verb constructions (§3.8.5.2). The serial verbs are mostly formed by a productive process, whereas the adjunct plus verb constructions tend to be lexicalized forms.

Some verbs have roots that are very similar to nouns. Especially in Austronesian languages the question arises whether these roots are originally nouns, verbs, or unspecified as to the grammatical category (Bugenhagen 1995: 162–165). This question for Mauwake is discussed in the section on verb derivation (§3.8.2).

Mauwake has no passive voice. The subject demotion strategy is described in §3.8.4.3.3.

There is a distinction in Mauwake between medial (§3.8.3.5) and final verbs (§3.8.3.4).[53] This distinction is very important on both sentence and discourse levels.

The verbs can be divided into two conjugation classes based on the past tense suffix vowel. Semantically these classes are arbitrary; the division is made on the basis of morphophonology and is discussed in §2.3.3.3. But the classification done according to transitivity (§3.8.4.2) and that based on semantic characteristics (§3.8.4.4) are more interesting grammatically and reveal more of the nature of the language.

3.8.1.3 Verb structure

A verb consists of a root optionally preceded by a derivational prefix (366) and followed by various derivational and inflectional suffixes (367), (368), as shown in the diagram below (Figure 3.1). Only tense and person/number suffixes are obligatory in a finite verb in the INDICATIVE mood. The obligatory elements are bolded in the diagrams.

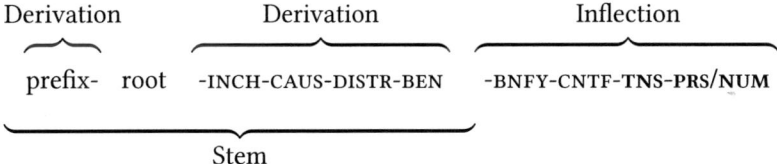

Figure 3.1: Verb derivation and finite inflection (indicative)

(366) *Soomia wia amap-ep-om-i-ya.*
spoon 3p.ACC BPX-go-BEN-Np-PR.3s
'He takes spoons to them.'

(367) *Iwera pun wiar aw-omak-e-k.*
coconut too 3.DAT burn-DISTR/PL-PA-3s
'Many of his coconut palms burned too.'

---

[52] Adjunct is here used in the sense of "a secondary element in a construction [, which] may be removed without the structural identity of the rest of the construction being affected" (Crystal 1997: 9).
[53] Sometimes they are also called dependent and independent verbs (e.g. Foley 1986:11).

3 Morphology

(368) *Lawiliw akena* **um-ek-a-m**.
nearly very die-CNTF-PA-1s
'I very nearly died.'

The IMPERATIVE verb structure Figure 3.2 is understandably different in that it cannot take counterfactual, tense or indicative person/number suffixes. Instead, an imperative person/number suffix needs to be attached as the final suffix of the verb (369), (370).

prefix – ROOT – INCH – CAUS – DISTR – BEN – BNFY – IMP.PRS/NUM

Figure 3.2: Verb derivation and imperative inflection

(369) *Ni* **ekap-omak-eka**.
2p.UNM come-DISTR/PL-IMP.2p
'Come!' (said to several people together)

(370) *Muuka* **arim-ow-e**.
son grow-CAUS-IMP.2s
'Bring up the boy.'

MEDIAL verbs likewise can have only the medial suffix after the derivational suffixes, if there are any. The medial suffix distinguishes between sequentiality (371) and simultaneity (372) of the actions when the subject stays the same; with a different subject (373) the actions are understood to be sequential, and simultaneity needs to be marked through continuous aspect form (§3.8.5.1.1.2).

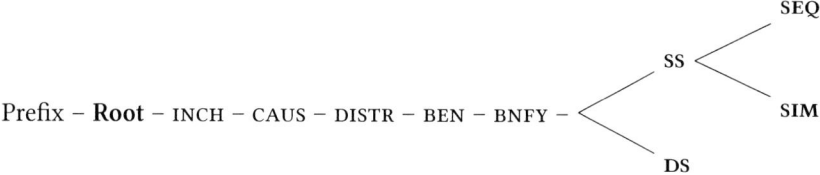

Figure 3.3: Medial verb inflection

(371) *Oposia* **pu-puuk-ap** *uup-e-mik*.
meat RDP-cut-SS.SEQ cook-PA-1/3p
'They cut the meat in many pieces and cooked it.'

(372) *Ewar=ke* **wuun-ow-ami** *epia faker-a-k, mukuna*.
wind=CF blow-CAUS-SS.SIM firewood raise-PA-3s fire
'The wind blew and raised the fire(wood), the fire.'

(373) **Kees-om-a-ya** *en-e-k*.
spit-BEN-BNFY2-2/3s.DS eat-PA-3s
'He spat/regurgitated it for her and she ate.'

3.8.2 Verb derivatives

This section deals with derivational processes in which the end result is always a verb. Verbs can be derived from other word classes through two category-CHANGING strategies. In category-MAINTAINING derivations affixes are added to the verb root to change the semantics of the root. Among the latter, the semantic changes can be considerable especially in cases where the valence changes, whereas in category-changing derivations the semantic difference is not always so great (Bybee 1985: 83).

3.8.2.1 Derivation vs. inflection

According to Bybee (1985: 81), "an inflectional morpheme ... is a bound non-root morpheme whose appearance in a particular position is compulsory." It is "required by syntax". In contrast, derivational affixes are non-obligatory (Greenberg 1954 [1960]: 191). In Mauwake, all the derivations are non-obligatory. Of the inflections, the beneficiary suffix and the counterfactual suffix as such are not required by syntax like the tense and person marking, but they have an interdependence relationship with other suffixes: the beneficiary suffix has to occur in a past tense or imperative form of a verb that also has the benefactive suffix, and the counterfactual suffix restricts the tense marking to past tense.

In Mauwake verb structure the derivational suffixes always precede the inflectional ones. This agrees with one of Greenberg's universals: "If the derivation and inflection follow the root ... the derivation is always between the root and the inflection" (1966 [1963]: 93).

Inflectional suffixes in Mauwake form paradigms, even if in some cases the paradigms only have two members.

The greater syntagmatic freedom of derivational affixes (Malkiel 1978: 128–129) is shown in Mauwake by the fact that a verb with any of the derivations can be nominalized with the nominalizing suffix -*owa*, whereas one with inflectional suffixes cannot.[54] This ability of verb stems with derivational suffixes to be nominalized is the main distinction between derivation and inflection in Mauwake.

A special feature in Mauwake is the dividing point between the derivational and inflectional suffixes: the benefactive suffix is derivational, whereas the beneficiary suffix is inflectional. The latter can only be present when there are other verbal suffixes following, whereas the former can also be followed by a nominaliser suffix. Other differences between the two suffixes are described below (§3.8.2.3.3), (§3.8.3.1). In the following section, the derivational suffixes are introduced in the order that they occur following the verb root; the prefixes are discussed last.

There is clear iconicity in the linear ordering of the derivational suffixes (Table 3.32): the closer the suffix is to the root, the more profound the change it effects on it. The verbalizing suffixes change the word class; the causative adds an argument; the distributive pluralizes an argument, and the benefactive adds a peripheral.

---

[54] It is possible to nominalize whole *clauses* where the main verb has inflectional suffixes, by adding the demonstrative *nain* 'that' after the clause, but this strategy is not available for individual verbs (§5.7.2).

3 Morphology

Table 3.32: Verbal derivation

Prefix	Root	Verbalizer	Causative	Distributive	Benefactive
p-		-Ø	-ow	-omak	-om
amap-		-ar		-urum	
aap-					
RDP					

3.8.2.2 Category-changing derivation: verb formation

There are two strategies in Mauwake whereby words from other word classes can be changed into verbs. Zero verb formation is less productive than the inchoative. Also the meanings of the verbs resulting from zero verb formation are in some cases more lexicalized, or less transparent, than the meanings of the verbs formed with the inchoative suffix. Often roots can be used for both the strategies, but not always: words like *amisa* 'knowledge' and *ewur* 'quickly, fast' only allow the inchoative suffix.

3.8.2.2.1 Zero verb formation Mauwake has a number of verbs where the root is originally a noun, an adjective or an adverb, and the verb is formed without any overt morpheme to mark the category change. Hopper & Thompson (1984: 745) remark that "languages often possess rather elaborate morphology whose sole function is to convert verbal roots into N's, but no morphology whose sole function is to convert nominal roots into V's". Zero verb formation is here understood, not as adding a zero morpheme, but as a lexical process (following Payne 1997: 224). A noun (Table 3.33), an adjective (Table 3.34) or an adverb (Table 3.35) is used as a root for the verb, and in this process it becomes a true verb, unlike nominalizations which are nouns but retain a lot of their verbal nature as well (Hopper & Thompson 1984: 747).[55]

The resulting verb is usually transitive (374), with a few exceptions. The final vowel of a noun or an adjective, usually /a/, is deleted before the verbal inflection (375).

(374)   Yo   aakisa inasina Rubaruba **nanar-i-yem**.
        1s.UNM now   spirit Rubaruba story-Np-PR.1s
        'Now I tell about spirit Rubaruba.'

(375)   Aruf-ami me **samor-eka**!
        hit-ss.SIM not bad-IMP.2p
        'Don't hit/beat and destroy it.'

---

[55] Hopper & Thompson (1984) propose that a word root is unspecified as to the grammatical category, and that discourse function assigns categoriality. This fits many Austronesian languages in which there are plenty of words where only the non-root morphology, or else syntactic behaviour, shows what class the word belongs to. Mauwake has relatively few forms like this and it is reasonable to assign words to specific word classes even without reference to discourse function.

3.8 Verbs

Table 3.33: Verbs from nouns

akuwa	'knot'	*akuw-*	'knot/bind/tie with a knot'
anima	'blade'	*anim-*	'sharpen'
eneka	'tooth, flame'	*enek-*	'light (a fire)'
ilen	'sign'	*ilen-*	'recognise sign'
nanar	'story'	*nanar-*	'tell a story'

Table 3.34: Verbs from adjectives

dubila	'smooth'	*dubil-*	'smoothen'
enuma	'new'	*enum-*	'renew'
iiwa	'short'	*iiw-*	'shrink'
itita	'soft'	*itit-*	'smash'
kaken	'straight'	*kaken-*	'straighten'
maneka	'big'	*manek-*	'enlarge'
momora	'fool'	*momor-*	'confuse'
samora	'bad'	*samor-*	'destroy'
siina	'tight'	*siin-*	'diminish' (intr.)[a]

[a] Another intransitive verb can be derived from *siina* with the inchoative suffix: *siin-ar-* 'become tight / narrow'.

Table 3.35: Verbs from adverbs

bilik	'mixed'	*bilik-*	'mix'
ikum	'illicitly'	*ikum-*	'speculate'
kerew	'strongly'	*kerew-*	'be angry at'
fan	'here'	*fan-*	'be/come here'
nan	'there'	*nan-*	'be/come here'

3 Morphology

Semantically the resulting verb is usually very close to the word that serves as the root, but in a few instances like (376) the semantic link is not very strong.

(376) *Nefa **ikum-am-ika-iwkin** nan kerer-e-n.*
2s.ACC illicitly-ss.SIM-be-2/3p.DS there appear-PA-2s

'They were just speculating about you when you arrived.'

3.8.2.2.2 Inchoative suffix   The second verb formation process in Mauwake takes a noun, adjective or adverb root and adds an inchoative suffix *-ar* (§2.3.3.4) to form a new verb usually meaning 'become n'.[56] Although in the majority of the cases a word from one of the other word classes is made into a verb, the basic meaning is inchoative rather than verbalizing, as the same suffix can also be added to a few verbs. The suffix has been grammaticalized from the verb *ar-* 'become', 'enter into a state', and there are a few cases where it is difficult to decide with certainty which one it is. The differences between the full verb and the suffix are listed below.

The full resultative verb *ar-* 'become' is more common with nouns, and the meaning of the verb is transparent (377). It is also used with numerals (378). Both words retain their word stress.

(377) *Arim-emi mu'a **ar-'e-k**.*
grow-ss.SIM man become-PA-3s

'He grew up and became man/adult.'

(378) *Aruf-owa e'repam **ar-'e-m**.*
hit-NMZ four become-PA-1s

'I hit it four times.' (Lit: 'Hitting it I became four.')

The inchoative suffix *-ar* can occur with nouns (379), but is more common with adjectives (380) and adverbs (381), and can attach to a few verb roots too (382). Since the result is one word it only has one word stress.

(379) *Yiena opaimika me baliwep **a'mis-ar-e-mik**.*
1p.GEN talk not well knowledge-INCH-PA-1/3p

'They don't know our language well.'

(380) *Miiw-aasa **sa'mor-ar-ek**.*[57]
land-canoe bad-INCH-PA-3s

'The car broke.'

(381) *Kau pun weeser-owa **e'wur-ar-ek**.*
cow too finish-NMZ quickly-INCH-PA-3s

'The beef finished quickly too.'

---

[56] The term 'inchoative' is used for derivation; 'inceptive' for aspect, following Payne (1997: 95).

[57] *Miiw-aasa samor-a-k* 'He broke the car' would be a corresponding sentence with zero verbalization.

(382) Mua *i'men-ar-ep* opora pun *i'men-ar-ek*.
man find-INCH-SS.SEQ talk too find-INCH-PA-3s

'When man appeared, talk/language appeared too.'

Verbs derived from adjectives are often used rather than adjectives in the predicative position (383), (384). And instead of a modifying adjective, a whole relative clause with a verb derived from an adjective may be used (385). This happens especially when the property denoted by the adjective is not static.

(383) Sia nain senam **pin(a)-ar-e-k**.
netbag that1 too.much heavy-INCH-PA-3s

'The netbag is/was (lit: became) very heavy.'

(384) Muuka nain op-iya **dubil(a)-al-e-k**.
boy that1 hold-2/3s.DS slippery-INCH-PA-3s

'When he₁ held the boy₂, he₂ was slippery.'

(385) [Konima **supuk(a)-ar-e-k** nain] yasuw-e.
cloth wet-INCH-PA-3s that1 wash-IMP.2s

'Wash the wet cloth.' (Lit: 'Wash the cloth that has become wet.')

The consonant /r/ in the suffix is lateralized into /l/ when the root has /l/ in the immediately preceding syllable. Lateralization takes place arbitrarily in a few other cases as well (388).

(386) Yo *damol(a)-al-e-m* oo.
1s.UNM bad-INCH-PA-1s oh

'I feel terrible.' (Lit: 'I'm destroyed/ruined.')

(387) Epa *dabel(a)-al-ek*.
place cold-INCH-PA-3s

'It is cold.'

(388) Opaimika efa *masi(a)-al-i-ya*.
mouth 1s.ACC bitter-INCH-Np-PR.3s

'It tastes bitter to me / in my mouth.'

If two preceding syllables contain /l/, the consonant in the verbaliser is not lateralized (389).[58]

(389) Aasa puuk-ap *ilel(a)-ar-i-ya*.
canoe cut-SS.SEQ gouge-INCH-Np-PR.3s

'He has cut the canoe (length from a tree) and is gouging/carving it'

---

[58] This rule is very tentative, as *ilelar-* is the only example found so far.

3 Morphology

The suffix *ar-* often retains its original verbal meaning 'become' when adjectives are made into verbs (390), but when the other word classes are used as the root the original meaning tends to become more opaque or get lost (391).

(390) ***Dubil(a)-al-e-k.***
slippery/smooth-INCH-PA-3s
'It became slippery/smooth.'

(391) *No* ***wadol(a)-al-i-n.***
2s.UNM lie-INCH-Np-PR.2s
'You are lying.'

Most of the verbs formed with the inchoative suffix are intransitive, but some are active, transitive verbs (392), (393):

(392) *Muuka kuisow* ***muuk(a)-ar-e-k.***
son one son-INCH-PA-3s
'She gave birth to one son.'

(393) *Epa* ***mores-ar-ep*** *ikiw-o-k.*
place like(ADV)-INCH-SS.SEQ go-PA-3s
'He made the place ready and went.'

The inchoative verb formation is also used with verb loans from other languages (395), especially Tok Pisin (394).[59] Both of the loan words below also have a vernacular synonym.

(394) *Muuka wia* ***was-ar-e-mik.*** *(from Tok Pisin was 'look after')*
son 3p.ACC look.after-INCH-PA-1/3p
'They were looking after the boys/children'

(395) ***Nading-ar-ep*** *uf-e-mik.* *(from Mala nading 'decoration')*
decoration-INCH-SS.SEQ dance-PA-1/3p
'We decorated ourselves and danced.'

3.8.2.3 Category-maintaining derivation: suffixes

3.8.2.3.1 Causative suffix The causative suffix *-ow* (or *-aw*) transitivizes an intransitive verb (Peterson 2007: 2): the clause gets a new subject, and the subject of the intransitive verb becomes the direct object. Usually it adds a causative meaning 'cause someone to do something', or 'cause something to happen'. The object of a causative construction has no control, or only minimal control, over the action or event indicated by the verb.

---

[59] The Tok Pisin loans often originally come from English.

3.8 Verbs

In many verbs there is free variation between -*ow* and -*aw*. Some verbs seem to prefer one or the other, but there is no clear pattern. There is also some dialectal and possibly age-based variation depending on the speaker. -*ow* is taken here as the basic form, since it is the more common of the two, and because in "double causatives" it is always used at least as the first one. Table 3.36 lists some causative verbs.

Table 3.36: Causative verbs and their bases

arim-ow-	'bring up / raise'	arim-	'grow'
in-aw-	'put to bed'	in-	'lie down'
bagiwir-ow	'cause to be angry'	bagiwir-	'be angry'
iimar-ow-	'make sth. stand up'	iimar-	'stand up'
imenar-ow-	'create/cause to appear'	imenar-	'appear'
waki-ow-aw-	'cause to stumble'	waki-	'stumble'
ook-ow-	'place alongside'	ook-	'follow'

Sometimes the causative suffix occurs reduplicated as a "double causative", but these still add only one argument. Many of the short directional verbs (§3.8.4.4.5) take a double causative instead of a single one (396).

(396) *Eewua ir-**ow-aw**-ap osaiwa ar-e-k.*
wing climb-CAUS-CAUS-SS.SEQ bird.of.paradise become-PA-3s
'She put the wing up (on herself) and became a bird of paradise.'

A single or double causative can be added to the intransitive verb *reen-* '(become) dry' with the result of two different meanings, but both of these still only add one more argument: *reenow-* 'dry (something)', *reenowaw-* 'smoke (something)'.

The only two transitive verbs that have been found to take the causative are *mik-* 'spear/hit' and *op-* 'hold/grab', with the causative forms *mik-ow-aw-* 'join (the ends of two long items)' and *op-aw-* 'accuse falsely'.

Table 3.37 lists some verbs that have are derived from other verbs with the causative suffix but which do NOT have any causative meaning (397), (398). The causative as a valence-increasing device is discussed in §3.8.4.3.1.

Table 3.37: "Causative" verbs without causative meaning

aakun-ow-	'grumble (at)'	from:	aakun-	'speak'
baun-ow-	'bark (at)'		baun-	'bark'
kirir-ow-	'shout (about)'		kirir-	'shout'
op-aw-	'accuse falsely'		op-	'hold'

3 Morphology

(397) *Mukuna kuuf-ap kirir-e-k.*
fire see-SS.SEQ shout-PA-3s
'She saw the fire and shouted.'

(398) *Yiok-ami naap **yia** kirir-ow-am-ik-ua.*
follow.us-SS.SIM thus 1p.ACC shout-CAUS-SS.SIM-be-PA.3s
'She was following us and shouting about us like that.'

3.8.2.3.2 Distributive suffix A distributive suffix pluralizes one of the verbal arguments. There are two distributive suffixes: *-urum* 'all' and *-omak* 'many'. They are fully productive in the whole verb class, as long as the semantics of the verb allows multiple arguments.

The hierarchy of which argument the distributive applies to is as follows: if there is a recipient (400) or beneficiary (401), the distributive applies to that; if there is no recipient or beneficiary but an object, the distributive applies to the object (402); and in case the clause has neither a recipient or beneficiary nor an object, the distributive applies to the subject (403). Since transitive verbs need an object, the subject can be pluralized with the distributive only when the verb is intransitive.

(399) REC/BEN > O > S

(400) *Mua teeria opaimika wia sesek-**omak**-e-mik.*
man family talk 3p.ACC send-DISTR/PL-PA-1/3p
'They sent word to (many members of) the man's family.'

(401) *Wiena wiawi=ke amia wia keraw-om-**omak**-e-mik.*
3p.GEN 3s/p.father=CF spear 3p.ACC carve-BEN-DISTR/PL-PA-1/3p
'Their fathers carved spears for them (*many* beneficiaries).'

(402) *Emeria unowa fain nia aaw-**urum**-i-kuan.*
woman many this 2s.ACC take-DISTR/A-Np-FU.3p
'They will take all you women.'

(403) *Emeria teeria koka ikiw-**urum**-e-mik.*
woman group jungle go-DISTR/A-PA-1/3p
'The whole group of women / all the women went to the jungle.'

In verbal groups (§3.8.5.1) the distributive suffix usually attaches to the last verb root (404), (405), but it can occasionally also attach to the first root, i.e. the main verb in a verb+AUX combination (406).

(404) *Iinan aasa ikiw-emi paran-em-**mi**-omak-e-k.*
sky canoe go-SS.SIM rumble-SS.SIM-go.around-DISTR/PL-PA-3s
'Many planes went rumbling around.'

(405) *Iinan aasa fan or-om-**ik-omak**-eya* ...
sky canoe here1 descend-SS.SIM-be-DISTR/PL-2/3S.DS
'When many planes were coming down here ...'

(406) *Wi ifa saarik **in-urum-ep**-ik-e-mik.*
3p.UNM snake like sleep-DISTR/A-SS.SEQ-be-PA-1/3p
'They all slept/lay like snakes.'

Both suffixes can be attached to the same verb but it is rare. In that case *-urum* precedes *-omak* (407).

(407) *Wia ifakim-**urum-omak**-e-mik.*
3p.ACC kill-DISTR/A-DISTR/PL-PA-1/3p
'They killed each and every one of them.' (There were many of those killed.)

3.8.2.3.3 Benefactive suffix The benefactive suffix, indicating the fact that the action of the verb is done FOR SOMEONE, for their benefit or detriment, is a borderline case among the derivations. It is the last one of the derivational suffixes, and the BENEFICIARY SUFFIX (§3.8.3.1) following it and marking the person that the action is done for, is inflectional even if the two suffixes go together semantically. The position of the benefactive is not as stable as that of the other suffixes: it comes after the distributive when the beneficiary is first person singular (408), (409) but occurs preceding it with the other persons (410), (411).

(408) *Mua Maneka=ke maa maneka on-**omak-om**-e-k.*
Man Big=CF thing big do-DISTR/PL-BEN-BNFY1.PA[60] -3s
'God did great things to/for me.'

(409) *Buk aaw-**omak-om**-e!*
book get-DISTR/PL-BEN-BNFY1.IMP.2s
'Get the books for me!'

(410) *Buk aaw-**om-omak**-e!*
book get-BEN-DISTR/PL-IMP.2s
'Get the books for him!'

(411) *Wiena wiawi=ke amia wia keraw-**om-omak**-e-mik.*
3p.GEN 3s/p.father=CF bow 3p.ACC carve-BEN-DISTR/PL-PA-1/3p
'Their fathers carved bows for them.'

---

[60] The vowel of the beneficiary suffix deletes the vowel of the past tense suffix. The relationship between the beneficiary suffix and the suffix following it is discussed in detail in §3.8.3.1, and the medial suffix forms are discussed in §3.8.3.5.

3 Morphology

In verbal groups the benefactive suffix is usually attached to the finite verb or auxiliary (412) but can occasionally occur on the non-finite root (413) or even on both of the two (414).

(412) *Iwera wia uruk-am-ik-**om**-a-mik.*
coconut 3p.ACC drop-SS.SIM-be-BEN-BNFY2.PA-1/3p
'We kept dropping coconuts for them.'

(413) *Maamuma wia p-ikiw-**om**-ap-pu-ap* ...
money 3p.ACC textscbpx-go-BEN-BNFY2.SS.SEQ-CMPL-SS.SEQ
'Having taken money to them, ... '

(414) *Moro mua wia wu-**om**-am-ik-**om**-a-mik.*
Moro man 3p.ACC put-BEN-BNFY2.SS.SIM-be-BEN-BNFY2.PA-1/3p
'They put them (=carts) for the Moro men.'

The benefactive form does not always mean that something happens for someone's BENEFIT. The benefactive may be strengthened with the adverb *orawin* 'for the benefit' (415), which makes it unambiguous.

(415) *Iwera **orawin** kais-**om**-e-mik.*
Coconut for.the.benefit husk-BEN-BNFY1.PA-1/3p
'They husked coconuts for me (for free).'

By using a suffix completely unrelated to the verb 'give', Mauwake shows itself different from all of those reasonably closely related languages that have grammatical descriptions available. A serial verb construction involving the verb 'give' is a very common way of expressing benefactive in Papuan languages (Foley 1986: 141). Waskia (Ross and Paol 1978:45) and Maia (Hardin 2002: 125) employ this strategy, and in Usan it is behind one of the two strategies: the benefactive verb form has been grammaticalized from a serial verb with the verb 'give' (Reesink 1987:110–111). The other strategy for Usan is to use a postposition with the appropriate noun phrase (ibid. 154). Bargam is similar to it (Hepner 2002:65–66, 99), but Amele utilizes an indirect object clitic attached to the verb to express the beneficiary as well as other semantic relations (Roberts 1987: 167).

3.8.2.4 Derivational prefixes

Although Mauwake is very strongly a suffixing language, it makes use of some derivational prefixes as well. Reduplication is the most common among these.

3.8.2.4.1 Reduplication The morphophonological aspect of reduplication was already described in §2.3.3.2. In §6.4.2, reduplication is discussed as one of the many quantification strategies in Mauwake.

Reduplication in verbs is used in Mauwake to indicate continuity or iterativity of action and/or plurality of the resulting object. Mostly the reduplication is done only once, but especially motion verbs can have several identical reduplicative prefixes.

In verbs of motion reduplication means continuity (416), and the passing of time may be shown by the number of reduplications (417).

(416) **Biri-birin-emi** wia   akim-omak-e-mik.
      RDP-fly-SS.SIM 3p.ACC try-DISTR/PL-PA-1/3p
      'They were flying and teasing them.'

(417) Ne **oro-oro-oro**-oro-mi   **oro-oro**-or-o-k,   onoma.
      and RDP-RDP-RDP-descend-SS.SIM RDP-RDP-descend-PA-3s horizon.
      'And it went down and down and down all the way to the horizon.'

In other intransitive verbs reduplication indicates either iterative action (418) or occasionally continuity (419).

(418) Nomokowa **ku-ku-ep**   or-om-ik-ua.
      tree   RDP-break-SS.SEQ descend-SS.SIM-be-PA.3s
      'The timber (in a bridge) kept breaking and falling down.'

(419) Epa **wii-wiim-ik-ua**, ...
      place RDP-dawn-be-PA.3s
      'It was dawning, ...'

Both of these meanings fit in well with Moravcsik's (1978: 319) description of the various meanings that reduplication in verbs can have. In transitive verbs reduplication indicates iterative action as well as the plurality of an inanimate object (420). The form is used especially when the action RESULTS in a plural object (421).

(420) Iinan aasa=ke   maifa **fu-fuurk-ikiw-o-k**.
      sky   canoe=CF paper RDP-throw-go-PA-3s
      'The plane went throwing paper slips down'

(421) Oposia nain **pu-puuk-ap**   uup-e-mik.
      meat   that1 RDP-cut-SS.SEQ cook-PA-1/3p
      'We cut up the meat (into many pieces) and cooked it.'

Usan differs from Mauwake in that it does not use reduplication very much in verbs, and never in main clause final verbs (Reesink 1987: 116). Also, when reduplication is used to indicate duration or repetition the whole verb word is reduplicated (ibid. 117). In Bargam reduplication occurs but is not very productive. In transitive verbs reduplication indicates plurality of objects, in intransitive verbs plurality of subjects (Hepner 2002: 19). In Maia "verb roots may be partially or completely reduplicated. Verb reduplication broadly indicates an augmented action which may include a greater, more massive, more intensified or very often repetitive form of the action" (Hardin 2002: 50).

3 Morphology

3.8.2.4.2 Bring-prefixes The prefixes in this group change the directional verbs (§3.8.4.4.5) into transitive verbs with the meaning 'bring' or 'take'. *p-* is a neutral prefix and by far the most common one (422), *amap-* is used when something is brought out in the open, often with the meaning 'bring forth'. Usually there is a clear goal, a person or a place, which may not be mentioned in the clause itself but occurs in an earlier one (423), or is understood from the context (424). If the goal is explicitly mentioned in the clause, the neutral prefix is used (422), (425). The prefix *aap-* (426) is very rare and I have been unable to establish whether it really differs from *amap-* or whether it is just a matter of idiolectal use.[61]

(422) *Amina aaw-ep   Liisa ame   wia   **p-er**-om-a.*
    pot   take/get-SS.SEQ Liisa others 3p.ACC BPX-go-BEN-BNFY2.IMP.2s
    'Get the pot and take it to Liisa and the others.'

(423) *Pita pensil wiar or-op   ik-ua   nain aaw-ep   **amap-ikiw**-om-aka.*
    Pita pencil 3.DAT fall-SS.SEQ be-PA.3s that1 take-SS.SEQ BPX-go-BEN-BNFY2.IMP.2p
    'Take to Pita his pencil that has dropped.'

(424) *Wiipa   oko   **amap-ora**-iwkin   ma-e-k   ...*
    daughter other BPX-descend-2/3p.DS say-PA-3s
    'When they took another daughter down (from the house out in the open), he said...'

(425) *Ni   auwa maa **p-urup**-om-aka.*
    2p.UNM father food BPX-ascend-BEN-BNFY2.IMP.2p
    'Take food (up) to father.'

(426) *Iwera   ir-ap   erup op-ap   **aap-or**-e.*
    coconut go.up-SS.SEQ two grab-SS.SEQ BPX-descend-IMP.2s
    'Climb the coconut palm, grab two coconuts and bring them down.'

3.8.3 Verb inflection

The inflectional suffixes are discussed in the order that they occur following the verb stem.

---

[61] The bring-PRefixes may have been grammaticalized from a medial verb construction involving the verb *aaw-* 'take'. It is easy to see how *aawep ekap-* 'take (and) come' could have developed into *aapekap-* 'bring' and possibly also into *pekap-*. Another possibility is that it is a result of a related process to that in Usan where the verb *ba* 'take' has contracted into *b-*, which has combined with verbs of motion and been lexicalized with the meaning of bringing or taking (Reesink 1987:144–145). The *amap-*prefix may have its origin in the expression *ama-PA* 'in the sun', which implies 'in the open'. There is also a very slight possibility that the *p-*prefix might be an Austronesian loan, as p(V)- is a common causative or transitivizer prefix in Austronesian languages (Bugenhagen 1995: 61). But all of this is just conjecture at this point.

3.8.3.1 Beneficiary

The beneficiary suffix indicates the person the action is done for. Its position is directly after the benefactive suffix, or after the distributive suffix in those few cases where the benefactive comes before the distributive (§3.8.2.3.3). It is inflectional rather than derivational because 1) when it is used, nominalization is blocked and 2) it has a paradigm for different persons, even if the paradigm only consists of two members.

The only two forms for the beneficiary are -*e* for first or second person singular (427) and -*a* for all the other persons (428). The context often provides more person distinctions, as the plural requires accusative pronouns to precede the verb to indicate the beneficiary, like third person plural in (429).

(427)   *Wafur-om-e!*
        throw-BEN-BNFY1.IMP.2s
        'Throw it to me!'

(428)   *Marasin wu-om-a-mik=na   weetak.*
        medicine put-BEN-BNFY2.PA-1/3p=TP no
        'They put medicine on him but no (it didn't help).'

(429)   *Na-iwkin   wia   uf-om-a-mik.*
        say-2/3p.DS 3p.ACC dance-BEN-BNFY2.PA-1/3p
        'They said so and we danced for them.'

When the beneficiary suffix is followed by a vowel, a mid vowel is deleted adjacent to a low vowel (430) and both a mid and a low vowel are deleted preceding a high vowel (431). In the latter case the person distinction gets neutralized in the singular (432), but not in the plural where the obligatory accusative pronouns maintain the distinction (433). The examples (434)-(436) below show how the beneficiary suffix affects the past tense suffix. In (436) a sequence of two identical vowels is reduced to one vowel.

(430)   *aaw-om-**ak**-a-m*   < *aaw-om-**a**-ek-a-m*
        get-BEN-BNFY2.CNTF-PA-1s
        'I would have gotten it for him'

(431)   *aaw-om-**i**-non*   < *aaw-om-e-i-non, aaw-om-a-i-non*
        get-BEN-BNFY.NPS-FU.3s
        'he will get it for me/you/him/her'

(432)   *aaw-om-**uk***   < *aaw-om-e-uk, aaw-om-a-uk*
        get-BEN-BNFY.IMP.3p
        'let them get it for me/you/him/her'

(433)   *Panewowa maa **wia**   p-ikiw-om-**uk**.*
        old   food 3p.ACC BPX-go-BEN-BNFY.IMP.3p
        'Let them take food for the old people.'

3 Morphology

(434) *Uf-**o**-k.*
   dance-PA-3s
   'He danced.'

(435) *Uf-om-**e**-k.*
   dance-BEN-BNFY1.PA-3s
   'He danced for me/you.'

(436) *Uf-om-**a**-k.*
   dance-BEN-BNFY2.PA-3s
   'He danced for him.'

3.8.3.2 Counterfactual

The counterfactual modality is the only modal distinction made in the verb morphology. It is an expression of the truth value of the statement: something could or would have happened, but did not, or something might be the case but for some reason is not. The counterfactual is marked by the suffix *-ek* (437) and is only used with the past tense suffix even if the verb refers to the present (438) or future (439) time. The counterfactual is used in both hypothetical and counterfactual conditional clauses (§8.3.5).

(437) *Lawiliw akena waki-**ek**-a-m.*
   nearly very fall-CNTF-PA-1s
   'I very nearly fell.'

(438) *Yena aamun aakisa uruf-**ek**-a-m=na kemel-**ek**-a-m.*
   1s.GEN yonger.brother now see-CNTF-PA-1s=TP rejoice-CNTF-PA-1s
   'If I saw my younger brother now, I would be happy.'

(439) *Morauta fan ik-**ek**-a-k=na uurika ikiw-ep maak-**ek**-a-mik.*
   Morauta here be-CNTF-PA-3s=TP tomorrow go-SS.SEQ tell-CNTF-PA-1/3p
   'If Morauta were here, tomorrow we would go and tell him.'

If there is a beneficiary suffix *-a* preceding the counterfactual, the vowel /e/ of the counterfactual suffix is deleted (440):

(440) *Maifa yia aaw-om-**ak**-a-k=na...*
   paper 1p.ACC get-BEN-BNFY2.CNTF-PA-3s=TP
   'If he had gotten tickets for us...'

3.8.3.3 Mood

Mood in Mauwake is defined as a morphological category of the verb, relating to the pragmatic function of the sentence (cf. Palmer 1986: 21). Mauwake has a mixed tense-mood system, where the indicative present, past and future, and the imperative are in contrast.

The mood distinctions only show in the finite verb. Same-subject medial verbs take the interpretation of their mood from the following finite verb, but different-subject medial verbs may be independent of the final verb as to their mood.

3.8.3.3.1 Indicative The indicative is the neutral, morphologically unmarked mood. It is characterized by the tense distinctions between present, past (441) and future (442), and the person/number distinctions of first, second, and third person in singular and plural.

(441) I   me yia   damol-a-mik.
       1s.UNM not 1s.ACC harm-PA-1/3p
       'They didn't harm us.'

(442) Aria,   iperowa   opora wiar ook-i-yen.
       alright, middle-aged   talk   3.DAT follow-Np-FU.1p
       'Alright, we'll follow the advice of the middle-aged men.'

3.8.3.3.2 Imperative The term imperative is used for "mands" (Lyons 1977: 745)[62] showing in the verbal morphology, regardless of person. In Mauwake the imperatives form a full paradigm (with the first person singular being replaced with the first person dual), and their syntactic behaviour is similar. So there is no valid reason to divide them into different categories such as imperatives, jussives and hortatives, just because semantically giving orders to oneself differs from giving orders to an addressee or to a third person (443)–(445).[63]

There are no tense distinctions in the imperative forms. The initial (or only) vowel in the second person imperatives is usually <e>, but in very few cases it is <a>.[64] The imperative suffixes are listed in Table 3.38.

Table 3.38: Imperative suffixes

	person/number
-u	1d
-e / (-a)	2s
-inok	3s
-ikua	1p
-eka / (-aka)	2p
-uk	3p

---

[62] Lyons borrows the term from B.F. Skinner as a useful cover term, without subscribing to Skinner's behaviouristic position.
[63] For a discussion on this question, see Palmer (1986: 109–111).
[64] The only verbs found with -a in the imperative are iw- 'go', mik- 'spear, hit', op- 'hold' and pok- 'sit'.

3 Morphology

(443) *Or-op   mua nain uruf-**e**.*
descend-SS.SEQ man that1 see-IMP.2s
'Go down and see that man.'

(444) *Ikoka amap-urup-eya   op-**ikua**.*
later BPX-ascend-2/3s.DS hold-IMP.1p
'Later when he comes up, let's hold/grab him.'

(445) *Wi   urup-ep   mukuna nain umuk-**uk**.*
3p.UNM ascend-SS.SEQ fire   that1 extinguish-IMP.3p
'Let them go up and extinguish the fire.'

The imperative differs from the other moods in that in the first person it has a dual form, rather than a singular form (446), (447).

(446) *Aria,   i   owowa=ko or-**u**.*
alright, 1p.UNM village=NF descend-IMP.1d
'Alright, let's (d.) go down to the village.'

(447) *Yiena   ikos   akena iw-**u**.*
1p.GEN two.together truly go-IMP.1d
'Let's just the two of us go together.'

The initial (or only) vowel in the second person imperative forms is deleted after the beneficiary suffix (448)–(451).

(448) *Iwera   ir-**e**.*
coconut ascend-IMP.2s
'Climb up the coconut palm (to get coconuts).'

(449) *Iwera   ir-om-**e**.*
coconut ascend-BEN-BNFY1.IMP.2s
'Climb up the coconut palm for me.'

(450) *Iwera   ir-om-**a**.*
coconut ascend-BEN-BNFY2.IMP.2s
'Climb up the coconut palm for him.'

(451) *Iwera   yia   ir-om-**aka**.*
coconut 1p.ACC ascend-BEN-BNFY2.IMP.2p
'Climb up (plural) the coconut palm for us.'

The semantics of the imperative and the functional aspects of commands are discussed in §7.3. On the use of subject pronouns with imperatives, see §3.5.11. The imperative forms of the verbs are also used in desiderative and conative (§8.3.2.1) constructions.

3.8.3.4 Tense and person/number in final verbs

Tense is a "grammaticalized expression of location in time" (Comrie 1985: 9). Mauwake has a straightforward three-tense system in the finite verbs marking past, present and future time reference. The tense system is simple compared with most other Papuan languages, many of which have more than three genuine tense distinctions and/or interaction between tense and status[65] resulting in several "tenses" (Foley 1986:158–163). Of the most closely related languages well studied so far, Usan has five tenses (Reesink 1987: 98) out of which one, uncertain future/subjunctive, is semantically related to irrealis. Maia has a complete status system instead of a tense system, and temporal relations are inferred from the realis or irrealis status and the aspects (Hardin 2002: 55). According to Foley, "most Papuan languages are tense-dominated [rather than status-dominated]" 1986: 162. In Mauwake the status hardly plays any role at all.

Portmanteau morphemes of the tense and person/number markers are very common in Papuan languages, but having the two distinct from each other is not uncommon either (Foley 1986: 137). The tense and person suffixes are separate morphemes in Mauwake, but have an interesting interplay with each other.

The speech event is taken as the reference point. The tense suffixes in themselves only distinguish between two tenses, past and non-past, and the further distinction between present and future is made by the person/number suffixes (452). The person/number suffixes, on the other hand, are the same in past and present tense except for the first and third person singular forms.

(452) Unan **aakun-e-mik**, aakisa **aakun-i-mik** ne uurika nainiw
yesterday talk-PA-1/3p now/today talk-Np-PR.1/3p ADD tomorrow again
aakun-i-yen.
talk-Np-FU.1p
'Yesterday we talked, now/today we talk and tomorrow we'll talk again.'

The NON-PAST marker in the second person plural future form is -o instead of -i possibly because of assimilation to the labial consonant /w/ in the person/number suffix.

The verb conjugation classes determining the past tense suffix vowels are discussed in the section on morphophonology (§2.3.3.3). The beneficiary and the counterfactual suffixes influence the past tense suffix in the following way. After the counterfactual the past tense suffix is always -a. When the beneficiary suffix is present, the vowel of the past tense suffix is assimilated to it. Table 3.39 presents the full paradigms for the tense and person/number suffixes.

The person/number marking in the verb distinguishes three persons in both singular and plural. There is no dual number, nor is there inclusive-exclusive distinction in the first person plural form. The plural is marked only for humans, spirits and important animals. The singular form is used for less important and small animals as well as all inanimates (453).

---

[65] 'Status' here refers to the distinction between realis and irrealis.

3 Morphology

Table 3.39: Tense and person/number suffixes

	Non-past	Present & person	Non-past	Future & person	Past	Person
1s	-i	-yem	-i	-nen	-a/E	-m
2s	-i	-n	-i	-nan	-a/E	-n
3s	-i	-ya	-i	-non	-a/E	-k
1p	-i	-mik	-i	-yen	-a/E	-mik
2p	-i	-man	-o	-wen	-a/E	-man
3p	-i	-mik	-i	-kuan	-a/E	-mik

(453) *Waa muuka arow ekap-o-**k**.*
pig boy three come-PA-3s
'Three piglets came.'

Besides their primary meaning, the present and future tenses also have secondary meanings. The present tense form of the first or third person plural is used for generic or time-neutral statements (454). For the habitual aspect in the present, the simple present tense (455) is an alternative to the full habitual aspect form.[66]

(454) *Ifa yia keraw-i-ya nain miira **saawirin-i-mik**.*
snake 1p.ACC bite-Np-PR.3s that1 face become.round-Np-PR.1/3p
'When a snake bites us, we become dizzy.'

(455) *Nos=ke anane urema efar **ikum-ar-i-n**.*
2s.FC=CF always bandicoot 1s.DAT illicitly-INCH-Np-PR.2s
'You always steal bandicoots from me.'

The future tense in any person form is used for habitual or generic conditionals (456) (§8.3.5). The example (457) refers to a traditional custom and is generic, even if the first person form of the verb is used, and the first person pronoun as well.

(456) *Waaya **ika-i-non**, waaya **uup-i-nan**, naap.*
pig   be-Np-FU.3s pig   cook-Np-FU.2s thus
'If there is a pig, you will cook it - it is like that.'

(457) *Ikoka yo **um-i-nen**, muuka nain nainiw wiena **aaw-i-kuan**.*
later 1s.UNM die-Np-FU.1s son that1 again 3p.GEN take-Np-FU.3p
'Later, if I die (without paying the bride price) they will take the son back.'

The second person singular form of the future tense has two other usages as well. It can be used when referring to generic or habitual situations, especially in process

---
[66] Continuous aspect form is required for the past habitual (§3.8.5.1.1.2).

descriptions which can also be understood as instructions. For these, the first person plural form of the present tense is much more common, but often the two alternate. The following example (458) describes work involved in harvesting taro roots (and the addressee that the story was told to, had no garden, so the speaker did not refer to her personally).

(458) *Perek-ami   en-ow(a) gelemuta **on-i-nan**.*
      harvest-SS.SIM eat-NMZ little   make-Np-FU.2s

'When you harvest it, you make a feast.'

It is also used for a command, or a statement of obligation (459):

(459) *Ikoka kuisow kuuma kuisow **yi-i-nan**.*
      later one   stick one   give.me-Np-FU.2s

'Very soon you have to give me 10 kina.' Or: 'Give me 10 kina very soon.'

3.8.3.5 Medial verb marking

The distinction between medial and final verbs is common in Papuan languages (Foley 1986: 11). Especially in the TNG languages the medial verbs are "very common, universal over a wide area [and the] systems often highly complex" (Wurm 1982: 63, also Roberts 1997). The medial verbs typically lack the full tense and person/number marking of the finite verbs. Instead, they usually indicate whether the subject is the same as the subject of the following verb, and/or whether the action of the verb is simultaneous or sequential with the action of the following verb.[67] As for person reference, the verbs in the simplest systems only show whether the two subjects are the same or different, but in the most elaborate systems the subjects of both the medial verb and that of the following verb are shown in the medial verb, which is thus even more specific than the finite verb.[68]

In Mauwake the medial verb system is relatively simple. The suffixes indicate whether the subject of the medial verb stays the same in the following verb as well, and in the "same subject following" (SS) verbs there is a further distinction between simultaneous and sequential action. The "different subject following" (DS) verbs indicate sequential action; for simultaneous action one needs to use the continuous or stative aspect (§3.8.5.1.1). The DS verbs also have some person marking but not as detailed as the finite verbs have.

---

[67] This is called the "switch-reference system". The question whether the system really tracks the topic (pragmatic subject) or the syntactic subject is discussed further in §8.2.3.
[68] Usan makes a distinction between neutral and future medial verbs, and in both of these there is a division between same-subject and different-subject forms, but not between sequentiality and simultaneity (Reesink 1987:87–92). Maia only uses medial verbs when a clause has the same subject as the following clause; a distinction is made between simultaneous and sequential actions. When the following clause has a different subject, finite forms plus the contrast clitic *-(d)i* is used (Hardin 2002: 87). Amele makes the basic distinction between the same-subject and different-subject medial verbs, and has simultaneous and sequential forms in both. But it also has different-subject simultaneous irrealis forms (Roberts 1987: 275). Particularly the East New Guinea Highlands languages are known for marking the anticipatory subject in their medial verbs. See Franklin (1983: 40–41) for a succinct list of switch-reference characteristics in Papuan languages, and Roberts (1997) for a more comprehensive overview.

3 Morphology

The two sections below give a general outline of the person reference in medial clauses, but it is discussed in more detail in §8.2.3.

Typically, medial verbs have much fewer inflectional possibilities than finite verbs (Foley 1986: 11). This is the case in Mauwake too: mood or tense and full person/number marking cannot be suffixed to the medial verbs. Derivational suffixes, on the other hand, can freely occur on the medial verbs. In Tail-Head linkage a new sentence begins with a medial verb copy of the finite verb that ended the previous sentence (§8.2.3.5). Often the derivational morphology of the two verbs is the same, and sometimes the medial verb has less derivation than the final verb; very rarely it has even MORE (460):

(460) *Ikiwosa wiar pepekim-ep kaik-a-m. Kaik-**om**-ap...*
 head 3.DAT measure-SS.SEQ tie-PA-1s tie-BEN-BNFY2.SS.SEQ
 'I measured her head and tied it (=headdress). I tied it for her and ...'

3.8.3.5.1 Same-subject marking When the subject of the medial clause is the same as that of the following clause, the verb itself does not give any indication of the person and number of the subject, only that the same subject continues in the next clause.[69] If the actions are sequential, i.e. the action indicated by the verb in the medial clause precedes that of the following clause, the suffix is *-ap* or *-ep* (461) depending on the conjugation class (§2.3.3.3).[70]

(461) *Owowa or-**op**, wuailal-**ep** akia ik-e-k.*
 village go.down-SS.SEQ be.hungry-SS.SEQ banana roast-PA-3s
 'He went (down) to the village, was hungry and roasted bananas.'

If the verb has the beneficiary suffix *-a* or *-e* (§3.8.3.1), the vowel of the medial verb suffix gets assimilated to it (462), (463).

(462) *...eka=pa merena yasuw-om-**ep**... (cf. yasuw-**ap**)*
 water=LOC foot wash-BEN-BNFY.1-SS.SEQ
 '... she washed my feet in water (and) ...'

(463) *...waaya nain uup-om-**ap** samapora=pa wu-ap maak-e-mik...*
 pig that1 cook-BEN-BNFY2.SS.SEQ floor=LOC put-SS.SEQ tell-PA-1/3p
 *(cf. uup-**ep**)*

 '... they cooked the pig for him, put it on the floor and told him, ...'

When the medial clause subject is the same as the subject in the following clause but the two actions are simultaneous, or at least overlapping, the suffix is *-ami* or *-emi* (or *-omi*) according to the conjugation class of the verb. Even if the action of the medial verb

---

[69] For exceptions to this, see §8.2.3 where the functional aspects of switch reference are discussed.
[70] For the second conjugation class verb *or-* 'descend' the suffix is *-op*.

may often be INTERPRETED as continuous (464), the suffix in itself only indicates simultaneity (465). Continuous aspect marking may be needed for clarity when continuity is in focus (466).

(464) Wi   sawur ir-**ami**   fan yiar   pok-a-mik.
      3p.UNM spirit go-SS.SIM here 1p.DAT sit.down-PA-1/3p
      'As the spirits were going they sat down here with us.'

(465) ...ekap-**emi** koora=pa yia   wua-i-mik.
      come-SS.SIM house=LOC 1p.ACC put-Np-PR.1/3p
      '...coming (=upon arrival) they put us in the house.'

(466) **Soomar-em-ik-ok** ifara oko   uruf-a-k.
      walk-SS.SIM-be-SS vine other see-PA-3s
      'He was walking and saw another vine.'

The verb *ik-* 'be' is different from other verbs in that there is no differentiation between the simultaneous and sequential forms in the same-subject medial verb: in example (467) the actions are simultaneous, in (468) sequential. Also, the verb does not take either one of the normal same-subject suffixes.

(467) Owowa=pa neeke   **ik-ok** mua maak-ek...
      village=LOC there.CF be-SS man tell-PA-3s
      'While they were there in the village she told her husband, ...'

(468) No   kaaneke **ik-ok** kerer-e-n?
      2s.UNM where.CF be-SS appear-PA-2s
      'Where have you been and now come?'

3.8.3.5.2 Different-subject marking If the subject of the medial clause is different from that of the following clause, the suffix of the DS verb reflects this. There are some person/number distinctions in these suffixes, even though not as many as in the finite verbs. The first person singular and plural are distinguished from all the other forms; in the other persons the distinction is based on the number: second and third person singular share the same suffix, and second and third person plural likewise (469), (470).[71] Table 3.40 shows the different subject suffixes.

(469) Imen-ap   maak-**iwkin** o   miim-o-k.
      find-SS.SEQ tell-2/3p.DS 3s.UNM precede-PA-3s
      'They found him and told him, and he went ahead of them.'

---

[71] There is great variation in this area in Papuan languages. Some only have one form to indicate that the subject changes, others have partial or full differentiation according to the person, some even show the subject of the following clause in the medial verb.

3 Morphology

Table 3.40: Suffixes marking a different subject in the following clause

	Singular	Plural
1	-Vmkun	
2	-eya	-iwkin
3		

(470) *Mik-**amkun** me um-o-k, wiowa onaiya ikiw-em-ik-**eya** Olas=ke*
spear-1s/p.DS not die-PA-3s spear with go-SS.SIM-be-2/3s.DS Olas=CF
war-ek.
shoot-PA-3s

'When I speared it, it didn't die, (but) as it was going with the spear Olas shot it.'

The suffix is *-aya* instead of *-eya* in a few short conjugation class 1 verbs (§3.8.4.1) (471)[72] and in those benefactive verbs where the first vowel of the suffix is assimilated to the preceding vowel of the beneficiary suffix (472).

(471) *Iw-**aya** nan miira saawirin-e-k.*
enter-2/3s.DS there face become.round-PA-3s

'As [the poison] entered [his liver], he became dizzy.'

(472) *Aaya=ko yia aaw-om-**aya** enim-i-yan.*
sugarcane=NF 1p.ACC get-BEN-BNFY2.2/3s.DS eat-Np-FU.1p

'Get us sugarcane and we'll eat it.'

The different-subject marking *-eya* is also used with some non-verbs. This seems to be uncommon in PNG languages: in Roberts' (1997:137) survey the very few examples where the switch-reference marking was on non-verbs these were pro-clausal substitutes like a demonstrative or vocative. In Mauwake the DS suffix can be added to nouns (473) or adjectives (474), or the negative adverbs *weetak* and *marew* (475) functioning as predicates in verbless clauses. When it is added to words ending in *-a*, the first vowel in the suffix gets assimilated to this vowel (473).

(473) *Enakiwa-**ya** me aaw-e-m.*
half-2/3s.DS not take-PA-1s

'There was (only) half (left), so I didn't take any/it.'

(474) *Mauwow maneka-**ya**=na yia maak-i-non.*
work big-2/3s.DS=TP 1p.ACC tell-Np-FU.3s

'If the work is big, she will tell us.'

---

[72] The vowel *-a* is somewhat more common in the Muaka dialect group where the 2/3s.DS marker is *-era* instead of *-eya*.

(475) *Soomia marew-**eya** amap-ep-om-a-m.*
spoon none-2/3s.DS BPX-come-BEN-BNFY2.PA-1s

'She has/had no spoons (lit: there are/were no spoons) so I brought them to her.'

When the different subject marking *-eya* is added to the adverb *naap* 'thus', the outcome is a consecutive connective 'therefore, so' (§3.11.2).

3.8.3.5.3 Tense and medial verbs The medial verbs have no tense marking, so the tense in a medial clause is interpreted in relation to that of the next finite clause. When the finite clause is in the past tense, both a simultaneous (476) and a sequential medial clause (477) are also understood to be in the past tense.

(476) *Iwera uruk-am-ika-iwkin wi ikiw-emi aaw-em-ik-e-mik.*
coconut drop-SS.SIM-be-2/3p.DS 3p.UNM go-SS.SIM take-SS.SIM-be-PA-1/3p

'They$_i$ kept dropping coconuts, and they$_j$ went and got them.'

(477) *Owowa **or-op**, **wailal-ep**, akia ik-e-k.*
village descend-SS.SEQ be.hungry-SS.SEQ banana roast-PA-3s

'He came down to the village, was hungry and roasted bananas.'

Since a sequential verb indicates that the action takes place before another action, a sequential medial clause preceding a present tense final clause has to be interpreted to be in the past tense, whereas a simultaneous clause is interpreted to be in the present tense like the final verb (478).

(478) *Iperuma nain=ke mua **puuk-ap** owora **en-emi** afura*
eel that1=CF man change.into-SS.SEQ betelnut eat-SS.SIM lime.container
buan-em-ika-i-ya.
knock-SS.SIM-be-Np-PR.3s

'The eel has become man, and is eating betelnut and knocking the lime container.'

Both a sequential and a simultaneous medial clause preceding a future final clause are also understood as future clauses. The action in a sequential medial clause takes place before that in the final clause, but it is still in the future (479). The action in a simultaneous clause is partly or fully overlapping with that in the final clause (480).

(479) *Is=ke maa uup-emkun wi **ekap-ep** enim-i-kuan.*
1p.FC=CF food cook-1s/p.DS 3p.UNM come-SS.SEQ eat-Np-FU.3p

'We'll cook the food and they'll come and eat it.' Or: 'When we have cooked the food they will come and eat it.'

(480) *Wi **ir-ami** nia **aaw-emi** efa ifakim-i-kuan.*
3p.UNM come-SS.SIM 2p.ACC take-SS.SIM 1s.ACC kill-Np-FU.3p

'They will come and take you and kill me.'

3 Morphology

The medial verb form cannot be used in the following example, because the first verb refers to time preceding the speech event and the second verb to time following it. Final verbs with different tenses have to be used, and in this case it is most natural to place the past tense verb in a relative clause (481).

(481) *Mukuna kerer-e-k   nain kamenap umuk-i-yan?*
        fire   appear-PA-3s that1 how   extinguish-Np-FU.1p
        'How shall we extinguish the fire that started?'

The medial verbs acquire more absolute-relative tense character of "past in the past" (Comrie 1985: 65) in those cases where sequential medial clauses are either right-dislocated and placed after the final clause (482) or placed inside another medial clause (483), or when there is a separate time expression referring to earlier time than that indicated by the final verb (484).

(482) *Rubaruba nain=ke ona   emeria nain aaw-ep   p-ikiw-o-k,*
        Rubaruba that1=CF 3s.GEN woman that1 take-ss.SEQ BPX-go-PA-3s
        iw-iwkin.
        give.him-2/3p.DS
        'That Rubaruba took his wife and took her (away), when they had given her to him.'

(483) *Um-eya   merena ere-erup [**ifara aaw-ep**] kaik-ap   nabena*
        die-2/3s.DS leg   RDP-two vine   get-ss.SEQ tie-ss.SEQ carrying.pole
        suuw-ap   akua   aaw-ep   or-o-m.
        push-ss.SEQ shoulder take-ss.SEQ descend-PA-1s
        'It died, and I tied its legs in pairs with a vine that I had gotten, and pushed it to the carrying pole and carried it down on my shoulder.'

(484) ***Iiriw** inasin mua nain=ke naap wia   **maak-eya** wi   naap on-a-mik.*
        earlier spirit man that=CF thus 3p.ACC tell-2/3p.DS 3p.UNM thus do-PA-1/3p
        'The spirit man had earlier told them like that and they did so.'

3.8.4 Verb classes

Verbs can be divided into classes on the basis of various criteria. Conjugation classes based on morphological/inflectional criteria are usually arbitrary and unrelated to other parts of the grammar (Anderson 1985a: 191). They are only touched on briefly in the next subsection. Transitivity as a basis of verb classes is discussed in §3.8.4.2, and valence-changing operations in §3.8.4.3. Verb classes based on semantic features are described in §3.8.4.4.

3.8.4.1 Conjugation classes

In the Mauwake lexicon the verbs are divided into classes 1 and 2 depending on whether they have *-a* or *-E* as the past tense suffix. There are morphophonological rules for deriving the past tense marking for most verbs (§2.3.3.3), but since some of the rules are rather complicated, and because they do not cover a number of cases like (485) and (486) below, the division into two separate classes is maintained.

(485) *miim-a-k*
hear-PA-3s
'he heard'

(486) *miim-o-k*
precede-PA-3s
'he went ahead'

In Class 1, transitive verbs outnumber intransitive verbs over four times, but Class 2 is divided almost equally between transitive and intransitive verbs.[73]

(487) *puuk-a-k* vs. *puk-o-k*
cut-PA-3s   burst-PA-3s
'he cut (it)' 'it burst'

(488) *teek-a-k* vs. *ten-e-k*
pluck-PA-3s   collapse-PA-3s
'he plucked (it)' 'it collapsed' (also: 'it broke away')

3.8.4.2 Verb classes based on transitivity

With the term TRANSITIVITY of a verb I refer to its SYNTACTIC transitivity, i.e. "the number of overt morpho-syntactically coded arguments it takes" (Van Valin & LaPolla 1997: 147).

Intransitive verbs in Mauwake only require a subject, whereas transitive verbs require a direct object as well. This definition differs slightly from that of Crystal (1997: 397), who defines as transitive verbs those that CAN take a direct object, and as intransitive those that CANNOT (emphasis mine). Crystal's definition works for Mauwake when considering prototypical patient/undergoer objects, but it fails in the cases where the syntactic object manifests other roles not required by the semantic structure of the verb.[74]

In some languages verb roots can be neutral as to transitivity (Kittilä 2002: 53), but in Mauwake each verb has a basic transitivity value. Most verbs are either intransitive (§3.8.4.2.1) or transitive (§3.8.4.2.2). There are only a few ambitransitives (§3.8.4.2.3). Mauwake does not have a regular class of ditransitive verbs that would require two objects.

---

[73] For this count, the verbs formed with the verbalizer *-ar* and the causative *-ow* were deleted from the total of 857 verbs, since both these suffixes influence the choice of the past tense vowel.

[74] The syntactic transitivity of a verb can differ from both its semantic and macrorole transitivity (Van Valin & LaPolla 1997).

3 Morphology

Instead, some verbs that are transitive easily allow a second object. And in the small class of the object cross-referencing verbs (§3.8.4.2.4), in which the pronominal object is in the verb root, two of the verbs require a second object as well.

The basic transitivity of a verb can be changed with valence-changing strategies (§3.8.4.3). Causative (§3.8.2.3.1) and benefactive morphology (§3.8.2.3.3) as well as possessor raising (§5.3.2.3) are processes that increase the number of syntactic objects in a clause.

3.8.4.2.1 Intransitive verbs In Mauwake the class of basic, or "ordinary", intransitive verbs consists of a semantically very diverse group including involuntary processes (489), many motion verbs (490), and some bodily function verbs (491).

(489) *Fikera* **aw-o-k**.
kunai.grass burn-PA-3s
'The kunai grass burned.'

(490) *Kuuten ikos* **karu-e-mik**.
Kuuten with run-PA-1/3p
'I ran with Kuuten.'

(491) *Niir-emi* **pisi-e-k**.
laugh-SS.SIM fart-PA-3s
'He laughed and farted.'

Some experience verbs expressing physiological states are also regular intransitive verbs (492):

(492) *Maa enowa nopa-yiaw-ep* **wuailal-ep** *ma-e-mik*, "..."
food eat-NMZ search-move.around-SS.SEQ get.hungry-SS.SEQ say-PA-1/3p
'They searched around for food and got hungry and said, "..." '

The verbs derived with the inchoative suffix *-ar* (§3.8.2.2.2) are mostly intransitive (493), (494), but a few of them are transitive (495).

(493) *Uuw-ap uuw-ap* **lebum-ar-e-m**.
work-SS.SEQ work-SS.SEQ lazy-INCH-PA-1s
'I worked and worked and got tired.'

(494) *Nan teeria* **manek-ar-e-k**, *owowa pun manek-ar-e-k*.
there family big-INCH-PA-3s village also big-INCH-PA-3s
'The family grew big there, and the village grew big too.'

(495) *Maa unowa oram me* **amis-ar-i-mik**, *weetak*.
thing many just not knowledge-INCH-Np-PR.1/3p no
'We don't just gain knowledge of many things (without learning them), no.'

3.8 Verbs

Climate expressions often use intransitive verbs. There is no separate class of verbs for climate expressions (496).[75]

(496) Aapereka **paran-em-ika-i-ya**.
 cloud rumble-ss.SIM-be-Np-PR.3s
 'It is thundering.'

Intransitive clauses are discussed in §5.4.

3.8.4.2.2 Transitive verbs Transitive verbs require a subject and an object. A [+human] object needs to be marked with an accusative pronoun (§3.5.3) regardless of the presence or absence of a separate object NP (497).

(497) Yaapan wia *ifakim-e-mik*.
 Japan 3p.ACC kill-PA-1/3p
 'They killed the Japanese.'

Besides the prototypical transitive verbs with an agent subject and a patient-of-change object (Givón 1984: 96) like (498) and (499), also many verbs of perception (500), cognition (501) and emotion (502) are transitive.

(498) Wiipa erup wia **sesek-a-mik**.
 girl two 3p.ACC send-PA-1/3p
 'They sent the two girls.'

(499) Yo me efa **enim-uk**.
 1s.UNM not 1.ACC eat-IMP.3p
 'Let them not eat me.'[76]

(500) Nomokowa unowa aakisa wia **uruf-i-n**.
 2s/p.brother many now 3p.ACC see-Np-PR.2s
 'Now you see many brothers of yours.

(501) Nefa **amis-ar-ep** ma-i-yem.
 2s.ACC knowledge-INCH-SS.SEQ say-Np-PR.1s
 'I am saying (this) because I know you.'

(502) Yena mua=ke efa **kookal-ep** manin(a) uuw-owa efa asip-i-ya.
 1s.GEN man 1s.ACC like-ss.SEQ garden work-NMZ 1s.ACC help-Np-PR.3s
 'My husband likes me and helps me in the garden.'

---

[75] Climate expressions also use directional verbs (*ipia oraiya* 'the rain descends'), inchoative verbs (*kokomarek* 'it got dark') and transitive verbs (*ama fookak* 'the sun split (tr.)').

[76] This was said in a traditional story by a spirit that was able to change into a man or into an eel, which the people in the story were preparing to eat.

3 Morphology

If there is no other overt object available for a transitive verb, the maximally generic noun *maa* 'thing'[77] is used as a dummy object (503), (505). Compare the next two examples: in (503) *maa* is added because of syntactic requirements, whereas in (504) the lack of an overt object indicates a third person singular object.

(503) *(Yo)* **maa** *uruf-i-yem.*
    I   thing see-Np-PR.1s
    'I see.' (=I see something, or: I can see.)

(504) *(Yo) uruf-i-yem.*
    I   see-Np-PR.1s
    'I see him/her/it.'

(505) *Iir   oko   maa enim-i-yem, iir   oko   maa me enim-i-yem.*
    time other thing eat-Np-PR.1s time other thing not eat-Np-PR.1s
    'Sometimes I eat, sometimes I don't eat.'

The language-specific characteristic of syntactic transitivity (Kittilä 2002: 49–51) is illustrated by a number of verbs that are transitive in Mauwake but intransitive in English: *aner-* 'aim (at), refer (to)' (506), *ikum-* 'wonder (about)' (507), *kerew-* 'be angry (at)'.

(506) *Wi   wia   amukar-emi me nefa   **aner-a-m**.*
    3p.UNM 3p.ACC scold-SS.SIM not 2s.ACC refer.to-PA-1s
    'When I scolded them I didn't refer to you.'

(507) *Nefa   **ikum-am-ika-iwkin**   nan   kerer-e-n.*
    2s.ACC wonder.about-SS.SIM-be-2/3p.DS there arrive-PA-2s
    'As they were wondering about you, you arrived there.'

There are a few verbs that require an undergoer object, but usually have recipient object as well. The verbs *ofakow-* 'show, teach' (508) and *maak-* 'tell' (509) are the most common of these.[78]

(508) *Tunde   urera   Liisa ame=ke   [**epa**]ₒ [**yia**]ₒ **ofakowa-yiaw-e-mik**.*
    Tuesday afternoon Liisa ASSOC=CF place   1p.ACC show-move.around-PA-1/3p
    'On Tuesday afternoon Liisa and the othes showed us around the place.'

(509) *Nena   panewowa pun [**wadol opora**]ₒ [**yia**]ₒ **maak-i-n**.*
    2s.GEN old   also lie   talk   1p.ACC tell-Np-PR.2s
    'You yourself – an old person too! – tell us lies.'

---

[77] The semantic area of *maa* is at least as wide that of its English equivalent 'thing'. Because it is used so often with verbs denoting eating and preparing food, it has acquired a secondary meaning 'food'.

[78] The verb 'send' is cross-linguistically typically ditransitive, but in Mauwake it requires the benefactive suffix in order to be able to take a second object.

3.8 Verbs

The verb *wu-* 'put' requires both an undergoer object and a locative adverbial (510):

(510)   [*Sosora   nain*]$_O$ [*pona=pa*]$_{AdvP}$ *wu-a-mik.*
    grass.skirt that1   riverbank=LOC put-PA-1/3p

    'They put those grass skirts on the riverbank.'

The directional verbs (§3.8.4.4.5) could be treated as weakly transitive, in which case the goal NP, which is never marked with the locative clitic *-pa*, could be a locative object. There are two main reasons against this analysis. When the goal of a directional verb is a personal pronoun, the dative case is used rather than the accusative (511).

(511)   ...*ona wiawi   wiar ikiw-o-k.*
    3s.GEN 3s/p.father 3.DAT go-PA-3s

    '...she went to her father.'

Also, if the directional verbs were considered weakly transitive and the the goal a locative object, the locative adverb *nan* 'there' in the following clauses would be treated as a locative adverb in (512) but as a locative object in (513):

(512)   *Kerer-ep   nan soomare-miaw-e-mik.*
    arrive-ss.SEQ there walk-move.around-PA-1/3p

    'They arrived and walked around there.'

(513)   *Or-op   nan ikiw-ep wia   uruf-a-k.*
    descend-ss.SEQ there go-ss.SEQ 3p.ACC see-PA-3s

    'He went down and went there and saw them.'

3.8.4.2.3 Ambitransitive verbs Although most verb roots in Mauwake are clearly transitive or intransitive, there are a few that are ambitransitive (514)–(519). Many of their English equivalents would be intransitive. Only the following roots have been found to be neutral with regard to transitivity (Table 3.41). Of them *ofof-* and *taan-* are of the S=O type, where the intransitive subject is an undergoer; the others are of the S=A type, where the intransitive subject is an actor (Dixon 2010b: 124).

Table 3.41: Ambitransitive verbs

ofof-	'shake'
taan-	'become full'; 'fill (a place)'
karu-	'run'; 'visit'
om(om)-	'cry'; 'mourn (for)'
pepek er-	'be enough'; 'suffice'
aakun-	'speak, talk'; 'discuss'

(514) *Ifar(a) makena wulewul **ofof-i-ya**.*
vine fruit wulewul shake-Np-PR.3s
'The vine fruit (called) *wulewul* shakes.'

(515) *Maa-ofofona saarik **wia** ofof-a-k.*
earthquake like 3p.ACC shake-PA-3s
'It shook them like an earthquake.'

(516) *Ifa uruf-ap baurar-ep **karu-or-o-mik**.*
snake see-SS.SEQ flee-SS.SEQ run-descend-PA-1/3p
'We saw a snake and fled and ran down (to the village).'

(517) *Epasia=pa ik-omkun me **efa** karu-e-mik.*
far=LOC be-1s/p.DS NEG 1s.ACC run/visit-PA-1/3p
'When I lived far away, they didn't visit me.'

(518) *En-em-ika-eya ona wiamun=ke uruf-ap om-o-k.*
eat-SS.SIM-be-2/3s.DS 3s.GEN younger.sibling=CF see-SS.SEQ cry-PA-3s
'When he was eating it his younger sibling saw it/him and cried.'

(519) ***Efa** om-em-ik-eya epa wiim-o-k.*
1s.ACC cry-SS.SIM-be-2/3s.DS place dawn-PA-3s
'While she was mourning for me it dawned.'

The subject of the adjunct plus verb *pepek er-* 'be enough, suffice' is typically inanimate (520), whereas the object, when there is one, is usually human (521).

(520) *Kemuka nain **pepek er-eya** onak ona wiar puuk-a-k.*
string that1 enough go-2/3s.DS 3s/p.mother 3s.GEN 3.DAT cut-PA-3s
'When the string was (long) enough, their mother herself cut it.'

(521) ***Wia** pepek er-a-k.*
3p.ACC enough come/go-PA-3s
'It was enough for them.'

3.8.4.2.4 Object cross-referencing verbs   One feature very common to a small group of verbs in the Trans-New Guinea languages is that the "verb stem undergoes changes according to the person of the object or beneficiary" (Wurm 1982: 62).[79] In Mauwake this group consists of only five members.

I call these verbs object cross-referencing because, besides marking the subject with a suffix like all other verbs do, they also OBLIGATORILY mark the object in the verb root.

---

[79] Wurm actually seems to be referring to *recipient* rather than beneficiary, as 'give' is the most common of these verbs, and the verb stem changes according to the recipient.

3.8 Verbs

What has clearly been a prefix[80] earlier has been grammaticalized as part of the verb itself: there is no neutral root that would not be linked to any particular person (522)–(524).[81] In this respect these verbs differ from all the other verbs in Mauwake. In the case of 'give' the verb root *i-* has assimilated into the prefix, so currently the person marking of the recipient object is the only root that there is. Four of the object cross-referencing verbs are listed in Table 3.42.

Table 3.42: Object cross-referencing verbs

'give'	'feed'	'follow'	'shoot'
yi- 'give me'	enak 'feed me'	yook- 'follow me'	enar- 'shoot me'
ni- 'give you'	nenak- 'feed you'	nook- 'follow you'	nenar- 'shoot you'
iw- 'give him'	onak- 'feed him'	ook- 'follow him'	war- 'shoot him'
yi- 'give us'	yienak- 'feed us	yiok- 'follow us	yiar- 'shoot us'
ni- 'give you'	nienak- 'feed you'	niok- 'follow you'	niar- 'shoot you'
wi- 'give them'	wienak- 'feed them'	wiok- 'follow them'	wiar- 'shoot them'

(522) Maa fain me **iw**-o-k.
thing this not give.him/her-PA-3s
'He did not give this thing to him/her.'

(523) Waaya pun **enak**-e-mik.
pig too feed.me-PA-1/3p
'They also gave me pork to eat.'

(524) Amia=iya **nenar**-e-mik=i?
bow=COM shoot.you-PA-1/3p=QM
'Did they shoot you with a gun?'

The cross-referenced objects are semantically quite different. In the verbs *iw-* 'give (him)' and *onak-* 'feed (him)' it is the recipient,[82] in *war-* 'shoot (him)' and *ook-* 'follow (him)' the undergoer. The verb *wionar-*[83] 'hide among (them)' is a special case in two ways: the cross-referenced argument 'among a group' is quite untypical as a verbal argument; and only plural forms of this verb can be used because of semantic restrictions: *yionar-* 'hide among us', *nionar-* 'hide among you (pl)', *wionar-* 'hide among them' (525).

---

[80] Phonetically this prefix is closer to the unmarked pronouns than the accusative pronouns.
[81] When a "neutral" form is required, the third person singular is used.
[82] *onak-* 'feed (him)' requires a food term as the undergoer object, so a better translation, but longer, would be 'give him (something) to eat'.
[83] A possible origin for this is PRON+*onaiya*+*ar-* 'become together-with PRON' (Kwan, p.c.)

3 Morphology

(525) Wi **wionar**-ep pok-ap ik-ua.
3p.UNM hide.among.them-SS.SEQ sit.down-SS.SEQ be-PA.3s
'He sat hiding among them.'

Maia does not have any verbs behaving like this (Hardin 2002), and Hepner only reports one for Bargam: -g 'give' (2002:87). Usan has three verbs involving a stem change of this kind: *utâb* 'give (him)', *wâb* 'shoot' and *wâramb* 'hit'(Reesink 1987: 44). *Utâb*, which coreferences the recipient, has quite strict co-occurrence restrictions with other arguments or even with peripheral elements in the same clause (ibid. 129–30).

Unlike Usan, in Mauwake the clauses with object cross-referencing verbs can easily have a locative or instrument phrase, and the verb itself can take a benefactive suffix. A sentence like (526) would be possible for instance when sending money to people travelling in the same vehicle as the addressee.

(526) *Miiw-aasa=pa* **wi-om-e**.
land-canoe=LOC give.them-BEN-BNFY1.IMP.2s
'Give it to them for me in the car.'

3.8.4.3 Valence changes

The term VALENCE refers to the number of arguments that have a grammatical relation with the verb. As was mentioned above, almost all of the verb roots in Mauwake have a basic valence of one or two: they take either a subject only (intransitive verbs §3.8.4.2.1) or a subject and an object (transitive verbs §3.8.4.2.2) as their arguments. There are some ways to change the valence of verbs, even if strategies like passivization and dative shift are not possible in Mauwake. The valence is increased, when an intransitive verb is made into transitive or a transitive verb into causative with the addition of an causative suffix, or when a benefactive suffix is added to a verb. There are no processes to decrease the syntactic valence of a verb. The SEMANTIC valence is decreased when the object of a transitive verb is a reflexive or reciprocal pronoun, since the subject and object have the same referent(s). Subject demotion is another way to decrease the semantic valence.

3.8.4.3.1 Causatives The causative always increases the number of arguments a verb can take: the subject of an intransitive verb (527) becomes the object of a transitive verb (528), and a new subject is added. The causative suffix *-ow* was described above in §3.8.2.3.1. In most cases the meaning of a causative is 'to cause someone or something to do something'. The caused 'doing' is usually NOT agentive (529).

(527) *Iwera nainiw kaken iimar-e-k.* (Intransitive)
coconut again straight stand-PA-3s
'The coconut palm stood straight again.'

(528) *[Eka napia]ₒ koor miira=pa iimar-ow-a-mik.*
water bamboo house face=LOC stand-CAUS-PA-1/3p
'We made the bamboo water containers stand in front of the house.'

(529) [Wiowa erup]$_O$ ar-**ow**-amkun um-o-k.
 spear two become-CAUS-1s/p.DS die-PA-3s

 'I speared it a second time and it (=the pig) died.' (Lit: 'I caused a spear to become two and it died.')

The mental state of being angry is expressed via a verb in Mauwake (530), and it can take the causative suffix (531).

(530) *Kema bagiwir-a-m.*
 liver be.angry-PA-1s

 'I was angry.'

(531) *Yo kema [efa]$_O$ bagiwir-ow-a-n, yaa!*
 1s.UNM liver 1s.ACC be.angry-CAUS-PA-2s INTJ

 'Boy, have you made me angry!'

In some cases the causative suffix acts simply as a transitivizer. The subject in (532) does not actually cause the children to grow. Also in this case the suffix increases the valency of the verb: *arim-* 'grow' in (533) is intransitive, but *arimow-* in (532) is transitive and takes an object.

(532) *Aakisa arim-o-n, aakisa muew-o-n.*
 now grow-PA-2s now marry-PA-2s

 'Now you have grown, now you have married.'

(533) *No nena maa fariar-ep [muuka nain]$_O$ arim-ow-e.*
 2s.UNM 2s.GEN food abstain-SS.SEQ son that1 grow-CAUS-IMP.2s

 'You yourself have to abstain from (certain) food(s) and bring the son up.'

When the causative suffix is added to the intransitive verb *sail-* '(tell a) lie', its meaning changes into 'lie to someone', 'cheat' (534).

(534) *Opor(a) makena ma-i-yem, me [nia]$_O$ sail-ow-iyem.*
 talk true say-Np-PR.1s not 2p.ACC lie-CAUS-PR.1s

 'I am telling the truth, I am not cheating you.'

Bring-prefixes (§3.8.2.4.2) are another causative strategy, used only with the directional verbs (535), (536) (§3.8.4.4.5) and a couple of other motion verbs (537). The subject of the verb causes the object to move by undertaking the transfer himself/herself.

(535) *Maa unowa ifer aasa=ke **p**-urup-o-k.*
 thing many sea canoe=CF BPX-ascend-PA-3s

 'A lot of things were brought/taken up by ships.'

3 Morphology

(536) O   mua imen-ap=na   feeke wia   **p**-ekap-eka.
       3s.UNM man find-ss.SEQ=TP here.CF 3p.ACC BPX-come-IMP.2p
       'If/when you find a/any man, bring them/him here.'

(537) Gomi   kawus **p**-irapar-i-ya.
       east.wind smoke BPX-move.to.and.fro-Np-PR.3s
       'The east wind moves the smoke around.'

Forming a causative from an agentive verb (INDUCIVE CAUSATIVE, Talmy 2007: 112) is not done morphologically with an affix but SYNTACTICALLY with a verbal construction involving the nominalized form of the main verb and *suuw-* 'push' as the causative auxiliary (538), (539) (§5.7.1).

(538) O   uruf-ap   op-ap   Yeesus nomokowa moke
       3s.UNM see-ss.SEQ hold-ss.SEQ Jesus tree   slanting
       akua-aaw-om-owa   suuw-a-mik.
       shoulder-take-BEN-NMZ push-PA-1/3p
       'They saw him and took hold of him, and made him carry Jesus' cross on his shoulder.'

(539) Sira   enuma **ook-owa** nia   **suuw-i-mik**.
       custom new   follow-NMZ 2p.ACC push-Np-PR.1/3p
       'They make you follow new customs/ways.'

In the following examples the three different causative strategies have been applied to the same verb *ikiw-* 'go', and in all of them the patient is [+human]. In (540) and (541) the object of the causative verb has no influence on what happens to him/her, but in (542) the object of the inducive causative is active and becomes the actor of the verb resulting from the causation.

(540) Ipamsika mua=ke **ikiw-ow-a-k**.
       nail   man=CF go-CAUS-PA-3s
       'A sorcerer (lit: nail man) killed him (lit: caused him to go).'

(541) Kes   tepak=pa   wu-ap   **p-ikiw-e-mik**.
       coffin inside=LOC put-ss.SEQ BPX-go-PA-1/3p
       'They put him inside the coffin and took him (away).'

(542) Yo   mua oko   **ikiw-owa suuw-amkun** ikiw-i-non.
       1s.UNM man other go-NMZ   push-1s/p.DS go-Np-FU.3s
       'I make a man go and he goes.'

3.8.4.3.2 Benefactive

The benefactive form of a verb (§3.8.2.3.3) is used when an action is done FOR someone, for their benefit (543), or in some cases for their detriment (544). With the addition of the benefactive suffix to the verb, the beneficiary becomes an obligatory argument. The beneficiary is always animate, and usually human.

(543) Wi   owow mua=ke wilkar wia   muf-em-ik-**om**-a-mik.
      3p.UNM village man=CF cart   3p.ACC pull-SS.SIM-be-BEN-BNFY2.PA-1/3p
      'The village men kept pulling carts for them.'

(544) Epia   wilin-owa uruf-ap   bom yia   fuurk-**om**-i-kuan.
      fire(wood) shine-NMZ see-SS.SEQ bomb 1p.ACC throw-BEN-Np-FU.3p
      'When they see the light from the fire(s), they will throw bombs at us.'

More than one valency-increasing strategy can be applied to a verb simultaneously. In both (545) and (546) the valency of the verb increases from one to three: besides the subject of the original verb, the derived verbs also have both an object and a beneficiary.

(545) Koor poka iimar-**ow-om**-e.
      house post stand.up-CAUS-BEN-BNFY1.IMP.2s
      'Stand up the house posts for me.'

(546) Ona   soomia marew-eya   **amap**-ep-**om**-a-m.
      3s.GEN spoon no(ne)-2/3s.DS BPX-come-BEN-BNFY2.PA-1s
      'She has/had no spoons of her own, so I brought them for her.'

3.8.4.3.3 Decreasing semantic valence

There are no morphological means in Mauwake for decreasing syntactic valence. A verb that is inherently reflexive, like *yaki-* 'wash oneself', is intransitive. But the semantic valence of transitive verbs is decreased when they are made either reflexive (547) or reciprocal (548). Syntactically the reflexive/reciprocal pronoun is an object, but the pronoun refers to the same referent(s) as the subject.

(547) Birin-ep   nomokowa iinan akena ikiw-ep   wame   pipilim-ep
      fly-SS.SEQ tree   top   very go-SS.SEQ 3s.REFL hide-SS.SEQ
      aakun-em-ika-i-non.
      speak-SS.SIM-be-Np-FU.3s
      'It will fly and hide (itself) in the very top of a tree and keep making noise.'

(548) Osaiwa   aalbok   ikos   uf-owa   na-ep   ofa
      bird.of.paradise black.cuckoo-shrike together dance-NMZ say-SS.SEQ colour
      wiam   if-e-mik.
      3p.REFL paint-PA-1/3p
      'A bird of paradise and a black cuckoo-shrike wanted to dance together and painted each other with colour.'

3 Morphology

A common valence-decreasing device in many languages is the passive voice, which demotes or deletes the subject. In Mauwake verbs there is no passive voice. The standard way of demoting the subject is to have the verb in third person plural form and leave the subject NP unexpressed (549), (550) .[84] None of the arguments change their syntactic function. The example (549) comes from a story where the main point was that the people responsible for the fire were never found, and it was not known if only one person was involved or many.

(549) *Fikera   ikum   **kuum-e-mik** nain ma-i-yem.*
      kunai.grass illicitly burn-PA-1/3p that1 say-Np-PR.1s

      'I tell about when the kunai grass was burned (by arson).'

(550) *Nefa   **war-iwkin**   naap ma-e.*
      2s.ACC shoot-2/3p.DS thus say-IMP.2s

      'If/when you are shot, then say like that.' (Or: 'If they shoot you, then say like that.')

Another strategy to demote the subject is to use the same-subject sequential form of the main verb and the auxiliary *ik-* 'be' agreeing with the object of the verb (551) . This can only be used when the end result is a state.

(551) *Nomokowa puuk-ap   ik-ua.*
      tree   cut-SS.SEQ be-PA.3s

      'The tree is cut.'

3.8.4.4 Semantically based verb classes

Even though the following classification is based on semantic characteristics of the verbs, the verbs within the resulting groups tend to have similarities in their syntactic behaviour as well.

3.8.4.4.1 Stative/existential verb *ik-*   The basic meaning of the stative verb *ik(a)-* is 'be'. The vowel /a/ gets deleted elsewhere except in the present tense and the medial different-subject non-first plural form; in the corresponding singular form the vowel may be optionally deleted (552).

(552) *Nan mukuna=pa **ik(a)-eya** o   nan samor aaw-o-k.*
      there fire=LOC be-2/3s.DS 3s.UNM there badly get-PA-3s

      'They (=bananas) were there on the fire and he really got bad there.'

Like intransitive verbs, it may form a complete clause by itself. Example (553) is from a situation where the speaker was in a plane for the first time, refused to eat and declined any help offered to him.

---

[84] Cf. the English impersonal "they": *They say it is going to be cold tomorrow.*

(553) **Ika-i-nen.**
       be-Np-FU.1s
       'I will just be (like this).'

Often it is used for 'be/live (somewhere)', and in this use it naturally co-occurs with a locative adverbial (554):

(554) I   naap koora=pa   **ik-e-mik.**
       1p.UNM thus house=LOC be-PA-1/3p
       'We were in the house like that.'

Together with the dative pronouns *ik-* is used to form possessive constructions (555) (§§3.5.5, 5.5.2).

(555) Yo   waaya arow **efar**   **ik-ua.**
       1s.UNM pig   three 1s.DAT be-PA.3s
       'I have three pigs.'

The function of *ik-* as a copular verb is very restricted. In equative or descriptive clauses it is normally not used in the present tense finite form, but in the past (556) and future (557) tenses it is employed. It could be said, following Givón (1984: 92), that in these clauses its primary function is to be the carrier of the tense.

(556) Yo   um-ep   ik-owa saarik **ik-e-m.**
       1s.UNM die-SS.SEQ be-NMZ like   be-PA-1s
       'I was like dead.'

(557) Ikoka maa   marew, eliw manek=iw **ika-i-nan.**
       later thing none   well big=LIM   be-Np-FU.2s
       'Later there will be no problem, you will just be very well.'

In Mauwake it can also be used when the non-verbal predicate is understood to be transitory (558) rather than stable over time:

(558) No   kamenap **ika-i-n?**
       2s.UNM how   be-Np-PR.2s
       'How are you?'

The verb *ik-* 'be' is in a class of its own for several reasons. Its morphology is irregular, and so are the semantics of some of its morphology. In (555) the past tense and the person/number marker in the third person singular form are merged into one portmanteau morpheme. An alternative form for the different-subject first person form *ikemkun* is *ikomkun* (559). The same-subject medial form is *ikok* (560), not **ikep* and **ikemi*.[85] There is no formal differentiation between a simultaneous (560) and a sequential (561) form in the same-subject medial verb.

---

[85] *ikep* and *ikemi* are the same subject medial forms of the homophonous verb *ik-* 'roast'.

3 Morphology

(559) *Siowa nain kakalt-am-**ik**-emkun   arim-o-k.*
dog   that1 look.after-ss.SIM-be-1s/p.DS grow-PA-3s
'I was looking after the dog and it grew.'

(560) *Naap **ik-ok** uruf-am-ika-iwkin   wia.*
thus be-SS see-ss.SIM-be-2/3p.DS no
'As he was/stayed like that they were watching him (but) no (=he didn't get better).'

(561) *Owowa ekap-o-k,   amia mua=pa **ik-ok**.*
village come-PA-3s bow man=LOC be-SS
'He came to the village, having been in the police (force).'

It also differs from ordinary intransitive verbs in that in a verb+auxiliary construction it cannot be the main verb, but can be used as the aspectual auxiliary (559) (see also §3.8.4.5). But it is like other intransitive verbs in that it can take an causative suffix (562).[86]

(562) *Nomokowa war-ep   miiwa=pa **ik-ow-a-mik**.*
tree   cut-ss.SEQ ground=LOC be-CAUS-PA-1/3p
'We cut trees and laid them on the ground'

The tense distinction is partly neutralized: the past tense form is used for past (563) and present (564). The present tense form is not very common and is mainly used for less time-stable situations (558), (565), or to replace the missing continuous aspect form (566). The verb *ik-* is used as the regular continuous aspect auxiliary (§3.8.5.1.1.2), and as a main verb *ik-* 'be' cannot take this auxiliary.

(563) *Yo   unan   koka=pa   **ik-e-m**.*
1s.UNM yesterday jungle=LOC be-PA-1s
'Yesterday I was in the jungle.'

(564) *Ni   kaaneke **ik-e-man** oo, ni   ekap-omak-eka   oo!*
2p.UNM where   be-PA-2p oh 2p.UNM come-DISTR-IMP.2p oh
'Wherever you are, come!'

(565) *Mesa   asia fiker   gone=pa **ika-i-ya**   nain*
winged.bean wild kunai.grass middle=LOC be-Np-PR.3s that1
aaw-em-ik-e-m.
take-ss.SIM-be-PA-1s
'I was picking wild winged bean that was (lit: is) in the middle of the kunai grass.'

---

[86] Reesink (1987: 142) notes that in Usan the corresponding verb *igo* 'be' cannot occur with the causative suffix. In Mauwake there is no similar restriction.

(566) *Yo   nan **ika-i-yem** nain yo   nia   asip-i-yem,*   ...
      1s.UNM there be-Np-PR.1s that1 1s.UNM 2p.ACC help-Np-PR.1s

      'Now that I am living there I help you, ...'

The verb *ik-* mainly functions in intransitive clauses, but it is also needed as a copula for those cases where a non-verbal predicate is in a non-present tense (567).

(567) *O   ikoka somek mua maneka **ika-i-non**.*
      3p.UNM later song man big   be-Np-FU.3s

      'He will later be the headmaster.'

An equative or descriptive medial clause requires *ik-* as a copula regardless of the tense of the final verb (568).

(568) *Koora naap **ik-eya**   uruf-i-mik.*
      house thus be-2/3s.DS see-Np-PR.1p

      'We see the house as it is like that.'

3.8.4.4.2 Position-taking verbs The three position-taking verbs are among the most frequently used verbs in Mauwake: *pok-* 'sit down', *iimar-* 'stand up' and *in-* 'lie down/fall asleep'. They are essentially punctiliar verbs with an inceptive meaning (569), but they are most typically used in the same-subject sequential form together with the auxiliary *ik-* (§3.8.4.5) to convey stative meaning: 'sit' (570), 'stand', and 'lie/sleep'.

(569) *Kokom-ar-eya   **in-e-mik**.*
      darkness-INCH-2/3s.DS lie.down-PA-1/3p

      'When it got dark we went to bed.'

(570) *Ona   koora=pa arew-ap   **pok-ap**   ik-e-mik.*
      3s.GEN house=LOC wait-SS.SEQ sit.down-SS.SEQ be-PA-1/3p

      'We sat and waited (lit: waited and sat) in his house.'

The verb *pok-* is occasionally used even without the auxiliary to mean 'sit' (571).

(571) *Neek(e) **pok-aka**.*
      there   sit-IMP.2p

      'Sit there/Keep sitting there.' (Commonly used as a conversational "filler" for people that are already sitting, when there is a lull in the conversation.)

The continuous aspect form of the position-taking verbs is not used with progressive meaning, only with the meaning 'habitual' (572) (§3.8.5.1.1).

(572) *Irak-ow   epa=pa   koka=pa   **in-em-ik-e-mik**.*
      fight-NMZ time=LOC jungle=LOC lie.down-SS.SIM-be-PA-1/3p

      'During the war we used to sleep in the jungle.'

3 Morphology

3.8.4.4.3 Location verbs The two verbs that have been verbalized from the demonstrative adverbs *fan* 'here' and *nan* 'there' (§3.8.2.2.1), are very restricted in their use. The original meaning of the verbs must refer to arrival at some place, but since they are only used in the past tense, they currently tend to indicate presence at a place rather than movement (573)–(575).[87] They can even be used with immobile objects (576).

(573) *No   ikiw-e,   irak-owa   maneka **fan-e-k**   a.*
       2s.UNM go-IMP.2s fight-NMZ big   here-PA-3s INTJ
       'Go (home), the big war is here.'

(574) *Aakisa i   **fan-e-mik**.*
       Now   1p.UNM here-PA-1/3p
       'Now we are / have come here.'

(575) *No   niawi   akena **nan-e-k**.*
       2s.UNM 2s/p.father true   there-PA-3s
       'Your real father is there.'

(576) *Aa, o   koora **fan-e-k**   a.*
       INTJ 3s.UNM house here-PA-3s INTJ
       'Ah, his house is here.'

3.8.4.4.4 Resultative verbs The resultative verbs with the meaning 'become' are another small group of intransitive verbs. Besides the semantic similarity they also share the syntactic characteristic that, in addition to the subject, they require another argument expressing the result of change. This other obligatory argument is a noun with the verbs *ar-* 'become' (577), (578) and *puuk-* 'change into' (579),[88] and a colour adjective with the verb *kir-* 'turn' (580).

(577) *Takira arim-ep   mua **ar-e-k**.*
       boy   grow-SS.SEQ man become-PA-3s
       'The boy grew and became a man.'

(578) *Emeria nain afa   **ar-e-mik**.*
       woman that1 flyng.fox become-PA-1/3p
       'Those women became flying foxes.'

(579) *Inasin mua ifa   **puuk-ap**   solon-ep   ...*
       spirit man snake change.into-SS.SEQ glide-SS.SEQ
       'The spirit man changed into a snake, glided and ...'

---

[87] This may indicate that the past tense used to encode perfectivity (Malcolm Ross, p.c.)
[88] This verb is homonymous with the transitive verb *puuk-* 'cut'. They may be historically related, but synchronically the meanings are quite different.

(580) Oona kia **kir-em-ik-eya**   uruf-ap ma-e-k   ...
       bone white turn-SS.SIM-be-2/3s.DS see-SS.SEQ say-PA-3s
       'She saw that the bones were turning white and said, ...'

The verb *ar-* is mostly used when the subject stays essentially the same but undergoes some change (577). However, it can also be used when the subject changes into something else (578). The verb *puuk-* is only used in the latter context (579), and it is always an intentional action. It is most common in traditional stories where spirits change into various inanimate things or animate beings. The verb *kir-* is used with most colour terms (580), but for 'black' there is a separate verb formed with the inchoative suffix *-ar* : *sepenar-*[89] 'become black'. The inchoative suffix (§3.8.2.2.2) is the standard device used for verbalizing adjectives.

3.8.4.4.5 Directional verbs The verbs indicating coming and going are among the most frequent verbs in Mauwake. These verbs have the direction inherent in the verb root. Verbs of this kind are quite common among Papuan languages: in some languages the directional is an affix, in others it is part of the meaning of the root itself (Foley 1986: 149); Mauwake is of the latter type. The directional verb group contains verbs that in many languages would be prototypically intransitive (581), (582). The directional verbs are listed in Table 3.43.

Most of these verbs can be translated into English as either 'go' or 'come', depending on the context. Since the elevation of the goal, the direction of the compass and the distance all influence the choice of the verb, and may conflict with each other, the speaker has some freedom of choice. Also, with regard to proximity, it is a very relative notion how close or far away something is.

Table 3.43: Directional verbs

ikiw-	'go', 'leave' (away from the deictic centre; generic)
iw-	'go' (away from the deictic centre)[a]
ekap-	'come' (towards the deictic centre; generic)
urup-	'go/come up', 'ascend' (uphill/away from sea)
or(a)-	'go/come down', 'descend' (downhill/towards sea)
ek-	'go (close/east)'
ep-	'come (close/west)'
er-	'go (not close/west/downriver)'
ir-	'come/go (not close/east/upriver)', 'climb'

[a] In the Moro area *iw-* also has the meaning 'enter': *Marasin kema wiar iwak* 'The poison entered his liver.'

---

[89] This is related to the adjective *sepa* 'black'.

(581) *Manina **urup-ep**   nan uuw-ap   owowa **or-o-k**.*
garden ascend-ss.SEQ there work-ss.SEQ village descend-PA-3s

'She went up to the garden, worked there and came down to the village.'

(582) *Fofa   **er-ap**   ir-i-mik.*
market go-ss.SEQ come-Np-PR.1/3p

'We are coming back from the market.' (Lit: 'We went west to the market and are coming east.')

The deictic orientation of *ikiw-* 'away from speaker/deictic centre' and *ekap-* 'towards the speaker/deictic centre' is stricter in Mauwake than in many European languages where the deictic centre especially for 'come' can vary considerably. The sentence (583) is all right in Finnish regardless of the location of the speaker, but the corresponding sentence in Mauwake would be acceptable only if the speaker were in Tampere at the time of speaking.

(583) *Isoisäni tuli Tampereelle vuonna 1912.* (Finnish)

'My grandfather CAME to Tampere in 1912.'

The equivalent of the English 'come' in (584) has to be 'go' in Mauwake (585). This is discussed further in (§6.3).

(584) *I'll COME to your place tomorrow.*

(585) *Uurika   nefa   uruf-owa **ikiw-i-nen**.*
tomorrow 2s.ACC see-NMZ go-Np-FU.1s

'Tomorrow I'll go to see you.'

When these verbs occur with a locative phrase containing the locative marker (§3.12.4), the phrase almost always refers to either source (586), or location/path (587). The goal is very seldom marked with the locative marker *-pa*; this happens when the goal is important mainly as the location of the next event (588). Also, in (588) *mukuna* 'fire' is an untypical goal for a directional verb.

(586) ***Manina=pa ekap-ep**   maa uup-e-mik.*
garden=LOC come-ss.SEQ food cook-PA-1/3p

'We came from the garden and cooked food.'

(587) *Iinan aasa   **iinan=pa** fan **ekap-emi** ...*
sky   canoe sky=LOC   here come-ss.SIM

'The airplane came here in the sky and...'

(588) *Ne soran-emi* **epia** **mukuna=pa or-omi** *aw-o-k.*
ADD get.startled-ss.SIM firewood fire=LOC descend-ss.SIM burn-PA-3s

'And he got startled and fell on the fire and burned himself.'

The directional verbs differ from other verbs in Mauwake in that they can be transitivized with the bring-prefixes *p-* (589), *amap-* and *aap-* (§3.8.2.4.2) to indicate either bringing or taking something somewhere.

(589) *Ona owowa **p-ikiw-ep** soop-i-yan.*
3s.GEN village BPX-go-ss.SEQ bury-Np-FU.1p

'We'll take him (=his body) in his village and bury him (there).'

The causative suffix *-ow* (§3.8.4.3.1) can be added to the roots; when following a one-syllable root the suffix is often reduplicated (590), but the meaning is still the same as with a single causative suffix.

(590) *Purowa ir-**ow**-(**ow**)-eya siin-ar-e-k.*
armband go.up-CAUS-CAUS-2/3s.DS tight-INCH-PA-3s

'She pushed the armband up and it got tight.'

The directional verbs are very frequent as the second root in serial verbs (591) (§3.8.5.1.2) and as the main verb in verb plus auxiliary constructions (592) (§3.8.5.1.1). Some of them also enter into adjunct plus verb constructions (593) (§3.8.5.2).

(591) *Wi Amerika "epa eliwa" nae-**ekap**-e-mik.*
3p.UNM America time good say-come-PA-1/3p

'The Americans came saying, "peace".'

(592) *Wi Yaapan saa=iw **ir**-am-ika-i-mik.*
3p.UNM Japan sand=INST go-ss.SIM-be-Np-PR.1/3p

'The Japanese are going along the beach.'

(593) *Kemuka **pepek er**-eya puuk-a-k.*
string enough go-2/3s.DS cut-PA-3s

'When the string was (long) enough she cut it.'

The meaning of the verbs *ekap-* 'come' and *ikiw-* 'go' can be metaphorically extended to time, to signal time spans. The former is used when the time span is extended from the past to the present (594), the latter is more common when the time extends from the present to the future (595), but it can also refer to the past (596).

(594) *Naap on-am-ik-e-mik,* **ekap-ep** *aakisa.*
thus do-ss.SIM-be-PA-1/3p come-ss.SEQ now

'We have been doing like that (all the time) up until now.'

3 Morphology

(595) *No   naap ik-ok **iki(w-e)p** mokoma enuma iiwawun   aakun-i-nan.*
       2s.UNM thus be-SS go-SS.SEQ year   new   altogether talk-Np-FU.2s
       'You will be like that (long time) but next year you will talk.'

(596) *Buren   **ife-iki(w-e)p** aakisa arim-o-n.*
       ceremonial.liquid rub-go-SS.SEQ now   grow-PA-2s
       'You have kept rubbing the BUREN liquid on (for years), and now you have grown up.'

On the fringe of directional verbs are *kerer-* 'arrive', *yiaw-/miaw-* 'walk/move around, wander' and *irapar-* 'move back and forth (aimlessly)', which share some of their grammatical characteristics but not all of them. Of these three verbs, *kerer-* cannot be prefixed with the bring-prefixes, but it mainly occurs with an unmarked goal instead of a locative phrase (597).

(597) *Emeria mua manina **kerer-e-mik**.*
       woman man garden arrive-PA-1/3p
       'The people arrived in the garden.'

With the other two, a bring-prefix is acceptable (598), but they do not take a goal/path argument. If a locative phrase occurs with them it requires a locative clitic (599).

(598) *Gomi   kawus **p-irapar-i-ya**.*
       east.wind smoke BPX-move.back.and.forth-Np-PR.3s
       'The east wind moves/blows the smoke around.'

(599) *Soora=pa   nan   **yiaw-e-mik**.*
       jungle=LOC there walk.around-PA-1/3p
       'They walked around in the jungle.'

3.8.4.4.6 Utterance verbs   Utterance verbs may be either intransitive (600), ambitransitive (601), (602), or transitive (603). They may be used to introduce a quote complement, but not to close it. They often occur with one of the 'saying' verbs described below (601).

(600) *Takira niir-emi   **kirir-i-mik**.*
       boy   play-SS.SIM shout-Np-PR.1/3p
       'The boys are playing and shouting.'

(601) *Wi   iperowa=ke **aakun-ep**   ma-e-mik, "..."*
       3p.UNM middle.aged=CF discuss-SS.SEQ say-PA-1/3p
       'The middle-aged men discussed (it) / talked and said, "..." '

(602) *Maapora kamenap **aakun-i-yan**?*
       feast   how   discuss-Np-FU.1p
       'How shall we discuss the feast?'

3.8 Verbs

(603) *Yena mua **far-e-m**, "Sarak oo, ..."*
1s.GEN man call-PA-1s Sarak oh

'I called to my husband, "Oh Sarak,..." '

The 'SAYING VERBS' described in this section below include three, or four, verbs that between them divide the semantic area of 'tell/say/speak/think' (Table 3.44). They are frequently used as frame verbs in quote formulas, but they have other functions as well.

Table 3.44: 'Saying verbs'

maak-/naak-	'tell'
ma-	'say/speak'
na-	'say/speak/think'

The verb *maak-* 'tell' is used in the same two main senses as its English equivalent: telling someone ABOUT something (604) and telling someone TO DO something (605). In direct quote formulas it is used mainly preceding a quote (606), not directly following it as a short closing formula. It is not used in indirect quotes at all.

(604) *Ne **maak-e-mik**, "Ifa yia keraw-i-ya nain, ..."*
and tell-PA-1/3p snake 1p.ACC bite-Np-PR.3s that1

'And they told him, "When a snake bites us, ..." '

(605) *Moma yia **maak-i-mik**.*
taro 1p.ACC tell-Np-PR.1/3p

'They are telling us (to get them) taro roots.'

(606) *Efa **maak-ek**, "Opora tep=pa wu-e."*
1s.ACC tell-PA-3s talk tape.recorder=LOC put-IMP.2s

'She told me, "Put the talk on a tape recorder." '

When *maak-* closes a direct quote, it requires the manner adverb *naap* 'thus' to precede it (607):

(607) *"Aaw-ep p-ekap-eka," **naap** yia **maak-em-ik-e-mik**.*
get-SS.SEQ BPX-come-IMP.2p thus 1p.ACC tell-SS.SIM-be-PA-1/3p

' "Bring it", they were telling us like that.'

The default object for *maak-* is the addressee (606) and a possible second object is the speech itself (608).

(608) *[Wadol opora]_O [yia]_O **maak-i-n**.*
lie talk 1p.ACC tell-Np-PR.2s

'You are telling us lies.'

177

3 Morphology

The status of the verb *naak-* is unclear. It is infrequent, and in natural texts only occurs in closing formulas (609). It may have developed as an analogy to the verb pair *ma-/na-*.

(609) *"No   bom fain=iw   mera kuum-e,"   **naak-e-mik**.*
2s.UNM bomb this=INST fish burn-IMP.2s tell-PA-1/3p
' "Blast fish with this bomb," they told him.'

With the verb *ma-* 'say/speak/tell' the addressee is not in focus, and is hardly ever even mentioned. Instead, the verb requires either an object referring to the speech content (610) or an adverb *naap* 'thus' (611) preceding the verb, or a quote complement following it (612).

(610) *Yo   yena   yaaya   ifa   ku-o-k   nain opora **ma-i-yem**.*
1s.UNM 1s.GEN 1s/p.uncle snake bite-PA-3s that1 talk say-Np-PR.1s
'I am telling a story about my uncle that was bitten by a snake.'

(611) *Momora, no   naap me **ma-e**.*
Fool   2s.UNM thus not say-IMP.2s
'Fool, don't say like that.'

(612) *En-e-mik   na⁹⁰ **ma-e-mik**, "Eliwa, aara oposia saarik."*
eat-PA-1/3p ADD say-PA-1/3p good hen meat   like
'They ate it and said, "It is good, like chicken meat." '

Occasionally the verb can occur without any of the above objects (613):

(613) *Yena   oram **ma-i-yem**.*
1s.GEN just say-Np-PR.1s
'I'm just speaking (without any reason).'

The difference between the verbs *maak-* and *ma-* in regard to the semantic role of a person object is shown clearly in (614):

(614) *Naap **yia   ma-i-kuan**   na-ep   yo   ariman **nefa   maak-i-yem**.*
thus 1p.ACC say-Np-FU.3p think-ss.SEQ 1s.UNM openly 2s.ACC tell-Np-PR.1s
'Thinking that they will SAY like that ABOUT US I'm openly TELLING YOU (this).'

The verb *na-* 'say/speak/call/think' is the most interesting of the speech verbs. In quote formulas it is only used for closing the quote, with (615) or without another utterance verb (616) in an opening formula.

(615) *...**ma-em-ik-e-mik**,   "Oo, ..." **na-em-ik-e-mik**.*
...say-SS.SIM-be-PA-1/3p oh ... say-SS.SIM-be-PA-1/3p
'...they kept saying, "Oh...", they kept saying (like that).'

---

⁹⁰ Tok Pisin *na* 'and' is increasingly used instead of the vernacular additive connective *ne*.

(616) *Amerika fan* "*Epa eliwa*" **nae-ekap-e-mik**.
America here time good say-come-PA-1/3p

'The Americans came saying "peace".'

In a tail-head type construction (§8.2.3.5) it is often used as a generic verb to replace another utterance verb, when normally the first verb would be repeated (617).[91]

(617) *Wia* **maak-e-mik**, "*Yia uf-om-aka.*" *Na-iwkin*...
3p.ACC tell-PA-1/3p 1p.ACC dance-BEN-BNFY2.IMP.2p say-2/3p.DS

'They told them, "Dance for us." When they said (that)...'

When *na-* replaces another utterance verb in that way, the replaced verb may influence what semantic argument becomes the object. In (618) *maak-* requires the addressee of the verb as the default object, and in the following sentence with *na-* the same accusative pronoun *wia* still refers to the addressees, even if with *na-* it would normally refer to the people spoken about.

(618) *Ekap-emi wia* **maak-e-mik**, "*Maa iiw-eka.*" *Wia na-iwkin*
come-SS.SIM 3p.ACC tell-PA-1/3p food dish.out-IMP.2p 3p.ACC say-2/3p.DS
ma-e-mik, ...
say-PA-1/3p

'They_i came and told them_j, "Dish out food." They_i said to them_j like that and they_j said, ...'

The verb *na-* is also used in a somewhat different sense 'call (by some name)'. In (619) the speaker tells that the word used by the Japanese soldiers for 'coconut' was *yasi*, a foreign word for her.[92]

(619) *Iwera* "*yasi*" *yia* **na-em-ik-e-mik**.
coconut yasi 1p.ACC say-SS.SIM-be-PA-1/3p

'They kept calling coconut (by the name) "yasi" to us.'

The "speaking" expressed by *na-* can also be internal speech, i.e., thinking (620). This characteristic is quite common to speech verbs in Papuan languages. When the thinking PROCESS itself is more in focus, an adjunct plus verb construction *kema suuw-* 'think' (literally: 'push the liver') is used.

(620) *Maa eliwa=ke* **na-ep** *aaw-e-m*.
thing good=CF say-SS.SEQ get-PA-1s

'I thought it was a good thing and got it.'

---

[91] Other types of verbs, when not repeated in a tail-head construction, are replaced with the generic verb *on-* 'do'.

[92] The verb *unuf-* is used when the calling by name or giving a name is emphasized.

3 Morphology

Related to the inner speech is another usage typical of verbs for 'saying' in Papuan languages: to convey desire, intention or plan (621)–(623). For this function only the same subject sequential form *naep* is used, and the verb that indicates the desired or intended action is in a preceding speech complement clause. This is discussed more fully in the section on complements of utterance verbs (§8.3.2.1).

(621) [*Yo   manina urup-i-nen*]   ***na-ep***.
1s.UNM garden ascend-Np-FU.1s say-SS.SEQ
'I want to go to the garden.'

(622) [*Irak-u*]   ***na-ep***   *ikiw-e-mik*.
fight-IMP.1d say-SS.SEQ go-PA-1/3p
'They went to fight.' (Lit: ' "Let's fight" they said/thought and went.')

(623) [*Ununa   owowa p-or-owa*]   ***na-ep***   *maa eno-wa maneka*
slit.gong village BPX-descend-NMZ say-SS.SEQ food eat-NMZ big
on-i-kuan.
make-Np-FU.3p
'When they want to take the slit gong down to the village they make a big feast.'

In this function *naep* is becoming less like a regular medial verb. It can occur in sentence-final position, without being right-dislocated (621). It usually does retain its word stress, but there is a tendency to un-stress and shorten it by dropping the vowel /a/ in speech (624). When the verb in the speech complement clause is in the counterfactual form, all that is sometimes left of *na-ep* is only the suffix, which is then added as a suffix to the other verb (625).

(624) *Ifana wu-am-ika-i-kuan,*   [*unuma wia   miim-u*]   ***n-ep***.
ear   put-ss.SIM-be-Np-FU.3p name   3p.ACC hear-1d.IMP say-SS.SEQ
'They$_i$ are listening carefully (lit: putting their ear), wanting to hear their$_j$ names.'

(625) *Yo   aakisa nanar nain **ma-ek-a-m-Ø-ep***.
1s.UNM now   story that1 say-CNTF-PA-1s-Ø-SS.SEQ
'Now I would like to tell that story.'

The verb *na-* quite freely combines with sound words (626), and a number of these combinations have been lexicalized (627), (628). The onomatopoeic word has become part of the verb, and the vowel /a/ has been deleted from the verb in the process.

(626) *Oro-mi*   ***bulak na-i-ya***.
drop-ss.SIM plop   say-Np-PR.3s
'When it drops it says "plop".'

(627) Siowa **baun-i-ya**. (< bau na-i-ya)
  dog bark-Np-PR.3s (bau say-Np-PR.3s)
  'The dog barks.'

(628) Ema   **buun-eya**   mua erup um-e-mik. (< buu na-eya)
  mountain erupt-2/3s.DS man two die-PA-1/3p (buu say-2/3s.DS)
  'The mountain (=volcano) erupted and two men died.'

In fast speech *na-* is often reduced to *a-* when the verb follows a consonant-final word (629).

(629) *"Uruf-a-mik" a-e-k*.
  see-PA-1/3p   say-PA-3s
  ' "They saw it," he said.'

The medial form *na-eya* is also used as resultative connective 'so, therefore' (630) (§3.11.2).

(630) Iwera   yia   na-em-ik-e-mik.   **Naeya** iwera   wia
  coconut 1p.ACC say-SS.SIM-be-PA-1/3p So   coconut 3p.ACC
  uruk-am-ik-om-a-mik.
  drop-SS.SIM-be-BEN-BNFY2.PA-1/3p
  'They kept speaking to us about coconuts /asking us for coconuts. So we kept dropping coconuts for them.'

3.8.4.4.7 Impersonal experience verbs This very small group mainly consists of verbs indicating some kind of pain. They look like transitive verbs, but the syntactic subject is inanimate, usually a body part, and the human experiencer is the object (631), (632) (Table 3.45).

Table 3.45: Impersonal experience verbs

gilin-	'smart (v.)'
kokas-	'itch'
liilin-	'sting'
tiitin-	'hurt, ache (generic)'
tukun-	'throb'
sirir-	'ache'

(631) Maara efa   **tiitin-i-ya**.
  forehead 1s.ACC hurt-Np-PR.3s
  'My head hurts.'/ 'I have a headache.' (Lit: 'It hurts my forehead.')

3 Morphology

(632) Uuw-ap   uuw-ap   oona=ke efa   sirir-i-ya.
       work-SS.SEQ work-SS.SEQ bone=CF 1s.ACC ache-Np-PR.3s
       'I have worked and worked, and my bones ache.'

Most of the experience verbs in Mauwake are adjunct plus verb constructions (§3.8.5.2.1), a few are ordinary intransitive verbs (§3.8.4.2.1).

3.8.4.5 Auxiliary verbs

The small group of auxiliary verbs in Mauwake consists of two ordinary verbs that have also grammaticalized as auxiliaries indicating aspect. In this function the lexical meaning of the verbs is somewhat bleached. The auxiliary is the last verb in a verbal group (§3.8.5.1).

The paradigms of the auxiliaries are similar to those of main verbs. Table 3.46 shows the auxiliary verbs.

Table 3.46: Auxiliary verbs

AUX	MEANING	MAIN VERB FORM
ik-	'continuous'	SS.SIM
	'stative'	SS.SEQ
pu- (<wu-)	'completive'	SS.SEQ

The auxiliary *ik-* is very frequent and has several functions. When it is used with a main verb in the same-subject simultaneous form (SS.SIM), it indicates continuous aspect, which can have either progressive (633) or habitual (634) meaning. For position-taking verbs (§3.8.4.4.2) and other semantically punctiliar verbs the habitual interpretation is the only possible one, but for other verbs the context is needed to determine the correct interpretation.

(633) Fikera   aw-em-**ik**-eya   uruf-a-k. (progressive)
       kunai.grass burn-SS.SIM-be-2/3s.DS see-PA-3s
       'When the kunai grass was burning she saw it.' (Or: 'She saw the kunai grass burning.')

(634) I   yabuela aaw-ep   ... wi-em-**ik**-e-mik.   (habitual)
       1p.UNM papaya get-SS.SEQ ... give.them-SS.SIM-be-PA-1/3p
       'We kept getting papayas and ... giving them to them.'

When the main verb is in the same-subject sequential form (SS.SEQ), the auxiliary *ik-* indicates stativity (635). With non-punctiliar verbs this form can often be translated into English with a past perfect (636).

(635) *Pok-ap-**ik**-emkun*　　　*epa wiim-o-k.* (stative)
　　　sit.down-ss.seq-be-1s/p.ds place dawn-pa-3s

　　　'As I was sitting it became light.'

(636) *Ikiw-ep-**ik**-eya*　　　*ona emeria=ke ekap-o-k.* (perfect)
　　　go-ss.seq-be-2/3s.ds 3s.gen woman=cf come-pa-3s

　　　"After he was/had gone his wife came.'

The auxiliary *pu-* 'completive', is obviously derived from *wu-* 'put'[93] through assimilation with the final /p/ of the same-subject sequential form in the main verb preceding it (637), (638) . Synchronically, the Mauwake speakers do not recognise the origin of the auxiliary.

(637) *Maa en-ep-**pu**-ap*　　　*soomar-eka.*
　　　food eat-ss.seq-cmpl-ss.seq walk-imp.2p

　　　'Having finished eating you may go.' (Lit: 'Eat the food and go'.)

(638) *Nan efa wu-ap-**pu**-ami*　　*o*　　*Ulingan ikiw-o-k.*
　　　there1 1s.acc put-ss.seq-cmpl-ss.sim 3s.unm Ulingan go-pa-3s

　　　'He left (lit: put) me there and went to Ulingan.'

3.8.5 Verbal clusters

The verbal clusters are described here under verb morphology, because they function as a unit very much like single verbs. There are two kinds of verbal clusters: verbal groups and adjunct plus verb constructions. The definition of a verbal group is from Halliday (1994: 175): "a sequence of words in the primary class of verb" (639).

(639) *Ifara **mokak-ikiw-em-ik-ok** ifara oko uruf-a-k.*
　　　vine stare-go-ss.sim-be-ss　vine other see-pa-3s

　　　'He kept looking for a vine and saw one vine.'

Adjunct plus verb combinations[94] contain a verb (or a verbal group) plus an element from another word class that is obligatory and contributes to the meaning of the verb (640).

(640) *Owora efar **ikum aaw-iwkin** wia maak-e-m.*
　　　betelnut 1s.dat illicitly get-2/3p.ds 3p.acc tell-pa-1s

　　　'They stole my betelnut and I talked to them.'

The status of a verb phrase in Mauwake is somewhat questionable. It is discussed in §4.5.

---

[93] 'Put' is one of the verbs commonly used in Papuan languages to indicate completion (Foley 1986: 145).
[94] Halliday (1994: 184) calls these "phrasal verbs".

3 Morphology

3.8.5.1 Verbal groups

A verbal group consists of two or more verbs that function grammatically and semantically as one unit. The semantic unity within the group varies between different types of verbal groups.

The verbal groups containing a main verb plus auxiliary have developed by merging clauses as can still be seen from the verbs involved. But since they synchronically function as a unit very much like an individual verb they are treated on the word level. Features that identify them as one close-knit unit are as follows:

- Shared subject (and object, if relevant)
- No non-verbal elements intervening between the parts
- Scope of negation spans over the whole group
- No coordinators are allowed between the parts
- Phrasal intonation and pause structure, i.e. no pauses between the words.

Mauwake has two kinds of verbal groups. The verbs in the first group consist of a main verb and an aspectual auxiliary. The second group consists of serial verbs, where all the verb stems contribute to the semantic, rather than grammatical, meaning of the verb.

3.8.5.1.1 Main verb plus auxiliary: aspect The importance of tense as a verbal category in Mauwake shows in its obligatory morphological marking, but aspect is a relatively important category as well. Aspects are 'different ways of viewing the internal temporal constituency of a situation' (Comrie 1976: 3).

Aspect in Mauwake is expressed periphrastically, through verbal groups that have a main verb and an auxiliary. The main verb, which is in the medial form, largely gives the semantic content to the whole, and the auxiliary adds the grammatical meaning of aspect. In the continuous and stative aspects also the medial form of the MAIN verb contributes to the aspectual meaning. What distinguishes these constructions from medial clauses (§8.2) is that the two verbs function as a unit rather than individual verbs, and their phonological stress, intonation and pause pattern is that of a word or phrase rather than a medial clause.

As is typical of sov languages, the auxiliary follows the main verb (Greenberg 1966 [1963]: 85; Dryer 2007b: 90). The more common of the aspectual auxiliaries is *ik-* 'be', which can combine with two different medial forms. The other aspectual auxiliary is *pu-* 'completive' (§3.8.4.5).

The neutral, aspectually unmarked verb form is used in Mauwake whenever the speaker chooses not to pay special attention to the internal structure of the situation. It could be claimed that this is a neutral perfective, since the situation is viewed as a whole, but that term would be confusing, as the neutral forms can also be used in clauses that are aspectually habitual (cf. Payne 1997: 239). The majority of the verb forms used in all kinds of texts in Mauwake are aspectually neutral.

The marked completive aspect is only used when completion of an action is stressed. The continuous aspect is used for both progressive and habitual actions, and the stative aspect for a state continuing over some time.

3.8.5.1.1.1 Completive aspect When the COMPLETION of an action is in focus, the completive aspect is used. It is formed by a main verb in the same-subject sequential form, followed by the auxiliary *pu-* 'completive' (641) (§3.8.4.5).

(641) Ifakim-ep nomokow ekeka=pa **sererim-ep-pu-a-k**.
kill-ss.SEQ tree branch=LOC hang-ss.SEQ-CMPL-PA-3s
'He killed it and hung it on a tree branch.'

The completive aspect verb is often used in a medial same-subject sequential form, which in itself only indicates sequentiality but often implies completion of the first action as well (642)–(644).

(642) **Sererim-ep-pu-ap** owowa or-o-k.
hang-ss.SEQ-CMPL-ss.SEQ village descend-PA-3s
'He hung it up and went/came down to the village.'

(643) Manina **nop-ap-pu-ap** nomokowa war-i-mik.
garden burn-ss.SEQ-CMPL-ss.SEQ tree cut-Np-PR.1/3p
'We burn (the undergrowth for new) garden and (when it is done we) cut the trees.'

(644) Nomokowa **war-ep-pu-ap** arew-i-mik.
tree cut-ss.SEQ-CMPL-ss.SEQ wait-Np-PR.1/3p
'We cut the trees and wait.'

But it is not uncommon either to have the completive aspect with a simultaneous action medial form, when the second action coincides with the completion of the first one (645)–(647).

(645) Wia **maak-ep-pu-ami** i ikiw-e-mik.
3p.ACC tell-ss.SEQ-CMPL-ss.SIM 1p.UNM go-PA-1/3p
'We told them and went.'

(646) Aria yo nan efa **wu-ap-pu-ami** o Ulingan ikiw-o-k.
alright 1s.UNM there 1s.ACC put-ss.SEQ-CMPL-ss.SIM 3s.UNM Ulingan go-PA-3s
'Alright he put me there and he went to Ulingan.'

(647) Maa en-owa **wakesim-ep-pu-ami** ikiw-o-k.
thing eat-NMZ cover-ss.SEQ-CMPL-ss.SIM go-PA-3s
'Covering the food she left.'

3 Morphology

The completive aspect form is also used when MOMENTANEITY of the action is emphasized (648):

(648) **En-ep-pu-ap**   ikiw-e!
eat-SS.SEQ-CMPL-SS.SEQ go-IMP.2s
'Get done with your eating and go!'

The origin of the auxiliary, the verb 'put', shows in the fact that it cannot be used with non-controlled actions (649).[95]

(649) * Waki-ep-pu-a-k
fall-SS.SEQ-CMPL-PA-3s

In process descriptions a medial verb, followed by the verb *weeser-* 'finish', which stresses the endpoint of the action, is used more than the completive aspect (650). This, however, is a case of clause chaining (§8.2), not a verbal group.

(650) Uup-ep   **weeser-eya** wienak-e-m.
cook-SS.SEQ finish-2/3s.DS feed.them-PA-1s
'I finished cooking it and fed it to them.' [Lit: 'I cooked it and when it (=the cooking) was finished I fed it to them.']

3.8.5.1.1.2 Continuous aspect: progressive and habitual

Continuity, or duration, is the semantic component shared by the aspects called progressive and habitual in many languages: continuation of the same action or of repeated actions of the same kind (Comrie 1976: 26). The continuous aspect form in Mauwake can have either progressive (651), (652) or habitual (653), (654) interpretation. The main verb is in the same-subject simultaneous medial form, but with the final /i/ deleted, and the auxiliary *ik-* 'be' is inflected for tense and person/number (653).

(651) Maa **en-em-ik-omkun**   ama or-o-k.
food eat-SS.SIM-be-1s/p.DS sun descend-PA-3s
'As I was eating the sun went down.'

(652) Fikera   **aw-em-ik-eya**   nain umuk-i-nen   na-ep
kunai.grass burn-SS.SIM-be-2/3s.DS that1 extinguish-Np-FU.1s say-SS.SEQ
urup-o-k.
ascend-PA-3s
'The kunai grass was burning, and she went up in order to extinguish it.'

(653) Iwera=ke   wia   aruf-eya   **ma-em-ik-e-mik,**   "..."
coconut=CF 3p.ACC hit-2/3s.DS say-SS.SIM-be-PA-1/3p
'When coconuts hit them, they kept saying, "..."'

---

[95] In general, control vs. non-control is not a prominent feature in the verb system in Mauwake, unlike many other Papuan languages (Foley 1986: 127, Reesink 1987: 128).

(654) Wi   Yaapan naap kuisow=iw **ekap-em-ik-e-mik**.
3p.UNM Japan thus one=INST come-ss.SIM-be-PA-1/3p
'The Japanese kept coming like that, one by one.'

For punctiliar verbs the habitual interpretation (655) is the only one possible, whereas for non-punctiliar (656) verbs both habitual and progressive interpretations are possible.

(655) Koka=pa   nan   **in-em-ik-e-mik**.
jungle=LOC there lie.down-ss.SIM-be-PA-1/3p
'We kept sleeping in the jungle'

(656) Owowa oko   wiam=iya   **irak-em-ik-e-mik**.
village other 3p.ACC=COM fight-ss.SIM-be-PA-1/3p
'We were fighting (or: kept fighting repeatedly) with the other village.'

When the verbal group is in the medial form, the progressive interpretation (657) is the more common:

(657) Waaya **urup-em-ik-eya**   mik-a-m.
pig   ascend-ss.SIM-be-2/3s.DS spear-PA-1s
'As the pig was going/coming up I speared it.'

Often the context provides the only clue as to whether the continuous aspect form should be interpreted as progressive or habitual. The example (658) describes a situation where the villagers kept feeding the Japanese soldiers who asked them for food; the sentence (659) is from a text describing a coconut plantation fire and its consequences.

(658) Waaya yia   na-iwkin   waaya **wienak-em-ik-e-mik**.
pig   1p.ACC say-2/3p.DS pig   feed.them-ss.SIM-be-PA-1/3p
'They asked us for pigs and we kept giving them pigs to eat.'

(659) Kawus **ir-am-ik-eya**   kuuf-a-k.
smoke rise-ss.SIM-be-2/3s.DS see-PA-3s
'The smoke was rising and she saw it.'

Cross-linguistically the habitual aspect more commonly receives overt marking in the past tense than in the present (Cristofaro 2006: 154). In Mauwake the continuous aspect can be used for habitual in any of the three tenses. The example (660) was said about particular work that the speaker was not involved in continuously; he used to do it time to time because of his position as need arose. The example (661) refers to a couple needing to keep visiting an ailing father.

(660) Yo   anane maneka naap **mauw-am-ika-i-yem**.
1s.UNM always very   thus work-ss.SIM-be-Np-PR.1s
'I always/forever keep working like that.'

3 *Morphology*

(661) O   me sariar-i-non-(na)   neeke **in-em-ika-i-kuan**.
3s.UNM not get.well-Np-FU.3s-(TP) there.CF sleep-ss.SIM-be-Np-FU.3p
'If he doesn't get well, they will keep sleeping/staying *there*.'

For a clause to have habitual interpretation it is not obligatory to use the continuous aspect form in the verb. For instance in process descriptions, which tell how something is habitually done, the unmarked, aspectually neutral present tense form is more common than the continuous aspect. Three of the four verbs in (662) are aspectually unmarked, although all the clauses have habitual interpretation, describing seclusion customs.

(662) *Moma ik-owa* **enim-i-mik**. *Eka me* **enim-i-mik**, *iwer eka me*
taro roast-NMZ eat-Np-PR.1/3p water not eat-Np-PR.1/3p coconut water not
enim-i-mik. *Aaya muutiw* **en-em-ika-i-mik**.
eat-Np-PR.1/3p sugarcane only eat-ss.SIM-be-Np-PR.1/3p
'We do not eat roasted taro. We do not drink water or coconut water. We only eat / keep eating sugarcane.'

3.8.5.1.1.3 Stative aspect   The same semantic component of continuity is also shared by the other aspect using the auxiliary *ik-* 'be': this time it is a STATE rather than activity that continues the same over time. In the stative aspect, the auxiliary is combined with a main verb that is in the same-subject sequential form. This usage is most common with the position-taking verbs like *pok-* 'sit down' (663), *iimar-* 'stand up' (664) and *in-* 'lie down/ fall asleep'.

(663) **Pok-ap-ik-omkun**   *epa wiim-o-k*.
sit.down-ss.SEQ-be-1s/p.DS place dawn-PA-3s
'As we were sitting it dawned.'

(664) *Yena koor miira=pa* **iimar-ep-ik-e-m**, ...
1s.GEN house face=LOC stand.up-ss.SEQ-be-PA-1s
'I was standing in front of my house, ...'

Other punctiliar verbs (665), as well as non-punctiliar verbs, can be used in this aspect to indicate the state resulting from an action (666), or process (667), but they are less frequent.

(665) *Ifakim-eya* **pu-ep-ik-eya** *om-em-ik-ua*.
kill-2/3s.DS die-ss.SEQ-be-2/3s.DS cry-ss.SIM-be-PA.3s
'When she killed him and he was dead, she was crying.'

(666) **Ikiw-ep-ik-eya** *ona emeria=ke ekap-o-k*.
go-ss.SEQ-be-2/3s.DS 3s.GEN woman=CF come-PA-3s
'While he was gone his wife came.'

(667) *Ewar   pun wuun-e-k ne epa **reen-ep-ik-ua**.*
       west.wind too blow-PA-3s and place dry-SS.SEQ-be-PA.3s

       'The west wind blew, too, and the ground was dry.'

In (668) the continuous form indicates more active waiting process than is the case in (669) with the stative aspect. In (668) the people were getting impatient with the vehicle that should already have come to get them. The example (669) is from a description of garden work, and part of the work process is the state of patiently waiting for the felled trees and undergrowth to dry.

(668) *Arew-**am**-ik-omkun   ama ikur miiw-aasa kerer-ek.*
       wait-SS.SIM-be-1s/p.DS sun five land-canoe arrive-PA-3s

       'As we were waiting the car arrived at five.'

(669) *Nomokowa war-ep-pu-ap   arew-**ap**-ika-iwkin   reen-eya*
       tree   cut-SS.SEQ-CMPL-SS.SEQ wait-SS.SEQ-be-2/3p.DS dry-2/3s.DS
       saama   kuum-i-mik.
       cleared.bush burn-Np-PR.1/3p

       'They cut the trees and while they are waiting it dries and then they burn the cleared bush.'

3.8.5.1.2 Serial verbs Verbal groups called serial verbs are very common in Papuan languages (Foley 1986: 116). Finding a cross-linguistic definition for serial verbs has proved to be an extremely hard task (Sebba 1987: 5, Lord 1993: 1). Instead of one definition covering all the possible serial verbs, Crowley (2002: 19) suggests defining these verbs within "specific typological and linguogenetic groupings" for comparative purposes.

For a working definition I borrow one given by James (1983: 28) describing the serial verbs in Siane, another Papuan language:

> A serial verb construction consists of two or more verbs which occur in series with neither normal coordinating nor subordinating markers, which share at least some core argument (normally subject and/or object/goal), and which in some sense function together semantically like a single predication.

Typically, even if not obligatorily, one of the verbs in the series is finite and the other(s) more or less "stripped-down". In a verb-final language the finite verb is the last one in the series. After describing the serial verb construction in Mauwake, I will discuss the question whether serial verbs are actually compound verbs, and the relationship of the serial verbs to main verb + auxiliary verbal groups and medial clauses.

In Mauwake a non-final verb in a serial construction consists of a bare root without any inflection at all. This restriction is tighter than those given for serial verbs in many other languages (Crowley 2002: 19; Sebba 1987: 86–87; James 1983: 28). Each of the verbs in a serial construction contributes to the overall semantic meaning of the predicate. Even if the meaning is not exactly the same as the combination of the same verbs would have in a tight medial verb chain (670) (cf. Payne 1997: 310), it does not get bleached either, like that of the auxiliaries.[96]

(670) *Sama=pa   oro-boon-ek.*
ladder=LOC descend-get.loose-PA-3s
'He fell from the ladder.'

The last verb in a series is either a finite verb with tense and person/number inflection, or a medial verb. The arguments are shared by the whole verbal complex, even if they would originally have been associated with only one of the verbs (671). Also negation and obliques (672) are shared. All this points to serial verbs being a nuclear-level phenomenon in Mauwake, rather than a core-level one (Foley & Van Valin 1984: 189–193).

(671) *Yo   Amerika wia   akup-ikiw-i-yem.*
1s.UNM America 3p.ACC search-go-Np-PR.1s
'I am going to look for the Americans. / I go searching the Americans.'

(672) *Neeke   aw(e)-or-om-ik-eya   ...*
there.CF burn-descend-SS.SIM-be-2/3s.DS
'As it was burning (towards) down *there...*'

Semantically the verb combinations are of two types. In the more common one a directional or another motion verb follows another verb stem, giving the meaning of MOVEMENT to the whole (671)-(673), and often the meaning of DIRECTIONALITY as well (672)-(674).[97] This is a productive process, as long as the verbs are semantically compatible.

(673) *Wia   mokak-urup-o-k, wia   mokak-or-o-k.*
3p.ACC stare-ascend-PA-3s 3p.ACC stare-descend-PA-3s
'He stared them up and down.'

(674) *Aasa suuw-or-o-mik.*
canoe push-descend-PA-1/3p
'We pushed the canoe down (towards the sea).'[98]

If the first stem is also a motion verb, it indicates the MANNER of movement (675):

(675) *Merena kir-ep   segen-ikiw-o-k.*
foot   turn-SS.SEQ limp-go-PA-3s
'He twisted his foot and limped.'

---

[96] Since a serial verb construction has only one main stress it is written as one word in the orthography, but the verb stems are separated by hyphens to make reading easier.
[97] Cross-linguistically motion and location verbs are very common in serial verbs (Lord 1993: 9).
[98] Compare this with a medial construction: *Aasa suuw-ap or-o-mik* 'We pushed the canoe and went down (to sea)'

3.8 Verbs

A motion verb in a serial construction can also indicate TEMPORAL CONTINUITY over a long period of time. In (676) the length of time is emphasized even more by the repetition of the motion verb.

(676) **Ife-iki(w-e)p iki(w-e)p** aakisa arim-o-n.
rub-go-SS.SEQ go-SS.SEQ now grow-PA-3s

'You kept rubbing it (over the years) and now you have grown up.'

In the second type, any two verbs can, in principle, combine into a serial verb. But this process is less productive, and both the type and token frequency of this type is low when compared with the frequency of the first type. Usually, like in (677) the meaning of the whole is transparent and can be inferred from the meanings of the component roots, but sometimes the semantics are more opaque (678).

(677) Emera **kue-puuk-ap** okaiwi siowa onak-e-k.
sago bite-cut-SS.SEQ other.side dog feed.him-PA-3s

'He bit off half of the sago cake and fed it to the dog.'

(678) Aakun-emi **mika-kof-a-m.**
speak-SS.SIM spear-knock-PA-1s

'I stumbled in my speech.'

This type of serialization in Mauwake is very close to what James (1983: 1–5) calls LEXICAL serialization.

A special case among the roots forming serial verbs is *afur-* 'do well'/'augmentative', which is not used as an independent verb, only as a second element in a serial verb structure (679).[99]

(679) Koora ku-owa **amis-ar-afur-a-k.**
house build-NMZ knowledge-INCH-do.well-PA-3s

'He really knew how to build a house.'

It is quite possible even if not very common to form a three-root serial verb by combining the two types (680):

(680) **Mika-fien-ikiw-o-k.**
hit-push.aside-go-PA-3s

'He went on countering (an attack).'

It is far more common to have three verbs in a combination where an auxiliary is attached to a serial verb (681):

(681) Naap **amis-ar-ikiw-em-ik-o-wen.**
thus knowledge-INCH-go-SS.SIM-be-Np-FU.2p

'That way you will gain more and more knowledge.'

---
[99] See James (1983: 32) for the use of a similar verb, *ito,* in Siane.

3 Morphology

Combining four or more roots into one verbal group is more of a theoretical possibility than a practical reality. Examples are easy enough to obtain through elicitation, but very rare in non-elicited texts.

Mauwake does NOT use serial verbs for a benefactive like many languages do (Sebba 1987: 174–80); it utilizes benefactive morphology for that purpose (§3.8.2.3.3, §3.8.3.1). Neither is the serial verb structure used for aspect, as a verb plus auxiliary construction takes care of that. Another function often associated with serial verbs is that of instrument marking, but for that Mauwake uses either an ordinary switch-reference construction or an adverbial phrase (§4.6.3).

Distinguishing serial verbs from compound verbs on the one hand and medial clauses on the other is not a problem for Mauwake only, as serial verbs can behave very much like either (Crowley 2002: 17). Crowley suggests the following continuum of gradually loosening syntactic juncture: verbal compounds > nuclear serial verbs > core serial verbs > clause chains > subordinate clauses > coordinate clauses (ibid. 18). In the following I will briefly discuss the relationship of serial verbs to adjunct plus verb constructions, to verbal groups consisting of a main verb plus auxiliary, and to medial clauses in Mauwake.

The serial verbs in Mauwake show the following characteristics of compounding (cf. James 1983: 69 regarding Papuan languages). The first verb appears as a mere root (or as a stem, if it has undergone derivation); secondly, the verbs obligatorily share the same arguments; thirdly, the meaning of the whole may differ from the combined meanings of the parts. Furthermore, the stress and intonation contour of a serial verb is that of a single word rather than that of a phrase or a clause. There are two main reasons for calling them serial verbs. The first one is that especially the first type is productive. I also want to link them to a typologically widespread phenomenon instead of looking at them from a strictly language-specific point of view. In this I follow Margetts (1999: 101), who maintains that "the term 'compound' does not by definition contradict an analysis as serialization". A similar position is also strongly defended by Crowley (2002: 16) and by Givón (1991: 17).

Because of the tight restriction of "root only" for the first element in a serial verb in Mauwake, the main verb plus auxiliary combinations are left outside the group by definition. Another reason for this differential treatment is the fact that different processes seem to be going on in the two groups: grammaticalization in the main verb + AUX group, lexicalization in the true serial verbs.[100]

In Mauwake the clause chaining is structurally midway between serialization and main clause coordination, and may consequently be used instead of either in some cases. The instrumental may in Mauwake be expressed by a 'take-instrument-do' structure (682) which in many serializing languages is a serial verb construction (Sebba 1987: 162–74); but in Mauwake there is no good reason to call the structure anything other than a combination of a medial and final clause. This shows more clearly in example (683),

---

[100] In some other languages main verb +AUX constructions are included among serial verbs (e.g. James 1983: 29; Crowley 2002: 178). Farr (1999: 174) notes the "staging" aspects of the two constructions: in medial verbs the temporal relationship of the two verbs may be specified, but as "the verbal constituents of SVCs [serial verb constructions] do not specify temporal borders or overlapping relationships, the events they represent can blend into a unit ... and present the SVC is a complex but integrated event".

which does not pass the rule for verbal groups: "no non-verbal elements between the parts".

(682) Fura **aaw-ep** puuk-a-m.
knife take-ss.SEQ cut-PA-1s

'I took a knife and cut it.' Or: 'I cut it with a knife.'

(683) Burir **aaw-ep** nomokowa unowa war-e-mik.
axe take-ss.SEQ tree many fell-PA-1/3p

'We took an axe and felled many trees.' Or: 'We felled many trees with an axe.'

For Mauwake, I propose the following continuum where the syntactic juncture gradually loosens: serial verb > verb + AUX group > subordinate + main clause > clause chain > coordinate main clauses.

The borderline between serial verbs and medial verbs on the one hand, and between verb + AUX groups and medial verbs on the other is not absolutely clear-cut. In (684) the medial verb structure is used instead of a serial verb, even though the two actions are simultaneous, not sequential as indicated by the form of the medial verb.[101]

(684) Wi Malala=ke **muf-ep** ekap-emi...
3p.UNM Malala=TP pull-ss.SEQ come-ss.SIM

'The Malala people came pulling it and...'

Likewise, the four verbs in (685) describe ONE protracted action in spite of the sequential form in the medial verbs:

(685) Ifa nain **murar-ep** wiok-ap ekap-ep ekap-ep owowa
snake that1 follow-ss.SEQ follow.them-ss.SEQ come-ss.SEQ come-ss.SEQ village
kerer-ek.
arrive-PA-3s

'The snake kept following them and arrived in the village.'

The main verb in verb plus AUX combinations has to be in medial form. The only exception found is the continuous aspect form of the verb *wiaw-* 'move around'. The mere root of this verb is used when it is the second verb in a serial structure which then takes an aspectual auxiliary (686):

(686) Ifara mufe-**wiaw**-ik-ok...
vine pull-move.around-be-ss

'As he was pulling the vine around...'

---

[101] Mauwake does not allow same subject simultaneous forms following each other except in a strictly coordinate structure where the verbs do not so much indicate simultaneity with each other as with the final verb.

3 Morphology

3.8.5.2 Adjunct plus verb constructions

Papuan languages typically enlarge their verb inventories through adjunct plus verb combinations (Foley 1986: 127). Foley only discusses nominal adjuncts, but adverbial adjuncts are commonly used in these structures as well.

Mauwake is not nearly as productive in the use of the adjunct plus verb construction as many other Papuan languages. Some of them use almost exclusively generic verbs (Foley 1986: 117; Roberts 1987: 309; Whitehead 2004: 145), whereas others employ a larger set of verbs (Farr 1999: 62–66) in these constructions.[102]

3.8.5.2.1 Nominal adjunct plus verb The nominal adjuncts look like object NPS, and the origin of at least some of them probably is in object NPS, but currently there are syntactic and semantic differences between the two. An object NP may be separated from the verb by the negator adverb *me* or by an accusative or a dative pronoun, but a nominal adjunct must immediately precede the verb (687). The meaning of the nominal adjunct plus verb construction often cannot be derived from the meanings of its constituent parts.

(687) *Meta yia   miim-ap   yia   miira puuk-ekap-e-mik.*
       fame 1p.ACC hear-SS.SEQ 1p.ACC face cut-come-PA-1/3p

      'They heard about us and came to greet us.'

An object NP only occurs with a transitive verb, but a nominal adjunct can also occur with an intransitive verb (688):

(688) *Uura or-op   arua karu-e-mik.*
       night descend-SS.SEQ torch run-PA-1/3p

      'At night we went down to sea and fished with a torch.'

Those nominal adjunct plus verb structures where the verb is transitive look like two-object clauses, and in a few cases behave like them syntactically. In (689) the nominal adjunct *kema* 'liver' is in its normal adjunct position, but in (690) it is in object NP position. The basic meanings of the two sentences are the same, but with a different prominence: (689) encodes marked negative focus and (690) verb focus. The clause (691) with an initial theme pronoun *yo* 'I' is pragmatically more neutral than the others except in cases where the initial pronoun receives extra stress. Note the intervening negator also in (697) below.

(689) *Me efa   kema suuw-a-k.*
       not 1s.ACC liver push-PA-3s

      'He did NOT think of me.'

---

[102] Farr divides the nominals in these constructions into 'complements' an 'adjuncts'. Korafe does not seem to use adverbial adjuncts in these structures.

(690) ***Kema** me efa   suuw-a-k.*
 liver not 1s.ACC push-PA-3s
 'He didn't THINK of me.'

(691) *Yo   me efa   **kema** suuw-a-k.*
 1s.UNM not 1s.ACC liver   push-PA-3s
 'He didn't think of me.'

In cases where the adjunct only occurs with a certain verb it is difficult to give it a specified meaning apart from the verb (692). The same is true for verbs that do not occur independently, only with an adjunct (693).

(692) ***Naruw** ir-a-mik.*
 ?   ascend-PA-1/3p
 'They acted silly.'

(693) *Naap **kema tuup**-am-ika-i-ya.*
 thus liver ?-SS.SIM-be-Np-PR.3s
 'He is hoping so.'

Most of the verbs in Mauwake indicating physiological or psychological states and cognition are nominal adjunct plus verb constructions. The verb takes the person marking from the experiencer. Table 3.47 gives only a small sample of these constructions, where the most common nominal is *kema* 'liver'.[103] The second column provides a literal translation. A few more examples of these constructions are in the sentences (694)-(697).

Table 3.47: Nominal adjunct plus verb constructions

kema enekar-	liver catch.fire	'be thirsty'
kema kaalal-	liver float	'be enthusiastic'
kema korin-	liver get.stuck	'be confused'
kema peelal-	liver rot	'be grieved'
kema ten-	liver collapse	'be relieved'
eneka maayar-	tooth become.long	'be hungry for meat'
miira ikiw-	face go	'feel dizzy'

(694) *Uura **uroma** ikiw-e-m.*
 night stomach go-PA-1s
 'Last night I had diarrhea.'

---

[103] A good list of these is in Kwan (1989: 47–63), where she has described a large number of body image concepts formed with *kema* from semantic point of view. For that study the syntactic characteristics of the structures were not relevant.

3 Morphology

(695) **Kema samor-ar-ep** maa me enim-i-yem.
 liver spoil-INCH-SS.SEQ food not eat-Np-PR.1s
 'I am sad and don't eat.'

(696) ...oko **emina urur-ep** soomar-ikiw-i-kuan.
 ...other occiput drop-SS.SEQ walk-go-Np-FU.3p
 '...lest they feel ashamed and walk away.'

(697) Muuka gelemuta akena **kema me puk-e-mik**.
 son small very liver not burst-PA-1/3p
 'Little boys/children do not think well (yet).'

3.8.5.2.2 Adverbial adjunct plus verb Adverbial adjuncts also have to precede the verb without any intervening words (698), (699).

(698) Maamuma efar **ikum aaw-e-mik**.
 money 1s.DAT illicitly get-PA-1/3p
 'They stole money from me.'

(699) Maa me efa **pepek er-a-k**.
 food not 1s.ACC enough go-PA-3s
 'The food wasn't enough for me.'

Some of the adverbial adjuncts, like *ikum* 'illicitly' (698) and *pepek* 'enough' (699), also function as independent adverbs, shown by an intervening pronoun (700) and/or negator (701).

(700) Yo oram **ikum** efa wu-a-n.
 1s.UNM for.nothing illicitly 1s.ACC put-PA-2s
 'You accused me for theft without grounds.'

(701) No **pepek** me ma-e-n.
 2s.UNM enough not say-PA-2s
 'You didn't say right.'

Other adjuncts like *ane* 'together' (702) and *anu* 'apart' (703), only combine with verbs to form verbal groups, and it is hard to give them an exact meaning; the glosses below are just approximations.

(702) Apura **ane** suuw-am-ika-iwkin pok-ap ik-ok om-o-k.
 widow together push-SS.SIM-be-2/3p.DS sit.down-SS.SEQ be-SS cry-PA-3s
 'They were supporting the widow (sitting against her back) and she sat and wailed.'

(703) Opora **anu**   **fien-owa**   me pepek.
       talk apart/aside brush.off-NMZ not enough
       'He wasn't able to disregard the talk.'

It was mentioned above that the meanings of the adjunct plus verb combinations are often idiomatic rather than analytically derivable from the meanings of the parts. But this is a somewhat dangerous statement for one to make who comes from outside the speech community. For example, how literally *kema* 'liver', which figures very strongly in the adjunct plus verb constructions, is understood to be really involved in the emotional and cognitive processes would need to be established in a separate study.

3.9 Adverbs

Adverbs in Mauwake are a heterogeneous class morphologically, syntactically and semantically. Schachter's (1985: 20) definition of adverbs as words functioning "as modifiers of constituents other than nouns" is quite usable for Mauwake. Functionally the adverbs can be divided into four groups. The MATERIAL adverbs (Ahlman 1933)[104] form the largest group, which contains the subgroups of locative, temporal and manner adverbs. The second group, that of INTENSITY adverbs,[105] consists of a small group of adverbs that function on phrase level and modify an adjective or adverb. SENTENTIAL (or MODAL) adverbs modify a whole sentence. The last group consists of the two FREE adverbs *pun* 'also' and *muutiw* 'only'.

A material adverb may function as the head of an adverbial phrase. In this respect, however, adverbs differ from most other word classes: whereas the head of a noun phrase is usually a noun, that of a verb phrase a verb, and an adjective phrase an adjective, an adverbial phrase typically either consists of an adverb only, or does not contain an adverb word at all (§4.6).

The position of adverbs within a clause is also discussed under adverbial phrase (§4.6).

3.9.1 Material adverbs

The material adverbs function as peripherals in a clause. They are divided into locative, temporal, and manner adverbs. The temporal and manner adverbs may be subdivided into deictic and non-deictic adverbs, and the locative adverbs are practically all deictic; in this they differ from the intensity and modal adverbs, which cannot be deictic.

---

[104] Ahlman used the term in classifying adverbs in Finnish, and I find it useful in describing the adverbs in Mauwake as well, since the temporal, locative and manner adverbs share some characteristics which differentiate them from the other adverbs.

[105] In some grammars these form a class of their own, called "intensifiers". But that name is somewhat misleading as it may contain words like *somewhat* or *hardly* which do not intensify the meaning of the adjacent adjective or adverb.

3 Morphology

3.9.1.1 Locative adverbs

All the non-controversial locative adverbs are deictic (704), (705), and they were discussed above in section on spatial deictics (§3.6.3).

(704) ...mokoma kuisow naap ***fan*** yiam=iya ik-e-mik.
 year one thus here 1p.REFL=COM be-PA-1/3p
 '...for about a year they were here with us.'

(705) ...mua owawiya ***neeke*** ik-ok uruf-ap... kiiriw ep-i-kuan.
 man with there.CF be-SS see-SS.SEQ again come-Np-FU.3p
 '...having been with her husband there and seeing [her father] they will come (back) again.'

The words that are formed with a noun plus the locative clitic -*pa* are treated as (adverbial) locative phrases, since they are expandable.

The words *epasia* [106] 'far (away)' (706) and *mamaiya* 'near, close' (707), (708) are actually locative nouns, but may be in the process of becoming adverbs. They optionally take the locative clitic -*pa*, but its presence or absence causes no semantic difference. *Tiil* 'edgewise, close' (709) cannot take the locative clitic. Its use is quite restricted, and it might be more accurately classified as a manner adverb.

(706) ***Epasia*** ikiw-em-ik-omkun yia far-e-k.
 far go-SS.SIM-be-1s/p.DS 1p.ACC call-PA-3s
 'As we were (still) walking at a distance, he called us.'

(707) Fikera ***mamaiya=pa*** nan pok-ap ...
 kunai.grass near=LOC there sit-SS.SEQ
 'Having sat there near the kunai grass ...'

(708) Mua oko=ke ***mamaiya*** pok-a-k.
 man other=CF near sit-PA-3s
 'Another man slept with her (lit: sat near).'

(709) Saapipia baliwep me wu-a-m, ***tiil*** wu-a-m.
 trap well not put-PA-1s on.edge put-PA-1s
 'I didn't put the trap well, I put it right on the edge (of the reef).'

Locative expressions that in some other languages would be expressed through pre- or postpositions or adverbs are formed with locative phrases containing locative relational nouns in Mauwake (710).

(710) koor ***kuenuma=pa***
 house underside=LOC
 'underneath (lit: in/on the underside of) the house'

---

[106] *Epasia* has probably developed from *epa asia* 'wild place'.

3.9.1.2 Temporal adverbs

The temporal adverbs can be classified semantically as deictic or non-deictic. The meaning of the former is tied to the time of the utterance, whereas the meaning of the latter is independent of it. Both the deictic and non-deictic temporal adverbs are either specific or non-specific. This grouping is relevant on the syntactic level, as it influences the ordering of multiple temporal adverbials within a clause (§4.6.2).

Deictic specific temporal adverbs refer to a certain day in relation to the time of the utterance (711), (712).[107] They are given in Table 3.48.

Table 3.48: Deictic specific temporal adverbs

aakisa[a]	'today'
unan	'yesterday'
erekema	'the day before yesterday'
uurika	'tomorrow'
ere	'the day after tomorrow'
arowona	'third day from today'

[a] *Aakisa* 'today, now' may be either specific or non-specific.

(711) **Unan** nainiw yiam fiirim-e-mik.
Yesterday again 1p.REFL gather-PA-1/3p
'Yesterday we met again.'

(712) **Uurika** emeria manina ikiw-ep en-owa nop-ap or-eka.
tomorrow woman garden go-SS.SEQ eat-NMZ fetch-SS.SEQ descend-IMP.2p
'You women, go to the garden tomorrow and fetch food (and come) down.'

The DEICTIC NON-SPECIFIC TEMPORALS (Table 3.49) refer to a time that is related to the time of the utterance (or in some cases to the time of the event), but is not restricted to a certain day (713)–(715).

(713) Aria, no **aakisa** maa enim-e.
alright 2s.UNM now thing/food eat-IMP.2s
'Alright, eat now.'

(714) **Eewuar,** eka me saanar-owa ik-ua.
not.yet water not dry-NMZ be-PA.3s
'Not yet, the water hadn't dried.'

---

[107] The only exception to this in the data is *uurika*, which in the forms *uurik ona* (lit: 'tomorrow place') and *uurika naap nain* (lit: 'tomorrow thus that') means 'the following day' and takes the time of the event as the deictic centre.

3 Morphology

Table 3.49: Deictic non-specific temporal adverbs

aakisa	'now'
aakisa fain	'nowadays, now', literally: 'now this'
aakisa fan	'just a while ago, just now (past)', literally: 'now here'
aakisa kuisow	'right now, in a minute' (future), literally: 'now one'
eewuar	'not yet'
iirakuma	'a few days ago'
iiriw	'already, earlier, long ago'
iiriwiw	'long time ago'
ikoka	'later'
ikoka kuisow	'right now' (future), literally: 'later one'
uurik ona	'the following day', literally: 'tomorrow place'
wiimar	'later, some other time'

(715) No   emeria **iiriw**   sesek-a-mik.
       2s.UNM woman already send-PA-1/3p
       'We already sent your wife (away).'

Both *ikoka* and *wiimar* mean 'later', and they can occasionally be used interchangeably. *Ikoka* is the more common of the two, and has to be used when referring to a later time the same day (716). *Wiimar* always refers to a less specific time somewhere in the future, but the use of *ikoka* is spreading to cover that too. The sentence (717) is from a wedding speech, and it was unlikely that the young couple would be fighting later the very same day.

(716) **Wiimar** ikiw-i-yan, **ikoka** weetak.
       later   go-NP-FU.1p later   no
       'We'll go some other time, not later today.'

(717) No   **ikoka** mua ikos irak-ep   me efar kerer-e.
       2s.UNM later   man with fight-SS.SEQ not 1s.DAT arrive-IMP.2s
       'Later when you fight with your husband, don't come to me.'

Aakisa 'now' can be modified to further specify the meaning, as the exact present moment is so short that a word referring to it only is practically useless. *Aakisa kuisow* (lit: 'now one') refers to something that WILL TAKE PLACE 'just now', in a moment (718), *aakisa fan* (lit: 'now here') refers to something that HAS HAPPENED just now (719) and *aakisa fain* (lit: 'now this') compares the present situation with earlier times (720).

(718) **Aakisa kuisow** on-e,   ikoka weetak.
       now   one   do-IMP.2s later no
       'Do it right now, not later.'

(719) *Muuna kirip-owa   ma-e-mik   nain **aakisa fan** kirip-a-mik.*
      debt   return-NMZ say-PA-1/3p that1 now   here return-PA-1/3p
      'They (only) just now returned the debt they have talked about returning.'

(720) *Iiriw   miiw-aasa marew, **aakisa fain** miiw-aasa nepik akena.*
      earlier land-canoe none   now   this land-canoe crowd real
      'Earlier there were no cars, now(adays) there are lots of cars.'

The NON-DEICTIC SPECIFIC temporals (721), (722) refer to a specific time, but their interpretation is not tied to the time of the utterance (Table 3.50).

(721) ***Amirika** ama kekan-eya   uurar-i-mik.*
      day   sun strong-2/3.DS rest-Np-PR.1/3p
      'During the day (or: at noon) when the sun is strong, we take a rest.'

(722) *Yaapan=ke **uura**   ifera=pa nan pok-om-ow-a-mik.*
      Japan=CF evening/night sea=LOC there sit-BEN-CAUS-PA-1/3p
      'In the evening the Japanese made him sit in the sea.'

The temporal adverbs in Table 3.51 are both NON-DEICTIC and NON-SPECIFIC (723), (724).

(723) *Yo **anane** naap mauw-am-ika-i-yem.*
      I always thus work-SS.SIM-be-Np-PR.1p
      'I always work like that.'

(724) *Irak-owa maneka **ewur**   me imen-ar-e-k.*
      fight-NMZ big   quickly not find-INCH-PA-3s
      'The big fight/war didn't start quickly.'

Table 3.50: Non-deictic specific temporal adverbs

uuriw	'morning'
amirika	'day(time), noon'
urera	'(late) afternoon'
uura	'evening/night'
uur gonegon[a]	'midnight'
epa wiiwim[b]	'close to dawn'

[a] The word *gonegon*, which I have not come across elsewhere, is a partial reduplication of the locative noun *gone* 'middle'. As a reduplication it is unusual in that the partial reduplication follows rather than precedes the root.

[b] This is a back-formation of the expression *epa wii-wiim-ik-ua* [place RDP-dawn-be-PA.3s] 'It is/was beginning to dawn'.

3 Morphology

Table 3.51: Non-deictic non-specific temporal adverbs

aawurun	'forever'
anane	'always', 'every day'
ewur	'soon, quickly, fast'
ewursow	'soon, at once'
iir oko	'once upon a time, at some point' (lit: '(an)other time')
kiikir	'first'
kiiriw	'again'
mokomokoka	'first'
nainiw	'again' (<nain=iw)
muri[a]	'later, behind'

[a] This is an Austronesian borrowing (M. Ross, p.c.). It also occurs in the verb *murar-* 'follow', which has grammaticalized from the adjunct plus verb compound *muri ar-* 'behind become'.

Nainiw (725) and *kiiriw* (726) both mean 'again', and they can be used interchangeably when referring to repeated action.

(725) Ne **nainiw** sande uura yiam fiirim-e-mik.
 ADD again Sunday evening 1p.REFL gather-PA-1/3p
 'And again on Sunday evening we gathered together.'

(726) Ne **kiiriw** enuma on-am-ik-e-mik.
 ADD again new make-SS.SIM-be-PA-1/3p
 'And again they kept making a new one.'

When some action or event results in a state that is the same or similar as before, even if the action itself is not repeated, only *kiiriw* can be used. Thus, only *kiiriw* is possible in (727). *Kiiriw* indicates that Jesus is alive again, as he had been before, whereas *nainiw* would indicate that he had risen from the dead earlier too.

(727) Yeesus **kiiriw** iikir-a-k.
 Jesus again rise-PA-3s
 'Jesus rose again (= rose from the dead).'

Also, if the action is the same but the situation changes, *kiiriw* is used. The example (728) describes a situation where a grandmother first sent her younger grandchild, a girl, to listen to a sound. Later she sent the grandson for the same errand; the act of sending was repeated but the person who was sent changed:

(728) **Kiiriw** morena iperowa nain sesek-a-k.
 again male older that1 send-PA-3s
 'Again she sent the elder male (grandchild).'

Occasionally, *kiiriw* and *nainiw* can be used together (729):

(729) *Ar-ep ik-eya aria **kiiriw** mua nain **nainiw** urup-o-k.*
become-SS.SEQ be-2/3s.DS alright again man that1 again ascend-PA-3s
'When she had become like that, alright the man came up again.'

3.9.1.3 Manner adverbs

The manner adverbial phrase is often manifested by just an adverb word rather than a longer phrase. The same distinction between deictic and non-deictic adverbs that was made with the other material adverbs can be made with the manner adverbs as well. The description of the deictic manner adverbs (730), (731) is in §3.6.4.

(730) *...maa oposia pun **naap** sesek-a-mik.*
thing meat also thus sell-PA-1/3p
'...like that they also sold meat.'

(731) *Soo nain **feenap**: era erup ik-ua.*
fishtrap that1 like.this way two be-PA.3s
'The fishtrap (custom) is like this: there are two ways.'

Most of the non-deictic manner adverbs are non-derived (732)–(734), but a few have been derived from adjectives by the deletion of word-final <a> (735). This process is not productive. Table 3.52 gives a list of some of the more common non-deictic manner adverbs.

(732) *Naap yia ma-i-kuan na-ep yo **ariman** nefa*
thus 1p.ACC say-Np-FU.3p say/think-SS.SEQ 1s.UNM openly 2s.ACC
maak-i-yem.
tell-Np-PR.1s
'I am telling you this openly, thinking that they will say like that about us.'

(733) *Opaimika **baliwep** me wiar amis-ar-e-m.*
talk well not 3.DAT knowledge-INCH-PA-1s
'I don't/didn't know their language well.'

(734) *Fikera **ikum** kuum-e-mik nain ma-i-yem.*
kunai.grass illicitly burn-PA-1/3p that1 say-Np-PR.1s
'I tell about that when the kunai grass was burned by arson.'

(735) ***Samor** akena aruf-a-mik.*
badly very hit-PA-1/3p
'They beat him very badly.'

3 Morphology

Table 3.52: Non-deictic manner adverbs.

ariman	'openly, publicly'
baliwep/balisow	'well'
damol/samor	'badly, poorly' (from *damola/samora* 'bad')
ewur/ewuriw	'quickly'
ikum	'illicitly'
kapi	'askew'
kaken/kakeniw	'straight, correctly'
kekelka	'quietly, gently'
kerew	'strongly'
kokot	'secretly'
momasia	'slowly' (cf. adjective *momasia* 'slow')
momor	'indiscriminately', 'foolishly' (from *momora* 'foolish')
pepek	'correctly'
oram/moram	'without reason', 'without doing anything'[a]
orawin	'for the benefit'

[a] This word is difficult to gloss in English; its meaning is close to that of Tok Pisin *nating*.

3.9.2 Intensity adverbs

Intensity adverbs are a small and heterogeneous group of adverbs that modify a verb, an adjective, a quantifier or another adverb (736), (737). Some of them (*akena, maneka*) are also adjectives, some others (*lawisiw, iiwawun, wenup*) are non-numeral quantifiers (§3.4.2) with a second function as intensity adverbs. The distribution is different for each of the intensity adverbs (Table 3.53).

Table 3.53: Intensity adverbs

akena	'very, really, truly'
iiwawun	'altogether'
kakeniw	'exactly'
lawisiw/lawiliw	'somewhat'
maneka	'very'
oram	'very, just'
pepek	'enough'
wenup	'very'

3.9 Adverbs

(736) *Moma fain eliw(a)* **oram**.
 taro this good just/very
 'This taro is very good.'

(737) *Koora nain maala* **pepek**.
 house that long enough
 'That house is long enough.'

Akena 'really, truly' is more flexible than the other intensity adverbs in that it can modify a word belonging to almost any word class (738)– (742).

(738) *Eka mamaiya* **akena** *i yoowa me aaw-i-yen*
 river near very 1p.UNM hot not get-Np-FU.1p
 'Very near the river we'll not get hot.'

(739) *Iikamin* **akena**=*ko imen-ar-i-non?*
 when really=NF find-INCH-Np-FU.3s
 'Exactly when is it going to appear?'

(740) *Sira samora piipu-eka* **akena**.
 habit bad leave-IMP.2p really
 'You (pl) must really leave (your) bad habits.'

(741) *Yiena ikos* **akena** *iw-u*.
 1p.GEN two.together really go-IMP.1d
 'Lets's go JUST the two of us together.'

(742) *Weetak* **akena**, *i=ko me kuum-e-mik*.
 no really, 1p.UNM=NF not burn-PA-1/3p
 'REALLY NO, we did not burn it.'

Lawisiw 'somewhat' is different from the rest in that it precedes the expression it modifies, rather than following it (743).

(743) *Uuw-owa nain* **lawisiw** *yoowa*.
 work-NMZ that1 somewhat hot/hard
 'That work is somewhat hard.'

As an adjective *maneka* 'big' is very common, but as an intensity adverb 'very' it is very restricted in its distribution. *Maneka* cannot modify a verb, but it can intensify some non-numeral quantifiers like *unowa* 'many' and *iiwawun* 'altogether', as well as the temporal adverb *anane* 'always' (744).

(744) *Yo anane* **maneka** *naap mauw-am-ika-i-yem*.
 I always very thus work-ss.SIM-be-Np-PR.1s
 'I ALWAYS keep working like that.'

3 Morphology

3.9.3 Modal adverbs

The two modal adverbs in Mauwake differ from each other not only semantically, but morphologically and syntactically as well. Modality of a predication is discussed in §6.1.

Eliw 'all right, well'[108] is a DEONTIC adverb and expresses permission or desirability: 'it is all right/good that...'. It can often be translated with the auxiliary 'may' in English. It follows the subject, if there is any, but precedes the other clause constituents (745). It may also be in the tail position after the clause, either following a clause that already has *eliw* in it (746), or by itself (747).

(745) *Wie   wi   **eliw** wiar op-i-kuan.*
 3s/p.uncle 3p.UNM well 3.DAT hold-Np-FU.3p
 'Her uncles may get (lit: hold) them (=clay pots) from her.'

(746) ***Eliw** Kululu ma-e-man, **eliw**.*
 well Kululu say-PA-2p well
 'It is all right that you mentioned Kululu, that is OK.'

(747) *Nomokowa, nie   owowa=pa fan pok-a-n, **eliw**.*
 2s/p.brother 2s/p.uncle village=LOC here sit-PA-2s well
 'It is good/OK that you settled here in your brother's and uncle's village.'

An EPISTEMIC modal adverb is the clitic *-yon* (with an alternative form *-nion*), expressing hesitation or non-committal assumption: 'perhaps', 'maybe', 'I suppose'. It is attached to the predicate, which usually is a verb (748), (749), but can also be non-verbal (750). The question word *kamenion* 'or what' is related to the modal adverb *-yon* (§3.9.3).

(748) *Maa   me wu-om-a-mik=**yon**.*
 thing/food not put-BEN-BNFY2.PA-1/3p-perhaps
 'Perhaps they didn't put food (aside) for him.'

(749) *Yo   me efa   ma-e-n=**yon**   aa?*
 1s.UNM not 1s.ACC say-PA-2s-perhaps aa
 'I suppose you weren't saying it about me?'

(750) *Ni   kema puk-owa marewa=ke=**yon**!*
 2p.UNM liver burst-NMZ none=CF-perhaps
 'You must be crazy!' (Lit: 'I suppose your liver hasn't burst (yet).')

3.9.4 Free adverbs

The adverbs *muut(a)/muutiw* 'just/only' and *pun* 'also, too' are called free adverbs, as they can move around quite freely and attach themselves to various elements in a clause.

---

[108] The manner adverb 'well' is *baliwep* (§3.9.1.3).

3.9 Adverbs

Muutiw is a combination of *muut(a)* and the limiter clitic *-iw*, and it restricts the scope of a preceding noun phrase or adverbial phrase (751)–(756). *Muut(a)* is used almost exclusively with noun phrases (757), (758).

(751) *Aaya   muutiw en-em-ika-i-mik.*
sugarcane only   eat-ss.SIM-be-Np-PR.1/3p
'They are only eating sugarcane.'

(752) *Ofa sepa muutiw (if-o-k).*
paint black only   paint-PA-3s
'He painted with only black paint.'

(753) *Ewar wuun-i-ya   nain muutiw miim-i-nan.*
wind blow-Np-PR.3s that only   hear-Np-FU.2s
'You will hear only the wind blowing.'

(754) *Lotu   koora Ulingan=pa muutiw ik-ua=i?*
worship house Ulingan=LOC only   be-PA.3s=QM
'Is there a church only at Ulingan?'

(755) *Aakisa muutiw niir-i-mik.*
today only   play-Np-PR.1/3p
'They play only today.'

(756) *Eliw muutiw.*
well only
'It's just all right.'

(757) *Yo   opora muut naap.*
1s.UNM talk   only   thus
'That's my talk.'

(758) *Uf-owa   erup muuta naap uf-e-mik.*
dance-NMZ two only   thus dance-PA-1/3p
'We only danced two dances like that.'

Pun 'also' has even wider distribution than *muutiw*: it can occur following almost any element in a clause (759)–(763).[109]

(759) *Ne waaya nain pun afila   marew, waaya asia pun.*
and pig   that1 also grease no(ne) pig   wild also
'And that pig also didn't have fat, (as) it was a wild pig too.'

---
[109] *Pun* may be in the process of developing into a clitic. As a one-syllable word it it often has a weak stress, and some speakers also write it attached to the preceding word with a hyphen, the way clitics are written in the Mauwake orthography.

3 Morphology

(760) Yos **pun** wie   opora nainiw ma-i-yem.
1s.FC too 3s/p.uncle talk again say-Np-PR.1s
'I, too, will again give "uncle-talk" (=cultural instruction).'

(761) Ne **pun** aakisa iperowa   korokor or-owa   sira   iiriw
and also now middle.aged initiation descend-NMZ custom earlier
wafur-a-mik.
throw-PA-1/3p
'Also, now the middle-aged people have already rejected the initiation custom.'

(762) Iiriw **pun** miiwa muuta   nain irak-owa marew.
earlier also ground because.of that1 fight-NMZ no(ne)
'Earlier there were also no fights over ground' (or: 'Earlier, too, there were no fights over ground.')

(763) Teeria maneka wadol opora mik-a-mik **pun** naap, …
group big   lie   talk hit-PA-1/3p also thus
'(When) the big group lied it was also like that, …'

3.10 Negators

Mauwake has four negators: *weetak, wia, me* and *marew*. They are morphologically free and syntactically heterogeneous, each one having its specific position. Of the four negators *me* is positioned before the negated element (764), (765), while *marew* follows the negated element (766). *Weetak* and *wia* either form a complete utterance by themselves, or they are sentence-initial when used as negative interjections (767) but clause-final when functioning as non-verbal predicates (768), and when replacing full clauses they take the position of the clause they replace (769), (770).

(764) Maamuma **me** tuun-owa   ik-e-mik.
money   not count-NMZ be-PA-1/3p
'They haven't counted the money (yet).'

(765) Mukuna **me** op-a,   nefa kuum-i-non!
fire   not touch-IMP.2s 2s.ACC burn-Np-FU.3s
'Don't touch the fire, it will burn you!'

(766) I   muuka **marew**.
1p.UNM son   no(ne).
'We have no son.'

(767) **Wia**, me kookal-i-yem.
No   not like-Np-PR.1s
'No, I don't like it.'

(768) Yo   uuw-owa oko **weetak**.
     1s.UNM work-NMZ other no

  'I have no other work.'

(769) Wafur-a-k   na **weetak**, ufer-a-k.
     throw-PA-3s but no,   miss-PA-3s

  'He threw it (a spear), but no (=he didn't succeed), he missed (the pig).'

(770) Akup-a-mik,   akup-a-mik,   **wia**.
     search-PA-1/3p search-PA-1/3p no

  'We searched and searched, but no (=we did not find it).'

According to a rough generalization, the most frequent negator *me* is basically a clause and constituent negator. It is also used to negate imperatives. *Weetak* and *wia* are negative interjections or predicates in verbless clauses, and *marew* can negate non-verbal predicates and occasionally noun phrase constituents. *Marew* often has the meaning 'none at all' (771).

Weetak (742), *wia* and occasionally *marew* (771), may be intensified by a postposed intensity adverb *akena* 'truly, very'. *Me* can only be intensified as a verbal negator, in which case *akena* comes after the verb rather than after the negator (772).

(771) Ni   niam   erup kema **marew akena**!
     2p.UNM 2p.REFL two liver no(ne)   really

  'The two of you have REALLY NO sense at all!'

(772) **Me** on-a-m   **akena**.
     not do-PA-1s really

  'I REALLY DIDN'T do it.'

A fuller treatment of the negators is in §6.2, where negation as a functional category is discussed.[110]

3.11 Connectives

The inventory of connectives in Mauwake is small. They are called connectives rather than conjunctions, because conjunctions are normally understood as a class of words, but in Mauwake a connective may be a word or a phrase. The term CONJUNCTION is reserved for the conjunctive coordination construction (§8.1.1). Many of the connectives also have another primary function.

The main division is into pragmatic and semantic connectives; all of them are coordinate. Subordination is discussed in §8.3. The connectives mostly operate on sentence

---

[110] Berghäll (=Järvinen) (2006) gives a somewhat more comprehensive treatment of negation in Mauwake, but some of the analysis has changed since the writing of the article.

3 Morphology

level, joining clauses (§8.1). Almost all of the coordinators also conjoin sentences. Only the pragmatic connectives and the disjunctive connective *e* 'or' are able to conjoin elements on the word and phrase levels as well.

The most typical way of combining clauses is clause chaining through medial verbs, with no connective words at all (§8.2). When there are connectives, they are always placed between the two clauses.

3.11.1 Pragmatic connectives

Instead of clearly specifying the semantic relationship between the units they connect, like semantic connectives do, the pragmatic connectives signal a pragmatic relationship between them.[111] In Haspelmath's (2007: 8) terms they are 'medial [and] prepositive', meaning that they occur between the items they conjoin, and are linked more closely to the following constituent rather than the preceding one.

The connective *ne* 'additive' only indicates that something is added to what has just been said. It can connect word and phrase level units (§4.1.2), but is mostly used between clauses (§8.1) and even sentences. It is semantically neutral. When it conjoins words (773) or phrases (776), and often when it coordinates clauses (774) or sentences (775), it can be translated into English with 'and'.

(773) *kumin,   wutkekela **ne** mera ...*
      hermit.crab calamari   ADD   fish

   'hermit crabs, calamari and fish ...'

(774) *Inawera sira   unowa, **ne** kemena unowa.*
      dream   custom many   ADD inside many

   'There are many kinds of dreams, and (they have) many meanings.'

(775) ***Ne** yo   aakisa tep=pa   ma-i-yem.*
      ADD   1s.UNM   now   tape.recorder=LOC say-Np-PR.1s

   'And now I say it to a tape recorder.'

Words or phrases in lists are most commonly joined by juxtaposition only. If a connective is used, *ne* usually joins the last two (776) coordinands. It is also possible to place the connective(s) closer to the beginning of the list.

(776) *Sesa nain waaya erup arow **ne**   maamuma kuuma erepam ikur **ne***
      price that1 pig two three ADD   money   stick four   five ADD
      manar   kuisow, waa eneka, naap muuka sesenar-i-nen.
      forehead.ornament one   pig tooth thus son   buy-Np-FU.1s

   '(As for) the price, I will buy my son with two-three pigs and forty-fifty kina and a forehead ornament (and) pig's tusk(s), like that.'

---

[111] For this distinction on pragmatic and semantic connectives I am indebted to Stephen Levinsohn.

3.11 Connectives

There is no emphatic coordinate connective of the type 'both ... and' in Mauwake.

If the propositions connected by *ne* contrast with each other in some way, it may be interpreted as adversative and translated into English with 'but' (777), (778).[112] In these cases it is always a "weak" adversative in contrast to the demonstrative *nain* used in "strong" adversative clauses (§8.1.3).

(777) *Maa en-owa iw-e-mik,   **ne** rais weetak.*
       thing eat-NMZ give.him-PA-1/3p ADD rice no
       'They gave him food, but not rice.'

(778) *Wi   me kuum-e-mik, **ne** wi   murar-owa=pa   mukuna nain*
       3p.UNM not burn-PA-1/3p ADD 3p.UNM follow-NMZ=LOC fire   that
       kerer-e-k.
       appear-PA-3s
       'They didn't burn it, but the fire started after them.'

In a number of cases either neutral additive or contrastive interpretation is possible (779):

(779) *Wiam erup irak-ep   puk-e-mik,   aalbok=ke   ifera*
       3p.REFL two fight-SS.SEQ disperse-PA-1/3p black.cuckoo-shrike=CF sea
       or-o-k   ne osaiwa=ke   soor(a) asia ikiw-o-k.
       descend-PA-3s ADD bird.of.paradise=CF forest wild go-PA-3s
       'The two of them fought and went their separate ways, the black cuckoo-shrike went down to the coast and/but the bird of paradise went to the wild (rain)forest.'

There are two DISCOURSE-MARKING pragmatic connectives, *aria* and *ne aria*. They both mark discontinuity in the text.

Aria 'alright'[113] usually comes sentence-initially, but can also or occur sentence-medially. Its main function is to indicate a break in the topic chain. In (780) the topic changes from the snake to the man, and in (781) from a health extension officer to a group of men:

(780) *Keraw-eya **aria** nomokowa gelemuta puuk-ap ifa   nain ifakim-o-k.*
       bite-2/3s.DS alright tree   small   cut-SS.SEQ snake that kill-PA-3s
       'It (=the snake) bit him, and he cut a small tree and killed the snake.'

(781) *... miim-o-k. **Aria**   wi   kiiriw neeke ...*
       ...3s.UNM   precede-PA-3s. Alright 3p.UNM again there.CF ...
       '... he went ahead. (When) they were THERE again ...'

---

[112] Many Papuan languages have a connective that is glossed 'and/but'. I suggest it is an additive connective like *ne*, interpreted as either 'and' or 'but' according to the content of the clauses conjoined.

[113] The translation reflects the Tok Pisin word *orait*, which sometimes has a similar discourse function. *Aria* occurs in many Madang languages, and the speakers of those languages tend to use *aria* in Tok Pisin too.

3 Morphology

It often signals the beginning of a turn in a conversation (782), or beginning of a speech (783), again indicating a break with the preceding text.

(782) ***Aria*** *wiipa, i   yia   uruf-e.*
alright daughter, 1p.UNM 1p.ACC see-IMP.2s
'Daughter, look at us.'

(783) ***Aria****, i   owowa=ko urup-u.*
alright, 1p.UNM village=NF ascend-IMP.1d
'Alright, let's go back to the village.'

Even if the topic stays the same, *aria* can be used, especially when there is a contrast between alternatives (784), or sometimes when an expected sequence of events is broken (785).

(784) *Mua maneka maamuma erup,* ***aria*** *wi   suule takira maamuma kuisow,*
man big   money   two   alright 3p.UNM school child   money   one
naap omopora sesenar-e-mik.
thus door   buy-PA-1/3p
'The grown men paid two coins (=20 toea) for entrance, the schoolchildren one coin.'

(785) *Wiawi   onak   urera   maa uup-e-mik,* ***aria*** *maa me*
3s/p.father 3s/p.mother evening food cook-PA-1/3p alright food not
wu-om-a-mik=yon.
put-BEN-BNFY2.PA-1/3p-perhaps
'In the evening his parents cooked food, (but) perhaps they didn't put any food for him.'

Ne aria 'and alright' occurs less often than *aria*, and only sentence-initially (786). It marks major points of development in the plot of a story. Sometimes it also signals return to foreground text (i.e. main story line) after some backgrounded material.

(786) *Naap wia   maak-e-mik.* ***Ne aria****, ifa   nain murar-ep...*
thus 3p.ACC tell-PA-1/3p ADD alright snake that follow-SS.SEQ
'They told them like that. Now, the snake followed them and ...'

3.11.2 Semantic connectives

The semantic connectives specify the relationship between two propositions. The DIS-JUNCTIVE connective *e* 'or' can connect not only propositions but words or phrases as well. It is used both for standard (787) and interrogative (788) disjunction[114] (§§8.1.2, 7.2.2). When there are two alternatives, the connective occurs between them. It is also common

---

[114] This terminology is from Haspelmath (2007).

3.11 Connectives

to have the question marker *-i* cliticized to the end of the first alternative, especially in questions, but also elsewhere.

(787)　*ama arow naap,* **e** *erepam naap, ...*
　　　　sun three thus　or four　　thus
　　　　'at about three o'clock, or at about four ...'

(788)　*Emeria=ko efar　uruf-a-man=i* **e** *weetak?*
　　　　woman=NF 1s.DAT see-PA-2p=QM or no
　　　　'Did you see my wife or not?'

When there are more alternatives than one and the question clitic is present, the connective may be left out altogether (789), or it may occur between the first two alternatives (790).

(789)　*maa oposia=i moma, emera, naap*
　　　　thing meat=QM taro,　sago,　thus
　　　　'meat, or taro, or sago, (things) like that'

(790)　*iwer　eka=ki　* **e** *mauwa=ki, a episowa=ki,　ufia=ki*　　　...
　　　　coconut water=CF.QM or what=CF.QM ah tobacco=CF.QM, betel.pepper=CF.QM
　　　　'coconut juice or - ummm - tobacco, or betel pepper ...'

The following CONSECUTIVE connectives marking effect or result[115] are used in sentences where the clauses have a consecutive, i.e. a cause-effect or reason-result relationship: *naapeya/naeya*, *neemi*, and *naap nain*. They can all be glossed with 'therefore, (and) so'.

Naapeya/naeya is the most generic and frequently used of the four. *Naapeya* has developed from the manner adverb *naap* 'thus' followed by the different-subject marker *-eya* (§3.8.3.5.2);[116] the resulting meaning is 'it being thus'. The origin of *naeya* is in the medial different-subject form of the verb *na-* 'say, think'. The difference between the two is mainly dialectal, or areal: *naapeya* (791), (792) is used more on the coast, *naeya* (793), (794) in the inland. They are used for marking the effect or result clause in a consecutive sentence.

(791)　*I　　 maamuma marew,* **naapeya** *ifera=ko me sesenar-e-mik.*
　　　　1p.UNM money　　no(ne), so　　　salt=NF not buy-PA-1/3p
　　　　'We didn't have money, so we didn't buy salt.'

(792)　*Ben uuw-owa piipu-a-k.* **Naapeya** *emina　urur-ep　me ekap-o-k.*
　　　　Ben work-NMZ left-PA-3s therefore occiput fall-SS.SEQ not come-PA-3s
　　　　'Ben has left the work. Therefore he was ashamed to come.'

---

[115] It is typical for Papuan languages to mark the effect/result clause rather than the cause/reason clause. For a Papuan language which has several connectives both for result and for reason, see Farr (1999: 267–273).

[116] Actually this connective in the coastal villages is *naapera*, but because of the language committee's decision to use *-eya* for the 2/3s.DS marker, this form is used here too.

213

(793) *Pika oona me kekan-ow-a-k.* **Naeya** *uura ewar=ke teek-a-k.*
wall bone not strong-CAUS-PA-3s therefore night wind=CF tear-PA-3s

'He didn't strengthen the wall studs. So at night the wind tore it (the house) down.'

(794) *I miiw-aasa=pa ekap-e-mik,* **naeya** *o me yook-a-k.*
1p.UNM land-canoe=LOC come-PA-1/3p therefore 3s.UNM not follow.us-PA-3s

'We came in a car, so he didn't follow/come with us.'

The origin of *naeya* is so transparent that there are many cases where two different interpretations for *naeya* are acceptable (795).

(795) *"Yo koka=pa ik-e-m."* **Na-eya** *Magerka=ke (ma-e-k)...*
1s.UNM jungle=LOC be-PA-1s say-2/3s.DS MacArthur (say-PA-3s)

' "I was in the jungle." He said that, and (or: So) MacArthur said, ...'

But in (796) *naeya* clearly means 'therefore' and cannot be interpreted as a medial verb, as the correct verb form in this case would be plural *naiwkin* 'they said and...', not singular *naeya* 'you/(s)he said and...'.

(796) *Iwera yia na-em-ik-e-mik.* **Naeya** *iwera wia*
coconut 1s.ACC say-SS.SIM-be-PA-1/3p So coconut 3p.ACC
uruk-am-ik-om-a-mik.
drop-SS.SIM-be-BEN-BNFY2.PA-1/3p

'They kept asking us for coconuts. So we kept dropping coconuts for them.'

The originally dialectal difference may be developing into a semantic one. In the original text data from three decades ago there is no clear semantic distinction between the use of *naapeya* and *naeya*, but fairly recently when a group with members from different dialects, discussing language matters, produced consecutive clauses, nearly all of the sentences with *naapeya* were cases of cause-effect (797), and all of the sentences with *naeya* were cases of reason and result (798).

(797) *I fiirim-owa=pa ik-emkun ama or-o-k,* **naapeya** *epa*
1p.UNM gather-NMZ=LOC be-1s/p.DS sun descend-PA-3s therefore place
kokom-ar-e-k.
dark-INCH-PA-3s

'When we were in the meeting the sun went down, so it became dark.'

(798) *I fiirim-owa=pa ik-emkun ama or-o-k,* **naeya** *maa me wiar*
1p.UNM gather-NMZ=LOC be-1s/p.DS sun descend-PA-3s therefore food not 3.DAT
en-owa ikiw-o-k.
eat-NMZ go-PA-3s

'When we were in the meeting the sun went down, so he went without eating the food.'

3.11 Connectives

Naapeya can also co-occur with the conjunctive coordinators *ne* or *aria*. In argumentation, *ne naapeya* or *aria naapeya* has to be used, when the reason is not confined to one clause but extends to a longer stretch of the discourse (799).

(799) **Aria naapeya** niena soomar-owa ne aakun-owa pun sira yi-e-k
alright therefore 2p.GEN walk-NMZ ADD talk-NMZ also custom give.us-PA-3s
nain kaken=iw ook-ap soomar-eka.
that1 straight=LIM follow-SS.SEQ walk-IMP.2p

'So therefore, as concerns your walk and talk too, follow straight the behaviour that he gave us and walk that way.'

Neemi is used only in reasoning. It requires some point of similarity between the antecedent and the result clause (800).

(800) *Teeria fain K10 wu-a-mik.* **Neemi** wi teeria nain pun K10 wu-a-mik.
group this K10 put-PA-1/3p therefore 3p.UNM group that1 too K10 put-PA-1/3p

'This group put down K10. Therefore that group put down K10, too.'

Naap nain can be translated into English with 'therefore', 'in that case', 'if so, then'. It is made up of the manner adverb *naap* 'thus' and the distal demonstrative *nain* 'that'. It is a strong connective, stressing the fact that the proposition following the connective is a logical conclusion from the preceding proposition (801).

(801) *Ni moma uup-i-man=i?* **Naap nain** yo saa uup-i-nen.
2p.UNM taro cook-Np-2p=QM thus that 1s.UNM rice cook-Np-FU.1s

'Are you cooking taro? In that case I'll cook rice.'

It is much less common in Mauwake to mark the reason clause than the result clause with a connective. When the reason clause is emphasized, it is marked with the connective *moram (wia)* 'because' and always follows the result clause rather than preceding it. The origin of the reason connective is in the question word *moram* 'why?' and the negator *wia* 'no(t)'.[117] The difference between *moram wia* and *moram* is that the former is mainly used across sentence boundary (802), and the latter within a sentence (803).

(802) *Maamuma senam aaw-e-mik.* **Moram wia**, maa ele-eliwa sesek-a-mik.
money a.lot get-PA-1/3p why not thing RDP-good sell-PA-1/3

'They got a lot of money. (That's) because they sold good things/foods.'

(803) *Miiw-aasa muf-owa me ikiw-e-mik,* **moram** os=ke naap ar-eya.
land-canoe pull-NMZ not go-PA-1/3p why 3s.FC=CF thus become-2/3s.DS

'We didn't go to fetch a truck, because she had become like that (=died).'

---

[117] *Moram* as a reason connective is probably a calque on Tok Pisin *bilong wanem* 'why, because'. The negator, which does not influence the meaning of the connective, may have been added in Mauwake to help distinguish the connective from the question word.

3 Morphology

3.12 Postpositions and clitics

Since Mauwake is an SOV language, it is natural that it has postpositions rather than prepositions. But their number is small: besides the comitative postpositions there are only two others, one for comparison and one indicating reason.

Unlike the postpositions, which are both phonological and grammatical words, clitics are grammatical words that together with the preceding word form one phonological word. The stress assignment rule does not affect them: they are always unstressed. If there are any derivational and inflectional suffixes in the host word, the clitics are added after all of them (Dixon 2010a: 221–222).

The nominal clitics associate with noun phrases and attach themselves phonologically to the last element of the noun phrase. They mark either the case role or the pragmatic function of the NP. The only sentential clitic is the question marker -*i*. The modal clitic -*yon* 'perhaps' was discussed above in §3.9.3.

The postpositions and clitics are discussed together because of their shared origin in some cases, causing similarity in form, and because some of them have similarities in function.

3.12.1 Comitative clitic and postpositions

Accompaniment, or a COMITATIVE relationship may be expressed by one clitic or by five different postpositions, three of which are formed with the clitic.

The comitative clitic is -*iya* 'with, and, both … and'. The clitic may be attached to either of the two related noun phrases (804), (805), or to both (806).

(804) *Nan pok-ap-ik-e-mik,*   ***mua=iya emeria.***
       there sit-SS.SEQ-be-PA-1/3p man=COM woman.
       'They were sitting there, (both) husband and wife.'

(805) ***Muuka wiip=iya***   *kerer-e-mik.*
       son   daughter=COM appear-PA-1/3p
       '(Both) a son and a daughter appeared.'

(806) ***Bom=iya kateres=iya, bom=iya kateres=iya*** *(fuurk-a-mik).*
       bomb=COM cartridge=COM bomb=COM cartridge=COM drop-PA-1/3p
       'They dropped (both) bombs and cartridges, (both) bombs and cartridges.'

It combines with pronouns to form comitative pronouns (§3.5.9), and the word for 'all', *unowiya*, is made up of *unowa* 'many' plus the comitative clitic.

Occasionally the clitic can also be used to indicate instrument (807).

(807) *Mauwa ar-e-n,*   ***amia=iya*** *nenar-e-mik=i?*
       what   become-PA-2s bow=COM shoot.you-PA-1/3p=QM
       'What happened to you, did they shoot you with a gun?'

Owawiya/owawik 'with, together with' is used only for humans; it can refer to two or more people (808). It can also occur by itself (809). The origin of the first part *owaw-* is unknown. The second part is either the comitative clitic *-iya* or the root of the existential verb *ik-* 'be', a reflection of an earlier construction *owawiya ik-* 'be together' (810).

(808) Yoli onak   ***owawiya*** efa   amukar-e-mik.
       Yoli 3s/p.mother with   1s.ACC scold-PA-1/3p

       'Yoli and his mother scolded me.'

(809) ***Owawiya*** feeke   pok-ap   ik-ok soomar-ek-eka.
       with   here.CF   sit-SS.SEQ be-SS walk-go-IMP.2p

       '(First) sit here with us and (then) go.'

(810) Iikir-ami   onak   ***owawik*** soomar-e-mik.
       get.up-SS.SIM 3s/p.mother with   walk-PA-1/3p

       'He got up and walked with his mother.'

The postposition *onaiya/onaria/onaiyik* may be based on the third person singular genitive pronoun *ona* and the clitic *-iya*; *onaiyik* also includes the root of the verb *ik-* 'be'. This postposition is more generic and can be used with noun phrases referring to people (811) but is also common when referring to things (812). When the relationship between the two noun phrases is unequal, *onaiya* may used, like in (813), where the other people carried the sick man. The subject marking on the verb is influenced by how active part the referents of the comitative noun phrase take in the action. When all the participants are active, the subject marking on the verb is plural. The speech in (814) was directed towards the villagers who were instructed to stay away from the Japanese troops.

(811) Mua unowa ***onaiya*** ikiw-e-mik.
       man many   with   go-PA-1/3p

       'We went with many people.'

(812) Urom(a) ***onaiya*** ik-ua.
       stomach with   be-PA.3s

       'She is/was pregnant.'

(813) Mua napuma ***onaiya*** Medebur ek-a-mik.
       man sick   with   Medebur go-PA-1/3p

       'They went to Medebur with the sick man.'

(814) No   ara   sepa ara   kia   ***onaiyik*** bilik   ar-i-nan=na   ...
       2s.UNM trunk black trunk white together mixed   become-Np-FU.2s=TP

       'If you, a black person, are together with the white people mixed with them ...'

3 Morphology

Another comitative postposition that mainly refers to things is *feekiya* 'with' (815)–(817). It originates from the combination of *feeke* 'here' and *-iya* 'comitative', but the meaning does not reflect the deictic origin of the initial part. In those rare cases when it is attached to a [+human] noun phrase, the referent of this NP is subordinate to the referent of the other NP and not in control, but still influencing the subject marking of the verb (816).

(815) *Mokok urupa kaik-i-man   nain **feekiya** baurar-eka.*
      eye   cup   tie-Np-PR.2p that1 with   flee-IMP.2p
      'Flee with your "eye cups" (a singsing decoration) still on.'

(816) *Wiamun   gelemuta pun aaw-ep   **feekiya** ikiw-e-mik.*
      3s/p.brother small   also take-SS.SEQ with   go-PA-1/3p
      'He took his little brother too, and went with him.'

(817) *Maa eliw akena nain aaw-ep   **feekiya** ikiw-o-k.*
      thing good very that1 take-SS.SEQ with   go-PA-3s
      'He took the very good thing and went with it.'

The DUAL comitative *ikos* 'with, together (with)' can only be used when two human participants are referred to (818). It can also occur alone, without a preceding noun phrase, when the participants are known from the person/number suffix in the verb, or from the context (819). The parties are considered equally active, so the verb is always in the plural.

(818) *Wekera   **ikos** irak-e-mik.*
      3s/p.sister with fight-PA-1/3p
      'He fought with his sister.'

(819) ***Ikos** ikiw-i-yen.*
      with go-Np-FU.1p
      'Let's go together (just the two of us).'

ASSOCIATIVE *ame* 'with others' is different from the comitative postpositions above in that only one of the parties is specified. The identity of 'the others' is left unspecified (820), (821).

(820) *Auwa   **ame** wia   maak-eya   res   aaw-ep   merena puuk-a-mik.*
      1s/p.father ASSOC 3p.ACC tell-2/3s.DS razor take-SS.SEQ leg   cut-PA-1/3p
      'He told my father and the others, and they took a razor and made a cut on his leg.'

(821) *Kuuten **ame**=ke   miim-e-mik.*
      Kuuten ASSOC=CF precede-PA-1/3p
      'Kuuten with (some) others went ahead of them.'

3.12.2 Reason postposition *muuta (nain)*

Muuta (nain) 'because of, for' gives a reason for an action, when the reason is expressed in a noun phrase rather than a full clause. It has developed from the adverb *muuta* 'a little, only', and in some cases the meaning 'only' is retained with the new function as well (822), (823). The distal-1 demonstrative *nain* 'that' is optional, and is left out especially when there is another demonstrative *nain* preceding *muuta* (824).

(822) Iiriw miiwa **muuta nain** irak-owa marew, oram momor
 earlier land for that1 fight-NMZ no(ne) just indiscriminately
 mauw-am-ik-e-mik.
 work-SS.SIM-be-PA-1/3p

 'Earlier there was no fighting for land, they just worked indiscriminately (on any land).'

(823) Yia amukar-owa **muuta nain** nan iiriw ifakim-e-mik.
 1p.ACC scold-NMZ for that1 there earlier kill-PA-1/3p

 'We killed her earlier (only) because she scolded us (lit: ...for her scolding of us).'

(824) Opora ara nain **muuta** ifakim-u na-ep on-a-mik.
 Talk section that1 for kill-IMP.1d say-SS.SEQ do-PA-1/3p

 '(Only) because of that talk they tried to kill him.'

3.12.3 Comparison postposition *saarik*

Saarik 'like' occurs with noun phrases (825) and with nominalized clauses (826). It indicates a point of similarity between two essentially DIFFERENT things.

(825) Mua eliwa **saarik** aakun-e-k.
 man good like speak-PA-3s

 'He spoke like a good man.'

(826) No sia on-owa **saarik** magimal puuk-a-n.
 2s.UNM netbag make-NMZ like vine.sp. cut-PA-2s

 'You cut *magimal* vine as if you were going to make a netbag.'

For the functional category of comparison, see §6.5.

3.12.4 Locative clitic *-pa*

The locative clitic *-pa* mainly marks locative in noun phrases (827). The most common verb that it collocates with is *ik-* 'be' (828). When it occurs with the directional verbs (§3.8.4.4.5), it often indicates source (829), but it can also be used for path (830), or for instrument in cases where it has a strong locative meaning as well (831). It is rarely used for goal (832); this is possible in cases where the goal is the location for an event taking place immediately.

3 Morphology

(827) *Pon piipa unowa=**pa** soomar-em-ik-eya mik-a-m.*
turtle seaweed many=LOC walk-ss.SIM-be-2/3s.DS spear-PA-1s
'The turtle was walking among the seaweeds and I speared it.'

(828) *Ona owowa=**pa** ik-eya epa wiim-o-k.*
3s.GEN village=LOC be-2/3s.DS place dawn-PA-3s
'When he was in his village it dawned.'

(829) *Ifa maneka=ke iinan=**pa** or-o-k.*
snake big=CF on.top=LOC descend-PA-3s
'A big snake dropped from above.'

(830) *Saa=**pa** ir-am-ika-i-mik.*
sand=LOC come/go-ss.SIM-be-Np-PR.1/3p
'They are coming on/along the beach.'

(831) *Miiw aasa=**pa** ikiw-e-mik.*
land canoe=LOC go-PA-1/3p
'We went by car/in a car.'

(832) *Mua nain ... eka kapa=**pa** ir-ap eka nain up-o-k.*
man that1 ... river top=LOC come/go-ss.SEQ river that1 block-PA-3s
'The man went to the top/source of the river and blocked the river.'

As temporal phrases locate an event in time, they also use the same locative clitic (833).

(833) *Fraide=**pa** maapora puk-o-k, urera.*
Friday=LOC celebration burst-PA-3s, afternoon.
'On Friday the celebration started, in the afternoon.'

It can also be used with an essive meaning, when referring to people's jobs (834):

(834) *Yena mua owowa ekap-o-k, amia mua=**pa** ik-ok.*
1s.GEN man village come-PA-3s bow man=LOC be-SS
'My husband came back to the village, having been a policeman.'

The locative clitic has its origin in the word *epa* 'place'; the transition vowel [e] can sometimes be heard between the clitic and its host, when the host word ends in a consonant (835).

(835) *Ne Sarak ikos Gawar=(e)**pa** ik-emkun yia maak-e-mik ...*
ADD Sarak with Gawar=LOC be-1s/p.DS 1p.ACC tell-PA-1/3p
'And as Sarak and I were in Gawar, they told us, ... '

3.12.5 Instrumental clitic -*iw*

The instrumental clitic -*iw* is used both for concrete (836) and abstract (837) instruments.[118]

(836) *Nomokowa galua-galua nain=iw   biiris on-am-ik-e-mik*
tree   soft-soft   that1=INST bridge make-SS.SIM-be-PA-1/3p
'They kept making bridges with soft timber.'

(837) ...*wiena opaimik=iw yia   maak-em-ik-e-mik.*
3p.GEN mouth=INST 1p.ACC tell-SS.SIM-be-PA-1/3p
'They talked to us in their language.'

It is also used for PATH and has the meaning 'along'; the verb indicates action that continues for some time (838).

(838) *Saa=iw   ir-am-ika-i-mik,*   ...
sand=INST ascend-SS.SIM-be-Np-PR.3p
'They are coming along the beach...'

The difference between (838) and (830) above is that in (830) the people were coming along the beach at least some of the way, and more specifically at the time of the speaking; whereas (838) indicates that they travelled along the beach more or less the whole way.

The instrumental may also be utilized to indicate MANNER (839)–(842):

(839) *Uurik   ona   naap=iw iw-ap   poka   aaw-e-mik.*
tomorrow place thus=INST go-SS.SEQ housepost get-PA-1/3p
'The following day they went in the same way and got houseposts.'

(840) *Karu-(o)w=iw ekap-o-k.*
run-NMZ=INST come-PA-3s
'He came running.'

(841) *Ne   ikoka maa   marew eliw manek=iw ika-i-nan.*
ADD later thing none well big=INST be-Np-FU.2s
'And later you will have no problems, you will just be very well.'

(842) *Waaya=ke anane wiar en-ow=iw   ika-i-ya.*
pig=CF   always 3.DAT eat-NMZ=INST be-Np-PR.3s
'A pig stays eating their (taro) all the time.'

Another usage is in those temporal phrases that refer to something taking place repeatedly at the same time (843):

---

[118] A less emphasized way to add an instrument is to use the chaining structure: 'take instrument do something' (682), (683).

(843) I   amirik=**iw**   ... Gawar wiar ikiw-e-mik.
       1p.UNM daytime=INST ... Gawar 3.DAT go-PA-1/3p

       'In the daytime we always went to Gawar ...'

3.12.6 Limiter -*iw*

The limiter clitic -*iw* 'only, just' is homophonous with the instrumental. The two probably are of common origin, but synchronically their meanings and positions in the word are distinct (§3.12.9). The limiter does not mark a case but restricts the applicability of the predication to the element that it is attached to (844), (845).

(844) [Maa eka]_{NP}=***iw*** en-ep   en-ep   lebum-ar-i-nan.
       food water=LIM eat-SS.SEQ eat-SS.SEQ lazy-INCH-Np-FU.2s

       'When you keep eating only food cooked with water you become tired of it.'

(845) Mua=***iw*** pok-aka.
       man=LIM sit-IMP.2p

       'Sit just among the men.'

The limiter clitic may attach itself to genitive and focal pronouns, resulting in restrictive pronouns (§3.5.7).

The free adverb *muutiw* 'only' is a combination of *muut(a)* 'only' and the limiter clitic -*iw* (§3.9.4).

3.12.7 Topic and focus markers

The topic and focus markers indicate the discourse function of the noun phrases that they are attached to.

3.12.7.1 Topic markers

Of the two topic markers *ena* is fairly low in frequency, and the description given here is only tentative. It seems that *ena* as an independent word originally had a topic marking function, but later the topic clitic -*(e)na* developed from it and is now used for highlighted topic (§9.2.4) in main clauses. *Ena* still marks a topic, but mainly in relative clauses. It often has a specifying function as well: 'the/that (particular one)' (846).

(846) [***Mua ena*** ma-e-k   nain] makena yos.
       man SPEC say-PA-3s that1 true   1s.FC

       'The man that he talked about is I.'

In long relative clauses, where it is attached to the RELNP, it helps to distinguish it from all the other NPs in the clause (847), (848).

3.12 Postpositions and clitics

(847) [***Mua papako ena*** Australia=ke wia aaw-ep wiena feekiya
man other SPEC Australia=CF 3p.ACC take-SS.SEQ 3p.GEN with
yiaw-e-mik nain] me epa fan irak-owa uruf-a-mik ...
walk.around-PA-1/3p that1 not place here fight-NMZ see-PA-1/3p

'Those other (particular) men whom the Australians took and with whom they walked around did not see the war here in this place ...'

(848) [*I* mua owowa=pa ik-ok ***ena*** irakowa uruf-a-mik nain] nanar nain
1p.UNM man village=LOC be-SS SPEC fight-NMZ see-PA-1/3p that1 story that1
yo fan ma-i-yem.
1s.UNM here say-Np-PR.1s

'I am telling the story of us (particular) people who stayed in the village and saw the fighting.'

If the head noun of the NP is is recoverable from the context, it may be deleted, leaving behind only *ena*. In (849) the head noun *epira* 'bowl(s)' has been omitted.

(849) [*Aakisa fan **ena** maneka wu-a-mik nain*] eliw, wie wi eliw wiar
now here SPEC big put-PA-1/3p that1 well 3s/p.uncle 3p.UNM well 3.DAT
op-i-kuan.
grab-Np-FU.3p

'Those big (bowls) that we put just now, all right, the uncles may take those from them.'

The example (850), taken from Bible translation, has a highlighted topic marker *-na* on the sentence-initial topic NP, which is part of the main clause, and *ena* inside the relative clause:

(850) *Ni Samaria=na* [*o **ena** me baliwep amis-ar-e-man nain*]$_{RC}$ *lotu*
2p.UNM Samaria=TP 3s.UNM SPEC not well knowledge-INCH that1 worship
on-i-man.
do-Np-PR.2p

'You Samaritans worship [the one that you do not know well].'

Without *ena* in the relative clause the sentence would mean 'You Samaritans do not know him well but (still) worship him.'

The more common topic clitic *-(e)na*[119] is used to highlight a changed topic, to which attention is drawn. The topic may have been introduced in the immediately preceding clause. The use of this device is infrequent in texts. It can often be glossed with 'as for X'. Highlighted topics are discussed in §9.2.4.

Example (851) is from a traditional story, where a man has gone hunting and the spirit of his lover comes to his home. When the wife sees her, she knows what the spirit woman has come to look for and comments:

---

[119] The clitic has mostly lost the phoneme /e/, but it can sometimes be heard when the host word ends in a voiceless consonant.

3 Morphology

(851) Nena mua=**na** urema   osarena ikiw-o-k.
       2s.GEN man=TP bandicoot path   go-PA-3s
       '(As for) your husband, he went to catch bandicoots.'

In (852) the answer to the question reveals the identity of the person asked about; the topic marker may be used even in a short exchange like this but especially if the text continues to tell more about the topic.

(852) Mua nain naareke? Mua nain=**na** owow   saria   maneka=ke.
       Man that1 who.CF man that1=TP village headman big=CF
       'Who is that man? -That man is the big village headman.'

In (853) the speaker changes the topic to the addressee after a discussion on something else:

(853) Nos=**na**?
       2s.FC=TP
       '(So,) what about you?'

An important function for the topic marker -na is to mark conditional clauses (854), (855) (§8.3.5). This is a common function for topic markers in Papuan languages (Haiman 1978; Reesink 1983a, 1987: 242; Foley 1986: 203).

(854) Opora wiar ika-i-ya=**na**   eliw urup-ep   wia   maak-uk.
       talk 3.DAT be-Np-PR.3s=TP well ascend-SS.SEQ 3p.ACC tell-IMP.3p
       'If they have something to say, they can get up and tell them.'

(855) O   emeria aaw-owa kookal-ek-a-k=**na** iw-ek-a-mik.
       3s.UNM woman get-NMZ like-CNTF-PA-3s=TP give.him-CNTF-PA-1/3p
       'If he had liked to get a wife, they would have given him one.'

It is also used in adversative subordinate clauses (§8.3.4) when the main clause expresses a frustrated effort or a cancelled expectation (856), or surprise.

(856) Ikiw-ep   mukuna nain umuk-a-mik=**na**   me pepek.
       go-SS.SEQ fire   that1 extinguish-PA-1/3p=TP not enough/able
       'We went and (tried to) extinguish the fire, but couldn't.'

3.12.7.2 Focus clitics

There are two focus clitics, the CONTRASTIVE FOCUS marker -(e)ke and the neutral focus marker -ko, which has developed from the indefinite oko 'a certain, other'.[120] The main candidate for the contrastive focus marker is the subject of a noun phrase (857). When the object is fronted as a theme (§9.1), the subject usually gets the contrastive focus marking to distinguish it from the object (858).

---

[120] Most of this section is based on Järvinen (1988b:81–96).

(857) *Iiriw ifa marasin=**ke** kekan-e-k.*
earlier snake poison=CF be.strong-PA-3s
'The snake poison had already taken effect.'

(858) *Episowa ifa nain atua=**ke** en-e-k.*
tobacco leaf that1 worm=CF eat-PA-3s
'The tobacco leaves were eaten by worms.'

Another possible host is the non-verbal predicate of a verbless clause (859) (§5.6).

(859) *Iperuma nain me enim-eka, inasin mua=**ke**.*
eel that1 not eat-IMP.2p spirit man=CF
'Do not eat that eel, it is a spirit man.'

There are a few isolated cases where it occurs on some other contrasted element of a clause (860).

(860) *Amirika=**ke** eliw ika-i-yem, uura=**ke** napum-ar-i-yem.*
noon=CF well be-Np-PR.1s night=CF sickness-INCH-Np-PR.1s
'At noon I'm well, at night I am sick.'

Contrastive focus as a pragmatic device in a text is discussed in §9.3.1.

The NEUTRAL FOCUS clitic *-ko* mostly occurs in irrealis-type clauses:[121] questions (861), commands (862), negative clauses (863), or those with future tense (864). Unlike the contrastive focus marker, the neutral focus marker can be attached to almost any element of a clause except the final verb. Neutral focus as a textual device is discussed further in §9.3.2.

(861) *Mukuna=**ko** op-a-man=i?*
fire=NF hold-PA-2p=QM
'Did you hold any fire?'

(862) *Mua nain=**ko** onak-e!*
man that1=NF give.to.eat-IMP.2s
'Give it to that man to eat!'

(863) *Oposia en-e-man nain yo=**ko** me uruf-a-m.*
meat eat-PA-2p that1 1s.UNM=NF not see-PA-1s
'I didn't (even) see the meat that you ate.'

(864) *Akim-ap=**ko** uruf-i-yen.*
try-SS.SEQ=NF see-Np-FU.1p
'We'll try and see.'

---

[121] Because of this, it was called *Irrealis focus clitic* in Järvinen (1988b).

3 Morphology

3.12.8 Question marker

The question marker -*i* is a sentential clitic, used to form polar questions, and it attaches itself to the clause-final verb (865) or another clause-final element (866). Its relationship to the alternative connective *e* 'or' (§3.11.2) is unclear; it is possible that *i* was originally an alternative connective but was also employed as a question marker and became so established in this function that a new alternative connective *e* developed. It is not uncommon in TNG Madang languages that the question marker and the alternative connective are either the same or closely related.[122]

(865) Sira nain piipua-i-nan=**i**?
       habit that1 leave-Np-FU.2s=QM
       'Will you give up that habit?'

(866) Nobonob ikiw-e-man nain, owowa eliwa=**i**?
       Nobonob go-PA-2p   that1 village good=QM
       'You went to Nobonob, is it a good village?'

The question marker can also be used in statements, when two or more ALTERNATIVES are given (867):

(867) Mua kuisow manina erup=**i** (e) arow=**i**   (e) naap.
       man one   garden two=QM (or) three=QM (or) thus
       'A man can have two gardens, or three, like that.'

3.12.9 Co-occurrence of the clitics

It is possible to have two or more clitics attached to the same word; only the topic marker does not allow other clitics with it. A case marking clitic, forming a constituent with the preceding noun phrase, is placed first. Next comes the focus clitic (868), with the scope over a phrase but not forming a constituent. The limiter -*iw* may have a phrase with the focus marking in its scope, so it follows the focus marker. When the limiter follows another clitic, there is a transition consonant <r>between the clitics (869), (870). The modal clitic -*yon* 'perhaps' (§3.9.3) may have a scope over a whole predication, so its position is after the limiter (871). The sentential clitic, with a scope over the whole sentence, comes last. When the contrastive focus marker -*ke* and the question marker -*i* are adjacent, they become a portmanteau clitic -*ki* (872).

(868) Fura=**iw**=**ko** me puuk-a-mik.
       knife=INST=NF not cut-PA-1/3p
       'They didn't cut it with a knife.'

---

[122] In Usan and Amele the alternative connector and the question marker are the same (Reesink 1987: 293, Roberts 1987: 99). Maia has -*i* 'QM' and *e* 'or' like Mauwake (Hardin 2002: 83,159). Bargam has borrowed the Tok Pisin *o* as an alternative connector but has retained the clitic -*e* as the question marker (Hepner 2002: 53,122). Kobon may use the alternative interrogative connector *aka* 'or' sentence-finally in leading polar questions, where the speaker expects the addressee to agree with the proposition.

(869) *Fikera=**pa**-r=**iw**   fiirim-eka.*
kunai.grass=LOC-Ø=LIM gather-IMP.2p
'Gather them right at the *kunai* grass.'

(870) *Os=**ke**-r=**iw**   maa en-emi   ewur-ar-e-k.*
3s.FC=CF-Ø=LIM food eat-SS.SIM haste-INCH-PA-3s
'Only he rushed with his food.'

(871) *Wi   anim onoma pun o   makena Krais=ke*
3p.UNM blade basis   also 3s.UNM truly   Christ=CF
*na-i-mik=**yon**=i?*
say-Np-PR.1/3p=perhaps=QM
'Are also the authorities perhaps saying that he truly is Christ?'

(872) *Mua fain Saror muuka=**ki**?*
man this Saror son=CF.QM
'Is this man Saror's son?'

3.13 Interjections

There are a lot of interjections in Mauwake; the following Table 3.54 is not even nearly exhaustive. The pronunciation of interjections may differ from that of other words: intonational variations are greater, and lengthening, even extreme lengthening, of the final vowel is common. Interjections are not part of the normal clause structure, and they usually occur either sentence-initially or finally (873)–(877). Some can also be placed between clauses in a coordinate sentence (878). The glosses given in Table 3.54 for the interjections are just rough approximations.

(873) ***Aa**, kema=ko kir-ek-a-n   **aa**!*
oh liver=NF turn-CNTF-PA-2s oh
'Oh, if only you had changed your ways (lit: turned your liver)!'

(874) ***Arika**, takira, yo   yook-eka.*
let's.go boy   1s.UNM follow.me-IMP.2p
'Alright boys, follow me (and will get going).'

(875) *Laman tapala wu-a-k,   **aiyoo**!*
Laman hat   put-PA-3s INTJ
'My goodness, Laman put a hat on (and exposed himself and us to the fighter pilots)!'

(876) ***Emawa**, nena   niawi   um-o-k.*
sorry   2s.GEN 2s/p.father die-PA-3s
'Sorry, your father is dead.'

3 Morphology

Table 3.54: Interjections

a		impatience, also used as a filler
aa	'oh'	emphasizes what has been said
ae	'yes'	agreement[a]
aiyoo		distress, disapproval
arika[b]	'OK, let's go'	exhorting others to get going
awue	'wow'	any strong emotion, surprise
ee		delight
ei	'hey!'	being surprised or startled
emawa	'sorry'	expression of empathy, especially grief or pity
emawik	'excuse me'	speech opening in a controversial situation
faa		disgust or astonishment
maa senam	'watch out!'	grave warning (lit: 'thing too.much')
oo	'o'	calling someone
oo [*oo??*]	'yes'	agreement
na		strengthens an imperative
nii?	'really? oh?'	response to hearing something surprising
nom	'please'	when repeating a request or command
noma	'oh dear'	
sa, se		impatience, disapproval
se-ek	'wow'	great happiness
wiisak	'sorry'	mild regret, for minor losses
yaa		impatience
yee	'oh'	recognition, emphasis
yii	'eek', 'oh'	ear, sorrow

[a] The negators *weetak* and *wia* 'no' also function as interjections but are not listed here, because they have other functions as well (see §3.10 and §6.2).
[b] This is obviously an imperative derived from the discourse-marker *aria* (§3.9.1), as it is only used with second person plural, whereas *aria* is used with all other persons. Elsewhere *aria* has no verb-like qualities.

(877) *Naap ma-emi om-em-ika-i-nan,* **na.**
thus say-SS.SIM cry-SS.SIM-be-Np-FU.2s INTJ
'You must cry saying like that.'

(878) *Yo damol-al-e-m* **oo**, *fiker fufa iw-a-m* **oo**.
1s.UNM bad-INCH-PA-1s oh kunai.grass old.grass enter-PA-1s oh
'Oh, I'm in a bad way, I am hiding among the grass.'

(879) *Ni kaaneke ik-e-man* **oo**, *ni ekap-omak-eka* **oh**
2p.UNM where be-PA-2p oh 2p.UNM come-DISTR/PL-IMP.2p oo!
'O where are you? – come!'

(880) *Yii, ifa=ke yee!*
Eek snake=CF INTJ
'Eek, that's a snake oh!

4 Phrase level syntax

4.1 Noun phrase

The noun phrase in Mauwake functions as subject, object or non-verbal predicate in a clause. It can also function as a head in an adverbial phrase, or as a possessor, qualifier or post-modifier in another noun phrase.

4.1.1 Basic noun phrase

The most common noun phrase structure consists of the head noun only. That is slightly more frequent than a head noun plus one or more attributive elements. The head noun may have either pre- or postmodifiers, or both. The relative order of the NP constituents is as follows:[1]

(1) Unmarked/Genitive pronoun – Temporal phrase – Possessive NP – Genitive pronoun – Qualifying NP – HEAD NOUN – Modifying NP – Adjective phrase^n – Quantifier phrase^n / Indefinite – Demonstrative – Dative pronoun

The relative clause, in which the head noun is modified by an entire clause, is discussed in §8.3.1.

The order of NP constituents following the head noun agrees with a cross-linguistic generalization of SOV languages: noun-adjective-numeral-demonstrative (Dryer 2007b: 112).

Theoretically it is possible, and grammatically correct, to have a NP like the one in (2), but natural language data seldom has any NPs with more than two modifiers. Example (3) is one of those.

(2) *auwa   ona   mera   sia maala erup nain*
    1s/p.father 3s.GEN fish   net long   two that1
    POSSNP   GENPR QUALNP HN AP   QP DEM

   'my father's two long fish nets' / 'the/those two long fish nets of my father'

(3) *iiriw   Naawura miiw-aasa awona nain*
    earlier Naawura land-canoe old   that1
    TMPP   POSSNP   HN   AP   DEM

   'the/that earlier truck of Naawura's'

---

[1] The superscript ^{n} indicates that it is possible to have more than one of these constituents within a single NP.

(4) *yiena iiriw kae sira nain*
1p.GEN earlier 1s/p.grandfather custom that1
'that traditional custom of ours'

The only modifier in a noun phrase is most typically either a possessor (5), a deictic (6) or a qualifying noun or noun phrase. The qualifying noun in (7) is a compound noun.

(5) *ona siowa*
3s.GEN dog
'his/her dog'

(6) *ifa nain*
snake that1
'the/that snake'

(7) *owow(a) maneka mua*
village big man
'townsman'

In the following, each NP position is discussed in turn, starting with the leftmost one.

An UNMARKED THIRD PERSON PLURAL PRONOUN is used as an optional plural marking for humans and other human-like beings in (8) and (9).

(8) **Wi** *sawur=ke kuura puuk-a-mik.*
3p.UNM spirit=CF fly change.into-PA-1/3p
'The spirits changed into flies.'

(9) *Ne nan* **wi** *owow mua wia maak-e-mik, ...*
ADD there 3p.ACC village man 3p.ACC tell-PA-1/3p
'And there they told the village men, ...'

The plural-marking pronoun differs from the appositive use (10) of the unmarked pronoun in that the former is unstressed, whereas the latter is stressed. Furthermore, the appositive use is not restricted to the third person plural pronoun. (For appositional NPs, see §4.1.4.)

(10) *'Yo nena niawi=ke nefa maak-i-yem.*
1s.UNM 2s.GEN 2s/p.father=CF 2s.ACC tell-Np-PR.1s
'I, your father, tell you...'

A special case of the plural-marking unmarked pronoun is its occurrence in connection with a place name to refer to the people of that place (11). The head noun *mua* 'men, people' or *emeria mua* 'people' is not needed. It may be used, but is usually left out.

(11) **Wi**   Lasen=ke ekap-e–mik.
    1p.UNM Lasen=CF come-PA-1/3p
    'The Lasen (village) people came.'

A TEMPORAL PHRASE is rare as a NP constituent. It is mainly the temporal words *aakis* 'present-day' from *aakisa* 'now, today' (12) and *iiriw* 'earlier' (13) that are used. A temporal phrase is also allowed but uncommon.

(12) ni   **aakis**   takira
    2p.UNM present-day young.person
    'you young people of today'

(13) wi   [*iiriw akena*] mua
    3p.UNM earlier truly   man
    'the people of long ago'

The structure of the two pre-modifying NPS, possessive NP and qualifying NP, is similar to that of the basic NP. It is because of their position and function inside another NP that they are named differently here.

The head noun of a POSSESSIVE np can only be [+human], with 'human' including spirits (14) and sometimes some domestic animals like dogs or pigs (15). The humanness of the POSSNP is stressed by the fact that it may be followed by a pronoun copy in the genitive (14).

(14) **sawur emeria** ona   onak   wiawi
    spirit   woman 3s.GEN 3s/p.mother 3s/p.father
    'the spirit woman's parents'

(15) **siowa** wiawi
    dog   3s/p.father
    'the dog's owner'

The head noun of the POSSNP may itself be possessed (16), (17):

(16) **yiena kae**   sira
    1p.GEN 1s/p.grandfather custom
    'our ancestors' (lit: grandfathers') custom'

(17) *i*   emeria apura yiena   mua weria   emeria nain=ke
    1p.UNM   woman widow 1p.GEN   man planting.stick woman that1=CF
    [Poss NP   [Poss NP   [HN]]] Dem
    'the wives of the "weria-men"[2] of us widows'

---

[2] The *weria*-men are relatives responsible for a person's burial. For more information see §1.3.6.

4 Phrase level syntax

The semantic relation of the "possessor" to the "possessed" may be that of real ownership, paraphrasable with 'have' (18), a human relationship (14), origin (16) or subjecthood (19).

(18) ona   koora
      3s.GEN house
      'his house'

(19) takira niir-owa
      youth play-NMZ
      'young people's play(ing)'

Either an unmarked pronoun or a genitive pronoun may be used as a POSSESSIVE PRONOUN (20). Often the two can be used interchangeably, but the following rules and tendencies have been observed. First, when the pronoun is a pronoun copy of a preceding possessive NP, it must be in the genitive (21).

(20) **Ona** apura maa oposia me enim-i-non.
      3s.GEN widow thing meat not eat-Np-FU.3s
      'His widow will not eat meat.'

(21) sawur emeria **ona** onak   wiawi
      spirit woman 3s.GEN 3s/p.mother 3s/p.father
      'the spirit woman's parents'

Second, an unmarked pronoun is used especially with things that are closely related to a person (22), whereas the genitive pronoun tends to be used more when the ownership is emphasized (23).

(22) Oo, **no** emeria iiriw   sesek-a-mik.
      Oh 2s.UNM woman already send-PA-1/3p
      'Oh, we already sent your wife away.'

(23) Nep(a) opaimika me amis(a)-ar-ep   **wiena opaimik(a)**=iw yia
      bird   talk   not knowledge-INCH-SS.SEQ 3p.GEN talk=INST   1p.ACC
      maak-em-ik-e-mik.
      tell-SS.SIM-be-PA-1/3p
      'They did not know Tok Pisin and talked to us in their (own) language.'

Third, an unmarked pronoun used possessively often receives extra stress in speech (24).

(24) Nain '**i**   sira=ke.
      that1 1p.UNM custom=CF
      'That is our custom.'

4.1 Noun phrase

In recursive genitive structures like (17), more than one possessive pronoun may occur as a pronoun copy, so (25) is a possible alternative for (17):

(25) i emeria apura **yiena** mua weria **wiena** emeria nain=ke
1p.UNM woman widow 1p.GEN man planting.stick 3p.GEN woman that1=CF
'the wives of the "weria-relatives" of us widows'

A QUALIFYING NOUN PHRASE usually consists of the head noun only (26)–(28). If it has other elements, the structure is that of the basic noun phrase. The distinction between a qualifying NP and a possessive NP on the one hand, and between a qualifying NP and a N+N compound on the other, is often hard to make. (See §3.2.5 for a discussion on the distinction between compound nouns and NPs.) Unlike a possessive NP, a qualifying NP may not take a genitive pronoun copy.

(26) **Fiker(a)** epia nain aw-i-non.
kunai.grass fire that1 burn-Np-FU.3s
'The grass fire will burn.'

(27) **Mua** takira unowa ne **emeria** wiip-takira=ke me unowa akena.
man youth many ADD woman daughter-youth=CF not many very
'There are many young boys but not very many young girls.'

(28) Epa kokom-ar-eya urera **siowa** mua ookinon.
place dark-INCH-2/3s.DS afternoon dog man follow-Np-FU.3s
'When it gets dark in the afternoon he will follow the "dog man" (a certain nominated person in the *singsing* traditions).'

A place name may be a qualifier for a locative noun functioning as head noun (29), (30).

(29) **Bogia** era
Bogia road
'the Bogia road'

(30) **Malala** owowa
Malala village
'Malala village'

The qualifying NP can also be a nominalized clause. This is most common when the head noun is an abstract noun like *sira* 'custom' (31) or *opora* 'talk, story'.

(31) [garanga oko muuka wiar aaw-owa]_{NP} sira
family other son 3.DAT get-NMZ custom
'adoption custom (lit: the custom of getting a son from another family)'

4 Phrase level syntax

The HEAD NOUN is either a single or a compound noun. If the head noun is replaced by a pronoun, it can only take post-modifiers (32):

(32) **wi(am)** arow nain
 3p.UNM(REFL) three that1
 'the three of them / those three'

A POST-MODIFYING NOUN PHRASE often expresses qualities that in many European languages would be expressed by true adjectives (33), or via adjectivalized (34) or comitative expressions (35).

(33) labuel(a) **mua**
 pawpaw man
 'male pawpaw'

(34) takira **emin(a) kekanowa**
 boy occiput strong
 'pig-headed boy'

(35) mua **bug maala** nain
 man wind long that1
 'the man with good lungs'

A noun phrase can have one or more ADJECTIVE PHRASES as modifiers. The adjective phrase typically consists of an adjective only. If there are more APs than one, the order is as follows: colour - physical property or human propensity - size/age - value (36).

(36) Waa(ya) muuka **kia gelemuta** op-a-m.
 pig son white small catch-PA-1s
 'I caught a small white piglet.'

In recorded texts the maximum number of adjective phrases per NP is two, but the speakers have no difficulty producing NPs with more APs (37):

(37) Emer(a) **itita enum(a) eliwa** nain enak-e.
 sago soft new good that1 feed.me-IMP.2s
 'Give me the good new soft sago/bread to eat.'

The position of either a QUANTIFIER PHRASE or an INDEFINITE is after the adjective phrase (38).

(38) Siowa morena **oko** aruf-a-k.
 dog male another hit-PA-3s
 'He hit another male dog.'

The last regular post-modifier in a noun phrase is a DEMONSTRATIVE. Especially the distal demonstrative *nain* 'that' is very common (39), and in many cases it is no more than a marker for given information.

(39) koora erepam **nain**
 house four that1
 'the/those four houses' or 'the fourth house'

The DATIVE PRONOUN (§3.5.5) is unusual as a modifier. Semantically, it belongs to the noun phrase, marking a possessive relationship, but syntactically it still reflects its origin as a [+human] locative adverbial (§4.6.1) of the verb. It is often non-contiguous with the rest of the NP, which can be fronted for a theme while the dative pronoun needs to stay in its pre-verbal position (41). Other elements that can separate the dative pronoun from the rest of the NP are *me* 'not' (42), and the free adverbs *muutiw* 'only' and *pun* 'also' (43).

(40) Owow emeria mua unowa **sira** eliwa wiar uruf-ap ...
 village woman man many custom good 3.DAT see-SS.SEQ ...
 'The many villagers saw his good manners and ...'

(41) **Pina gelemuta** eliw owowa=pa **nefar** kaken-ami welaw-i-kuan.
 guilt small well village=LOC 2S.DAT straighten-SS.SIM finish-NP-FU.3p
 'Your small guilt they can well straighten and finish in the village.'

(42) **Amina fain** me **wiar** op-aka.
 pot this not 3.DAT hold-IMP.2p
 'Don't hold/touch these pots of hers.'

(43) Yo miira me uruf-a-m, afifa muutiw **wiar** uruf-a-m.
 1s.UNM face not see-PA-1s hair only 3.DAT see-PA-1s
 'I didn't see the face, I only saw his hair.'

4.1.2 Coordinate noun phrase

Joining noun phrases into a coordinate noun phrase can be done either by simple juxtaposition or with connectives. Juxtaposition is the default strategy (44), (45). In spoken texts the juxtaposed noun phrases are separated by a longer pause, in written texts by a comma.

(44) **Amina, wiowa, eka napia** koor miira=pa iimar-ow-a-mik.
 pot spear, water bamboo house face=LOC stand-CAUS-PA-1/3p
 'We placed the pots, spears and water bamboos in front of the house.'

(45) I **mua unowa, emeria papako** ikiw-e-mik.
 1s.UNM man many woman some go-PA-1/3p
 'Many men (including the narrator) and some women went.'

4 Phrase level syntax

The pragmatic connective *ne* 'additive' (§3.11.1) is used rather infrequently to connect the parts of a coordinate noun phrase (46). When it is used, and when there are more than two noun phrases to connect, it is usually placed between the last two noun phrases (47), but other positions are possible too, see (3.776).

(46) Nie   **ne** neke   nomokow fiira=ke.
     2s/p.maternal.uncle ADD 2s/p.grandfather tree root=CF

  'Your maternal uncle and your grandfather are the most important relatives.'

(47) Mera kas,   mulamul **ne** popotimaw aaw-i-mik.
     fish mackerel trevally.sp ADD trevally.sp get-Np-PR.1/3p

  'We catch mackerel, *mulamul* trevally and *popotimaw* trevally.'

A focus clitic (48) or a case marking clitic (49) is only added to the last noun phrase in a coordinate noun phrase.

(48) Manin koora nain **koka ne** *ifara=ke* wakesim-o-k.
     garden house that1 jungle ADD vine=CF cover-PA-3s

  'The garden house was covered by jungle and vines.'

(49) **Wiena merena ne wapen=iw** era akup-a-mik.
     3p.GEN foot ADD hand=INST road search-PA-1/3p

  'They felt (lit: searched) for the road with their feet and hands.'

The pragmatic connective *aria* 'alright', too, can occasionally join the elements of a coordinate noun phrase (50), (51). As a sentential or clausal connective it indicates a break in the discourse, but when it joins two noun phrases there does not seem to be a significant difference between that and *ne* 'additive.' It may be that *aria* draws more attention to the separate noun phrases being joined than either juxtaposition or *ne* does.

(50) Yos, yena auwa,   **aria** wi   emer en-ow(a) mua kuisow ikiw-e-mik.
     1s.FC 1s.GEN 1s/p.father alright 3p.UNM sago eat-NMZ man one go-PA-1/3p

  'I, my father, and one Sepik man went.'

(51) Moma, **aria** emera naap lawisiw eeyar-e-k.
     taro, alright sago thus rather last-PA-3s

  'Taro, and sago, lasted a little (longer).'

The disjunctive connective *e* 'or' (52) (§3.11.2), and/or the question marker *-i* (53) is used in a coordinate noun phrase if the noun phrases are presented as alternatives.

(52) Mera aaw-owa sira   **e** era ikur okaiwi=pa   kuisow ik-ua.
     fish get-NMZ custom or way five other.side=LOC one be-PA.3s

  'There are six means, or ways, of catching fish.'

(53) Maa oposia=**i** moma, emera, naap sesek-a-mik.
     thing meat=QM taro   sago thus sell-PA-1/3p

  'They sold meat, or taro, (or) sago, (things) like that.'

4.1.3 Comitative noun phrase

A comitative noun phrase is made up of one or two basic noun phrases plus a comitative postposition or clitic (§3.12.1). A comitative pronoun (§3.5.9) can also form a comitative phrase either by itself or attached to a NP (54)–(56). When there is only one overt noun phrase and if it is unmarked for number, the plurality is shown both by the comitative marking and in the verb person marking (57). The choice of the comitative marker and the number marking in the verb, when relevant, reflect whether the noun phrases in the comitative relationship are co-subjects/co-objects of the same verb (58), or whether one is a dominant member (59).

(54) *Ikoka **mua owawiya** irak-ep me efar kerer-e.*
     later man with   fight-ss.seq not 1s.dat appear-imp.2s
     'Later when you fight with your husband, do not come to me.'

(55) ***Wi**   Yaapan oos   onaiya Madang ikiw-e-mik.*
     3p.unm Japan horse with   Madang go-pa-1/3p
     'The Japanese went with horses to Madang.'

(56) *Parosifa siisim-ep   **muuka feekiya** sesek-i-nen.*
     letter   write-ss.seq son   with   send-Np-fu.1s
     'I will write a letter and send it with my son.'

(57) ***Ona**   siowa ikos* manina ikiw-e-mik, ...
     3s.gen dog   with garden go-pa-1/3p
     'He went to the garden with his dog, ...' or: 'He and his dog went to the garden, ...'

(58) *Rabaul kemena=pa naap pok-ap   ik-e-mik, **mua=iya emeria**.*
     Rabaul bay=loc   thus sit-ss.seq be-pa-1/3p man=com woman
     'They are now sitting in the Rabaul bay, the husband and/with the wife.'

(59) ***Wiamiya** irak-owa na-ep   ikiw-e-mik.*
     3p.com   fight-nmz say-ss.seq go-pa-1/3p
     'We went to fight with them.'

With the dual comitative postposition *ikos* there may be an additive connective *ne* between the two noun phrases (60). It seems to be more common with younger speakers.

(60) ***Osaiwa**   *ne aalbok*   *ikos womar   wiam op-a-mik.*
     bird.of.paradise add black.cuckoo.shrike with 3s/p.friend 3p.refl hold-pa-1/3p
     'The bird of paradise and/with the black cuckoo-shrike were friends.'

4 Phrase level syntax

4.1.4 Appositional noun phrase

An appositional noun phrase consists of two noun phrases which have identical or similar reference (Crystal 1997: 24). Very commonly, the first noun phrase is either a personal pronoun (61) or a kinship term (62), (65), the second one a proper name, but there are other possibilities as well (63), (64).

(61) Yo   nena nie=ke   nefa   maak-i-yem.
     1s.UNM 2s.GEN 2s/p.uncle 2s.ACC tell-Np-PR.1s
     'I, your uncle, am telling you this.'

(62) **Yena yaiya   Tup** ifa=ke   keraw-a-k.
     1s.GEN 1s/p.uncle Tup snake=CF bite-PA-3s
     'My Uncle Tup was bitten by a snake.'

(63) **Inasina Rubaruba nain=ke** ona   emeria aaw-ep   p-ikiw-o-k.
     spirit   Rubaruba that1=CF 3s.GEN woman take-SS.SEQ BPX-go-PA-3s
     'The spirit Rubaruba took his wife and went.'

(64) **Manina gelemuta, esewa,** nena   kookal-owa=pa perek-i-nan.
     garden small   esewa 2s.GEN like-NMZ=LOC   pull.out-Np-FU.2s
     'You may harvest the little garden, "esewa", at your desire.'

(65) Wokome=ke   **wiimasip**   oko, **suwina gelemuta nain** maak-e-k ...
     3s/p.grandmother=CF 3s/p.grandchild other female small   that tell-PA-3s
     'The grandmother told her other grandchild, the little girl ...'

4.2 Adjective phrase

The head of an adjective phrase (AP) is an adjective. Most commonly it occurs alone, but it can be intensified by an intensity adverb either preceding or following it, or both (66). The negator *marew* 'none, no' when following the adjective, negates its quality, thus creating its opposite (67).

(66) Owowa nain **lawiliw manek(a) akena**.
     village that1 rather   big   very
     'The village is rather big'

(67) Koora **eliw(a) marew** nan   ik-e-mik.
     house good   none   there be-PA-1/3p
     'They live in the bad (lit: no-good) house.'

When the adjective *masia* 'bitter' takes a nominalized verb as its modifier, the meaning of the adjective changes to indicate that one is doing a lot of some action (68).

(68) Mua **manin(a) mauw-ow(a) masia** nain emeria wi-i-mik.
man garden work-NMZ compulsive that1 woman give.him-Np-PR.1/3p

'We give a wife to a hard-working man.'

The adjective phrase functions as a post-modifier in a noun phrase (67), or as a non-verbal predicate (66).

A coordinate adjective phrase is also possible (69). The additive *ne* is used instead of juxtaposition.

(69) Oka keraw-a-k nain **efefa ne eliwa akena**.
hand.drum carve-PA-3s that1 light ADD good very

'The hand drum that he carved is light and very good.'

The pragmatic function of adjectives in discourse[3] seems to vary according to the language. In Mauwake, the modification of a new participant is the main function of adjective phrases.[4] Also, a known participant is modified by an adjective especially in cases where the adjective is needed for contrast: *manin(a) maneka* 'big garden' and *manin(a) gelemuta* 'small garden', referring to two different TYPES of garden (also called *ekina* and *esewa*, respectively), were repeated several times in a text describing garden work.

4.3 Quantifier phrase

A quantifier phrase (QP) usually only consists of a quantifier head (70) (§3.4), but it can be modified by a few intensity adverbs (71) (§3.9.2).

(70) I koora **kuisow** yiar aw-o-k.
1p.UNM house one 1p.DAT burn-PA-3s

'One of our houses burned.'

(71) Koora **arow akena** ku-a-mik.
house three truly build-PA-1/3p

'We built exactly three houses.'

A quantifier phrase most commonly functions as a post-modifier in a noun phrase (72), but it can also be used as a non-verbal predicate (73).

---

[3] For the function of adjectives in English and Mandarin Chinese spoken text see Thompson (1988) and Croft (1991). The former claims their main function is to predicate the property of an established discourse referent; attributive function, or modification, is secondary and used almost exclusively for new participants. Croft, however, considers modification the main discourse function of the adjectives. As for Papuan languages, Roberts reports that in Amele the adjective normally functions as a modifying (lit: attributive) element in a NP (1987: 318).

[4] In the text data nearly half of the occurrences (48%) of adjectives were in attributive positions where the adjective modified a *new* participant.

4 *Phrase level syntax*

(72) *Maamuma **unowa akena**   aaw-e-mik.*
money   much truly/very get-PA-1/3p
'They got very much money.'

(73) *Yo   muuka **arow**.*
1s.UNM son   three.
'I have three sons.' (Lit: 'My sons are three.)

Quantifier phrases may also be coordinated. The most plausible coordination semantically is disjunction (74):

(74) *Waaya maneka wiowa **erup-i** **e** **arow** naap mik-iwkin   um-i-ya.*
pig   big   spear two=QM or three thus spear-2/3p.DS die-Np-PR.3s
'They spear a big pig with two or three spears and it dies.'

4.4 Possessive phrase

The possessive phrase[5] is a very specific and rare structure (75). It consists of an unmarked or genitive pronoun, followed by the long form of the dative pronoun (§3.5.5), which has developed from the dative pronoun and the verb *ik-* 'be'. The verb has lost all inflection and only retains the root, which has merged into the dative pronoun. The possessive phrase only functions as a non-verbal predicate. It is always without a head noun. A co-referential noun or pronoun is encoded in an earlier NP in the same clause.

(75) *Auwa maa unowa nain pun **yo/yena**   **efarik**.*
father thing many that1 also 1s.UNM/1s.GEN 1s.DAT
'My father's possessions, too, are mine.'

4.5 Verb phrase

There is no justification in Mauwake for a verb phrase as it is understood in the generative sense, i.e. as a constituent including almost everything else than the subject of the sentence.[6] But there is one structure that can be called a verb phrase: an accusative pronoun plus a verb. In this structure, nothing can come between the two elements, not even a verbal negation, which is usually placed immediately before the verb.

Every transitive verb requires an accusative pronoun for a [+human] object, regardless of whether there is an object noun phrase or not (76)–(79). The accusative pronoun is also required, when the verb is in benefactive form and the beneficiary is plural (80).

---

[5] Not to be confused with the Possessive NP.
[6] The verb phrases in the traditional sense of the word, a group of verbs functioning as one unit, are treated under verbal clusters (§3.8.5).

(76) *Nan wi   owow mua **wia**   maak-e-mik*, ...
there 3p.UNM village man 3p.ACC tell-PA-1/3p

'There they told the village men, ... '

(77) ***Nefa war-iwkin**   naap ma-e.*
2s.ACC shoot-2/3p.DS thus say-IMP.2s

'When they shoot you, say like that.'

(78) *Mua me **wia**   imen-a-mik.*
man not 3p.ACC find-PA-1/3p

'We did not find the men.'

(79) *Yaapan=ke i   emeria **yia**   aaw-urum-i-kuan.*
Japan=CF 1p.UNM woman 1p.ACC take-DISTR/A-Np-FU.3p

'Japan will take all of us women.'

(80) *Takira enow gelemuta **wia**   on-om-a-mik.*
child meal small   3p.ACC make-BEN-BNFY2-PA-1/3p

'We made a feast for the children.'

4.6 Adverbial phrases

An adverbial phrase may consist of an adverb word alone, or it may be modified by an intensity adverb, a noun phrase plus a clitic or a postposition, or a dative pronoun functioning as a [+human] locative phrase.

The main function of an adverbial phrase is to modify the verb. An ADVP is an optional constituent in a clause, not an obligatory argument.

The default position of the adverbial phrase depends on the semantic type of the ADVP. Recursion is possible, and is more common in the case of locative and temporal phrases than the others.

4.6.1 Locative phrases

The number of locative adverbs is small (§3.6.3). Most locative phrases are made up of a noun phrase plus a clitic if they indicate a location, source or path, and of a noun phrase only if they indicate a goal. Givón (1984: 78, 110–112) distinguishes between the locative adverbials and the locative objects of certain verbs. The former have the whole clause in their scope, the latter only the verb. While there is this scope difference between the two, they are syntactically similar in Mauwake.

The locative adverbs (§3.6.3), all of which are deictic, occur by themselves, without modifiers (81)–(83). The same form can be used for location, source, or goal, depending on the verb.

4 *Phrase level syntax*

(81) *Miiw-aasa **nan** ik-eya mua nain nabena suuw-a-mik.*
land-canoe there be-2/3s.DS man that1 carrying.pole push-PA-1/3p
'The car stayed there, and they carried the man on their shoulders.'

(82) *Fura op-ap ik-o-n nain **feeke** wu-e.*
knife hold-ss.SEQ be-PA-2s that1 here.CF put-IMP.2s
'Put here the knife that you are holding.'

(83) *Manin(a) onoma maa en-owa **nan** aaw-i-ya.*
garden basis thing eat-NMZ there get-Np-PR.3s
'An owner of a garden (lit: the garden basis) gets his food from there.'

When the locative phrase is based on a noun phrase, one form is used both for a location where something takes place and a source, but a goal is marked differently. The phrases indicating a location are formed by adding the locative clitic -*pa* to a noun phrase (84)–(86).

(84) *Pon **sisina=pa** ik-eya mik-a-m.*
turtle shallow.water=LOC be-2/3s.DS spear-PA-1s
'The turtle was in shallow water and I speared it.'

(85) ***Sapara=pa** nan suusa iw-e-mik.*
Sapara=LOC there needle give.him-PA-1/3p
'There in Sapara he was given an injection.'

(86) *Nomokowa unowa serer-iw-ap **Takora=pa** nan or-o-mik.*
tree many hang-go-ss.SEQ Takora=LOC there descend-PA-1/3p
'They went hanging to many trees, and at Takora they got down.'

Source is also marked as a location, with the clitic -*pa* (87)–(89). In some cases there is possible ambiguity as to the interpretation, but the context usually provides a clue.

(87) *Parosifa siisim-ep **iinan aasa=pa** wafur-a-mik.*
paper write-ss.SEQ sky canoe=LOC throw-PA-1/3p
'They wrote papers and threw them from airplanes.'

(88) *Aite=ke **manina=pa** yia aaw-om-iwkin enim-i-mik.*
1s/p.mother=CF garden=LOC 1p.ACC get-BEN-1s/p.DS eat-Np-PR.1/3p
'Our mothers get (it) from the garden for us and we eat (it).'

(89) *Me fan **Madang kame=pa** ekap-e-mik.*
not here Madang side=LOC come-PA-1/3p
'They didn't come here from the Madang side.'

4.6 Adverbial phrases

The noun phrase indicating a goal normally does not take the locative clitic or any other marking. The directional verbs are the most common ones used with goal (90), (91), but other verbs of motion can be used as well (92), (93).

(90) Ae, o **fiker gone** urup-o-k.
yes 3s.UNM kunai.grass middle ascend-PA-3s
'Yes, he went up to the middle of the *kunai* grass area.'

(91) [*Manina=pa nan*]_{Source} [**koka**]_{Goal} iw-a-mik.
garden=LOC there   jungle   go-PA-1/3p
'From the garden there the day they went into the jungle.'

(92) **Medebur** karu-eka, baurar-eka.
Medebur run-IMP.2p flee-IMP.2p
'Run to Medebur, flee!'

(93) **Ulingan nan** bom fu-fuurk-ikiw-e-mik.
Ulingan there bomb RDP-throw-go-PA-1/3p
'They went throwing bombs to Ulingan.'

It is possible to mark the goal with the locative clitic if the goal is mainly important as the location of the following verb. The frequency of this usage for the clitic is low. Example (3.588) is repeated below as (94):

(94) Ne soran-emi **epia mukuna=pa** or-omi   aw-o-k.
ADD get.startled firewood fire=LOC   descend-ss.SIM burn-PA-3s
'And he got startled and fell on the fire and burned himself.'

When the locative phrase is [+human], the dative pronoun (§3.5.5) must be used (95), (96).

(95) Mua oko=ke waaya nain mik-ap **nefar** aaw-i-non.
man other=CF pig   that1 spear-ss.SEQ 2s.DAT take-Np-FU.3s
'Another man will spear the pig and take it from you.'

(96) Feeke **wiar** ik-ok kiiriw mua **wiar** urup-e.
here.CF 3.DAT be-ss again man 3.DAT ascend-IMP.2s
'Stay here with him and (then) go (back) to your husband again.'

The dative pronoun is also commonly added when the location is a village or a larger area, which is seen mainly as a setting for the people. In both (92) and (93) above it is the LOCATION which is in focus, in the former as the closest village to flee to, and in the latter as an object of bombing, so the dative pronoun is not used. In (97) a certain culturally important place referred to is in the area of the Koran village people and considered their property:

(97) *Koran epa=pa* **wiar** *ik-ua.*
Koran place=LOC 3.DAT be-PA.3s

'It is in Koran area.'

The noun phrase indicating a path is marked with the instrumental clitic *-iw* (98), (99), or occasionally with the locative clitic *-pa* (3.830).

(98) **Iinan=iw** **iinan=iw** *wu-ami feenap ... ikiw-o-k.*
on.top=INST on.top=INST putss.SIM like.this ... go-PA-3s

'They (airplanes) flew (lit: put) high up, high up, and went like this...'

(99) **Saa=iw** *ir-am-ika-i-mik,* *oos ono-onaiya.*
sand=INST ascend-ss.SIM-be-Np-PR.1/3p, horse RDP-with

'They are coming along the beach, with horses.'

When a clause has more locative phrases than one, the following rules apply. If the phrases have a different function, source is placed before goal (91). When they have the same function and a deictic locative adverb strengthens another locative phrase, the adverb follows the other locative (85), (93). But the dative pronoun, when used locatively, has to be placed even after the locative adverb (96). When both of the phrases have an independent meaning, the phrase indicating the more general location comes first, and the one marking the more specific location follows (100), (101).

(100) *Mia aka nain aaw-ep p-ikiw-ep* **manina=pa upuna=pa** *wu-a-k.*
body blood that1 take-ss.SEQ BPX-go-ss.SEQ garden=LOC row=LOC put-PA-3s

'She took the menstrual blood with her and put it in a (plant) row in a garden.'

(101) *Ikiw-ep* **eeneke wiena owowa=pa** *uruf-a-mik, ...*
go-ss.SEQ there 3p.GEN village=LOC see-PA-1/3p

'They went and there, in their village, they saw, ...'

4.6.2 Temporal phrase

Temporals mark location in time, so it is natural that temporal phrases behave very similarly to locative phrases. They can consist of a temporal adverb (§3.9.1.2), possibly modified by an intensity adverb (§3.9.2) or of a noun phrase (§4.1) with a head noun indicating time (102), plus a locative clitic with some nouns (103) (§3.12.4).

(102) **Uuriw akena** *mukuna nain kerer-e-k.*
morning truly/very fire that1 appear-PA-3s

'The fire started early in the morning.'

(103) *Ne* **fraide=pa** *maapora puk-o-k,* **urera.**
ADD Friday=LOC feast burst-PA-3s afternoon

'And on Friday the feast started, in the afternoon.'

4.6 Adverbial phrases

Recursion of temporal phrases is possible and quite common. When there are two or more temporal phrases in the same clause, the order is determined by whether the temporals are deictic and/or specific (105)–(108) (§3.9.1.2). Their default order relative to each other is as follows:

(104) *(non-deictic non-specific) > deictic non-specific > deictic specific > TempNP (day) > non-deictic specific > TempNP (time of day) > (non-deictic non-specific)*

The position of the non-deictic non-specific temporal is either as the first (105) or the last element (108) of the group of temporals.

(105) Ne **nainiw sande uura** yiam fiirim-e-mik.
ADD again Sunday night 1p.REFL gather-PA-1/3p
'And we gathered again on Sunday night.'

(106) **Uurika mande uuriw** amia mua feeke kerer-i-non.
tomorrow Monday morning bow man here.CF appear-Np-FU.3s
'Tomorrow Monday a policeman will come here in the morning.'

(107) **Unan urera ama ikur naap** on-a-mik.
yesterday afternoon sun five thus do-PA-1/3p
'We did it yesterday afternoon around five o'clock.'

(108) **Ikoka trinde=pa nainiw** aakun-i-yen.
later Wednesday=LOC again talk-Np-FU.1p
'We'll talk again later on Wednesday.'

When a noun phrase acts as a temporal phrase, the locative clitic *-pa* is attached to it (108), unless it is followed by another temporal phrase specifying it further or it includes a demonstrative (106). If there are several of these temporal noun phrases, their relative order is from the larger time unit to the smaller one (109).

(109) **Mokoma fain siiwa Mas=pa** weeser-i-non.
year this month March=LOC finish-Np-FU.3s
'It will finish in March this year.'

A temporal phrase may be formed with the instrumental clitic *-iw* (§3.12.5) when something takes place repeatedly at the same time of the day. The example (3.843) is here repeated as (110):

(110) I **amirik=iw** ... Gawar wiar ikiw-e-mik.
1p.UNM daytime=INST ... Gawar 3.DAT go-PA-1/3p
'In the daytime we (always) went to Gawar ...'

4.6.3 Manner phrase

An adverbial phrase indicating manner most often consists of just a manner adverb (111) (§3.9.1.3). That is occasionally intensified by an intensity adverb (112), (113)(§3.9.2).

(111) *Iwera   nainiw **kaken** iimar-e-k.*
coconut again   straight stand.up-PA-3s
'The coconut palm stood up straight again.'

(112) *Koran wiena **balisow akena**   epa   nain amis-ar-e-mik.*
Koran 3p.GEN well   truly/very place that1 knowledge-INCH-PA-1/3p
'The Koran people themselves know that place very well.'

(113) *O   iiwawun samor aaw-o-k.*
3p.UNM altogether badly get-PA-3s
'He got it really bad (= he got into a very bad condition).'

A manner phrase can also be formed by a noun phrase plus a clitic, either instrumental *-iw* (114) or, less frequently, with locative *-pa* (115).

(114) *Siowa wiawi=ke siowa aluowa miim-ap   **karu-(o)w(a)=iw** ekap-o-k.*
dog   3s/p.father dog   noise hear-SS.SEQ run-NMZ=INST   come-PA-3s
'The dog's master heard its noise and came running.'

(115) ***Yiena kae   sira=pa**   mauw-owa ik-ua.*
1p.GEN grandfather custom=LOC work-NMZ be-PA.3s
'We have to work according to the custom of our grandfathers.'

If there are more manner phrases than one, one of them is usually deictic *naap* 'thus, like that' (116), or *feenap* 'like this' either preceding or following the other manner phrase(s).

(116) *Wi   Yaapan **naap kuisow=iw** ekap-em-ik-e-mik.*
3p.UNM Japan thus one=INST come-SS.SIM-be-PA-1/3p
'The Japanese came like that one by one.'

When comparison is indicated in the manner phrase, the postposition *saarik* 'like, as' follows the noun phrase (117).

(117) *Wie,   wiawi   nain **ifa   saarik** in-urum-ep-ik-e-mik.*
3s/p.uncle 3s/p.father that1 snake like   sleep-DISTR/A-SS.SEQ-be-PA-1/3s
'His uncles and fathers were all sleeping like snakes.'

One type of a manner phrase is one that indicates instrument. It is always formed with a noun phrase plus one of three clitics: instrumental *-iw* (§3.12.5), locative *-pa* (§3.12.4) or comitative *-iya* (§3.12.1). The instrumental clitic is the most common (118), (119).

4.6 Adverbial phrases

(118) *Ifa mia nain **fura=iw** lalat-em-ik-om-a-mik.*
snake skin that1 knife=INST sweep-SS.SIM-be-BEN-BNFY2.PA-1/3p
'They kept scraping the snake skin off her with a knife.'

(119) *...**wiena opaimik=iw** yia maak-em-ik-e-mik.*
...3p.GEN mouth/language=INST 1p.ACC tell-SS.SIM-be-PA-1/3p
'...they kept telling us in their language.'

When a coordinate noun phrase is made into an instrumental manner phrase, the instrumental clitic only follows the last noun phrase (120).

(120) ***Wiena merena ne wapen=iw*** *era akup-amik.*
3p.GEN foot ADD hand=INST way search-PA-1/3p
'With their feet and hands they felt (lit: searched) for the road.'

The use of locative clitic is restricted almost exclusively to those cases where the instrument is a vehicle (121), so they could also be understood as locatives. In other cases it is used rarely (122).

(121) *Yo iiriw **iinan aasa=pa** karu-owa erup ar-ep me keker*
1s.UNM earlier sky canoe=LOC run-NMZ two become-SS.SEQ not fear
op-a-m.
hold-PA-1s
'I had already travelled by plane twice, and was not afraid.'

(122) ***Sureka=pa*** *owora nain teek-ap aaw-e-mik.*
harvesting.stick=LOC betelnut that1 pluck-SS.SEQ get-PA-1/3p
'They picked the betelnuts with a harvesting stick.'

The comitative clitic is also possible but infrequent in instrumental manner phrases (123). Its use in this function may be influenced by Tok Pisin, where *wantaim* 'together (with)' is used not only for accompaniment, but for instruments as well.

(123) *Mauwa ar-e-n, **amia=iya** nenar-e-mik=i?*
what become-PA-2s bow/gun=COM shoot.you-PA-1/3p=QM
'What happened to you, did they shoot you with a gun?'

In Mauwake texts, manner phrases are much less frequent than either locative or temporal phrases.

5 Clause

A clause,[1] or simple sentence, typically expresses one predication and is a minimal utterance that can stand alone.

In Mauwake the predicate is the only obligatory element in those clauses that have a verbal predicate. Verbless clauses need to have both an overt subject and a predicate. The different clause types are discussed in §§5.3–5.6.

Instead of the common two-way distinction between main and subordinate clauses, in Trans New Guinea languages it is practical to talk about main, medial and subordinate clauses. Main clauses have a finite verb, and most commonly it is the last element in a sentence. Medial clauses (§8.2.1) are coordinate with the main clauses but dependent on them, and the verbs are in medial form (§3.8.3.5). The default position for a medial clause is non-final, but for pragmatic purposes it may be postposed to follow the main clause. Also a subordinate clause (§8.3) usually precedes the main clause.

5.1 Order of constituents

Two seemingly conflicting statements about the clausal constituent order in Papuan languages have been given by Wurm (1982) and Foley (1986). Wurm (1982: 64) maintains that they have a rigid SOV order; Foley (1986: 167) claims that the order in most Papuan languages is relatively free, and therefore he prefers to call them just verb-final (ibid. 10). But it seems that the two linguists are talking about somewhat different things, and both of them are correct in what they say. The DEFAULT constituent order in neutral sentences is SOV, as Wurm claims, but Foley is right in that the INTERPRETATION of the arguments of a verb as subject or object does not rely heavily on the constituent order. Especially in languages with extensive verb morphology marking the syntactic roles on the verb itself the order of the nominals can be relatively free, and is mainly constrained by pragmatic factors.

The basic constituent order in Mauwake clauses is quite rigid SOV, even if the verb morphology cross-references the syntactic roles to some extent. Although only a fraction of the clauses in the text corpus – less than 10% – have an overt subject and object NP it is possible to establish the dominant order. About nine out of ten of those clauses that do have an overt subject and object NP manifest SOV order.[2] They are also pragmatically

---

[1] I use the separate terms *clause* and *sentence* to avoid confusion. A simple sentence consists of just one clause, but most of the sentences in Mauwake have more than one clause in either coordinate, chaining or subordinate relationship.

[2] SOV: 210 clauses, OSV: 22 clauses

5 Clause

neutral (1), whereas the other possible order, OSV, only occurs when the object is fronted as a theme (2).

(1) [Owow mua]$_S$ [kau kuisow]$_O$ aaw-e-mik.
    village man   cow one   get-PA-1/3p
    'The village men got one cow.'

(2) [Yena aamun]$_O$ [ariwa=ke]$_S$ aaw-o-k.
    1s.POSS 1s/p.younger.sibling arrow=CF   get-PA-3s
    'My younger brother was killed by an arrow.'

As was described in §1.4.2.2, Mauwake exhibits many typological characteristics associated with SOV languages.

The basic constituent order is always based on the structure of a transitive clause. Intransitive clauses (§5.4) do not have objects, but otherwise the structure is the same as that in the transitive clauses. The structure of other types of clause is described in the relevant sections.

The constituent order in an extended predication is harder to establish, because a clause typically has very few constituents, the average being only 1.2 non-verb constituents per clause; because any non-verbal element can be fronted as topic; and because the subject is often shown only by a verbal suffix and the object by an accusative pronoun in the VP. A clause formula for a maximally extended predication is hypothetical, and mainly shows the order of the constituents on the basis of their attested orders in relation to each other:

(3) $S\ X_1\ O_1\ X_2\ O_2\ X_3\ V$

There are two object positions[3] and three X-positions for adverbial phrases. Depending on the grammatical model, the adverbial phrases may be called peripherals, obliques, satellites or adjuncts. I call them *peripherals* and reserve the term *adjunct* for the non-verb part of an adjunct plus verb construction. If a clause has only one object, it occupies the O$_2$ position immediately preceding the verb regardless of whether the semantic function is that of a patient, a recipient or a beneficiary. When there are two objects, their position is dictated mainly by their relative topicality. A [+human] argument tends to be more topical than a [-human] one, so an object that is semantically a recipient (4), (5), or a beneficiary (6), typically occupies the first object position, and the other object, typically a [-human] patient, fills the second object position.

(4) [Muuka]$_{O1}$ [sira]$_{O2}$ iw-i-mik.
    son   custom   give.him-Np-PR.1/3p
    'They teach the right behaviour to the son.'

(5) Sarak=ke [wi   takira]$_{O1}$ [inglis]$_{O2}$ [wia]$_{O1}$ ofakow-i-ya.[4]
    Sarak=CF 3p.UNM child   English   3p.ACC   teach-Np-PR.3s
    'Sarak teaches the children English.'

---

[3] The two objects are discussed further in the next sections §5.2 and §5.3.

(6) Ni   [auwa]$_{O1}$ [maa]$_{O2}$ p-ikiw-om-aka.
    2p.UNM 1s/p.father food   BPX-go-BEN-BNFY2.IMP.2p
    'Take food to/for father.'

If a [-human] patient object is more topical than a [+human] object, it can occupy the first object position. A more topical [+human] object in (7) would have an unmarked third person plural pronoun before the [-human] object.[5]

(7) Onak=ke   [aaya]$_{O1}$ [wia]$_{O2}$ aaw-om-aya
    3s/p.mother sugarcane 3p.ACC get-BEN-BNFY2.2/3s
    enim-or-om-ik-e-mik.
    eat-descend-SS.SIM-be-PA-1/3p
    'Their mother got sugarcane for them and they went down eating it.'

If both the objects are [-human], the one that is more clearly the patient, i.e. more profoundly affected by the action, occupies the O$_2$ position (8). Usually the object in O$_1$ position has a more locative-type meaning (9).

(8) [Epira]$_{O1}$ [lolom]$_{O2}$ if-e-mik.
    plate   mud   smear-PA-1/3p
    'They smeared the plate with mud' or: 'They smeared mud on the plate.'

(9) [Wut   makena nain]$_{O1}$ [ona]$_{O2}$ puuk-a-m.
    Derris.root.tree seed that1   hole   cut-PA-1s
    'I cut a hole in the seed of a derris root tree.'

The normal position of the peripherals is between the subject and the object NP, if any (10), or between the first and second object (11).

(10) Yo   **uura** arua isim-ap   ...
     1s.UNM night torch light-SS.SEQ
     'I lighted a torch in the night and ...'

(11) [Wiipa   nain]$_{O1}$ [**samapora iinan=pa**]$_{AdvP}$ [epia]$_{O2}$ ururum-om-ap...
     daughter that   floor   top=LOC   fire   light-BEN-BNFY2.SS.SEQ
     'They lighted a fire for the daughter on top of the floor, and ...'

A locative adverbial can also come between an object NP and a verb. A deictic locative phrase (12) or another short locative phrase (13) is common in this position.

---

[4] Compare this with: *Sarak=ke inglis wia ofakowiya* 'Sarak teaches (them) English' and *Sarak=ke wi takira wia ofakowiya* 'Sarak teaches the children.' Both the recipient and the patient are coded in the same way as an object.

[5] More examples of can be found in §5.3.2.

5 Clause

(12) *Emer en-ow(a) mua=ko* [*emeria*]_O [***fan***]_{AdvP} *aaw-o-k.*
sago eat-NMZ man=NF woman here get-PA-3s
'A Sepik man got a wife here.'

(13) *Yo* [*maa unowa*]_O [***koora=pa***]_{AdvP} *wu-a-m.*
1s.UNM thing many house=LOC put-PA-1s
'I put (the) many things in the house.'

The position immediately before the verb is also the only possible place for a [+human] locative adverbial, manifested by a dative pronoun (§3.5.5). In both (14) and (15) there are two locative adverbials, a [-human] and a [+human] one. The [+human] locative adverbial refers to the people of the location. If it is left out, the other locative refers to the location but not the people.

(14) [*Ni* [*koka-pa*]_{AdvP} [***wiar***]_{AdvP} *in-em-ik-e-man nain*]_{RC}
2p.UNM jungle=LOC 3.DAT sleep-ss.SIM-be-PA-2p that1
kerer-omak-eka.
appear-DISTR/PL-IMP.2p
'You(pl.) who have slept in the jungle (villages), come!'

(15) *I amirk=iw* [*Gawar*]_{AdvP} [***wiar***]_{AdvP} *urup-e-mik.*
1p.UNM day=INST Gawar 3.DAT ascend-PA-1/3p
'During the day we went to Gawar.'

If there are more adverbial phrases than one, a temporal phrase normally precedes any others (16). The relative order of the other adverbial phrases is syntactically quite free and depends on their relative topicality (16), (17).

(16) *I **amirika owowa ewur** me ekap-em-ik-e-mik.*
1p.UNM day village quickly not come-ss.SIM-be-PA-1/3p
'In the daytime we didn't come quickly to the village.'

(17) *Niena **ikoka oram neeke** ika-i-non.*
2s/p.mother later for.nothing there.CF be-Np-FU.3s
'Your mother will later just be there (without you).'

(18) ***Mokoma kuisow naap fan** yiam=iya ik-e-mik.*
year one thus here 1p.REFL=COM be-PA-1/3p
'They were here with us for about a year.'

Both transitive (19) and intransitive clauses (20) are negated with the verbal negator *me* 'not' placed immediately before the verb phrase.[6]

---
[6] For the placement of *me* as a constituent negator, see §6.2.2.

(19) I   **me** wia amukar-e-mik.
      1p.UNM not 3.ACC scold-PA-1/3p
      'We didn't scold them.'

(20) Nain yo   **me** baurar-em-ik-e-m.
      but 1s.UNM not run.away-SS.SIM-be-PA-1s
      'But I didn't keep running away.'

As was mentioned above, pragmatic factors influence the constituent order. A constituent that is fronted as a theme to the beginning of the clause is still part of the constituent structure of the clause (21) (for theme, see §9.1).[7]

(21) [***Oposia gelemuta***]$_{O1}$ [wiam erup fain wia]$_{O2}$ wu-om-a-m.
      meat   little   3p.REFL two this 3p.ACC put-BEN-BNFY2.PA-1s
      'A bit of the meat I put (aside) for these two.'

A left-dislocated theme (§9.1) and an afterthought are outside the clause proper. A left-dislocated theme (22) is separated from the clause by a short pause and a comma intonation, slightly rising pitch at the end of the utterance. An afterthought (23), right-dislocated, is also separated from the rest of the clause by a short pause.

(22) ***Irak-owa fa***, opora unowa akena.
      fight-NMZ INTJ talk much very
      'The war, now - there is much to talk about.'

(23) Inasin opaimika eliwa me yia   maak-e-mik, **wi**   Yaapan=ke.
      spirit talk   good not 1p.ACC tell-PA-1/3p 3p.UNM Japan=CF
      'They didn't speak good Pidgin to us, the Japanese (didn't).'

5.2 Syntactic arguments

Syntactic arguments together with the verb form the core of a clause. They differ from the peripherals in that they have a grammatical relation to the verb (Foley & Van Valin 1984: 77–80), and therefore have to do with the valence of the clause. The basic syntactic structure is influenced by the arguments but not by the peripherals. In Mauwake the only syntactic arguments are subject and object.

Since Mauwake is very clearly a nominative-accusative type language, the grammatical role of SUBJECT and the semantic role of AGENT or ACTOR normally converge on the same constituent, which usually, but not always, also has the pragmatic role of TOPIC.

---

[7] In Amele the pre-verbal position is a focus position (Roberts 1987: 142), but in Mauwake this does not seem to be the case. Focus is indicated by a heavier stress and sometimes by focus markers.

Another semantic role the subject may have is that of EXPERIENCER, and in verbless clauses that of "THEME".[8]

The syntactic coding of the subject includes both the clausal constituent order and cross-referencing on the verb (24). In pragmatically neutral clauses the subject is the first of two argument noun phrases. It is also obligatorily marked on the person/number suffix of the verb. The same distinctions are made in the subject marking of the verb as in the personal pronouns: first, second or third person and singular or plural number.

(24) *Komori emeria wu-a-k.*
Komori woman put-PA-3s
'Komori buried his wife.'

The subject governs reflexivization. A noun phrase itself is marked as subject only when the subject NP is a pronoun: then it has to be unmarked (25) (§3.5.2.1) or in the genitive case (§3.5.4).

(25) *Tirinde uura i nainiw yiam fiirim-e-mik.*
Wednesday evening 1p.UNM again 1p.REFL gather-PA-1/3p
'On Wednesday evening we gathered again.'

The switch-reference system (§8.2.3) basically tracks the subject (26).[9]

(26) *...imen-ap maak-iwkin o miim-o-k.*
find-SS.SEQ tell-2/3p.DS 3s.UNM precede-PA-3s
'...when they found him and told him, he went ahead.'

In (27), the object/topic/theme of the first clause is the Australians; in the second clause they become the subject.

(27) *Wi Australia Amerika=ke wia asip-iwkin irak-owa nomak-e-mik.*
3p.UNM Australia America=CF 3p.ACC help-2/3p.DS fight-NMZ win-PA-1/3p
'Australians were helped by Americans and won the war.'

Syntactic operations like passivization and dative shift do not apply to Mauwake and consequently cannot be used to define either the subject or other syntactic arguments.

Although the prototypical subject is a [+human] agent, also an instrument that is unable to initiate an action can become a metaphorical agent, thus the subject (Givón 1984: 106). This is very common in expressions describing cases where one involuntarily hurts oneself with some instrument (28). (In the following example, there is also possessor raising (§5.3.2.3) resulting in two objects.)

---

[8] This semantic role "theme" is different from the pragmatic function (§9.1) and refers to the participant which is said to be in some state, or located in some place (Andrews 2007b: 140). Because of a possible confusion with the pragmatic role of theme, the term for the semantic role is written inside double quotes.

[9] Roberts maintains that in Amele and most other Papuan languages the switch reference system tracks the thematic notion of topic across clauses (1988: 105, 1997). But his definition of topic (1988: 16) is such that in Mauwake it practically excludes all other clause constituents except the subject.

(28)   [***Fura=ke***]$_S$ [*merena*]$_{O1}$ [*efa*]$_{O2}$ *puuk-a-k.*
       knife=CF   leg   1s.ACC   cut-PA-3s

   'I cut my leg / myself in the leg.' (Lit: 'A knife cut my leg.')

Because the subject is so often marked by only a verbal suffix, it would be possible to treat the subject marking on the verb as the real subject, as Van Valin & LaPolla (1997: 33–34) suggest for those languages that mark the core arguments on the verb. Although this approach would have some advantages,[10] I choose the more traditional way of treating the NP as the subject, both because 1) an object is not marked in the verb inflection but requires either a separate NP or an accusative pronoun outside the verb proper,[11] and because 2) the constituent order, based on the position of the subject and object NPs, has many interconnections with various parts of the syntax.

The OBJECT as a syntactic role is not coded on the verb word except in the few object cross-referencing verbs (§3.8.4.2.4). A [+human] object must be referenced by an accusative pronoun (§3.5.3) preceding the verb in the verb phrase (§4.5), even if the object is also expressed by a full noun phrase earlier in the clause (29). The position of the object NP in the argument structure of the clause is between the subject and the verb (30), but this syntactic definition is not very useful, as subject and object do not co-occur very often, and sometimes when they do, the object is fronted to the clause-initial theme position (31).

(29)   ***Emeria*** *naap* ***wia***   *aruf-i-nen*   *na-ep*   *on-a-k.*
       woman   thus 3p.ACC   hit-Np-FU.1s   say-SS.SEQ   do-PA-3s

   'He tried to hit women that way.'

(30)   *Amia mua=ke* ***wiam***   *erup nain* ***wia***   *nokar-e-k.*
       bow   man=CF 3p.REFL   two   that1 3p.ACC   ask-PA-3s

   'The policeman asked those two.'

(31)   ***Mua emeria muuka wiipa***   *eka=ke* ***wia***   *mu-o-k.*
       man woman son daughter   river=CF 3p.ACC   swallow-PA-3s

   'A man and his wife and children were drowned by the river.'

There is not enough basis in Mauwake for positing a separate syntactic category INDIRECT OBJECT. In many languages the most typical verb requiring an indirect object for the semantic role of recipient is 'give'. But in Mauwake the verbs 'give' and 'feed/give to eat' are among the few object cross-referencing verbs (§3.8.4.2.4), which change their stem according to the patient or recipient object. The verb 'send', another cross-linguistically typical verb taking an indirect object, in Mauwake requires the benefactive suffix on the verb (§3.8.4.3.2), rather than a marking on the NP. In (32) the verb *maak-* 'tell' has two objects, the patient object *moma* 'taro' and the recipient object *yia* 'us', which is marked by an accusative pronoun in the VP in the same way as a [+human] undergoer/patient.

---

[10] The main advantage would be having an overt subject in every clause, regardless of the presence of a separate subject NP.

[11] The small group of object cross-referencing verbs (§3.8.4.2.4) are an exception.

5 *Clause*

(32) Wi   [***moma***]ᴏ [***yia***]ᴏ *maak-i-mik.*
     3p.UNM taro   1p.ACC tell-Np-PR.1/3p
     'They are telling us (to get them) taro.'

This is consistent with Whitehead's (1981: 51) survey results showing that "a large number of [Papuan] languages ... do not differentiate between Patient and Recipient". Rather, there are verbs that are capable of taking two objects (ibid. 52).[12] Amele is one of those Papuan languages that clearly have indirect object as a syntactic category (Roberts 1987: 69).

It could be argued that a locative adverbial is an argument rather than a peripheral clause constituent with the directional verbs[13] (§3.8.4.4.5) and with the verb *ik-* 'be/live (somewhere)' (§3.8.4.4.1), as these verbs so often co-occur with a locative. But these verbs also occur without a locative so often that it would be both unnatural to interpret all of those instances as elliptical constructions and sometimes difficult to posit the "deleted" locative (33), (34).

(33) *Maak-e-mik, "No   ikiw-e,   irak-owa maneka fan-e-k   a."*
     tell-PA-1/3p 2s.UNM go-IMP.2s fight-NMZ big   here-PA-3s INTJ
     'They told him, "Go, the war is here."'

(34) *Iwera   uruk-am-ika-iwkin   wi   ikiw-emi aaw-em-ik-e-mik*   ...
     coconut drop-ss.SIM-be-2/3p.DS 3p.UNM go-ss.SIM get-ss.SIM-be-PA-1/3p
     'When they$_i$ kept dropping coconuts, they$_j$ kept going and getting them ...'

The verb *ik-* 'be' seldom occurs alone (35). This is probably due to its very neutral semantic character. When it denotes being or living somewhere, it is accompanied by a locative adverbial phrase (36). Another very common adverbial phrase accompanying the verb is a manner phrase, especially the adverb *naap* 'thus' (37). Rather than positing separate clause types with adverbials as arguments it seems reasonable to subsume clauses like these under intransitive clauses.

(35) *Ika-i-nen.*
     be-Np-FU.1s
     'I will just be like this.'

(36) *Siiwa erepam naap **nan** ik-ok napuma sariar-e-k.*
     moon four   thus there be-ss sickness heal-PA-3s
     'He was there about four months and his sickness was healed.'

---

[12] Usan behaves in the same way as Mauwake (Reesink 1987: 160).
[13] For Usan, where motion verbs have either the goal or locative as a nuclear argument, see Reesink (1987: 130).

(37)　*Komor(a) muuka nain memel-am-ik-emkun* **naap ik-ok** *iir oko uura*
　　　cuscus　son　that1　tame-ss.SIM-be-1s/P.DS　thus　be-ss　time　other　night
　　　baurar-e-k.
　　　escape-PA-3s

　　　'I was taming the cuscus and it was like that and then one night it escaped.'

5.3 Transitive clauses

Transitivity is an important characteristic of both a verb and a clause; which of these is primary has been an object of a great deal of discussion.[14] This may be language-specific. In languages like English where an intransitive verb like *sneeze* can be made transitive in a construction *He sneezed the napkin off the table* (Goldberg 1995: 9), it makes sense to say that the verb combines with a transitive argument structure construction (Goldberg 2006: 6). But in Mauwake it can be claimed that the transitivity of the verb is primary. The claim is supported by the clear distinction between transitive and intransitive verbs and the fact that transitive verbs often require a dummy object when there is no real object available.

Clauses are here looked at from the point of view of SYNTACTIC TRANSITIVITY: clauses that have an overt object are treated as transitive clauses, regardless of the semantic role of the object.

Linguistically the most interesting transitive clauses are those that have two or possibly even three objects. These can be divided into three different groups: clauses where a transitive verb can take more than one object without requiring any morphological or syntactic operation (§5.3.2.1) and those where an object has been added by a valence-increasing operation (§5.3.2.2) or by possessor raising (§5.3.2.3).

5.3.1 Monotransitive clauses

Monotransitive clauses have a transitive verb and one object, which is prototypically a patient (38), (39).

(38)　[*Sawur emeria nain=ke*]$_S$ [**ona soma mua nain**]$_O$ *ifakim-o-k.*
　　　spirit　woman　that1=CF　3s.GEN　lover　man　that1　kill-PA-3s

　　　'The spirit woman killed her lover.'

---

[14] In transformational grammar (EST) verbs had to be subcategorized in the lexicon according to whether they allowed a NP-object or not (Radford 1981: 120). Also Van Valin & LaPolla (1997: 147–157) consider transitivity essentially a characteristic of a verb, distinguishing between the semantic, syntactic and macrorole transitivity of each verb. Givón (1995: 76), Kittilä (2002: 25) and Dixon (2010a: 115), among others, maintain that transitivity is primarily a characteristic of a whole clause. Taking still another angle, Hopper and Hopper & Thompson (1980: 294) claim that transitivity is very closely bound with discourse features, namely background and foreground.

(39) Amirika [i]ₛ   [**maa eneka fain**]_O uup-ep   enim-i-yen.
     noon   1p.UNM thing tooth this cook-ss.SEQ eat-Np-FU.1p
     'At noon we'll cook and eat this (edible) animal.'

If there is only one NP argument in a transitive clause, it is usually the object rather than subject (40), unless marked with the contrastive focus marker -*ke* (41).

(40) [**Wiawi**]_O kuum-eya   aw-ep   eka iw-a-k=na   wia.
     3s/p.father burn-2/3.DS burn-ss.SEQ river go-PA-3s=TP no
     '(It) burned their father and when he burned he went into the river but it didn't help.'

(41) Ufer-iwkin   urup-em-ik-eya   [yos=ke]ₛ mik-a-m.
     miss-2/3p.DS ascend-ss.SIM-be-2/3s.DS 1s.FC=CF shoot-PA-1s
     'When they missed and it was going up, I shot it.'

But in (42) the contrastive focus marker is not needed to disambiguate the subject from the object: *wiam arow* 'the three of them' has to be the subject. If it were the object, it would require the third person plural accusative pronoun *wia* in the NP.

(42) [Ne wiam   arow]ₛ miim-ap   ...
     and 3p.REFL three hear-ss.SEQ
     'And the three of them heard it, and ...'

Clauses with an impersonal experience verb (§3.8.4.4.7) as the predicate are also transitive. The subject is inanimate, usually a body part where the pain is felt, and the human experiencer is the object (43), (44). The possibility of adding the contrastive focus clitic to the noun indicating a body part shows that it is the subject rather than a second object (43).

(43) Uuw-ap   uuw-ap   [oona=ke]ₛ [efa]_O sirir-i-ya.
     work-ss.SEQ work-ss.SEQ bone=CF   1s.ACC hurt-Np-3s
     'I have worked and worked, and my bones hurt (me).'

(44) Yo   [uroma]ₛ [efa]_O op-am-ik-eya   yo   haussik me ikiw-e-m.
     1s.UNM stomach 1s.ACC hold-ss.SIM-be-2/3s.DS 1s.UNM aidpost not go-PA-1s
     'I was having birth pains (lit: My stomach was holding/grabbing me) but I did not go to the aidpost.'

5.3.2 Ditransitive clauses

A number of ditransitive clauses (4)–(7) were already listed under §5.1. They belong to the three different groups below.

5.3.2.1 Inherent ditransitivity

Some ditransitive clauses are called inherently ditransitive, because they do not require a morphological or syntactic process to make them ditransitive. The most common verbs in ditransitive clauses of this type are the object cross-referencing verbs and the utterance verb *maak-* 'tell', and the verb *ofakow-* 'show, teach'.

The (recipient) object is marked in the verb root of the object cross-referencing verbs denoting giving and feeding (§3.8.4.2.4), but it may appear as a separate NP as well (45):

(45) [*Mua yiar   ekap-e-mik   nain*]$_O$ [*pura kui-kuisow*]$_O$ *wi-e-mik.*
       man 1p.DAT come-PA-1/3p that   bunch RDP-one   give.them-PA-1/3p

       'We gave a bunch each to the men who came to us.'

The section on utterance verbs (§3.8.4.4.6) describes in some detail how these verbs behave in clauses. *Maak-* 'tell' requires the addressee/recipient to be a [+human] obligatory object, and as a second object it often has a NP denoting the speech itself (46) or the contents of that speech (47).

(46) *I*   [*opora muut nain*]$_O$ [*nefa*]$_O$ *maak-u   na-ep   ep-a-mik.*
       1p.UNM talk   only thus   2s.ACC   tell-IMP.2d say-SS.SEQ come-PA-1/3p

       'We came wanting to tell you just that (talk).'

(47) *Wi*   [*moma*]$_O$ [*yia*]$_O$ *maak-i-mik,   moma=ko wi-i-yan.*
       3p.UNM taro   1p.ACC   tell-Np-PR.1/3p taro=NF give.them-Np-FU.1p

       'They tell us (to get them) taro, (so) we'll give them taro.'

Na- 'say, speak, call, think' most commonly has the quotation as a speech complement, but it may also have up to two nominal objects instead (48).

(48) [*Waaya*]$_O$ [*yia*]$_O$ *na-iwkin   waaya wienak-em-ik-e-mik.*
       pig   1p.ACC   say-2/3p.DS pig   feed.them-SS.SIM-be-PA-1/3p

       'They spoke about pigs to us and we kept giving them pigs to eat.'

There are a few verbs that are ordinary transitive verbs but which can take semantically different objects. It is also possible to have one of each kind in the same clause. The verb *if-* 'paint, spread' can have a patient or goal object; the sentence in example (49) includes both. Another such verb is *mik-* 'spear, hit' (57).

(49) [*Yena aasa*]$_O$ [*ofa*]$_O$ *if-e-m.*
       1s.GEN canoe   colour   paint-PA-1s

       'I painted my canoe with paint.' Or: 'I spread paint on my canoe.'

5 Clause

5.3.2.2 Derived ditransitivity

When the transitivity is increased by one of the valence-increasing strategies (§3.8.4.3), a recipient or beneficiary (50), (51) becomes a second object. The linear order of the two objects depends on their relative topicality.

(50) [*Moma pura oko*]$_O$ [*Kuuten*]$_O$ *amap-urup-om-a-mik.*
 taro bunch other Kuuten BPX-ascend-BEN-BNFY2.PA-1/3p
 'They took another bunch of taro up for Kuuten.'

(51) *Ne* [*mua nain*]$_O$ [*waaya*]$_O$ *mik-om-a-mik.*
 ADD man that1 pig spear-BEN-BNFY2.PA-1/3p
 'And they speared that man a pig.'

5.3.2.3 Possessor raising

There are also cases with two patient-type objects, either one of which could be the single patient of the same verb. One of these objects has resulted from possessor raising: the possessor of the initial object NP, which has to be a semantic patient, has been "raised" to become a second object (Van Valin & LaPolla 1997: 258; Payne 1997: 194–196). Especially when something is done to a body part (52) or name (53), or something closely identified with a person (54)–(56), both the person and the other noun occur as objects.

(52) [*Merena*]$_O$ [*efa*]$_O$ *keraw-a-k.*
 leg 1s.ACC bite-PA-3s
 'It bit me in the leg.' Or: 'It bit my leg.'

(53) [*No unuma*]$_O$ [*nefa*]$_O$ *faker-i-kuan.*
 2s.UNM name 2s.ACC raise-Np-FU.3p
 'They will praise (lit: raise) your name.'

(54) [*Opaimika*]$_O$ [*efa*]$_O$ *fien-a-man.*
 talk 1s.ACC push.aside-PA-2p
 'You disregarded/disobeyed my talk.'

(55) *Era=pa* [*ekera wiam erup*]$_{O1}$ [*kukusa*]$_{O2}$ [*wia*]$_{O1}$ *aaw-o-k.*
 way=LOC 1s/p.sister 3p.REFL erup picture 3p.ACC take-PA-3s
 'On the way he took a picture of my two sisters.'

(56) *Mua papako=ke* [*irak-owa*]$_O$ [*wia*]$_O$ *puuk-a-mik.*
 man some=CF fight-NMZ 3p.ACC cut-PA-1/3p
 'Some men$_i$ stopped their$_j$ fight.'

Even three objects are allowed, but this is rare (57): the verb *mik-* 'spear, hit' itself allows two different objects, and the third one is added via possessor raising. The objects have to be in this order. Note that in the English translation, only one direct object is allowed, and the other two phrases have to be either possessive or oblique.

(57) **[Keema-muuna, umakuna]**₀ **[meta]**₀ **[yia]**₀ **mik-i-mik.**
 knee-joint neck ritual.paste 1p.ACC hit-Np-PR.1/3p

'They stick the *meta* paste on our knees and necks' or: 'They mark our knees and necks with the *meta* paste.'

As the preferred clause structure in Mauwake is short and because it is harder to process a verb with many arguments, a common strategy is to divide the arguments between more than one clause, so that each clause has only one or two arguments (58).

(58) I dabuela aaw-ep Yaapan wi-em-ik-e-mik.
 1p.UNM pawpaw take-ss.SEQ Japan give.them-ss.SIM-be-PA-1/3p

'We took pawpaws and gave them to the Japanese' or: 'We gave pawpaws to the Japanese.'

Even if having more than one NP in non-subject argument or peripheral positions in the same clause is not preferred, it is still reasonably common. But having more than one pronoun as arguments or peripherals is unusual. In the rare case that that does happen, the accusative pronoun occupies the position closest to the verb (59), (60), next the dative pronoun (61), then the others. The first two of the following three examples have been elicited.

(59) Mua nain teeria muutiw **wame wia** ofakow-a-k.
 man that group only 3s.REFL 3p.ACC show-PA-3s

'He only showed himself to that man's group.'

(60) O **wiar nefa** sesek-i-yem.
 3s.UNM 3.DAT 2s.ACC send-Np-PR.1s

'I am sending you to him.'

(61) Emeria ikoka Yaapan **wiena niar** aaw-i-kuan
 woman later Japan 3p.GEN 2p.DAT take-Np-FU.3p

'Later the Japanese will take your wives as their own.'

5.4 Intransitive clauses

An intransitive clause in Mauwake is a verbal clause that does not have an object. It normally indicates an event of some kind (action or process), or a state. This differs from the definition used for typological studies of an intransitive predication consisting of "a one-place predicate and its argument" (Stassen 1997: 9) in that in Mauwake those predications that indicate some property or quality, or designate a class, are not treated as intransitive but as verbless clauses (§5.6). Any of the intransitive verbs (§3.8.4.2.1) can be the predicate in an intransitive clause, whereas a verbless clause characteristically has no verb. The only negation strategy for clauses with a verbal predicate is the negator *me* 'not', whereas verbless clauses have more negator options.

The following clauses (62)–(68) are typical intransitive clauses:

(62) *Epa wiim-eya   mua karer-omak-e-mik.*
place dawn-2/3s.DS man gather-DISTR/PL-PA-1/3p
'When it got light a lot of people gathered.'

(63) *O   koora=pa   naap ik-ok um-o-k.*
3s.UNM house=LOC thus be-SS die-PA-3s
'She was in the house like that and died.'

(64) *Uuriw   akena mukuna nain kerer-e-k.*
morning truly fire   that1 appear-PA-3s
'The fire started early in the morning.'

(65) *Iiwawun iwera   pun wiar aw-omak-e-k.*
altogether coconut also 3.DAT burn-DISTR/PL-PA-3s
'His many coconut trees too burned altogether.'

(66) *I   Sarak ikos owowa ekap-em-ik-e-mik.*
1p.UNM Sarak with village come-SS.SIM-be-PA-1/3p
'Sarak and I kept coming back to the village.'

(67) *Fikera   mamaiya=pa nan pok-ap   ik-e-mik.*
kunai.grass close=LOC   there sit-SS.SEQ be-PA-1/3p
'We were sitting near the *kunai* grass.'

(68) *Ne kiiriw miiw-aasa nan ik-eya   ...*
and again land-canoe there be-2/3s.DS
'And again the car was/stayed there, and ...'

Many climate expressions (69)–(71) are normal intransitive clauses.

(69) *Moram **ewar**   pun **wuun-e-k** ne ...*
why   west.wind too blow-PA-3s and
'Because wind blew too, and ...' Or: 'Because it was windy too, and ...'

(70) ***Ipia or-om-ik-eya***   owora   aaw-ep   up-o-k.
rain descend-SS.SIM-be-2/3s.DS betelnut take-SS.SEQ plant-PA-3s
'When it was raining he took betelnuts and planted them.'

(71) ***Epa kokom-ar-eya***   *in-e-mik.*
place dark-INCH-2/3s.DS sleep-PA-1/3p
'It became dark and we slept.'

5.5 Existential and possessive clauses

The resultative verbs (§3.8.4.4.4) require a nominal argument, i.e., a noun (73) or an adjective (72), expressing the result of change:

(72) Mua eneka, woosa **kia kir-em-ik-ua**.
 man tooth head white turn-ss.SIM-be-PA.3s
 'The people's teeth and skulls were turning white.'

(73) Arim-emi **emeria ar-e-k**.
 grow-ss.SIM woman become-PA-3s
 'She grew and became a woman.'

A few intransitive verbs can occur with a syntactic object or object-like element whose semantic role is not a patient. These differ from true patient objects in that the range of possible "objects" for those verbs is very restricted, they cannot be substituted with an accusative pronoun, and the verb cannot occur with the dummy object *maa* 'thing'. The first type can be called a "content object" (74) (Hakulinen & Karlsson 1979: 179):

(74) Wis pun wiisa uf-e-mik.
 3p.FC too wiisa dance-PA-1/3p
 'They, too, danced "wiisa".'

The second type is an object-like adverbial, as it functions in the same way as an adverbial phrase (75).

(75) Era maala soomar-e-mik.
 way long walk-PA-1/3p
 'We walked a long way.'

5.5 Existential and possessive clauses

Existential clauses and possessive clauses are distinguished from the intransitive clauses. Only the verb *ik-* 'be' is used as the predicate in both of them.

5.5.1 Existential clauses

Existential clauses are not very common in Mauwake. Givón (1990: 741) names these clauses as one of the main devices for introducing a new topic into a discourse, but in Mauwake they are not used very much in that function (§9.2.1). Existential clauses use the verb *ik-* 'be' as their predicate, and they often contain a locative phrase (76), but it is not necessary (77), (79).

(76) **Aaya=ko feeke ik-eya** nefa aaw-ep enim-i-yen.
 sugarcane=NF here.CF be-2/3s.DS 2s.ACC take-ss.SEQ eat-Np-FU.1p
 'If there is (any) sugarcane here, we'll take and eat you (the sugarcane).'

(77) Aakisa Malala suule ik-ua, …
      now   Malala school be-PA.3s
      'Now there is the Malala school, …'

Both the past (78) and future tense forms (79) can be used; the past tense may be used for both present and past meaning.

(78) Kuisow owowa=pa=ko me ik-ua.
      one   village=LOC=NF not be-PA.3s
      'There was/is not even one in the village.'

(79) Waaya ika-i-non-(na)   waaya uup-i-nan.
      pig   be-Np-FU.3s-(TP) pig   cook-Np-FU.2s
      'If there is a pig, you will cook a pig.'

When an existential clause of this type is negated with a negator other than *me*, it becomes a verbless clause (§5.6.3).

A special type of existential clause has one of the two location verbs (§3.8.4.4.3) as the predicate. These verbs are only used in the past tense, even with the present tense meaning (80), (81).

(80) Nomokowa unowa **fan-e-mik**, aakisa wia   uruf-i-n.
      2s/p.brother many here-PA-1/3p now   3p.ACC see-Np-PR.2s
      'Many of your brothers are here, now you see them.'

(81) No   niawi   akena **nan-e-k**, no   fain me nena niawi
      2s.UNM 2s/p.father real there-PA-3s   2s.UNM this not 2s.GEN 2s/p.father
      akena=ke.
      real=CF
      'Your real father is there, this isn't your real father.'

5.5.2 Possessive clauses

Possessive clauses, or so-called 'have' clauses, are formed with a dative pronoun and the verb *ik-* 'be' (82). This is a grammaticalization from [+human] locative constructions with the semantic function of goal or locative (Heine 1997: 50–61), as was already mentioned in §3.5.5.

The possessee is the patient-of-state subject, which is shown by the fact that it may take the contrastive focus clitic *-ke* (83) and it determines the person inflection on the verb as well (84). The possessor is a HABITIVE ADVERBIAL, like a corresponding construction in Finnish is called (Hakulinen & Karlsson 1979: 209). Givón calls it a dative object (1984: 104), but I prefer to keep the term "object" for those arguments in a transitive clause that can take an accusative form when they are [+human].[15]

---

[15] Dixon (2010b: 302) calls the initial argument position copula subject (CS) and the second one copula complement (CC), regardless of whether the position is filled by the possessor or the possessee.

(82) Aaya **efar ikua**,   ifera wia.
      sugar 1s.DAT be-PA.3s salt no
      'I have sugar, but no(t) salt.'

(83) Apu maa epira marok maneka=ke **wiar ik-ua**.
      Apu food plate prawn big=CF   3.DAT be-PA.3s
      'Apu has/had big prawns on his food plate.' (Lit: 'Apu's food plate_Theme he has/had big prawns.')

(84) Woos(a) mua **yiar   ik-e-mik**, wis=ke eliw nia   kaken-i-kuan.
      head   man 1p.DAT be-PA-1/3p 3p.FC=CF well 2p.ACC straight-Np-FU.3p
      'We have leaders, they can straighten you out.'

Because the possessee is typically inanimate and often indefinite whereas the possessor is human and definite, this causes a violation to the universal discourse-pragmatic principle, according to which animate/human and definite participants tend to precede inanimate and indefinite participants (Heine 1997: 135). In order to follow the principle, Mauwake often makes the possessor a theme by moving the possessor noun phrase to sentence-initial position. Only the dative pronoun keeps its position immediately preceding the verb (86). If there is no other possessor NP, an unmarked pronoun is used as a theme (85). In these two sentences, moving part of the NP to the theme position causes the NP to be non-contiguous. In the example (82) the possessee subject *aaya* 'sugar' is also the theme, and in (84) the possessee is animate/human, so in those clauses there is less pressure to make the possessor into the theme.

(85) [*I*]_Theme sira   naap me **yiar   ik-ua**.
      1p.UNM custom thus not 1p.DAT be-PA.3s
      'We do not have a custom like that.'

(86) [**Mua oko**]_Theme ona   koor miira=pa nan waaya unowa **wiar ik-ua**.
      man   other   3s.GEN house face=LOC there pig   many 3.DAT be-PA.3s
      'Another man has many pigs there in front of his house.'

Clauses like the example (87), where the possessed noun is [+human] and [+plural], triggering the plural form of the verb, are quite rare, and it seems that the singular verb form is also becoming possible in these cases:

(87) Mua nain pun muuka wiipa   **wiar ik-ua**.
      man that1 also son   daughter 3.DAT ik-PA.3s
      'That man also has children/son(s) and daughter(s).'

All the tenses are possible. The past tense form normally covers both present and past meaning.

(88) Naap on-i-non=na   pina **wiar ika-i-non**.
      thus do-Np-FU.3s=TP guilt 3.DAT be-Np-FU.3s
      'If he does like that he will have guilt.'

When the present tense form is used, it indicates a more transitory possession (89):

(89) Wis   pun maa eliwa=ko wiar **ika-i-ya=na**   iw-i-mik.
      3p.UNM too thing good=NF 3.DAT be-Np-PR.3s=TP give.him-Np-PR.1/3p
      'They too, if they (happen to) have good things, give to him.'

A possessive clause may be elliptical, with the verb deleted, in cases where the possessed NP has at least one post-modifier, which most commonly is a quantifier (90).

(90) Yo   muuka arow, wiipa   kuisow muuta Ø.
      1s.UNM son   three, daughter one   only
      'I have three sons, (and/but) only one daughter.'

When the possessor is not human, the possessive clause is made with the existential verb *ik-* 'be' plus a comitative construction rather than the dative pronoun, and the possessor always precedes the possessee (91), (92). These are cross-linguistically typical features for the grammaticalization strategy that uses a comitative phrase for a possessive predication (Heine 1997: 53–57). As was noted in §3.5.4, in this case the third person singular genitive pronoun *ona* is used for a non-human possessor.

(91) Parina ona   wakesim-owa **onaiya** ika-i-ya.
      lamp   3s.GEN cover-NMZ   with   be-Np-PR.3s
      'The lamp has a cover.'

(92) Miiwa ona   mua **onaiya** ik-ua.
      land 3s.GEN man with   be-PA.3s
      'The land has its men.' (Each piece of ground "has" men whose responsibility it is to see how the land is allocated for gardens.)

Possessive clauses are similar to existential clauses in that when a possessive clause is negated with a negator other than *me*, it becomes a verbless clause (§5.6.3 and §6.2.1).

5.6 Verbless clauses

The predicate of a verbless clause belongs to some other phrase class than the verbs. The two subtypes below, equative (93) and descriptive clauses (94), are very similar syntactically; their differences are mainly in the semantics of the predicates. Their negation strategies are also slightly different from each other.

(93) *Mua nain yena kae panewowa=ke.*
man that1 1s.GEN 1s/p.grandfather old=CF
'That man is my old grandfather.'

(94) *Waaya nain me maneka, muuka kia gelemuta.*
pig that1 not big son white small
'The pig wasn't big, it was a small white piglet.'

In certain cases the verb *ik-* 'be' is required as a copula. This happens mainly in the future (95) or sometimes in the past tense, or when the clause requires a medial form to indicate that it is a medial clause (96).

(95) *Ikoka mua eliwa ne mua oona ika-i-nan.*
later man good and man bone be-Np-FU.2p
'Later you will be a good and strong man.'

(96) *No gelemuta ik-eya ...*
2s.UNM little be-2/3s.DS
'When you were little, ...'

5.6.1 Equative and classifying clauses

Syntactically equative and classifying clauses are identical. The non-verbal predicate typically has contrastive focus marking *-ke*, even though it is not absolutely necessary.

In an equative clause the subject and the non-verbal predicate have the same reference, so their order can be reversed with the basic meaning staying the same (97), (98).

(97) *Dogimaw yiena owow saria=ke.*
Dogimaw 1p.GEN village headman=CF
'Dogimaw is our village headman.'

(98) *Yiena owow saria Dogimaw(=ke).*
Our village headman Dogimaw(=CF)
'Our village headman is Dogimaw.'

An equative clause is only negated with the verbal negator *me* (99):

(99) *Dogimaw me yiena owow saria=ke.*
Dogimaw not 1p.GEN village headman=CF
'Dogimaw is not our village headman.'

In classifying clauses,[16] the reference of the subject is not identical with the reference of the predicate (100), (101).

---

[16] Dryer (2007a: 233) calls them "clauses with a true nominal predicate".

(100) *Yo   inasin mua=ke.*
1s.UNM spirit man=CF

'I am a spirit man.'

(101) *Oo Kululu takira=ke,   o   me amis-ar-e-k.*
oh Kululu young.person=CF 3s.UNM not knowledge-INCH-PA-3s

'Oh, Kululu is a youth (compared to us), he doesn't know.'

The classifying clauses are negated with the verbal negator *me* (102) or with a clause-final negator *weetak/wia* (103).[17]

(102) *Nain me inasin mua=ke, iperuma=ke.*
that1 not spirit man=CF eel=CF

'That is not a spirit man, it is an eel.'

(103) *O somek mua weetak/wia.*
he song man no

'He is not a teacher (lit: song man).'

The predicates of both these clauses are more time-stable compared both with verbal predicates and those in the descriptive clauses (Givón 1984: 51; Stassen 1997: 16).

5.6.2 Descriptive clauses

A descriptive clause is very much like an equative clause, but the predicate is an adjective phrase (104), a noun phrase with an adjective (108), or less frequently a numeral (105) or an adverbial phrase (106). On the time-stability scale these predicates are in between verbal and nominal predicates.

(104) *Irak-owa nain kekanowa akena.*
fight-NMZ that1 strong very

'The fighting was very fierce.'

(105) *Yiena miiwa kuisow.*
1p.GEN land one

'Our land is one.'

(106) *Nain pun sira   naap=iw, mua me kerer-e-mik.*
that1 too custom thus=INST man not appear-PA-1/3p

'That, too, was like that: people didn't arrive.'

A descriptive clause can use any of the negation strategies available in Mauwake (107)–(109) (§3.10, 6.2).

---

[17] Berghäll (=Järvinen) (2006: 272) also gives *marew* 'no(ne)' as a possible negator for equative clauses, but actually the equative clauses do not use it, only the descriptive clauses.

(107) Biiris me eliwa, damo-damola=ko.
       bridge not good RDP-bad=NF
       'The bridges were not good, they were bad.'

(108) Yo   (mua) maala marew.
       1s.UNM (man) long   no(ne)
       'I am not (a) tall (man).'

(109) Awuliak   nain eliwa weetak/wia.
       sweet.potato that1 good no
       'That sweet potato is not good.'

5.6.3 Negated existential and possessive clauses

The existential (§5.5.1) and possessive clauses (§5.5.2) are different from the other verbal clauses with regard to negation. Besides the standard verbal negation they can use all the other negators as well (110) (111) (§6.2.1). The verb *ik-* 'be' is retained only with the verbal negator *me*. With all the other negators the negator itself replaces the verb, and the clause becomes a verbless clause:

(110) Iiriw   miiwa muuta nain irak-owa **marew**.
       earlier land   for   that1 fight-NMZ no(ne)
       'Earlier there was no fighting for land.'

(111) I   urupa **weetak**, i   soomia **wia**, i   epira **marew**.
       1p.UNM cup   no   1p.UNM spoon no   1p.UNM plate no(ne)
       'We had no cups, no spoons, no plates.'

5.7 Nominalized clauses

Lexical nominalization, where an action nominal is a regular noun, was discussed in §3.2.6.1; in this section nominalization as an operation on the whole clause is described.

Action nominals and infinitives are usually assumed to be two separate non-finite categories.[18] Cross-linguistically, the two often tend to be identical in form (Ylikoski 2003: 224), and there is apparently a separate tendency for their functions to look rather similar as well (ibid. 196–197). It seems that the origin of the infinitive in many languages is in a nominalized verb (Noonan 2007: 69).

In Mauwake there is just one form, and rather than positing two homonymous forms with different functions, I maintain that action nominals function both like prototypical

---

[18] Ylikoski (2003; 2009) discusses the similarities and differences between various non-finite verb forms and presents insightful definitions based mainly on their syntactic functions. Many of the details are not relevant to Mauwake, however, as there are no verb forms that would easily fit under the categories of converbs or participles in Mauwake, and because it seems that infinitives and action nominals may be collapsible into one category.

nouns or adjectives AND in functions typically associated with infinitives: as complements[19] of certain verbs, in goal/purpose and deontic structures among others.

Structurally there are two kinds of nominalized clauses in Mauwake. They may occur as complements of the same verbs, with somewhat different semantics. The first type is what the term NOMINALIZED CLAUSE most commonly refers to: the verbal predicate of a clause is nominalized, and consequently the whole clause becomes a noun phrase. The second type retains the form of a verbal clause, but the distal deictic *nain* 'that' after the finite verb nominalizes it. The first type has a wider distribution.

5.7.1 Type 1: with a nominalized verb

When verbs are nominalized, the action or event referred to still keeps some of its verbal characteristics (Hopper & Thompson 1985: 177). Languages differ as to how verbal or nominal in character their nominalized verbs are, and also within one language the outcomes of different nominalization strategies may vary in regard to this (Comrie & Thompson 2007: 344). In this respect Mauwake is a very VERBAL language: the nominalized verbs retain a number of their verbal characteristics.

Neutralization of tense or aspect distinctions, as well as the loss of other than just one argument are common features associated with nominalization (Hopper & Thompson 1984: 737–738). In Mauwake the nominalized verb forms may keep all of the derivational suffixes but not the inflectional ones, which include tense and person/number marking (112).

(112) *Aakisa=ko me kerer-em-ika-i-ya,   wia   bala   op-aw-ap*
now=NF   not appear-SS.SIM-be-Np-PR.3s 3p.ACC decoration hold-CAUS-SS.SEQ
*wia   **wiim-om-owa** nain.*[20]
3p.ACC escort-BEN-NMZ that1

'Now it doesn't take place (any more), decorating them and escorting them for them (i.e. escorting girls to their prospective husbands).'

Verbal groups showing aspect may be nominalized as well, so the aspectual distinction is retained (113):

(113) [*Mua papako maa **ik-em-ik-owa**]   nain kawus wiar   uruf-i-kuan.*
man some   food roast-SS.SIM-be-NMZ that1 smoke 3.DAT see-Np-FU.3p

'They will see the smoke from some men's roasting of food.'

The nominalized verb in itself is neutral in regard to modality, even if it often gets deontic interpretation. But it can be, and frequently is, used in cases where modality is intentionally left unspecified. In (114) the reason for not coming may be that one is not allowed, or able, or willing, to come.

---

[19] Ylikoski widens the definition of complement to cover "obligatory and argumental adverbials as well" (2003: 209).
[20] The long subject NP consisting of a nominalized clause has been right-dislocated.

5.7 Nominalized clauses

(114) Yo   **ekap-owa** wia.
      1s.UNM come-NMZ no
      'I won't come.'

But note (121) where the contrastive focus marker added to the nominalized verb forces a deontic interpretation. See also §6.1.2.

The nominalized verb can keep all the arguments and peripherals that a corresponding finite verb would have. This sometimes results in very long noun phrases. In (115) there is lexical nominalization of the verb *kookal-* 'like' as well, besides the clausal nominalization.

(115) [*Manin(a) maneka, ekina, naisow nena   kookal-owa=pa perek-owa*]
      garden   big   ekina   2s.ISOL 2s.GEN like-NMZ=LOC   pull.out-NMZ
      weetak.
      no
      'You are not allowed to harvest the big garden, called ekina, at your own liking.'

In (116) and (117) only the nominalized verb is within the scope of the negation. The nominalized clauses are in brackets.

(116) [*Maa eneka **me** en-owa*] maa   marew.
      thing tooth not eat-NMZ thing none
      'Not eating meat is all right / is not an issue.'

(117) Wi   mua [*naap **me** on-owa*] nain=ko   ik-e-mik=i?
      3p.UNM man thus   not do-NMZ that1=NF be-PA-1/3p=QM
      'Are there people who wouldn't do / keep doing like that?'

Any of the four negators (§6.2.1) may be used to negate the nominalized clause (114)–(117).

Cross-linguistically nominalized clauses also vary as to whether they retain a manner adverbial of the corresponding verbal clause or change it into an adjective (Comrie & Thompson 2007: 374). Mauwake keeps the adverbial (118).

(118) [*Wiena teeria **baliwep wia**   kakalt-owa*] sira   nain wia   maak-e-k.
      3p.GEN family well   3p.ACC look.after-NMZ custom that1 3p.ACC tell-PA-3s
      'He talked to them about the custom of looking after their families well.'

One common feature in nominalized clauses is that the arguments, instead of taking the morphology they would have in a finite clause, tend to follow typical NP morphology in their marking (Hopper & Thompson 1984: 738). This is perhaps clearest with the subject, which in many languages gets possessive/genitive marking in a nominalized clause. In Mauwake this criterion is not very helpful. The pronominal subject of this first type of nominalized clause, if present, is often genitive (119), but may be nominative as well. But also the subject of a finite clause can be nominative or genitive in form, depending on whether it is neutral or emphatic; and if the subject of a nominalized clause is also the theme, it is nominative rather than genitive (114). A pronominal object in a nominalized clause is in the accusative (118).

(119) *Yiena owow maneka ikiw-owa nain ma-i-yem.*
1p.GEN village big go-NMZ that1 say-Np-PR.1s
'I am talking about our going to town.'

The nominalized verb may take an adjective as a modifier (120):

(120) *Kema suuw-owa eliwa aaw-ep kekan-e-k.*
liver push-NMZ good get-SS.SEQ get.strong-PA-3s
'He got good thinking and became strong.'

Another structural indicator of the nominal status of a nominalized clause is the focus marking, which can be attached to the verb (121).

(121) *I uuw-owa yi-iwkin baliwep uuw-owa=ke ik-ua.*
1p.UNM work-NMZ give.us-2/3p.DS well work-NMZ=CF be-PA.3s
'When they give us work, working well is our duty.'

Nominalized clauses, like other noun phrases, use the far deictic *nain* 'that' as a determiner (122), (123).

(122) [*Ona epa maneka or-owa*] *nain fofa=pa ... unow-iya taan-e-mik.*
3s.GEN place big descend-NMZ that1 day=LOC ... many=COM fill-PA-1/3p
'On the day of his coming down to the big place ... all of them filled (the place).'

(123) [*Niena waaya mik-owa*] *nain on-ami kuep-i-man, niena maa=ke,*
2p.GEN pig spear-NMZ that1 do-ss.SIM break-Np-PR.2p 2p.GEN thing=CF
niena wiowa=ke.
2p.GEN spear=CF
'If you break (the spears) (while) doing your pig-hunting (lit: pig-spearing), that is your business, they are your spears.'

An interesting structure, and not much described in Papuan languages, is one where a same-subject medial clause is in the scope of the nominalization. In Mauwake this tends to happen when the medial verb shares an object with the following verb and there is no, or very little, intervening material between the verbs (124), (125).

(124) *Dabe wiawi* [*maa ik-ep en-owa*] *na-ep manin(a) koora*
Dabe 3s/p.father food roast-SS.SEQ eat-NMZ say-SS.SEQ garden house
iw-a-k.
go-PA-3s
'Dabe's father wanted to roast and eat food and went to the garden house.'

5.7 Nominalized clauses

(125) *Toiyan iiriw maak-ep-pu-a-mik,* [*uuriw yia aaw-ep Madang*
Toiyan already tell-SS.SEQ-CMPL-PA-1/3p morning 1p.ACC take-SS.SEQ Madang
ikiw-owa] nain.
go-NMZ that1

'We already told Toiyan about taking us in the morning and going to Madang.'

Medial clauses preceding nominalized clauses do not automatically fall within the scope of the nominalization. Just looking at the linguistic form it would be possible to analyse the following examples so that the medial clause is outside the nominalization. In that case the free translation of (126) would be 'Having worked on the garden alone it is not acceptable to leave it there', and (127) 'Hold the planting stick and keep practising the making of planting holes'. But culturally these alternative interpretations are not valid. Even starting to work on a big garden without previous negotiations and proper rituals is not acceptable, and the holding of the planting stick and making planting holes form a cultural 'expectancy chain' and belong together conceptually.

(126) [*Manina waisow mauw-ap neeke wafur-ap-pu-owa*] nain weetak.
garden 3s.ISOL work-SS.SEQ there.CF throw-SS.SEQ-CMPL-NMZ that1 no

'Working on the garden alone and leaving it there (=without proper rituals) is not (acceptable/customary).'

(127) [*Weria op-ap wiinar-owa*] nain akim-am-ik-e.
planting.stick hold-SS.SEQ make.planting.holes-NMZ that1 try-SS.SIM-be-IMP.2s

'Keep practising the making of planting holes with the planting stick.'

In (128) the medial clause has to be within the scope of the nominalization for the sentences to make sense. The speaker had seen a possum in a tree and would have liked to shoot it, but since he had not taken his bow and arrows with him, he did not climb up the tree either.

(128) [*Nomokowa ir-ap mik-owa*] nain yena amia me aaw-e-m.
tree climb-SS.SEQ shoot-NMZ that 1s.GEN bow not take-PA-1s

'(For) climbing the tree and shooting (an animal), I hadn't taken my bow (and arrows).'

An intervening overt object may block a same-subject medial clause from being within the scope of a following nominalized verb (129). A different-subject medial clause does not fall within the scope of a nominalized verb.

(129) [*Irak-ep*] *luuwa niir-owa piipu-a-mik.*
fight-SS.SEQ ball play-NMZ leave-PA-1/3p

'We fought and stopped (lit: left) playing football.'

The nominalized clause has several different functions. Like any other noun phrase, it may function as an argument (130) or in the periphery of a clause (131), or in another noun phrase (132).

(130) [*Epia wilin-owa*]$_O$ uruf-ap bom yia wafur-om-i-kuan
firewood shine-NMZ see-SS.SEQ bomb 1p.ACC throw-BEN-Np-FU.3p
na-e-mik.
say-PA-1/3p

'They$_i$/we said that when they$_j$ see the light (lit: shining) of the fire they$_j$ will throw bombs at us.'

(131) *Wiena oram niir-emi* [*wiam kookal-owa=pa*]$_{Advl}$ *nan wiam*
3p.GEN just play-SS.SEQ 3p.REFL like-NMZ=LOC there 3p.REFL
aaw-i-mik.
take-Np-PR.3s

'They just play together and (on the basis of) liking each other they marry each other.'

(132) [[*garanga oko muuka wiar aaw-owa*]$_{NP}$ *sira*]$_{NP}$
family other son/child 3.DAT get-NMZ custom

'the adoption custom' (Lit: the custom of getting a child from another family')

The following functions are often associated with infinitives in languages that distinguish between infinitives and nominalizations (Ylikoski 2003: 207).

Expressions of obligation (§6.1.2) use the nominalized form of the main verb. It is followed by the contrastive focus clitic, when it is either a non-verbal predicate (133), (135) or the subject of the verb *ikua* 'is' (134).

(133) *Yo uurika owow maneka ikiw-owa=ke.*
1s.UNM tomorrow village big go-NMZ=CF

'I have to go to town tomorrow.'

(134) *Wi iperowa ekima wia op-ap baliwep ik-owa=ke ik-ua.*
3p.UNM middle-aged forehead 3p.ACC hold-SS.SEQ well be-NMZ=CF be-PA.3s

'One has to respect[21] the middle-aged/elderly and behave well.'

(135) *Inasina wia patir-a-mik nain me wiar en-owa=ke.*
bush.spirit 3p.ACC sacrifice-PA-1/3p that1 not 3.DAT eat-NMZ=CF

'One must not eat what has been sacrificed to the bush spirits.'

Directional verbs (§3.8.4.4.5) may take a nominalized clause as the goal. In many of these cases it is hard to distinguish between goal and purpose, which can be expressed via nominalization as well (136).

(136) *Yo emeria aaw-owa urup-e-m.*
1s.UNM woman take-NMZ ascend-PA-1s

'I came up to take my wife.'

---

[21] The verbal expression for respecting someone is *ekima opowa* 'holding someone's forehead'.

5.7 Nominalized clauses

Nominalized clauses are used as complements of various complement-taking verbs (137), (138) (§8.3.2).

(137)   **Miiw-aasa muf-owa ikiw-owa** na-em-ik-omkun   o   ar-e-k.
        land-canoe pull-NMZ go-NMZ say-SS.SIM-be-1s/p.DS 3s.UNM die-PA-3s
        'As we were talking about going to get a vehicle, she died.'

(138)   **Maa uup-owa** paayar-ep   ep-a-n.
        food cook-NMZ know-SS.SEQ come-PA-2s
        'You know cooking and you came.'

A nominalized clause is sometimes used to express habituality. It indicates a more deliberate and permanent habit than that expressed by the continuous aspect, which is the default marking for the habitual (139), (140) (§3.8.5.1.1).

(139)   Wi   mua **naap me onowa nain**=ko ik-e-mik=i?
        3p.UNM man thus not do-NMZ that1=NF be-PA-1/3p=QM
        'Are there people who wouldn't keep doing like that?'

(140)   Mua papako **opor(a) makena me ookowa**,   sira   samora
        man other talk   true   not follow-NMZ custom bad
        on-am-ika-i-mik.
        do-SS-SIM-be-Np-PR.1/3p
        'Some people (as a rule) do not follow the true talk (but) keep doing bad things.'

Mauwake verbs may take a causative suffix, which often indicates causation (§3.8.4.3.1). When the causation is less mechanical and requires the cooperation of the object of the causation, the verb *suuw-* 'push' is used together with a nominalized clause (141):

(141)   Mua naareke **naap on-owa** nefa   suuw-a-k?
        man who.CF thus do-NMZ 2s.ACC push-PA-3s
        'Who made you do like that?'

Ability is expressed via a nominalized clause followed by the intensity adverb *pepek* 'enough, able' (142).

(142)   **Ariwa perek-owa**   me pepek.
        arrow pull.out-NMZ not enough/able
        '(He was) not able to pull out the arrow.'

One strategy for purposives is to use the nominalized form of the main verb followed by the same-subject sequential form *naep* of the verb 'say/think'. This strategy is used especially when the purpose is understood to be somewhat generic (143) or when the purpose clause is right-dislocated (144). For purpose clauses, see §8.3.2.1.4.

5 Clause

(143) *Weniwa=pa* **en-owa na-ep** *uuw-i-mik.*
hunger.time=LOC eat-NMZ say-SS.SEQ plant-Np-PR.1/3p

'We/they work in order to eat during the time of hunger.'

(144) *Ona siowa ikos manina ikiw-e-mik,* **pika on-owa** *na-ep.*
3s.GEN dog together.with garden go-PA-1/3p fence make-NMZ say-SS.SEQ

'He went together with his dog to the garden (in order) to make a fence.'

Mauwake has an idiosyncratic clausal structure for the expression 'not yet'. The negated verb is nominalized, and it is followed by an appropriate form of the verb *ik-* 'be' (145). The presence of the negative temporal adverb *eewuar* 'not yet' indicates expectation that what hasn't happened yet will, or should, take place in not too distant future (146).

(145) *Aakisa baliwep* **me amis-ar-owa** *ik-e-mik.*
now well not knowledge-INCH-NMZ be-PA-1/3p

'Now we do not yet know it well.'

(146) *Iwera popoka wafur-am-ika-iwkin or-op 'bulak',* **eewuar,** *eka*
coconut unripe throw-SS.SIM-be-2/3p.DS descend-SS.SEQ plop not.yet water
me saan-ar-owa ik-ua.
not dry-INCH-NMZ be-PA.3s

'They$_i$ kept throwing unripe coconuts$_j$ and when they$_j$ dropped they$_j$ said 'plop' (so they$_i$ knew:) not yet, the water had not dried yet.'

Unlike many other languages, in Mauwake a nominalized clause does not function as a complement of an adjective. Rather, the nominalized clause functions as the subject and it takes the adjective as a non-verbal predicate (147), (148):

(147) **Maa wiar ikum aaw-owa** *eliwa=ki?*
thing 3.DAT illicitly take-NMZ good=CF.QM

'Is it good to steal?'

(148) **Galasim-owa**[22] *lawisiw yoowa.*
spear.fish-NMZ rather hot/hard

'Spearing fish is rather hard.' Or: 'It is rather hard to spear fish.'

5.7.2 Type 2: with a finite verb

The second strategy for nominalizing a clause is to end an ordinary verbal clause with the far demonstrative *nain* 'that' used as a determiner. The demonstrative is the only

---

[22] The verb for spear-fishing is a loan from Tok Pisin, which refers to the goggles used when diving to spear fish.

5.7 Nominalized clauses

element marking the clause as nominalized. Comrie & Thompson call this type "clausal nominalization" (2007:376–377). Givón (1990: 506) suggests that there may be a correlation "between the DEGREE OF NOUNHOOD of a nominalized expression and its ability to take determiners". In Mauwake this is clearly not the case, as the demonstrative is obligatory in this second type of nominalized clause but only optional in the first type, which is otherwise more like a noun phrase.

The distribution of finite clauses nominalized only with a demonstrative is more restricted than that of clauses with a nominalized verb. They function as complement clauses (149) (§8.3.2), relative clauses (150) (§8.3.1), or temporal clauses (151) (§8.3.3.1), but not in the many other specific functions where the other type can occur. Forming complement clauses and relative clauses by adding a demonstrative pronoun after a finite verb is a common strategy in Papuan languages (Reesink 1983a; 1987: 228; Farr 1999: 77; Whitehead 2004: 192).

(149) [*Takira en-ow(a) gelemuta wia on-om-a-mik nain*]$_{CC}$
child eat-NMZ small 3p.ACC make-BEN-BNFY2.PA-1/3p that1
ma-i-yem.
say-Np-PR.1s
'I tell about our making/having made a feast for the children.'

(150) [*Akia ik-e-k nain*]$_{RC}$ *me en-e-k.*
banana roast-PA-3s that1 not eat-PA-3s
'He did not eat the bananas that he roasted.'

(151) [*Koora ikiw-i-mik nain*]$_{TempC}$ *mera eka me enim-i-mik.*
house go-Np-PR.1/3p that1 fish water not eat-Np-PR.1/3p
'When/After we go into the house, we do not eat fish soup.'

6 Functional domains

This chapter describes various functional systems that affect the clause or the sentence as a whole. Most of them are touched upon in various other parts of the grammar where they are relevant, but here they are treated in a more systematic manner.

6.1 Modality

Modality, or mode – expressing the speaker's attitude to a situation – relates not just to the verb but to the whole proposition. Because of this it is typically not expressed via verbal inflection (Bybee 1985: 22). In Mauwake the counterfactual modality is manifested by a suffix on the verb §3.8.3.2; more often the modality is conveyed via various other strategies outlined below.

Many Papuan languages make a distinction between realis and irrealis mode,[1] and tense. Foley (1986: 162) estimates that, on the whole, tense is more prominent than mode, but there are also languages like Hua (Haiman 1980) and Maia (Hardin 2002) which do not have tense as a verbal category at all, only mode. But in Mauwake the realis-irrealis dichotomy is not grammatically relevant.

6.1.1 Epistemic modality

Epistemic modality has to do with certainty, probability and possibility: it "relates to the speaker's … commitment to the probability that the situation is true" (Payne 1997: 234).

The default and unmarked mood in statements is indicative, when something is stated as a fact. If the speaker wants to strengthen the proposition more, the intensity adverb *akena* 'truly, very' is added to the end of the statement (1), (2).

(1) Wi   owow oko   oko pun wia   maake-miaw-i-yem   **akena**.
     3p.UNM place other other also 3p.ACC tell-wander-NPS-PR.1s truly
     'I really walk around telling people in many other places too.'

(2) Wi   o   ook-owa   nain me pepek **akena**.
     3p.UNM 3s.UNM follow.him-NMZ   that1 not able truly
     'They really are not able to follow him.'

When the proposition is considered less than certain, either probable or just possible, the modal adverb clitic -*yon* 'probably/perhaps/I think' (§3.9.3) is attached to the last

---

[1] Foley (1986: 158) calls it *status*.

word in the statement, usually either a verb (3) or non-verbal predicate (4). An interjection can still follow the word with -*yon* (5).

(3) *Mua Maneka=ke lawisiw wia amukar-e-k=**yon**.*
man big=CF somewhat 3p.ACC scold-PA-3s-perhaps
'Perhaps God reproached/punished them a little.'

(4) *Nis pun kema puk-owa marewa=ke=**yon** aa!*
2p.UNM also liver burst-NMZ none=CF-perhaps INTJ
'Ah, I think you don't have any sense at all (lit: your liver hasn't burst)!'

(5) *Naap=**yon**.*
thus-perhaps
'I think/suppose it is like that.'

The counterfactual form of the verb (§3.8.3.2) is used in speculative statements where the situation mentioned in the proposition DID NOT happen, although it could have (6)–(8).

(6) *Lawisiw akena um-**ek**-a-m.*
somewhat very die-CNTF-PA-1s
'I very nearly fell (but in reality didn't).'

(7) *Yena kookal-owa=pa uuw-**ek**-a-m=na sesa na-**ek**-a-m.*
1s.GEN like-NMZ=LOC work-CNTF-PA-1s=TP price say-CNTF-PA-1s
'If I had worked on my own will, I would have required payment.'

(8) *Naap wiar amis-ar-**ek**-a-mik oo!*
thus 3.DAT knowledge-INCH-CNTF-PA-1/3p INTJ
'Oh, if only we had known that about him/them!'

Abilitative is expressed by the adverb *pepek* 'enough, correctly, able' as a non-verbal predicate. In affirmative statements the verb that the adverb refers to often occurs in the following clause (9):

(9) *No **pepek**, eliw on-i-nan.*
2s.UNM able well do-Np-FU.2s
'You are able, you can do it.'

The verb may also be in the same clause but in the nominalized form; this is more common in negative statements (10):

(10) *... mukuna nain **umuk**-owa me **pepek**.*
... fire that1 extinguish-NMZ not able
'... (we were) not able to extinguish the fire.'

Evidentials are an important feature in some Papuan languages, but Mauwake does not have them as a grammatical category.

6.1.2 Deontic modality

The deontic modality indicates obligation or permission. Deontic expressions can vary from a statement of a strong obligation to a polite request or to expressions of permission or denying permission.

The syntactic strategy for expressing strong obligation is to use the nominalized form of the verb followed by the contrastive focus clitic, and optionally an appropriate form of the verb 'be' (11).

(11) Yo   uurika   owow maneka *ikiw-owa=ke (ik-ua)*.
     1s.UNM tomorrow village big   go-NMZ=CF   be-PA.3s
     'I have to go to town tomorrow.'

A nominalized clause structure may may be interpreted to express obligation even without the contrastive focus clitic, and in a medial clause. A dative pronoun is added if clarification is needed to state who is obligated to do something (12).

(12) **Ekap-owa efar   ika-eya   ekap-e-m.**
     come-NMZ 1s.DAT be-2/3s.DS come-PA-1s
     'I had to come, so I came.'

A polite request can also take the form of a question (13).

(13) No   maa nain=ko eliw yi-i-nan=i?
     2s.UNM thing that=NF well give.me-Np-FU.2s=QM
     'Will/would you give that to me (please)?'

Permission is indicated by the adverb *eliw* 'well/all right' placed before the verb, which is in the future form (14), (15).

(14) Yiena   miiwa kuisow, **eliw** feeke   soop-i-yen.
     1p.GEN land one   well here.CF bury-Np-FU.1p
     'Our land is one, we may bury him here.'

(15) **Eliw** ek-ap   fook-i-nan,   fook-ap   ep-i-nan.
     well   come-SS.SEQ split-Np-FU.2s split-SS.SEQ go-Np-FU.2s
     'You may come and split (coconuts), and having split them, go.'

Prohibition or denial of permission is done with a negated nominalized form of a verb (16), (17).

(16) Manin   maneka na-isow nena   kookal-owa=pa **perek-owa weetak**.
     garden big   2s.ISOL 2s.GEN like-NMZ=LOC harvest-NMZ no
     'You are not allowed to harvest the big garden by yourself when your like.'

(17) I **me** sira samora **on-owa=ke**, weetak.
    1p.UNM not custom bad do-NMZ=CF no
    'We must not do bad things.'

In sentences expressing disobedience to a prohibition, it is particularly common to have the prohibition in a relative clause where the nominalized verb is negated with the verbal negator *me* (18), (19). Here the contrastive focus clitic is not used.

(18) *Maa=ko* [***me on-owa*** *nain*] *nis=ke on-i-man.*
    thing=NF not do-NMZ that1 2p.FC=CF do-Np-PR.2p
    'You do things that must not be done.'

(19) *Sabat fofa=pa* [***me uuw-owa*** *nain*] *emeria nain saliw-a-k.*
    sabbath day=LOC not work-NMZ that1 woman that1 heal-PA-3s
    'He healed the woman on a Sabbath day when it was forbidden to work.'

6.2 Negation

Mauwake has more variety in negation than many other Papuan languages.[2] There are four negators in Mauwake instead of only one or two: *me, weetak, wia* and *marew*, which have somewhat overlapping functions (§3.10). Negation can also express frustration or be used as a verb root with certain suffixes; its scope can vary from one constituent to a whole sentence; and it may be emphasized. Double negation results in cancellation of the negation rather than emphasizing it.

6.2.1 Clausal negation

Verbal clauses are negated with the negator *me* 'not', placed before the verb (20), verbal group (21) or verb phrase (22).

This type of negation, also called standard negation, is symmetric in Mauwake: the negative clause is similar to the corresponding affirmative clause apart from the presence of the negator (Miestamo 2005: 61–67). The negation strategy is the same for transitive and intransitive, independent and dependent clauses, and for imperatives (23) as well.

(20) I iinan aasa **me kuuf-a-mik**.
    1p.UNM sky canoe not see-PA-1/3p
    'We did not see the airplanes.'

(21) Yo **me keker op-a-m**, Kedem=ke makena.
    1s.UNM not fear hold-PA-1s, Kedem=CF true
    'I was not afraid, true, Kedem was.'

---

[2] The contents of this §6.2 is mostly based on Berghäll (=Järvinen) (2006).

(22) *Mua **me wia** kuuf-a-mik, **me wia** furew-a-mik, ne **me wia***
man not 3p.ACC see-PA-1/3p not 3p.ACC sense-PA-1/3p and not 3p.ACC
imen-a-mik.
find-PA-1/3p
'We did not see, sense, or find the men.'

(23) *Ni uf-ep=na maadara **me** iirar-eka.*
2p.UNM dance-SS.SEQ=NF forehead.ornament not remove-IMP.2p
'If/when you have danced, do not remove your forehead ornaments.'

The non-verbal predicate in equative (24) and descriptive clauses (25) can be negated with any of the four negators.

(24) *O somek mua **weetak/wia**.*
3s.UNM song man no
'He is not a teacher.'

(25) *O **me** somek mua=ke.*
3s.UNM not song man=CF
'He is not a teacher.'

However, *marew* is possible in these clauses only if the predicate contains an adjective (26).

(26) *Awuliak fain afila **weetak/wia/marew**.*
sweet.potato this sweet no
'This sweet potato is not sweet.'

(27) *Awuliak fain **me** afila(=ke).*
sweet.potato this not sweet=CF
'This sweet potato is not sweet.'

When the possessive and existential clauses are negated with the verbal negator *me*, they are like other verbal clauses (28), (30). But if any of the other negators is used, the negator replaces the verb and becomes a non-verbal predicate, so these clauses become verbless clauses (29), (31) (§5.6.3).

(28) *I sira naap **me** yiar ik-ua.*
1p.UNM custom thus not 1p.DAT be-PA.3s
'We do not have a custom like that.'

(29) *Wi Yaapan emeria **weetak**, mua manek=iw.*
3p.UNM Japan woman no, man big=LIM
'The Japanese had no women/wives, (they were) only men.'

285

(30) Iiriw   miiwa muuta nain irak-owa **me ik-ua.**
     earlier land   for   that1 fight-NMZ not be-PA.3s
     'Earlier there was no fighting for land.'

(31) Iiriw   miiwa muuta nain irak-owa **marew,** ...
     earlier land   for   that1 fight-NMZ no(ne)
     'Earlier there was no fighting for land, ...'

With so many possible alternatives, the speaker has a choice of repeating the same negator (32) or using different ones (33) when several items are negated. Either strategy is used by good language users.

(32) I   muuka **marew** a, i   wiipa   **marew** a.
     1p.UNM son   no(ne) oh 1p.UNM daughter no(ne) oh
     'We have no son, and we have no daughter.'

(33) I   urupa **weetak**, i   soomia **wia**, i   epira **marew**.
     1p.UNM cup   no   1p.UNM spoon no   1p.UNM plate no(ne)
     'We had no cups, we had no spoons, we had no plates.'

In a few cases the choice of a negator indicates a difference in meaning. The example (35) is the Mauwake equivalent for the common Tok Pisin idiom *nogat tok* 'I do not have anything against it'.

(34) Yo   opora **weetak/wia**.
     1p.UNM talk   no
     'I have no talk. (= I do not have anything to say.)'

(35) Yo   opora **marew**.
     1p.UNM talk   no(ne)
     'I have no talk. (= It is OK / I do not have anything against it.)'

The predicate function of the negators *weetak* and *marew* is also shown in the fact that they take a medial different-subject suffix, when the verbless negative possessive or existential-presentative clauses occur sentence-medially in a chaining structure (36). *Wia* cannot be suffixed with the medial verb suffix.

(36) Maa pela **marew**-eya   / **weetak**-eya fofa   er-a-m.
     thing leaf no(ne)-2/3s.DS / no-2/3s.DS   market go-PA-1s
     'I had no greens and went to the market.'

6.2.2 Constituent negation

Papuan languages typically do not have lexicalized constituent negation of the type 'nothing', 'nobody' etc., and even syntactic constituent negation may be lacking (Reesink 1987: 271–272). But in Mauwake it is possible to negate various constituents within a clause, and, although very rarely, even inside a noun phrase. The basic constituent negator is *me* 'not'. It precedes the negated element, which receives extra stress. Position of the negator, stress, and sometimes the neutral focus clitic all interact in constituent negation (37)–(41).

(37) **Me napuma=ke** *ifakim-o-k.*
 not sickness kill-PA-3s
 'It wasn't sickness that killed him.'

(38) *Maa oposia* **me ewur** *enim-i-mik.*
 thing meat not soon eat-Np-PR.1/3p
 'Meat we will not eat soon (after spouse's death).'

(39) **Me epa fan** *irak-owa uruf-a-mik.*
 not place here fight-NMZ see-PA-1/3p
 'It was not here that they saw the fighting.'

(40) *Nepa opaimika* **me baliwep** *miim-a-mik.*
 bird talk not well hear-PA-1/3p
 'They did not hear (understand) Tok Pisin well.'

(41) **Me nomokowa eliwa** *aaw-e- mik.*
 not tree good take-PA-1/3p
 'It wasn't good trees that they took.'

In clauses with QUANTIFIERS, constituent negation has an important function disambiguating the meaning. If the subject or object noun phrase has a quantifier, the negation is done in different ways depending on whether the quantifier is in the scope of the negation or not. In (42) the noun phrase with the particular quantifier *kuisow* 'one' is not in the scope of the negation, but in (43) it is. The neutral focus clitic is required to clarify the meaning; it can even be attached to some other constituent between the quantifier and the negator (44).

(42) *Mua* **kuisow me** *ekap-o-k.*
 man one not come-PA-3s
 'One (particular) man did not come.'

(43) *Mua* **kuisow=ko me** *ekap-o-k.*
 man one=NF not come-PA-3s
 'Not (even) one man came.'

(44) Mua **kuisow** owowa=pa=**ko** me ik-ua.
    man one   village=LOC=NF not be-PA.3s
    'Not (even) one man stayed in the village.'

The example (45) is ambiguous as to whether only one man did not go down or whether it is negated that only one man went. The first alternative is the more likely meaning, and if one wants to make sure to give the second meaning, the standard strategy for constituent negation (46) is used.

(45) Mua kuisow muuta **me** ekap-o-k.
    man one   only not come-PA-3s
    'Only one man did not come.' Or: 'Not only one man came (but more).'

(46) **Me** mua kuisow (muuta) ekap-o-k.
    not man one   (only)   come-PA-3s
    'Not only one man came.'

Similarly, with the universal quantifier *unowiya* 'all', the scope of the negation may be ambiguous. The preferred interpretation for (47) is that the statement about not following God's talk refers to all people, thus NO ONE follows it; but it may also be understood that even if all the people do not follow it, some do.

(47) Emeria mua **unowiya** Mua Maneka opora **me** ook-i-mik.
    woman man all   Man Big   talk not follow-Np-PR.1/3p
    'All the people do not follow God's talk.'

If the negator is in the constituent negation position, the statement is unambiguous (48). In this respect Mauwake behaves differently from Usan, which does not allow a constituent negation structure (Reesink 1987: 275–277).

(48) Nain **me** mua **unowiya** opora wiar op-i-mik.
    but not man all   talk 3.DAT hold-Np-PR.1/3p
    'But not all men/people believe in him (= some do).'

Stress may also be employed to give a constituent negation interpretation to a negated clause. When the clausal stress is on the negator, the whole clause is negated (49). In order to negate the universal quantifier rather than the verb, the main stress needs to be on the quantifier (50). This type of negation is used in Usan as well (ibid. 277).

(49) Mua **unow=iya** 'me ikiw-e-mik.
    man many=COM not go-PA-1/3p
    'All the men *didn't go* (=none of them went).'

(50) Mua '**unow=iya** me ikiw-e-mik.
    man many=COM not go-PA-1/3p
    '*All* the men didn't go (=only some went).'

6.2 Negation

When a clause with the universal quantifier *unow onaiya* 'all' is negated, it tends to be interpreted as a constituent negation of the quantifier, possibly because *unow onaiya* is a heavier structure than *unowiya* and as such more prominent (51).

(51) **Unow onaiya me** *ikiw-e-mik.*
many with not go-PA-1/3p
'Not all of them went (= only some went)'

The example (52) is not a case of *unowa* negated separately inside a NP; instead, *mua* 'man' is fronted as a theme (§9.1):

(52) *Mua* **me unowa** *ekap-e-mik.*
man not many come-PA-1/3p
'There were not many men that came.' Or: 'As for men, not many came.'

Eliwa 'good' may be the only adjective that can be negated by itself inside a noun phrase. These structures are very rare and would need a more careful study (53), (54). (53) may also be a combination of a non-verbal clause and a transitive clause where the object NP only retains the adjective; the noun is deleted because it occurs in the previous clause.

(53) *Maa en-owa* **eliw(a) marew** *p-or-o-mik.*
thing eat-NMZ good no(ne) BPX-descend-PA-1/3p
'They brought down not-good food.'

(54) *Biiris* **me eliwa**, *damo-damola=ko on-a-mik.*
bridge not good RDP-bad=NF make-PA-1/3p
'They did not make good bridges (but) bad ones.' (Or: The bridges were not good, they made bad ones.)

The example (55) looks like a constituent negation attached to the noun *mokoka* 'eye(s)', but actually *me* here is a clausal negator negating the whole idiomatic sentence of 'keeping one's eyes shut' (i.e. being ignorant).

(55) **Me** *mokoka op-ar-ep ik-e.*
not eye(s) closed-CAUS-SS.SEQ be-IMP.2s
'Do not have your eyes closed.'

Those cases of constituent negation where *me* precedes a verb can be distinguished from clausal negation only in spoken language on the basis of extra stress on the verb (56).

(56) *Ni iperuma fain* **me** *e'nim-eka, wafur-eka!*
2p.UNM eel this not eat-IMP.2p throw-IMP.2p
'*Don't eat* this eel, throw it away!'

6.2.3 Negative interjection

A negative interjection is used as a one-word reply to a question or a statement. It stands as a complete sentence by itself or is preposed and syntactically independent of the rest of the sentence. Two of the negators are used as negative interjections: *weetak* and *wia* (57), (58). They are synonymous and usually interchangeable, but in a few environments one or the other is preferred. For the use of *weetak/wia* as an answer to a negative question, see §7.2.7.

(57) No   aaya sesenar-e-n=i? -***Weetak/wia*** *(me sesenar-e-m).*
      2s.UNM sugar buy-PA-2s=QM -no   (not buy-PA-1s)
      'Did you buy sugar?' –'No (I didn't).'

(58) *Yomar   owora   efar   aaw-o-k. -**Weetak/wia**, me os=ke   aaw-o-k.*
      1s/p.cousin betelnut 1s.DAT take-PA-3s -no   not 3s.FC=CF take-PA-3s
      'My cousin took my betelnut. –No, it wasn't he who took it.'

6.2.4 Other cases of negation

When an affirmative clause is followed by a negative one, and the two only differ by the contrasted element, the whole clause apart from the contrasted element is replaced by *weetak* or *wia* (59), (60). A full clause is possible instead of *weetak/wia*, but it is not as common.

(59) *Mua bug   maala nain=ke mera unowa isak-i-non,   mua bug iiwa nain*
      man wind long that1=CF fish many spear-Np-FU.3s man wind short that1
      weetak/wia.
      no.
      'A man with long breath (=big lungs) will spear many fish, a man with short breath will not.'

(60) *Mera papako unowa, papako **weetak/wia**.*
      fish some   many   some   no
      'Some fish there are many, some not.'

Also when an affirmative question is followed by a negative alternative, *weetak* or *wia* is used (61), (62).

(61) *Sira nain piipua-i-nan=i   e   **weetak**?*
      habit that leave-Np-FU.2s=QM or no
      'Will you stop that habit or not?'

(62) *Yo   emeria=ko efar   uruf-a-man=i   e **weetak**?*
      1s.UNM woman=NF 1s.DAT see-PA-2p=QM or no
      'Have you seen my wife or not?'

6.2 Negation

If an action fails to have the expected result, again one of the two negative interjections is used either by itself (63), (64) or followed by a full clause (65).

(63) *Marasin wu-om-a-mik=na* **weetak**.
medicine put-BEN-BNFY2.PA-1/3p=TP no
'They put medicine in him but no (=with no result).'

(64) *Naap ik-ok uruf-am-ika-iwkin* **wia**.
thus be-ss see-ss.SIM-be-2/3p.DS no
'They were thus watching him (but) no (he did not revive).'

(65) *I unan maa en-e-mik en-e-mik* **wia**, *ipoka taan-ep*
1p.UNM yesterday food eat-PA-1/3p eat-PA-1/3p no stomach become.full-ss.SEQ
enakiwa wu-a-mik.
half put-PA-1/3p
'Yesterday we ate and ate, (but) no (=we could not finish the food), our stomachs were full and we put half of it aside.'

When the clause expressing frustration of an effort starts a new sentence and begins with the additive connective *ne* 'and/but', the negator is always *wia*, and an explanatory clause follows (66).

(66) **Ne wia**, *papako=ke ma-e-mik,* "*Weetak, moram owowa p-ikiw-i-yan?*"
ADD no other=CF say-PA-1/3p no why village BPX-go-Np-FU.1p
'But no, others said, "Why take him to the village?" '

Mauwake has two different kinds of double negation. In both cases the negation is cancelled and the result is affirmative, but not an emphatic affirmative. A negated verb (67) or an inherently negative verb (68) may occur with the clausal negator *me* 'not':

(67) *Ona muuka* **me** *sesek-owa=ke* **me** *ma-e-k*.
3s.GEN son not send-NMZ=CF not say-PA-3s
'He did not say that he wouldn't send (lit: say about not sending) his son.'

(68) *Maamuma* **me** *marew-ar-e-mik*.
money not no(ne)-INCH-PA-1/3p
'We/They did not lack money.'

In the second type of double negation a speaker's negative statement is challenged by another speaker. In this case a different negator is used to challenge the original negation (69).

(69) *Yo episowa weetak*. -**Weetak wia**.
1s.UNM tobacco no. -no no
'I have no tobacco.' 'Don't say you don't have any.'

The negation can be emphasized with the intensity adverb *akena* 'very' (70), (71):

(70) **Weetak akena**, i   me kuum-e-mik.
 no   very   1p.UNM not burn-PA-1/3s
 'No, we did not burn it.'

(71) I   **me** kuum-e-mik **akena**.
 1p.UNM not burn-PA-1/3p very
 'We did NOT burn it.'

Another possible strategy for emphasizing a negative statement or command is to attach the neutral focus clitic *-ko* to the verbal negator *me* 'not' (72)–(74). In (73) the neutral focus clitic appears twice, as the speaker wants both to emphasise the negation and to distance himself from the situation (without implying that someone else did see what he did not).

(72) I   **me=ko** miim-a-mik.
 1p.UNM not=NF hear-PA-1/3p
 'We did NOT hear it.'

(73) Yo=ko   **me=ko** uruf-a-m.
 1s.UNM=NF not=NF see-PA-1s
 'I did NOT see it.'

(74) **Me=ko** niir-e   sa, kae   napum-ar-e-k.
 not=NF laugh-IMP.2s INTJ grandfather sick-INCH-PA-3s
 'Do NOT laugh, grandfather is sick.'

Negative spreading is fairly common in languages that have a medial verb system. The negation can spread forwards or backwards, or both, depending on the language. In Mauwake both forward (75) and backward (76) spreading is possible across medial clause boundaries, but only with the same-subject medial verbs.[3] The spreading is not common, but it is more acceptable if the verbs form a logical sequence, an "expectancy chain".

(75) Nain yo   **me ep-ap**   nefa   aaw-e-m.
 but 1s.UNM not come-SS.SEQ 2s.ACC get-PA-1s
 'But I did not come and get you.'

(76) Nainiw **ekap-ep**   maa me sesek-a-mik.
 again   come-SS.SEQ food not sell-PA-1/3p
 'They did not come back and sell food again.'

---

[3] In Usan, the negation of a final clause can spread backwards even with a different subject medial verb (Reesink 1987: 282), but Hua, like Mauwake, requires a same subject medial verb (Haiman 1980: 408).

But negative spreading is not automatic; even with a same-subject medial verb two clauses can have different polarity (77), (78). If the speaker wants to avoid ambiguity, finite clauses can be used when the polarity is different (79).

(77) *Nepa opaimika **me baliwep amis-ar-ep***   *wiena opaimik=iw yia*
bird talk   not well   knowledge-INCH-SS.SEQ 3p.GEN talk=INST 1p.ACC
maak-em-ik-e-mik.
tell-SS.SIM-be-PA-1/3p

'They did not know Tok Pisin well and talked to us in their own language.'

(78) *Mua lebuma **me arim-ep** takira ik-ok emeria wia aaw-i-mik.*
man lazy   not grow-SS.SEQ young be-SS.SIM woman 3s.ACC take-Np-PR.1/3p

'Lazy men, not having grown and (still) being young, take wives.'

(79) *Nainiw ekap-e-mik, nain maa **me** sesek-a-mik.*
again come-PA-1/3p that1 food not sell-PA-1/3p

'They came back again, but did not sell any food.'

If the context is not clear enough, the negator can be repeated for each negated verb in a medial verb construction. In (80), if only the first verb is negated, the sentence could mean that many people do not know the person but follow him nevertheless; whereas if only the second verb is negated, the sentence might be taken to mean that many people do know the person but do not follow him.

(80) *Mua unowa o **me** amis-ar-ep **me** ook-i-mik.*
man many 3s.UNM not knowledge-INCH-SS.SEQ not follow-Np-PR.3p

'Many people do not know him and do not follow him.'

Different-subject marking blocks negative spreading in both directions. Thus in (81) the polarity changes with each new clause:

(81) *Soomar-em-ika-iwkin **me wia** far-eya nefa ma-i-kuan, ...*
walk-SS.SIM-be-2/3p.DS not 3p.ACC call-2/3s.DS 2s.ACC say-Np-FU.3p

'When they walk past, and you do not call them, they will say about you that ...'

Negative transportation from a complement clause to a main clause does not take place in Mauwake.[4]

6.3 Deixis

Different parts in the grammar interact to produce the deictic system, the spatio-temporal and personal orientation related to the speech situation or another situation specified in the text. The default deictic centre is the speaker, the speaker's location and the present time.

---

[4] This is true of Amele as well (Roberts 1987: 44), but Usan allows it (Reesink 1987: 278–280).

6.3.1 Person deixis

Only the first and second person are inherently deictic, as they get their whole meaning, apart from the number, from the speech situation. The person marking is done by pronouns (§3.5) and by person/number suffixes on the verbs (§3.8.3.4, §3.8.3.5). The special status of the first person as against both the second and third persons shows in the imperative and the switch-reference marking. In the imperative the dual number is only possible in the first person (82) (§3.8.3.3.2):

(82) *Aria, i   owowa=ko urup-u.   Auwa   aite   wia*
     alright 1p.UNM village=NF ascend-IMP.1d 1s/p.father 1s/p.mother 3p.ACC
     karu-i-yan,   owowa=pa wia   uruf-u.
     visit-Np-FU.1p village=LOC 3p.ACC see-IMP.1d

   'Alright, let's (dl) go up to the village. We'll visit father and mother, let's (dl) see them in the village.'

In the different-subject medial verbs the first person singular and plural share the same suffix, whereas the second and third persons are grouped together and the distinction is made according to number, between singular and plural (83) (§3.8.3.5.2).

(83) *I   ikoka urup-ep   nia   **maak-omkun ora-iwkin,**   aria*
     1p.UNM later ascend-ss.SEQ 2p.ACC tell-1s/p.DS   descend-2/3p.DS alright
     owawiya feeke   pok-ap   ik-ok ...
     together here.CF sit-ss.SEQ be-ss

   'Later when we come up and tell you and (then) you come down and we sit down together here and ...'

Even though the first and second person pronouns are already deictic in themselves, their unmarked plural forms can both co-occur with the proximate demonstrative *fain* 'this', (84) and the second person also with the distal demonstrative *nain* 'that'. As only one of the people referred to by these plural forms typically is a speech act participant and the others may or may not be present, the addition of the demonstrative makes it clear that all the people referred to are present in the situation:

(84) *Ikoka Yaapan=ke ekap-emi   **ni**   emeria unowa **fain** nia*
     later Japan=CF come-ss.SIM 2p.UNM woman many this 2p.ACC
     aaw-urum-i-kuan.
     take-DISTR/A-Np-FU.3p

   'Later the Japanese will come and take all of you many women [here in this village].'

Mauwake has no separate system of social deixis, as there are no honorifics, nor are there special pronouns used for particular kin or social groups or the like.

Emotional deixis, associating the speaker with the topic of conversation or distancing him from it, is a possible use for demonstratives in Papuan languages and worldwide

6.3 Deixis

(Farr & Whitehead 1982: 72–78, Lakoff 1974: 347–355). In Mauwake that possibility is not utilized: the demonstratives are neutral in this respect.

6.3.2 Locative deixis

Locative deixis, which relates the location to the speech act participants, utilizes several different word classes. The proximate demonstrative *fain* 'this' (85) (§3.6.2) and the corresponding locative adverb *fan* 'here' (86) (§3.6.3) are truly deictic, as their meaning is based on the location of the speaker. The distal-1 demonstrative *nain* 'that' and the adverb *nan* 'there' are more neutral, and the less common distal-2 and -3 deictics have other defining features besides the distance to the speaker.

(85) *Ep-ap   owora fain aaw-ep   enim-eka, iwer(a) eka fain enim-eka.*
come-SS.SEQ betelnut this take-SS.SEQ eat-IMP.2p coconut water this eat-IMP.2p
'Come and take this betelnut and eat it, (and) drink this coconut water.'

(86) *Yo   wia   wiim-urup-ep   fan wia   wu-ap   kiiriw iw-a-m.*
1s.UNM 3p.ACC escort-ascend-SS.SEQ here 3p.ACC put-SS.SEQ again go-PA-1s
'I escorted them up here and went (back) again.'

In the location verbs *fan-* 'arrive/be here' (87) and *nan-* 'arrive/be there' (§3.8.4.4.3) the deictic goal forms the verb root.

(87) *Auwa   afura fan-e-k   a,   no=ko   wiar akim-ap=ko uruf-e.*
1s/p.father lime here-PA-3s INTJ 2s.UNM=NF 3.DAT try-SS.SEQ=NF see-IMP.2s
'Ah, father's lime is here, you try it and see.'

In the directional verbs (88) (§3.8.4.4.5) as well as the related bring-verbs (89) (§3.8.2.4.2) the verb root gives indication as to the direction of the movement. Only those directional verbs where the direction is clearly related to the speaker are deictic. The second person is not a possible alternative deictic centre for the verb *ekap-* 'come'.

(88) *Uurika   nefar ikiw-i-nen.*
tomorrow 2s.DAT go-Np-FU.1s
'Tomorrow I'll come to you.' (Lit: '...I'll go (from my present place) ...')

(89) *Mua imen-ap=na   feeke wia   p-ekap-eka.*
man find-SS.SEQ=TP here.CF 3p.ACC BPX-come-IMP.2p
'If you find the men, bring them here.'

Although the prototypical deictic centre is close proximity to the speaker, it may be extended to quite a large area. In (90) where the coming of the Japanese troops is described, it covers the whole North Coast of the New Guinea island:

6 Functional domains

(90) Ne **ekap-ep** Numbia=pa nan urup-e-mik.
ADD come-SS.SEQ Numbia=LOC there ascend-PA-1/3p

'And they came and landed at Numbia.'

In narratives it is more typical that the verbs *ekap-* 'come' and *ikiw-* 'go', as well as the related verbs for 'bring' and 'take', get their deictic centre from the main character (91), not the narrator, since the narrator often is not even a participant in the story.

(91) Sawur emeria nain ikiw-eya o iikir-ami owowa ekap-o-k.
spirit woman that go-2/3s.DS 3s.UNM get.up-SS.SIM village come-PA-3s

'When the spirit woman went (away), he came to the/his village.'

6.3.3 Temporal deixis

Temporal deixis relates time to the speech act, or alternatively to the time of a specific event. Tense marking (§3.8.3.4) is the most important device for this in Mauwake, as tense is an obligatory category in verbs.[5] The present tense marks the default deictic centre, the past tense refers to the time before that point, and the future tense to the time after it. The example (3.452) is repeated here as (92):

(92) Unan **aakun-e-mik**, aakisa **aakun-i-mik** ne uurika nainiw
yesterday talk-PA-1/3p now/today talk-Np-PR.1/3p ADD tomorrow again
aakun-i-yen.
talk-Np-FU.1p

'Yesterday we talked, now/today we talk and tomorrow we'll talk again.'

Papuan languages in general favour presenting a narrative in strictly chronological order, so a relative tense, where the deictic centre is shifted either to the past or to the future, is not utilized widely. This is true of Mauwake as well. When a shift to the past is needed, it can be done by right-dislocating a medial clause after a past-tense marked final clause (93):

(93) Wilkar wia muf-em-ik-om-a-mik, **mua kui-kuisow wia**
cart 3p.ACC pull-SS.SIM-be-BEN-BNFY2.PA-1/3p man RDP-one 3p.ACC
maak-iwkin.
tell-2/3p.DS

'They₁ pulled carts for them₂, after they₂ had told the men₁ one by one.'

The same-subject sequential forms of the directional verbs *ekap-* 'come' and *ikiw-* 'go' also have temporal deictic use, the former referring to time extending to the present moment, the latter mainly to time from the present moment onward. The examples (3.594) and (3.595) are repeated below as (94) and (95).

---

[5] In some Papuan languages tense markers and demonstratives are morphologically related (Cindi Farr, p.c.), but this is not the case in Mauwake.

(94) *Naap on-am-ik-e-mik,* **ekap-ep** *aakisa.*
thus do-ss.SIM-be-PA-1/3p come-ss.SEQ now
'We have been doing like that (all the time) up until now.'

(95) *No naap ik-ok **iki(w-e)p** mokoma enuma iiwawun aakun-i-nan.*
2s.UNM thus be-ss go-ss.SEQ year new altogether talk-Np-FU.2s
'You will be like that (long time) but next year you will talk.'

The two groups of deictic temporal adverbs (§3.9.1.2) behave differently as to what the deictic centre is. The specific temporal adverbs, which refer to a certain day in relation to the utterance, always take the time of the speech act as their deictic centre (96).

(96) *...i **uurika** ora-i-yan, ifera un-owa ora-i-yan.*
...1p.UNM tomorrow descend-Np-FU.1p sea(water) fetch-NMZ descend-Np-FU.1p
'...we will go down tomorrow, we will go down to fetch sea water.'

The non-specific temporals normally do this too (97):

(97) *Nain **iiriw** me kerer-e-k, **aakisa fan** Ø.*
that1 earlier not appear now here
'That didn't appear ealier/long ago but just now (lit: now here).'

But their time reference may also be relative, with the time of the event taken as the deictic centre. This is especially true of *aakisa* 'now', which is used for perspectivization.[6] In the following two examples, the temporal adverbs *aakisa* 'now' and *aakisa fan* 'just now', do not refer externally to the time close to the speech event; instead, they are text-internal perspectivization devices to highlight the importance of the event to the main characters in the text. (98) is from an old traditional story and (99) tells about events that took place over four decades before the recording.

(98) *Nain or-op "buu" (na-e-k), **aakisa** eka saanar-e-k.*
that1 fall-ss.SEQ buu say-PA-3s now water dry-PA-3s
'It fell with a thud (and they knew that) now the water had dried up.'

(99) *Ekap-ep, ekap-ep, **aakisa fan** unowa Wewak=pa nan urup-e-mik.*
come-ss.SEQ come-ss.SEQ now here many Wewak=LOC there ascend-PA-1/3p
'They came and came, and just now many came up there in Wewak.'

For the deictic shift that takes place in indirect speech, see §8.3.2.1.2.

---

[6] The "WAS-NOW paradox" occurs in "free indirect style" when "[t]he deictic centre of the utterance is the writer/narrator, but certain deictic elements are relativized to give the impression of direct access to the character's mental states: these include temporal and spatial expressions such as *now, here, today* ... but not tense or person." (Mushin & Stirling 2000).

6.4 Quantification

Nouns are not inflected for number in Mauwake, and in the whole noun phrase the number may be left unspecified (100). The verbs are marked for either singular or plural, but the plural form can be used also for unspecified number (101). The pronouns must be either singular or plural. Besides these two obligatory number marking devices the language has several other means for quantification.

(100) *Waaya kiikir=iw uruf-i-mik,   owowa=pa.*
       pig   first=INST see-Np-PR.1/3p village=LOC
       'First they look at the pig(s) in the village.'

(101) *Nain pun sira   naap=iw, mua=ko me kerer-e-mik.*
       that1 too custom thus=INST man=NF not appear-PA-1/3p
       'That was like that too, the (guilty) person/people did not appear.'

6.4.1 Quantification in the noun phrase

Numerals (§3.4.1) are used when the exact number is relevant (102), (103), non-numeral quantifiers (§3.4.2) are used elsewhere (104).

(102) **Masin erup** *nainiw wu-owa epa   ik-ua.*
       engine two   again put-NMZ place be-PA.3s
       'There is a place for putting two more engines.'

(103) **Waa muuka arow** *ekap-o-k.*
       pig son   three come-PA-1s
       'Three piglets came.'

(104) **Emeria unow=iya** *ikiw-ep   eka   nain imar-e-mik.*
       woman many=COM go-SS.SEQ river that1 catch.fish-PA-1/3p
       'All the women went and fished at the river.'

The third person plural unmarked pronoun functions as a pluraliser both in an ordinary non phrase (105) and with place names when the population of the place is referred to (106) (§4.1.1).

(105) *Nain* **wi**   *mua sira=ke, emeria soop-owa sira.*
       that1 3p.UNM man custom=CF woman bury-NMZ custom
       'That is the men's custom, the custom of burying wife/wives.'

(106) *Irak-owa weeser-eya aria   * **wi**   *Simbine baurar-e-mik.*
       fight-NMZ finish-2/3s.DS alright 3p.UNM Simbine flee-PA-1/3p
       'When the fighting was finished, alright the Simbine people fled.'

6.4 Quantification

Even without the pluralizing pronoun, the word for, or a name of, a village may occasionally, as a subject of a clause, refer to the population and thus be interpreted as plural. In (107) this shows in the plural marking in the verb.

(107) Ne owowa oko nain=ke maak-e-mik, ...
 ADD village other that1=CF tell-PA-1/3p

 'And (the people of) that other village told him, ...'

Reduplication is another pluralizing device used in the noun phrase. Only a small group of nouns can undergo reduplication (108) (§3.2.6.2), but in adjectives it is somewhat more common (109) (§3.3).

(108) Waaya pa-ep **kio-kiowa** naap uup-e-mik.
 pig butcher-SS.SEQ RDP-piece thus cook-PA-1/3p

 'We butchered the pig and cooked the pieces like that.'

(109) Owow(a) saria=ke kiikir perek-i-mik, **mua or-oram** fain
 village headman=CF first pull.out-Np-PR.1/3p man RDP-insignificant this
 weetak.
 no

 'The village headmen harvest it first, not common people like this/us.'

Comitative noun phrases (§4.1.3) are used to indicate duality (110), (111) or plurality (112), (113).

(110) **(Yo/I)** auwa ikos fan ik-e-mik.
 1s/1p.UNM 1s/p.father together.with here be-PA-1/3p

 'I and my father are here.'

(111) No ikoka **mua owawiya** irak-ep me efar kerer-e.
 2s.UNM later man with fight-SS.SEQ not 1s.DAT appear-IMP.2s

 'Later when you and your husband fight, don't come to me.'

(112) Ne **bom=iya kateres=iya bom=iya kateres=iya** Ø.
 and bomb=COM cartridge=COM bomb=COM cartridge=COM

 'And bombs and cartridges, bombs and cartridges (kept dropping).'

(113) **Pauli ame** era=pa wia uruf-ap ...
 Pauli ASSOC road=LOC 3p.ACC see-SS.SEQ

 'I saw Pauli and the others on the road, and ...'

Personal pronouns have to mark the number,[7] but in cases where the number is unknown or unspecified, the plural is used (114).

---

[7] Except for third person dative pronoun, which is *wiar* for both singular and plural.

6 Functional domains

(114) Ikiw-ep   mua **wia**   uruf-a-k na weetak, mua=ko me **wia**   furew-a-k.
go-ss.SEQ man 3p.ACC see-PA-3s but no   man=NF not 3p.ACC sense-PA-3s

'She went and looked for anyone/people but no, she did not sense (there was) anyone (there).'

6.4.2 Quantification devices in the verbs

The person/number suffix in the finite verbs (§3.8.3.4) is the most frequently used device to indicate quantification: it shows whether the subject is singular or plural. Often the person/number suffix in the verb is the only element in a clause overtly showing number (115).

(115) Mauw-am-ik-ok   ik-ok mauw-owa weeser-eya   urera   ekap-e-**mik**.
work-ss.SIM-be-ss be-ss work-NMZ finish-2/3s.DS afternoon come-PA-1/3p

'They came and landed there at Numbia.'

But if the subject noun is [-human], even the person/number suffix may not indicate the number, since plural marking is only used for humans and occasionally for large animals, and only very rarely for inanimates. In (116), the verbs in both sentences refer to airplanes, but because the action in the first sentence is attributed to the soldiers inside the planes, the finite verb is in plural form.

(116) Amerika irak-ow(a) iinan aasa ekap-ep   Ulingan nan bom
America fight-NMZ sky   canoe come-ss.SEQ Ulingan there bomb
fu-fuurk-ikiw-e-mik. Iinan=iw iinan=iw wu-ami   feenap Wewak kame
RDP-drop-go-PA-1/3p   sky=INST sky=INST put-ss.SIM like.this Wewak side
naap **ikiw-o-k**.
thus go-PA-3s

'American fighter planes came and went on dropping bombs there in Ulingan. They were really high up and went like this to Wewak.'

Reduplication is more common in verbs than in nouns or adjectives (§3.8.2.4.1). In transitive verbs the reduplication indicates plurality of the resulting object (117), (118).

(117) Kau nain pa-ep,   gele-gelemuti-tik **pu-puuk-ap**   uup-e-mik.
cow that1 butcher-ss.SEQ RDP-small-RDP   RDP-cut-ss.SEQ cook-PA-1/3

'They butchered the cow and cut it into small pieces and cooked it/them.'

(118) Aruf-irapar-emi   meren(a) suuw-owa wiar **pere-perek-a-mik**.
hit-to.and.fro-ss.SIM leg   pull-NMZ 3.DAT RDP-tear-PA-1/3p

'They hit him all over and tore his trousers to pieces.'

Both the distributive suffixes (§3.8.2.3.2) mark plurality; the argument that the marking pluralizes depends on the type of verb (119)–(122).

6.4 Quantification

(119) Iinan aasa fan **or-om-ik-omak-i-ya**.
sky canoe here descend-ss.sim-be-distr/pl-Np-pr.3s
'Many planes are descending here.'

(120) Koora pun ariwa=ke kuum-eya **aw-omak-e-k**.
house also arrow=cf burn-2/3s.ds burn-distr/pl-pa-3s
'Also many houses burned down when the ammunition burned them.'

(121) Owowa wia **wi-urum-e-p** naap ikiw-i-kuan.
village 3p.acc give.them-distr/a-ss.seq thus go-Np-fu.3p
'They give villages to all of them and then they go like that.' (Certain villages are designated for certain people to go to.)

(122) O iiriw maa bala wiar **aaw-urum-ep** ona
3s.unm earlier thing ornament 3.acc get-distr/a-ss.seq 3s.gen
mia=pa-r=iw wu-a-k.
body=loc-Ø=lim put-pa-3s
'Earlier he had received ornaments from all of them and (now) he put them on his own body only.'

In the object cross-referencing verbs (§3.8.4.2.4) the root shows singularity (124) or plurality (123) of the object that is cross-referenced.

(123) Iperowa opora **wiok-i-yan**.
middle.aged talk follow.them-Np-fu.1p
'We'll follow/obey the talk of the middle-aged men.'

(124) Maa eneka kes mane-maneka oram **iw-e-mik**.
thing tooth case RDP-big just give.him-pa-1/3p
'They gave him big meat (tin) cases for free.'

When a numeral follows a nominalized verb form and precedes the resultative verb ar- 'become' (§3.8.4.4.4), that indicates how many times an action was performed (125), (126).

(125) Ewar maneka **muf-owa erup ar-e**.
wind big pull-nmz two become-imp.2s
'Breathe deeply twice.'

(126) Kiikir iinan=pa **akim-owa arow ar-e-mik**.
first top=loc try-nmz three become-pa-1/3p
'First they tried it three times on top.'

6.5 Comparison

6.5.1 Comparison of inequality: comparative constructions

As the inventory of adjectives is typically small in Papuan languages (Haiman 1980: 268, Reesink 1987: 63, MacDonald 1990: 105–107), it is no surprise that regular morphological or syntactic forms to express comparative and superlative are rare, or even non-existent. In Mauwake comparison can be expressed in various ways, but there are no specific forms that could be called comparative or superlative. Since the overall frequency of comparative constructions is very low, it is not possible here to call any of them the preferred strategy.

One way to express comparison is to conjoin two structurally similar clauses, where the adjective in the first one functioning as the non-verbal predicate is not intensified, but in the second clause it has an intensifier. The first clause contains the standard of comparison (127).

(127) Poka fain **maala**, ne oko **maala akena**.
       stilt this long ADD other long very

       'This stilt is long but the other one is longer (lit: very long).'

Although the clauses usually are descriptive, as above, they do not have to be. In the following example the locative noun *iinan* 'top', functioning like an adjective here, modifies the head noun in both the clauses (128).

(128) Ema   **iinan** urup-e-m, ne no   ema   **iinan akena**
       mountain top   ascend-PA-1s ADD 2s.UNM mountain top   very
       urup-o-n.
       ascend-PA-2s

       'I climbed a high mountain, but you climbed a higher (lit: very high) mountain.'

Another way is to use adjectives that are antonymous (129). As a comparative structure this is problematic in that it is arbitrary to call the subject of one clause the standard and the subject of the other the object of comparison.

(129) Waaya nain **gelemuta**, oko nain **maneka**.
       pig   that1 small   other that1 big

       'That pig is smaller than the other one.' Or: 'That other pig is bigger than that one.' (Lit: That pig is small, the other one is big.)

The same caveat applies to the following structure, where the adjective is negated for comparison (130):

(130) Auwa   uuw-owa **eliwa**, mua oko   fain **wia**.
       1s/p.father work-NMZ good   man other this no

       'My father's work is better than this other man's. (Lit: My father's work is good, this other man's is not.)'

According to Stassen (2008) this CONJOINED COMPARATIVE strategy, exemplified above, is prevalent in Australia and New Guinea. But the sample of New Guinean languages used for the generalization is very small (and includes both Austronesian and Papuan languages), and I suggest that at least for TNG languages the EXCEED COMPARATIVE, the strategy represented in that sample only by Amele (Roberts 1987: 134–135), is a possible alternative and may actually be as common as, or more common than, the Conjoined Comparative strategy.[8] There are two clauses in this pattern too: one may be equative and contain an adjective, the other is a transitive clause containing the verb *nomak-* 'exceed/surpass' as the predicate and the standard of comparison as the object (131)–(133). The order of the two clauses is free.

(131) Maa mane-maneka, maa fain **nomak-ep** ik-ua.
 thing RDP-big thing this surpass-SS.SEQ be-PA.3s
 'They are big things, greater than these.'

(132) No yiena nembesir **nomak-ep** maneka ar-ek-a-m
 2s.UNM 1p.GEN ancestor surpass-SS.SEQ big become-CNTF-PA-1s
 na-ep=i?
 say-SS.SEQ=QM
 'Do you want to become greater than our ancestors?'

(133) Nomokowa kakawa fain iiwa, oko **nomak-ep** puuk-a-m.
 tree strip this short other surpass-SS.SEQ cut-PA-1s.
 'This piece of timber is short, I cut the other one longer.'

A transitive clause with *nomak-* is also used, when a noun rather than an adjective describes the characteristic under comparison (134), (135).

(134) O kekan-owa=ke yo kekan-owa efar **nomak-e-k.**
 3s.UNM be.strong-NMZ=CF 1s.UNM be.strong-NMZ 1s.DAT surpass-PA-3s
 'He is stronger than I. (Lit: His strength surpasses my strength.)'

(135) Mua oko=ke ikiwosa/amisa efar **nomak-e-k.**
 man other=CF head/knowledge 1s.DAT surpass-PA-3s
 'Someone else is more intelligent than I. (Lit: …surpasses my head/knowledge.)'

In (136), *nomak-* is employed to compare arrival times:

(136) …wia **nomak-ep** me miim-ep … urup-i-yen, weetak.
 3p.ACC surpass-SS.SEQ not precede-SS.SEQ … ascend-Np-FU.1p no
 '… we'll not go up earlier than they, no.'

---

[8] My opinion is mainly based on the experience of working with national translators. When searching for translation equivalents for comparison forms, they often start with the Conjoined Comparative pattern, but very soon after realising that they do not have to stay within the limits of stative clauses only or stick to the adjective class, many actually tend to prefer the Exceed Comparative as the more natural and accurate expression for comparison. Reesink (1987: 68) mentions both of these mechanisms for Usan.

For superlatives, the quantifier *unowiya* 'all' may be used in the object NP (137).

(137) No   unuma nain mua **unow=iya** wia   nomakek.
      2s.UNM name that1 man many=COM 3p.ACC surpass-PA-3s

'You are the most important of all people.' (Lit: 'Your name surpasses all people.')

In (138), the two comparison strategies are employed in the same sentence, and the intensifier *akena* 'very' indicates superlative:

(138) Poka fain **maala**, nain **nomak-e-k**, ne oko nain **maala akena**.
      stilt this long   that1 surpass-PA-3s ADD other that1 long   very

'This stilt is longer than that one, and/but that other one is the longest.'

When there is a difference between things that are compared, but the difference is not graded, the phrase *sira oko* 'different (lit: another kind)' is used to modify the noun (139), (140).

(139) Iwakara **sira oko** miim-ap   baurar-e-mik.
      neck   kind other hear-SS.SEQ flee-PA-1/3p

'They heard a different voice and ran away.'

(140) Takira   opor(a) **sira oko**=ko me wia   maak-e.
      youngster talk   kind other=NF not 3p.ACC tell-IMP.2s

'Don't tell different things to the youngsters (from what you are supposed to tell them).'

6.5.2 Comparison of similarity: equative constructions

A possible outcome of comparison is that the compared items, or actions, are identical or similar rather than different. Mauwake has several equative constructions,[9] ways of expressing similarity.

For an equivalent of 'as ADJ as' structure, the intensity adverb *pepek* 'enough' is used, often together with another intensifier (141), (142).

(141) No   merena **maneka** yo   merena **iiwawun pepek**.
      2s.UNM foot   big   1s.UNM foot   altogether enough

'Your feet are big, just as big as my feet.' Or: 'Your big feet are just as big as mine.'

(142) Urauwa maala Moro owowa **maala pepek   akena**.
      hole   long Moro village long   enough very

'The hole (is) as deep as Moro village is long.'

---

[9] The term "equative construction" is not to be confused with equative clauses discussed in §5.6.1

The two most common words used in equative constructions are the deictic manner adverb *naap* 'thus, like that' (§3.9.1.3) and the postposition *saarik* 'like' (§3.12.3). *Naap* is used to compare things that are essentially the same, even identical (143)–(145).

(143) *Auwa   mia maneka, muuka pun **naap**.*
      1s/p.father body big   son   also like.that
      'The father is big, (and) the son is like that too.'

(144) *Muuka nain (ona)   wiawi **naap**.*
      boy   that1 3s/p.GEN father like.that
      'The boy/son is like his father.'

(145) *I   maa en-owa **naap**   nain yienak-e.*
      1p.UNM food eat-NMZ like.that that1 feed.us-IMP.2s
      'Give us food like that.'

Also the corresponding proximal manner adverb *feenap* 'like this' is used occasionally (146):

(146) *Uura **feenap** nain, wi   wilkar nain muf-e-mik.*
      night like.this that1 3p.UNM cart   that1 pull-PA-1/3p
      'On nights like this they pulled the carts.'

The postposition *saarik* 'like' expresses some similarity between two essentially different things. The actual point of similarity may be expressed explicitly (147) or left implied (148).

(147) *Pon   oposia eliwa, aara   oposia **saarik**.*
      turtle meat   good   chicken meat   like
      'Turtle meat is good, like chicken meat.'

(148) *Mera iperuma ifa   **saarik**.*
      fish eel   snake like
      'An eel is like a snake.'

The similarity may not be a particular quality, expressible with an adjective. In (149) it is the number of different things that is compared.

(149) *Ulingan fa=na   iinan aasa nepa **saarik**, unow(a) akena.*
      Ulingan INTJ=TP sky   canoe bird like   many   very
      'Ulingan – wow – the airplanes were like birds, there were lots of them.'

When *saarik* is postposed after a nominalized verb, it indicates pretension. This is a case of a similarity of action, but not "the real thing" (150), (151).

6 Functional domains

(150) *Moram era **paayar-owa** saarik fan yia p-or-o-n?*
       why   road understand-NMZ like here 1p.ACC BPX-descend-PA-2s
       'Why did you bring us down here as if you knew the road?'

(151) *O   Menamura **or-owa** saarik iwera fook-a-k.*
       3s.UNM Manam   descend-NMZ like coconut split-PA-3s
       'He split coconuts (for copra), as if he were going to Manam.'

In other cases it may not indicate pretension but a false or ungrounded expectation (152):

(152) *Yo   **efa** sesenar-owa saarik oram   maneka uuw-owa yoowa*
       1s.UNM 1s.ACC buy-NMZ   like   for.nothing big   work-NMZ hot
       on-a-m.
       do-PA-1s
       'I worked hard for nothing, as if they would pay me for it (lit: buy me).'

The phrase **nainiw akena** 'exactly like' is reserved for the cases of striking similarity (153).

(153) *Wiipa nain onak   miikapura **nainiw akena**.*
       girl that1 3s/p.mother face   again   very
       'The girl's face is exactly like her mother's.'

7 Sentence types

The basic speech acts are mostly expressed by the functional sentence types typical of them: a statement by a declarative sentence, a question by an interrogative sentence and a command by an imperative sentence.

7.1 Statements

The declarative sentence, used to make a statement/assertion, is the unmarked sentence type, default in narrative, descriptive and procedural texts and common in other text types as well. The final verb has full tense and person/number marking. The intonation pattern in declarative sentences is falling (§2.1.3.2).

7.2 Questions

The basic function of questions, or interrogative sentences, is to request either information or some action from the addressee(s). Rhetorical questions have other functions as well. Structurally the two basic types are non-polar, or content, questions and polar, or yes-no, questions. Echo questions and confirmation questions are modifications of these.

7.2.1 Non-polar questions

Non-polar questions, or content questions, require the use of question words (§3.7.1). There is no question-word fronting: a question word occupies the same position that the questioned element would have in a statement.[1] The intonation is falling like in a statement, but the stressed syllable of the question word has a slightly higher pitch than the words before and/or after it (§2.1.3.2).

Any argument or peripheral in a clause can be questioned, as well as its constituents (1)–(7).

(1) *(Mua) naareke koora ku-am-ika-i-ya?*
 (man) who.CF house build-SS.SIM-be-Np-3s
 'Who is building a house?'

(2) *Muuka nain maa mauwa enim-i-non?*
 son that1 thing what eat-Np-FU.3s
 'What will the son eat?'

---
[1] This is typical of Papuan SOV languages (Reesink 1987: 294).

7 Sentence types

(3) No   muuka wiipa   **kamin**   (nefar ik-ua)?
    2s.UNM son   daughter how.many (2s.DAT be-PA.3s)
    'How many children (lit. son daughter) do you have?'

(4) Mua napuma   **moram** owowa p-ikiw-i-yan?
    man sick/body why   village BPX-go-Np-FU.1p
    'Why should we take the body to the village?'

(5) Mukuna aw-o-k   nain **kamenap** umuk-i-yen?
    fire   burn-PA-3s that1 how   extinguish-Np-FU.1p
    'How could we extinguish the fire that was burning?'

(6) Maa nain epa   **kain=pa**   imenar-i-non?
    thing that1 place which=LOC appear-Np-FU.3s
    'Where (lit: in which place) will that thing appear?'

(7) Wi   **kaakew**   mua=ke uf-e-mik?
    3p.UNM which.village man=CF dance-PA-1/3p
    'The men of which village danced?'

The kind of ambiguity between a subject and an object that Usan has, which arises from the fronting of a topicalized element[2] (Reesink 1987: 294), is not possible in Mauwake. This is because the question words take the contrastive focus marker -*ke* when functioning as a subject. Because of elision, and the merging of the contrastive focus marker with the question word, the word for 'who' in Mauwake actually has a contrasted/nominative (1), (9) and an accusative form (8). The object is fronted in (9) as a theme; in (10) the object is not fronted.

(8) [Mua nain]s [**naarew**]o aruf-a-k?
    man that1 who(ACC) hit-PA-3s
    'Who did that man hit?'

(9) [Mua nain]o [**naareke**]s aruf-a-k?
    man that1 who.CF   hit-PA-3s
    'Who hit that man?'

(10) [(**Mua**) **naareke**]s [mua nain]o aruf-a-k?
     (man) who.CF   man that1 hit-PA-3s
     'Who hit that man?'

It is most common to have the question in a main clause, but medial clauses also easily allow non-polar questions. The scope of the question word only extends to the clause which contains it. In (11) the fact that the people ran away is not questioned.

---

[2] A THEME in my terminology here.

(11) **Mua naareke wia** *aruf-eya* baurar-e-mik?
man who.CF 3p.ACC hit-2/3s.DS run.away-PA-1/3p
'Who hit them (so that) they ran away?'

A constituent in a complement clause (with a nominalized verb) can be questioned (12), but not in a relative clause (13).

(12) **Ama kamin** *ikiw-owa* ma-e-mik?
sun/time how.much go-NMZ say-PA-1/3p
'At what time did they say to go?'

(13) *****Wi** *iikamin ekap-e-mik nain* wia *uruf-a-n?*
3p.UNM when come-PA-1/3p that1 3p.ACC see-PA-2s

Multiple constituents in the same clause can be questioned with a question word. This is not common, but the following elicited sentences are considered completely natural (14), (15).

(14) Emeria **naareke** ama **kamin=pa** ekap-o-k?
woman who.CF sun/time how.much=LOC come-PA-3s
'Who (woman) came at what time?'

(15) Mua **kain=ke** emeria **kain** aaw-o-k?
man which=CF woman which take-PA-3s
'Which man took/married which woman?'

When there is a lot of hesitation in the question, the question clitic *-i*, which normally marks a polar question, is added to the end of the question (16). This is the same form that the echo questions have (§7.2.3).

(16) Auwa efa amukar-e-k nain yo **kamenap** ar-i-nen=i?
father 1s.ACC scold-PA-3s that 1s.UNM how become-Np-FU.1s=QM
'(I wonder) what will happen to me because father scolded me?'

7.2.2 Polar questions

Polar questions, also called nexus questions, or yes-no questions, expect either confirmation or negation of the questioned proposition. According to Wurm (1982: 63), a polar question in TNG languages is often marked by an affix which is part of the verb complex. In Mauwake it is coded by the question clitic *-i* (§3.12.8) and slightly rising intonation (§2.1.3.2), both occurring sentence-finally. Because Mauwake is an SOV language, the clitic most often attaches itself to a verb (17), but it can attach to another word class as well, when there is no final verb (18), (19):

7 Sentence types

(17) *Ni   nain me=ko uruf-a-man=**i**?*
     2p.UNM that1 not=NF see-PA-2p=QM
     'Didn't you see that?'

(18) *Nos=**i**?*
     2s.FC=QM
     'You?'

(19) *Maa nain eliwa=**ki**?*
     thing that1 good=CF.QM
     'Is that thing good?'

When the polar question is in the negative, a one-word answer may be ambiguous. Traditionally the answer either affirmed or negated the affirmative or negative POLARITY of the question, but because of the influence of Tok Pisin and English, Mauwake is changing so that the answer tends to either affirm or negate the VERB (§6.2.4).

Alternative questions can be closed or open.[3] The former give two, or sometimes more, alternatives, one of which has to be chosen; the latter also allow the possibility that none of the alternatives is chosen. The two types differ in Mauwake as to the nature of the last alternative.

The non-final alternatives in a closed question take the question marker *-i*. The final alternative, usually preceded by the disjunctive coordinator *e* 'or' (§3.11.2), may be just a negation particle *weetak* or *wia* (20), a full statement (21), or an elliptical clause with only the questioned item (22).

(20) *Yo   emeria=ko efar   uruf-a-man=**i** e weetak?*
     1s.UNM woman=NF 1s.DAT see-PA-2p=QM or no
     'Did you see my wife or not?'

(21) *Nain kema suuw-i-man=**i**   e kema irin-ar-e-man?*
     that1 liver push-Np-PR.2p=QM or liver stuck-INCH-PA-2p
     'Do you remember (lit: push the liver) that, or have you forgotten (lit: liver is stuck) it?'

(22) *No   Matukar ikiw-i-nan=**i**   Dylup=**i** e Sarang?*
     2s.UNM Matukar go-Np-FU.2s=QM Dylup=QM or Sarang
     'Will you go to Matukar, Dylup, or Sarang?'

When the alternative question is open, the question marker *-i* marks not only the non-final alternatives but also the final one (23), (24).

---

[3] Haspelmath (2007) calls only the former an alternative (or disjunctive) question, and the latter a question with standard disjunction.

(23) *Matukar ikiw-i-nan=i   e Dylup ikiw-i-nan=i?*
Matukar go-Np-FU.2s=QM or Dylup go-Np-FU.2s=QM
'Will you go to Matukar or Dylup (or perhaps neither)?'

(24) *Mukuna=ko wu-a-man=i   e mua=ko wia   uruf-a-man=i?*
fire=NF   put-PA-2p=QM or man=NF 3.ACC see-PA-2p=QM
'Did you light a fire or did you feel (that there was) a man?'

An alternative question is left open also when the last alternative is replaced with the question word *kamenion* '(or) what?'/ '(or) how is it?' (25), (26).

(25) *Maa en-owa=ko p-ekap-e-mik=i   kamenion?*
food eat-NMZ=NF BPX-come-PA-1/3p=QM or.what
'Did they bring food, or what?'

(26) *Beel(a)-al-i-non=i   kamenion, naap uruf-am-ik-ua.*
rotten-INCH-Np-FU.3s=QM or.what   thus see-SS.SIM-be-PA.3s
'He was watching whether it would rot or what would happen.'

Leading questions are another subtype of polar questions. The person asking wants to guide the answer in a certain direction. This is done in Mauwake by adding the epistemic modal adverb clitic *-yon* 'perhaps' to the predicate of the question clause. The slightly rising intonation in the question distinguishes it from a statement (27).

(27) *Me ikiw-o-k=**yon**?*
not go-PA-3s-perhaps
'He didn't go, did he?'

7.2.3 Echo questions

Echo questions are used when an original statement or question is questioned, either because it was not properly heard in the first place or because the addressee has some doubts about it. Structurally all echo questions are polar questions.

Echo question of a STATEMENT is like a normal polar question, except that the questioned element receives an extra stress (28).

(28) *A:Paapa   Goroka ikiw-i-non. - B: Goróka ikiw-i-non=i?*
A:elder.sibling Goroka go-Np-FU.3p - B: Goroka go-Np-FU.3p=QM
'A: Big brother is going to Goroka. B: Is he going to GOROKA?'

When the validity of a NON-POLAR QUESTION (29) is questioned, the question clitic is attached directly to the end of the question already containing a question word (30).

(29) *A: Mua naarew wia   maak-e-k?*
A: man who   3.ACC tell-PA-3s
'Who did he tell?'

7 Sentence types

(30) B: *Mua naarew wia   maak-e-k=**i**?*
B: man who   3.ACC tell-PA-3s=QM
'Who did he tell???'

But if the addressee wants to check if (s)he heard correctly, the echoed question is made into a complement of a sentence-final utterance verb, to which a question clitic is attached (31).

(31) B: *Mua naarew wia   maak-e-k **na-i-n=i**?*
B: man who   3.ACC tell-PA-3s say-Np-PR.2s=QM
'Are you asking who he told?'

Since POLAR QUESTIONS already have a clause-final question clitic, an echo question cannot be formed by adding the same clitic a second time. Instead, the original question is made into a complement of the utterance verb *ma-* 'say' or *na-* 'say/think' (32).

(32) A: *Nain eliwa=ki?*   B: *Nain eliwa-ki   **ma-e-n=i**?*
A: that1 good=CF.QM B: that1 good=CF.QM say-PA-2s=QM
'A: Is that good? B: Did you ask if that is good?'

7.2.4 Confirmation questions

Confirmation questions are mainly used in argumentation. The question word *naap-i* '(is it) like that?' is tagged to a statement, which may be preceded by another question (33).

(33) *Ni   kema maneka naap efa   wu-i-man=i,   yo   eliw nia*
2p.UNM liver big   thus 1s.ACC put-Np-PR.2p=QM 1s.UNM well 2p.ACC
*saliw-i-nen,   **naap=i**?*
heal-Np-FU.1s thus=QM
'Do you believe about me that I can heal you, is that so?'

7.2.5 Indirect questions

Indirect questions (34), (35) are a subgroup of complement clauses and are discussed under INDIRECT SPEECH in §8.3.2.1.2.

(34) [*Yo   maa   mauwa uruf-a-m*] *efa   na-e-k.*
1s.UNM thing what   see-PA-1s   1s.ACC say-PA-3s
'He asked me what I saw.'

(35) [*Kamin   wu-a-mik(-yon)*], *yo   me wiar amis-ar-e-m.*
how.much put-PA-1/3p-perhaps 1s.UNM not 3.DAT knowledge-INCH-PA-1s
'I don't know how much they put.'

7.2.6 Rhetorical questions

Traditionally the Mauwake speakers lived in a society where everyone more or less knew everybody's business and there was not much need for eliciting information by asking questions. Consequently, many questions in normal speech are rhetorical in nature. The question form may be used to emphasize the opposite of what is said (36), (37) or sometimes just to prompt the addressee to think more clearly, but very often rhetorical questions have an element of reproach or assigning blame as well (38), (39).

(36) *Maamuma kaaneke ika-eya ni-i-yan?*
money where.CF be-2/3s.DS give.you-Np-FU.1p
'Where would we have that kind of money to give you? (=We do not have money to give you.)'

(37) *Yo anane niam=iya ika-i-nen=i?*
1s.UNM always 2p.REFL=COM be-Np-FU.1s=QM
'Will I be with you forever? (= I will not.)'

(38) *No moram naap om-em-ika-i-n?*
2s.UNM why thus cry-SS.SIM-be-Np-PR.2s
'Why are you crying like that? (=You should not cry like that.)'

(39) *Mua naareke nia maak-eya ekap-e-man?*
man who.CF 2p.ACC say-2/3p.DS come-PA-2p
'Who told you to come? (=You shouldn't have come)'

Implied reproach or accusation is particularly common with questions including the word *moram* 'why?' (40), but it is not limited to them. Especially accusations of theft are couched in neutral-looking questions (41).

(40) *Aa muuka, no moram naap yia on-a-n?*
oh son 2s.UNM why thus 1s.ACC do-PA-2s
'Oh son, why did you do this to us?'

(41) *Yo seewa gelemuta uruma or-o-k nain uruf-a-man=i?*
1s.UNM rat small valley descend-PA-3s that1 see-PA-2p=QM
'Have you seen my "little rat" (pig) that went down to the valley? (implying: I have no doubt that you have stolen my pig.)'

Because questions are so easily understood as reproaches or accusations, real questions are often preceded by a preamble to prevent this interpretation (42)–(44).

(42) [*Ama arow=pa mauw-owa weeser-eya*] *maa mauwa on-a-man?*
sun three=LOC work-NMZ finish-2/3s.DS thing what do-PA-2p
'After your work finished at three, what did you do?'

(43) [Yo   oram nefa   nokar-i-yem], soomia=ko efar   uruf-a-n=i?
     1s.UNM just   2s.ACC ask-Np-PR.1s spoon=NF 1s.DAT see-PA-2s=QM
     'I'm just asking: have you seen my spoon?'

(44) Anane maneka ewur   me urup-i-n   nain moram?
     always big   quickly not ascend-Np-PR.2s that1 why
     'What is the reason why you never come up quickly?'

7.2.7 Answers to questions

Apart from rhetorical questions, a verbal answer is often expected. An affirmative answer to a polar question (45) may be just an affirmative interjection (46) or the verb from the question by itself or preceded by the interjection (47). A negative answer must have at least one negator (§6.2), whether only a negative interjection (§6.2.3), or any of the other negators, or both (48). Less commonly the answer may also be a full statement with or without a preceding affirmation (49) or negation.

(45) No   uurika   owow maneka ikiw-i-nan=i?
     2s.UNM tomorrow village big   go-Np-FU.2s=QM
     'Are you going to town tomorrow?'

(46) Ae/Oo.
     yes
     'Yes.'

(47) (Ae,) ikiw-i-nen.
     yes   go-Np-FU.1s
     '(Yes,) I am going.'

(48) (Weetak,) me ikiw-i-nen.
     no   not go-Np-FU.1s
     '(No,) I am not going.'

(49) (Ae,) yo   uurika   owow maneka ikiw-i-nen.
     yes   1s.UNM tomorrow village big   go-Np-FU.1s
     '(Yes,) I'll go to town tomorrow.'

The reply to a non-polar question most typically includes an answer to the questioned item and often the verb of the original question too (50)–(51).

(50) Maa   sira kamenap nain en-em-ik-e-man?
     thing/food kind how   that1 eat-ss.SIM-be-PA-2p
     'What kind of food did you eat?'

(51) Wi   mia kia   en-owa   nain   (en-em-ik-e-mik).
      3p.UNM body white eat-NMZ that1 (eat-SS.SIM-be-PA-1/3p)
      '(We ate) the white people's food.'

If the speaker wants to negate the presupposition in the question (52), (s)he begins with a negator, and then goes on to answer the question itself (53).

(52) Neremena   kamenap nefa   on-a-k?
      2s/p.nephew how   2s.ACC do-PA-3s
      'What did your nephew do to you?'

(53) **Weetak**, yo   mauw-a-m   ne o   me efa   uruf-a-k.
      no   1s.UNM work-PA-1s ADD 3s.UNM not 1s.ACC see-PA-3s
      'I worked but he did not even look at me.' (Implying: Your presupposition is wrong; he did not do anything indecent to me.)

If the question or statement itself is negative, a one-word answer is ambiguous in present-day usage, and a full clause is needed to disambiguate it (54). Traditionally an answer to a question affirmed or negated the affirmative or negative POLARITY of the question or statement (55).

(54) O   aakun-owa marew=yon.   -**Wia**, aakun-owa wiar   ik-ua.
      3s.UNM   talk-NMZ no(ne)-perhaps -no talk-NMZ   3.DAT   be-PA.3s
      'Perhaps he doesn't have anything to say. –No, he DOES have something to say.'

(55) Auwa   me ekap-o-k=i?   -**Weetak** (ekap-o-k).
      1s/p.father not come-PA-3s=QM -no   (come-PA-3s)
      'Didn't father come? –Yes (he DID).'

But Mauwake is changing to become more like English in that the negative answer stands for a negative statement regardless of the polarity of the question or statement that it is a reply to (56):[4]

(56) Auwa   me ekap-o-k=i?   -**Weetak** (me ekap-o-k).
      1s/p.father not come-PA-3s=QM -no   (not come-PA-3s)
      'Didn't father come? –No (he didn't).'

7.3 Commands

The simple imperative is the default way of expressing a command in Mauwake. It shows in the verb inflection (57) (§3.8.3.3.2). In a prohibition the verbal negator *me* 'not' precedes the simple imperative (58).

---

[4] A similar change is taking place in Tok Pisin, and it is likely that this is causing the development in Mauwake too.

7 Sentence types

(57) *Ni   Medebur **karu-eka, baurar-eka**.*
      2p.UNM Medebur run-IMP.2p flee-IMP.2p
      'Run(pl.) to Medebur, flee.'

(58) *Momora, no   naap **me ma-e**.*
      fool   2s.UNM thus not say-IMP.2s
      'Fool, don't say like that.'

The simple imperative can be strengthened with the intensity adverb *akena* 'very, truly' following the verb (59).

(59) *Ni   sira samora **piipu-eka akena**.*
      2p.UNM habit bad   leave-IMP.2p   truly
      'Really get rid of your bad habits.'

Another way to intensify it is with the clause-final interjection *nom* 'PLEASE!', which is only used when a person has already been told to do something at least once and has not complied (60).

(60) ***Pootin-e,   nom!***
      stop.crying-IMP.2s please
      'Stop crying, PLEASE!'

The imperative marking on verbs shows only in the finite forms. When a command or request is in a medial clause, and the final clause verb is in the indicative mood and future tense, there is nothing in the medial verb to indicate the mood (61).

(61) *No   opaimika pon   aaw-o-n nain **ma-eya**   i   miim-i-yen.*
      2s.UNM talk   turtle get-PA-3s that1 tell-2/3s.DS 1p.UNM hear-Np-FU.1p
      'Tell us about your catching a turtle, and we'll listen.' (Or: 'You will tell us about your catching a turtle and we'll listen.')

This type of clause combination has given rise to a softer, less direct command, which is given with a medial different-subject form of a verb; the final clause is left out altogether (62).[5] This form is particularly common when commands are given to children.

(62) ***P-ekap-eya!***
      BPX-come-2/3s.DS
      'Bring it!'

The imperative of the final clause may have an influence on the medial clause(s) so that they are also interpreted as belonging within the scope of the command. This happens very easily with same-subject medial verbs (63); it is also possible but much less likely

---

[5] This fairly common use of a medial verb form in Papuan languages is probably the origin of the use of *pastaim* 'first' in Tok Pisin commands, e.g. *Kam pastaim* 'Come!'

when the subject changes (64).[6] Example (65) is ambiguous: in the situation where it was said, the medial clause was not in the scope of the final clause imperative; in some other situation it could be. When the medial verb has a first person form, imperative interpretation is not possible (66).

(63) *Emeria manina **ikiw-ep** en-owa **nop-ap** **or-eka**.*
woman garden go-SS.SEQ eat-NMZ search-SS.SEQ descend-IMP.2p
'Women, go to the garden, look for food and come down.'

(64) *Mua emeria wia **maak-eya** me efa **enim-uk**.*
man woman 3p.ACC tell-2/3s.DS not 2s.ACC eat-IMP.3p
'Tell the people and let them not eat me.'

(65) *Feeke wiar **ik-ok** kiiriw mua wiar **urup-e**.*
here.CF 3.DAT be-SS again man 3.DAT ascend-IMP.2s
'Having been here with him (=your brother), go up to your husband again.'

(66) *I or-op ununa **anum-amkun ma-eka**, "..."*
1p.UNM descend slit.gong beat-1s/p.DS say-IMP.2p
'When we go down and beat the slit gong, say, "..."'

A special feature in Mauwake commands is that they occur with a pronominal subject more often than statements do (§§3.5.2.1, 3.5.11).

Although a command is usually directed towards one or more people in the second person, it can also be directed towards the speaker as part of a group of two (67) or more (68), or towards a third person in singular (69) or plural (70).

(67) *Aria, i owowa=ko **or-u**.*
alright 1p.UNM village=NF descend-IMP.1d
'Alright, let's go down to the village.'

(68) *Ikiw-ep=ko wia **uruf-ikua**.*
go-SS.SEQ=NF 3p.ACC see-IMP.1p
'Let's go and see them.'

(69) *Womokowa me wia **maak-inok**.*
3s/p.brother not 3p.ACC tell-IMP.3s
'Let her not talk to her brothers.'

(70) *Ona mua owawiya ek-ap uruf-am-ik-ok **ep-am-ika-uk**.*
3s.GEN man with go-SS.SEQ see-SS.SIM-be-SS come-SS.SIM-be-IMP.3p
'Let her keep going with her husband, seeing him (= her father) and coming back.'

---

[6] This example may also be interpreted to have two commands: a "soft" one, expressed with a medial verb, and a regular one.

7 Sentence types

Imperatives cannot have tense distinctions, but aspectual distinctions are possible. The continuous aspect form is used for habitual aspect in (70) above, and for continuous aspect in (71). Completive aspect is used in (72) and stative aspect in (73).

(71) Sira   naap **on-am-ik-eka**.
custom thus do-ss.SIM-be-IMP.2p
'Keep doing like that.'

(72) Aakisa naap **on-ap-pu-e**.
now   thus do-ss.SEQ-CMPL-IMP.2s
'Now do that.'

(73) No   me mokoka **opar-ep-ik-e**.
2s.UNM not eye   close-ss.SEQ-be-IMP.2s
'Don't have/keep your eyes closed.'

The second person future tense form is also used for a command, but this is not very common. It is used in a specific situation, not for giving generic commands or rules. The sentence (74) was said to a person who was suspected of lying, and in (75) parents give instructions to their daughter how to mourn.

(74) No   **me sail-i-nan**!
2s.UNM not lie-Np-FU.2s
'Don't lie!'

(75) Naap ma-emi   **om-em-ika-i-nan**   na.
thus say-ss.SIM cry-ss.SIM-be-Np-FU.2s INTJ
'Say like that and wail.'

8 Clause combinations

Some linguistic models, the mainstream generative grammar in particular, disregard the distinction between a clause and a sentence, but here the distinction is maintained. One of the main reasons is the medial clause system operating in Mauwake. A simple sentence in Mauwake consists of one clause, but if that is a verbal clause, it must be a finite clause, not a medial one, as medial clauses only function within a sentence in combination with other clauses. Their distribution is restricted to non-final position in a sentence – they may occur sentence-finally only if they are dislocated or the final clause is ellipted. Medial clauses also add the chaining structure to the clause combination possibilities (§8.2), besides regular coordination (§8.1) and subordination (§8.3).

A sentence has the following features. It consists of one or more clauses. The end of a sentence is marked in speech by a falling intonation, or by a slightly rising intonation in polar questions, and normally a pause. The sentence-final falling intonation is clear, and can be distinguished from a less noticeable fall at the end of a non-final finite clause. In writing the end of a sentence is marked by a full stop, a question mark or an exclamation mark.

A simple sentence is the same as a clause, and was discussed in Chapter 5. When two main clauses are joined in a coordinate sentence, they are independent of each other as to their functional sentence type. In (1) the first clause is declarative and the second one interrogative; in (2) the first clause is imperative and the second one declarative, but the order could also be reversed.

(1) Yo   owora=ko   me aaw-e-m, no   moram efa   ma-i-n?
    1s.UNM betelnut=NF not take-PA-1s 2s.UNM why   1s.ACC say-NP-PR.2s
    'I didn't take the betelnut, why do you accuse me?'

(2) Ni   uf-owa   ikiw-eka, yo   miatin-i-yem.
    2p.UNM dance-NMZ   go-IMP.2p 1s.UNM dislike-NP-PR.1s
    '(You) go to dance, I don't want to.'

In clause chaining (§8.2) and in complex clauses involving main and subordinate clauses (§8.3), the situation is more complicated. Formally almost all of the subordinate and medial clauses are neutral/declarative. A subordinate clause typically lacks an illocutionary force of its own (Cristofaro 2003: 32) and conforms to the functional sentence type of the main clause. In the examples (3)–(5), the subordinate clauses are in brackets.

(3) [Ni   ifa   nia   keraw-i-ya   nain] sira   kamenap on-i-man?
    2p.UNM snake 2p.ACC bite-NP-PR.3s   that1 custom   what.like do-NP-PR.2p
    'When a snake bites you, what do you do?'

(4) Ni   [yapen ... wiar   in-em-ik-e-man   nain]   kerer-omak-eka!
    2p.UNM inland ... 3.DAT sleep-SS.SIM-be-PA-2p that1 arrive-DISTR/PL-2p.IMP

    'Those (many) of you, who have stayed inland, arrive (back in your villages)!'

(5) [Ni   uf-ep-na]   ni   maadara   me iirar-eka.
    2p.UNM dance-SS.SEQ=TP 2p.UNM forehead.ornament not remove-2p.IMP

    'If/when you have danced, do not remove your forehead ornaments.'

The non-polar questions are an exception, since the question word may also be in a subordinate clause (6). When a subordinate clause contains a question word, the illocutionary force of a question spreads to whole sentence.

(6) No   [kaaneke ikiw-owa] efa   maak-i-n?
    2s.UNM where.CF go-NMZ   1s.UNM tell-NP-PR.2s

    'You are telling me to go where?'

A medial clause is coordinate with the main clause but dependent on it (§8.2). The imperative form is only possible in finite verbs, and the polar question marker only occurs sentence-finally.[1] Because of these formal restrictions, it is impossible to have an imperative or interrogative medial clause coordinated with a declarative main clause. A medial clause commonly conforms to the illocutionary force of the final clause, but it does not need to do so. In the examples (7) and (8) the bracketed medial clause is questioned with the main clause, in (9) and (10) it is not.

(7) [Maamuma uruf-ap]   ma-i-n-i?
    money   see-SS.SEQ say-PA-2s=QM

    'Have you seen the money and (so) ask?'

(8) [Yo   pina on-amkun=ko] efa   uruf-a-man=i?
    1s.UNM guilt do-1s/p.DS=NF 2s.ACC see-PA-2p=QM

    'Did I do wrong and you saw me?'

(9) [Sande erup weeser-eya]   owowa ekap-e-man=i?
    week two finish-2/3s.DS village come-PA-2p=QM

    'When two weeks were finished, did you (then) come to the village?'

(10) [...ikoka ekap-ep]   sira   nain piipua-i-nan=i   e weetak?
     later   come-SS.SEQ habit that1 leave-NP-FU.2s=QM or no

     '...later when you come, will you drop that habit or not?'

When a medial clause itself contains a question word, the illocutionary force spreads to the whole sentence (11), (12).

---

[1] As an alternative marker, the QM is used in non-final clauses as well (§3.12.8, §8.1.2).

(11) [*No   maa mauwa uruf-ap*] *soran-ep   kirir-e-n?*
    2s.UNM thing what   see-ss.SEQ be.startled-ss.SEQ shout-PA-2s
    'What did you see and (then) got startled and shouted?'

(12) [*Naareke nia   maak-eya*] *ekap-e-man?*
    who.CF   2p.ACC tell-2/3s.DS come-PA-2p
    'Who told you to come?' (Lit: 'Who told you and you came?')

When the final clause is in the imperative mood, the implication of a command often extends backwards to a medial verb marked for the same subject (13), but not so easily to one marked for a different subject. In (7.64) above, the command/request extends to the medial clause, whereas in (14) it does not. For more examples, see (7.63)–(7.66) above.

(13) [*No   nena maa fariar-ep*]   *muuka nain arim-ow-e.*
    2s.UNM 2s.GEN food abstain-ss.SEQ son   that1 grow-CAUS-IMP.2s
    'Abstain from (certain) food(s) and bring up the son.'

(14) [*Nefa war-iwkin*]   *naap ma-e.*
    2s.ACC shoot-2/3p.DS thus say-IMP.2s
    '(If/when) they shoot you, (then) say like that.'

Although it is impossible to have an imperative verb form in a medial clause, a "soft" command/request (§7.3) may be used in medial clauses, as it takes the medial verb form. In (15), the first clause is a request, the second one a statement.

(15) *Aite,*   [*i   aaya=ko   yia   aaw-om-aya*]   *enim-i-yan.*
    1s/p.mother 1p.UNM sugarcane=NF 1p.ACC get-BEN-BNFY2.2/3s.DS eat-NP-FU.1p
    'Mother, get us sugarcane and we will eat it.'

8.1 Coordination of clauses

Coordination links units of "equivalent syntactic status" (Crystal 1997: 93). Clausal coordination commonly refers to the coordination of main clauses, as that is much more frequent than the coordination of subordinate clauses. In the following, it is assumed that the discussion is about main clause coordination unless stated otherwise.

The main clauses joined by coordination are independent in the sense that they could stand alone as individual sentences. Examples (1) and (2) above show that they can even manifest different functional sentence types. But they are called clauses firstly because they are coordinated within one sentence, and secondly for the sake of consistency, since the coordinated medial (§8.2.1) and subordinate clauses (§8.3.7) could not be called sentences.

As Givón (1990: 848) points out, no clause in a text is truly independent from its context. Likewise, the coordination vs. subordination of clauses is in many languages a matter of degree rather than a clear-cut distinction.

8 Clause combinations

Although the chaining of medial and final clauses (§8.2) is the main strategy for combining clauses in Mauwake, coordination of main clauses is also common. It is used not only for the cross-linguistically typical cases of conjunction, disjunction, and adversative relations between clauses, but also for causal and consecutive relations.

8.1.1 Conjunction

Conjunction is the most neutral form of coordination: two or more clauses are joined in a sentence, with or without a link between them. If there is a link, it is a pragmatic additive that does not specify the semantic relationship between the clauses. This sometimes allows different interpretations for the relationship, but usually the context constrains the interpretation considerably.

8.1.1.1 Juxtaposition

In juxtaposition[2] two or more clauses are joined without any linking device at all. According to Haspelmath (2007: 8) unwritten languages tend to lack their own coordinators and therefore use more juxtaposition and/or coordinators borrowed from other, more prestigious languages.

In Mauwake, juxtaposition is the most typical strategy for conjunction overall. Especially the coordination of verbless clauses is often symmetrical: the reversal of the conjuncts is possible without a change of meaning (16), (17).

(16) Wi   Yaapan emeria weetak, mua manek=iw.
     3p.UNM Japan   woman no   man big=LIM
     'The Japanese didn't have any wives, (they were) just the men.'

(17) Kuuten wiawi   iperowa, yo   auwa   kapa=ke.
     Kuuten 3s/p.father firstborn 1s.UNM 1s/p.father lastborn=CF
     'Kuuten's father was the firstborn (son), my father was the lastborn.'

When one of the conjuncts is a verbless clause and another is a verbal one, symmetrical conjunction is quite common (18):

(18) I   uruwa   miim-i-mik,   ni   sosora=ke.
     1p.UNM loincloth precede-NP-PR.1/3p 2p.UNM grass.skirt=CF
     'We father's side of the family (lit: loincloth) go first, you are mother's side (lit: grass skirt).'

Symmetrical conjunction of verbal clauses may be used, when there is parallelism between the clauses (19), (20):

---

[2] Also called "zero strategy" by Payne (1985: 25).

(19) *Na-emi wi afa ar-omak-e-mik, osaiwa*
say-SS.SIM 3p.UNM flying.fox become-DISTR/PL-PA-1/3p bird.of.paradise
ar-e-mik, biri-birin-e-mik.
become-PA-1/3p RDP-fly-PA-1/3p

'Saying so, they became many flying foxes, they became birds of paradise, they flew (away).'

(20) *Aria makera miirifa okaiwi soo=pa kaik-i-mik, okaiwi pia*
alright cane end other.side trap=LOC tie-NP-PR.1/3p other.side bamboo
kaik-i-mik.
tie-NP-PR.1/3p

'Alright we tie one end of the cane to the trap, the other to a (piece of) bamboo.'

In (21) the medial clause relates to both of the final clauses, not just to the first one:

(21) *Koora=pa efa uruf-am-ik-eya **ikiw-i-nen ekap-i-nen.***
house=LOC 1s.ACC see-SS.SIM-be-2/3s.DS go-NP-FU.1s come-NP-FU.1s

'You see me from the house and/as I will go and come.'

When the coordination is not symmetrical, the clause in the second conjunct is an example or an explanation of the first clause (22), or it follows the first one in a temporal sequence (23).

(22) *Auwa aite wia karu-i-yen, owowa=pa wia uruf-u.*
1s/p.father 1s/p.mother 3p.ACC visit-NP-FU.1p village=LOC 3p.ACC see-1d.IMP

'We'll visit my parents, let's see them in the village.'

(23) *Miiw-aasa um-eya miiw-aasa nain on-am-ika-iwkin epa*
land-canoe die-2/3s.DS land-canoe that1 do-SS.SIM-be-2/3p.DS place
kokom(a)-ar-e-k, epa iimeka tuun-e-k.
dark-INCH-PA-3s place ten count?-PA-3s

'The truck broke and while they were fixing the truck it became dark, (then) it was midnight.'

A fairly common structure is one where the first conjunct is not directly followed by another finite clause but by one or more medial clauses before the final clause (24):

(24) ***Ikemika kaik-ow(a) mua nain nop-a-mik,** imen-ap maak-iwkin o*
wound tie-NMZ man that1 search-PA-1/3p find-SS.SEQ tell-2/3p.DS 3s.UNM
miim-o-k.
precede-PA-3s

'They looked for the medical orderly, and when they found him and told him, he went ahead of them.'

Juxtaposition in itself is neutral and only shows that the two or more clauses are somehow connected with each other, but it can be used when propositions joined by it have different semantic relationships with each other (25), (26).

(25) *Waaya maneka marew pun, mua unowa me wia pepek-er-a-k.*
pig big no(ne) also man many not 3p.ACC enough-INCH-PA-3s
'Also, the pig was not big, (so) it was not enough for many people.'

(26) *Ni iperuma fain me enim-eka, inasin(a) mua=ke.*
2p.UNM eel this not eat-IMP.2p spirit man=CF
'Don't eat this eel, (because) it is a spirit man.'

8.1.1.2 Conjunction with coordinating connectives

Two of the three pragmatic connectives (§3.11.1) are used as clausal coordinators: the additive *ne* and *aria*, 'alright' which marks a break in the topic chain. *Ne* can be used in some of the contexts where mere juxtaposition is also used, but it is less frequent. If the second conjunct is an explanation or example of the first one, conjoining the clauses with *ne* is not allowed. Example (27) is a case of symmetrical coordination, but if the order of the two conjuncts were reversed, the adverbial *pun* 'also', which has to be in the second conjunct, would not move to the first conjunct with the rest of the clause.

(27) *I mua=ko me wia furew-a-mik, **ne** yiena pun mukuna=ko me*
1p.UNM man=NF not 3p.ACC sense-PA-1/3p ADD 1p.GEN also fire=NF not
op-a-mik.
hold-PA-1/3p
'We didn't sense anyone there and we ourselves did not hold fire either.'

The example (28) is syntactically neutral, but semantically it is interpreted as both temporal and consecutive sequence.

(28) *...maa wiar fe-feef-omak-e-mik, **ne** wi ikiw-e-mik ...*
food 3.DAT RDP-spill-DISTR/PL-PA-1/3p ADD 3p.UNM go-PA-1/3p
'... they$_i$ spilled their$_j$ food, and (so/then) they$_j$ went (away) ...'

When there are more than two coordinated clauses in a sentence without any intervening medial clauses, it is common to have *ne* joining the last two clauses (29):

(29) *Mua kuum-e-mik nain me wia kuuf-a-mik, me wia furew-a-mik, **ne***
man burn-PA-1/3p that1 not 3p.ACC see-PA-1/3p not 3p.ACC sense-PA-1/3p ADD
me wia imen-a-mik.
not 3p.ACC find-PA-1/3p
'We didn't see the men who burned it, we didn't sense them and we didn't find them.'

The connective *ne* is also used in sentences where an adversative interpretation can be applied.[3] Example (30) describes a couple that stayed in the village during the war and placed some of their belongings outside their house to show that there were people living in the village, while many others ran away into the rainforest.

(30) *Amina, wiowa, eka napia koor(a) miira=pa iimar-aw-ikiw-e-mik,* **ne**
 pot spear water bamboo house front=LOC stand-CAUS-go-PA-1/3p ADD
 wi unowa baurar-e-mik.
 3p.UNM many flee-PA-1/3p

 'We placed the pots, spears and bamboo water containers in line in front of the house, but many ran away.'

The connective *aria* 'alright' may be used when there is a change of topic or an unexpected development within the sentence (31), (32).

(31) *Epa wii-wiim-ik-ua,* **aria** *wi sawur=ke ekap-ep takira nain*
 place RDP-dawn-be-PA.3s alright 3p.UNM spirit=CF come-SS.SEQ boy that1
 samapora onaiya akua aaw-e-mik.
 bed with shoulder take-PA-1/3p

 'It was getting light, and spirits came and carried the boy with his bed (away) on their shoulders.'

(32) *Iiriw muuka oko wiawi onak urera maa uup-e-mik,* **aria**
 earlier boy other 3s/p.father 3s/p.mother afternoon food cook-PA-1/3p alright
 maa me wu-om-a-mik yon...
 food not put-BEN-BNFY2.PA-1/3p perhaps

 'Long ago, the parents of a boy cooked food in the afternoon, (but) perhaps they did not put any food for him ...'

It is also the default coordinator when a non-verbal constituent in two or more otherwise very similar conjuncts are contrasted (33), or emphasized (34), in coordinated clauses.

(33) *Yo Malala mauw-owa nia asip-i-yem,* **aria** *yena owowa, Moro*
 1s.UNM Malala work-NMZ 2p.ACC help-NP-PR.1s alright 1s.GEN village Moro
 owowa wia asip-i-yem.
 village 3p.ACC help-NP-PR.1s

 'I help you Malala people with your work, and I help my village, Moro village.'

---

[3] Using Haspelmath's (2007: 28) terms, *ne* in the adversative function could be called an *oppositive* coordinator, as the second coordinand does not cancel an expectation like it does in adversative clauses formed with either the demonstrative *nain* or the topic marker *-na* (§8.3.4).

(34) *Eema pun ekap-ep yia maak-e-k, **aria** buburia ona pun ekap-ep*
Eema also come-ss.SEQ 1p.ACC tell-PA-3s alright bald 3s.GEN also come-ss.SEQ
yia maak-e-k.
1p.ACC tell-PA-3s

'Eema came and told us, and the bald man himself too came and told us.'

8.1.2 Disjunction

The speech of the Mauwake people tends to be rather concrete in the sense that they do not speculate much on different abstract alternatives. So disjunction of clauses, although possible, is not common. Disjunction is marked by the connective *e* 'or' placed between the conjuncts (35) (§3.11.2).

(35) *Nain=ke napum-ar-i-mik e um-i-mik, mua oko*
that1=CF sickness-INCH-NP-PR.1/3p or die-NP-PR.1/3p man other
napum-ar-e-k nain erewar-e-n.
sickness-INCH-PA-3s that1 foresee-PA-2s

'That is about people becoming sick or dying, you foresaw (in a dream) that some man became sick.'

Sometimes the question marker *-i* replaces the connective (36).

(36) *Aria no ikoka mua owawiya irak-ep=i kamenap on-ap*
alright 2s.UNM later man with fight-ss.SEQ=QM how do-ss.SEQ1s.UNM
yo me efar kerer-e, no nomokowa Kululu fan-e-k a.
not 1s.DAT arrive-IMP.2s 2s.UNM 2s/p.brother Kululu here-PA-3s INTJ

'Alright, later when you fight with your husband or do something like that, do not come to me, your brother Kululu is right here.'

Alternative questions (§7.2.2) have the question marker *-i* cliticized to the end of the clause at least in the first conjunct. Closed alternative questions leave the question mark out of the last conjunct (37).

(37) *Ikoka ekap-ep feeke sira nain piipua-i-nan=i e weetak?*
later come-ss.SEQ here.CF habit that1 leave-NP-FU.2s=QM or no

'Later when you come, will you here leave that habit or not?'

Open alternative questions have the question marker in all the conjuncts (38).

(38) *Mua oko miira inawera=pa uruf-ap ma-i-mik, mua oko=ke napuma*
man other face dream=LOC see-ss.SEQ say-NP-PR.1/3p man other=CF sickness
aaw-o-k=i e um-o-k=i?
get-PA-3s=QM or die-PA-3s=QM

'When we see some man's face in a dream we say, "Has some other man become sick or died (or possibly neither)?" '

8.1.3 Adversative coordination

There is no adversative coordinator in Mauwake. It was mentioned above (§3.11.1, 8.1.1.2) that the pragmatic additive connective *ne*, which is semantically neutral, is possible when there is a relationship between clauses that may be interpreted as contrastive (39).

(39) Iir   nain Kedem manek akena keker op-a-k   **ne** Yoli weetak.
      time that Kedem big   very fear hold-PA-3s ADD Yoli no
      'That time Kedem was very scared but Yoli wasn't.'

There are two strategies that can be used when a strong adversative is needed. A 'but'-protasis (Reesink 1983a: 237) may be marked by either the distal demonstrative *nain* 'that' (§3.6.2), or the topic marker *-na* (§§3.12.7.1, 8.3.4), added to a finite clause. Adversative clauses with the demonstrative *nain* differ from nominalized clauses functioning as complement clauses or relative clauses in the following respects. Intonationally, *nain* is the initial element in the second one of the contrasted clauses, rather than a final element in a subordinate clause, and it is often preceded by a short pause (40). The protasis may even be a separate sentence (41).

(40) *Panewowa nain, wi   iiriw   eno-wa   en-e-mik,   **nain** me onak-e-mik.*
      old.person that1 3p.UNM earlier eat-NMZ eat-PA-1/3p that1 not give.3s-PA-1/3p

      'As for the old woman, they (aready) ate the meal earlier but did not give (any of it) to her to eat.'

(41) *Yo   bom koor miira=pa efar   or-om-ik-ua.   **Nain** yo   me*
      1s.UNM bomb house face=LOC 1s.DAT fall-SS.SIM-be-PA.3s that1 1s.UNM not
      baurar-em-ik-e-m.
      flee-SS.SIM-be-PA-1s
      'Bombs kept dropping in front of my house. But I didn't keep running away.'

The examples (42) and (43) are structurally very similar to sentences with relative clauses (§8.3.1.2). But here the demonstrative *nain* is part of the adversative clause and is preceded by a pause.

(42) *Mera eka   enim-i-mik,   **nain** i   mangala me enim-i-mik,   waaya me*
      fish water eat-NP-PR.1/3p that1 1p.UNM shellfish not eat-NP-PR.1/3p pig   not
      enim-i-mik.
      eat-NP-PR.1/3p
      'We eat fish soup, but we don't eat shellfish, (and) we don't eat pork.'

(43) *I   nan   soomar-e-mik, **nain** i   mukuna=ko me op-a-mik.*
      1p.UNM there walk-PA-1/3p that1 1p.UNM fire=NF not hold-PA-1/3p
      'We walked there, but we did not hold/have any fire.'

Compare (43) with the relative clause (44), where the demonstrative functions as a relative marker and comes at the end of the clause. This is shown by the slightly rising intonation on *nain*, as well as a pause following it in spoken text:[4]

(44) I   nan   soomar-e-mik **nain**, i   mukuna=ko me op-a-mik.
      1p.UNM there walk-PA-1/3p that1 1p.UNM fire=NF   not hold-PA-1/3p

'We who walked there didn't hold/have any fire.' (Or: 'When we walked there, we didn't hold/have any fire.')

The adversative sentences formed with the topic marker -*na* are complex rather than coordinate sentences (§8.3.4).

8.1.4 Consecutive coordination

Within a sentence, clauses are typically connected by one of the syntactically neutral strategies, which leave the semantic relationship implied. Some sentences using juxtaposition (26), the pragmatic additive *ne* (28) or clause chaining (97) can be interpreted as having a consecutive relationship between the clauses, although this does not show in the syntax. This section deals with the cases where the consecutive relationship is marked overtly.

Relationships of cause and effect, or reason and result,[5] are central in the discussion of causal and consecutive clauses. It seems that currently Mauwake may be developing a distinction between cause and reason on one hand, and between effect and result on the other. But the tendency, if there, is not very strong (§3.11.2).

Both the clauses in a sentence expressing a cause-effect or reason-result relationship are main clauses and are in a coordinate relationship with each other. It is common for the two clauses to form separate sentences rather than be within the same sentence.

The tendency to present events in the same order that they occur, common to languages in general, is very strong in Papuan languages. Consequently, there is a strong preference to present a cause clause before an effect clause (Haiman 1980: 409, Roberts 1987: 59, Reesink 1987). In Mauwake consecutive coordination is the default, unmarked strategy for those sentences that express cause-effect or reason-result relationships overtly, because their structure follows this principle (45), whereas in causal coordination sentences the effect is stated before the cause.

(45) Emar,   nos=ke   yo   efa   kemal-ep   iripuma fain ifakim-o-n, **naapeya**
      1s/p.friend 2s.CF=CF 1s.UNM 1s.ACC pity-SS.SEQ iguana this kill-PA-2s   therefore
      iripuma fain ik-ep   *enim-e.*
      iguana this roast-SS.SEQ eat-IMP.2s

'Friend, it was you who pitied me and killed this iguana, therefore you roast and eat this iguana.'

---

[4] This similarity creates a problem with written texts that do not have adequate punctuation. Sometimes either interpretation is acceptable.
[5] Reason-result relationship presupposes the presence of reasoning in the process, cause-effect relationship does not.

8.1 Coordination of clauses

Effect and result clauses use *naapeya/naeya* 'therefore, (and) so' (§3.11.2) as their connective (46)–(50).

(46) *Koora fuluwa unowa marew,* **naapeya** *in-i-mik   nain dabela me*
house hole   many no(ne) therefore sleep-NP-PR.1/3p that1 cold   not
senam   furew-i-mik.
too.much sense-NP-PR.1/3p

'The houses do not have many windows, so those who sleep (there) do not sense/feel the cold too much.'

(47) *Pita weke   wiar um-o-k,* **naapeya** *o   suule me iw-a-k.*
Pita 3s/p.grandfather 3.DAT die-PA-3s therefore 3s.UNM school not go-PA-3s

'Pita's grandfather died, so he (Pita) didn't go to school.'

(48) *...pika oona   me kekan-ow-a-k,   **naeya**   uura ewar maneka=ke*
...wall support not be.strong-CAUS-PA-3s therefore night wind big=CF
kerer-emi   koora nain wiar teek-a-k.
appear-SS-SIM house that1 3.DAT tear-PA-3s

'He did not strengthen the wall supports, so at night a big wind arose and tore down his house.'

(49) *No   nena   pun pina sira   naap nain on-i-n,   **naeya**   nos   pun*
2s.UNM 2s.GEN also guilt custom thus that1 do-NP-PR.2s therefore 2s.FC also
opora=pa ika-i-nan.
talk=LOC be-NP-FU.2s

'You yourself do bad things like that too, therefore you too will be under accusation.'

Naapeya can also co-occur with the conjunctive coordinator *ne* (50).

(50) *Epa   nan   soomar-em-ik-ok or-o-mik,   **ne naapeya** pina wi   wiar*
place there walk-SS.SIM-be-SS descend-PA-1/3p ADD therefore guilt 3p.UNM 3.ACC
korin-e-k.
stick-PA-3s

'They were walking there in that place and came down, and so the guilt (for starting a forest fire) stuck to them.'

The use of *naapeya* and *naeya* is both external and internal, i.e., they connect events in a situation and ideas in a text. The internal use of *ne naapeya* and *aria naapeya* is restricted to intersentential use. They refer to a longer stretch in the preceding text as their protasis (51).

8 *Clause combinations*

(51) ***Aria naapeya*** wi   inasina ook-i-mik   sira   nain me wiar
     alright therefore 3p.UNM spirit follow-NP-PR.1/3p custom that1 not 3.DAT
     ook-eka.
     follow-IMP.2p
     'So therefore do not follow the behavior of those who follow/believe in spirits.'

As an internal connective *naeya* mainly connects full sentences (52), only seldom clauses within a sentence (53):

(52) No   mua woos reen-owa=ke, ***naeya*** no   kema kir-owa
     2s.UNM man head dry-NMZ=CF   therefore   2s.UNM liver turn-NMZ
     miatin-i-n.
     dislike-NP-PR.2s
     'You are hard-headed, therefore you do not like to change your (bad) ways.'

(53) Ni   sira-sira   naap on-i-man. ***Naeya*** opora iiriw ma-e-k   nain
     2p.UNM RDP-custom thus do-NP-PR.2p therefore talk   earlier say-PA-3s that1
     pepek   akena nia   ma-e-k.
     enough very 2p.ACC say-PA-3s
     'You do (bad) things like that. Therefore the talk that he already said about you is very accurate.'

Neemi is a consecutive coordinator that almost exclusively conjoins full sentences rather than clauses within a sentence: (55) is from translated text but considered natural. (3.800) is repeated here as (54). *Neemi* is an internal connective, only used in reasoning. It requires some point of similarity between the two conjuncts.

(54) Teeria fain K10 wu-a-mik. ***Neemi*** wi   teeria nain pun K10 wu-a-mik.
     group this K10 put-PA-1/3p therefore 3p.UNM group that1 too K10 put-PA-1/3p
     'This group put down ten kina. Therefore that group put down ten kina, too.'

(55) Krais sirir-owa aaw-omak-e-k,   ***neemi*** is   pun unowiya naap
     Christ hurt-NMZ get-DISTR/PL-PA-3s therefore 1p.FC also all   thus
     aaw-i-mik.
     get-NP-PR.1/3p
     'Christ received a lot of pain, so we all too get (pain) like that.'

The connective *naap nain* is used almost only inter-sententially (56). Between clauses in a sentence it is possible but rare (57):

(56) Naeya   nokar-e-mik, "***Naap nain*** no   naareke?"
     therefore ask-PA-1/3p   thus   that1 2s.UNM who.CF
     'Therefore they asked, "So then, who are you?" '

(57) *Wiam arow pepek nan urup-e-mik nain, **naap nain** yo moram*
 3p.REFL three enough there ascend-PA-1/3p that1 thus that1 1s.UNM why/in.vain
 urup-e-m.
 ascend-PA-1s

 '(Since it is the case that) those three are enough and came up, so then why did I have to come up? (or: ...so then I came up in vain).'

8.1.5 Causal coordination, "afterthought reason"

The causal coordination is a very marked structure, which shows in the unusual ordering of the clauses: the causal clause follows rather than precedes the consequent clause. The causal clause in Mauwake begins with the connective *moram* 'because' (§3.11.2), which is originally the interrogative word for 'why'. There are two possible origins for this untypical structure. It may be a recent calque on the Tok Pisin causal construction, which uses *bilong wanem* 'why/because' as the connector and the same ordering of the two clauses. The ordering of the clauses shows that it may also have originated as an "afterthought reason",[6] even though currently it is used when the cause or reason is emphasized (58), (59).

(58) *Owowa mamaiya soora weetak, **moram** iwera isak-omak-e-mik.*
 village near forest no because coconut plant-DISTR/PL-PA-1/3p

 'There is no forest near the village, because we have planted a lot of coconut palms.'

(59) *Poh San uruf-ap kema ten-e-mik, **moram** i kema naap suuw-a-mik,*
 Poh San see-SS.SEQ liver fall-PA-1/3p because 1p.UNM liver thus push-PA-1/3p
 napuma me sariar-owa ik-ua.
 sickness not heal-NMZ be-PA.3s

 'We saw Poh San and were relieved (lit: liver fell), because we had thought that (her) sickness hadn't healed yet (but it had).'

Moram wia is used almost exclusively between full sentences (60); the example (61) is the only intra-sentential instance of *moram wia* in the data. I have not noticed any semantic difference caused by the addition of the negator.

(60) *...maamuma senam aaw-e-mik. **Moram wia**, maa ele-eliwa*
 money too/very.much get-PA-1/3p why not thing/food RDP-good
 sesek-a-mik.
 sell-PA-1/3p

 '...they got a lot of money. (That's) because they sold good food.'

---

[6] The term suggested by Ger Reesink.

(61) *Ir   nain yo   owowa=pa=ko me mauw-a-m, **moram wia** yo*
time that1 1s.UNM village=LOC=NF not work-PA-1s because not 1s.UNM
Ukarumpa urup-owa=ke   na-ep   mauw-owa miatin-e-m.
Ukarumpa ascend-NMZ=CF say-SS.SEQ work-NMZ dislike-PA-1s

'That time I did not work in the village, because I thought that I was due to go up to Ukarumpa, and (so) I didn't like to work.'

Both a causative and a consecutive connective can co-occur in the same sentence. When that happens, the consecutive clause occurs twice: first without a connective and after the causal clause with a connective (62), (63). This underlines the strong preference to keep the cause-effect (or reason-result) order.

(62) *I   epa   unowa=ko me soomar-e-mik, **moram** owowa maneka, **naapeya***
1p.UNM place many=NF not walk-PA-1/3p because village big   therefore
soomar-owa lebum(a)-ar-e-mik.
walk-NMZ   lazy-INCH-PA-1/3p

'We didn't walk in many places, because the village/town was big, therefore we didn't care to walk.'

(63) *Mua lebuma emeria me wi-i-mik,   **moram** emeria muukar-eya*
man lazy   woman not give.them-NP-PR.1/3p because woman give.birth-2/3s.DS
*muuka nain maa mauwa enim-i-non, **naapeya** mua lebuma emeria me*
son   that1 food what   eat-NP-FU.3s therefore man lazy   woman not
wi-i-mik.
give.them-NP-PR.1/3p

'We do not give wives to lazy men, because when the woman bears a child what would it eat, therefore we do not give wives to lazy men.'

8.1.6 Apprehensive coordination

A less common clause type, that of apprehensive clauses (Roberts 1987: 61), also called negative purpose clauses (Haiman 1980: 444, Thompson & Longacre 1985: 188), is perhaps more commonly subordinate than coordinate. But in Mauwake the apprehensive clauses are coordinated finite clauses (64), (65), originally separate sentences (66). The apprehension clause is introduced by the indefinite *oko* 'other' (§3.7.2), which has also developed the meaning 'otherwise'.

(64) *Ni   maa uru-uruf-ami ik-eka, **oko** mua oko=ke   nia*
2p.UNM thing RDP-see-SS.SIM be-IMP.2p other man other=CF 2p.ACC
peeskim-i-kuan.
cheat-NP-FU.3p

'Watch out, otherwise/lest you get cheated.'

(65) *Naap on-owa weetak,* **oko** *yiena sira puuk-i-yen.*
 thus do-NMZ no other 1p.GEN custom cut-NPS-FU.1p

 'We must not do like that, otherwise/lest we break our custom/law (or: ... lest we ourselves break the custom/law).'

(66) *Naap yo aakisa efa uruf-i-n.* **Oko** *neeke*
 thus 1s.UNM now 1s.ACC see-NP-PR.2s other there.CF
 soomar-ekap-em-ik-omkun ma-i-nan, "... "
 walk-come-SS.SIM-be-1s/p.DS say-NP-FU.2s

 'So you see me now. Otherwise I'll be walking there and you will say, "..."'

8.2 Clause chaining

Clause chaining is a feature typical of Papuan languages, and of the Trans-New Guinea languages in particular.[7] A sentence may consist of several medial clauses[8] where the verbs have medial verb inflection (§3.8.3.5), and a final clause where the verb has "normal" finite inflection (§3.8.3.4). Clause chaining indicates either temporal sequence or simultaneity between adjacent clauses.

The division into just medial and final clauses is not adequate for describing the system. Haiman & Munro (1983: xii) call the medial clauses MARKING CLAUSES and the clauses following them REFERENCE CLAUSES.[9] Marking clause is simply another name for a medial clause and will not be used here. But a reference clause may be medial or finite[10] – what is important is that both the temporal relationship of the medial verb, and the person reference, is stated in relation to the reference clause. When a reference clause for a preceding medial clause is also a medial clause, it again has its own reference clause following it.

The medial clauses linked by clause chaining are sometimes called COSUBORDINATE (Olson 1981, Foley & Van Valin 1984: 257[11] or COORDINATE-DEPENDENT (Foley 1986: 177), because they share features with both coordinate and subordinate clauses. Their relationship with each other and with the following finite clause is essentially coordinate,[12] but the medial clauses are dependent on the finite clause both for their absolute tense, and, in the case of "same subject" forms, also for their person/number specification.

---

[7] Wurm (1982: 36) seems to consider clause chaining a genetic feature of the TNG languages, but Haiman (1980: xlvii) suggests that it is an areal feature. Roberts (1997: 122), with the most data to date, suggests that there is a combination of both, but leaves the final decision open.
[8] The terms *medial* and *final* clauses are well established in Papuan linguistics.
[9] Comrie (1983) and Roberts (1997) call them *marked clauses* and *controlling clauses*, respectively.
[10] I prefer the term *finite* to *final* clauses (and verbs), as it is the finiteness rather than the position in the sentence that is important in their relation with medial clauses. Subordinate clauses are the most typical *non-final* finite clauses, and they may also have medial clauses preceding them and relating to them.
[11] This is cosubordination at the *peripheral* level; verb serialization is cosubordination at core or nuclear level.
[12] Roberts (1988a) brings several syntactic arguments to show that basically switch reference is indeed coordination rather than subordination. But he also argues for a separate subordinate switch reference in Amele and some other languages.

8 Clause combinations

Another term commonly used for the chained clauses, SWITCH-REFERENCE CLAUSES (SR),[13] is related to their other function as a reference-tracking device (Haiman & Munro 1983: ix). They typically indicate whether their topic/subject is the same as, or different from, the topic/subject of the following clause. This is discussed below in §8.2.3. In this grammar the two terms are used interchangeably, as in Mauwake the medial verbs not only indicate a temporal relationship but are used for reference tracking as well.

8.2.1 Chained clauses as coordinate clauses

It is widely accepted that the relationship of medial clauses to their reference clauses is basically coordinate, but with some special features and exceptions.[14] In Mauwake medial clauses are subordinate only if subordinated with the topic/conditional marker *-na*; otherwise they are coordinate.

Instead of giving background information like subordinate clauses do, medial clauses are predications that carry on the foreground story line (67). But they are also different from coordinate finite clauses. The similarities and differences are discussed in this section.

The pragmatic additives *ne* (68) and *aria* (69) (§3.11.1) can occur between a medial clause and its reference clause, as between normal coordinate clauses. This is uncommon, however.

(67) *Wiawi   ikiw-ep maak-eya, **ne** wiawi=ke   maak-e-k ...*
     3s/p.father go-SS.SEQ tell-2/3s.DS ADD 3s/p.father=CF tell-PA-3s

  'She went to her father and told him, and her father told her ...'

(68) *... wiena en-emi,   epira lolom if-emi   **ne** owowa*
     ... 3p.GEN eat-SS.SIM plate mud spread-SS.SIM ADD village
     p-urup-em-ik-e-mik.
     PBx-ascend-SS.SIM-be-PA-1/3p

  'They ate it themselves, spread mud on the plates, and brought them up to the village.'

(69) *I   ikoka yien=iw   urup-ep   nia   maak-omkun ora-iwkin,*
     1p.UNM later 1p.GEN=LIM ascend-SS.SEQ 2p.ACC tell-1s/p.DS descend-2/3p.DS
     aria** owawiya feeke pok-ap   ik-ok eka   liiwa muuta en-ep   **aria
     alright together here.CF sit-SS.SEQ be-SS water little only eat-SS.SEQ alright
     ni   soomar-ek-eka.
     2p.UNM walk-go-2p.IMP

  'Later we (by) ourselves will come up and tell you (to come), and when you come down we will sit here together and eat a little bit of soup and then you can walk back.'

---

[13] Clause chaining and switch reference are two separate strategies, but in Papuan languages the two very often go together (Roberts 1997: 104).

[14] E.g., Reesink (1987: 175, 193), Roberts (1988a: 51), Roberts (1988a: 51, 1997).

8.2 Clause chaining

Coordinated main clauses are free in regard to their mood and, related to that, their functional sentence type. The medial clauses do not have any marking for mood. They usually conform to that of the finite clause, but this is a pragmatic matter, not a syntactic requirement.

When either the medial clause or the finite clause is a question, the whole sentence is interrogative, even if the other clause is a statement. In (70) the finite clause is a polar question, but the medial clause is not questioned. In the story that (71) is taken from, the killing is not questioned, only the manner. But since a medial clause cannot take the question marker, the verb in the finite clause has to carry the marking.

(70) *Sande erup weeser-eya   owowa ekap-e-man=i?*
 week two finish-2/3s.DS village come-PA-2p=QM

 'Two weeks were finished, and did you (then) come to the village?'[15]

(71) *Naap on-ap   ifakim-i-nen=i?*
 thus do-SS.SEQ kill-NP-FU.1s=QM

 'Shall I do like that and kill her?' (Or: 'Is it in that way that I shall kill her?')

A non-polar question can be in either a medial (72) or in a finite clause (73).

(72) *No   sira   kamenap on-eya   napuma fain nefar   kerer-e-k?*
 2s.UNM custom how   do-2/3s.DS sickness this 2s.DAT appear-PA-3s

 'What did you do (so that) this sickness came to you?'

(73) *No   karu-emi kame kaanek ikiw-o-n?*
 2s.UNM run-SS.SIM side where go-PA-2s

 'You ran and where did you go?'

For more examples, see (7.63)–(7.66) in §7.3 and the introductory section to Chapter 8.

In regard to the scope of negation, the same-subject medial clauses differ from all other clauses. Negative spreading (§6.2.4) in both directions is allowed only between ss medial clauses and their reference clauses, and even there it is not very common. Backwards spreading is especially rare. In the following examples, negative spreading takes place in (74) and (75), but not in (76) and (77). Between other types of clauses negative spreading is not permitted at all.

(74) *Nainiw ekap-ep   maa me sesenar-e-mik.*
 again   come-SS.SEQ food not sell-PA-1/3p

 'They did not come back and sell food.'

---

[15] Another possible translation is 'When the two weeks were finished, did you (then) come to the village?' but this does not reflect the coordinate relationship of the clauses in the original.

(75) *Ikiw-em-ik-ok* **me kir-ep**   *uruf-e,*   *no*   *oram*
go-ss.sim-be-ss not turn-ss.seq look-imp.2s 2s.unm just
woolal-ikiw-em-ik-e.
paddle-go-ss.sim-be-imp.2s

'While going, don't turn and look back, just keep paddling.'

(76) *Yaapan=ke urup-em-ika-iwkin*   *wi*   *Australia=ke wia*   *uruf-ap*
Japan=cf   ascend-ss.sim-be-2/3p.ds 3p.unm Australia=cf 3p.acc see-ss.seq
baurar-emi **me yia**   *maak-e-mik.*
flee-ss.sim not 1p.acc tell-pa-1/3p

'When the Japanese were coming up the Australians saw them and ran away and/but did not tell us.'

(77) *Iiriw   auwa=ke   sira   fain* **me paayar-ep**   *muuka momor*
earlier 1s/p.father=cf custom this not understand-ss.seq son   indiscriminately
wiar   aaw-em-ik-e-mik.
3.dat get-ss.sim-be-pa-1/3p

'Earlier our (fore)fathers didn't understand this custom, and (so) they adopted (lit: got/took) children indiscriminately.'

Like coordinated main clauses and unlike subordinate clauses, medial clauses are not embedded as constituents in other clauses. However, a medial clause may interrupt its reference clause and appear inside it, if the subject or object noun phrase of the reference clause is fronted as the theme and thus precedes the interrupting medial clause (78). For more examples, see (3.171) and (3.172). In the examples, the reference clause is bolded and the intervening medial clause is placed within square brackets.

(78) *Aria*   **yena mua pun** [*irak-owa kerer-owa   epa   weeser-em-ik-eya*]
alright 1s.gen man too fight-nmz appear-nmz time finish-ss.sim-be-2/3s.ds
iirar-iwkin   *owowa ekap-o-k,   o   amia mua=pa ik-ok.*
remove-2/3p.ds village come-pa-3s 3s.unm bow man=loc be-ss

'Alright, the war was getting close and they dismissed my husband and he came to the village, after he had been a soldier.'

In (79), both the object and the subject are fronted. After the first medial clause, the object of the finite clause is fronted as the theme of the remainder of the sentence, and it pulls with it the subject, marked with the contrastive focus marker. In the free translation, passive is used, because the object is fronted as a theme.

(79) *Sisina=pa*   *wu-ap*   **papako**$_O$ **mua=ke**$_S$ [*mera saa   urup-eya*]
shallow.water=loc put-ss.seq some   man=cf fish   sand ascend-2/3s.ds
patopat=iw   *mik-i-mik.*
fishing.spear=inst spear-np-pr.1/3p

'They drive (lit: put) them to the shallow water and the fish ascend to the beach and (then) some are speared by men with a fishing spear.'

8.2 Clause chaining

The examples (80)–(82) show that some of the same-subject medial clauses interrupting the reference clause, especially those that have a directional verb or the verb *aaw-* 'take, get', may be in the process of grammaticalizing into serial verbs:

(80)   *I   iwer(a) eka   [iki(w-e)p]   nop-a-mik.*
       1p.UNM coconut water go-SS.SEQ fetch-PA-1/3p

       'We went and fetched coconut water.'

(81)   *Yo   merena [fura aaw-ep]   puuk-a-m.*
       1s.UNM leg   knife take-SS.SEQ cut-PA-1s

       'I took a knife and cut (into) the leg. (Or: I cut into the leg with a knife.)'

(82)   *Um-eya   merena ere-erup [ifara aaw-ep]   kaik-ap nabena*
       die-2/3s.DS leg   RDP-two rope take-SS.SIM tie-SS.SEQ carrying.pole
       suuw-ap   akua   aaw-ep   or-o-m.
       push-SS.SEQ shoulder take-SS.SEQ descend-PA-1s

       'It (=a pig) died and I took a rope and tied its legs two and two together and pushed it to a carrying pole and carried it down on my shoulder.'

RIGHT-DISLOCATION of a medial clause is not unusual. One reason commonly given for right-dislocations is an afterthought: the speaker notices something that should be part of the sentence and adds it to the end (83). Another reason is giving prominence to the dislocated clause, since the end of a sentence is a focal position. The right-dislocation of same-subject sequential medial clauses in particular breaks the iconicity between the events and the sentence structure, and has this effect. Consequently, the right-dislocated ss sequential clauses, like the ones in examples (84) and (85), are much more prominent than medial clauses in their normal position.

(83)   *Or-op   naap wia   uruf-a-mik, [mua oona, eneka, woosa kia*
       descend-SS.SEQ thus 3p.ACC see-PA-1/3p man bone tooth head white
       kir-em-ik-eya].
       turn-SS.SIM-be-2/3s.DS

       'They went down and saw them like that, the people's bones, teeth and heads turning white.'

(84)   *Aw-iki(w-e)m-ik-eya   wiena mua unowa fiker(a)   epia nain*
       burn-go-SS.SIM-be-2/3s.DS 3p.GEN man many kunai.grass fire that1
       ook-i-kuan,   [wiowa aaw-ep].
       follow-NP-FU.3p spear take-SS.SEQ

       'It keeps burning and many men follow the kunai grass fire, having taken spears.'

8 Clause combinations

(85) *Aaya muuna kuisow enim-i-mik,* [*aite=ke manina=pa yia*
sugarcane joint one eat-NP-PR.1/3p 1s/p.mother=CF garden=LOC 1p.ACC
aaw-om-iwkin].
get-BEN-2/3p.DS

'We eat one joint of sugarcane, when/after our mothers have gotten it for us from the garden.'

8.2.2 Temporal relations in chained clauses

Clause chaining in Mauwake distinguishes between sequential and simultaneous actions in the clauses joined by chaining, but only when the clauses have the same subject (§3.8.3.5.1). The sequential action verb in (86) indicates that one action is finished before the next one starts.

(86) *No nainiw kir-**ep** ikiw-**ep** owow mua wia maak-eya*
2s.UNM again turn-SS.SEQ go-SS.SEQ village man 3p.ACC tell-2/3s.DS
*urup-**ep** mukuna nain umuk-uk.*
ascend-SS.SEQ fire that1 extinguish-IMP.3p

'Turn around, go and tell the village men and let them come up and extinguish the fire.'

When a clause has a simultaneous action medial verb (87), it indicates at least some overlap with the action in the following clause.

(87) *Or-**omi** yo koka koora=pa nan efa wu-**ami** ma-e-k,* "..."
descend-SS.SIM 1s.UNM jungle house=LOC there 1s.ACC put-SS.SIM say-PA-3s

'As he went down, he put me in the jungle house and said, "..."'

Simultaneity vs. sequentiality is not always a choice between absolutes; sometimes it is a relative matter. Example (88) refers to a situation where a man came back home from a period of labour elsewhere and got married upon arrival. In actual life, there may have been a time gap of at least a number of days, possibly longer, but because the two events were so closely linked in the speaker's mind, the simultaneous action form was used when the story was told decades after the events took place.

(88) *Ekap-**emi** yo efa aaw-o-k.*
come-SS.SIM 1s.UNM 1s.ACC take-PA-3s

'He came and married me.'

The simultaneous action form is less marked than the sequential action form: when the relative order of the actions or events is not relevant, the simultaneous action form is used. In example (89), the order of the preparations for a pighunt is not crucial, but the sequential action form on the last medial verb indicates that all the actions take place before leaving, rather than just at the time of leaving.

(89) Maa en-ep-pu-**ami**   top aaw-**emi** moma unukum-**emi** kapit,
      food eat-SS.SEQ-CMPL-SS.SIM trap take-SS.SIM taro wrap-SS.SIM   trap.frame
      wiowa aaw-**ep**   fikera   iw-i-**mik**.
      spear take-SS.SEQ kunai.grass go-NP-PR.1/3p

      'We eat, take the trap, wrap taro, take the the trap frame and spear(s) and go to the kunai grass area.'

A medial verb takes its temporal specification from the tense of the closest following finite clause (90)–(92), or in the case of a right-dislocated medial clause, from the preceding finite clause (83).

(90) Nomokowa maala war-ep   ekap-ep   ifa   nain ifakim-**o-k**.
      tree   long cut-SS.SEQ come-SS.SEQ snake that1 kill-PA-3s

      'He cut a long stick, came and killed the snake.'

(91) Mua=ke kais-ap   neeke   wu-ap   miiw-aasa nop-ap   miiw-aasa=ke
      man=CF husk-SS.SEQ there.CF put-SS.SEQ land-canoe fetch-SS.SEQ land-canoe=CF
      iwer(a) ififa nain aaw-ep   p-ekap-ep   epia koora mamaiya=pa
      coconut dry that1 take-SS.SEQ BPX-come-SS.SEQ fire house near=LOC
      wu-eya   fook-**i-mik**.
      put-2/3s.DS split-NP-PR.1/3p

      'Men husk them (coconuts) and put them there and fetch a truck, and the truck takes the dry coconuts and brings them close to the drying shed (lit: fire house), and we split them.'

(92) Ikoka mua ar-ep   emeria aaw-ep   kamenap on-**i-nan**?
      later man become-SS.SEQ woman take-SS.SEQ how   do-NP-FU.2s

      'Later when you become a man and take a wife, what will you do?'

The DS medial verbs (§3.8.3.5.2) do not differentiate between sequential and simultaneous action. Sequential action (93) is the default interpretation for verbs other than *ik-* 'be', which is interpreted as simultaneous with the verb in the reference clause (94). So in order to specify that two or more actions by different participants took place at the same time, the speaker needs to use the continuous aspect form (95):

(93) Maa unowa ifer-aasa=ke p-urup-**eya**   miiw-aasa=ke fan
      thing many sea-canoe=CF BPX-ascend-2/3s.DS land-canoe=CF here
      p-ir-am-ik-ua.
      BPX-come-SS.SIM-be-PA.3s

      'The cargo was brought up (to the coast) by ship(s), and (then) trucks kept bringing it here.'

(94) Wi   yapen=pa   **ik**-omak-**iwkin**   Amerika kerer-e-mik.
      3p.UNM inland=LOC be-DISTR/PL-2/3p.DS America appear-PA-1/3p

      'Many people were inland and the Americans arrived.'

8 Clause combinations

(95) *Ek-ap   umuk-i-nen   na-ep   on-am-**ik-eya**   ifa=ke*
go-ss.SEQ extinguish-NP-FU.1s say-ss.SEQ do-ss.SIM-be-2/3s.DS snake=CF
keraw-a-k, ...
bite-PA-3s

'He went and as he was trying to extinguish it (a fire), a snake bit him, ...'

Although the chaining structure itself only specifies the temporal relationship between the clauses and is otherwise neutral, it is open especially for causal/consecutive interpretation. Reesink (1983a: 237) notes this for different-subject medial verbs in Usan, and although not very common in Mauwake in general, it is more frequent with DS predicates (96), (97) than with ss verbs.

(96) *Yo   maamuma marew-**eya**   maak-e-m, "Iir oko=pa   ni-i-nen."*
1s.UNM money   no(ne)-2/3s.DS tell-PA-1s time other=LOC give.you-NP-FU.1s

'I had no money and I told him (or: Because I had no money I told him), "I'll give it to you another time." '

(97) *Iperowa=ke   kekan-**iwkin**   ma-e-mik, "Aria, ..."*
middle.aged=CF be.strong-2/3p.DS say-PA-1/3p alright

'The elders insisted, and (so) we said, "All right, ..." '

The causal/consecutive interpretation is most common when the object of a transitive medial clause becomes the subject in an intransitive reference clause: in example (98) 'the son' is the object of the first two clauses and the subject of the final clause.

(98) *[**Muuka**]ₒ p-or-op   **p-er-iwkin**   yak-i-ya.*
son   BPX-descend-ss.SEQ BPX-go-2/3p.DS bathe-NP-PR.3s

'They bring the son down (from the house) and take him (to the well) and (so) he bathes.'

Cognition verbs and feeling or experiential verbs seem to be the only ones that allow a causal/consecutive interpretation when a medial clause has a ss verb (99)–(101):

(99) *Siiwa, epa   maak-e-mik nain **paayar-ep**   ma-e-k,   "Amerika aakisa*
moon place/time tell-PA-1/3p that1 understand-ss.SEQ say-PA-3s America now
irak-owa kerer-e-mik."
fight-NMZ appear-PA-1/3p

'He understood the month and time/place that they (had) told him, and (so) he said, "Now the Americans have come to fight." '

(100) *... ne   wi   ikiw-e-mik, **kerewar-ep**   ikiw-e-mik.*
... ADD 3p.UNM go-PA-1/3p become.angry-ss.SEQ go-PA-1/3p

'... and they went; they were angry and (so) they went.'

(101) *Mua oko=ko **napum-ar-ep**   ikemika kaik-ow(a) mua wiar ikiw-o-k.*
man other=CF sickness-INCH-ss.SEQ wound   tie-NMZ   man 3.DAT go-PA-3s

'A man got sick and (so) he went to a doctor.'

8.2.3 Person reference in chained clauses

The switch-reference marking tracks the referents in a different way from the person/number marking in finite verbs. The medial verb suffix indicates whether the clause has the same subject/topic as the reference clause that comes after it, and the DS suffixes also have some specification of the subject (§3.8.5.2). In (102), the subjects are a man and his wife in the first two clauses and in the last one, and a spirit man in all the others:

(102) *Ikiw-ep$_i$ nan ika-iwkin$_i$ inasina mua$_j$ ifa puuk-ap$_j$ solon-ep$_j$*
go-SS.SEQ there be-2/3p.DS spirit man snake change.into-SS.SEQ crawl-SS.SEQ
urup-ep$_j$ manina=pa waaya puuk-ap$_j$ moma wiar
ascend-SS.SEQ garden=LOC pig change.into-SS.SEQ taro 3.DAT
en-em-ik-eya$_j$ uruf-a-mik$_i$.
eat-SS.SIM-be-2/3s.DS see-PA-1/3s

'They went and were there, and a spirit man came and changed into a snake and crawled up and in the garden it changed into a pig and as it was eating their taro they saw it.'

Because the switch reference marking relates to the subject/topic in two different clauses at the same time, this sometimes causes ambiguities that need to be solved. If the subjects in adjacent clauses are partially same and partially different, a choice has to be made whether they are marked as SS or DS; only a few Papuan languages have a choice of marking both SS and DS on the same verb (Roberts 1997). Also, if the SR marking is considered to track the syntactic subject, there are a number of apparent irregularities in the marking. These have been discussed in particular by Reesink (1983b) and Roberts (1988b) with reference to Papuan languages. The next three subsections describe how Mauwake deals with these questions.

8.2.3.1 Partitioning of the participant set

When one of the subjects is plural and the other is singular included in the plural, this mismatch theoretically allows for a number of different choices in the switch-reference marking, but in practice each language limits this choice in a way peculiar to it.[16] The following table Table 8.1 shows this for Mauwake.

When a plural subject changes into a singular, the suffix is always the one used for same subject (103).

(103) *...owowa urup-e-mik. Owowa urup-ep o koora ikiw-o-k.*
...village ascend-PA-1/3p village ascend-SS.SEQ 3s.UNM house go-PA-3s

'...We came up to the village. After we came up to the village he went into the house.'

---

[16] For a summary of how different Papuan languages treat this area of ambiguity, see Reesink (1983b), Reesink (1987: 201–202) and Roberts (1988b: 87–91).

8 Clause combinations

Table 8.1: Switch-reference marking with partial overlap of subjects

Singular to plural		Plural to singular	
1s > 1p	ss	1p > 1s	ss
2s > 1p	ds	1p > 2s	ss
2s > 2p	ss/ds	1p > 3s	ss
3s > 1p	ss/ds	2p > 2s	ss
3s > 2p	ss/ds	2p > 3s	ss
3s > 3p	ss/ds	3p > 3s	ss

When a singular subject changes into a plural there is more variation. First person singular changing into plural calls for same-subject marking (104), but second person singular switching into first person plural requires different-subject marking even when this second person singular is part of the group denoted by the first person plural (105).

(104) *Mik-ap,   patot=iw   mik-ap,   aaw-ep,   aasa=pa   wu-ap,*
spear-ss.SEQ fishing.spear=INST spear-ss.SEQ take-ss.SEQ canoe=LOC put-ss.SEQ
amap-urup-ep,   yena   koora=pa   wu-ap,   uuriw   epa   wiim-eya
BPX-ascend-ss.SEQ 1s.GEN house=LOC put-ss.SEQ morning place get.light-2/3s.DS
*or-op,   saa=pa   pa-**ep**   uup-e-mik.*
descend-ss.SEQ sand=LOC butcher-ss.SEQ cook-PA-1/3p

'I speared it, I speared it with a fishing spear, and took it and put it in the canoe, brought it up and put it in my house, and in the morning when it was light I went down and butchered it on the beach, and WE cooked it.'

(105) *Ekap-**eya**   ikiw-i-yen.*
come-2/3s.DS go-NP-FU.1p

'When you come we (including you) will go.'

When a second person plural switches into a first person plural (including the people indicated by the 2p), the marking has to be for different subject, but in the opposite case, the first person plural changing into the second person plural (again included in the 1p), the marking can be either for same or different subject. Both of these are exemplified in (106). Here the switch from first person plural to second person plural is marked with the ss marking.

(106) *I   ikoka yien=iw   urup-ep   nia   maak-omkun ora-**iwkin***
1p.UNM later 1p.GEN=LIM ascend-ss.SEQ 2p.ACC tell-1s/p.DS descend-2/3p.DS
*aria   owawiya feeke   pok-ap   ik-ok eka   liiwa   muuta en-**ep**   aria*
alright together here.CF sit-ss.SEQ be-ss water a.little only   eat-ss.SEQ alright

ni   soomar-ek-eka.
2p.UNM walk-go-IMP.2p

'Later we (by) ourselves will come up and tell you (to come), and when you come down we will sit here together and eat a bit of something and then you (can) walk back.'

With the rest, the speaker has a choice between the two forms. This choice is probably pragmatic and depends on whether the speaker wants to stress the change or the continuity of the referents (Franklin 1983: 47).

8.2.3.2 Tracking a subject high in topicality

Haiman & Munro (1983: xi) claim that it is strictly the syntactic subject whose reference is tracked, but this statement has been challenged and modified by several others.[17] If it is accepted as such, both Mauwake and other Papuan languages present a number of irregularities that have to be explained somehow.

Reesink (1983b: 242–243) suggests that the switch-reference system does monitor the subject co-referentiality in the medial clause and its reference clause, but topicality considerations cause apparent "anomalies" to the basic system. Roberts (1988b) makes a well supported claim for Amele that in fact it is the topic that is tracked rather than the syntactic subject, or semantic agent, and he tentatively extends the claim to cover other Papuan languages as well. His later survey (Roberts 1997) presents a more balanced view that SR can be either agent-oriented or topic-oriented, while maintaining that in most Papuan languages it is topic-oriented.

In a nominative-accusative language like Mauwake the syntactic subject, the semantic agent and the pragmatic topic coincide most of the time. The SR marking tracks the subject, but when there is competition between a more topical and less topical subject in clause chains, it is the more topical one that is tracked. An object, even if it is the topic, does not participate in the SR marking.

Competition between a more topical subject with a less topical one most commonly occurs when a clause with an inanimate subject intervenes between clauses where there is an animate/human subject. Even here the "normal" SR strategy is used, if the inanimate subject is topical enough to control the SR marking in the same way as animate subjects do. In the following examples, the drying of the soup (107) and the bending of the coconut palm (108) are important events in the development of the story and so the regular SR marking is maintained. In (108), the coconut palm can also be interpreted as a volitional participant, as it bends and straightens itself according to the needs of the people.

(107)   *Uup-em-ika-**iwkin**   maa eka saanar-em-ik-**eya**   iki(w-e)p eka*
cook-SS.SIM-be-2/3p.DS food water dry-SS.SIM-be-2/3s.DS go-SS.SEQ water
un-ep   ekap-ep   amina=pa feef-am-ik-e-mik.
draw-SS.SEQ come-SS.SEQ pot=LOC   pour-SS.SIM-be-PA-1/3p

'They were cooking it and the soup kept drying and they kept going and drawing water and coming and pouring it in the pot.'

---

[17] Givón (1983); Reesink (1983b; 1987); Roberts (1988b; 1997) and Farr (1999) among others.

8 *Clause combinations*

(108) *Emeria panewowa nain wiimasip   erup wia   aaw-ep   owow*
      woman old   that1 3s/p.grandchild two 3p.ACC take-ss.SEQ village
      uruma   or-op   iimar-ep   ika-iwkin iwera   oko
      open.place descend-ss.SEQ stand.up-ss.SEQ be-2/3p.DS coconut other
      mekemkar-ep or-eya   wi   iwera   ir-iwkin   nainiw kaken
      bend-ss.SEQ   descend-2/3s.DS 3p.UNM coconut climb-2/3p.DS again straight
      iimar-e-k.
      stand.up-PA-3s
      'The old woman took the two grandchildren and they went down to the village square and were standing there, and a coconut palm bent down and they climbed up the coconut palm and it stood up straight again.'

When an inanimate subject is low in terms of topicality, the SR marking of the previous clause disregards it and indicates same-subject continuation, but the verb in the inanimate clause has to indicate a change of subject, if a more topical subject follows. This structure in many Papuan languages is typical of temporal and climate expressions and other impersonal predications (Reesink 1983b, Roberts 1988b), which are often used for giving backgrounded[18] information. In examples (109) and (110) the verb in the initial medial clause predicating the action of human participants is marked with same subject following even when the following clause mentions the coming of darkness or dawn. Returning to the main line action requires different-subject marking. In the examples, the "skipped" medial clauses are in brackets.

(109) *Aria   maa en-ep   naap ik-ok [kokom-ar-eya]   in-e-mik.*
      alright food eat-ss.SEQ thus be-ss dark-INCH-2/3s.DS sleep-PA-1/3p
      'Alright we ate and stayed like that and (then) it became dark and we slept.'

(110) *In-ep   [epa wiim-eya]   onak   maak-e-mik, "..."*
      sleep-ss.SEQ place dawn-2/3s.DS 3s/p.mother tell-PA-1/3p
      'They slept, and when it dawned they told their mother, "..." '

If the impersonal predicate is important for the main story line, rather than providing backgrounded information, the impersonal verb itself is placed as a final verb, and the verb in the preceding medial clause is marked for different subject (111). Reesink (1987: 206) notes a similar rule for Usan.

(111) *Kir-ep   ekap-em-ika-iwkin   epa   wiim-o-k.*
      turn-ss.SEQ come-ss.SIM-be-2/3p.DS place dawn-PA-3s
      'They turned and as they were coming, it dawned.'

In many Papuan languages, the impersonal predications include a number of experiential verbs (Reesink 1987: 204, Roberts 1997). In Mauwake, most of the experiential

---

[18] Farr (1999: 244) calls this *on-line background* to distinguish it from the off-line background information of subordinate clauses.

expressions are adjunct plus verb constructions (§3.8.5.2.1), where the experiencer is a subject rather than an object; in chained clauses these behave in a regular manner. But those few experiential expressions that are impersonal do not trigger DS marking in the preceding medial clause, because the inanimate subject in the experiential clause is not topical enough to do it. In (112), the first person singular subject of the medial clauses becomes the object of the final clause, but the medial clause has same subject marking:

(112) *Uuw-ap uuw-ap oona=ke efa sirir-i-ya.*
work-SS.SEQ work-SS.SEQ bone=QF 1s.ACC hurt-Nc-PR.3s
'I worked and worked and my bones hurt.'

The verb *weeser-* 'finish' is often used in chained clauses to indicate the finishing of an action. In this function, its low-topicality subject, the nominalized form of the preceding verb, is never mentioned overtly, and the preceding medial clause has ss marking (113):

(113) *Uup-ep [weeser-eya] aria oposia gelemuta wiam erup fain wia*
cook-SS.SEQ finish-2/3s.DS alright meat small 3p.REFL two this 3p.ACC
wu-om-a-m.
put-BEN-BNFY2.PA-1s
'I cooked it and when it was finished, all right, I put (aside) a little of the meat for these two (women).'

In (114), there are two intervening clauses with different low-topicality inanimate subjects. The same-subject marking of the first clause "jumps over" these two clauses and refers to the subject in the last clause. The two clauses in between both have DS marking.

(114) *Maa uup-ep [fofola urup-eya] [maa op-iya] iiw-o-k.*
food cook-SS.SEQ foam rise-2/3s.DS food be.done-2/3s.DS dish.out-PA-3s
'She cooked the food and when it boiled and was done she dished it out.'

Although human subjects are typically high on the topicality hierarchy (Givón 1984: 364), even a human subject may occasionally be so low in topicality that it gets overlooked in the SR marking (115), (116).[19] What is particularly striking with the example (115) is that the clause that is overlooked has a subject in first person singular, which is usually considered to be topically the highest possible subject. A plausible explanation is that politeness and hospitality requires the host of a big meal to downplay his own importance in this way.

(115) *Efa arew-ap [maa eka liiwa muuta on-amkun] en-ep-pu-ami*
1s.ACC wait-SS.SEQ food water little only make-1s/p.DS eat-SS.SEQ-CMPL-SS.SIM
soomar-ek-eka.
walk-go-IMP.2p
'Wait for me, and when I have made just a little soup you eat it and then you (may) go.'

---
[19] Reesink (1983b: 236–237) gives similar examples from other Papuan languages.

(116) *Ikiw-ep* [*mua nain urema   osarena=pa iimar-ep   ik-eya*] *ona   mua*
       go-ss.seq man that1 bandicoot path=loc stand-ss.seq be-2/3s.ds 3s.gen man
       nain ifakim-o-k.
       that1 kill-pa-3s

   'She went and as the man was standing on the bandicoot path she killed that husband of hers.'

In process descriptions, the identity of people performing the actions is not important, and their topicality is low. In (117), the person watching the fire in the coconut drying shed is not mentioned in any way. This example is also like (114) above, in that there are two clauses with a different low-topicality subject, here one of them [+human], intervening between the second ss clause and the final clause, where the original subject is picked up.

(117) *Epia wu-ap   ikiw-ep*   [*iwera kuuf-am-ik-eya*]   [*iwera   reen-eya*]
       fire put-ss.seq go-ss.seq coconut watch-ss.sim-be-2/3s.ds coconut dry-2/3s.ds
       iwer   urupa anum-i-mik.
       coconut shell knock-Np-pr.1/3p

   'We/they put them (the coconuts) on the fire and go, and (someone) keeps watching the coconuts and they dry and (then) we/they knock the shells away.'

Even an inanimate subject may override an animate/human one in sr marking, if its topicality is high enough. In (118) the subject/topic is *kunai* grass and the burning of the grass, which is such an important part of a pighunt that the hunt itself is called *fiker(a) kuumowa* 'kunai-burning'. The grass is a continuing topic from the previous several sentences, so a noun phrase is not used for marking it.

(118) *Kuum-iwkin aw-emi*   [*mua unow maneka iiwawun   fikera*
       burn-2/3p.ds burn-ss.sim man many very   altogether kunai.grass
       kuum-emi   saawirin-ow-iwkin] *aria   fiker   epia aw-i-non.*
       burn-ss.sim round-caus-2/3p.ds alright kunai.grass fire burn-Np-fu.3s

   'They burn it and it burns and all the men burn and surround the kunai grass, (and) alright the kunai fire will burn.'

8.2.3.3 Apparent mismatches of reference

A medial verb with ds marking is used in two instances where it does not indicate a change of subject. Both types have two or more clauses with identical ds marking even though the subject is the same; only the last of those clauses really indicates a change of subject. One of them is recursion of a ds verb (119), indicating continuity; the identification of the subject is suspended until the repetition ends (Reesink 1987: 201).

(119) *Wiawi   kuum-**eya**   kuum-**eya**   kuum-**eya**   aw-ep   eka*
3s/p.father burn-2/3s.DS burn-2/3s.DS burn-2/3s.DS burn-SS.SEQ river
iw-a-k   na wia, eka=ke   saanar-e-k.
enter-PA-3s but no   river=CF dry-PA-3s

'It kept burning and burning their father and he burned and entered the river but no, the river dried.'

A medial clause that has the same subject as the following medial clause may have DS marking if both the medial clauses relate to the same finite clause as their reference clause, and the first of the medial clauses gets expanded or defined more closely in the second one. The DS verbs may be identical (120), but they do not need to be (121), (122).

(120) *Efa   uruf-am-ik-**eya**,   koora=pa efa   uruf-am-ik-**eya**   ikiw-i-nen*
1s.ACC see-SS.SIM-be-2/3.DS house=LOC 1s.ACC see-SS.SIM-be-2/3.DS go-NP-FU.1s
ekap-i-nen.
come-NP-FU.1s

'You will keep seeing me, you will keep seeing me from the house, and I will come and go.'

(121) *...pon sisina=pa   ik-**eya**,   piipa   unowa=pa*
...turtle shallow.water=LOC be-2/3s.DS seaweed many=LOC
*soomar-em-ik-**eya**   mik-a-m.*
walk-SS.SIM.be-2/3s.DS spear-PA-1s

'... the turtle was in the shallow water, it was walking among a lot of seaweed and I speared it.'

(122) *No   ikoka era=pa   wia   far-**eya**,   owora   wia   maak-**eya**, aria*
2s.UNM later road=LOC 3p.ACC call-2/3s.DS betelnut 3p.ACC tell-2/3s.DS alright
mua=ke naap me nefa   ma-i-nok,   "..."
man=CF thus not 2s.ACC say-NP-FU.3s

'Later, when you see them on the road, when you ask them for betelnut, alright let your husband not say about you that ...'

The SS medial form of the verb 'be' is used in the expression *naap ikok* 'it is/was thus (and)', regardless of the following subject/topic (123), (124). The construction seems to have grammaticalized as an expression of an indefinite time span.

(123) ***Naap ik-ok** wi   Saramun=ke wiisa   uf-e-mik.*
thus   be-SS 3p.UNM Saramun=CF dance.name dance-PA-1/3p

'It was like that and (then) the Saramun people danced *wiisa*.'

(124) ...*mua me wia imen-a-mik.* **Naap ik-ok** *sarere uura buburia ona amia*
...man not 3p.ACC find-PA-1/3p thus be-SS Saturday night bald 3S.GEN bow
mua wiar kerer-ep opaimika=pa yia wu-a-k.
man 3.DAT appear-SS.SEQ talk=LOC 1p.ACC put-PA-3s

'... we didn't find the men. It was like that, and on Saturday evening the bald man himself went to the police and accused us.'

Even when the final clause is verbless (125), (126), or missing completely because of ellipsis (127), a medial clause is still possible. In both cases, the SR marking is based on what the expected subject would be, if there were one.

(125) *Naap ik-ok uruf-am-ika-iwkin wia.*
thus be-SS see-SS.SIM-be-2/3p.DS no

'He was like that and they were watching him, but no (he didn't get any better).'

(126) *Iinan aasa gurun-owa miim-**ap** eka=iw umuk-owa ewur.*
sky canoe rumble-NMZ hear-SS.SEQ water=INST extinguish-NMZ quickly

'We heard the rumble of the airplane(s) and quickly extinguished (the fires) with water (lit: and the extinguishing with water quickly).'

The two sentences preceding the example sentence (127) mention American airplanes that flew over and dropped messages during the Second World War. The "same subject" needs to be picked from there – as the story continues without another reference to the Americans for a while – and the elliptical clause construed as something like *naap onamik* 'and they did so'.

(127) *Wi Yaapan nan ik-e-mik nain wia uruf-**ap**.*
3p.UNM Japan there be-PA-1/3p that1 3p.ACC see-SS.SEQ

'They had seen that the Japanese were there (and so they [the Americans] did so).'

8.2.3.4 Medial clauses as a complementation strategy for perception verbs

Perception verbs in Mauwake mostly use a medial clause as a complementation strategy (Dixon 2010a: 371), when the object of the perception verb is an ACTIVITY (128)–(130).[20] Regular, nominalized complement clauses are only used with perception verbs when a FACT is reported (§8.3.2.2).

(128) *Moma wiar **en-em-ik-eya** uruf-a-mik.*
taro 3.DAT eat-SS.SIM-be-2/3s.DS see-PA-1/3p

'It was eating their taro, and they saw it.' (Or: 'They saw that it was eating their taro.')

---

[20] Reesink (1983a: 237) notes this for Usan too.

(129) Aara **muuk-ar-ep** **ik-eya** uruf-a-mik.
hen son-INCH-SS.SEQ be-2/3s.DS see-PA-1/3p

'The hen had laid an egg and we saw it.' (Or: 'We saw that the hen had laid an egg.')

(130) Yo me baliwep paayar-e-m, oram iperowa=ke **nanar-iwkin**
1s.UNM not well understand-PA-1s just middle.aged=CF tell.story-2/3p.DS
miim-a-m.
hear-PA-1s

'I do not understand it well, I have just heard the older people tell stories about it.'

8.2.3.5 Tail-head linkage

Tail-head linkage is a typical feature especially in oral texts[21] in Papuan languages. It is an inter-sentential cohesive device and could be understood to belong outside "syntax proper", if syntax is defined very narrowly. It is mentioned here as it is an important linking device, and the chaining structure is used for it. In narratives and in descriptions of processes, tail-head linkage is utilized to tie sentences together within a thematic paragraph.

The tail-head link is formed when one sentence ends in a finite clause ("tail"), and the next sentence begins with a medial clause ("head") that copies the verb but changes it into a medial one. The information in this medial clause is given rather than new, unlike in most other medial clauses. Foley (1986: 200–201) claims for Yimas, and assumes for the rest of Papuan languages, that these medial clauses are subordinate, but at least in Mauwake they are not – they are coordinate like other medial clauses. In a narrative, the final verbs, which then get recapitulated in the next sentence, carry the core of the story line (131).

(131) Wafur-a-k na weetak, **ufer-a-k. Ufer-ap** nainiw burir aaw-ep
throw-PA-3s but no miss-PA-3s miss-SS.SEQ again axe take-SS.SEQ
woosa=pa aruf-eya waaya nain **in-e-k.** **In-eya** yena
head=LOC hit-2/3s.DS pig that1 lie.down-PA-3s lie.down-2/3s.DS 1s.GEN
ikiw-emi nainiw wiowa erup ar-ow-amkun iiwawun **um-o-k.**
go-SS.SIM again spear two become-CAUS-1s/p.DS altogether die-PA-3s
Um-eya merena ere-erup kaik-ap ...
die-2/3s.DN leg RDP-two tie-SS.SEQ

'He threw it (=a spear) but no, he missed. He missed it and again took an axe and hit it on the head and the pig fell down. It fell down and I myself went and speared it twice and it died completely. It died and I tied its legs two and two together and ...'

---

[21] With the development of written style, this feature is becoming less prominent.

8 Clause combinations

The repeated verb retains its arguments, but there is a choice in how overtly they and the peripherals are marked in the medial clause. Retaining them makes the medial clause more emphatic, and the first element becomes a theme for the new sentence (§9.1). In (131) only the verbs are copied; (132) copies the subject as well, (133) the object and (134) the locative adverbial.

(132) *Miiw-aasa samor-ar-e-k. Miiw-aasa samor-ar-eya...*
land-canoe bad-INCH-PA-3s land-canoe bad-INCH-2/3s.DS
'The car broke. The car broke and ...'

(133) *Owowa or-op, wuailal-ep* **akia ik-e-k.** *Akia*
village descend-SS.SEQ be.hungry-SS.SEQ banana roast-PA-3s banana
ik-ep *en-em-ik-ok, ...*
roast-SS.SEQ eat-SS.SIM-be-SS
'He came down to the village, was hungry and roasted bananas. He roasted bananas and was eating them, and ...'

(134) *P-ikiw-ep* **Bogia=pa nan wu-a-mik.** *Bogia=pa nan wu-ap i*
BPX-go-SS.SEQ Bogia=LOC there put-PA-1/3p Bogia=LOC there put-SS.SEQ 1p.UNM
kiiriw ekap-e-mik.
again come-PA-1/3p
'We took it (=his body) and put/buried it in Bogia. We put it in Bogia and came back again.'

Most commonly the derivational morphology in the two verbs is identical, but sometimes the derivation in the finite verb is dropped from the medial verb (135), (136). In (135), there is a good reason for dropping the benefactive marking from the repeated verb: the spear was thrown for someone's benefit, but it missed, and consequently there was no benefit for anyone.

(135) *Olas=ke ekap-emi wiowa* **wafur-om-a-k.** **Wafur-a-k** *na weetak,*
Olas=CF come-SS.SIM spear throw-BEN-BNFY2.PA-3s throw-PA-3s but no
ufer-a-k.
miss-PA-3s
'Olas came and threw a spear for him. He threw it but no, he missed.'

(136) *Epa wiim-eya mua* **karer-omak-e-mik.** *Karer-a-p ma-e-mik, "..."*
place dawn-2/3s.DS man gather-DISTR/PL-PA-1/3p gather-SS.SEQ say-PA-1/3p
'It dawned and many men gathered. They gathered and said, "..."'

Adding new derivation to the medial verb is possible, but rare: the example (3.460) is repeated below as (137).

(137) *Ikiwosa wiar pepekim-ep* **kaik-a-m. Kaik-om-ap...**
head 3.DAT measure-SS.SEQ tie-PA-1s tie-BEN-BNFY2.SS.SEQ
'I measured her head and tied it (=headdress). I tied it for her and ...'

8.2 Clause chaining

Similarly, aspect marking normally stays the same in both the verbs, but it is also possible to have aspect marking on the medial verb, although the finite verb is without any aspect marking (138), (139). When new information is added to the verb either by derivation or aspect marking, it is less clear if this still is a true case of tail-head linkage.

(138) ...*nomokowa maala war-ep,   ekap-ep   ifa   nain **ifakim-o-k.***
       ...tree   long cut-SS.SEQ come-SS.SEQ snake that1 beat-PA-3s
       Ifakim-em-ik-eya   *ifa   nain=ke siowa wasirk-a-k.*
       beat-SS.SIM-be-2/3s.DS snake that1=CF dog   release-PA-3s
       '...he cut a long stick, came, and beat up the snake. As he was beating it, the snake released the dog.'

(139) *Moma manina mokomokoka **nop-i-mik.**   **Nop-ap-pu-ap***
       taro garden first   clear-NP-PR.1/3p clear-SS.SEQ-CMPL-SS.SEQ
       nomokowa war-i-mik.
       tree   cut-NP-PR.1/3p
       'First we clear (the undergrowth for) taro garden. When we have cleared it we cut the trees.'

The tail-head linkage disregards right-dislocated items that come between the two verbs (140), (141).

(140) *Ne   kiiriw nan   Medebur **ek-a-mik**, mua napuma onaiya. **Ek-ap***
       ADD again there Medebur go-PA-1/3p man sick   with   go-SS.SEQ
       Medebur=pa   neeke   ...
       Medebur=LOC there.CF
       'And again from there they went to Medebur, with the sick man. They went and there in Medebur ...'

(141) ...*pok-ap   ika-iwkin mua wiar **ekap-e-mik**, wiinar-ep.*
       sit.down-SS.SEQ be-SS.SEQ man 3.DAT come-PA-1/3p make.planting.holes-SS.SEQ
       Ekap-emi   *wia   maak-e-mik, "Maa iiw-eka."*
       come-SS.SIM 3p.ACC tell-PA-1/3p food dish.out-IMP.2p
       '... they were sitting and their husbands came, having made the planting holes. They came and told them, "Dish out the food." '

A summary tail-head linkage with a generic verb (142), a common feature in many TNG languages, is used very little in Mauwake.

(142) *Or-omi   **ma-em-ik-e-mik**,   "Eka mamaiya akena i   yoowa me*
       descend-SS.SIM say-SS.SIM-be-PA-1/3p river near   very 1p.UNM hot   not
       *aaw-i-yen." **Naap on-am-ika-iwkin**   eka   owowa kerer-ep   ...*
       get-NP-FU.1p thus do-SS.SIM-be-2/3p.DS river village appear-SS.SEQ
       'They went down and were saying, "Very near the river we won't get hot." They were doing like that and (then) the river reached the village and ...'

8.3 Subordinate clauses: embedding and hypotaxis

Subordinate clauses are a problematic area to define both cross-linguistically (Haiman & Thompson 1984, Mathiessen & Thompson 1988: 317) and even within one language (Givón 1990: 848). It seems that there is a continuum from fully independent to embedded clauses (Reesink 1987: 207, Lehmann 1988: 189).

Rather than treating subordinate clauses as one group, it is helpful to differentiate between embedding and hypotaxis. Embedded clauses have a function in the main clause: relative clauses as qualifiers within a NP, complement clauses as objects or subjects, and adverbial clauses as adverbials. Hypotactic clauses are also dependent on the main clause, but they do not function as a constituent in it (Halliday 1994: 219, Lehmann 1988). Even though subordination is "a negative term which lumps together all deviations from some 'main clause' norm" (Haiman & Thompson 1984: 510), the term still has limited usefulness, as there are some rules that affect both embedded and hypotactic clauses.

In Mauwake, subordinate clauses usually precede the main clauses, and they have a non-final intonation pattern. The initial position is related to the pragmatic function of topic that these clauses often have (Lehmann 1988: 187); but when the subordinate clause is right-dislocated, it does not have a topic function.[22] The semantic function varies according to the type of subordinate clause.

Embedded clauses in Mauwake are nominalized clauses: relative clause nominalization (RC) (§8.3.1) is always done with the demonstrative *nain* 'that' added to a finite clause, whereas complement clauses (CC) (§8.3.2) can use either one of the two nominalization strategies (§5.7). The locative and temporal adverbial clauses (§8.3.3), like the relative clauses, are Type 2 nominalized clauses (§5.7.2). All of these clauses bear out Reesink's (1983: 236) claim that "subordinate clauses, especially in sentence-initial position, are natural vehicles for the speaker's presuppositions".[23] Reesink (1983a: 230) also suggests that the origin of the relative clause is in a paratactic construction. At least in Mauwake this seems to be true not only of the relative clause but of the complement clause (§8.3.2) as well.

The hypotactic conditional and concessive clauses are dependent on their main clause, but not embedded in it.

8.3.1 Relative clauses

I define a restrictive relative clause (RC),[24] following Andrews (2007a: 206), as a "subordinate clause which delimits the reference of a NP by specifying the role of the referent of that NP in the situation described by the RC".

---

[22] For a discussion on the topic function of subordinate clauses see, e.g., Reesink (1983a; 1987), Mathiessen & Thompson (1988), Lehmann (1988), and Thompson, Longacre & Hwang (2007).
[23] "Presuppositions" here refer to pragmatic, not logical-semantic presuppositions.
[24] This definition only applies to restrictive relative clauses; non-restrictive RCs (§8.3.1.4) are not real RCs although they are structurally similar to the real RCs.

8.3 Subordinate clauses: embedding and hypotaxis

The relative clause is a statement about some noun phrase in the main clause. That NP is here called the antecedent NP (ANTNP),[25] since it is the unit that the the coreferential NP in the relative clause derives its meaning from (Crystal 1997: 20). The coreferential NP in the RC is called the relative NP (RELNP).[26]

Often the referent of the ANTNP is assumed to be known to the hearer but not necessarily easily accessible, so the RC gives background information to help the hearer identify the referent.

The relative marker is the distal-1 demonstrative *nain* 'that' (§3.6.2) occurring clause-finally in the relative clause (143). It has a slightly rising non-final intonation indicating that the sentence continues; right-dislocated RCs have sentence-final falling intonation. Givenness is an essential part of the meaning of the demonstrative, which is also used in NPs (144). The demonstrative in effect makes the RC into a noun phrase. The similarity of the two structures can be seen in the examples below.

(143) [*Takira gelemuta nain*]_{NP} *uruf-a-m.*
boy   small   that1   see-PA-1s
'I saw that/the small boy.'

(144) [*Takira me arim-o-k   nain*]_{RC} *uruf-a-m.*
boy   not grow-PA-3s that1   see-PA-1s
'I saw the boy that has not grown.'

8.3.1.1 The type and position of the relative clause

In typological terms, relative clauses in Mauwake are mostly replacive, also called internal (145)–(148). A normal finite clause is made into a noun phrase by the addition of the demonstrative *nain*, and the RELNP inside the RC replaces the ANTNP. Pre-nominal RCs, where the RC precedes the ANTNP, are cross-linguistically more typical of OV languages than replacive ones (Keenan 1985: 144), but the latter are also common in Papuan languages (Reesink 1983a: 229 and Reesink 1987: 219, Roberts 1987: 49, Farr 1999: 281, Whitehead 2004: 193). Often both pre-nominal and replacive RCs are possible, with one or the other being the dominant type.

(145) [*Ni   nomona unuf-a-man nain*], *aria   iimeka kuisow na-e-man.*
2p.UNM stone   call-PA-2p that1 alright ten   one   say-PA-2p
'The money that you mentioned, alright you said ten (kina).'

(146) *Ne* [*eka opora biiris marew nain*] *wiena on-am-ik-e-mik.*
ADD river mouth bridge no(ne) that1 3p.GEN do-SS.SIM-be-1/3p
'And they themselves kept making bridges to river channels that didn't have them.'

---

[25] This is often called Head NP, but because it is not grammatically a "head" of anything, I prefer to call it antecedent NP. The name "antecedent" is also somewhat of a misnomer, as in Mauwake it does not *precede* the RELNP.

[26] Keenan (1985: 142) calls it a domain noun.

(147) [**Mua** kuum-e-mik nain] me wia kuuf-a-mik.
man burn-PA-1/3p that1 not 3p.ACC see-PA-1/3p

'We/They did not see the men that burned it.'

(148) Ne [**akia** ik-e-k nain] me en-e-k.
ADD banana roast-PA-3s that1 not eat-PA-3s

'And/but he did not eat the banana(s) that he roasted.'

It is possible to retain the antecedent NP, in which case the relative clause is not replacive but pre-nominal. In Mauwake this is not common; it is used when the noun phrase that is relativized is given extra emphasis (149).

(149) [**Fofa** ikiw-e-mik nain], **fofa** nain yo me paayar-e-m.
day go-PA-1/3p that1 day that1 1s.UNM not know-PA-1s

'The day that they went, I do not know the day/date.'

Even though the RC is usually embedded in the main clause, it can be right-dislocated. In that case the main clause contains the antecedent NP, and the relative NP is deleted from the RC. This way the first one of the coreferential NPs is retained for easier processing. Reasons for right-dislocating a relative clause are firstly, a long RC, which would be hard to process sentence-medially (150), secondly, focusing on the RC, or thirdly, an afterthought: something that the speaker still wants to add (151).

(150) **Wi teeria papako** o asip-a-mik, [ona eka sesenar-ep
3p.UNM group other 3s.UNM help-PA-1/3p 3s.GEN water buy-SS.SEQ
wienak-e-k nain].
feed.them-PA-3s that1

'Another group helped him, (those) that he had bought and given beer to.'

(151) **I mua** yiam ikur, [fikera ikiw-e-mik nain].
1p.UNM man 1p.REFL five kunai.grass go-PA-1/3p that1

'There were five of us men that went to the kunai grass (=pig-hunting).'

In a very rare case the antecedent NP is deleted and the relative NP is retained in the right-dislocated RC. What makes it possible in example (152) may be that the verb in the main clause can only have some food (or medicine/poison) as its object, so the object, although usually present, may also be left out.

(152) Wi mua ... ekap-iwkin wienak-e-mik, [**maa** nop-a-mik nain].
3p.UNM man ... come-2/3p.DS feed.them-PA-1/3p food search-PA-1/3p that1

'The men ... came, and we gave it to them to eat, (that is,) the food that we had searched for.'

8.3 Subordinate clauses: embedding and hypotaxis

Comrie (1981: 144–146) presents another typology based on how the role of the relative NP is presented in the RC. Basically Mauwake is of the "gap type", which "does not provide any overt indication of the role of the head within the relative clause". Noun phrases get very little case marking for their clausal role, and this is reflected in the RC too. This results in ambiguous relative clauses when both a third person subject NP and a third person object NP are present in the RC and the context does not make the meaning clear enough (153):

(153) [*Siowa kasi keraw-a-k nain*] *um-o-k.*
      dog   cat bite-PA-3s that1 die-PA-3s
      'The dog that bit the cat died.' Or: 'The dog that the cat bit died.'

The ambiguity can be avoided by adding the contrastive focus marker to the subject when the object is fronted to the theme position.[27] Although this is not case marking, it can function as such, because the subject is the best candidate for contrastive focus marking (154) (§3.12.7.2).

(154) [*Mua ona   emeria=ke aruf-a-k nain*] *uruf-a-m.*
      man 3s.GEN woman=CF hit-PA-3s that1 see-PA-1s
      'I saw the man whose wife hit him.'

Comrie's (1981: 140) "non-reduction type" is exhibited in Mauwake by those few cases where the relative NP keeps its oblique case marking. With overt case marking on the RELNP, the ANTNP has to be retained (155):

(155) [*Burir=iw nomokowa war-e-m nain,*] *burir nain duduw-ar-e-k.*
      axe=INST tree   cut-PA-1s that1 axe that blunt-INCH-PA-3s
      'The axe with which I cut trees became blunt.'

But when the case marking does not appear in the RC, the ANTNP is not present in the main clause either, and the RC is a gapping-type relative clause (156):

(156) [*Burir nomokowa war-e-m nain=ke*] *duduw-ar-e-k.*
      axe   tree   cut-PA-1s that1=CF blunt-INCH-PA-3s
      'The axe with which I cut trees became blunt.'

8.3.1.2 The structure of the relative clause

In Mauwake, the most typical relative clause is syntactically like a finite main clause, plus the distal-1 deictic *nain* functioning as a clause final relative marker. It was mentioned in §5.7.2 that this is one strategy for nominalizing clauses in Mauwake. The demonstrative as a possible origin of a relative marker is well attested cross-linguistically (e.g. Dixon 2010b: 342).

---

[27] For some reason this is done in relative clauses mainly with human subjects, although the contrastive focus marker can be added to non-human subjects as well.

8 Clause combinations

The verb of the relative clause is a fully inflected finite verb. But when a non-verbal clause is a relative clause, it has no verb and is structurally like other non-verbal clauses (157).

(157) *Ne [eka opora biiris marew nain] wiena on-am-ik-e-mik.*
ADD river mouth bridge no(ne) that1 3p.GEN do-SS.SIM-PA-1/3p
'And they themselves kept making bridges to rivers that didn't have them.'

The relative NP tends to be initial in the RC regardless of its syntactic function. This is because it often has the pragmatic function of theme, which takes the clause-initial position. The initial position is easy to have also because a typical clause in Mauwake has so few noun phrases: in many RCs the RELNP is the only noun phrase (158).

(158) *[Moma p-or-o-mik nain] wiar sesenar-e-mik.*
taro BPX-descend-PA-1/3p that1 3.DAT buy-PA-1/3p
'They$_i$ bought from them$_j$ the taro that they$_j$ brought down.'

When a personal pronoun functions as a subject and the relative NP in some other syntactic role, the pronoun tends to keep its initial position, thus maintaining the basic constituent order. The personal pronouns are high on the topicality hierarchy (Givón 1976: 166), so it is natural that they tend to keep the clause-initial and also sentence-initial position. Since the object *sirirowa* 'pain' in (159) is not fronted, a temporal adverbial also keeps a place it would have in a neutral main clause.

The tense in the RC can be past (158) or present (162), but not future. For future meaning, the present tense form has to be used (159).

(159) *[Yo ikoka sirir-owa aaw-i-yem nain], nis pun eliw aaw-owen=i?*
1s.UNM later hurt-NMZ get-NP-PR.1s that1 2p.FC also well get-FU.2p=QM
'Is it all right that you will also get the pain that I (will) later get?'

As was mentioned above, the antecedent NP only rarely occurs overtly. But a relative NP can also be deleted if it is generic (160), or recoverable from situational (161) or textual context (162). In (161), the deleted RELNP can either be generic 'what/whatever' or it may be *opora* 'talk'; in (162), the speaker is describing the process of making a fishtrap, which has already been mentioned in previous sentences.

(160) *[Iinan aasa=pa or-omi kiikir furew-a-mik nain] dabela.*
sky canoe=LOC descend-SS.SIM first sense-PA-1/3p that1 cold
'What we first sensed/felt when we descended from the plane was the cold.'

(161) *[Kululu ma-e-k nain] kirip-i-yem.*
Kululu say-PA-3s that1 turn/reply-NP-PR.1s
'I reply to what Kululu said.'

8.3 Subordinate clauses: embedding and hypotaxis

(162) *Aria [malol=pa ifemak-i-mik nain] aana puuk-i-mik.*
alright deep.sea=LOC press-NP-PR.1/3p that1 cane cut-NP-PR.1/3p
'Alright for those that we lower to the deep sea we cut cane.'

In (163), there is no other indication of the relative NP than the person suffix of the verb. The group of women referred to were mentioned as a noun phrase only near the beginning of the story, whereas the example is from close to the end:

(163) *Domora=pa or-omi nan ik-e-mik, [afa ar-e-mik nain].*
Domora=LOC descend-SS.SIM there be-PA-1/3p flying.fox become-PA-1/3p that1
'They went down from Domora and were there, those (women) who became flying foxes.'

In the following two examples the RCs are identical, but they have a different relative NP. The RELNP of (164) is *mukuruna* 'noise', but the RELNP of (165), *wi* 'they', only shows in the verbal suffix. The obligatory accusative pronoun in the main clause provides a key for the interpretation of (165).

(164) *[Mukuruna wua-i-mik nain] ikiw-ep miim-eka.*
noise put-NP-PR.1/3p that1 go-SS.SIM hear-IMP.2p
'Go and listen to the noise that they are making.'

(165) *[Mukuruna wua-i-mik nain] ikiw-ep wia miim-eka.*
noise put-NP-PR.1/3p that1 go-SS.SEQ 3p.ACC hear-IMP.2p
'Go and listen to those who are making the noise.'

The antecedent in most relative clauses has a specific reference. In Mauwake, when the reference is generic, a very generic noun is chosen as the head of the relativized NP and is modified by a question word (166), (167). So-called free (Andrews 2007a: 213) or condensed (Dixon 2010b: 359) relative clauses, which usually replace the whole NP with a generic or interrogative pronoun, are not used in Mauwake.

(166) *[Maa mauwa maak-i-n nain] me nefa miim-i-non.*
thing what tell-NP-PR.2s that1 not 2s.ACC hear-NP-FU.3s
'Whatever you tell him, he will not hear.'

(167) *[Mua naareke kema enek-ar-i-ya nain] eka dabela enim-i-nok.*
man who.CF liver tooth-INCH-NP-PR.3s that1 water cold eat-NP-IMP.3s
'Whoever is thirsty must drink (cold) water.'

When the antecedent is generic and human, there are two more possibilities for the RELNP: it may be *mua* 'man, person' (168) or the third person singular pronoun, plus the specifier *ena* (169) (§3.12.7.1).

357

8 Clause combinations

(168) [*Mua ena kema enek-ar-i-ya   nain*] ...
      man SPEC liver tooth-INCH-NP-PR.3s that1

   'Whoever is thirsty...'

(169) [*O   ena kema enek-ar-i-ya   nain*] ...
      3s.UNM SPEC liver tooth-INCH-NP-PR.3s that1

   'Whoever is thirsty...'

Non-verbal descriptive clauses can be made into relative clauses, but it is only in the negative that they are recognizable as such. In the affirmative, they are exactly like noun phrases with a demonstrative (170), and because the meanings are so similar, it can be questioned whether there is such a thing as an affirmative non-verbal descriptive RC at all in Mauwake.

(170) [*Mua eliwa nain*] *kookal-i-yem.*
      man good that1 like-NP-PR.1s

   'I like the good man.' Or 'I like the man that is good.'

In the negative, these clauses are different from the noun phrases because the negation is placed before the non-verbal predicate (171).

(171) [*Koora* **me** *maneka nain*] *uruf-a-m.*
      house   not   big   that1   see-PA-1s

   'I saw the house that is not big.'

8.3.1.3 Relativizable noun phrase positions

Several NP functions can be relativized, and Mauwake conforms to Keenan & Comrie's (1977) Noun Phrase Accessibility Hierarchy:[28] the higher up an NP is in the hierarchy, the easier it is to relativize. Noun phrases with the following functions can be relativized: subject, object, recipient, beneficiary, instrument, comitative, object of genitive, temporal and locative.

Subject (172) and object (173) are the most frequent functions of the RELNP.

(172) [**Mesa**   *asia fiker(a)   gone=pa   ika-i-ya   nain*] *aaw-em-ik-e-m.*
      wingbean wild kunai.grass middle=LOC be-NP-PR.3s that1   get-SS.SIM-be-PA-1s

   'I kept picking wild wingbeans that are/grow in the middle of the kunai grass.'

(173) *Muuka,* [*yo*   **opora** *nefa   maak-i-yem nain*] *miim-ap   ook-e.*
      son   1s.UNM   talk   2s.ACC tell-NP-PR.1s that1   hear-SS.SEQ follow-IMP.2s

   'Son, listen to and follow the talk that I am telling you.'

---

[28] As Mauwake adjectives do not have comparative forms there can be no relativization for an object of comparison, which in Keenan and Comrie's hierarchy is the hardest to relativize.

8.3 Subordinate clauses: embedding and hypotaxis

Recipient (174) and beneficiary (175) are possible to relativize, but in natural texts beneficiary is very infrequent.

(174) [*Takira iwoka iw-e-m* nain] yena aamun=ke.
boy yam give.him-PA-1s that1 1s.GEN 1s/p.younger.sibling=CF
'The boy that I gave yam to is my younger brother.'

(175) Ne [*wi emeria papako* iiriw sawur wia iirar-om-a-k
ADD 3p.UNM woman some earlier bad.spirit 3p.ACC remove-BEN-BNFY2.PA-3s
nain] ...
that1
'And some women, from (lit: for) whom he had removed bad spirits, ...'

When an instrument is relativized, the RELNP either takes the instrumental case marking (155) or has no case marking (176):

(176) Aria [*maa unowa* wakesim-e-mik nain] sererk-a-mik.
alright thing many cover-PA-1/3p that1 distribute-PA-1/3p
'Alright they distributed the many things with which they had covered her (body).'

A comitative NP (§4.1.3) containing a comitative postposition may be relativized (177), but one formed with a comitative clitic may not.

(177) [*Mua nain ikos* ikiw-e-mik nain] napum-ar-e-k.
man that1 with go-PA-1/3p that1 sick-INCH-PA-3s
'That man with whom I went became sick.'

The object of genitive, or object of POSSESSIVE as it should be called when describing Mauwake grammar, only uses the dative pronoun (§3.5.5) when relativized (178), not the unmarked (§3.5.2.1) or genitive (§3.5.4) pronoun.

(178) [*Mua emeria wiar* um-o-k nain=ke] baurar-ep owowa oko ikiw-o-k.
man woman 3.DAT die-PA-3s that1=CF flee-SS.SEQ village other go-PA-3s
'The man whose wife died went away[29] to another village.'

Temporal (179) and locative (180) RCs are structurally identical to the other RCs when the relativized temporal or locative NP does not have an adverbial function in the main clause.

(179) [*Fofa ikiw-e-mik nain*] me paayar-e-m.
day go-PA-1/3p that1 not understand-PA-1s
'I don't know the day that they went.'

---

[29] Moving to another village after some misfortune is quite common, and the verb 'flee' is used in this context but here it does not have a strongly negative connotation; this is reflected in the free translation.

(180) [*Koora maneka wiena opora siisim-i-mik   nain*] *uruf-a-mik.*
       house big   3p.GEN talk write-NP-1/3p that1 see-PA-1/3p

       'We saw the big house where they write their talk (=printshop).'

When the relativized temporal NP is a temporal in the main clause as well, the relative marker can optionally be replaced by the locative deictic *nan* or *neeke* 'there' (181).

(181) [*Aite   uroma   yaki-e-k   fofa nain/nan/neeke*]   *auwa*   *Madang*
       1s/p.mother stomach wash-PA-3s day that1/there/there.CF 1s/p.father Madang
       ikiw-o-k.
       go-PA-3s

       'The day that mother gave birth, father went to Madang.'

When the relativized locative NP is also a constituent in the main clause, the relative marker has to be replaced by *nan* or *neeke* (182).

(182) *Or-op*   [*i   koora ik-e-mik neeke*] *ekap-o-k.*
       descend-SS.SEQ 1p.UNM house be-PA-1p there.CF come-PA-3s

       'It descended and came to the house/building where we were.'

Temporal adverbial clauses, which are structurally close to relative clauses, are discussed below in §8.3.3.1, and locative adverbial clauses in §8.3.3.2.

8.3.1.4 Non-restrictive relative clauses

Non-restrictive, or appositional, relative clauses are structurally exactly like restrictive relative clauses, but their function is different. They do not delimit the reference of the antecedent NP. Instead, they give new information about it. Functionally they are like a coordinate clause added to the main clause.

Because of the structural and even intonational similarity, it is sometimes difficult to tell if a particular RC is restrictive or non-restrictive. When the ANTNP is a proper noun or when it includes a first or second person singular pronoun, the RC is usually non-restrictive (183), (184):

(183) *Bang=ke ekap-o-k,* [*Ponkila aaw-o-k   nain*].
       Bang=CF come-PA-3s Ponkila get-PA-3s that1

       'Bang came, (he) who married Ponkila.'

(184) *Yo   nena   owowa* [*moma marew nain*] *miatin-i-yem.*
       1s.UNM 2s.GEN village taro   no(ne) that1 dislike-NP-PR.1s

       'I don't like your village, which doesn't have taro.'

The proximate demonstrative *fain* 'this' can also function as a relative marker in the non-restrictive RCs but not in restrictive ones (185):

(185) Nomokowa   unowa fan-e-mik,   [Simbine ekap-omak-e-mik   fain].
      2s/p.brother many here-PA-1/3p Simbine come-DISTR/PL-PA-1/3p this

      'Your many (clan) brothers are here, these Simbine people who came.'

When the ANTNP is a pronoun other than first or second singular, the RC may be either restrictive or non-restrictive (186).

(186) I   mua yiam   ikur, [fikera   ikiw-e-mik nain].
      1p.UNM man 1p.REFL five   kunai.grass go-PA-1/3p that1

      'There were five of us men who went to the kunai grass (= pig-hunting).' Or:
      'We were five men, who went pig-hunting.'

8.3.2 Complement clauses and other complementation strategies

The prototypical function of a complement clause is as a subject or object in a main clause. In Mauwake, a complement clause proper functions as an object of a complement-taking verb (CTV), and occasionally as a subject in a non-verbal clause. Structurally it is a Type 2 nominalized clause: a finite clause that has the distal-1 demonstrative *nain* 'that' occurring as a nominaliser clause-finally (§5.7.2). The complement clause precedes the complement-taking verb. The complement clause differs from the relative clause in that none of the noun phrases inside it is an ANTNP or a RELNP.

The division of complements into different types, "Fact, Activity and Potential", that Dixon (2010b: 371) provides, is crucial for the use of the different complementation strategies in Mauwake. A complement clause is normally used when a CTV needs a fact-type object complement.

Besides the regular complement clause described above, Mauwake has other complementation strategies. The indirect speech clauses are ordinary sentences embedded in the utterance clause (§8.3.2.1.2). Medial clauses are used as the main complementation strategy for activity-type complements with perception verbs (§8.3.2.2). Clauses with a nominalized verb are used for potential-type complements with various CTVs. The regular complement clause and the clause with a nominalized verb may occur as a subject of a clause (§8.3.2.4).

Since one CTV can take more than one complementation strategy, the main grouping below is done according to the CTVs.

8.3.2.1 Complements of utterance verbs

Some utterance verbs (§3.8.4.4.6) are also used for thinking, so speech and thought are discussed as one group.

The status of direct quote clauses (§8.3.2.1.1) as complement clauses is questionable, but they are discussed here because of their co-occurrence with the utterance verbs and their similarity with the indirect quotes (§8.3.2.1.2), which are complement clauses.

The most important of the utterance verbs is *na-* 'say, think'. It is used as the utterance verb for indirect quote complements, which in turn have grammaticalized, together with

8 *Clause combinations*

the same subject sequential form of the verb, as desiderative (§8.3.2.1.3) and purpose clauses (§8.3.2.1.4) and the conative construction (§8.3.2.1.5)

8.3.2.1.1 Direct speech It seems to be a universal feature of direct quote clauses that they behave independently of their matrix clauses. If they are considered complement clauses of utterance verbs, their independence sets them apart from all the other complement clauses (Munro 1982: 303). Dixon (2010a: 398) maintains that direct speech quotes are not any kind of complementation.

A direct quote may be a whole discourse on its own, not just a clause within a sentence.

It is rather typical in Papuan languages to have a strict quote formula both before and after a quotation, or at least before it (Franklin 1971: 120, Davies 1981: 1, Roberts 1987: 12, Farr 1999, Hepner 2002: 128). It is also common that either there is no separate structure for indirect speech (Davies 1981: 2) or that direct and indirect speech are so similar that they are often hard to distinguish from each other (Roberts 1987: 14).

In the use of quote formulas, Mauwake is much freer than Papuan languages in general. A direct quotation in Mauwake is often preceded or followed by one of the utterance verbs. The verbs *na-* 'say/think' and *naak-* 'say/tell' are almost exclusively used after quotes. Enclosing a quote between two utterance verbs is not frequent (187):

(187) *Ne ona mua pun* **ma-e-k**, *"Eka maneka nain=ke iwa-mi ifakim-o-k,"*
ADD 3s.GEN man also say-PA-3s river big that1=CF come-SS.SIM kill-PA-3s
na-e-k.
say-PA-3s

'Her husband also said, "The big river came and killed her," he said.'

Most commonly, only a speech verb precedes the quote (188), (189):

(188) *Panewowa=ke* **ma-e-k**, *"Yo nia maak-emkun opaimika efa*
old=CF say-PA-3s 1s.UNM 2p.ACC tell-2/3p.DS talk 1s.ACC
fien-a-man."
disobey-PA-2p

'The old (woman) said, "When I told you, you disobeyed me."'

(189) *Iiw-ep wiipa muuka nain wia* **maak-e-k**, *"Auwa maa*
dish.out-SS.SEQ daughter son that1 3p.ACC tell-PA-3s 1s/p.father food
p-ikiw-om-aka.
BPX-go-BEN-BNFY2.IMP.2p

'She dished out (the food) and told the children, "Take the food to father."'

A single utterance verb (190) or a whole quote-closing clause (191) may follow the quote. A quote-closing clause has to be used when the quotation consists of several sentences.

362

8.3 Subordinate clauses: embedding and hypotaxis

(190) *"No bom fain=iw mera kuum-e,"* **naak-e-mik.**
2s.UNM bomb this=INST fish burn-IMP.2s tell-PA-1/3p
' "Blast fish with this bomb," they told him.'

(191) *"I muuka marew a, wiipa marew a,"* **naap wia maak-e-k.**
1p.UNM son no(ne) ah daughter no(ne) ah thus 3p.ACC tell-PA-3s
' "We have no son, we have no daughter," he told them like that.'

In narratives where there are several exchanges between the participants, it is possible to leave out the utterance verb (192), (193) and even the NP referring to the speaker of the utterance (192), if the speaker is clear enough from the context. A good speaker creates variety in the text by utilizing all these different possibilities.

(192) *Ne onak=ke Ø, "A, ifera feeke un-eka." Ne wi*
ADD 3s/p.mother Ø Ah, salt.water here.CF fetch(water)-IMP.2p ADD 3p.UNM
maak-e-mik, "Wia, i oro-or-op un-i-yan." "A,
tell-PA-1/3p No 1p.UNM RDP-descend-SS.SEQ fetch-NP-FU.1p Ah
neeke-r=iw un-eka." "Weetak, i oro-ora-i-yan."
there.CF-Ø=LIM fetch-IMP.2p no 1p.UNM RDP-descend-NP-FU.1p

'And their mother (said), "Ah, fetch the sea water (from) here." But they told her, "No, we'll go down (to the deep sea) and fetch it." "Ah, fetch it right there." "No, we'll go down a long way." '

(193) *"Mauwa ar-e-n, amia=iya nenar-e-mik=i?" Sarak=ke Ø.*
what become-PA-2s bow=COM shoot.you-PA-1/3p=QM Sarak=CF Ø
"'What happened to you, did they shoot you with a gun?" Sarak (asked).'

8.3.2.1.2 Indirect speech Indirect speech quotes, which report speech or thought, are objects of speech verbs.

Most indirect quotes in Mauwake are syntactically identical to direct quotes. There is an intonational difference: the indirect quote is part of the intonation contour of the main clause, rather than having a contour of its own as a direct quote has. The quote is almost always followed by the utterance verb *na-* 'say, think' (194); but it is also possible for the verb *ma-* 'say' to precede it, in which case both the utterance verb and the quote have their own intonation contour (195).[30] An indirect quote is never enclosed between two utterance verbs.

(194) *Aria, Kalina, [Amerika ekap-e-mik]* **na-i-mik.**
alright Kalina America come-PA-1/3p say-NP-PR.1/3p

'Alright, Kalina, they say that the Americans have come.'

---

[30] In Amele, the absence of the speech verb before the quote is the main criterion for indirect speech (Roberts 1987: 14). In Mauwake, this cannot be used as a criterion, as the occurrence of speech verbs with direct quotes varies so much.

8 Clause combinations

(195)   *Ma-e-m,* [*nena owowa=pa ik-o-n*].
say-PA-1s 2s.GEN village=LOC be-PA-2s
'I said (to her_i) that you_j are in your own village.'

As direct quotes behave independently of their matrix clauses, they often have a separate deictic centre. But indirect quotes vary in this respect. Deictic elements, which get part or all of their interpretation from the situational context, are often the same in indirect quotes as they would be in direct quotes (196), (197):

(196)   *Aite=ke*   [*manina yook-e*]   *na-eya*   *o*   *ook-e.*
1s/p.mother=CF garden   follow.me-IMP.2s say-2/3s.DS 3s.UNM follow.her-IMP.2s
'When mother tells you to follow her to the garden, follow her.'

(197)   *Ni*   *Krais* [*yena teeria efar   ik-eka*]   *na-ep*   *nia*   *far-eya*
2p.UNM Christ 1s.GEN family 1s.DAT be-IMP.2p say-SS.SEQ 2p.ACC call-2/3s.DS
ona   *teeria wiar ik-e-man.*
3s.GEN family 3.DAT be-PA-2p
'Christ called you to be his family and (now) you are his family.'

But the deictic centre may also shift partly or completely towards that of the matrix clause. When this happens, the pronouns are the easiest to change, next the adverbs. In (198) a second person pronoun has replaced the proper name or third person pronoun that would have been used in a direct quote.

(198)   *Sarak oo, Amerika ekap-ep   Ulingan nan ik-e-mik,* [***nefa***
Sarak INTJ America come-ss.SEQ Ulingan there be-PA-1/3p 2s.ACC
ikum-i-mik]   *na-i-mik*   *oo.*
wonder.about-NP-PR.1/3p say-NP-PR.1/3p INTJ
'Sarak! The Americans have come and are in Ulingan and they say that they are wondering where you are!'

When reported by the addressee of the example clause (199), only the pronoun in the reported clause (200) is different:

(199)   *No*   *owowa ikiw-ep buk   nain sesek-om-e.*
2s.UNM village go-ss.SEQ book that1 send-BEN-BNFY1.IMP.2s
'When you go to the village, send the book to me.'

(200)   [***Yo***   *owowa **ikiw-ep** buk   nain sesek-om-e*]   *efa*   *na-e-k.*
1s.UNM village go-ss.SEQ book that1 send-BEN-BNFY1.IMP.2s 1s.ACC say-PA-3s
'He told me to send that book to him (lit: me) when I would go to the village.'

The verbs are most resistant to deictic shift. In (201), even though the verb root changes, it still retains the tense and person marking of the direct quote (202). Both the temporal adverb and the pronoun are shifted to reflect the deictic centre of the matrix clause.

8.3 Subordinate clauses: embedding and hypotaxis

(201) *Uurika   nefar ikiw-i-nen.*
tomorrow 2s.DAT go-NP-FU.1s

'Tomorrow I'll come (lit: go) to you.'

(202) [*Ikoka   efar ekap-i-nen*]   *na-e-k   na weetak.*
Later(today) 1s.DAT come-NP-FU.1s say-PA-3s but no

'He said that he would come to me today, but he hasn't.'

Below in (204) also the person suffix is changed from that in (203) to reflect the situation of the new speech act participants.

(203) *Ona   owowa=pa ik-ua.*
3s.GEN village=LOC be-PA.3s

'She is in her own village.'

(204) *Ma-e-m,* [*nena   owowa=pa ik-o-n*].
say-PA-1s 2s.GEN village=LOC be-PA-2s

'I said (to her) that you are in your own village.'

The deictic shift would need more study to ascertain if there are specific rules governing this variation in indirect quotes.

When the verb *na-* 'say, think' indicates thinking, the complement clause is usually an indirect quote rather than a direct one (205), (206).

(205) [*Muuka ifera   me enim-i-non*]   *na-ep   me uruf-a-m.*
boy   salt.water not drink-NP-FU.3s think-SS.SEQ not look-PA-1s

'Thinking that the boy wouldn't drown I didn't watch him.'

(206) *Mua pepena=ke*   [*menat=ke ek-i-ya*]   *na-ep   menat*
man inexperienced=CF tide=CF   go-NP-PR.3s think-SS.SEQ tide
ora-i-nan.
descend-NP-FU.2s

'An inexperienced man will think that the tide is going down and will go to fish at low tide.'

Indirect non-polar questions are similar to the corresponding direct questions apart from possible adjustments to deictic elements (207), (208).

(207) [*Wi   uf-ow(a)   epa   kaaneke ik-ua*]   *na-e-k.*
3p.UNM dance-NMZ place where.CF be-PA.3s say-PA-3s

'He asked where their dancing place was.'

(208) [*O   ikoka sesa   kamenap aaw-i-non*]   *na-e-k.*
3s.UNM later price what.like get-NP-FU.3s say-PA-3s

'He asked what kind of wages he would get later.'

8 Clause combinations

Polar questions, when indirect, have to be alternative questions (209). The verb *naep* may be deleted, when the indirect question is sentence-final (210).

(209) [*Beel-al-i-non=i*   *kamenion*] *na-ep*   *uruf-am-ik-ua.*
rotten-INCH-NP-FU.3s=QM or.what think-SS.SEQ see-SS.SIM-be-PA.3s

'He was watching (thinking) whether it would rot or what would happen.'

(210) *Wi*   *iwera*   *iinan=pa ik-ok iwer(a) popoka wafur-am-ik-e-mik,*   [*eka*
3p.UNM coconut top=LOC be-ss coconut unripe throw-SS.SIM-be-PA-1/3p water
saanar-e-k=i   *eewuar*] Ø.
dry-PA-3s=QM not.yet

'They were at the top of the coconut palm and threw unripe coconuts (thinking) whether the water had dried or not yet.'

8.3.2.1.3 Desiderative clauses It is very common in Papuan languages that an indirect quote construction with the intended action verb in future tense, imperative or irrealis form expresses a want/wish[31], desire or intention to do something. (Reesink 1987: 254–259, Foley 1986: 157, Hardin 2002: 112, Hepner 2002: 76–77).

In Mauwake, the future, imperative, counterfactual and nominalized forms of the main verb are possible in the complement clause. In desiderative clauses, the verb *na-* 'say/think' is always in the medial same-subject sequential form *naep*; in purpose clauses, other forms are possible as well. Historically, there probably always used to be a clause with a finite verb following the clause expressing intention or desire (211); synchronically the finite clause is often missing (212), especially when the verb would be the same as in the complement.

(211) *Niena* [*maa enim-u*] *na-ep*   *iiw-eka.*
2p.GEN food eat-IMP.1d say-SS.SEQ dish.out-IMP.2p

'If you want/intend to eat food, dish it out (yourselves).'

(212) *Yo*   [*opora gelemuta=ko ma-i-nen*]   *na-ep.*
1s.UNM talk little=NF say-NPS-FU.1s say-SS.SEQ

'I want to tell a little story.' Or: 'I'm going to tell a little story.'

The main verb in the complement clause is either marked for first person[32] or is nominalized. Mauwake uses the future (212) or imperative form (213) of the main verb for intention or a clear/certain wish, and the counterfactual form for a wish that has less potential to be realized. The latter is also the most polite form to use, if the wish indicates a request (214).

---

[31] In Mauwake, the verb *kookal-* 'like, love, desire', is mostly used with an NP object, but it can take a clausal complement as well. It does not indicate intention or purpose. The complement is either type of nominalized clauses (§5.7).
[32] Purpose clauses may use other person forms as well (§8.3.2.1.4).

8.3 Subordinate clauses: embedding and hypotaxis

(213) [*Haussik p-ek-u*] *na-ep* *miiw-aasa nop-a-mik.*
aidpost BPX-go-IMP.1d say-SS.SEQ land-canoe search-PA-1/3p
'We/they wanted to take her to the aidpost and looked for a vehicle.'

(214) [*Yo=ko* *wia* *uruf-ek-a-m*] *na-ep.*
1s.UNM=NF 3p.ACC see-CNTF-PA-1s say-SS.SEQ
'I would like to see them.'

The nominalized form is mostly used in complement clauses that can also be interpreted as purpose clauses. In "pure" desiderative clauses it is practical to use the nominalized form especially if the first person marking in the verb might make it harder to process the meaning (215):

(215) *Ne* [*o* *uruf-owa*] *ne* [*maa en-owa asip-owa*] *na-ep=na* *eliw*
ADD 3s.UNM see-NMZ ADD food eat-NMZ help-NMZ say-SS.SEQ=TP well
asip-uk.
help-IMP.3p
'And if they want to see him and help him with food, let them help him.'

8.3.2.1.4 Purpose clauses Purpose is both conceptually close and structurally similar to desiderative, and in Mauwake many of the desiderative clauses can be interpreted as purpose clauses. This is particularly so when the main verb is in the nominalized form (216), (217). But a truly desiderative clause even with an action nominal is never right-dislocated, whereas a purpose clause (218) often is. The nominalized form in the main verb is common:

(216) [*Weniwa=pa en-owa*] *na-ep* *uuw-i-mik.*
famine=LOC eat-NMZ say-SS.SEQ work-NP-PR.1/3p
'We work in order to (be able to) eat during the time of hunger.'

(217) [*Wi* *Amerika wiam=iya irak-owa*] *na-ep* *ikiw-e-mik.*
3p.UNM America 3p=COM fight-NMZ say/think-SS.SEQ go-PA-1/3p
'They went to fight with the Americans.'

(218) *Ona* *siowa ikos manina ikiw-e-mik,* [*pika on-owa*] *na-ep.*
3s.GEN dog with garden go-PA-1/3p fence make-NMZ say-SS.SEQ
'He went to the garden with his dog, in order to make a fence.'

Future and imperative forms are also used in the purpose clause. When the subject in the purpose clause is the same as the subject of the utterance verb and the main clause, the first person future form is used for singular (219), (220) and first person dual imperative for plural (221).

8 *Clause combinations*

(219) [*Nain nefa maak-i-nen*] *na-ep yo ep-a-m.*
that1 2s.ACC tell-NP-FU.1s say-SS.SEQ 1s.UNM come-PA-1s
'I came to tell you that.'

(220) *No* [*owora sesenar-i-nen*] *na-ep Kainantu fofa ikiw-ep neeke*
2s.UNM betelnut buy-NP-FU.1s say-SS.SEQ Kainantu market go-SS.SEQ there.CF
aaw-i-nan.
get-NPS-FU.2s
'To buy betelnut you will (need to) go to Kainantu marker and get it THERE.'

(221) *Ne* [*haussik p-ek-u*] *na-ep miiw-aasa nop-a-mik.*
ADD aidpost BPX-go-IMP.1d say-SS.SEQ land-canoe search-PA-1/3p
'And they searched for a truck (in order) to take him to the aidpost.'

When the subject of the verb in the main clause differs from that of the purpose clause, the verb inside the purpose clause has to be in the imperative (222)–(228). The whole purpose clause is structurally like a direct quote of the "inner speech" verb *naep*, so there is no deictic shift of the kind that may take place in indirect quotes.

(222) [*Me yiar-uk*] *na-ep koka=pa ik-e-mik.*
not shoot.us-IMP.3p say-SS.SEQ jungle=LOC be-PA-1/3s
'We stayed in the jungle so that they would not shoot us.'

(223) [*Auwa=ke o=ko amukar-inok*] *na-ep maa naap*
1s/p.father=CF 3s.UNM=NF scold-IMP.3s say-SS.SEQ thing thus
sirar-em-ik-e-mik.
make-SS.SIM-be-PA-1/3
'They kept doing things like that so that father would scold HIM (and not them).'

(224) *Nain* [*ni amis-ar-eka*] *na-ep feenap on-i-yem.*
that1 2p.UNM knowledge-INCH-IMP.2p say-SS.SEQ like.this do-NP-PR.1s
'But I am doing this so that you would know.'

(225) [*Efa asip-e*] *na-ep ekap-e-m.*
1s.ACC help-IMP.2s say-SS.SEQ come-PA-1s
'I came so that you would help me.'

(226) [*Feenap nokar-eka*] *na-ep yia sesek-a-k.*
like.this ask-IMP.2p say-SS.SEQ 1p.ACC send-PA-3s
'He sent us to ask (you) like this.'

(227) [*Yo efa miim-eka*] *na-ep wapena wu-ami ma-e-k,...*
1s.UNM 1s.ACC hear-IMP.2p say-SS.SEQ hand put-SS.SIM say-PA-3s
'He raised his hand for them to listen to him and said, ...'

8.3 Subordinate clauses: embedding and hypotaxis

(228) *Ne wi popor-ar-urum-ep ik-ok ifana muutiw*
ADD 3p.UNM silent-INCH-DISTR/A-SS.SEQ be-SS ear only
wu-am-ika-i-kuan, [mua unuma wia miim-u] na-ep.
put-SS.SIM-be-NP-FU.3p man name 3p.ACC hear-IMP.1d say-SS.SEQ

'And they all will be quiet and listen carefully in order to hear the men's names.'

There is no raising of negation from the subordinate to the main clause (229).

(229) [*Yo me pina=pa nia wu-ek-a-m] na-ep ma-i-yem.*
1s.UNM not guilt=LOC 2p.ACC put-CNTF-PA-1s say-SS.SEQ say-NP-PR.1s

'I am not saying (this) to put guilt on you.' (=I am saying this, but not in order to put guilt on you.)

A purpose clause does not always have the auxiliary *naep*. A clause with just a nominalized verb is used especially with the directional verbs (230), (231):

(230) [*Yo yena emeria aaw-owa] urup-e-m.*
1s.UNM 1s.GEN woman take-NMZ ascend-PA-1s

'I came up to take my wife.'

(231) *Bogia ikiw-e-mik, [opaimika aakun-owa].*
Bogia go-PA-1/3p talk talk-NMZ

'We went to Bogia to talk.'

A clause with a nominalized verb plus a clause-final distal-1 demonstrative *nain* 'that' is also possible, but less common (232), (233). I have not observed a functional difference between the different purpose structures.

(232) *Tunde=pa [maa muutitik uruf-owa nain] soomar-e-mik.*
Tuesday=LOC thing all.kinds see-NMZ that1 walk-PA-1/3p

'On Tuesday we walked to see all kinds of things.'

(233) *Ifemak-ep nomona iinan=pa wua-i-nan, [ikoka ifera me p-ikiw-owa*
press-SS.SEQ stone on.top=LOC put-NP-FU.2s later sea not BPX-go-NMZ
nain].
that1

'You press it down and put stones on top (or: put it on top of stones/corals) so that the sea would not later take it away.'

8.3.2.1.5 Conative clauses: 'try' Instead of using a verbal construction with the verb 'see' for conative modality – expressing the attempt to do something – which Foley (1986: 152) claims as almost universal for Papuan languages, Mauwake makes use of a structure where the desiderative is followed by the verb *on-* 'do' as the verb in its reference clause (234). Usan uses an identical construction for the same purpose (Reesink 1987: 258).

(234) [*Mukuna umuk-u   na-ep   on-a-mik*]=*na me pepek.*
fire   extinguish-IMP.1d say-SS.SEQ do-PA-1/3p=TP not enough

'We tried to extinguish the fire but were not able to.'

When this structure is used, it is implied that somehow or other the effort fails (235), (236):

(235) [*Emeria aruf-i-nen   na-ep   on-am-ik-eya*]   *op-a-mik.*
woman hit-NP-FU.1s say-SS.SEQ do-SS.SIM-be-2/3s.DS hold-PA-1/3p

'When he was trying to hit the woman, they grabbed him.'

(236) [*Wia   uruf-ek-a-m   na-ep   on-a-k   on-a-k*] *weetak, o   me wia*
3p.ACC see-CNTF-PA-1s say-SS.SEQ do-PA-3s do-PA-3s no   3s.UNM not 3p.ACC
uruf-a-k.
see-PA-3s

'He tried and tried to see them, but no, he didn't see them.'

The conative structure is not used when the effort is successful (237), and also when the 'trying' is not so much an effort to do something as experimenting (238). In these cases the verb *akim-* 'try' is used, which is neutral as to the outcome. It requires a nominalized verb in the complement clause.

(237) [*Aasa keraw-owa*] *akim-ap   akim-ap   amis-ar-i-nan.*
canoe carve-NMZ   try-SS.SEQ try-SS.SEQ knowledge-INCH-NP-FU.2s

'After trying and trying to carve a canoe, you will know (how to do it).'

(238) [*Weria   op-ap   wiinar-owa   nain*] *akim-am-ik-e.*
planting.stick hold-SS.SEQ make.planting.holes-NMZ that1 try-SS.SIM-be-IMP.2s

'Keep trying/learning to make planting holes with the planting stick.'

8.3.2.1.6 Complements of other utterance verbs The verb *ma-* 'say, talk' can take a regular complement clause, which is of the fact type (Dixon 2010b: 389). This clause functions as an object of the verb in the same way as an NP with the head noun *opora* (or *opaimika*) 'talk/story' in (239):

(239) [*Opora gelemuta=ko*]$_{NP}$ *ma-i-nen   na-ep.*
talk   little=NF   say-NP-FU.1s say/think-SS.SEQ

'I want to tell a little story.'

The complement clause says something about the contents of the story and functions as a kind of title. This type of structure is quite common in Papuan languages[33] and is used mainly in an opening or closing formula in narrative texts (240):

---

[33] Reesink (1987: 231) treats them under relative clauses and considers them equivalents of English cleft sentences.

8.3 Subordinate clauses: embedding and hypotaxis

(240) *Aria   yo   aakisa [takira en-owa   gelemuta wia*
      alright 1s.UNM now   child   eat-NMZ   little   3p.ACC
      *on-om-a-mik   nain]*_{CC} *ma-i-yem.*
      make-BEN-BNFY2.PA-1/3p that1   say-NP-PR.1s

   'Alright now I tell about our making a feast for the children.'

The complement "clause" may actually be a whole sentence, since it is possible to have medial clauses preceding the finite clause of the complement (241):

(241) [*Tunde=pa   fikera   kuum-iwkin ikiw-ep   waaya mik-a-m   nain*]_{CC}
      Tuesday=LOC kunai.grass burn-2/3p.DS go-SS.SEQ pig   spear-PA-1s that1
      ma-i-yem.
      say-NP-PR.1s

   'I tell about that when they burned kunai grass on Tuesday and I went and speared a pig.'

Often the sentence has both a NP containing a word for 'story' and the complement clause (242). The relationship of these two NPs is not really appositional, because the nominalized clause modifies the other NP. But the nominalized clause is not a prototypical RC either, in spite of identical structure, because *opora* is neither an antecedent NP nor a relative NP that would have a function in the RC. I consider the nominalized clause a modifier of the other NP, and the whole comparable to the NP in (243).[34]

(242) *Aria   yo   aakisa [fikera   ikum   kuum-e-mik nain*]_{CC} *opora*
      alright 1s.UNM now   kunai.grass illicitly burn-PA-1/3p that1   story
      gelemuta=ko ma-i-yem.
      little=NF   say-NP-PR.1s

   'Alright now I tell a little story about the kunai grass that was burned by arson.'

(243) *manina uuw-owa   opora*
      garden work-NMZ talk

   'garden work talk / talk (n.) about garden work'

Another complementation strategy for utterance verbs is a clause with a nominalized verb. It is used when the event expressed in the clause is regarded as potential, rather than an actual activity or a fact. The following example has two levels of complementation, as the verb in the nominalized complement also takes a nominalized complement (244):

---

[34] Comrie & Horie (1995) present another alternative: treating complement clauses like this and relative clauses as a single construction, where the structure only indicates that the subordinate clause is connected to an NP, and the interpretation of their relationship is done pragmatically. This possibility would need more investigation in Mauwake.

8 Clause combinations

(244) I   [*yiena* [*miiw-aasa muf-owa*] *ikiw-owa*] *na-em-ik-omkun*   *o*
1p.UNM 1p.GEN land-canoe pull-NMZ go-NMZ   say-SS.SIM-be-2/3p.DS 3s.UNM
ar-e-k.
become-PA-3s

'While we were talking about our going to fetch a vehicle, she died (lit: became).'

The same strategy is used with the verb *maak-* 'tell' when it is used in the sense of ordering someone to do something (245):

(245) *Emar,* [*no   muut fain uf-owa*]   *nefa   maak-e-m.*
friend 2s.UNM only this dance-NMZ 2s.ACC tell-PA-1s

'Friend, I told you to dance only this.'

8.3.2.2 Complements of perception verbs

It was mentioned above (§8.2.3.4) that the chaining structure is used with perception verbs in Mauwake as the main complementation strategy for perception verbs, when the complement is an activity (246) or event (247). These are not genuine complement clauses, as they are not embedded in the main clause, but they perform the same function as regular complement clauses do.

(246) [*Mukuruna wu-am-ika-iwkin*]   *i*   *miim-a-mik.*
noise   put-SS.SIM-be-2/3p.DS 1p.UNM hear-PA-1/3p

'We heard you making (the) noise.'

(247) [*Urema   maneka um-ep   ika-eya*]   *uruf-a-mik.*
bandicoot big   die-SS.SEQ be-2/3s.DS see-PA-1/3p

'They saw the big bandicoot dead (=having died).'

A regular complement clause is only used with perception verbs about a past activity, when the complement clause reports a fact rather than an activity (248), (249).

(248) *Iikir-ami*   [*iwera   nain emeria ar-e-p   ik-ua   nain*]_{CC} *uruf-ap*   ...
get.up-SS.SIM coconut that1 woman become-PA-3s be-PA.3s that1   see-SS.SEQ

'He got up and saw that the coconut had become a woman, and ...'

(249) [*Yeesus owow   iinan urup-o-k   nain*]_{CC} *uruf-ap   kemel-a-mik.*
Jesus village above ascend-PA-3s that1   see-SS.SEQ rejoice-PA-1/3p

'They saw that Jesus ascended into heaven, and rejoiced.'

When a perception verb takes an indirect question as a complement, it has to be a regular complement clause (250):

(250) *Ni*   [*kakala sira   kamenap eliw-ar-i-ya   nain*]_{CC} *uruf-eka.*
2p.UNM flower custom what.like good-INCH-NP-PR.3s that1   see-IMP.2p

'See how the flowers grow.'

8.3 Subordinate clauses: embedding and hypotaxis

8.3.2.3 Complements of cognitive verbs

The verbs for knowing, *amisar-* and *paayar-* together cover the cognitive area of knowing facts and skills, coming to realize, and understanding. When the complement clause indicates contents of factual knowledge, it is usually a regular complement clause (251).

(251) O [kaanek aaw-ep p-ekap-om-a-mik nain] me
 3s. where.CF get-SS.SEQ BPX-come-BEN-BNFY2.PA-1/3p that1 not
 amis-ar-e-k.
 knowledge-INCH-PA-3s
 'He didn't know where they got it from and brought to him.'

It seems that a clause with a nominalized verb is also used as a "fact" complement but only when it refers to pre-knowledge of an event (252). It could also be understood as a "potential" type complement, in which case it is natural that it uses this complementation strategy. This requires more investigation.

(252) [O ikiw-owa nain] amis-ar-e-n=i?
 3s.UNM go-NMZ that1 knowledge-INCH-PA-2s=QM
 'Did you know about his going?'

When the complement is about knowing a skill, the verb in the complement clause is in nominalized form, or a medial clause is used (253), (254):

(253) [Nain on-owa (nain)] me amis-ar-e-m.
 that1 do-NMZ that1 not knowledge-INCH-PA-1s
 'I don't know how to do that.'

(254) [Sawiter inera on-ap] amis-ar-e-k.
 Sawiter basket make-SS.SEQ knowledge-INCH-PA-3s
 'Sawiter knows how to make baskets.'

When the complement indicates lack of some experience, a construction with a medial clause is used. In this case, the main clause is in the negative, and the scope of the negation has to extend to the medial clause (255):

(255) [Owora en-ep] me paayar-e-m.
 betelnut eat-SS.SEQ not understand-PA-1s
 'I'm not used to eating betelnut.' Or: 'I don't know how to eat betelnut.'

8.3.2.4 Complement clauses as subjects

Both types of a nominalized clause (§§5.7.1, 5.7.2) may be used as subjects in verbless clauses, even though this function for complement clauses is not common. A clause with a nominalized verb is used when the activity is potential (256), (257).

8 Clause combinations

(256) [*Maa wiar ikum aaw-owa*] *eliwa=ki?*
      thing 3.DAT illicitly take-NMZ good=CF.QM
      'Is stealing from others good?'

(257) [*Maa eneka me en-owa*] *maa marew.*
      thing tooth not eat-NMZ thing no(ne)
      'Not eating meat is all right.'

A regular complement clause with a finite verb is used when the activity is considered a fact (258):

(258) [*Ni   unuma niam p-ir-i-man   nain*] *eliw(a) marew.*
      2p.UNM name   2p.REFL BPX-ascend-NP-PR.2p that1 good no(ne)
      'That you praise yourselves (lit: lift up your own name) is not good.'

8.3.3 Adverbial clauses

Adverbial clauses are a very small group of subordinate clauses. They are Type 2 nominalized clauses (§5.7.2), and they perform the same function in a clause as a temporal or locative adverbial phrase.

8.3.3.1 Temporal clauses

The presence of the distal-1 demonstrative *nain* 'that' indicates the pragmatic difference between the temporal clauses and those medial clauses that may get a temporal interpretation: the temporal clauses are presented as given information (259)–(261), whereas the medial clauses usually present new information (262), except when they occur in tail-head constructions.

(259) *Ni*   [*ifa nia keraw-i-ya   nain*] *sira   kamenap on-i-man?*
      2p.UNM snake 2p.ACC bite-NP-PA.3s that1 custom what.like do-NP-PR.2p
      'When a snake bites you, what do you do?'

(260) [*Maa fain pakak na-e-k   nain*] *yo   soran-e-m.*
      thing this bang say-PA-3s that1 1s.UNM be.startled-PA-1s
      'When this thing went "bang!" I got startled.'

(261) [*Yo   napum-ar-e-m   nain*] *eneka maay-ar-e-m.*
      1s.UNM sick-INCH-PA-1s that1 tooth long-INCH-PA-1s
      'When I got sick, I became hungry for meat (lit: my teeth got long).'

(262) *Yo   napum-ar-ep   eneka maay-ar-e-m.*
      1s.UNM sick-INCH-SS.SEQ tooth long-INCH-PA-1s
      'I got sick and became hungry for meat.'

8.3 Subordinate clauses: embedding and hypotaxis

8.3.3.2 Locative clauses

Locative adverbial clauses use a clause-final deictic locative *nan* (263) or *neeke* (264) 'there' instead of the demonstrative *nain* 'that'. Note that in (263) the locative noun *manina* 'garden' is not a relative NP; if there were one, that would be *epa* 'place' immediately preceding *nan* 'there'.

(263) I   naap ikiw-ep   [yiena manina on-a-mik   nan] ik-e-mik.
      1p.UNM thus go-SS.SEQ 1p.GEN garden make-PA-1p there be-PA-1p
      'We went there and stayed where we had made our gardens.'

(264) [Luuwa niir-i-mik   neeke]   soomar-e-mik.
      ball   play-NP-PR.1/3p there.CF walk-PA-1/3p
      'We walked (to) where they play football.'

The following example is actually a locative relative clause, since it has a relative NP *kame* 'side' that has a function in both clauses (265):

(265) [No   in-i-n   kame nan] urup-ep   tepak iw-a-mik.
      2s.UNM sleep-NP-PR.2s side there ascend-SS.SEQ inside go-PA-1/3p
      'They climbed up on the side where you sleep and went inside.'

8.3.4 Adversative subordinate clause

Coordinate adversative clauses were discussed in §8.1.3.

The topic marker *-na* (§3.12.7.1) marks an adversative clause when the main clause cancels an expectation, either expressed in the text or assumed to be in the hearer's mind. Because of this, this construction is used when some effort is frustrated (266), or when there is a strong element of surprise (267) in the main clause.

(266) Mukuna nain umuk-a-mik=**na**   me pepek.
      fire   that1 quench-PA-1/3p=TP not able
      'They tried to quench the fire, but couldn't.'

(267) Ekap-ep   uruf-a-k=**na** ifa   maneka=ke siowa
      come-SS.SEQ see-PA-3s=TP snake big=CF   dog
      wasi-ep-pu-eya   ...
      tie.around-SS.SEQ-CMPL-2/3s.DS
      'He came and looked, but a snake had tied itself around the dog, and/but ...'

In (268), what the boys expect to see is a crocodile, but it turns out to be a turtle.

(268) Takir(a) oko=ke pon   muneka wu-ek-a-m   na-ep
      boy   other=CF turtle egg   put-CNTF-PA-1s say-SS.SEQ
      urup-em-ika-eya   uruf-ap   tuar=ke   na-ep   alu-emi
      ascend-SS.SIM-be-2/3s.DS see-SS.SEQ crocodile=CF say-SS.SEQ shout-SS.SIM

> baurar-e-k. Takir(a) unowa ekap-ep uruf-a-mik=***na*** pon=ke, ne
> flee-PA-3s boy many come-SS.SEQ see-PA-1/3p=TP turtle=CF ADD
> unow=iya op-ap kirip-a-mik.
> many=COM hold-SS.SEQ turn-PA-1/3p

'A boy saw a turtle coming up (to the beach) to lay eggs and thought it was a crocodile, and shouted and fled. Many boys came and saw/looked, but it was a turtle, and they all together grabbed and turned it.'

In (269), a man talks to his son whom he wanted and expected to be a good person:

(269) Aakisa yo nefa uruf-i-yem=***na*** no mua eliw marew.
now 1s.UNM 2s.ACC look-NP-PR.1s=TP 2s.UNM man good no(ne)

'I now look at you but you are not a good man.'

Because these clauses express a cancellation or frustration of an expectation, a negator commonly follows as the first element in the main clause, and often the negator is the only element left of the main clause, as in (270).

(270) Marasin wu-om-a-mik=***na*** weetak.
medicine put-BEN-BNFY2.PA-1/3p=TP no

'They injected medicine in him, but no (it had no effect).'

8.3.5 Conditional clauses

Haiman (1978) was the first one to clearly describe the close connection between conditionals and topics, and it has since then been attested in various languages (Thompson, Longacre & Hwang 2007: 292). In many Papuan languages, the connection is very evident (Reesink 1987: 235–244, MacDonald 1990: 304–308, Farr 1999: 263. The protasis – the subordinate clause expressing the condition – provides the presupposition for the apodosis, the asserted main clause. In other words, "it constitutes the framework which has been selected for the following discourse" (Haiman 1978: 585).

The conditional clauses in Mauwake can be grouped into three main groups on semantic and structural grounds: imaginative, predictive, and reality conditionals.[35] Imaginative and predictive conditionals together belong to the unreality conditionals. Reality conditionals only include habitual/generic conditionals, as there are no present or past conditionals.

The protasis clause, expressing the condition, is placed before the apodosis clause, which gives the consequence. Right-dislocation of the protasis is possible but rare. The verb forms in the protasis and the apodosis depend on the type of conditional. The topic marker -na is used as the conditional marker in the unreality conditional clauses, where it is cliticized to the last element of the protasis clause, usually the verb. Reality conditional clauses do not have a conditional marker, so structurally the protasis and

---

[35] The terminology is from Thompson, Longacre & Hwang (2007: 255).

8.3 Subordinate clauses: embedding and hypotaxis

apodosis are ordinary juxtaposed clauses. The intonation in the protasis has a slight rise towards the end, stronger with the topic marker *-na* than without it.

In IMAGINATIVE CONDITIONAL CLAUSES, the verb in both the protasis and the apodosis is in the counterfactual mood, which is marked by the suffix *-ek*. The conditional/topic marker *-na* is always present. The same form is used for semantically counterfactual and hypothetical conditionals. The counterfactual interpretation (271) is more common, but especially if there is a reference to present (272) or future time (273), it forces a hypothetical interpretation.

(271) [Yo   Sek haussik ikiw-**ek**-a-m=**na**]   miiw-aasa=pa   uroma
      1s.UNM Sek hospital go-CNTF-PA-1s=TP land-canoe=LOC stomach
      yaki-**ek**-a-m.
      wash-CNTF-PA-1s
      'If I had gone to the Sek hospital, I would have given birth in the truck.'

(272) [Yena aamun   aakisa uruf-**ek**-a-m=**na**] kemel-**ek**-a-m.
      1s.GEN 1s/p.younger.sibling now   see-CNTF-PA-1s=TP   be.happy-CNTF-PA-1s
      'If I saw my younger brother now, I would be happy.'

(273) [Morauta iimar-ow(a)   mua ik-**ek**-a-k=**na**,] uurika   ikiw-ep
      Morauta stand.up-NMZ   man be-CNTF-PA-3s=TP   tomorrow go-SS.SEQ
      maak-**ek**-a-mik.
      tell-CNTF-PA-1/3p
      'If Morauta were the leader, we would go and talk to him tomorrow.'

Usually the context determines the interpretation, but without a clear context the sentence may be ambiguous (274):

(274) [Inasin   napuma ik-**ek**-a-k=**na**]   sariar-**ek**-a-k.
      spirit/white.man sickness be-CNTF-PA-3s=TP   recover-CNTF-PA-3s
      'If it were the white man's sickness[36] he would recover.' Or: 'If it had been the white man's sickness, he would have recovered.'

PREDICTIVE CONDITIONALS are the most frequently used and show the greatest variation morphologically. The apodosis, and consequently the whole sentence, may be either a statement with a future tense verb, or a command with an imperative verb. The verb in the protasis may be in either present or future indicative, in imperative, or in medial form. The conditional/topic marker at the end of the protasis is obligatory.

When the predictive conditional is a statement, the verb in both the protasis and in the apodosis is usually in the future tense (275).

---

[36] This is contrasted with *owow napuma* 'village sickness', caused by sorcery.

8 *Clause combinations*

(275) [*No   oram mokok=iw **ika-i-nan=na**] ikoka mua lebuma **ika-i-nan**.
       2s.UNM just eye=INST be-NP-FU.2s=TP later man lazy be-NP-FU.2s

       'If you just watch with your eyes (without joining the work) you will be(come) a lazy man.'

The protasis may have a medial verb form if the condition is likely to be fulfilled (276), or when the protasis consists of two or more clauses that are in a medial-final relationship (277).

(276) [*Emeria **sesenar-ek-a-m na-ep=na**]   waaya ten erup naap
       woman buy-CNTF-PA-1s say/think-SS.SEQ=TP pig   ten two thus
       wienak-i-non.
       feed.him-NP-FU.3s

       'If/when he wants to buy a wife, he will give him (=the bride's father) twenty or so pigs.'

(277) [*Yaapan me **piipu-ap=na**   anane epaskun ika-i-nan=na*]   no
       Japan not leave-SS.SEQ=TP always together be-NP-FU.2s=TP 2s.UNM
       iiwawun   weeser-i-nan.
       altogether finish-NP-FU.2s

       'If you don't leave the Japanese but are always together, you will be finished altogether.'

Predictive conditionals allow right-dislocation of the protasis, but it is uncommon (278):

(278) *Owora   fain aite   panewowa onak-e,   [ekap-ep   **kerer-eya=na**].*
       betelnut this 1s/p.mother old   feed-IMP.2s come-SS.SEQ arrive-2/3s.DS=TP

       'Give these betelnuts to old mother to eat, if she comes and arrives here.'

In those instances where the conditional marker is attached to a predicate that is not originally a verb, the predicate needs to have medial verb marking (279), (280) (§3.8.3.5).

(279) [**Weetak-eya=na**] *weetak*.
       no-2/3s.DS=TP   no

       'If not, then not.'

(280) [*Mauw-owa **manek-aya=na**] *yia   maak-i-non*.
       work-NMZ big-2/3s.DS=TP   1p.ACC tell-NP-FU.3s

       'If the work is big, he will tell us.'

When the apodosis is in the imperative, there is normally some expectation that the the condition is to be fulfilled. When the likelihood is high, the medial form is used in the protasis (281), (282). Present tense (283) and imperative (284) indicate less, and future tense (285) the least likelihood for the condition to be fulfilled.

8.3 Subordinate clauses: embedding and hypotaxis

(281) [*Wia* **uruf-ap=na**] *wia maak-e.*
3p.ACC see-SS.SEQ=TP 3p.ACC tell-IMP.2s
'If/when you see them, tell them.'

(282) [*Maa mauwa nefa* **maak-iwkin=na**] *opaimika miim-e.*
thing what 2s.ACC tell-2/3p.DS=TP talk listen-IMP.2s
'Whatever they may tell you, listen to the talk.' (Lit: 'If they tell you what(ever), listen to the talk.')

(283) *Koora pun naap:* [*mua oko naareke koora* **kua-i-ya=na**] *o*
house also thus man other who.CF house build-NP-PR.3s=TP 3p.UNM
asip-e.
help-IMP.2p
'A house is like that too: if/when any man builds a house, help him.'

(284) [*Ni kirip-owa* **ika-inok=na**] *kirip-eka.*
2p.UNM reply-NMZ be-IMP.3s=TP reply-IMP.2p
'If you have something to reply, then reply.'

(285) [*Wia* **uruf-i-nan=na**] *wia maak-e.*
3p.ACC see-NP-FU.2s=TP 3p.ACC tell-IMP.2s
'If you (happen to) see them, tell them.'

REALITY CONDITIONAL CLAUSES are morpho-syntactically different from the other conditional clauses in that they are not marked with the topic marker. The protasis and apodosis are juxtaposed main clauses in future tense (286), but this construction is mainly used to encode habitual or generic conditions. The protasis can never be right-dislocated, since it does not have the topic marker.

(286) [*No inasin(a) unuma me unuf-i-nan*], *mua oko=ke waaya nain*
2s.UNM spirit name not call-NP-FU.2s man other=CF pig that1
mik-ap nefar aaw-i-non.
spear-SS.SEQ 2s.DAT take-NP-FU.3s
'If you don't call the spirit name, another man will spear the pig and take it from you.'

If there are two protasis clauses, they may be juxtaposed without a connective (287) or joined with the pragmatic additive *ne* (288).

(287) [*Nena kuuf-i-nan, parew-i-non*], *eliw perek-i-nan.*
2s.GEN see-NP-FU.2s mature-NP-FU.3s well harvest-NP-FU.2s
'If you see it yourself and it is matured you may harvest it.'

8 *Clause combinations*

(288) [*Yo   um-i-nen   ne yena emeria mua oko   aaw-i-non*],   *muuka*
1s.UNM die-NP-FU.1s ADD 1s.GEN woman man other take-NP-FU.3s son
onaiya me ikiw-i-non.
with   not go-NP-FU.3s
'If I die and my wife takes another husband, she will not go (to him) with the son.'

When a sentence contains alternatives expressed by two sets of reality conditional constructions, these are joined by the pragmatic additive *ne* (289).

(289) [*Yo auwa   miiwa=pa mauw-i-nen*], *irak-owa marew, ne* [*yo aite*
1s 1s/p.father land=LOC work-NP-FU.1s fight-NMZ no(ne) ADD 1s 1s/p.moher
miiwa=pa mauw-i-nen], *irak-owa ika-i-non.*
land=LOC work-NP-fu.1s fight-NMZ be-NP-FU.3s
'If I work on my father's land there is no fighting (over land), but if I work on my mother's land there will be fighting.'

The same construction can encode a simple coordinate relationship, but it is less common. In spoken text a slightly falling intonation at the end of the first clause indicates a coordinate sentence (290).

(290) *Oko=ke pusun-emi   feeke   **ikiw-i-non**, a mua oko=ke*
other=CF run.loose-SS.SIM here.CF go-NP-FU.3s ah man other=CF
mik-i-non.
spear-NP-FU.3s
'Another (pig) will run loose and run this way, ah, another man will spear it.'

8.3.6 Concessive clauses

Concessive clauses may look exactly like the predictive conditional clauses (291). If the context is not clear enough, the phrase *nain pun* 'that too' may be added between the protasis and the apodosis for clarification (292).

(291) [*Naapeya aara=ki   e kasi=ke um-inok=na*] *ni   nain kema*
therefore hen=CF.QM or cat=CF die-IMP.3s=TP 2p.UNM that1 liver
bagiw-ir-ap   malaria sevis   me wia   iirar-eka.
hatred-rise-SS.SEQ malaria service not 3p.ACC remove-IMP.2p
'Therefore, (even) if hens or cats die, do not get angry and drive away the Malaria Service people.'

(292) [*Naap yia   ma-ikuan=na*] **nain pun** *ni   kekan-ep   sira   eliwa*
thus 1p.ACC say-FU.3p=TP that too 2p.UNM be.strong-SS.SEQ custom good
ook-eka.
follow-IMP.2p
'Even if they talk about us like that, be strong and follow the good custom/ways.'

8.3 Subordinate clauses: embedding and hypotaxis

8.3.7 Coordination of subordinate clauses

Subordinate clauses may also be coordinated with each other, although in normal speech the frequency of these constructions is low. The only subordinate clauses in the natural text data conjoined either by juxtaposition or with the additive *ne* are relative clauses (293), (294). The distal demonstrative *nain*, functioning as a relative marker, is attached to the end of each relative clause.

(293) ...[*waaya koka=pa ika-i-ya nain*]$_{RC}$, [*sokowa maneka=pa ika-i-ya*
       pig   jungle=LOC be-NP-PR.3s that1   grove big=LOC be-NP-PR.3s
nain]$_{RC}$ *kanu-ep   aap-ekap-ep   fikera=pa-r=iw   fiirim-eka.*
that1   chase-SS.SEQ BPX-come-SS.SEQ kunai.grass=LOC-Ø=LIM gather-IMP.2p

'...chase the pigs that are in the jungle (and) that are in the big grove(s) and bring them and gather them right inside the kunai grass (area).'

(294) *Ne* [*o   maa kamenap on-eya   wiar uruf-i-n   nain*]$_{RC}$ *ne* [*wiar*
     ADD 3s.UNM thing how   do-SS.SEQ 3.DAT see-NP-PR.2s that1   ADD 3.DAT
miim-i-n   nain]$_{RC}$ *wia   maak-em-ika-i-nan.*
hear-NP-PR.2s that1   3p.ACC tell-SS.SIM-be-NP-FU.2s

'And you will keep telling them that which you see and which you hear him do.'

The chaining structure is also used to coordinate relative clauses (295) and complement clauses that have a nominalized verb (5.125), copied as (296) below:

(295) [*Ni   manina urup-ep   episowa perek-a-man nain*]$_{RC}$ *auwa*
     2p.UNM garden ascend-SS.SEQ tobacco pick-PA-2p   that   1s/p.father
p-ikiw-om-aka.
BPX-go-BEN-BNFY2.IMP.2p

'Take to father the tobacco that you went up to the garden and picked.'

(296) *Toiyan iiriw   maak-ep-pu-a-mik,   [uuriw yia   aaw-ep   Madang*
Toiyan already tell-SS.SEQ-CMPL-PA-1/3p morning 1p.ACC take-SS.SEQ Madang
ikiw-owa]$_{CC}$ *nain*
go-NMZ   that1

'We already told Toiyan about taking us in the morning and going to Madang.'

9 Theme, topic, and focus

Three features of textual prominence, the pragmatic functions theme, topic, and focus, are discussed in this chapter. All of them play an important role in Mauwake, and they show up in morphology and/or syntax. They are not mutually exclusive: a clausal constituent may have more than one pragmatic function.

Theme, topic, and focus have been defined in linguistic literature in different and sometimes conflicting ways, so they need a definition of how they are used here.

The definitions of topic are mainly divided along two questions: whether the topic needs to be an entity – more specifically an argument – or not, and whether it functions on the clause or the discourse level, or both.

One classic definition describes the topic as "the entity about which something is said, whereas the further statement made about this entity is the comment" (Crystal 1997: 391, see also Dik 1978: 19). This definition treats the topic as a clause-level function and an entity, but does not specify whether this entity needs to be an argument of the verb or not. Chafe's (1976: 50) well-known definition also discusses the topic at the sentence level. Any constituent may be a topic, in fact it need not even be an entity: "the topic sets a spatial, temporal or individual framework within which the main predication holds" (see also Li & Thompson 1976: 461). Haiman's (1978) analysis of conditionals as topics is based on this definition, as the protasis in the conditional clauses provides the presupposition for the assertion in the apodosis.

The definitions above do not touch upon topic continuity, which is an important object of study for those linguists who consider topic mainly from discourse point of view (Givón 1976; 1983; 1990). In this case, the topic function can only be assigned to an argument of a clause. Also Dixon (2010a: 340) defines topic as "an argument which occurs in a succession of clauses in a discourse and binds them together".[1] A single sentence can be said to have a topic only if the sentence constitutes at least a clause chain or a paragraph (Givón 1990: 902).

In the following, TOPIC is understood in the sense that Givón advocates, whereas the term THEME is used to refer to Chafe's "topic", for which a sentence-initial position is crucial.[2] What Dik (1978: 19) calls a theme is here called a LEFT-DISLOCATED THEME.

---

[1] In some other approaches, this discourse topic has also been called *theme* or *global topic*.
[2] Considering "topicality" in Chafe's sense, Mauwake is basically a subject-prominent language (Li & Thompson 1976). It has the following characteristics: surface coding for the subject as the first argument and as the argument that governs verb agreement; scarcity of "double subject" constructions, even though they are possible; the subject controls co-referential constituent deletion; there are constraints on the "topic" constituent; and the frequency of topic-comment clauses is low. But Mauwake shares the following features with topic-prominent languages: there is no passivization, nor are there any empty or dummy subjects.

9 Theme, topic, and focus

Mauwake is a SOV language and the default topic is also the syntactic subject and the semantic agent/actor, and yet the first noun phrase in a clause often is not the topic. This is because once the topic has been established, it is normally only marked by verbal suffixes, and the clause-initial position is taken by another constituent.

9.1 Theme

The position as the leftmost non-verb constituent in a sentence defines the theme in Mauwake. It may be an argument or a peripheral clause participant. When a sentence – or the first clause in a multi-clause sentence – consists of a verb alone, there is no theme in the sense adopted here. When the theme is an argument, it introduces what the sentence is about (1). When it is not an argument but a peripheral clause participant, it provides a circumstantial setting for the sentence, most commonly a locative or temporal setting (2). A theme forms one intonation contour with the rest of the clause.

(1) *Wi   owow mua=ke* wilkar wia   muf-em-ik-om-a-mik.
    3p.UNM village man=CF cart   3p.ACC pull-SS.SIM-be-BEN-BNFY2.PA-1/3p
    'The village men pulled carts for them.'

(2) Ne *fraide=pa* maapora puk-o-k,   urera.
    ADD Friday=LOC party   burst-PA-3s afternoon
    'And on Friday the party started, in the afternoon.'

When the theme coincides with the subject/topic (1), the clause has the default word order. But when another argument is the theme, it takes the initial position, and if there is also a subject NP in the same clause, it follows the theme NP (3):

(3) [I   yar]ₒ   [i]s   uruf-am-ik-omkun   o   koora=pa
    1p.UNM 1s/p.brother.in.law 1p.UNM see-SS.SIM-be-1s/p.DS 3s.UNM house=LOC
    pok-ap   ik-ua.
    sit.down-SS.SEQ be-PA.3s
    'Our brother-in-law, as we are seeing him, is sitting in his house.' (Lit: 'Our brother-in-law we are seeing and he is sitting in his house.')

The sentence (4) is from the middle of a description about the arrival of the Japanese troops, and the goods that they brought are only mentioned in this one sentence, and the theme is neither the subject nor the topic.

(4) [*Maa unowa*]ₒ ifer aasa=ke   p-urup-eya   miiw-aasa=ke fan
    thing many   sea canoe=CF BPX-ascend-2/3s.DS land-canoe=CF here
    p-ir-am-ik-ua.
    BPX-come-SS.SIM-be-PA.3s
    'Many things were brought up (to the coast) by ships and brought here by trucks.'

9.1 Theme

In a text about a school party, dancing is first mentioned in a final verb, and then the dance becomes the theme for the following sentence (5):

(5) *Naap ik-ok wi Saramun=ke wiisa uf-e-mik.* [*Uf-owa eliwa*]$_O$
 thus be-ss 3p.UNM Saramun=CF dance.name dance-PA-1/3p dance-NMZ good
 i wiar uruf-a-mik.
 1p.UNM 3.DAT see-PA-1/3p
 'Then the Saramun people danced *wiisa*. It was a good dance we saw from them.'

Very commonly, the subject only shows in the verbal suffixation, and the theme position is taken either by an object – which may or may not be a topic – or by an adverbial phrase. In (6) the theme *auwa ame* 'father and the others' becomes a topic that continues for the next five clauses, whereas the themes of (7) and (8) do not become topics and are not mentioned any more. (In the free translation it is often not possible to reflect the theme naturally.)

(6) ***Auwa ame*** *wia maak-eya res aaw-ep merena ifa keraw-a-k*
 1s/p.father ASSOC 3p.ACC tell-2/3s.DS razor take-ss.SEQ leg snake bite-PA-3s
 nain puuk-a-mik.
 that1 cut-PA-1/3p
 'He told my father and the others, and they took a razor and made a cut into the leg that the snake had bitten.'

(7) ***Maa en-owa*** *nopa-yiaw-ep wailal-ep naap ma-e-mik...*
 thing eat-NMZ search-move.around-ss.SEQ hunger-ss.SEQ thus say-PA-1/3p
 'They searched around for food and were hungry and said like that...'

(8) ***Emeria*** *naap wia aruf-i-nen na-ep on-a-k.*
 woman thus 3p.ACC hit-NP-FU.1s say/think-ss.SEQ do-PA-3s
 'He tried to hit the women like that.'

In a tail-head linkage construction (§8.2.3.5) the final verb of a sentence is repeated in the beginning of the following sentence, but in a medial form. An argument (9), (10), or occasionally a peripheral (11), (12), from the final clause may be picked as the theme of the new sentence.

(9) *Owowa or-op, wailal-ep akia ik-e-k.* ***Akia*** *ik-ep*
 village descend-ss.SEQ hunger-ss.SEQ banana roast-PA-3s banana roast-ss.SEQ
 en-em-ik-ok...
 eat-ss.SIM-be-ss
 'He came down to the village, was hungry, and roasted bananas. He roasted bananas and was eating them and ...'

9 Theme, topic, and focus

(10) *Aria, wi kiiriw neeke Ø miiw-aasa um-o-k. **Miiw-aasa** um-eya*
alright 3p.UNM again there.CF Ø land-canoe die-PA-3s land-canoe die-2/3s.DS
miiw-aasa nain on-am-ika-iwkin...
land-canoe that1 do-SS.SIM-be-2/3p.DS

'Alright, again when they (were) there the truck broke down (lit: died). The truck broke down, and while they were working on the truck...'

(11) *Yaki-ep weeser-eya owowa urup-e-mik. **Owowa** urup-ep o*
bathe-SS.SEQ finish-2/3s.DS village ascend-PA-1/3p village ascend-SS.SEQ 3s.UNM
koora ikiw-o-k.
house go-PA-3s

'They bathed and when it was finished they came up to the village. They came to the village and he went into the house.'

(12) *...siowa wiawi nain=ke alu-owa miim-ap karu-(o)w=iw*
dog 3s/p.father that1=CF make.noise-NMZ hear-SS.SEQ run-NMZ=INST
*ekap-o-k. **Karu-(o)w=iw** ekap-ep uruf-a-k=na ...*
come-PA-3s run-NMZ=INST come-SS.SEQ see-PA-3s=TP

'The dog's owner heard the noise and came running. He came running and saw...'

It is more common to have tail-head linkage where only the final verb is repeated; when the speaker repeats an argument or a peripheral as well, there is a reason for it: to give it prominence as the theme in the new sentence.

When the theme position is taken by a locative (13) or temporal (14) adverbial phrase, it normally gives a setting for the the whole sentence:

(13) ***Eka mamaiya akena** i yoowa me aaw-i-yen.*
river close very 1p.UNM hot not get-NP-FU.1p

'Very close to the river we won't get hot.'

(14) ***Ikoka kuisow** miiw-aasa=ke karu-eya ku-ku-ep*
later one land-canoe=CF run-2/3s.DS RDP-break-SS.SEQ
or-om-ik-ua.
descend-SS.SIM-be-PA.3s

'Straight away when the trucks ran (over them) they kept breaking and falling down.'

But in (15), the first temporal phrase is a setting for only the first clause, and the final clause has another temporal phrase. Also, in the second sentence the object is both a new topic (§9.2.1) and fronted as the theme before the temporal adverbial. In neutral constituent order, a temporal adverbial precedes the object.

(15) **Uura feenap nain** i   me in-em-ik-e-mik,   amirika maa me
night like.this that1 1p.UNM not sleep-ss.SIM-be-PA-1/3p day   food not
en-em-ik-e-mik.   **Maa** uura uup-ep   en-em-ik-e-mik.
eat-ss.SIM-be-PA-1/3p food night cook-ss.SEQ eat-ss.SIM-be-PA-1/3p

'On nights like this we did not sleep, in the daytime we did not eat food. The food we used to cook and eat at night.'

Other adverbial phrases may also be used in the theme position to provide a circumstantial setting (16), (17). In particular, the deictic manner adverbial *naap* 'thus, like that' is relatively common.

(16) **Naap** maak-iwkin naap ik-ua.   **Naap** ik-ok uruf-am-ika-iwkin   wia.
thus tell-2/3p.DS thus be-PA.3s thus be-ss see-ss.SIM-be-2/3p.DS no

'Like that they told him and like that he was. Like that he was and they watched him, but no (he did not get better).'

(17) **Wiena merena ne   wapen**=iw era akup-ami   owowa ikiw-e-mik.
3p.GEN foot   ADD hand=INST road search-ss.SIM village go-PA-1/3p

'With their feet and hands they searched the road and went to the village.'

A sentence-initial adverbial phrase that is syntactically outside the clause and also has its own slightly rising intonation contour on the last syllable is here called a LEFT-DISLOCATED THEME. In written texts, it is separated from the rest of the clause by a comma. This clause-external pragmatic function is called theme by Dik (1978: 19). He defines its function as "specif[ying] the universe of discourse with respect to which the subsequent predication is presented as relevant".

In (18), the left-dislocated theme consists of a relative clause where the antecedent noun *soo* 'fish trap' has been deleted:

(18) Aria   [**Ø malol**=**pa**   **ifemak-i-mik   nain**]$_{RC}$, aana puuk-i-mik...
alright Ø   deep.sea=LOC press-NP-PR.1/3p that1   cane cut-NP-PR.1/3p

'Alright, as for those (=fishtraps) that we let down in the deep sea, we cut cane ...'

There can be more than one dislocated theme for the same clause. In (19), there are two dislocated themes – a temporal and a locative phrase – plus a clause-internal theme *moma* 'taro', which is the syntactic object of the clause:

(19) **Iiriw, owow(a) oko   mua manina**, *moma* waaya=ke anane   wiar
earlier village   other man garden   taro pig=CF always 3.DAT
en-ow(a)=iw   ika-i-ya.
eat-NMZ=INST be-NP-PR.3s

'Earlier, (in) the garden of a man from another village, his taro was always being eaten by a pig.'

9.2 Topic

Givón (1976: 152) posited a universal topicality hierarchy, which shows features affecting the likelihood of NPs being discourse topics:

1. human > non-human

2. definite > indefinite

3. more involved participant > less involved participant

4. 1st person > 2nd person > 3rd person

This hierarchy can be observed in Mauwake as well: the prototypical topic refers to a referent that is human and definite, and if the first person is involved in the text, it is often the topic. And the most involved participant, the grammatical subject, is typically also the pragmatic topic.

The following three sections discuss how a new topic is introduced and maintained in a narrative text, and how it is brought back after it has been absent for a while.

9.2.1 Introducing a new topic

Even when a new topic is introduced for the first time, it is often definite,[3] identifiable to the addressee: a personal pronoun (20), a proper name (21) or a relationship term (22), or a noun phrase (23).

(20) *I*   me amis-ar-em-ik-omkun   iinan aasa iinan=pa fan
      1p.UNM not knowledge-INCH-SS.SIM-be-1s/p.DS sky   canoe sky=LOC here
      ekap-emi   ...
      come-SS.SIM

  'We were not aware (that anything would happen) and planes came here on the sky and ...'

(21) ***Muakura=ke** ma-e-k,*   " ..."
      Muakura=CF say-PA-3s

  'Muakura said, " ... " '

(22) *Aria   **yena   mua** pun ... iirar-iwkin   owowa ekap-o-k.*
      alright 1s.GEN man also ... remove-2/3p.DS village come-PA-3s

  'Alright they also dismissed my husband ... and he came to the village.'

---

[3] Definiteness is not an obligatory category in Mauwake. A NP may be specifically marked as definite or indefinite when this feature is considered important enough, but often it is left unspecified.

(23) Iiriw **wi mua iperowa=ke** feenap ma-em-ik-e-mik, emeria=ke
earlier 3p.UNM man middle.aged=CF like.this say-SS.SIM-be-PA-1/3p woman=CF
osaiwa ar-e-mik.
bird.of.paradise become-PA-1/3p

'Earlier the elders kept telling this story that women had changed into birds of paradise.'

When a potential topic is introduced, it is indefinite – the addressee is not expected to be able to identify it – and one of the following strategies is used. The new topic may first be an object in a clause before becoming the subject in the following clause. (15) is repeated here as (24):

(24) Uura feenap nain i me in-em-ik-e-mik, amirika **maa** me
night like.this that1 1p.UNM not sleep-SS.SIM-be-PA-1/3p noon food not
en-em-ik-e-mik. **Maa** uura uup-ep en-em-ik-e-mik.
eat-SS.SIM-be-PA-1/3p food night cook-SS.SEQ eat-SS.SIM.be-PA-1/3p

'On nights like this we did not sleep, at noon we did not eat food. Food we used to cook and eat at night.'

Most commonly, the new topic is already a subject in the clause where it is introduced, and the NP is either modified with the indefinite *oko* 'other' (25) or marked by the neutral focus clitic *-ko* (26), which also has its origin in *oko*. Occasionally both of them occur on the same NP (27).

(25) Iiriw Malala suule maneka **uuw-owa mua oko** unuma Kila.
earlier Malala school big work-NMZ man other name Kila

'Earlier there was a workman at the big Malala school whose name was Kila.'

(26) **Emer(a) en-ow(a) mua=ko** emeria fan aaw-o-k.
sago eat-NMZ man=NF woman here take-PA-3s

'A Sepik man married a wife here.'

(27) Iiriw akena **mua oko=ko** fura aaw-ep koka iw-a-k.
earlier very man other=NF knife take-SS.SEQ jungle go-PA-3s

'Long ago a man took a knife and went into the jungle.'

The indefinite NP may even have contrastive focus marking (28):

(28) Pika ifara mufe-wiaw-ik-ok **ifa maneka=ke** siowa wiar aaw-o-k.
fence vine pull-move.around-be-ss snake big=CF dog 3.DAT take-PA-3s

'As he was pulling around vines for the fence, a big snake grabbed his dog.'

Existential clauses, which Givón (1990: 741) mentions as one of the major strategies for introducing important topics, are possible but not very commonly employed for this function in Mauwake (29). Note that the neutral focus clitic *-ko* is also present.

(29) **Iiriw mua iperowa=ko** nan Wakoruma owowa=pa ik-ua.
earlier man middle.aged=NF there Wakoruma village=LOC be-PA.3s

'Earlier there was a middle-aged man in Wakoruma village.'

9.2.2 Maintaining an established topic

When a potential topic, which is indefinite when first introduced, becomes established the next mention is often made with a NP marked as definite by the distal-1 demonstrative *nain* 'that'. The sentence following (29) in the text is (30).

(30) **Mua nain** emeria ne muuka wiipa marew.
man that1 woman ADD son daughter no(ne).

'The man had no wife or children.'

Another possibility is the mere subject marking on the verb: sentence (31) below is continuation to the sentence (26) above.

(31) Ne manina ikiw-o-**k**.
ADD garden go-PA-3s.

'And he went to the garden.'

When the topic is already definite when introduced, it is possible to make a second mention with a personal pronoun (32).[4]

(32) Yena yaiya Tup ifa ku-o-k nain opaimika ma-i-yem. Ae, **o**
1s.GEN 1s/p.uncle Tup snake bite-PA-3s that1 talk say-NP-PR.1s yes 3s.UNM
fiker(a) gone urup-o-k.
kunai.grass middle ascend-PA-3s

'I tell a story about that when my uncle Tup was bitten by a snake. Yes, he went up to the middle of the *kunai* grass (area).'

In (33) the personal pronoun *wi* 'they' in the second sentence refers to the "weria-relatives" (see §1.3.6), introduced as the object in the preceding sentence; a mere verbal suffix would indicate continuation with the old topic, i.e. those who sent the message.

(33) Wiena mua weria ... opaimika wia sesek-omak-e-mik. Ne
3p.GEN man planting.stick ... talk 3p.ACC send-DISTR/PL-PA-1/3p ADD
wi ekap-e-mik.
3p.UNM come-PA-1/3p

'They$_i$ sent word to their$_i$ many weria-relatives$_j$. And they$_j$ came.'

---

[4] This whole story is Text B.2 in the Appendix.

More commonly the topic, once established, is maintained as a continuing topic without an overt NP or a pronoun, only via subject marking on the verb. This minimal marking conforms to Givón's (1983: 67) claim that the heaviness of the topic marking is in inverse relation to topic continuity/predictability. The following example (34) is a section of a text where *sawur* 'spirits', introduced earlier, think that there is a boy on the bed they are carrying, but the boy has already escaped. The reference to the spirits is only made by medial and final verb suffixes.

(34) *Ne aria, samapora oram akua aaw-ep ikiw-e-**mik**. Ikiw-**ep** wiena*
ADD alright, bed just shoulder take-ss.SEQ go-PA-1/3p go-SS.SEQ 3p.GEN
*owowa=pa uruf-a-**mik**=na weetak, samapora muutiw akua aaw-e-**mik**.*
village=LOC see-PA-1/3p=TP no bed only shoulder take-PA-1/3p
*Aria nainiw kir-e-**mik**. Kir-**ep** ekap-em-ika-**iwkin** epa*
alright again turn-PA-1/3p turn-SS.SEQ come-SS.SIM-be-2/3p.DS place
wiim-o-k.
dawn-PA-3s

'Alright, they carried just the bed and went. They went and in their village they looked but (to their surprise) they only carried the bed. Alright they turned back again. They turned and as they were coming, it dawned.'

The switch-reference system (§§3.8.3.5, 8.2.3) together with the person/number marking in the finite verbs (§3.8.3.4) can easily keep track of two active topics alternating with each other (35).

(35) *O iiwawun samor aaw-o-k. Ne nan ik-e-**mik**. Nan ik-ok ik-ok*
3s.UNM altogether badly get-PA-3s ADD there be-PA-1/3p there be-ss be-ss
*neeke pu-o-**k**. Neeke pu-**eya** oram akua aaw-e-**mik**.*
there.CF die-PA-3s. there.CF die-2/3s.DS just shoulder take-PA-1/3p

'He got really bad. They stayed and stayed there and he died there. He died there and they just carried him on their shoulders.'

In (35) one of the topics is in the singular, the other in the plural. But in (3.665), repeated below as (36), there are two third person singular topics alternating, with only the verbal marking to indicate who is doing what:

(36) *Ifakim-**eya** pu-ep-ik-**eya** om-em-ik-**ua**.*
kill-2/3s.DS die-SS.SEQ-be-2/3s.DS cry-SS.SIM-be-PA.3s

'When she killed him and he was dead, she was crying.'

9.2.3 Re-activating an earlier topic

When a topic has not been active for some time in the text, there are two main strategies to re-activate it. A personal pronoun is mainly used for the major participants. For the third person singular pronoun this is the most common usage (§3.5.11). The following

9 *Theme, topic, and focus*

example is from a text where the main participant, a man, has been killed by his spirit lover. For several sentences, the topic position is taken by the spirit woman and her parents, but in the sentence (37) the man, as a re-activated topic, gets up and goes to his village.

(37) *Epa wiim-eya sawur emeria nain ikiw-eya o iikir-ami owowa*
place dawn-2/3s.DS spirit woman that1 go-2/3s.DS 3s.UNM get.up-ss.SIM village
ekap-o-k.
come-PA-3s

'It dawned and the spirit woman went, and he got up and came to the village.'

The sentence in (38) re-activates the topic, a grandmother and two grandchildren, after a gap of five clauses:

(38) *Iwera mekemkar-ep or-eya* **wi** *pikin-ep miiwa*
coconut bend-ss.SEQ descend-2/3s.DS 3p.UNM jump-ss.SEQ ground
or-o-mik.
descend-PA-1/3p

'The coconut tree bent down and they jumped down to the ground.'

In the following stretch, (39), the health officer, who is one of the main participants in this section of the story, is mentioned as an object noun phrase, and after two clauses he becomes the topic for just one clause. Afterwards, the men accompanying the sick man again resume as the topic.

(39) *...ikemika kaik-owa mua nain nop-a-mik, imen-ap maak-iwkin o*
wound tie-NMZ man that1 search-PA-1/3p find-ss.SEQ tell-2/3p.DS 3s.UNM
miim-o-k. Aria, **wi** *kiiriw neeke Ø miiw-aasa um-o-k.*
precede-PA-3s alright 3p.UNM again there.CF Ø land-canoe die-PA-3s

'... they searched for the health officer, and when they found him and told him, he went ahead of them (to the aidpost). Alright, again when they were there the truck broke down.'

A full noun phrase is used for reactivating major participants when there are several of them and pronouns are not adequate for disambiguating between them. A noun phrase is always used when minor participants and props[5] are brought back to the stage.

The example (40) is an extract from a story about the speaker's uncle, who was introduced with a kinship term at the very beginning of the story and only referred to by a verbal suffix or an occasional pronoun afterwards. An important prop, snake poison, which becomes a topic for a short stretch, is referred to by a full noun phrase.

---

[5] Participants are typically human and active in a narrative, props typically non-human and inactive.

(40) *Akia   ik-ep   en-em-ik-ok   **ifa   marasin nain=ke** kema wiar*
     banana roast-SS.SEQ eat-SS.SIM.be-SS snake poison that1=CF liver 3.DAT
     iw-a-k. Iw-aya   nan miira saawirin-e-k.   Ne auwa   ame wia
     go-PA-3s go-2/3s.DS there face become.round-PA-3s ADD 1s/p.father ASS 3p.ACC
     maak-eya res   aaw-ep   merena ... nain puuk-a-mik. Puuk-ap   marasin
     tell-2/3s.DS razor take-SS.SEQ leg   ... that1 cut-PA-1/3p cut-SS.SEQ medicine
     wu-om-a-mik.   Marasin wu-om-a-mik=na   weetak. Iiriw
     put-BEN-BNFY2.PA-1/3p medicine put-BEN-BNFY2.PA-1/3p=TP no   earlier
     ***ifa   marasin=ke** kekan-e-k.   Ne akia   ik-e-k   nain me en-e-k.*
     snake poison=CF be.strong-PA-3s ADD banana roast-PA-3s that1 not eat-PA-3s
     Nan mukuna=pa ik-eya   o   nan samor aaw-o-k.
     there fire=LOC be-2/3s.DS 3s.UNM there badly get-PA-3s

     'He roasted bananas and when he was eating them the snake poison entered his liver. It entered and he felt dizzy there. And when he told my father and others, they took a razor and made a cut into the leg… They made a cut and put medicine into it. They put medicine but no (it didn't help). The snake poison was already strong. And he didn't eat the bananas that he roasted. They were there on the fire and he really got bad there.'

9.2.4 Highlighted topic

The topic marker -(e)na (§3.12.7.1) is only used with a new topic that the speaker wants to highlight. The constituent may have been briefly mentioned in an earlier clause (41), (42), or it is known from the outset as a future topic (43), and now it is specified as the topic for the following section of text.

(41) *Mauw-owa kamenap nain on-a-man?* ***Mauw-owa=na** sira   yia*
     work-NMZ what.like that1 do-PA-2p work-NMZ=TP custom 1p.ACC
     nokar-e-mik, yiena kae   sira   nain.
     ask-PA-1/3p 1p.GEN 1s/p.grandfather custom that1

     'What kind of work did you do? - The work (was such that) they asked us about customs, our ancestral customs.'

(42) *…Filip uruf-ap   maak-e-k, "Ikos   ikiw-u." **Filip=na** ona   owowa Suaru, …*
     …Filip see-SS.SEQ tell-PA-3s together go-IMP.1d Filip=TP 3s.GEN village Suaru

     'He saw Filip and told him, "We'll go together." Filip is/was from Suaru, …'

(43) *Yo   efa   aaw-eya   i   owawiya ik-omkun **Yaapan=ena** Wewak*
     1s.UNM 1s.ACC take-2/3s.DS 1p.UNM together be-1s/p.DS Japan=TP Wewak
     kame=pa nan ir-a-mik.
     side=LOC there come-PA-1/3p

     'He married me, and while we were together the Japanese came from the Wewak side.'

Highlighted topics are more frequent in conversations than in narratives. Since the first and second persons are more topical than the third person (44), (45), they may even get marked as topic when the discussion itself is about something else (46). The second person singular pronoun with the topic marker, *nos-na*, has acquired the meaning somewhat like 'you know' in English (47). A highlighted topic of this kind need not be a constituent in a clause.

(44) ***Nos=na*?**
 2s.FC=TP
 'What about you?' or: 'What do you want?' or: 'Where are you going?'

(45) *Emar,* ***yos=na*** *amina=ke   weetak.*
 friend 1s.FC=TP saucepan=CF no
 'Friend, I do not have a saucepan.'

(46) ***Is=na*** *yoo, takira fain ifa=ke   ku-eya   akua   aaw-ep*
 1p.FC=TP INTJ boy this snake=CF bite-2/3s.DS shoulder take-ss.SEQ
 ekap-em-ika-i-mik   yoo!
 come-ss.SIM-be-NP-PR.1/3p INTJ
 'We - this boy was bitten by a snake and we are coming carrying him on our shoulders.'

(47) *Mauwa ar-e-n,   amia=iya nenar-e-mik=i?   -Wia,* ***nos=na****, yo*
 what become-PA-2s bow=COM shoot.you-PA-1/3p=QM No   2s.FC=TP 1s.UNM
 fiker   fufa iw-ap   nefa   far-i-yem.
 kunai.grass base go-ss.SEQ 2s.ACC call-NP-PR.1s
 'What happened to you, did they shoot you with a gun? -No, you know, I went inside the *kunai* grass and am calling you.'

9.3 Focus constructions

The term FOCUS, as used here, refers to special prominence given to some constituent in a clause (Dixon 2010a: 174). In Mauwake, focus is not the same as new information, as the focused element can be either new or given information. And it cannot be contrasted with topic, as the topic may receive focus marking as well.[6]

The main discussion concentrates on two focus clitics, but syntactic and phonological focusing devices are also briefly touched on.

Since focus refers to special prominence, it is possible to have clauses and sentences without any focus marking; in fact, most of the clauses do not have any. But it is also possible to have more than one focused item in a clause.

---

[6] This §9.3 is based on my earlier paper (Järvinen (=Berghäll) 1988a).

9.3.1 Contrastive focus

Chafe (1976) lists the following factors as necessary for focus of contrast: the knowledge that someone did something, a set of possible candidates in the addressee's mind, and the assertion as to which of these candidates is the correct one. Thus, there can be no contrast if the number of candidates is either unlimited or one. A contrastive sentence often contradicts the addressee's expectation(s), but this is not crucial; what is essential is that there is a set of possible candidates in the addressee's mind. Also, as Linde (1979: 348) remarks, marking a contrast is not obligatory. Even if there are more candidates than one in the addressee's mind, it is still the speaker who decides whether to overtly mark something as contrastive or not.

The contrastive focus marker in Mauwake is -*ke*, which cliticizes to a noun phrase (§3.12.7.2). It can also follow a temporal or location word, although this is rare. The domain of the contrastive focus is one constituent. It is used when the NP is in focus and is contrasted with something else (48), (49).

(48) **Os=ke** ikiw-o-k.
3s.FC=CF go-PA-3s

'It was he who went.'

(49) **Mua bug maala nain=ke** *mera unowa isak-i-non,*   *mua bug iiwa nain*
man wind long   that1=CF fish   many spear-NP-FI.3s man wind short that1
weetak.
no

'A man with big lungs will spear many fish, a man with small lungs no.'

Sometimes the use or non-use of the contrastive marker makes a difference in the interpretation of the meaning of a word. In (50), *maneka* 'big' refers to the size of the man as a neutral quality, but in (51) either his big size is contrasted with the size of other people, or he is set apart as one of a limited set of big men, i.e., chiefs.

(50) *Mua nain maneka.*
man that1 big

'That man is big.'

(51) *Mua nain* **maneka=ke**.
man that1 big=CF

'That man is BIG' or: 'That man is a big man/chief.'

The main position for the contrastive focus marking is the subject (48),[7] (49), or the non-verbal predicate of a verbless clause (51). In a few cases, some other constituent is marked, e.g., a contrasted object (52), (53) or an adverbial phrase (54), (55).

---

[7] Waskia has an identical morpheme *ke*, labeled as a subject marker (Ross & Paol 1978: 36). The examples cited are very similar to those cases in Mauwake where the contrastive focus marker cliticizes to the subject.

9 *Theme, topic, and focus*

(52) Ne **erepam nain=ke** wiena skul stua on-a-mik.
ADD four that1=CF 3p.GEN school store make-PA-1/3p
'And the fourth one they made into their school store.'

(53) Maa en-owa iw-e-mik, **rais=ke** weetak.
food eat-NMZ give.him-PA-1/3p rice=CF no
'They gave him food (root crops), but not rice.'

(54) **Amirika=ke** eliw ika-i-yem, **uura=ke** napum-ar-i-yem.
noon=CF well be-NP-PR.1s night=CF sick-INCH-NP-PR.1s
'At noon I am well, at night I am sick.'

(55) **Amiten=ke** ikiw-i-yem, **Susure=ke** me ikiw-i-yem.
Amiten=CF go-NP-PR.1s Susure=CF not go-NP-PR.1s
'I go to Amiten but I don't go to Susure.'

The contrastive focus marker is also used for subject disambiguation. When an object of a clause is fronted as the theme, the constituent order changes from SOV to OSV. If both the subject and object are in the third person and are realized as overt NPs, this creates a potential ambiguity as to which one is which argument. The contrastive focus marker, added to the subject, may first have been used to disambiguate clauses like (56) and later spread as an optional marking even to clauses where the verbal suffix distinguishes the two arguments and which would not need this extra marking (57). Without the contrastive focus marking, the example (56) would mean 'and my younger sibling got/took an arrow/a bullet'.

(56) Ne yena aamun **ariwa=ke** aaw-o-k.
ADD 1s.GEN 1s/p.younger.sibling arrow=CF get-PA-3s
'And my younger sibling was killed by a bullet (lit: arrow).'

(57) Fofa=pa maa mauwa on-i-mik nain **(yos=ke)** ma-i-yem.
market=LOC thing what do-NP-PR.1/3p that1 1s.FC=CF say-NP-PR.1s
'I tell what we do at the market.'

Although the contrastive focus marker is very common when both the subject and object in an OSV clause are NPs, it is not obligatory. See the second clause of (5) for an example.

In other situations where there is ambiguity about the subject, the CF marker is also used. If (58) did not have CF marking, Pita could be interpreted as the possessor of the betelnuts and so the meaning would be 'He stole Pita's betelnuts from me'.

(58) **Pita=ke** owora efar ikum aaw-eya ...
Pita=CF betelnut 1s.DAT illicitly take-2/3s.DS
'Pita stole my betelnuts, and ...'

9.3 Focus constructions

In (59), the second CF is necessary, because otherwise 'this other one' would be interpreted as an object; the real object in the second clause is marked by zero.

(59) Ikoka **masin kaanin=ke** samor-ar-eya   oko **fain=ke** asip-i-non.
later engine which=CF bad-INCH-2/3s.DS other this=CF help-NP-FU.3s
'Later when any of the engines breaks this other one will help it.'

A clause can only have one constituent with contrastive focus. In a verbless clause, either the subject (61) or the non-verbal predicate (60) can be marked with it, but not both.

(60) Yo   **owow(a) saria=ke**.
1s.UNM village headman=CF
'I am the village headman.'

(61) Wia, **yos=ke** owow saria   ika-i-yem.
no   1s.FC=CF village headman be-NP-PR.1s
'No, *I* am the village headman.'

Contrastive focus can be assigned to a constituent regardless of whether it is given or new (62), indefinite (63) or definite (64). Non-verbal predicates with CF are mostly new information, whereas for subjects neither givenness nor definiteness matters.

(62) Iperuma nain me enim-eka, **inasin mua=ke**.
eel   that1 not eat-IMP.2p spirit man=CF
'Don't eat the eel, it is a spirit man.'

(63) Iir oko **mua oko=ke** koora ku-ek-a-m   na-ep   maakara war-ep...
time other man other=CF house build-CNTF-PA-1s say-SS.SEQ timber cut-SS.SEQ
'Another time a man wanted to build a house and he cut timber and ...'

(64) **Aaya   nain=ke** ifa   puuk-a-k.
sugarcane that1=CF snake change.into-PA-3s
'The sugarcane changed into a snake.'

In non-polar questions, it is the questioned element that is in focus. This is reflected in the question words and in the answers. When the question word is the subject (65) or the non-verbal predicate (67), it takes the CF clitic, and the corresponding constituent in the answer usually gets the focus marking as well (66), (68).

(65) **Mua naareke** nefa   maak-e-k?
man who.CF   2s.ACC tell-PA-3s
'Who told you?'

9 Theme, topic, and focus

(66) ***Mua=ke*** *me efa maak-e-mik, yena mokok=iw uruf-a-m.*
man=CF not 1s.ACC tell-PA-1/3p 1s.GEN eye=INST see-PA-1s
'It wasn't people that told me, I saw it with my own eyes.'

(67) *Maa nain **mauwa=ke**?*
thing that1 what=CF
'What is that thing?'

(68) *Maa nain **posa=ke**.*
thing that1 turban.shell=CF
'That thing is a turban shell.'

The contrastive focus clitic and the question clitic *-i* merge into *-ki* when both are used with the same constituent. This happens when the non-verbal predicate of a verbless clause is questioned (69), in alternative questions (70), and sometimes in alternative statements (71).

(69) *Emeria fain **Eema=ki**?*
woman this Eema=CF.QM
'Is this woman Eema?'

(70) *Emeria fain **Eema=ki** e emeria oko=ke?*
woman this Eema=CF.QM or woman other=CF
'Is this woman Eema or another woman?'

(71) ***Iwer(a) eka=ki** e mauwa=ki, owora=ki, episowa=ki*
coconut water=CF.QM or what=CF.QM betelnut=CF.QM tobacco=CF.QM
ika-i-non ...
be-NP-FU.3s
'If there is coconut water, or something else, betelnut, or tobacco ...'

9.3.2 Neutral focus

The neutral focus clitic (§3.12.7.2) most commonly occurs in irrealis-type clauses, i.e., questions (72), commands (73), negated clauses (74) or those with future tense (75), hence its original name in Järvinen (=Berghäll) (1988a). But it is also used in a some realis-type clauses. Although the clitic has probably developed from the indefinite *oko* 'a (certain), (an)other', it is added to definite noun phrases as well.

(72) ***Aaya=ko** niar ik-ua=i?*
sugar=NF 2p.DAT be-PA.3s=QM
'Do you have (ANY) SUGAR?'

(73) *Ikiw-ep* **maa en-owa=ko** *nop-aka.*
go-SS.SEQ food eat-NMZ=NF fetch-IMP.2s
'Go and fetch (SOME) FOOD.'

(74) **Owowa oko=ko** *me uf-e-mik.*
village other=NF not dance-PA-1/3p
'OTHER VILLAGES did not dance.'

(75) *Yo aakisa* **opaimika=ko** *ma-i-nen.*
1s.UNM now talk/story=NF say-NP-FU.1s
'Now I will tell A STORY.'

In most of those few instances where the NF clitic marks a constituent in a clearly realis-type clause, that constituent is a new, indefinite NP introduced as a subject (76), (77).

(76) ...**emer en-ow mua=ko** *eka en-ep momor-ar-ep* ...
sago eat-NMZ man=NF water eat-SS.SEQ fool-INCH-SS.SEQ
'... A SEPIK MAN had drunk beer and became drunk and ...'

(77) *Nan iimar-ep ika-eya* **urema=ko** *ekap-eya miim-a-k.*
there stand.up-SS.SEQ be-2/3s.DS bandicoot=NF come-2/3s.DS hear-PA-3s
'He was standing there and he heard A BANDICOOT coming.' (Lit: '...a bandicoot came and he heard it').

Any constituent in a clause can be marked as focused with the neutral focus clitic. The subject (76) and object (75) have been exemplified above, but a recipient (78), adverbial (79), (80), comitative, (81) and instrument (82) are also possible:

(78) **Mua nain=ko** *onak-e.*
man that1=NF feed.him-IMP.1s
'Give it to THAT MAN to eat.'

(79) *Miiw-aasa* **era=pa=ko** *me yiar samor-ar-e-k.*
land-canoe road=LOC=NF not 1p.DAT bad-INCH-PA-3s
'Our truck did not break ON THE ROAD.'

(80) *Ne* **samor akena=ko** *aruf-a-mik.*
ADD badly very=NF hit-PA-1/3p
'And they beat him VERY BADLY.'

(81) **Ikos=ko** *niir-u.*
together=NF play-IMP.1d
'Let's play TOGETHER.'

(82) **Fura=iw=ko** me puuk-a-mik.
knife=INST=NF not cut-PA-1/3p
'They didn't cut it WITH A KNIFE.'

In a sentence the final, fully inflected verbs are already on the basis of their position more prominent than other verbs, and they cannot receive focus marking. But the medial verbs may be given extra prominence with the neutral focus clitic (83).

(83) Amerika kerer-e-mik na-i-ya, **ikiw-ep=ko** wia uruf-ik-ua.
America appear-PA-1/3p say-NP-PR.3s go-SS.SEQ=NF 3p.ACC see-be-PA.3s
'He says that the Americans have arrived, let's GO and see them.'

Even the verbal negation particle *me* 'not' can be marked with the NF clitic, in which case the focus is on negating the whole proposition (84).

(84) Takira **me=ko** wia aruf-a-mik.
boy not=NF 3p.ACC hit-PA-1/3p
'It is NOT the case that we hit the boys.'

A clause can only have one contrastive focus,[8] but negations and especially polite requests may contain two or even three constituents marked with the neutral focus (85).

(85) **No=ko era=ko imen-ap=ko** yia asip-e.
2s.UNM=NF way=NF find-SS.SEQ=NF 1p.ACC help-IMP.2s
'If you find a way, please help us.' Or: 'Please find a way to help us.'

Especially in spoken language, it is possible to reduplicate the NF clitic in a word for extra prominence (86).

(86) Wi kema ma-e-mik, "**O=ko=ko** amukar-ek-a-n nom. Moram me
3p.UNM liver say-PA-1/3p 3s.UNM=NF=NF scold-CNTF-PA-2s please why not
amukar-e-n?"
scold-PA-2s
'They said in their hearts, "C'mon, you should have scolded HIM. Why didn't you scold him?"'

The two focus markers are not mutually exclusive, and consequently they can co-occur in one clause (87).

(87) **Yos=ke** maa **nain=ko** me aaw-e-m.
1s.FC=CF thing that1=NF not take-PA-1s
'It wasn't I who took that thing.'

---

[8] Clauses with a locative adverb *neeke* or *feeke* (§3.6.3) are an exception.

The constituent with focus marking retains the same position in a clause that it has in a non-focused clause. When a personal pronoun in some other case than nominative receives neutral focus, an unmarked pronoun is added as a pronoun copy and marked with the NF clitic (88). When this pronoun gets fronted as a theme, it is the pronoun copy that is fronted (89).

(88) *Mua nain **i=ko** me yia   far-e-k.*
 man that1 1p.UNM=NF not 1p.ACC call-PA-3s
 'The man didn't call US.'

(89) ***I=ko**   mua nain-(ke) me yia   far-e-k.*
 1p.UNM=NF man that1-(CF) not 1p.ACC call-PA-3s
 'US the man didn't call.'

More research is needed in order to establish what kind of prominence the NF clitic marks. Of the following three examples, (90) is a low-prominence clause with no item marked for extra prominence, in (91) 'I' is contrasted with other people, and in (92) the prominence is neutral: the speaker emphasizes that (s)he didn't see, but there is no implied contrast.

(90) *Yo   me uruf-a-m.*
 1s.UNM not see-PA-1s
 'I didn't see it.'

(91) ***Yos=ke** me uruf-a-m.*
 1s.FC=CF not see-PA-1s
 'It wasn't I who saw it (but someone else).'

(92) ***Yo=ko**   me uruf-a-m.*
 1s.UNM=NF not see-PA-1s
 '*I* didn't see it (regardless of whether anyone else did or not)'

Introduction of an indefinite topic has already been mentioned as one of the functions of neutral focus. In questions and requests the focus marking indicates politeness. And especially in many negated clauses with NF marking, there is a sense of distancing oneself from the situation (93).

(93) *I   **mua=ko** me wia   furew-a-mik ne yiena pun **mukuna=ko** me*
 1s.UNM man=NF not 3p.ACC sense-PA-1/3p ADD 1p.GEN also fire=NF   not
 op-a-mik.
 hold-PA-1/3p
 'We didn't sense (ANY) PEOPLE (there) and we ourselves didn't carry fire either.'

401

9 Theme, topic, and focus

9.3.3 Other focusing devices

Cross-linguistically, the most common focusing device is possibly stress. Stress in Mauwake is not only a word-level feature (§2.1.3.1); it can be employed to give prominence to a word or phrase in a clause. Default, or neutral, clause stress is on the verb or the non-verbal predicate. An extra heavy stress is used for contrastive focus especially for those constituents that seldom or never take CF marking (94)–(97).

(94) *O'wowa=pa emeria unowa wia maak-e-mik.*
village=LOC woman many 3p.ACC tell-PA-1/3p

'IN THE VILLAGE they told it to many women.'

(95) *Owowa=pa e'meria unowa wia maak-e-mik.*
village=LOC woman many 3p.ACC tell-PA-1/3p

'In the village they told it to many WOMEN.'

(96) *Owowa=pa emeria u'nowa wia maak-e-mik.*
village=LOC woman many 3p.ACC tell-PA-1/3p

'In the village they told it to MANY women.'

(97) *Owowa=pa emeria unowa wia 'maak-e-mik.*
village=LOC woman many 3p.ACC tell-PA-1/3p

'In the village they TOLD it to many women (instead of hiding it from them).'

Note that in (97) it is only the loudness/intensity in the stressed word that distinguishes it from the neutral clausal stress.

Right-dislocation is often called a topicalizing device, but in Mauwake it can't be that, since only a few of the right-dislocated constituents are topics (98).

(98) *Maa nain aaw-ep iima=pa wu-om-ap om-em-ik-ua,*
thing that1 take-SS.SEQ chest=LOC put-BEN-BNFY2.SS.SEQ cry-SS.SIM-be-3s.PA
sawur emeria nain=ke.
spirit woman that1=CF

'She took the thing and put it on his chest, the spirit woman (did).'

Most of the right-dislocated elements are not topics. Right-dislocation seems to be a focusing device of a special kind: the speaker decides that some constituent needs clarification or more prominence than it received, and adds it as an afterthought after the clause (99)–(101).

(99) *Saapara=pa nan suusa iw-e-mik, wiena ifa suusa nain.*
Saapara=LOC there needle give.him-PA-1/3p 3p.GEN snake needle that1

'There in Saapara they gave him an injection, their snake (antivenene) injection.'

(100) *Aaya puuk-ap iimar-ep ik-ua,* **manin(a)**
sugarcane change.into-SS.SEQ stand.up-SS.SEQ be-PA.3s garden
afua=pa.
old(garden)=LOC

'It had changed into a sugarcane and was standing in the old garden.'

(101) *Ne fraide=pa maapora puk-o-k,* **urera**.
ADD Friday=LOC party burst-PA-3s afternoon

'And on Friday the party started, in the afternoon.'

Appendix

A List of main texts used

The texts marked with an asterisk (*) appear interlinearised in Appendix B. (S) indicates spoken, (W) written text.

No	Name	Code	Type		Author	Sent./Cl
1	Uncle Tup* (B.2)	NASRAB	Narrative	(S)	Saror Aduna	65 / 146
2	Turtle* (B.3)	NAECAB	Narrative	(S)	Kuuten	9 / 33
3	World War 2* (B.1)	HIKCCH	Narrative	(S)	Kalina Sarak	134 / 336
4	Boika's kunai	NASRGG	Narrative	(S)	Saror Aduna	62 / 149
5	Dog and snake* (B.5)	NASCAI	Narrative	(S)	Saror Aduna	13 / 30
6	School party	NASRBI	Narrative	(S)	Saror Aduna	56 / 101
7	Piglet* (B.6)	NASREJ	Narrative	(S)	Saror Aduna	31 / 90
8	Komori's wife	NACRDC	Narrative	(S)	Saror Aduna	30 / 57
9	Man's lover* (B.7)	LEHCAN	Trad.story	(S)	Kinangir Saror	16 / 50
10	Flood* (B.8)	LEYREG	Trad.story	(S)	Yaura	33 / 89
11	Eel	LESW09	Trad.story	(W)	Saror Aduna	49 / 144
12	Rubaruba	LEHCAO	Trad.story	(S)	Kinangir Saror	63 / 201
13	Boy and flies	LESCAM	Trad.story	(S)	Saror Aduna	20 / 62
14	Suun story	LEPRDA	Trad.story	(S)	Paul	28 / 89
15	Marus' wedding	HOURGC	Hortatory	(S)	Kululu Sarak	116 / 274
16	Copra* (B.9)	DESW01	Process	(W)	Saror Aduna	12 / 37
17	Garden work* (B.10)	DESW02	Process	(W)	Saror Aduna	35 / 68
18	Fishing customs* (B.4)	DESW03	Process	(W)	Saror Aduna	59 / 116
19	Headdress	DESW15	Process	(W)	Saror Aduna	17 / 38
20	Pighunt	DEWCCA	Process	(W)	Muandilam	31 / 100
21	Girls' initiation* (B.11)	DEKRDE	Descriptive	(S)	Kalina Sarak	21 / 58
22	Funeral customs* (B.12)	DEKRDF	Descriptive	(S)	Kalina Sarak	41 / 109
23	Adoption	DESW14	Descriptive	(W)	Saror Aduna	40 / 89
24	My family	DESCAH	Descriptive	(S)	Saror Aduna	23 / 38
25	Dreams	DESW16	Descriptive	(W)	Saror Aduna	15 / 30
26	Tidal wave* (B.13)	DESRBK	Descriptive	(S)	Saror Aduna	17 / 36

B Texts

B.1 World War 2

by Kalina Sarak (extract, edited by Saror Aduna)

(1) *I me amis-ar-em-ik-omkun iinan aasa iinan-pa fan*
1p.UNM not knowledge-INCH-SS.SIM-be-1s/p.DS sky canoe sky-LOC here
ekap-emi paran-em-yi-omak-e-k.
come-SS.SIM rumble-SS.SIM-wander-DISTR/PL-PA-3s

'We were not aware, when airplanes came here rumbling on the sky.'

(2) *I naap koora=pa ik-e-mik, koora=pa ik-e-mik.*
1p.UNM thus house-LOC be-PA-1/3p house-LOC be-PA-1/3p

'We were in the house like that, we were in the house.'

(3) *Aria yena mua pun irak-owa kerer-owa epa weeser-em-ik-eya*
alright 1s.GEN man too fight-NMZ appear-NMZ time finish-SS.SIM-be-2/3s.DS
iirar-iwkin owowa ekap-o-k, o amia mua=pa ik-ok.
dismiss-2/3p.DS village come-PA-3s 3s.UNM weapon man-LOC be-ss

'Alright my husband too, when the fighting time was getting close, was dismissed and came to the village, he having been a policeman.'

(4) *Maak-e-mik, "No ikiw-e, irak-owa maneka fan-e-k a," ne*
tell-PA-1/3p 2s.UNM go-IMP.2s fight-NMZ big be.here-PA-3s INTJ ADD
ekap-o-k.
come-PA-3s

'They told him, "Go, the big war is here," and he came.'

(5) *Ekap-emi yo efa aaw-o-k.*
come-SS.SIM 1s.UNM 1s.ACC take-PA-3s

'He came and married me.'

(6) *Yo efa aaw-eya i owawiya ik-omkun Yaapan=ena Wewak*
1s.UNM 1s.ACC take-2/3s.DS 1p.UNM together be-1s/p.DS Japan-TP Wewak
kame=pa nan ir-a-mik.
side-LOC there come-PA-1/3p

'He married me and when we were together the Japanese came from the direction of Wewak there.'

B Texts

(7) *Ne i   Emer Era=pa nan ik-e-mik, ne oos onaiya Nemuru*
ADD 1p.UNM sago road-LOC there be-PA-1/3p ADD horse with   Nemuru
lul   nan   ir-am-ik-e-mik.
black.sand there come-SS.SIM-be-PA-1/3p

'And we were there in Sago Road (hamlet), and they were coming with horses there along Nemuru black sand beach.'

(8) *Ir-am-ik-aiwkin   yena   mua Sarak=ke wia   uruf-ap   ma-e-k,*
come-SS.SIM-be-2/3p.DS 1s.GEN man Sarak-CF 3p.ACC see-SS.SEQ say-PA-3s
"Yaapan nan-e-mik.
Japan   come.there-PA-1/3p

'As they were coming my husband Sarak saw them and said, "The Japanese have come there.'

(9) *Saa=iw   ir-am-ika-i-mik,   oos   ono-onaiya*
sand-INST come-SS.SIM-be-Np-PR.1/3p horse RDP-with
ir-am-ika-i-mik."
come-SS.SIM-be-Np-PR.1/3p

'They are coming along the beach, they are coming with many horses."'

(10) *Ne i   owowa ir-a-mik.*
ADD 1p.UNM village come-PA-1/3p

'And we came to the village.'

(11) *Owowa=pa fan yia   maak-e-mik, "Yaapan fan ikiw-e-mik, oos   onaiya*
village-LOC here 1p.ACC tell-PA-1/3p Japan   here go-PA-1/3p horse with
Madang ikiw-e-mik.
Madang go-PA-1/3p

'Here in the village they told us, "The Japanese went this way, they went to Madang with horses.'

(12) *Wi   sawur nain ir-ami   fan yiar   pok-a-mik."*
3p.UNM spirit¹ that1 come-SS.SIM here 1p.DAT sit-PA-1/3p

'Those spirits came and sat here with us.'

(13) *Wi   Yaapan nain naap wia   ma-e-mik, "Sawur=ke fan ikiw-e-mik."*
3p.UNM Japan   that1 thus 3p.ACC say-PA-1/3p spirit-CF here go-PA-1/3p

'We said like that about the Japanese, "The spirits went this way."'

(14) *Aria   naap ik-ok i   baurar-e-mik.*
Alright thus be-ss 1p.UNM flee-PA-1/3p

'Alright we were like that and (then) we ran away.'

---

[1] *Inasina* 'a bush spirit' is commonly used for white-skinned outsiders, *sawur* 'spirit of long-ago dead' only rarely.

(15) *Muakura=ke ma-e-k,* "*Ikoka Yaapan=ke ekap-emi   ni   emeria unowa*
    Muakura-CF say-PA-3s later Japan-CF come-SS.SIM 2p.UNM woman many
    fain nia   aaw-urum-i-kuan."
    this 2p.ACC take-DISTR/A-Np-FU.3p

    'It was Muakura who said, "Later the Japanese will come and take all of you women."'

(16) *I   uura maa unowa op-ap   baurar-ep koka   ikiw-e-mik.*
    1p.UNM night thing many grab-SS.SEQ flee-SS.SEQ jungle go-PA-1/3p

    'At night we grabbed our belongings and fled and went into the jungle.'

(17) *Iki(w-e)p koka=pa   nan in-em-ik-e-mik,   ikoka Yaapan me yia*
    go-SS.SEQ jungle-LOC there sleep-SS.SIM-be-PA-1/3p later Japan not 1p.ACC
    aaw-uk   na-ep.
    take-IMP.3p say-SS.SEQ

    'We went and kept sleeping in the jungle so that the Japanese would not take us.'

(18) "*Ni   ikoka Yaapan=ke emeria niar   aaw-emi   ni   umakuna nia*
    2p.UNM later Japan-CF woman 2p.DAT take-SS.SIM 2p.UNM neck   2p.ACC
    puuk-i-kuan."
    cut-Np-FU.3p

    '"Later the Japanese will take your wives and cut your necks."'

(19) *I   nain kema tooton-ep, ikoka Yaapan me yia   aaw-uk   na-ep*
    1p.UNM that1 liver fear-SS.SEQ later Japan not 1p.ACC take-IMP.3p say-SS.SEQ
    uura kuisow baurar-e-mik, maa   unowa owowa=pa feeke   ika-eya.
    night one   flee-PA-1/3   thing many village-LOC here.CF be-2/3s.DS

    'We were afraid of that, (and) so that the Japanese would not take us we ran away right that night, (with) many belongings staying here in the village.'

(20) *Aakisa Malala suule ik-ua, i   naap ikiw-ep   yiena manina*
    now   Malala school be-PA.3s 1p.UNM thus go-SS.SEQ 1p.GEN garden
    on-a-mik   nan   ik-e-mik.
    make-PA-1/3p there be-PA-1/3p

    'Now there is the Malala school, we went like that and stayed where we (had) made our gardens.'

(21) *I   miiwa nan   aruf-am-ik-e-mik,   ne iki(w-e)p nan*
    1p.UNM ground there hit-SS.SIM-be-PA-1/3p ADD go-SS.SEQ there
    in-em-ik-e-mik.
    sleep-SS.SIM-be-PA-1/3p

    'We kept tilling the soil there, and we went and kept sleeping there.'

(22) *Emeria teeria unow=iya baurar-ep koka ikiw-urum-e-mik, kuisow*
woman group many-COM flee-SS.SEQ jungle go-DISTR/A-PA-1/3p one
owowa=pa=ko me ik-ua.
village-LOC-IF not be-PA.3s

'The whole group of women fled into the jungle, not even one stayed in the village.'

(23) *Mua muutiw owowa=pa ik-e-mik.*
man only village-LOC be-PA-1/3p

'Only men stayed in the village.'

(24) *Mua kuisow, Muakura=ke i yia p-ikiw-o-k.*
man one Muakura-CF 1p.UNM 1p.ACC Bpx-go-PA-3s

'One man, Muakura, was the one who took us (to the jungle).'

(25) *"Karu-eka, ikoka Yaapan ir-ami ni nia aaw-emi yo efa*
run-IMP.2p later Japan come-SS.SIM 2p.UNM 2p.ACC take-SS.SIM 1s.UNM 1s.ACC
ifakim-i-kuan," na-eya i karu-em-ik-e-mik.
kill-Np-FU.3p say-2/3s.DS 1s.UNM run-SS.SIM-be-PA-1/3p

' "Run, (otherwise) later the Japanese will come and take you and kill me," he said, and we kept running.'

(26) *Irak-owa maneka ewur me imen-ar-e-k, wi Yaapan naap kuisow=iw*
fight-NMZ big quickly not find-INCH-PA-3s 3p.UNM Japan thus one-LIM
ekap-em-ik-e-mik, owowa yiar kuuf-owa.
come-SS.SIM-be-PA-1/3p village 1p.DAT see-NMZ

'The big fight did not start quickly, the Japanese kept coming one by one to see/look at our village(s).'

(27) *Ekap-ep, ekap-ep, aakisa fan unowa Wewak=pa nan urup-e-mik.*
come-SS.SEQ come-SS.SEQ now here many Wewak-LOC there ascend-PA-1/3p

'The came and came, and just now many landed (lit: came up) there in Wewak.'

(28) *Ne ekap-ep Numbia=pa nan urup-e-mik.*
ADD come-SS.SEQ Numbia-LOC there ascend-PA-1/3p

'They came and landed there at Numbia.'

(29) *Maa unowa ifer aasa=ke p-urup-eya miiw-aasa=ke fan*
thing many sea canoe-CF Bpx-ascend-2/3s.DS land-canoe-CF here
p-ir-am-ik-ua.
Bpx-come-SS.SIM-be-PA.3s

'Many things were brought up by the ships and brought here by trucks.'

(30) *Yaapan feenap   Madang kame ikiw-e-mik.*
Japan   like.this Madang side   go-PA-1/3p

'The Japanese went towards Madang like this.'

(31) *Ikoka Yaapan=ke i   emeria yia   aaw-urum-i-kuan   na-eya,*
Later Japan-CF   1p.UNM woman 1p.ACC take-DISTR/A-Np-FU.3p say-2/3s.DS
i   amirika owowa ewur   me ekap-em-ik-e-mik,   Yaapan fan   naap
1p.UNM daytime village quickly not come-ss.SIM-be-PA-1/3p Japan   here thus
ekap-em-ika-iwkin.
come-ss.SIM-be-2/3p.DS

'He (had) said that the Japanese will take all of us women, and (so) we did not come quickly to the village in the daytime (i.e. we kept staying away from the village), as the Japanese kept coming here like that.'

(32) *Wi   Yaapan emeria weetak, mua manek-iw.*
3p.UNM Japan   woman   no   man big-LIM

'The Japanese had no women/wives, (they were) only men.'

(33) *Me fan Madang kame=pa ekap-e-mik,   Wewak kame=pa fan   naap*
not here Madang side-LOC come-PA-1/3p Wewak side-LOC here thus
ir-am-ik-e-mik.
come-ss.SIM-be-PA-1/3p

'They did not come here from the Madang side/direction, they came here like that from the Wewak side.'

(34) *Wilkar, miiw-aasa, Madang naap irak-owa   ikiw-em-ik-e-mik,   wi*
cart   land-canoe Madang thus   fight-NMZ go-ss.SIM-be-PA-1/3p 3p.UNM
Amerika wiamiya irak-owa na-ep.
America 3p.COM   fight-NMZ say-ss.SEQ

'Carts, trucks - they kept going like that to fight in Madang, to fight with the Americans.'

(35) *I   owowa=pa fan yiar   ik-e-mik.*
1p.UNM village-LOC here 1p.DAT be-PA-1/3p

'They were here in our village(s).'

(36) *Uura feenap nain, wi   wilkar nain muf-emi   "Wensa, wensa, wensa", naap*
night like.this that1 3p.UNM cart   that1 pull-ss.SIM wensa wensa wensa   thus
kirir-em-ik-e-mik.
shout-ss.SIM-be-PA-1/3p

'On nights like this they kept pulling the carts and shouting, "Wensa, wensa, wensa."'

B Texts

(37) *Wi   owow mua=ke wilkar wia   muf-em-ik-om-a-mik,   mua*
     3p.UNM village man-CF cart   3p.ACC pull-SS.SIM-be-BEN-BNFY2.PA-1/3p man
     kui-kuisow wia   maak-iwkin.
     RDP-one   3p.ACC tell-2/3p.DS

     'The village men pulled carts for them, when they (the Japanese) had talked to a few men.'

(38) *"I   wilkar yia   muf-om-aka,"   na-iwkin.*
     1p.UNM cart   1p.ACC pull-BEN-BNFY2.IMP.2p say-2/3p.DS

     'When they had said, "Pull our carts for us."'

(39) *Wi   Malala=ke muf-ep   ekap-emi   i   Moro mua wia*
     3p.UNM Malala-CF pull-SS.SEQ come-SS.SIM 1p.UNM Moro man 3p.ACC
     wu-om-am-ik-om-a-mik.
     put-BEN-BNFY2.SS.SIM-be-BEN-BNFY2.PA-1/3p

     'The Malala people kept pulling them and coming and putting them for the Moro men.'

(40) *Wilkar nain wiena   maa koorma unowa ipar-iwkin wia*
     cart   that1 3p.GEN thing cargo many fill-2/3p.DS 3p.ACC
     muf-em-ik-om-a-mik,   feenap Madang p-ikiw-em-ik-e-mik,
     pull-SS.SIM-be-BEN-BNFY2.PA-1/3p ike.this Madang Bpx-go-SS.SIM-be-PA-1/3p
     Australia wiamiya irak-owa nain.
     Australia 3p.COM fight-NMZ that1

     'They (J) filled the carts with lots of their cargo and they (=villagers) kept pulling them for them – this way they (J) kept taking it to Madang, for the fighting with Australians.'

(41) *Nepa opaimika me baliwep amis-ar-ep   wiena   opaimik=iw yia*
     bird talk   not well   knowledge-INCH-SS.SEQ 3p.GEN talk-INST 1p.ACC
     maak-em-ik-e-mik.
     tell-SS.SIM-be-PA-1/3p

     'They didn't know Tok Pisin well and kept telling us in their own language.'

(42) *Aria   'taro' yia   na-iwkin   miim-ap   ma-em-ik-e-mik,   "Wi   moma*
     alright taro   1p.ACC say-2/3p.DS hear-SS.SEQ say-SS.SIM-be-PA-1/3p 3p.UNM taro
     yia   maak-i-mik,   moma=ko wi-i-yen."
     1p.ACC tell-Np-PR.1/3p taro-IF give.them-Np-FU.1p

     'Alright when they said to us 'Taro', we heard and said, "They tell us (to get them) taro, (so) we'll give them taro."'

(43) *"Banana mau oo, yasi kongkang," iwera   yia   ir-om-aka,   "yasi*
     banana mau oo yasi kongkang   coconut 1p.ACC climb-BEN-BNFY2.IMP.2p yasi

kongkang."
kongkang

' "Banana mau oo (ripe bananas oo, T.P.) , yasi kongkang" - climb coconut palms for us - "yasi kongkang." '

(44) *Iwera "yasi" yia na-em-ik-e-mik.*
coconut yasi   1p.ACC say-SS.SIM-be-PA-1/3p

'They kept calling coconut "yasi" to us.'

(45) *Naeya iwera wia   uruk-am-ik-om-a-mik.*
so   coconut 3p.ACC drop-SS.SIM-be-BEN-BNFY2.PA-1/3p

'So they (=men) kept dropping coconuts for them.'

(46) *Iwera   uruk-am-ika-i-wkin   wi   ikiw-emi aaw-em-ik-e-mik,*
coconut drop-SS.SIM-be-2/3p.DS 3p.UNM go-SS.SIM take-SS.SIM-be-PA-1/3p
iwera=ke   wia   aruf-eya ma-em-ik-e-mik,   "Oo kanaka oo, yasi paitim
coconut-CF 3p.ACC hit-2/3s.DS say-SS.SIM-be-PA-1/3p "Oo kanaka oo, yasi paitim
mi oo," na-em-ik-e-mik.
mi oo" say-SS.SIM-be-PA-1/3p

'When they kept dropping the coconuts, they went and got them, and when the coconuts hit them they said (in Tok Pisin), "Oh savages, yasi hit me", they kept saying (like that).'

(47) *I   me wia   amukar-e-mik, wis   pun naap, i   me yia*
1p.UNM not 3p.ACC scold-PA-1/3p 3p.FC also thus 1p.UNM not 1p.ACC
damol-a-mik.
bad-PA-1/3p

'We didn't scold them / quarrel with them, and they too likewise, they did not do damage to us.'

(48) *Ne eka   opora biiris marew nain wiena   on-am-ik-e-mik.*
ADD river mouth bridge no(ne) RM   3p.GEN make-SS.SIM-be-PA-1/3p

'And they themselves kept making bridges to rivers that didn't have them.'

(49) *Nemuru biiris on-a-mik.*
Nemuru bridge make-PA-1/3p

'They made the Nemuru bridge.'

(50) *Biiris me eliwa, damo-damola=ko.*
bridge not good, RDP-bad-IF

'The bridge was not good, it was very bad.'

(51) *Dabuel poka-poka, nomokowa galua-galua, nain=iw biiris*
papaya RDP-trunk tree RDP-soft that1-INST bridge
on-am-ik-e-mik.
make-SS.SIM-be-PA-1/3p

'Papaya trunks, soft timber, that's what they kept making the bridges with.'

(52) *Ikoka kuisow miiw-aasa=ke karu-eya ku-ku-ep*
later one land-canoe-CF run-2/3s.DS RDP-break-SS.SEQ
or-om-ik-ua.
descend-SS.SIM-be-PA.3s

'Straight away when trucks ran (over them) they kept breaking and falling down.'

(53) *Ne uurika naap nain nainiw, mauw-am-ik-e-mik.*
ADD tomorrow thus that1 again work-SS.SIM-be-PA.1/3p

'And the following day it was like that again, they kept on working.'

(54) *Waaya yia na-iwkin waaya wienak-em-ik-e-mik.*
pig 1p.ACC say-2/3p.DS pig feed.them-SS.SIM-be-PA-1/3p

'When they talked to us about pig/pork, we kept giving them pigs to eat.'

(55) *Aria naap ik-ok wi Australia kerer-e-mik.*
alright thus be-SS 3p.UNM Australia arrive-PA-1/3p

'Alright it was like that and then the Australians arrived.'

(56) *Ne wi Yaapan ikiw-ep Ulingan=pa owowa war-e-mik.*
ADD 3p.UNM Japan go-SS.SEQ Ulingan-LOC village found-PA-1/3p

'And the Japanese (had) set up a village at Ulingan.'

(57) *Ne nan wi owow mua wia maak-e-mik, "Ni kanaka yia*
ADD there 3p.UNM village man 3p.ACC tell-PA-1/3p 2p.UNM kanaka 1p.ACC
uf-om-aka."
dance-BEN-BNFY2.IMP.2p

'And there they told the village men, "You kanakas (savages), dance for us." '

(58) *Na-iwkin wia uf-om-a-mik.*
say-2/3p.DS 3p.ACC dance-BEN-BNFY2.PA-1/3p

'They said (so) and we/they danced for them.'

(59) *I Moro wenup uf-e-mik, i bidaru uf-e-mik.*
1p.UNM Moro separately dance-PA-1/3p 1p.UNM bidaru dance-PA-1/3p

'We Moro people danced on our own, we danced "bidaru".'

(60) *Uf-em-ika-iwkin, Amerika irak-ow iinan aasa ekap-ep Ulingan*
dance-ss.SIM-be-2/3p.DS America fight-NMZ sky canoe come-ss.SEQ Ulingan
nan bom fu-fuurik-ikiw-e-mik.
there bomb RDP-drop-go-PA-1/3p
'As they were dancing, American fighter planes came and went dropping bombs at Ulingan.'

(61) *I iinan aasa me kuuf-a-mik.*
1p.UNM sky canoe not see-PA-1/3p
'We didn't see the planes.'

(62) *Iinan=iw iinan=iw wu-ami feenap Wewak kame naap ikiw-o-k.*
on.top-INST on.top-INST put-ss.SIM like.this Wewak side thus go-PA-3s
'They stayed really high up and went like this towards Wewak.'

(63) *Ne Sarak opaimika wiar paayar-e-k, siiwa, epa maak-e-mik nain*
ADD Sarak talk 3.DAT understand-PA-3s moon place tell-PA-1/3p RM
paayar-ep ma-e-k, "Amerika aakisa irak-owa kerer-e-mik," na-ep
understand-ss.SEQ say-PA-3s America now fight-NMZ arrive-PA-1/3p say-ss.SEQ
wi Yaapan wia uf-om-owa ikiw-e-mik nain wia maak-e-k,
3p.UNM Japan 3p.ACC dance-BEN-NMZ go-PA-1/3p RM 3p.ACC tell-PA-3s
"Ni uf-owa ikiw-eka, yo miatin-i-yem.
2p.UNM dance-NMZ go-IMP.2p 1s.UNM dislike-Np-PR.1s
'And/but Sarak understood their talk, and he knew the month and place/time that they had told, and he said, "The Americans have now arrived to fight" - he said that and told those who went to dance for the Japanese, "You go to dance, I don't like (to go).'

(64) *Irak-owa maneka ikoka kerer-i-non.*
fight-NMZ big later appear-Np-FU.3s
'The big fighting will start later.'

(65) *Ni uf-ep=na ni maadara me iirar-eka, mokok*
2p.UNM dance-ss.SEQ-TP 2p.UNM forehead.ornament not remove-IMP.2p eye
urupa kaik-i-man nain feekiya Nomon owowa, Medebur karu-eka,
cup tie-Np-PR.2p RM with stone/reef village Medebur run-IMP.2p
baurar-eka.
flee-IMP.2p
'If/when you have danced, don't remove your forehead ornaments, and, with your eye cups that you have tied on, run to the reef village, Medebur, flee (there).'

(66) *Ne wi ikiw-iwkin Amerika iinan aasa nainiw kir-e-k.*
ADD 3p.UNM go-2/3p.DS America sky canoe again turn-PA-3s
'And when they had gone the American planes turned again (and came back).'

(67) *Iinan=iw   iki(w-e)p   kirip-ap   enen=iw,   enen=iw   wu-a-k   ne*
on.top-INST go-SS.SEQ turn-SS.SEQ low.down-INST low.down-INST put-PA-3s ADD
i   fiker   gone=pa   ik-emkun   ekap-o-k.
1p.UNM kunai.grass middle-LOC be-1s/p.DS come-PA-3s

'They went high up and turned and flew down, and came when we were in the middle of the kunai grass.'

(68) *Malala suule ik-ua   nain, Siburten ema, oram tene-ten-ep   or-op*
Malala school be-PA.3s that1 Siburten hill just RDP-fall-SS.SEQ descend-SS.SEQ
epa   iiwawun   ifemak-ep   ekap-e-mik.
place altogether press-SS.SEQ come-PA-1/3

'Where the Malala school is, and Siburten hill - (the bombs) just fell down and came covering the whole place.'

(69) *Ne   bom=iya,   kateres=iya,   bom=iya,   kateres=iya.*
ADD bomb-COM, cartridge-COM, bomb-COM, cartridge-COM

'And boms and cartridges, bombs and cartridges.'

(70) *Koora pun ariwa=ke kuum-eya   aw-omak-e-k,   i   koora kuisow*
house also arrow-CF burn-2/3s.DS burn-DISTR/PL-PA-3s 1p.UNM house one
yiar   aw-o-k.
1p.DAT burn-PA-3s

'Many houses too were burned by their firing, one house burned from us.'

(71) *Ne yena aamun   ariwa=ke aaw-o-k, weepa   Aduna*
ADD 1s.GEN 1s/p.younger.sibling arrow-CF get-PA-3s 3s/p.elder.sibling Aduna
ikos iimar-ep   ika-iwkin, owow erepura=pa   fan.
with stand.up-SS.SEQ be-2/3p.DS village outskirts-LOC here

'And my younger brother was killed by a bullet, as he was standing with his elder brother Aduna, here on the outskirts of the village.'

(72) *Wi   Amerika=ke war-e-mik.*
3p.UNM America-CF shoot-PA-1/3p

'The Americans shot him.'

(73) *Yena   aamun   unuma Saawoka.*
1s.GEN 1s/p.younger.sibling name Saawoka

'The name of my younger brother was Saawoka.'

(74) *I   fiker   gone=pa   ik-emkun kiikir iinan aasa=ke maifa*
1p.UNM kunai.grass middle-LOC be-1s/p.DS first sky canoe-CF paper
fu-fuurk-ikiw-o-k, wi   Amerika=ke.
RDP-drop-go-PA-3s 3p.UNM America-CF

'When we were in the middle of the kunai grass, first the planes went dropping papers, the Americans (did that).'

(75) *Ulingan fa=na iinan aasa nepa saarik, unow akena.*
Ulingan INTJ-TP sky canoe bird like many very
'Ulingan, phew! There were planes like birds, very many.'

(76) *Wi Yaapan nan ik-e-mik nain wia uruf-ap.*
3p.UNM Japan there be-PA-1/3p RM 3p.ACC see-SS.SEQ
'They had seen the Japanese that were there (and came).'

(77) *I karan-e-mik, yena mua Sarak=na fiker gone nomokowa*
1p.UNM shake-PA-1/3p 1s.GEN man Sarak-TP kunai.grass middle tree
onoma=pa in-ep ik-ua.
base-LOC sleep-SS.SEQ be-PA.3s
'We were afraid, (but) my husband Sarak was asleep at the base of a tree in the middle of the kunai grass area.'

(78) *Ne yo iki(w-e)p mesa asia aaw-em-ik-e-m, mesa asia*
ADD 1s.UNM go-SS.SEQ winged.bean wild get-SS.SIM-be-PA-1s winged.bean wild
fiker gone=pa ika-i-ya nain aaw-em-ik-e-m.
kunai.grass middle-LOC be-Np-PR.3s RM get-SS.SIM-be-PA-1s
'And I went and was picking wild winged beans, I was picking those wild winged beans that grow in the middle of the kunai grass.'

(79) *Ne iinan aasa uruf-ap fiker tepak iw-ap naap ik-e-m, ne*
ADD sky canoe see-SS.SEQ kunai.grass inside enter-SS.SEQ thus be-PA-1s ADD
iinan aasa yia nomak-ep ikiw-eya Sarak far-e-m, "Sarak, yo
sky canoe 1p.ACC pass-SS.SEQ go-2/3s.DS Sarak call-PA-1s Sarak 1s.UNM
damol-al-e-m oo, fiker fufa iw-a-m oo!"
bad-INCH-PA-1s INTJ kunai.grass old.grass enter-PA-1s INTJ
'And when I saw the planes I went inside the kunai grass and stayed like that, and when the planes passed over us and went I called to Sarak, "Sarak, oh I'm in a bad way, I am hiding among the kunai grass!"'

(80) *"Mauwa ar-e-n, amia=iya nenar-e-mik=i?" Sarak=ke Ø.*
what become-PA-2s gun-COM shoot.you-PA-1/3p-QM Sarak-CF
'"What happened to you, did they shoot you with a gun?" Sarak (asked).'

(81) *"Wia, nos=na, yo fiker fufa iw-ap nefa far-i-yem."*
no 2s.FC-TP 1s.UNM kunai.grass old.grass enter-SS.SEQ 2s.ACC call-Np-PR.1s
'"No, you see, I went inside the kunai grass and am calling you (from there)."'

(82) *"Momora, no naap me ma-e.*
fool 2s.UNM thus not say-IMP.2s
'"Fool, don't say like that.'

B Texts

(83) *Nefa war-iwkin naap ma-e.*
2s.ACC shoot-2/3p.DS thus say-IMP.2s
'When they shoot you, (then) say like that.'

(84) *Yo kema efa bagiw-ir-ow-a-n, yaa."*
1s.UNM liver 1s.ACC anger-come-APPL-PA-2s INTJ
'You really made me angry."'

(85) *Yo me efa war-e-mik, yo iinan aasa fan*
1s.UNM not 1s.ACC shoot-PA-1/3p 1s.UNM sky canoe here
or-om-ik-omak-eya mesa fufa=pa fan
descend-SS.SIM-be-DISTR/PL-2/3s.DS winged.bean old.grass-LOC here
erewar-ep iima ifemak-ep ik-e-m.
shelter-SS.SEQ chest press-SS.SEQ be-PA-1s
'They didn't shoot me; when the many planes were coming down here, I sheltered among the winged bean grass and was lying face down.'

(86) *Irak-owa nain kekan-owa akena, Amerika kerer-e-k nain, ne irak-owa*
fight-NMZ that be.strong-NMZ very America arrive-PA-3s that1 ADD fight-NMZ
naap ik-ua.
thus be-PA.3s
'The fighting was very strong when the Americans came, and the fighting continued like that.'

(87) *Uura feenap nain, i me in-em-ik-e-mik, amirika maa me*
night like.this that1 1p.UNM not sleep-SS.SIM-be-PA-1/3p daytime food not
en-em-ik-e-mik.
eat-SS.SIM-be-PA-1/3p
'On nights like this we did not sleep, in the daytime we did not eat.'

(88) *Maa uura uup-ep en-em-ik-e-mik.*
food night cook-SS.SEQ eat-SS.SIM-be-PA-1/3p
'The food we used to cook at night.'

(89) *Ikoka epia wilin-owa uruf-ap bom yia fuurk-om-i-kuan*
later fire shine-NMZ see-SS.SEQ bomb 1p.ACC drop-BEN-Np-FU.3p
na-ep.
say/think-SS.SEQ
'We thought that later when they see the shine of the fire(s) they will drop bombs at us (and so we did like that).'

(90) *Iinan aasa gurun-owa miim-ap eka=iw umuk-owa ewur.*
sky canoe rumble-NMZ hear-SS.SEQ water-INST extinguish-NMZ quickly
'When we heard the rumble of the planes, we extinguished (the fires) quicky with water.'

420

(91) *Epia wilinowa urufap   bom yia   wafur-om-i-kuan   na-ep*
     fire shine-NMZ see-SS.SEQ bomb 1p.ACC throw-BEN-Np-FU.3p say/think-SS.SEQ
     naap on-am-ik-e-mik.
     thus do-SS.SIM-be-PA-1/3p

   'We thought that when they see the shine of the fire they will throw bombs at us, and we did like that.'

(92) *I   Sarak ikos owowa ekap-em-ik-e-mik.*
     1p.UNM Sarak with village come-SS.SIM-be-PA-1/3p

   'Sarak and I kept coming to the village.'

(93) *Yiena koora pun me aw-o-k.*
     1p.GEN house also not burn-PA-3s

   'Our house too did not burn.'

(94) *Wi   yapen=pa ik-omak-iwkin   Amerika kerer-ep   "Eliwa, eliwa"*
     3p.UNM inland-LOC be-DISTR/PL-2/3p.DS America arrive-SS.SEQ good good
     nae-ekap-e-mik, "irak-owa weeser-e-k."
     say-come-PA-1/3p fight-NMZ finish-PA-3s

   'When they (=other villagers) were inland the Americans arrived saying, "Good, good - the war is finished." '

(95) *Wi   Yaapan pun iiwawun   ikiw-urum-e-mik.*
     3p.UNM Japan   also altogether go-DISTR/A-PA-1/3p

   'Also, all the Japanese went.'

(96) *Wi   Yaapan Madang kame ikiw-iwkin Amerika irak-owa mua*
     3p.UNM Japan   Madang side go-2/3p.DS America fight-NMZ man
     urup-e-mik.
     ascend-PA-1/3p

   'When the Japanese went/had gone towards Madang, the American soldiers came up (here).'

(97) *Urup-ep   koka-koka=pa nan, "Yapen oo, Luluai, Tultul, ni   kaaneke*
     ascend-SS.SEQ RDP-jungle-LOC there inland INTJ Luluai Tultul 2p.UNM where
     ik-e-man oo, ni   ekap-omak-eka   oo!"
     be-PA-2p INTJ 2p.UNM come-DISTR/PL-IMP.2p INTJ

   'They came up and (shouted) all over the jungle: "You in the inland, local administrators, wherever you are – come!" '

(98) *Wi   Amerika fan "Epa eliwa" nae-ekap-e-mik, "Yaapan weeser-e-mik."*
     3p.UNM America here time good say-come-PA-1/3p Japan   finish-PA-1/3p

   'The Americans came here saying, "It is peace, the Japanese are finished." '

B Texts

(99) *Naap yia   maake-miaw-e-mik.*
      thus 1p.ACC tell-go.around-PA-1/3p
      'They went around telling us like that.'

(100) *I   amirik=iw   yapen yiena Gawar wiar ikiw-e-mik.*
      1p.UNM daytime-INST inland 1p.GEN Gawar 3.DAT go-PA-1/3p
      'In the daytime we went to our (relatives at) Gawar.'

(101) *Ne Sarak ikos Gawar=pa ik-emkun yia   maak-e-mik "Sarak oo, Amerika*
      ADD Sarak with Gawar-LOC be-1s/p.DS 1p.ACC tell-PA-1/3p Sarak INTJ America
      ekap-ep   Ulingan nan   ik-e-mik, nefa   ikum-i-mik
      come-SS.SEQ Ulingan there be-PA-1/3p 2s.ACC wonder.about-Np-PR.1/3p
      na-i-mik   oo."
      say-Np-PR-1/3p INTJ
      'And when Sarak and I were at Gawar they told us, "Sarak oh, the Americans have come and are there in Ulingan and they say that they are wondering about you." '

(102) *"Aria, Kalina, Amerika ekap-e-mik   na-i-mik.*
      alright Kalina America come-PA-1/3p say-Np-PR.1/3p
      ' "Alright, Kalina, they say that the Americans have come.'

(103) *I   or-u".*
      1p.UNM descend-IMP.1d
      'Let's go down.'

(104) *Aria i   yapen=pa ik-ok owowa or-o-mik.*
      alright 1p.UNM inland-LOC be-ss village descend-PA-1/3p
      'Alright, after having stayed inland we went down to the village.'

(105) *Or-omi   yo   koka koora=pa nan efa   wu-ami   ma-e-k,*
      descend-SS.SIM 1s.UNM jungle house-LOC there 1s.ACC put-SS.SIM say-PA-3s
      "No   feeke ik-e,   yo   Amerika wia   akup-ikiw-i-yem."
      2s.UNM here.CF be-IMP.2s 1s.UNM America 3p.ACC search-go-Np-PR.1s
      'When we were coming down he put me in (our) jungle house and said, "Stay here, I go and look for the Americans." '

(106) *Aria yo   nan efa   wu-ap-pu-ami   o   Ulingan ikiw-o-k.*
      alright 1s.UNM there 1s.ACC put-SS.SEQ-CMPL-SS.SIM 3s.UNM Ulingan go-PA-3s
      'Alright he put me there and went to Ulingan.'

(107) *Ikiw-o-k=na wi   Amerika maneka unuma Magerka,   o   kerer-ep*
      go-PA-3s-TP 3p.UNM America big   name MacArthur 3s.UNM arrive-SS.SEQ

nan ik-ua.
there be-PA.3s

'He went, and the chief of the Americans, whose name was MacArthur. he had arrived and was there.'

(108) *O   ik-ip   uruf-eya   maak-ek,   "O   Sarak, no   kaaneke ik-ok*
3s.UNM go-SS.SEQ see-2/3s.DS tell-PA-3s INTJ Sarak 2s.UNM where be-ss
kerer-e-n   a?
arrive-PA-2s INTJ

'He (Sarak) went and saw him, and he (MacA.) said, "Sarak, where have you been?"'

(109) *"Yo   koka=pa   ik-e-m."*
1s.UNM jungle-LOC be.PA-1s

'"I have been in the jungle."'

(110) *Na-eya   Magerka=ke   Ø, "No   kamenap ik-o-n   noma?*
say-2/3s.DS MacArthur-CF Ø 2s.UNM how be-PA-2s INTJ

'He said that and MacArthur asked, "Well, how are you?"'

(111) *Yo   irak-owa nomak-e-m.*
1s.UNM fight-NMZ win-PA-1s

'I won the war.'

(112) *Nomak-ep fan kerer-e-m."*
win-SS.SEQ here arrive-PA-1s

'I won and I arrived here."'

(113) *"Yo   bom yo   kateres   koor   miira=pa efar   or-om-ik-ua.*
1s.UNM bomb 1s.UNM cartridge house front-LOC 1s.DAT descend-SS.SIM-be-PA.3s

'"Bombs and cartridges kept dropping in front of my house.'

(114) *Nain yo   me baurar-em-ik-e-m.*
that1 1s.UNM not flee-SS.SIM-be-PA-1s

'But I did not keep running away.'

(115) *I   iinan aasa   ekap-em-ika-eya   uruwa   ain-ep   or-op*
1p.UNM sky canoe come-SS.SIM-be-2/3.DS loincloth tie-SS.SEQ descend-SS.SEQ
yena   koor   miira=pa   iimar-ep   ik-e-m,   yena   emeria sosora
1s.GEN house front-LOC stand.up-SS.SEQ be-PA-1s 1s.GEN woman grass.skirt
ain-ep   or-op   koor   miira=pa iimar-em-ik-ua.
tie-SS.SEQ descend-SS.SEQ house front-LOC stand-SS.SIM-be-PA.3s

'When the planes kept coming I tied the loincloth and went down and stood in front of my house, and my wife used to tie the grass skirt and go down and stand in front of the house.'

(116) *Ne i me yiar-e-mik, Amerika iinan aasa ekap-em-ik-ua nain.*
ADD 1p.UNM not shoot-PA-1/3p America sky canoe come-SS.SIM-be-PA.3s RM

'And/but they didn't shoot at us, the American planes that kept coming.'

(117) *Amina, woowa, eka napia koor miira=pa*
pot spear water bamboo.container house front-LOC
iimar-aw-ikiw-e-mik, yena emeria ikos, ne wi unowa
stand.up-APPL-go-PA-1/3p 1s.GEN woman with ADD 3p.UNM many
baurar-e-mik.
flee-PA-1/3p

'We lined up pots, spears and bamboo water containers in front of the house, (I) with my wife, but many people fled.'

(118) *I iisow naap ik-emkun Amerika kerer-e-mik."*
1p.UNM 1p.ISOL thus be-1s/p.DS America arrive-PA-1/3p

'When we were by ourselves like that, the Americans arrived."'

(119) *"Ni yapen koka-koka=pa wiar in-em-ik-e-man nain*
2p.UNM inland RDP-jungle-LOC 3.DAT sleep-SS.SIM-be-PA-2p RM
kerer-omak-eka."
arrive-DISTR/PL-IMP.2p

'Those (many) of you who have stayed in the inland villages, arrive (back to your villages)."'

(120) *Amerika fan ekap-ep Uligan=pa manua maneka urup-ep*
America here come-SS.SEQ Ulingan-LOC maneuver big ascend-SS.SEQ
irak-ow(a) mua wia wu-eya nan ik-e-mik.
fight-NMZ man 3p.ACC put-2/3s.DS there be-PA-1/3p

'The Americans came here and went up to Ulingan for a big maneuver and put soldiers to stay there.'

(121) *Palauwa tin, maa eneka kes mane-maneka fa, oram iw-e-mik, Sarak*
flour tin thing tooth case RDP-big INTJ just give.him-PA-1/3p Sarak
iw-e-mik.
give.him-PA-1/3p

'Flour tins, big cases of meat (tins), wow, they gave to him for nothing, they gave them to Sarak.'

(122) *"No fain wiim-ep amap-ikiw-e."*
2s.UNM this take.along-SS.SEQ Bpx-go-IMP.2s

' "Take these along and go." '

(123) O   wi   Laman, Malager naap wia   maak-e-k, "Arika, takira, yo
      3s.UNM 3p.UNM Laman Malager thus   3p.ACC tell-PA-3s alright boy 1s.UNM
      yook-eka."
      follow.me-IMP.2p
      'He (Sarak) had told Laman and Malager, "Alright boys, follow me.'

(124) Amerika kerer-e-mik   naeya ikiwep=ko   wia   uruf-ikua.
      America arrive-PA-1/3p so   go-SS.SEQ-IF 3p.ACC see-IMP.1p
      'The Americans have arrived, so let's go and see them.'

(125) O   Ulingan ikiw-eya   bom iw-e-mik.
      3s.UNM Ulingan go-2/3s.DS bomb give.him-PA-1/3p
      'When he went to Ulingan they gave him a bomb/bombs.'

(126) "No   bom fain=iw   mera kuum-e,"   naak-e-mik.
      2s.UNM bomb this-INST fish burn-IMP.2s tell-PA-1/3p
      ' "Blast fish with this bomb/these bombs," they told him.'

(127) Maa   en-owa iw-e-mik,   palauwa dram, bata   tin naap nain, ne rais
      thing eat-NMZ give.him-PA-1/3p flour   drum butter tin thus that1 ADD rice
      weetak.
      no
      'They gave him food, flour drums, and things like butter tins, but no rice.'

(128) Ne irak-owa weeser-eya   i   owowa or-o-mik.
      ADD figth-NMZ finish-2/3s.DS 1p.UNM village descend-PA-1/3p
      'And when the war ended we came down to the village.'

(129) Irak-owa fa, opaimika eeya   akena yaa, kamenap aakun-i-yen   yaa?
      fight-NMZ INTJ talk   long.lasting very INTJ how   talk-Np-FU.1p INTJ
      'Oh the war - the talk lasts very long - how can we talk about it?'

(130) Aakun-i-yen,   aakun-i-yen,   me pepek, me welaw-i-yen.
      talk-Np-FU.1p talk-Np-FU.1p not enough not finish-Np-FU.1p
      'We will talk and talk, but it is not enough, we won't finish it.'

I me amisarem-ikomkun iinan aasa iinan-pa fan ekapemi paranem-yiomakek. I naap koora-pa ikemik, koora-pa ikemik.

Aria yena mua pun irakowa kererowa epa weeserem-ikeya iirariwkin owowa ekapok, o amia mua-pa ikok. Maakemik, "No ikiwe, irakowa maneka fanek a," ne ekapok. Ekapemi yo efa aawok. Yo efa aaweya i owawiya ikomkun Yaapan ena Wewak kame-pa nan iramik.

Ne i Emer Era-pa nan ikemik, ne oos onaiya Nemuru lul nan iram-ikemik. Iram-ikaiwkin yena mua Sarak-ke wia urufap maek, "Yaapan nanemik. Saa-iw iram-ikaimik, oos ono-onaiya iram-ikaimik."

Ne i owowa iramik. Owowa-pa fan yia maakemik, "Yaapan fan ikiwemik, oos onaiya Madang ikiwemik. Wi sawur nain irami fan yiar pokamik." Wi Yaapan nain naap wia maemik, "Sawur-ke fan ikiwemik."

Aria naap ikok i bauraremik. Muakura-ke maek, "Ikoka Yaapan-ke ekapemi ni emeria unowa fain nia aawurumikuan." I uura maa unowa opap baurarep koka ikiwemik. Iki(we)p kokapa nan inem-ikemik, ikoka Yaapan me yia aawuk naep. "Ni ikoka Yaapan-ke emeria niar aawemi ni umakuna nia puukikuan." I nain kema tootonep, ikoka Yaapan me yia aawuk naep uura kuisow bauraremik, maa unowa owowa-pa feeke ikaeya. Aakisa Malala suule ikua, i naap ikiwep yiena manina onamik nan ikemik. I miiwa nan arufam-ikemik, ne iki(we)p nan inemikemik. Emeria teeria unowiya baurarep koka ikiwurumemik, kuisow owowapa-ko me ikua. Mua muutiw owowa-pa ikemik. Mua kuisow, Muakura-ke i yia pikiwok. "Karueka, ikoka Yaapan irami ni nia aawemi yo efa ifakimikuan," naeya i karuem-ikemik.

Irakowa maneka ewur me imenarek, wi Yaapan naap kuisowiw ekapem-ikemik, owowa yiar kuufowa. Ekapep, ekapep, aakisa fan unowa Wewak-pa nan urupemik. Ne ekapep Numbia-pa nan urupemik. Maa unowa ifer aasa-ke purupeya miiw-aasa-ke fan piramikua. Yaapan feenap Madang kame ikiwemik. Ikoka Yaapan-ke i emeria yia aawurumikuan naeya, i amirika owowa ewur me ekapem-ikemik, Yaapan fan naap ekapemikaiwkin. Wi Yaapan emeria weetak, mua manekiw. Me fan Madang kamepa ekapemik, Wewak kame-pa fan naap iram-ikemik. Wilkar, miiw-aasa, Madang naap irakowa ikiwemikemik, wi Amerika wiamiya irakowa naep. I owowa-pa fan yiar ikemik.

Uura feenap nain, wi wilkar nain mufemi "Wensa, wensa, wensa", naap kirirem-ikemik. Wi owow muake wilkar wia mufem-ikomamik, mua kui-kuisow wia maakiwkin. "I wilkar yia mufomaka," naiwkin. Wi Malalake mufep ekapemi i Moro mua wia wuomamikomamik. Wilkar nain wiena maa koorma unowa ipariwkin wia mufem-ikomamik, feenap Madang pikiwem-ikemik, Australia wiamiya irakowa nain.

Nepa opaimika me baliwep amisarep wiena opaimikiw yia maakem-ikemik. Aria 'taro' yia naiwkin miimap maem-ikemik, "Wi moma yia maakimik, moma-ko wiiyen." "Banana mau oo, yasi kongkang," iwera yia iromaka, "banana mau oo yasi kongkang." Iwera "yasi" yia naem-ikemik. Naeya iwera wia urukam-ikomamik. Iwera urukam-ikaiwkin wi ikiwemi aawem-ikemik, iwera-ke wia arufeya maem-ikemik, "Oo kanaka oo, yasi paitim mi oo," naem-ikemik. I me wia amukaremik, wis pun naap, i me yia damolamik.

Ne eka opora biiris marew nain wiena onam-ikemik. Nemuru biiris onamik. Biiris me eliwa, damo-damola-ko. Dabuel poka-poka, nomokowa galua-galua, nainiw biiris onamikemik. Ikoka kuisow miiw-aasa-ke karueya ku-kuep orom-ikua. Ne uurika naap nain nainiw, mauwam-ikemik. Waaya yia naiwkin waaya wienakem-ikemik.

Aria naap ikok wi Australia kereremik. Ne wi Yaapan ikiwep Ulingan-pa owowa waremik. Ne nan wi owow mua wia maakemik, "Ni kanaka yia ufomaka." Naiwkin wia ufomamik. I Moro wenup ufemik, i bidaru ufemik. Ufem-ikaiwkin, Amerika irakow iinan aasa ekapep Ulingan nan bom fu-fuurik-ikiwemik. I iinan aasa me kuufamik. Iinaniw iinaniw wuami feenap Wewak kame naap ikiwok.

Ne Sarak opaimika wiar paayarek, siiwa, epa maakemik nain paayarep maek, "Amerika aakisa irakowa kereremik," naep wi Yaapan wia ufomowa ikiwemik nain wia maakek,

B.1 World War 2

"Ni ufowa ikiweka, yo miatiniyem. Irakowa maneka ikoka kererinon. Ni ufep-na ni maadara me iirareka, mokok urupa kaikiman nain feekiya Nomon owowa, Medebur karueka, baurareka."

Ne wi ikiwiwkin Amerika iinan aasa nainiw kirek. Iinaniw iki(we)p kiripap eneniw, eneniw wuak ne i fiker gone-pa ikemkun ekapok. Malala suule ikua nain, Siburten ema, oram tene-tenep orop epa iiwawun ifemakep ekapemik. Ne bomiya, kateresiya, bomiya, kateresiya. Koora pun ariwa-ke kuumeya awomakek, i koora kuisow yiar awok. Ne yena aamun ariwa-ke aawok, weepa Aduna ikos iimarep ikaiwkin, owow erepura-pa fan. Wi Amerika-ke waremik. Yena aamun unuma Saawoka.

I fiker gone-pa ikemkun kiikir iinan aasa-ke maifa fu-fuurk-ikiwok, wi Amerika-ke. Ulingan fa-na iinan aasa nepa saarik, unow akena. Wi Yaapan nan ikemik nain wia urufap. I karanemik, yena mua Sarak-na fiker gone nomokowa onoma-pa inep ikua. Ne yo iki(we)p mesa asia aawem-ikem, mesa asia fiker gone-pa ikaiya nain aawem-ikem. Ne iinan aasa urufap fiker tepak iwap naap ikem, ne iinan aasa yia nomakep ikiweya Sarak farem, "Sarak, yo damolalem oo, fiker fufa iwam oo!" "Mauwa aren, amiaiya nenaremik-i?" Sarak-ke. "Wia, nos-na, yo fiker fufa iwap nefa fariyem." "Momora, no naap me mae. Nefa wariwkin naap mae. Yo kema efa bagiwirowan, yaa." Yo me efa waremik, yo iinan aasa fan orom-ikomakeya mesa fufa-pa fan erewarep iima ifemakep ikem.

Irakowa nain kekanowa akena, Amerika kererek nain, ne irakowa naap ikua. Uura feenap nain, i me inem-ikemik, amirika maa me enem-ikemik. Maa uura uupep enem-ikemik. Ikoka epia wilinowa urufap bom yia fuurkomikuan naep. Iinan aasa gurunowa miimap ekaiw umukowa ewur. Epia wilinowa urufap bom yia wafuromikuan naep naap onam-ikemik. I Sarak ikos owowa ekapem-ikemik. Yiena koora pun me awok.

Wi yapen-pa ikomakiwkin Amerika kererep "Eliwa, eliwa" nae-ekapemik, "irakowa weeserek." Wi Yaapan pun iiwawun ikiwurumemik. Wi Yaapan Madang kame ikiwiwkin Amerika irakowa mua urupemik. Urupep koka-koka-pa nan, "Yapen oo, Luluai, Tultul, ni kaaneke ikeman oo, ni ekapomakeka oo!" Wi Amerika fan "Epa eliwa" nae-ekapemik, "Yaapan weeseremik." Naap yia maake-miawemik.

I amirikiw yapen yiena Gawar wiar ikiwemik. Ne Sarak ikos Gawar-pa ikemkun yia maakemik, "Sarak oo, Amerika ekapep Ulingan nan ikemik, nefa ikumimik naimik oo." "Aria, Kalina, Amerika ekapemik naimik. I oru".

Aria i yapen-pa ikok owowa oromik. Oromi yo koka koora-pa nan efa wuami maek, "No feeke ike, yo Amerika wia akup-ikiwiyem."

Aria yo nan efa wuap-puami o Ulingan ikiwok. Ikiwok-na wi Amerika maneka unuma Magerka, o kererep nan ikua. O ikip urufeya maakek, "O Sarak, no kaaneke ikok kereren a? "Yo koka-pa ikem." Naeya Magerkake, "No kamenap ikon noma? Yo irakowa nomakem. Nomakep fan kererem." "Yo bom yo kateres koor miira-pa efar orom-ikua. Nain yo me baurarem-ikem. I iinan aasa ekapem-ikaeya uruwa ainep orop yena koor miira-pa iimarep ikem, yena emeria sosora ainep orop koor miira-pa iimarem-ikua. Ne i me yiaremik, Amerika iinan aasa ekapem-ikua nain. Amina, woowa, eka napia koor miirapa iimaraw-ikiwemik, yena emeria ikos, ne wi unowa bauraremik. I iisow naap ikemkun Amerika kereremik." "Ni yapen koka-kokapa wiar inem-ikeman nain kereromakeka."

Amerika fan ekapep Uliganpa manua maneka urupep irakow(a) mua wia wueya nan ikemik. Palauwa tin, maa eneka kes mane-maneka fa, oram iwemik, Sarak iwemik. "No fain wiimep amapikiwe." O wi Laman, Malager naap wia maakek, "Arika, takira, yo yookeka." Amerika kereremik naeya ikiwep-ko wia urufikua. O Ulingan ikiweya bom iwemik. "No bom fainiw mera kuume," naakemik. Maa enowa iwemik, palauwa dram, bata tin naap nain, ne rais weetak.

Ne irakowa weesereya i owowa oromik. Irakowa fa, opaimika eeya akena yaa, kamenap aakuniyen yaa? Aakuniyen, aakuniyen, me pepek, me welawiyen.

B.2 Uncle Tup

by Saror Aduna

(131) *Yo   yena yaiya Tup ifa   ku-o-k   nain opaimika ma-i-yem.*
1s.UNM 1s.GEN uncle Tup snake bite-PA-3s that1 talk   say-Np-PR.1s

'I tell a story about that when my uncle Tup was bitten by a snake.'

(132) *Ae, o   fiker   gone   urup-o-k.*
yes 3s.UNM kunai.grass middle ascend-PA-3s

'Yes, he went up to the middle of the kunai grass (area).'

(133) *Fikera   aw-em-ik-eya   nain umuk-i-nen   na-ep*
kunai.grass burn-SS.SIM-be-2/3s.DS that1 extinguish-Np-FU.1s say-SS.SEQ
urup-o-k.
ascend-PA-3s

'The kunai grass was burning and he went up to extinguish it.'

(134) *Urup-ep   ek-a-k.*
ascend-SS.SEQ go.eastwards-PA-3s

'He went up and eastwards.'

(135) *Ek-ap   umuk-i-nen   na-ep   on-am-ik-eya*
go.eastwards-SS.SEQ extinguish-Np-FU.1s say-SS.SEQ do-SS.SIM-be-2/3s.DS
ifa=ke   keraw-a-k, mamepaperuma gele-gelemuti-tik nain=ke.
snake-CF bite-PA-3s death.adder   RDP-small-RDP   that1-CF

'He went eastwards and when he was trying to extinguish the fire a snake bit him, the very small death adder.'

(136) *Keraw-eya, aria   nomokowa gelemuta puuk-ap   ifa   makena nain*
bite-2/3s.DS alright tree   small   cut-SS.SEQ snake being that1
ifakim-o-k.
kill-PA-3s.

'It bit him, and he cut a small tree and killed the snake.'

(137) *Ifakim-ep, nomokowa ekeka=pa sererim-ep-pu-a-k.*
kill-ss.SEQ tree branch-LOC hang-ss.SEQ-CMPL-PA-3s
'He killed it and hung it on a tree branch.'

(138) *Sererim-ep-pu-ap or-o-k, owowa or-o-k.*
hang-ss.SEQ-CMPL-ss.SEQ descend-PA-3s village descend-PA-3s
'He hung it and came down, he came down to the village.'

(139) *Owowa or-op, wuailal-ep, akia ik-e-k.*
village descend-ss.SEQ hunger-ss.SEQ banana roast-PA-3s
'He came down to the village and was hungry and roasted bananas.'

(140) *Akia ik-ep en-em-ik-ok, ifa marasin nain=ke kema wiar*
banana roast-ss.SEQ eat-ss.SIM-be-ss snake medicine that1-CF liver 3.DAT
iw-a-k.
enter-PA-3s
'He roasted bananas and when he was eating them the snake poison entered his liver.'

(141) *Iw-aya nan miira saawirin-e-k.*
enter-2/3s.DS there face become.round-PA-3s
'It entered his liver and he felt dizzy there.'

(142) *Ne auwa ame wia maak-eya res aaw-ep merena ifa*
ADD 1s/p.father ASS 3p.ACC tell-2/3s.DS razor take-ss.SEQ leg snake
keraw-a-k nain puuk-a-mik.
bite-PA-3s that1 cut-PA-1/3p
'And when he told my father and others, they took a razor and made a cut into the leg that the snake had bitten.'

(143) *Puuk-ap marasin wu-om-a-mik.*
cut-ss.SEQ medicine put-BEN-BNFY2.PA-1/3p
'They made a cut and put medicine into it.'

(144) *Marasin wu-om-a-mik na weetak.*
medicine put-BEN-BNFY2.PA-1/3p TP no
'They put medicine but no (it didn't help).'

(145) *Iiriw ifa marasin=ke kekan-e-k.*
earlier snake medicine-CF be.strong-PA-3s
'The snake poison was already strong.'

(146) *Ne akia ik-e-k nain me en-e-k.*
ADD banana roast-PA-3s that1 not eat-PA-3s
'And he didn't eat the bananas that he roasted.'

(147) *Nan mukuna=pa ik-eya o nan samor aaw-o-k.*
There fire-LOC be-2/3s.DS 3s.UNM there badly get-PA-3s
'They were there on the fire and he really got bad there.'

(148) *Miira saawirin-e-k.*
face become.round-PA-3s
'He felt dizzy.'

(149) *Ne wi emeria papako wia maak-e-k, "Ni ifa nia*
ADD 3p.UNM woman some 3p.ACC tell-PA-3s 2p.UNM snake 2p.ACC
keraw-i-ya nain sira kamenap on-i-man?"
bite-Np-PR.3s that1 custom what.like do-Np-PR.2p
'And he asked some women, "When a snake bites you, what do you do?" '

(150) *Ne maak-e-mik, "Ifa yia keraw-i-ya nain miira*
ADD tell-PA-1/3p snake 1p.ACC bite-Np-PR.3s that1 face
saawirin-i-mik, ookakim-i-nan."
become.round-Np-PR.1/3p vomit-Np-FU.2s
'And the told him, "When a snake bites us, we feel dizzy, you will vomit.'

(151) *Naap maak-iwkin naap ik-ua.*
Thus tell-2/3p.DS thus be-PA.3s
'They told him like that and he was like that.'

(152) *Naap ik-ok uruf-am-ika-iwkin wia.*
thus be-ss see-ss.SIM-be-2/3p.DS no
'He was like that and they watched him but no (he didn't get better.)'

(153) *Epa naap kokom-ar-eya o lawisiw samor aaw-o-k.*
place thus dark-INCH-2/3s.DS 3s.UNM somewhat badly get-PA-3s
'When it got dark he became worse.'

(154) *Ne haussik p-ek-u na-ep miiw-aasa nop-a-mik.*
ADD aidpost Bpx-go-IMP.1d say-ss.SEQ land-canoe search-PA-1/3p
'And they looked for a vehicle to take him to the aidpost.'

(155) *Miiw-aasa nop-ap, iiriw Naawura miiw-aasa awona nain wiar*
land-canoe search-ss.SEQ earlier Naawura land-canoe old that1 3.DAT
aaw-e-mik.
get-PA-1/3p
'They looked for a vehicle and got Naawura's earlier old vehicle/truck.'

(156) *Aaw-ep p-ikiw-e-mik, haussik.*
get-ss.SEQ Bpx-go-PA-1/3p aidpost
'They got it and took him to the aidpost.'

(157) *Saapara p-ek-ap, Saapara=pa neeke ikemika kaik-ow(a) mua pun*
Saapara Bpx-go-SS.SEQ Saapara-LOC there.CF wound tie-NMZ man also
iiriw ona owowa Medebur ek-a-k.
earlier 3s.UNM village Medebur go-PA-3s
'They took him to Saapara, and there in Saapara (they found that) the health officer too had already gone to his village, Medebur.'

(158) *Ne kiiriw nan Medebur ek-a-mik, mua napuma onaiya.*
ADD again there Medebur go-PA-1/3p man sick with
'And again from there they went to Medebur, with the sick man.'

(159) *Ek-ap Medebur=pa neeke ikemika kaik-owa mua nain nop-a-mik,*
go-SS.SEQ Medebur-LOC there.CF wound tie-NMZ man that1 search-PA-1/3p
imen-ap maak-iwkin o miim-o-k.
find-SS.SEQ tell-2/3p.DS 3s.UNM precede-PA-3s
'They went and there in Medebur they searched for the health officer, and when they found him and told him he went ahead of them (to the aidpost).'

(160) *Aria, wi kiiriw neeke miiw-aasa um-o-k.*
alright 3p.UNM again there.CF land-canoe die-PA-3s
'Alright, again when they were there the truck broke down.'

(161) *Miiw-aasa ume-ya miiw-aasa nain on-am-ikai-wkin epa*
land-canoe die-2/3s.DS land-canoe that1 do-SS.SIM-be-2/3p.DS place
kokom-ar-e-k, epa iimeka tuun-e-k.
dark-INCH-PA-3s place/time ten count-PA-3s
'The truck broke down and while they were working on the truck it became dark, it became past midnight.'

(162) *Ne kiiriw miiw-aasa nan ik-eya mua nain nabena suuw-a-mik.*
ADD again land-canoe there be-2/3s.DS man that1 carrying.pole push-PA-1/3p
'And again the truck stayed there and they carried the man on a carrying pole.'

(163) *Nabena suuw-ap ep-ap, Saapara=pa Ø.*
carrying.pole push-SS.SEQ go-SS.SEQ Saapara-LOC
'They carried him on a carrying pole, went (and arrived) at Saapara.'

(164) *Saapara=pa nan suusa iw-e-mik, wiena ifa suusa nain.*
Saapara-LOC there needle give.him-PA-1/3p 3p.GEN snake needle that1
'There in Saapara they gave him an injection, that snake injection of theirs.'

(165) *Nain iw-iwkin, weetak, me pepek.*
that1 give.him-2/3p.DS no not enough/able
'They gave him that but no, it was not enough.'

(166) *O   iiwawun samor aaw-o-k.*
3s.UNM altogether badly get-PA-3s

'He got really bad.'

(167) *Ne nan ik-e-mik.*
ADD there be-PA-1/3p

'And they stayed there.'

(168) *Nan ik-ok ik-ok neeke   pu-o-k.*
there be-SS be-SS there.CF die-PA-3s

'They stayed and stayed there and there he died.'

(169) *Neeke   pu-eya   oram akua   aaw-e-mik.*
there.CF die-2/3s.DS just shoulder take-PA-1/3p

'There he died and they just carried him on their shouders.'

(170) *Miiw-aasa samor-ar-e-k.*
land-canoe bad-INCH-PA-3s

'The truck broke/was broken.'

(171) *Miiw-aasa samor-ar-eya   oram akua   aaw-ep   ekap-e-mik.*
land-canoe bad-INCH-2/3s.DS just shoulder take-SS.SEQ come-PA-1/3p

'The truck was broken and they just carried him on their shoulders and came.'

(172) *Akua   aaw-ep   ekap-em-ika-iwkin   senam   pin-ar-e-k.*
shoulder take-SS.SEQ come-SS.SIM-be-2/3p.DS too.much heavy-INCH-PA-3s

'They carried him on their shoulders and as they were coming he got very heavy.'

(173) *Pin-ar-eya   aria   Kuten   ame=ke miim-e-mik.*
heavy-INCH-2/3s.DS alright Kuuten ASS-CF precede-PA-1/3p

'He got heavy and so Kuuten and (some) others walked ahead.'

(174) *Miim-ep   ekap-ep   owow   mua wia   maak-e-mik.*
precede-SS.SEQ come-SS.SEQ village man 3p.ACC tell-PA-1/3p

'They came ahead and told the village people.'

(175) *Ne owow   mua wia   aaw-ep   kiiriw kir-e-mik.*
ADD village man 3p.ACC get-SS.SEQ again turn-PA-1/3p

'And they got village men and turned back again.'

(176) *Kir-ep   ek-ap   nabena   suuw-ap ep-am-ika-iwkin,   miiw-aasa*
turn-SS.SEQ go-SS.SEQ carrying.pole push   come-SS.SIM-be-2/3p.DS land-canoe
oko,   wi   Manub miiw-aasa Ø.
other 3p.UNM Manub land-canoe

'They turned and went and as they were coming carrying him, another truck, Manub village truck (took them).'

(177) *Miiw-aasa awona nain miiw-aasa fa-owa mua=ke neeke wia*
land-canoe old that1 land-canoe drive-NMZ man-CF there.CF 3p.ACC
aaw-o-k.
take-PA-3s

'The driver of that old truck took them from there.'

(178) *Neeke wia aaw-ep ep-a-mik.*
there.CF 3p.ACC take-SS.SEQ come-PA-1/3p

'He took them from there and they came.'

(179) *Ep-ap ona koora=pa in-aw-ap naap arew-ap pok-ap*
come-SS.SEQ 3s.GEN house-LOC sleep-APPL-SS.SEQ thus wait-SS.SEQ sit-SS.SEQ
ik-e-mik.
be-PA-1/3p

'They came and laid him in his house and they/we sat and waited like that.'

(180) *Pok-ap ik-omkun epa wiim-o-k.*
sit-SS.SEQ be-1s/p.DS place dawn-PA-3s

'As we were waiting it dawned.'

(181) *Epa wiim-eya mua karer-omak-e-mik.*
place dawn-2/3s.DS man gather-DISTR/PL-PA-1/3p

'After it dawned many people gathered.'

(182) *Karer-ap ma-e-mik, mua iperowa=ke ma-e-mik, "I feeke me*
gather-SS.SEQ say-PA-1/3p man middle.aged-CF say-PA-1/3p 1p.UNM here.CF not
soop-i-yen, ona owowa p-ikiw-i-yan.
bury-Np-FU.1p 3s.GEN village Bpx-go-Np-FU.1p

'They gathered and said - the middle-aged men/elders said, "We will not bury him here, we'll take him to his own village." '

(183) *Ne wia, papako=ke ma-e-mik, "Weetak, moram owowa p-ikiw-i-yan?*
ADD no some-CF say-PA-1/3p no why village Bpx-go-FU.1p

'But no, others said, "No, why take him to his village?'

(184) *Yiena miiwa kuisow, eliw feeke soop-i-yen."*
1p.GEN land one well here.CF bury-Np-FU.1p

'Our land is one, we can well bury him here." '

(185) *Ne wia. Iperowa=ke senam kekan-e-mik.*
ADD no middle.aged-CF too.much be.strong-PA-1/3p

'But no. The elders insisted.'

(186) *Kekan-iwkin   ma-e-mik, "Aria, iperowa   opora wia*
be.strong-2/3p.DS say-PA-1/3p alright middle.aged talk 3p.ACC
ook-i-yen.
follow-Np-FU.1p

'They insisted and we said, "Alright, we'll follow the talk of the elders.'

(187) *Ona   owowa p-ikiw-i-yan."*
3s.GEN village Bpx-go-Np-FU.1p

'We'll take him to his village." '

(188) *Malala miiw-aasa wia   maak-e-mik.*
Malala land-canoe 3p.ACC tell-PA-1/3p

'We talked to the owners of the Malala truck.'

(189) *Miiw-aasa wia   maak-ep, ekap-eya,   kes   on-om-a-mik.*
land-canoe 3p.ACC tell-SS.SEQ come-2/3s.DS coffin make-BEN-BNFY2.PA-1/3p

'We talked to them about the truck and when it came we made a coffin for him.'

(190) *Kes   tepak=pa wu-ap   p-ikiw-e-mik.*
coffin inside-LOC put-SS.SEQ Bpx-go-PA-1/3p

'We put him inside the coffin and took him (away).'

(191) *P-ikiw-ep   Bogia=pa nan wu-a-mik.*
Bpx-go-SS.SEQ Bogia-LOC there put-PA-1/3p

'We took him and buried him in Bogia.'

(192) *Bogia=pa nan wu-ap   i   kiiriw ekap-e-mik.*
bogia-LOC there put-SS.SEQ 1p.UNM again come-PA-1/3p

'We buried him in Bogia and came back again.'

(193) *Ekap-ep   uura owowa kerer-e-mik.*
come-SS.SEQ night village arrive-PA-1/3p

'We came and arrived in the village at night.'

(194) *Opora nain muut naap, weeser-e-k.*
talk that1 only thus finish-PA-3s

'The talk/story is just like that, (it is) finished.'

Yo yena yaiya Tup ifa kuok nain opaimika maiyem.
Ae, o fiker gone urupok. Fikera awem-ikeya nain umukinen naep urupok. Urupep ekak. Ekap umukinen naep onam-ikeya ifa-ke kerawak, mamepaperuma gele-gelemutitik nain-ke. Keraweya, aria nomokowa gelemuta puukap ifa makena nain ifakimok. Ifakimep, nomokowa ekeka-pa sererimep-puak. Sererimep-puap orok, owowa orok. Owowa orop,

wuailalep, akia ikek. Akia ikep enem-ikok, ifa marasin nain-ke kema wiar iwak. Iwaya nan miira saawirinek.

Ne auwa ame wia maakeya res aawep merena ifa kerawak nain puukamik. Puukap marasin wuomamik. Marasin wuomamik na weetak. Iiriw ifa marasin-ke kekanek. Ne akia ikek nain me enek.

Nan mukuna-pa ikeya o nan samor aawok. Miira saawirinek. Ne wi emeria papako wia maakek, "Ni ifa nia kerawiya nain sira kamenap oniman?" Ne maakemik, "Ifa yia kerawiya nain miira saawirinimik, ookakiminan." Naap maakiwkin naap ikua. Naap ikok urufam-ikaiwkin wia.

Epa naap kokomareya o lawisiw samor aawok. Ne haussik peku naep miiw-aasa nopamik. Miiwaasa nopap, iiriw Naawura miiwaasa awona nain wiar aawemik. Aawep pikiwemik, haussik. Saapara pekap, Saapara-pa neeke ikemika kaikow(a) mua pun iiriw ona owowa Medebur ekak.

Ne kiiriw nan Medebur ekamik, mua napuma onaiya. Ekap Medebur-pa neeke ikemika kaikowa mua nain nopamik, imenap maakiwkin o miimok.

Aria, wi kiiriw neeke miiw-aasa umok. Miiwaasa umeya miiw-aasa nain onam-ikaiwkin epa kokomarek, epa iimeka tuunek. Ne kiiriw miiw-aasa nan ikeya mua nain nabena suuwamik. Nabena suuwap epap, Saapara-pa. Saapara-pa nan suusa iwemik, wiena ifa suusa nain. Nain iwiwkin, weetak, me pepek.

O iiwawun samor aawok. Ne nan ikemik. Nan ikok ikok neeke puok. Neeke pueya oram akua aawemik. Miiw-aasa samorarek. Miiw-aasa samorareya oram akua aawep ekapemik. Akua aawep ekapem-ikaiwkin senam pinarek. Pinareya aria Kuten ame-ke miimemik. Miimep ekapep owow mua wia maakemik.

Ne owow mua wia aawep kiiriw kiremik. Kirep ekap nabena suuwap epam-ikaiwkin, miiw-aasa oko, wi Manub miiw-aasa. Miiw-aasa awona nain miiw-aasa faowa muake neeke wia aawok. Neeke wia aawep epamik. Epap ona koorapa inawap naap arewap pokap ikemik. Pokap ikomkun epa wiimok. Epa wiimeya mua kareromakemik. Karerap maemik, mua iperowa-ke maemik, "I feeke me soopiyen, ona owowa pikiwiyan."

Ne wia, papako-ke maemik, "Weetak, moram owowa pikiwiyan? Yiena miiwa kuisow, eliw feeke soopiyen." Ne wia. Iperowa-ke senam kekanemik. Kekaniwkin maemik, "Aria, iperowa opora wia ookiyen. Ona owowa pikiwiyan."

Malala miiw-aasa wia maakemik. Miiw-aasa wia maakep, ekapeya, kes onomamik. Kes tepak-pa wuap pikiwemik. Pikiwep Bogia-pa nan wuamik. Bogia-pa nan wuap i kiiriw ekapemik. Ekapep uura owowa kereremik. Opora nain muut naap, weeserek.

B.3 Catching a turtle

by Kuuten

(195) *Yo aakisa opaimika=ko ma-i-nen, pon aaw-e-m nain.*
1s.UNM now speech-IF say-Np-FU.1s, turtle get-PA-1s that1
'I will now tell a story about that when I caught a turtle.'

(196) Yo   uura arua isim-ap   aasa=pa   karue-miaw-ik-ok pon
1s.UNM night lantern light-ss.SEQ canoe-LOC run-wander-be-ss turtle
sisina=pa   ik-eya, piipa unowa=pa   soomar-em-ik-eya
shallow.water-LOC be-2/3s.DS seaweed many-LOC walk-ss.SIM-be-2/3s.DS
mik-a-m.
spear-PA-1s

'At night I lighted a lantern and was paddling in the canoe and I saw a turtle in the shallow water, walking among a lot of seaweed, and I speared it.'

(197) Mik-ap,   patot=iw   mik-ap,   aaw-ep,   aasa=pa   wu-ap,
spear-ss.SEQ fishing.spear-INST spear-ss.SEQ take-ss.SEQ canoe-LOC put-ss.SEQ
amap-urup-ep,   yena   koora=pa   wu-ap,   uuriw   epa   wiim-eya
Bpx-ascend-ss.SEQ 1s.GEN house-LOC put-ss.SEQ morning place dawn-2/3s.DS
or-op,   saa=pa   pa-ep   uup-e-mik.
descend-ss.SEQ beach-LOC butcher-ss.SEQ cook-PA-1/3p

'I speared it, speared it with a fishing spear, took it, put it in the canoe, brought it up (to the beach), put it in my house, (and) in the morning when it dawned went down and butchered it on the beach and we cooked it.'

(198) Uup-ep   weeser-eya,   aria   oposia gelemuta wiam erup fain wia
cook-ss.SEQ finish-2/3s.DS alright meat little   3p.REFL two this 3p.ACC
wu-om-a-m.
put-BEN-BNFY2.PA-1s

'When the cooking was finished, alright I put a little (aside) for these two (women).'

(199) En-ep   uruf-ap   efa   maak-e-mik, "No   opaimika pon   aaw-o-n nain
eat-ss.SEQ see-ss.SEQ 1s.ACC tell-PA-1/3p 2s.UNM speech   turtle get-PA-2s that1
ma-eya   i   miim-i-yen.
say-2/3s.DS 1p.UNM hear-Np-FU.1p

'They ate and saw (what it was like) and told me, "Tell us the story of how you you caught the turtle, and we'll listen." '

(200) Ne   yo   aakisa tep=pa   ma-i-yem.
ADD 1s.UNM now   tape.recorder-LOC speak-Np-PR.1s

'And now I speak it on a tape recorder.'

(201) En-e-mik   na   ma-e-mik,   "Eliwa, aara   oposia saarik."
eat-PA-1/3p and(TP) say-PA-1/3p good   chicken meat   like

'They ate it and said, "(It is) good, like chicken meat." '

(202) Ne   yo   efa   maak-iwkin   yo   aakisa tep=pa   ma-e-m.
ADD 1s.UNM 1s.ACC tell-2/3p.DS 1s.UNM now   tape.recorder-LOC speak-PA-1s

'And they told me and now I spoke it on a taperecorder.'

(203) *Yo   opaimika muut nan-e-k.*
      1s.UNM speech   only be.there-PA-3s
      'My speech is there.'

Yo aakisa opaimika-ko mainen, pon aawem nain. Yo uura arua isimap aasapa karue-miawikok pon sisina-pa ikeya, piipa unowa-pa soomarem-ikeya mikam. Mikap, patotiw mikap, aawep, aasa-pa wuap, amapurupep, yena koora-pa wuap, uuriw epa wiimeya orop, saa-pa paep uupemik. Uupep weesereya, aria oposia gelemuta wiam erup fain wia wuomam. Enep urufap efa maakemik, "No opaimika pon aawon nain maeya i miimiyen. Ne yo aakisa tep-pa maiyem. Enemik na maemik, "Eliwa, aara oposia saarik." Ne yo efa maakiwkin yo aakisa tep-pa maem. Yo opaimika muut nanek.

B.4 Fishing customs

by Saror Aduna

(204) *Mera aaw-owa sira   e era wapen in-aw-i-ya   okaiwi=pa*
      fish get-NMZ custom or way hand sleep-APPL-Np-PR.3s other.side-LOC
      kuisow.
      one
      'There are six ways to do fishing.'

(205) *Kaul=iw   aaw-i-mik,   arua karu-i-mik,   maer   puuk-i-mik,*
      hook-INST get-Np-PR.1/3p torch run-Np-PR.1/3p surface cut-Np-PR.1/3p
      patopat=iw   mera urum-i-mik,   oko   galasim-i-mik.
      fishing.spear-INST fish watch-Np-PR.1/3p other dive.with.goggles-Np-PR.1/3p
      'They (or: we) catch them with hooks, fish with torches, hit the surface, search the fish with fishing spears and dive with goggles.'

(206) *Oko   soo.*
      other fishtrap
      'Another (way) is a fishtrap.'

(207) *Soo   nain feenap: era erup ik-ua.*
      fishtrap that1 like.this way two be-PA.3s
      'Fishtrap is like this: there are two ways.'

(208) *Oko   sisina=pa   ifemak-i-mik,   oko   malol=pa   ifemak-i-mik.*
      other shallow.water-LOC press-Np-PR.1/3p other deep.sea-LOC press-Np-PR.1/3p
      'One is that they let it down in the shallow water, the other is that they let it down in the deep sea.'

(209) *Ne sisina   nain me yoowa akena.*
      ADD shallow.water that1 not hard very
      '(Letting it down in) the shallow water is not very hard.'

(210) *Oo malol lawisiw yoowa.*
INTJ deep.sea a.little hard
'Oh the deep sea is a bit hard.'

(211) *Sisina nain, soo ika on-i-nan, soo ika=pa kaik-ap*
shallow.water that1 fishtrap stand make-Np-FU.2s fishtrap stand-LOC tie-SS.SEQ
otal opora=pa ifemak-i-nan.
reef mouth-LOC press-Np-FU.2s
'As for the shallow water (style), you make a stand for the fistrap, tie the trap to the stand and let it down at the mouth of the reef.'

(212) *Ifemak-ep nomona iinan=pa wua-i-nan, ikoka ifera me p-ikiw-owa nain.*
press-SS.SEQ stone on.top-LOC put-Np-FU.2s later sea not Bpx-go-NMZ that1
'You let it down and then put stones on top of it, so that later the sea won't take it away.'

(213) *Soo nain ona malin saana=pa ifemak-i-mik.*
fishtrap that1 3s.GEN calm season-LOC press-Np-PR.1/3p
'The fishtrap is let down during the calm season.'

(214) *Oo ifera ku-owa epa=pa weetak.*
INTJ sea break-NMZ time-LOC no
'Not during the stormy time.'

(215) *Aria malol=pa ifemak-i-mik nain aana puuk-i-mik, makera*
alright deep.sea-LOC press-Np-PR.1/3p that1 cane cut-Np-PR.1/3p makera.cane
unowa puuk-ap makera nain anetir-i-mik.
many cut-SS.SEQ cane that1 tie-Np-PR.1/3p
'Alright the one that is let down in the deep sea (is like this), they cut cane, and after cutting a lot of *makera* cane, tie the canes (making a long rope).'

(216) *Anetir-ikiw-ep uruf-i-mik, makera nain maaya pepek.*
tie-go-SS.SEQ see-Np-PR.1/3p cane that1 long enough
'They keep tying them and then see that the cane is long enough.'

(217) *Aria makera miirifa okaiwi soo=pa kaik-i-mik, okaiwi pia*
alright cane end other.side fishtrap-LOC tie-Np-PR.1/3p other.side bamboo
kaik-i-mik, piakina na-i-mik nain.
tie-Np-PR.1/3p piakina say-Np-PR.1/3p RM
'Alright one end of the cane is tied to the trap, to the other end they tie a (piece of) bamboo called *piakina*.'

(218) *Ne soo ifemak-owa epa=pa aasa suuw-i-mik.*
ADD fishtrap press-NMZ time-LOC canoe push-Np-PR.1/3p
'And at the time of letting the trap down they push the canoe out.'

B.4 Fishing customs

(219) *Aasa suuw-ap soo aasa iinan=pa wu-ap p-ora-i-mik.*
canoe push-ss.SEQ fishtrap canoe top-LOC put-ss.SEQ Bpx-descend-Np-PR.1/3p
'They push the canoe out and put the trap on top of the canoe and take it down (to the sea).'

(220) *Or-op malol=pa soo nain fuurk-i-mik.*
descend-ss.SEQ deep.sea-LOC fishtrap that1 throw-Np-PR.1/3p
'They go down and at the deep sea they throw the fishtrap down.'

(221) *Fuurk-ap makera nain op-ap ika-i-kuan.*
throw-ss.SEQ cane that1 hold-ss.SEQ be-Np-FU-3p
'They throw it and hold on to the cane.'

(222) *Op-ap lawiliw piipu-am-ika-i-kuan.*
hold-ss.SEQ a.little leave-ss.SIM-be-Np-FU.3p
'They hold it and let go a little.'

(223) *Or-op saa=pa pok-aya wi piipua-i-kuan.*
descend-ss.SEQ sand-LOC sit-2/3s.DS 3p.UNM leave-Np-FU.3p
'When it has gone down and sits on the sand they will let go of it.'

(224) *Ne soo nainiw muf-owa pun naap, aana=pa neeke mufimik.*
ADD fishtrap again pull-NMZ also thus cane-LOC there.CF pull-Np-PR-1/3p
'And the pulling (up) of the fishtrap is like that too, it is pulled by the cane there.'

(225) *Aana=pa neeke muf-ep, p-urup-ep aasa=pa wua-i-mik.*
cane-LOC there.CF pull-ss.SEQ Bpx-ascend-ss.SEQ canoe-LOC put-Np-PR.1/3p
'They pull it by the cane there, bring it up and put it in the canoe.'

(226) *Aasa=pa wu-ap, mera aaw-ep weeser-eya nainiw fuurk-i-mik.*
canoe-LOC put-ss.SEQ fish get-ss.SEQ finish-2/3s.DS again throw-Np-PR.1/3p
'They put it in the canoe, get the fish and when that is finished they throw it down again.'

(227) *Nain soo era=ke.*
that1 fishtrap way-CF
'That is the fishtrap way.'

(228) *Aria maer pun naap.*
alright surface also thus
'Alright (hitting the surface) is like that too.'

(229) *Wi emeria kaalal-i-mik, kaalal-ep or-op otal=pa maer*
3p.UNM woman wade-Np-PR.1/3p wade-SS.SEQ descend-SS.SEQ reef-LOC surface
ar-i-mik.
become-Np-PR.1/3p

'The women wade, they wade down and at the reef they start the surface-hitting.'

(230) *Maer ar-ep urup-ep urup-ep, pona.*
surface become-SS.SEQ ascend-SS.SEQ ascend-SS.SEQ shore

'They start hitting the surface and keep coming up towards the shore.'

(231) *Pona=pa neeke mera nomona ona iw-omak-eya, wi wapen=iw*
shore-LOC there.CF fish reef hole enter-DISTR/PL-2/3s.DS 3p.UNM hand-INST
ona nain suuw-i-mik.
hole that1 push-Np-PR.1/3p

'When they have reached the shore, a lot of fish have entered holes in the reef and they (the women) push their hands in the holes (and pull the fish out).'

(232) *Ne mua patopat aaw-ep saa=pa iimar-ep ika-i-kuan.*
ADD man fishing.spear take-SS.SEQ sand-LOC stand.up-SS.SEQ be-Np-FU.3p

'And the men will take the fishing spears and be standing on the beach.'

(233) *Mera sisina urup-eya patopat=iw mik-i-kuan.*
fish shallow.water ascend-2/3s.DS fishing.spear-INST spear-Np-FU.3p

'When the fish comes up to the shallow water they will spear it with a fishing spear.'

(234) *Ne oko galasim-owa.*
ADD other dive.with.goggles-NMZ

'And another (way) is diving with goggles.'

(235) *Nain iiriw me kerer-e-k, aakisa fan.*
that1 earlier not appear-PA-3s now here.

'That didn't come up in the old days, (but) just recently.'

(236) *Wiena galasim-owa amia on-i-mik, on-ap*
3p.GEN dive.with.goggles-NMZ gun make-Np-PR.1/3p make-SS.SEQ
galasim-i-mik.
dive.with.goggles-Np-PR.1/3p

'They make their own fishing guns, and having made them they fish diving with goggles.'

(237) *Ne oko, mera urum-i-mik, patopat=iw.*
ADD other fish search-Np-PR.1/3p fishing.spear-INST

'And another (way): they watch for fish (and spear them) with a fishing spear.'

(238) *Nain ona   mua taraka   nain=ke mera mik-i-nan,   patopat*
that1 3s.GEN man accuracy that-CF fish spear-Np-FU.2s fishing.spear
opo-wa   nain.
hold-NMZ that1.
'If you are an accurate man, you will spear the fish, (accurate in) holding the spear.'

(239) *O   mua naap nain ikoka ufer-i-nan.*
3s.UNM man thus that1 later miss-Np-FU.2s
'A man with poor aim (literally: so-so) will miss.'

(240) *Ne oko, afukar-i-mik.*
ADD other fish.with.torch-Np-PR.1/3p
'And another (way): they do torch-fishing.'

(241) *Parina isim-ap   afukar-i-mik.*
lamp light-ss.SEQ fish.with.torch-Np-PR.1/3p
'They light lamps and do torch-fishing.'

(242) *Parina isim-ap   afukar-ep,   nain ona   kak   saana=pa.*
lamp light-ss.SEQ fish.with.torch-ss.SEQ that1 3s.GEN flying.fish season-LOC
'They light lamps and do torch-fishing and – that (takes place) in the flying fish season.'

(243) *Kak   saana=pa wi   parina isim-ap   or-op   kak*
flying.fish season-LOC 3p.UNM lamp light-ss.SEQ descend-ss.SEQ flying.fish
isak-i-mik.
spear-Np-PR.1/3p
'In the flying fish season they light lamps and go down (to the sea) and spear flying fish.'

(244) *Kak,   pirit,   mera papako.*
Flying.fish longtom fish other
'Flying fish, longtom and other fish.'

(245) *Tokol   gelemutitik, kookari, nain isak-i-mik.*
dussumier's.garfish, small-RDP fish.sp that1 spear-Np-PR.3p
'They spear small dussumier's garfish, *kookari* fish, (all) those.'

(246) *Ne kak   saana=pa kak   ora-i-mik,   ne parina ona*
ADD flying.fish season-LOC flying.fish descend-Np-PR.3p ADD lamp 3s.GEN
wakesim-owa onaiya ika-i-ya.
cover-NMZ with   be-Np-PR.3s
'And in the flying fish season they go down for flying fish, and the lamp has a covering.'

(247) *Ikoka wakesim-eya mera mamaiya ekap-i-non,   aasa   mamaiya.*
later cover-2/3s.DS fish close   come-Np-FU.3s canoe close

'Later when you cover it the fish will come close, close to the canoe.'

(248) *Aasa   mamaiya ekap-eya   aria   parina kiiriw mauwa on-e.*
canoe close   come-2/3s.DS alright lamp   again what   do-IMP.2s

'When they come close to the canoe, then again do what (reveal the lamp).'

(249) *Mauwa on-ap   mera isak-e.*
what   do-SS.SEQ fish spear-IMP.2s

'Do that and spear the fish.'

(250) *Isak-ep   weeser-eya   kiiriw wakesim-i-nan.*
spear-SS.SEQ finish-2/3s.DS again cover-Np-FU.2s

'When you have finished spearing them you will cover it again.'

(251) *Nain arua karu-i-mik.*
that1 lamp run-Np-PR.1/3p

'That is how they fish with a lamp.'

(252) *Aria   oko, kaul wafur-owa.*
alright other hook throw-NMZ

'Alright another way is throwing the hook.'

(253) *Kumin   wiim-ep,   uuriw   or-op   kaul wafur-i-mik,*
hermit.crab gather-SS.SEQ morning descend-SS.SEQ hook throw-Np-PR.1/3p
aasa   suuw-ap,   o papako uura.
canoe push-SS.SEQ or some   night

'They gather hermit crabs and go down in the morning and throw the hook, having pushed the canoe out – or some (do it) at night.'

(254) *Kaul wafur-owa maa eneka, ona   mera maa eneka, kumin,   wutkekela,*
hook throw-NMZ food tooth 3s.GEN fish   food tooth hermit.crab, calamari
ne   mera gelemuti-tik, nain kaul   wafur-i-mik.
ADD fish   small-RDP   that hook throw-Np-PR.1/3p

'Fish-throwing bait, fish-bait, hermit crabs, calamari and small fish – with those they throw the hook.'

(255) *Ne emeria wiena pona=pa iimar-ep   kaul wafur-i-mik,   ifer*
ADD woman 3p.GEN shore-LOC stand.up-SS.SEQ hook throw-Np-PR.1/3p sea
pona=pa.
shore-LOC

'And the women themselves stand on the shore and throw the hook, on the seashore.'

(256) O   mua=ke aasa suuw-ap   kaul wafur-i-mik.
       3s.UNM man-CF canoe push-SS.SEQ hook throw-Np-PR.1/3p
       'The men push the canoe and throw the hook (out in the sea).'

(257) Ne   kaul wafur-owa mera aaw-owa eliw, maa   marew.
       ADD hook throw-NMZ fish get-NMZ well thing none
       'And the hook-throwing is a good way to get fish, there is nothing to it.'

(258) O   galasim-owa   lawisiw yoowa.
       INTJ dive.with.goggles-NMZ   a.little hot/hard
       'Diving with goggles is a bit hard.'

(259) Kemawisa puk-i-nan,   mua bug maaya nain=ke eliw mera unowa
       breath   break-Np-FU.2s   man wind long that1-CF well fish many
       isak-i-non,   mua bug iiwa nain weetak.
       spear-Np-FU.3s   man wind short that1 no
       'You will be out of breath, a man with big lungs will spear many fish, a man
       with small lungs won't.'

(260) Soo   eliw.
       fishtrap well
       'Fishtrap is good.'

Mera aawowa sira e era wapen inawiya okaiwi-pa kuisow. Kauliw aawimik, arua karuimik, maer puukimik, patopatiw mera urumimik, oko galasimimik.

Oko soo. Soo nain feenap: era erup ikua. Oko sisina-pa ifemakimik, oko malol-pa ifemakimik. Ne sisina nain me yoowa akena. Oo malol lawisiw yoowa.

Sisina nain, soo ika oninan, soo ika-pa kaikap otal opora-pa ifemakinan. Ifemakep nomona iinan-pa wuainan, ikoka ifera me pikiwowa nain. Soo nain ona malin saana-pa ifemakimik. O ifera kuowa epa-pa weetak.

Aria malol-pa ifemakimik nain aana puukimik, makera unowa puukap makera nain anetirimik. Anetir-ikiwep urufimik, makera nain maaya pepek. Aria makera miirifa okaiwi soo-pa kaikimik, okaiwi pia kaikimik, piakina naimik nain. Ne soo ifemakowa epa-pa aasa suuwimik. Aasa suuwap soo aasa iinan-pa wuap poraimik. Orop malol-pa soo nain fuurkimik. Fuurkap makera nain opap ikaikuan. Opap lawiliw piipuam-ikaikuan. Orop saa-pa pokaya wi piipuaikuan. Ne soo nainiw mufowa pun naap, aana-pa neeke mufimik. Aana-pa neeke mufep, purupep aasa-pa wuaimik. Aasa-pa wuap, mera aawep weesereya nainiw fuurkimik. Nain soo era-ke.

Aria maer pun naap. Wi emeria kaalalimik, kaalalep orop otal-pa maer arimik. Maer arep urupep urupep, pona. Pona-pa neeke mera nomona ona iwomakeya, wi wapeniw ona nain suuwimik. Ne mua patopat aawep saa-pa iimarep ikaikuan. Mera sisina uru-peya patopatiw mikikuan.

Ne oko galasimowa. Nain iiriw me kererek, aakisa fan. Wiena galasimowa amia onimik, onap galasimimik. Ne oko, mera urumimik, patopatiw. Nain ona mua taraka nainke mera mikinan, patopat opowa nain. O mua naap nain ikoka uferinan.

Ne oko, afukarimik. Parina isimap afukarimik. Parina isimap afukarep, nain ona kak saana-pa. Kak saana-pa wi parina isimap orop kak isakimik. Kak, pirit, mera papako. Tokol gelemutitik, kookari, nain isakimik. Ne kak saana-pa kak oraimik, ne parina ona wakesimowa onaiya ikaiya. Ikoka wakesimeya mera mamaiya ekapinon, aasa mamaiya. Aasa mamaiya ekapeya aria parina kiiriw mauwa one. Mauwa onap mera isake. Isakep weesereya kiiriw wakesiminan. Nain arua karuimik.

Aria oko, kaul wafurowa. Kumin wiimep, uuriw orop kaul wafurimik, aasa suuwap, o papako uura. Kaul wafurowa maa eneka, ona mera maa eneka, kumin, wutkekela, ne mera gelemutitik, nain kaul wafurimik. Ne emeria wiena pona-pa iimarep kaul wafurimik, ifer pona-pa. O mua-ke aasa suuwap kaul wafurimik. Ne kaul wafurowa mera aawowa eliw, maa marew. O galasimowa lawisiw yoowa. Kemawisa pukinan, mua bug maaya nain-ke eliw mera unowa isakinon, mua bug iiwa nain weetak. Soo eliw.

B.5 Dog and snake

by Saror Aduna

(261) *Yo   aakisa opora gelemuta=ko ma-i-yem.*
      1s.UNM now   talk   little-NF   say-Np-PR.1s
      'Now I tell a little story.'

(262) *Emer en-ow(a) mua=ko emeria fan aaw-o-k.*
      sago eat-NMZ man-NF woman here take-PA-3s
      'A Sepik man married a woman from here.'

(263) *Ne manina ikiw-o-k.*
      ADD garden go-PA-3s
      'And he went to the garden.'

(264) *Ona   siowa ikos manina ikiw-e-mik, pika on-owa   na-ep.*
      3s.GEN dog   with garden go-PA-1/3p fence make-NMZ say-SS.SEQ
      'He went to the garden with his dog, to make a fence.'

(265) *Manina=pa nan   koka   iw-a-mik,   pika ifara muf-owa na-ep.*
      garden-LOC there jungle go-PA-1/3p fence vine pull-NMZ say-SS.SEQ
      'From the garden there they went to the jungle to pull vines for the fence.'

(266) *Pika ifara mufe-wiaw-ikok   ifa   maneka=ke siowa wiar   aaw-o-k.*
      Fence vine pull-move.around-be.SS snake big-CF   dog   3.DAT take-PA.3s
      'When he was moving around (and) pulling the vines, a big snake grabbed his dog.'

(267) *Siowa ikos irak-em-ika-iwkin   siowa wiawi   nain=ke siowa*
dog   with fight-ss.sim-be-2/3s.ds dog   3s/p.father that1-cf dog
alu-owa   miim-ap   karu-(o)w(a)=iw ekap-o-k.
make.noise-nmz hear-ss.seq run-nmz-inst   come-pa-3s

'When it was fighting with the dog, the dog's owner heard the dog's noise and came running.'

(268) *Karu-(o)w(a)=iw ekap-ep uruf-a-k=na ifa   maneka=ke siowa*
run-nmz-inst   come   see-pa-3s-tp snake big-cf   dog
wasi-ep-pu-eya,   aria   nainiw baurar-ep ikiw-ep   nomokowa maaya
wrap-ss.seq-cmpl-2/3s.ds alright again flee-ss.seq go-ss.seq tree   long
war-ep,   ekap-ep,   ifa   nain ifakim-o-k.
cut-ss.seq come-ss.seq snake that1 kill-pa-3s

'He came running and saw (to his surprise) a big snake wrapped around the dog; alright he ran away again and cut a long stick, came and killed the snake.'

(269) *Ifakim-em-ik-eya   ifa   nain=ke siowa wasirk-a-k.*
kill-ss.sim-be-2/3s.ds snake that1-cf dog   release-pa-3s

'As he was killing it, the snake released the dog.'

(270) *Siowa wasirk-ap   ifa   nain baurar-e-k.*
dog   release-ss.seq snake that1 flee-pa-3s

'The snake released the dog and fled.'

(271) *Baurar-ep iki(w-e)m-ik-eya   siowa wiawi   ikos pun baurar-e-mik.*
flee-ss.seq go-ss.sim-be-2/3s.ds dog   3s/p.father with too flee-pa-1/3p

'As it was fleeing, the dog with its owner ran away too.'

(272) *Baurar-ep owowa or-o-mik.*
flee-ss.seq village descend-pa-1/3p

'They ran away and came down to the village.'

(273) *Opaimika muut nan-e-k,   weeser-e-k.*
talk   only be.there-pa-3s finish-pa-3s

'The talk/story is there, it is finished.'

Yo aakisa opora gelemuta-ko maiyem.
Emer enow mua-ko emeria fan aawok. Ne manina ikiwok. Ona siowa ikos manina ikiwemik, pika onowa naep. Manina-pa nan koka iwamik, pika ifara mufowa naep. Pika ifara mufe-wiaw-ikok ifa maneka-ke siowa wiar aawok. Siowa ikos irakem-ikaiwkin siowa wiawi nain-ke siowa aluowa miimap karuw-iw ekapok. Karuw-iw ekapep urufak-na ifa maneka-ke siowa wasiep-pueya, aria nainiw baurarep ikiwep nomokowa maaya warep, ekapep, ifa nain ifakimok. Ifakimem-ikeya ifa nain-ke siowa wasirkak. Siowa wasirkap ifa nain baurarek. Baurarep ikim-ikeya siowa wiawi ikos pun bauraremik. Baurarep owowa oromik. Opaimika muut nanek, weeserek.

B.6 Piglet

by Saror Aduna

(274) *Tunde=pa fikera kuum-iwkin ikiw-ep waaya mik-a-m nain*
Tuesday-LOC kunai.grass burn-2/3p.DS go-SS.SEQ pig spear-PA-1s that1
ma-i-yem.
say-Np-PR.1s

'I tell about that when on Tuesday they burned kunai grass and I went and speared a pig.'

(275) *Tunde uuriw kiikir akena iwera fook-ap ikiw-e-mik.*
Tuesday morning first very coconut split-SS.SEQ go-PA-1/3p

'On Tuesday morning we split a coconut[2] and (then) went.'

(276) *Ne iwera fook-owa garanga nain wiena owow ara=pa wiar ik-ua,*
ADD coconut split-NMZ family that1 3p.GEN village part-LOC 3.DAT be-PA.3s
ne fikera pun wiena nain=ke.
ADD kunai.grass also 3p.GEN that1-CF

'And the coconut splitting was in that family's section of the village, and the kunai grass (area) was theirs too.'

(277) *Iwera fook-owa epa=pa maa uup-e-mik.*
coconut split-NMZ place-LOC food cook-PA-1/3p

'They cooked food in the coconut splitting place.'

(278) *Maa en-emi iwera op-ap fook-a-mik.*
food eat-SS.SIM coconut hold-SS.SEQ split-PA-1/3p

'We ate and held a coconut and split it.'

(279) *Nain weeser-eya woowa akua aaw-ep ikiw-e-mik.*
that1 finish-2/3s.DS spear shoulder take-SS.SEQ go-PA-1/3p

'When that was finished, we carried spears on our shoulders and went.'

(280) *Ikiw-ep fikera onaiya=pa nan pok-ap, wi yapen mua unow=iya*
go-SS.SEQ kunai.grass with-LOC there sit-SS.SEQ 3p.UNM inland man many-COM
pok-ap, nainiw neeke iwera fook-a-mik, maa en-e-mik.
sit-SS.SEQ again there.CF coconut split-PA-1/3p food eat-PA-1/3p

'We went and sat down there among the kunai grass, we sat down together with the inland men, and again there we split a coconut and ate food.'

(281) *Weeser-eya ama kuisow naap mukuna enek-a-mik.*
finish-2/3s.DS sun one thus fire light-PA-1/3p

'When that was finished at about one o'clock the fire was lighted.'

---
[2] Coconut-splitting ceremony is part of pig hunting.

(282) *Uma kiikir mukuna enek-a-mik.*
      top/ridge first fire light-PA-1/3p
      'The fire was first lighted at the top/ridge.'

(283) *Neeke awe-or-om-ik-eya i fiker saakia or-op*
      there.CF burn-descend-be-2/3s.DS 1p.UNM kunai.grass ashes descend.SS.SEQ
      fikera epia ook-a-mik.
      kunai.grass fire follow-PA-1/3p
      'From there it was burning down and we went down (along) the ashes and followed the grass fire.'

(284) *Ook-ap or-op ema mamaiya=pa waaya gelemuta urup-o-k.*
      follow-SS.SEQ descend-SS.SEQ hill near-LOC pig small ascend-PA-3s
      'We followed it down and near the hill a small pig came up.'

(285) *Me maneka, muuka, kia gelemuta.*
      not big, child, white small
      'It was not big, it was a small light-coloured piglet.'

(286) *Mua arow akena epa nain iimar-e-mik, yos=ke erepam.*
      man three very place that1 stand-PA-1/3p 1s.FC-CF four
      'Exactly three men stood at that place, I was the fourth.'

(287) *Waaya gelemuta nain urup-em-ik-eya mua arow naap ufer-a-mik.*
      pig small that1 ascend-SS.SIM-be-2/3s.DS man three thus miss-PA-1/3s
      'When the small pig was coming up those three men missed it.'

(288) *Ufer-iwkin urup-em-ik-eya yos=ke mik-a-m.*
      miss-2/3p.DS ascend-SS.SIM-be-2/3s.DS 1s.FC-CF spear-PA-1s
      'When they missed it and it was coming up I speared it.'

(289) *Mik-ap yena inasina unuma unuf-a-m.*
      spear-SS.SEQ 1s.GEN spirit name call-PA-1s
      'I speared it and called my spirit name.'

(290) *Ne sira naap ik-ua: waaya mik-ap, inasina unuma unuf-eya mua*
      ADD custom thus be-PA.3s pig spear-SS.SEQ spirit name call-2/3s.DS man
      unowa miim-ap ma-i-kuan, "O waaya mik-a-k."
      many hear-SS.SEQ say-Np-FU.3p 3s.UNM pig spear-PA-3s
      'And the custom is like that: when you spear a pig and call your spirit name, many men will hear it and say, "He has speared a pig." '

(291) *No   inasina unuma me unuf-i-nan   mua oko=ke waaya nain mik-ap*
2s.UNM spirit name not call-Np-FU.2s man other-CF pig that1 spear.SS.SEQ
nefar   aaw-i-non.
2s.DAT take-Np-FU.3s

'If you do not call (your) spirit name, another man will spear that pig and take it from you.'

(292) *Nain opora marew, no   inasina unuma me unuf-a-n.*
that talk no(ne) 2s.UNM spirit name not call-PA-2s

'You have no say, (because) you did not call the spirit name.'

(293) *Aria mik-amkun   me um-o-k, woowa onaiya iki(w-e)m-ik-eya   Olas=ke*
alright spear-1s/p.DS not die-PA-3s spear with go-SS.SIM-be-2/3s.DS Olas-CF
ekap-emi   woowa wafur-om-a-k.
come-SS.SIM spear throw-BEN-BNFY2.PA-3s

'Alright when I speared it, it didn't die; when it was going with the spear Olas came and threw a spear for it.'

(294) *Wafur-a-k   na weetak, ufer-a-k.*
throw-PA-3s TP no   miss-PA-3s

'He threw but no, he missed.'

(295) *Ufer-ap   nainiw burir aaw-ep   woosa=pa aruf-eya   waaya nain*
miss-SS.SEQ again axe   take-SS.SEQ head-LOC hit-2/3s.DS pig   that1
in-e-k.
sleep-PA-3s

'He missed and again took an axe and when he hit it in the head the pig fell.'

(296) *In-eya   yena   ikiw-emi nainiw woowa erup ar-ow-amkun*
sleep-2/3s.DS 1s.GEN go-SS.SIM again spear two become-APPL-1s/p.DS
iiwawun   um-o-k.
altogether die-PA-3s

'It fell and I myself went and speared it again twice and it died altogether.'

(297) *Ume-ya   merena ere-erup ifara aaw-ep   kaik-ap   nabena*
die-2/3s.DS leg RDP-two vine take-SS.SEQ tie-SS.SEQ carrying.pole
suuw-ap   akua   aaw-ep   or-o-m.
push-SS.SEQ shoulder take-SS.SEQ descend-PA-1s

'It died, and having taken a vine I tied its legs two and two (together) and pushed it onto a carrying pole and carried it on my shoulder and came down.'

(298) *Or-om-ik-ok   Pauli ame era=pa wia   uruf-ap   Pauli ikos waaya*
descend-SS.SIM-be-SS Pauli ASS road-LOC 3p.ACC see-SS.SEQ Pauli with pig

    nain akua   aaw-e-mik.
    that1 shoulder take-PA-1/3p

    'Coming down I saw Pauli and others on the road and (then) I carried it with Pauli on our shoulders.'

(299) *Akua   aaw-ep   owowa or-o-mik.*
    shoulder take-SS.SEQ village descend-PA-1/3p

    'We carried it on our shoulders and came down to the village.'

(300) *Urera   waaya gelemuta nain pa-ep,   kio-kiowa naap aaw-ep*
    afternoon pig   small   that1 butcher-SS.SEQ RDP-piece thus take-SS.SEQ
    uup-ep   en-e-mik.
    cook-SS.SEQ eat-PA-1/3p

    'In the afternoon we butchered the small pig, took the pieces like that, cooked and ate.'

(301) *Waaya maneka marew pun, mua unowa me wia   pepek-er-a-k.*
    pig   big   no(ne) also man many not 3p.ACC enough-come-PA-3s

    'It wasn't a big pig either, it wasn't enough for many people.'

(302) *Yiena iisow yiena garanga muutiw aaw-ep   uup-ep   en-e-mik.*
    1p.GEN 1p.ISOL 1p.GEN family only   take-SS.SEQ cook-SS.SEQ eat-PA-1/3p

    'Just our family by ourselves took and cooked and ate it.'

(303) *Ne waaya nain pun afila   marew, waaya asia pun.*
    ADD pig   that1 also sweet/fatty no(ne) pig   wild also.

    'And the pig wasn't fatty/sweet either, it was a wild pig too.'

(304) *Opaimika muut naap, weeser-e-k.*
    talk   only thus, finish-PA-3s

    'The talk is only like that, it is finished.'

Tunde-pa fikera kuumiwkin ikiwep waaya mikam nain maiyem.

Tunde uuriw kiikir akena iwera fookap ikiwemik. Ne iwera fookowa garanga nain wiena owow ara-pa wiar ikua, ne fikera pun wiena nain-ke. Iwera fookowa epa-pa maa uupemik. Maa enemi iwera opap fookamik. Nain weesereya woowa akua aawep ikiwemik. Ikiwep fikera onaiya-pa nan pokap, wi yapen mua unowiya pokap, nainiw neeke iwera fookamik, maa enemik. Weesereya ama kuisow naap mukuna enekamik. Uma kiikir mukuna enekamik. Neeke awe-orom-ikeya i fiker saakia orop fikera epia ookamik. Ookap orop ema mamaiya-pa waaya gelemuta urupok. Me maneka, muuka, kia gelemuta. Mua arow akena epa nain iimaremik, yos-ke erepam. Waaya gelemuta nain urupem-ikeya mua arow naap uferamik. Uferiwkin urupem-ikeya yos-ke mikam. Mikap yena inasina unuma unufam.

Ne sira naap ikua: waaya mikap, inasina unuma unufeya mua unowa miimap maikuan, "O waaya mikak." No inasina unuma me unufinan, mua okoke waaya nain mikap nefar aawinon. Nain opora marew, no inasina unuma me unufan.

Aria mikamkun me umok, woowa onaiya iki(we)m-ikeya Olas-ke ekapemi woowa wafuromak. Wafurak na weetak, uferak. Uferap nainiw burir aawep woosa-pa arufeya waaya nain inek. Ineya yena ikiwemi nainiw woowa erup arowamkun iiwawun umok. Umeya merena ere-erup ifara aawep kaikap nabena suuwap akua aawep orom. Orom-ikok Pauli ame era-pa wia urufap Pauli ikos waaya nain akua aawemik. Akua aawep owowa oromik.

Urera waaya gelemuta nain paep, kio-kiowa naap aawep uupep enemik. Waaya maneka marew pun, mua unowa me wia pepekerak. Yiena iisow yiena garanga muutiw aawep uupep enemik. Ne waaya nain pun afila marew, waaya asia pun.

Opaimika muut naap, weeserek.

B.7 Man's lover

by Kinangir Saror

(305) *Mua nain ona emeria onaria ik-ua, ne mua nain urema osarena*
man that1 3s.GEN woman with be-PA.3s ADD man that1 bandicoot path
ikiw-o-k.
go-PA-3s

'There was that man with his wife, and the man went to hunt bandicoots.'

(306) *Ikiw-ep ik-eya ona soma emeria nain kukusa nain=ke ekap-ep*
go-SS.SEQ be-2/3s.DS 3s.GEN lover woman that1 spirit that1-CF come-SS.SEQ
ona emeria nain maa wiar wafu-fur-eya naap maak-e-k, "Nena
3s.GEN woman that1 thing 3.DAT throw-RDP-2/3s.DS thus say-PA-3s 2s.GEN
mua=na urema osarena ikiw-o-k".
man-TP bandicoot path go-PA-3s

'When he was gone and his lover's spirit came and threw around his wife's things she told her, "Your man went to hunt bandicoots." '

(307) *Naap maak-eya aria ona womar emeria nain kukusa nain miim-a-k.*
thus tell-2/3s.DS alright 3s.GEN friend woman that1 spirit that1 heard-PA-3s

'When she told her like that alright the spirit of his lady friend heard that.'

(308) *Miim-ap ikiw-o-k, ikiw-ep mua nain urema osarena=pa iimar-ep*
hear-SS.SEQ go-PA-3s go-SS.SEQ man that1 bandicoot path-LOC stand-SS.SEQ
ik-eya ona mua nain ifakim-o-k.
be-2/3s.DS 3s.GEN man that1 kill-PA-3s

'She heard it and went; she went and, as the man was standing on the bandicoot path, killed his man.'

(309) *Ifakim-eya pu-ep ik-eya om-em-ik-ua.*
kill-2/3s.DS die-SS.SEQ be-2/3s.DS cry-SS.SIM-be-PA.3s
'She killed him and as he was dead she was crying.'

(310) *Sawur emeria nain=ke ona soma mua nain ifakim-o-k.*
spirit woman that1-CF 3s.GEN lover man that1 kill-PA-3s
'The spirit woman killed her lover.'

(311) *Om-em-ik-eya sawur emeria ona wiawi onak=ke*
cry-SS.SIM-be-2/3s.DS spirit woman 3s.GEN 3s/p.father 3s/p.mother-CF
ekap-emi naap maak-e-mik, "No moram naap om-em-ika-i-n?
come-SS.SIM thus tell-PA-1/3p 2s.UNM why thus cry-SS.SIM-be-Np-PR.2s
'As she was crying the spirit woman's father and mother came and told her, "Why are you crying like that?'

(312) *A=na naap ma-emi omom-e na, 'Mua yii, mua yee.'*
INTJ-TP thus say-SS.SIM cry-IMP.2s INTJ man INTJ man INTJ
'Cry like that, 'Man yii, man yee.''

(313) *Naap ma-emi om-em-ika-i-nan na."*
thus say-SS.SIM cry-SS.SIM-be-Np-FU.2s INTJ
'Keep crying and saying like that."'

(314) *Naap maak-e-mik.*
thus tell-PA-1/3p
'They told her like that.'

(315) *Ne mauwa nain aaw-ep iima=pa wu-om-ap*
ADD what that1 take-SS.SEQ chest-LOC put-BEN-BNFY2-SS.SEQ
om-em-ik-ua, sawur emeria nain=ke.
cry-SS.SIM-be-PA.3s spirit woman that-CF
'And she took this thing whatever and put it on his chest and cried, the spirit woman (did).'

(316) *Om-em-ik-eya om-em-ik-eya epa wiim-o-k.*
cry-SS.SIM-be-2/3s.DS cry-SS.SIM-be-2/3s.DS place dawn-PA-3s
'As she was crying and crying it dawned.'

(317) *Epa wiim-eya sawur emeria nain ikiw-eya, o iikir-ami owowa*
place dawn-2/3s.DS spirit woman that1 go-2/3s.DS 3s.UNM get.up-SS.SIM village
ekap-o-k.
come-PA-3s
'When it dawned and the spirit woman went, he got up and came to the village.'

(318) *Ekap-emi ona emeria maak-e-k, "Yo soma emeria nain=ke efa*
come-SS.SIM 3S.GEN woman tell-PA-3S 1S.UNM lover woman that1-CF 1S.ACC
ifakim-eya pu-ep ik-omkun efa om-em-ik-eya epa wiim-o-k.
kill-2/3S.DS die-SS.SEQ be-1S/p.DS 1S.ACC cry-SS.SIM-be-2/3S.DS place dawn-PA-3S

'He came and told his wife, "My lover came and killed me, and when I was dead and she was crying over me it dawned.'

(319) *Ne yo aakisa fan epa wiim-eya uuriw ekap-i-yem."*
ADD 1S.UNM now here place dawn-2/3S.DS morning come-Np-PR.1S

'And just now that it has dawned in the morning I come." '

(320) *Opora muut naap.*
talk only thus

'The story is like that.'

Mua nain ona emeria onaria ikua, ne mua nain urema osarena ikiwok. Ikiwep ikeya ona soma emeria nain kukusa nain-ke ekapep ona emeria nain maa wiar wafufureya naap maakek, "Nena mua=na urema osarena ikiwok." Naap maakeya aria ona womar emeria nain kukusa nain miimak. Miimap ikiwok, ikiwep mua nain urema osarena-pa iimarep ikeya ona mua nain ifakimok. Ifakimeya puep ikeya omem-ikua.

Sawur emeria nain-ke ona soma mua nain ifakimok. Omem-ikeya sawur emeria ona wiawi onak-ke ekapemi naap maakemik, "No moram naap omem-ikain? A=na naap maemi omome-na, 'Mua yii, mua yee.' Naap maemi omem-ikainan na." Naap maakemik.

Ne mauwa nain aawep iima-pa wuomap omem-ikua, sawur emeria nain-ke. Omem-ikeya omem-ikeya epa wiimok. Epa wiimeya sawur emeria nain ikiweya, o iikirami owowa ekapok. Ekapemi ona emeria maakek, "Yo soma emeria nain-ke efa ifakimeya puep ikomkun efa omem-ikeya epa wiimok. Ne yo aakisa fan epa wiimeya uuriw ekapiyem." Opora muut naap.

B.8 A flood story

by Yaura

(321) *Yiena emeria mia damol-al-i-mik nain mia aka nain aaw-ep*
1P.GEN woman body bad-APPL-Np-PR.1/3P that1 body blood that1 take-SS.SEQ
p-ikiw-ep manina=pa upuna=pa wu-a-k, mia aka nain aaw-ep.
Bpx-go-SS.SEQ garden-LOC furrow-LOC put-PA-3S body blood that1 take-SS.SEQ

'We women have menstruation (and a woman) took that menstrual blood and took it to the garden and put it in a furrow, having taken that menstrual blood.'

(322) *Upuna=pa wu-eya muuka wiip=iya kerer-e-mik.*
furrow-LOC put-2/3S.DS son daughter-COM appear-PA-1/3P

'When she put it in the furrow both a son and a daughter appeared.'

(323) *Kerer-ep onak maak-e-mik, "Aite, i aaya=ko*
appear-SS.SEQ 3s/p.mother tell-PA-1/3p 1s/p.mother 1p.UNM sugarcane-NF
yia aaw-om-aya enim-i-yan."
1p.ACC get-BEN-BNFY2.2/3s.DS eat-NP-FU.1p

'They appeared and told their mother, "Mother, get sugarcane for us and we will eat it." '

(324) *Ne onak=ke aaya wia aaw-om-aya*
ADD 3s/p.mother-CF sugarcane 3p.ACC get-BEN-BNFY2.2/3s.DS
enim-or-om-ik-e-mik.
eat-descend-SS.SIM-be-PA-1/3p

'And their mother got sugarcane for them and they went down eating it.'

(325) *Onak owawiya owowa or-o-mik.*
3s/p.mother with village descend-PA-1/3p

'They went down to the village with their mother.'

(326) *Owowa or-op owowa=pa onak maa uup-o-k.*
village descend-SS.SEQ village-LOC 3s/p.mother food cook-PA-3s

'They went down to the village and in the village their mother cooked food.'

(327) *Maa uup-ep fofola urup-eya maa op-iya iiw-o-k.*
food cook-SS.SEQ foam rise-2/3s.DS food be.done-2/3s.DS dish.out-PA-3s

'She cooked the food and it boiled and was done and (then) she dished it out.'

(328) *Iiw-ep wiipa muuka nain wia maak-e-k, "Ni auwa maa*
dish.out-SS.SEQ daughter son that1 3p.ACC tell-PA-3s 2p.UNM 1s/p.father food
p-ikiw-om-aka."
Bpx-go-BEN-BNFY2.IMP.2p

'She dished it out and said to the son and daughter, "Take food to father." '

(329) *Maa p-ikiw-om-iwkin wiawi=ke wia mokak-urup-o-k wia*
food Bpx-go-BEN-2/3p.DS 3s/p.father-CF 3p.ACC stare-ascend-PA-3s 3p.ACC
mokak-or-o-k, "I muuka marew a, wiipa marew a", naap
stare-descend-PA-3s 1p.UNM son none INTJ daughter none INTJ thus
wia maak-e-k.
3p.ACC tell-PA-3s

'When they took food to him, their father stared them up and down, "We have no son, no daughter," he told them.'

(330) *Ne wiawi=ke maa nain aaw-emi mia iinan=pa wiar sawik-a-k.*
ADD 3s/p.father-CF food that1 take-SS.SIM body on.top-LOC 3.DAT pour-PA-3s

'And taking the food their father poured it on them.'

(331) *Sawik-eya ep-ap onak maak-e-mik, "I auwa=ke maa*
pour-2/3s.DS come-SS.SEQ 3s/p.mother tell-PA-1/3p 1p.UNM 1s/p.father-CF food
mia iinan=pa yiar sawik-a-k."
body on.top-LOC 1p.DAT pour-PA-3s

'When he poured (food on them) they came and told their mother, "Father poured food on top of us." '

(332) *Om-emi maak-e-mik.*
cry-SS.SIM tell-PA-1/3p

'Crying they told her (that).'

(333) *Ne naap ik-ok in-e-mik.*
ADD thus be-SS sleep-PA-1/3p

'And then they slept.'

(334) *In-ep, epa wiim-eya onak maak-e-mik, "Aite, i*
sleep-SS.SEQ place dawn-2/3s.DS 3s/p.mother tell-PA-1/3p 1s/p.mother 1p.UNM
kemuka=ko yia kemi-om-a."
string-NF 1p.ACC roll-BEN-BNFY2.IMP.2s

'They slept, and in the morning when it dawned they told their mother, "Mother, roll string for us." '

(335) *Na-iwkin onak kemuka wia kemi-om-a-k.*
say-2/3p.DS 3s/p.mother string 3p.ACC roll-BEN-BNFY2.PA-3s

'They said (like that) and their mother rolled string for them.'

(336) *Wia kemi-e-k kemi-e-k kemi-e-k, kemuka nain maay-ar-e-k.*
3p.ACC roll-PA.3s roll-PA.3s roll-PA.3s string that1 long-APPL-PA-3s

'She rolled and rolled and rolled it (for) them and the string became long.'

(337) *Maay-ar-eya wia maak-e-k.*
long-APPL-2/3s.DS 3p.ACC tell-PA-3s

'It became long and she told it to them.'

(338) *"Ae, aite, i uurika ora-i-yan, ifera un-owa*
Yes 1s/p.mother 1p.UNM tomorrow descend-Np-FU.1p saltwater fetch-NMZ
ora-i-yan."
descend-Np-FU.1p

'Yes, mother, tomorrow we'll go down, we'll go down to fetch saltwater.'

(339) *Ne onak=ke, "A, ifera feeke un-eka."*
ADD 3s/p.mother INTJ saltwater here.CF fetch-IMP.2p

'And their mother (said), "Oh, fetch the water (from) right here." '

(340) *Ne wi maak-e-mik, "Wia, i oro-or-op un-i-yan."*
ADD 3p.UNM tell-PA-1/3p no 1p.UNM RDP-descend-ss.SEQ fetch-Np-FU.1p
'But they told her, "No, we'll go right down (=out to the sea) and fetch it." '

(341) *"A neeke-r=iw un-eka."*
INTJ there.CF-Ø-INST fetch-IMP.2p
'Oh, fetch it (from) right there.'

(342) *"Weetak, i oro-ora-i-yan."*
no 1p.UNM RDP-descend-Np-FU.1p
'No, we'll go right down.'

(343) *Ne oro-oro-oro-or-omi oro-oro-or-o-k, onoma.*
ADD RDP-RDP-RDP-descend-ss.SIM RDP-RDP-descend-PA-3s horizon
'And going down and down and down it went down and down to the horizon.'

(344) *Kemuka feekiya op-ap or-om-ik-e-mik.*
string with hold-ss.SEQ descend-ss.SIM-be-PA.1/3
'They held onto the string and went down.'

(345) *Ne kemuka nain pepek-er-eya onak ona wiar puuk-a-k.*
ADD string that1 enough-go-2/3s.DS 3s/p.mother 3s.GEN 3.DAT cut-PA-3s
'And when the string was long enough their mother herself cut it.'

(346) *Puuk-eya wi erup nain onoma or-o-mik.*
cut-2/3s.DS 3p.UNM two that1 horizon descend-PA-1/3p
'She cut it and the two of them went down to the horizon.'

(347) *Or-op neeke ika-iwkin kokom-ar-e-k.*
descend-ss.SEQ there.CF be-2/3p.DS dark-APPL-PA-3s
'They went down and when they were there it became dark.'

(348) *Kokom-ar-eya in-e-mik.*
dark-APPL-2/3s.DS sleep-PA-1/3p
'It became dark and they slept.'

(349) *Aria epa wiim-eya ama urup-o-k.*
alright place dawn-2/3.DS sun rise-PA-3s
'Alright when it dawned the sun rose.'

(350) *Ama urup-emi wiawi kuum-o-k.*
sun rise-ss.SIM 3s/p.father burn-PA-3s
'The sun rose and burned their father.'

(351) *Wiawi   kuum-eya,   kuum-eya,   kuum-eya   aw-ep   eka iw-a-k*
3s/p.father burn-2/3s.DS burn-2/3s.DS burn-2/3s.DS burn-SS.SEQ river go-PA-3s
na wia, eka=ke saan-ar-e-k.
TP no   river-CF dry-PA-3s

'It burned and burned and burned their father and when he burned he went into a river but no, the river dried.'

(352) *Eka oko   iw-a-k   na wia, eka oko=ke   saan-ar-e-k.*
river other go-PA-3s TP no   river other-CF dry-PA-3s

'He went into another river but no, the other river dried.'

(353) *Ne wiawi   kuum-eya   kuum-eya   um-o-k, ama=ke kuum-eya.*
ADD 3s/p.father burn-2/3s.DS burn-2/3s.DS die-PA-3 sun-CF burn-2/3s.DS

'And when it burned and burned their father he died; when the sun burned him.'

Yiena emeria mia damolalimik nain mia aka nain aawep pikiwep manina-pa upuna-pa wuak, mia aka nain aawep. Upuna-pa wueya muuka wiipiya kereremik. Kererep onak maakemik, "Aite, i aaya-ko yia aawomaya enimiyan."

Ne onak-ke aaya wia aawomaya enim-orom-ikemik. Onak owawiya owowa oromik. Owowa orop owowa-pa onak maa uupok. Maa uupep fofola urupeya maa opiya iiwok. Iiwep wiipa muuka nain wia maakek, "Ni auwa maa pikiwomaka." Maa pikiwomiwkin wiawi-ke wia mokak-urupok wia mokak-orok, "I muuka marewa, wiipa marewa", naap wia maakek. Ne wiawi-ke maa nain aawemi mia iinan-pa wiar sawikak. Sawikeya epap onak maakemik, "I auwa-ke maa mia iinan-pa yiar sawikak." Omemi maakemik.

Ne naap ikok inemik. Inep, epa wiimeya onak maakemik, "Aite, i kemuka-ko yia kemioma." Naiwkin onak kemuka wia kemiomak. Wia kemiek kemiek kemiek, kemuka nain maayarek. Maayareya wia maakek. "Ae, aite, i uurika oraiyan, ifera unowa oraiyan." Ne onak-ke, "A, ifera feeke uneka." Ne wi maakemik, "Wia, i oro-orop uniyan." "A neek-eriw uneka." "Weetak, i oro-oraiyan."

Ne oro-oro-oro-oromi oro-oro-orok, onoma. Kemuka feekiya opap orom-ikemik. Ne kemuka nain pepekereya onak ona wiar puukak. Puukeya wi erup nain onoma oromik. Orop neeke ikaiwkin kokomarek. Kokomareya inemik.

Aria epa wiimeya ama urupok. Ama urupemi wiawi kuumok. Wiawi kuumeya, kuumeya, kuumeya awep eka iwak na wia, eka-ke saanarek. Eka oko iwak na wia, eka oko-ke saanarek. Ne wiawi kuumeya kuumeya umok, ama-ke kuumeya.

B.9 Copra work

by Saror Aduna

(354) *Yo   aakisa iwera   mauw-owa nain ma-i-yem.*
1s.UNM now   coconut work-NMZ that1 say-Np-PR.1s

'Now I talk about coconut/copra work.'

(355) *Kiikir akena iwera opa aaw-ep up-i-mik.*
first very coconut seedling get-SS.SEQ plant-Np-PR.1/3p
'First of all we³ get coconut seedlings and plant them.'

(356) *Up-ep mokoma ikur naap ikiw-eya maken-ar-i-ya.*
plant-SS.SEQ year five thus go-2/3s.DS fruit-APPL-Np-3s
'We plant them and when about five years have gone they bear fruit.'

(357) *Iwera maken-ar-ep ififa wua-i-ya, ne ififa ora-eya*
coconut fruit-APPL-SS.SEQ dry put-Np-PR.3s ADD dry descend-2/3s.DS
fiirim-i-mik.
gather-Np-PR.1/3p
'Coconut (trees) bear fruit and develop dry coconuts, and when dry coconuts drop we gather them.'

(358) *Emeria=ke fiir-im-ikiw-ep aria ikoka mua=ke kais-i-mik.*
woman-CF father-SS.SIM-go-SS.SEQ alright later man-CF peel-Np-PR.1/3p
'The women have go around and gather them, alright later the men husk them.'

(359) *Mua=ke kais-ap neeke wu-ap miiw-aasa nop-ap miiw-aasa=ke*
man-CF peel-SS.SEQ there.CF put-SS.SEQ land-canoe search-SS.SEQ land-canoe-CF
iwer ififa nain aaw-ep p-ekap-ep epia koora mamaiya=pa
coconut dry that1 take-SS.SEQ Bpx-come-SS.SEQ fire house close-LOC
wu-eya fook-i-mik.
put-2/3s.DS split-Np-1/3p
'Men husk them and leave them there and look for a truck, and when the truck takes the dry coconuts and brings them and puts them close to the to the drying shed we split them.'

(360) *Fook-ap p-urup-ep koora=pa wua-i-mik.*
split-SS.SEQ Bpx-ascend-SS.SEQ house-LOC put-Np-PR.1/3s
'We split them and take them up and put them in the shed.'

(361) *Koora=pa wu-ap weeser-eya uurikona=pa epia wua-i-mik.*
house-LOC put-SS.SEQ finish-2/3s.DS next.day-LOC fire(wood) put-Np-PR.1/3p
'When we put them in the shed and it is finished, the following day we light the fire.'

(362) *Epia wu-ap ikiw-ep iwera kuuf-am-ik-eya iwera reen-eya*
fire put-SS.SEQ go-SS.SEQ coconut look-SS.SIM-be-2/3s.DS coconut dry-2/3s.DS

---

³ The whole text could also be in the third person: '*they* get... and plant...' etc., but because this is familiar activity to the writer, translation in the first person was chosen.

>   *iwer   urupa anum-i-mik.*
>   coconut shell   knock-Np-PR.1/3p

'We light the fire and go and (the watchman) watches the coconuts, and when the coconuts have dried we knock (the copra out of) the coconut shells.'

(363) *Iwer   urupa anum-ap   weeser-eya   p-or-op,   owaruma*
      coconut shell   knock-ss.SEQ finish-2/3s.DS Bpx-descend-ss.SEQ outside
      p-or-op   mik-i-mik.
      Bpx-descend-ss.SEQ hit-Np-PR.1/3p

'We knock the coconut shells and when that is finished we take it (copra) down, we take it down outside and hit it (into the sacks).'

(364) *Mik-ap   weeser-eya   owow   maneka sesek-ap   maamuma aaw-i-mik.*
      hit-ss.SEQ finish-2/3s.DS village big   send-ss.SEQ money   get-Np-PR.1/3p

'We hit it and when it is finished we send it to town and get money.'

(365) *Aakisa opora muut naap, weeser-e-k.*
      now   talk only thus finish-PA-3s

'Now the talk is only like that, it is finished.'

Yo aakisa iwera mauwowa nain maiyem.
Kiikir akena iwera opa aawep upimik. Upep mokoma ikur naap ikiweya makenariya. Iwera makenarep ififa wuaiya, ne ififa oraeya fiirimimik. Emeria-ke fiirim-ikiwep aria ikoka mua-ke kaisimik. Mua-ke kaisap neeke wuap miiwaasa nopap miiwaasa-ke iwer ififa nain aawep pekapep epia koora mamaiya-pa wueya fookimik. Fookap purupep koora-pa wuaimik. Koora-pa wuap weesereya uurikona-pa epia wuaimik. Epia wuap ikiwep iwera kuufam-ikeya iwera reeneya iwer urupa anumimik. Iwer urupa anumap weesereya porop, owaruma porop mikimik. Mikap weesereya owow maneka sesekap maamuma aawimik. Aakisa opora muut naap, weeserek.

B.10 Garden work

by Saror Aduna

(366) *Yo   aakisa manina uuw-owa   opora ma-i-nen   na-ep.*
      1s.UNM now   garden work-NMZ talk   say-Np-FU.1s say-ss.SEQ

'Now I want/intend to talk about garden work.'

(367) *Kiikir akena emeria=ke manina nop-i-mik.*
      first very woman-CF garden clear.bush-Np-PR.1/3p

'First of all the women clear the bush for the garden.'

(368) *Nop-ap   weeser-eya   mua=ke ikiw-ep   nomokowa war-i-mik.*
      clear.bush-ss.SEQ finish-2/3s.DS man-CF go-ss.SEQ tree   cut-Np-PR.1/3p

'When they have finished clearing the bush the men go and cut the trees.'

B.10 *Garden work*

(369) *Nomokowa war-ep   or-omak-eya   naap ik-ok nomokowa*
tree   cut-ss.SEQ descend-DISTR/PL-2/3s.DS thus be-ss tree
reen-eya   saama   kuum-i-mik.
dry-2/3s.DS cleared.bush burn-Np-PR.1/3p

'When they have cut the many trees down and they have stayed like that and the trees have dried they burn the cleared bush.'

(370) *Saama   kuum-ep weeser-eya   kafa   ik-i-mik.*
cleared.bush burn-ss.SEQ finish-2/3s.DS unburnt.wood roast-Np-PR.1/3p

'When they have finished burning the cleared bush they burn the unburnt wood.'

(371) *Kafa   ik-ep   wakoria fo-fook-i-mik.*
unburnt.wood roast-ss.SEQ section RDP-split-Np-PR.1/3p

'They burn the unburnt wood and split the garden into sections.'

(372) *Wakoria fo-fook-ap   weeser-eya   weria   faker-i-mik.*
section RDP-split-ss.SEQ finish-2/3s.DS planting.stick raise-Np-PR.1/3p

'They split the sections and when it is finished they raise the planting sticks (to make planting holes).'

(373) *Weria   faker-ap mua unowa wiinar-iwkin   emeria*
planting.stick raise-ss.SEQ man many make.planting.holes-2/3p.DS woman
uupura   up-i-mik.
taro.seedling plant-Np-PR.1/3p

'They raise the planting sticks and many/all men make planting holes and women plant taro seedlings.'

(374) *Moma nan miiwa=pa   ik-ok siiwa erepam=i ikur naap moma parew-eya*
taro there ground-LOC be-ss moon four-QM five thus taro mature-2/3s.DS
perek-i-mik.
harvest-Np-PR.1/3p

'The taro is there in the ground and in about four or five months it matures and is harvested.'

(375) *Ne manina erup on-i-mik.*
ADD garden two make-Np-PR.1/3p

'And we make two (kinds of) gardens.'

(376) *Manin maneka, manin gelemuta.*
garden big   garden small

'Big garden(s) and small garden(s).'

(377) *Manin maneka unuma ekina, aria manin gelemuta unuma esewa.*
garden big   name ekina alright garden small   name esewa.

'The name of the big garden is 'ekina', the name of the small garden is 'esewa'.'

(378) *Esewa naap: mua kuisow erup, arow, naap on-i-mik.*
esewa thus man one   two three thus make-Np-PR.1/3p

' 'Esewa' is like that: one man (makes) two (or) three, we do/make like that.'

(379) *Aria manin maneka, ekina, pun naap: mua kuisow manina erup=i arow=i*
alright garden big   ekina also thus man one   garden two-QM three-QM
naap.
thus

'Alright the big garden, 'ekina', is also like that: one man (makes) two or three, like that.'

(380) *Ona mua oona ook-i-mik.*
3s.GEN man bone follow-Np-PR.1/3p

'We work according to (each) man's strength (lit: We follow man's bone(s))'

(381) *Ne manin gelemuti-tik, esewa, nena kookal-owa=pa perek-i-nan.*
ADD garden small-RDP esewa 2s.GEN like-NMZ-LOC harvest-Np-FU.2s

'And the small gardens, 'esewas', you will harvest at your own liking.'

(382) *Nena kuuf-i-nan, parew-i-non, eliw perek-i-nan.*
2s.GEN look-Np-FU.2s mature-Np-FU.3s well harvest-Np-FU.2s

'You watch it yourself, it will mature, (and) you may harvest it.'

(383) *Manin maneka, ekina, naisow nena kookal-owa=pa perek-owa[4] weetak.*
garden big   ekina 2s.ISOL 2s.GEN like-NMZ-LOC harvest-NMZ no

'you are not allowed to harvest the big garden, 'ekina', by yourself at your own liking.'

(384) *Nena owowa onaiya aakun-ep perek-owa=ke ik-ua.*
2s.GEN village with   talk-SS.SEQ harvest-NMZ-CF be-PA.3s

'The harvesting must take place (only) after you have talked with your village.'

(385) *Perek-ami en-ow(a) gelemuta on-i-nan.*
harvest-SS.SIM eat-NMZ small   make-Np-FU.2s

'When you harvest you will make a feast.'

---

[4] This refers to harvesting the first taros of the year's crop.

(386) *Waaya ika-i-non   waaya uup-i-nan   naap, e owowa oko*
pig   be-Np-FU.3s pig   cook-Np-FU.2s thus or village other
wienak-owa   pun naap, nena   waaya ik-ok eliw wienak-i-nan.
feed.them-NMZ also thus 2s.GEN pig   be-ss well feed.them-Np-FU.2s
'If you have a pig, you will cook pork, (it is) like that; or giving food to other villages is also like that: when you have a pig you may feed (it to) them.'

(387) *Ne   manina pun naap, manina mauw-ap   manina uruf-ow(a) mua onaiya*
ADD garden also thus garden work-ss.SEQ garden look-NMZ man with
ika-i-ya.
be-Np-PR.3s
'And the garden is like this too: when the garden is done, it has (lit: is with) a guardian.'

(388) *Manina waisow mauw-ap   neeke   wafur-ap-pu-owa   nain weetak.*
garden 3s.ISOL work-ss.SEQ there.CF throw-ss.SEQ-CMPL-NMZ that1 no
'You may not make the garden by yourself and (just) leave it there.'

(389) *Manina kuuf-owa mua onaiya ika-i-ya.*
manina look-NMZ man with   be-Np-PR.3s
'The garden has a guardian.'

(390) *Mua nain=ke, "Aakisa moma parew-o-k.*
man that1-CF now   taro mature-PA-3s
'That man (will say), "Now the taro has matured."'

(391) *Aria   opora fiirim-ep,   fofa wu-ap,   iir nain perek-i-yan."*
alright talk gather-ss.SEQ day put-ss.SEQ time that1 harvest-Np-FU.1p
'Alright, we will discuss it, set a date and at that time harvest it."'

(392) *Aria   ona   fofa kerer-eya   perek-i-mik.*
alright 3s.GEN day appear-2/3s harvest-Np-PR.1/3p
'Alright when the day comes we harvest it.'

(393) *Nain manin maneka ma-i-yem,   ekina.*
that1 garden big   say-Np-PR.1s ekina
'I am saying that about the big garden, 'ekina'.'

(394) *O   manin gelemuta, esewa, nain naap, ona   mua kookal-owa.*
INTJ garden small   esewa that1 thus 3s.GEN man like-NMZ
'The small garden, 'esewa', is like this, (it can be worked according to) man's own liking.'

(395) *Ona weniwa=pa en-owa na-ep uuw-i-mik.*
3s.GEN hunger.time-LOC eat-NMZ say-SS.SEQ work-Np-PR.1/3p
'It is worked for eating during the "hunger time" (when there is no taro).'

(396) *Ne esewa nain no aakisa feenap nain mauw-am-ika-i-nan.*
ADD esewa that1 2s.UNM now like.this that1 work-SS.SIM-be-Np-FU.2s
'And the 'esewa' you can be working around this time.'

(397) *O manin maneka, ekina=ke, ikoka mauw-owa pun eliw.*
INTJ garden big ekina-CF later work-NMZ also well
'The big garden, 'ekina', may also be made/worked later.'

(398) *Ne moma perek-owa pun naap, ona owow saria=ke kiikir perek-i-mik, mua oro-oram fain weetak.*
ADD taro harvest-NMZ also thus 3s.GEN village headman-CF first harvest-Np-PR.1/3p man RDP-insignificant this no
'And taro harvesting is also like that, the village headmen harvest it first, not these ordinary men.'

(399) *Owow saria=ke perek-iwkin aria mua oko pun perek-i-mik.*
village headman-CF harvest-2/3p.DS alright man other also harvest-Np-PR.1/3p
'When the village headmen have harvested first, other men harvest too.'

(400) *Opaimika muut nan-e-k, weeser-e-k.*
talk only there-PA-3s finished-PA-3s
'The talk is there, it is finished.'

Yo aakisa manina uuwowa opora mainen naep.

Kiikir akena emeria-ke manina nopimik. Nopap weesereya mua-ke ikiwep nomokowa warimik. Nomokowa warep oromakeya naap ikok nomokowa reeneya saama kuumimik. Saama kuumep weesereya kafa ikimik. Kafa ikep wakoria fo-fookimik. Wakoria fo-fookap weesereya weria fakerimik. Weria fakerap mua unowa wiinariwkin emeria uupura upimik. Moma nan miiwa-pa ikok siiwa erepam-i ikur naap moma pareweya perekimik.

Ne manina erup onimik. Manin maneka, manin gelemuta. Manin maneka unuma *ekina*, aria manin gelemuta unuma *esewa*. Esewa naap: mua kuisow, erup, arow, naap onimik. Aria manin maneka, *ekina*, pun naap: mua kuisow manina erup-i arow-i naap. Ona mua oona ookimik.

Ne manin gelemutitik, *esewa*, nena kookalowa-pa perekinan. Nena kuufinan, parewinon, eliw perekinan. Manin maneka, *ekina*, naisow nena kookalowa-pa perekowa weetak. Nena owowa onaiya aakunep perekowa-ke ikua. Perekami enow gelemuta oninan. Waaya ikainon waaya uupinan naap, e owowa oko wienakowa pun naap, nena waaya ikok eliw wienakinan.

Ne manina pun naap, manina mauwap manina urufow mua onaiya ikaiya. Manina waisow mauwap neeke wafurap-puowa nain weetak. Manina kuufowa mua onaiya ikaiya. Mua nain-ke, "Aakisa moma parewok. Aria opora fiirimep, fofa wuap, iir nain perekiyan." Aria ona fofa kerereya perekimik. Nain manin maneka maiyem, *ekina*. O manin gelemuta, *esewa*, nain naap, ona mua kookalowa. Ona weniwa-pa enowa naep uuwimik.

Ne *esewa* nain no aakisa feenap nain mauwam-ikainan. O manin maneka, *ekina*-ke, ikoka mauwowa pun eliw. Ne moma perekowa pun naap, ona owow saria-ke kiikir perekimik, mua or-oram fain weetak. Owow saria-ke perekiwkin aria mua oko pun perekimik. Opaimika mut nanek, weeserek.

B.11 Girls' initiation customs

by Kalina Sarak

(401) *I   wiipa siiwa me wia   kuuf-owa ik-ok wia   kuuf-i-ya   nain*
1p.UNM girl   moon not 3p.ACC look-NMZ be-ss 3p.ACC look-Np-PR.3s that1
aite=ke   koora=pa yia   kaik-i-mik.
mother-CF house-LOC 1p.ACC tie-Np-PR.1/3p

'When the moon hasn't yet looked at our girls and then looks at them (I.e. when they have their first menstruation) our mothers seclude us in the house.'

(402) *Koora=pa yia   kaik-iwkin nan   ika-i-mik.*
house-LOC 1p.ACC tie-2/3p.DS there be-Np-PR.1/3p

'They seclude us in the house and we stay there.'

(403) *Nan ik-ok aite=ke   moma yia   ik-om-i-ya,   akia   yia*
there be-ss mother-CF taro   1p.ACC roast-BEN-Np-PR.3s banana 1p.ACC
ik-om-i-ya.
roast-BEN-Np-PR.3s

'We stay there and mother roasts us taros, she roasts us bananas'

(404) *Koora=pa nan   yiam   kaik-ap   ik-ok omopora yiam   up-ep   ik-ok*
house-LOC there 1p.REFL tie-SS.SEQ be-ss door   1p.REFL close-SS.SEQ be-ss
akia   ik-owa   enim-i-mik,   moma ik-owa   enim-i-mik.
banana roast-NMZ eat-Np-PR.1/3p taro   roast-NMZ eat-Np-PR.1/3p

'We are secluded there in the house and have locked the door on ourselves and eat roasted bananas and taros.'

(405) *Eka   me enim-i-mik,   iwera   eka   me enim-i-mik.*
water not eat-Np-PR.1/3p coconut water not eat-Np-PR.1/3p

'We don't drink water, we don't drink coconut water.'

(406) *Aaya muutiw en-em-ika-i-mik.*
sugarcane only eat-ss.SIM-be-Np-PR.1/3p

'We only keep eating sugarcane (i.e. chew the sugarcane and "drink" the juice from it).'

(407) *Nain en-em-ik-ok in-i-mik, kokom-ar-i-ya, in-i-mik,*
that1 eat-ss.SIM-be-ss sleep-Np-PR.1/3p dark-APPL-Np-PR.3s sleep-Np-PR.1/3p
epa wiim-i-ya.
place dawn-Np-PR.3s

'We eat that and sleep, it becomes dark, we sleep, (then) it dawns.'

(408) *Aite nainiw maa yia ik-om-i-mik.*
mother again food 1p.ACC roast-BEN-Np-PR.1/3p

'Our mothers again roast food for us.'

(409) *Ik-om-iwkin enim-i-mik.*
roast-BEN-2/3p.DS eat-Np-PR.1/3p

'They roast it for us and we eat.'

(410) *Aaya muuna kuisow, muuna kuisow enim-i-mik, aite=ke*
sugarcane joint.length one joint.length one eat-Np-PR.1/3p mother-CF
manina=pa yia aaw-om-iwkin.
garden-LOC 1p.ACC get-BEN-2/3p.DS

'We eat one joint length of a sugarcane, one joint length, when our mothers have gotten it for us from the garden.'

(411) *Nan ika-i-mik.*
there be-Np-PR.1/3p

'We stay there.'

(412) *Ik-ok ik-ok aite ona siiwa ara onaria ma-i-ya, "Wiipa no*
be-ss be-ss mother 3s.GEN moon section with say-Np-PR.3s daughter 2s.UNM
aakisa ora-e, no nan pok-a-n, owowa uruma ora-e".
now descend-IMP.2s 2s.UNM there sit-PA-2s village open.place descend-IMP.2s

'We stay and stay and at the right time of the moon mother says, "Daughter, go down now, you have sat there, go down to the open."'

(413) *Yia na-eya, fofa yia wu-om-eya i yak-i-mik.*
1p.ACC say-2/3s.DS day 1p.ACC put-BEN-2/3s.DS 1p.UNM bathe-Np-PR.1/3p

'When she says so about us and sets the date for us we bathe.'

(414) *Yaki-ep urup-emi koora=pa nan pok-ap ika-i-mik.*
bathe.ss.SEQ ascend-ss.SIM house-LOC there sit-ss.SEQ be-Np-PR.1/3p

'We bathe and go (back) up and sit in the house.'

(415) *Sosora   a-i-mik,   aite=ke   fia   yia   aw-om-i-mik,   ofa*
grass.skirt tie-Np-PR.1/3p mother-CF hair 1p.ACC shave-BEN-Np-PR.1/3p red.dye
op-i-mik,   epa   maneka ora-i-mik.
hold-Np-PR.1/3p place big   descend-Np-PR.1/3p

'We tie a grass skirt on, our mothers shave our hair, we are painted with red dye and we go down to the open.'

(416) *Epa maneka or-op   maa ikina ewur me enim-i-mik,   mera eka.*
place big   descend-ss.SEQ food smell soon not eat-Np-PR.1/3p fish water

'We go down to the open but we do not eat meaty (lit: smelly) food soon, or fish soup.'

(417) *Nan ika-i-mik,   nan   ik-ok, siiwa oko   kerer-eya   i   maa ikina*
there be-Np-PR.1/3p there be-ss moon other appear-2/3s.DS 1p.UNM food smell
enim-i-mik.
eat-Np-PR.1/3p

'We stay there, we stay there and when another moon appears we eat meaty food.'

(418) *Aite=ke   ma-i-mik,   "No   aakisa maa ikina=ko enim-e", a   i*
mother-CF say-Np-PR.1/3p 2s.UNM now   food smell-NF eat-IMP.2s INTJ 1p.UNM
maa ikina enim-i-mik.
food smell eat-Np-PR.1/3p

'Our mothers say, "Now eat meaty food", so we eat meaty food.'

(419) *A   weeser-e-k, i   maa momor   enim-i-yen, waaya, maa*
INTJ finish-PA-3s 1p.UNM food indiscriminately eat-Np-FU.1p pig   food
mauwa, aara,   nepa enim-i-mik.
what   chicken bird eat-Np-PR.1/3p

'It is finished, and we eat any food, we eat pork, whatever, chicken, birds.'

(420) *I   ikoka ikoka wia, maa momor   enim-i-yen.*
1p.UNM later later no food indiscriminately eat-Np-FU.1p

'Not sometime in the future, we (can now) eat food indiscriminately.'

(421) *I   naap on-i-mik,   i   sira.   Weeser-e-k.*
1p.UNM thus do-Np-PR.1/3p 1p.UNM custom finish-PA-3s

'We do like that, it is our custom. The end.'

I wiipa siiwa me wia kuufowa ikok wia kuufiya nain nain aite-ke koora-pa yia kaikimik. Koora-pa yia kaikiwkin nan ikaimik. Nan ikok aite-ke moma yia ikomiya, akia yia ikomiya. Koora-pa nan yiam kaikap ikok omopora yiam upep ikok akia ikowa enim-imik, moma ikowa enimimik. Eka me enimimik, iwera eka me enimimik. Aaya muutiw enem-ikaimik. Nain enem-ikok inimik, kokomariya, inimik, epa wiimiya. Aite nainiw maa yia ikomimik. Ikomiwkin enimimik. Aaya muuna kuisow, muuna kuisow enimimik, aite-ke manina-pa yia aawomiwkin. Nan ikaimik.

   Ikok ikok aite ona siiwa ara onaria maiya, "Wiipa no aakisa orae, no nan pokan, owowa uruma orae." Yia naeya, fofa yia wuomeya i yakimik. Yakiep urupemi koora-pa nan pokap ikaimik. Sosora aimik, aite-ke fia yia awomimik, ofa opimik, epa maneka oraimik. Epa maneka orop maa ikina ewur me enimimik, mera eka.

   Nan ikaimik, nan ikok siiwa oko kerereya i maa ikina enimimik. Aite-ke maimik, "No aakisa maa ikina-ko enime", a i maa ikina enimimik. A weeserek, i maa momor enimiyen, waaya, maa mauwa, aara, nepa enimimik. I ikoka ikoka wia, maa momor enimiyen. I naap onimik, i sira. Weeserek.

B.12 Funeral customs

by Kalina Sarak

(422) *I   mua soop-owa sira,   i   yiena kae   sira,*
1p.UNM man bury-NMZ custom 1p.UNM 1p.GEN 1s/p.grandfather custom
kome   sira,   a   naap, i   wiipa   mauwa sira   saarik.
1s/p.grandmother custom INTJ thus 1p.UNM daughter what   custom like

'Our custom of burying our husbands – our grandfathers' custom, our grandmothers' custom – is like that, similar to the custom of our daughters' what (initiation) custom.'

(423) *I   mua um-iya, mua om-ep   om-ep   om-ep   mua napuma*
1p.UNM man die-2/3s.DS man cry-SS.SEQ cry-SS.SEQ cry-SS.SEQ man body
yiar   soop-i-mik.
1p.DAT bury-Np-PR.1/3p

'When the husband dies we cry and cry and cry and the man's body is buried.'

(424) *Ikiw-ep   eruwa=pa wia   wua-i-mik.*
go-SS.SEQ grave-LOC 3p.ACC put-Np-PR.1/3p

'It is taken and put in the grave.'

(425) *Eruwa=pa wia   wua-iwkin i   emeria apura yiena mua weria*
grave-LOC 3p.ACC put-2/3p.DS 1p.UNM woman widow 1p.GEN man weria.relative
emeria nain=ke yia   amap-ikiw-ep eka=pa   yia   yakuw-ap
woman that1-CF 1p.ACC Bpx-go-SS.SEQ water-LOC 1p.ACC wash-SS.SEQ
ekap-emi   koora=pa yia   wua-i-mik.
come-SS.SIM house-LOC 1p.ACC put-Np-PR.1/3p

'It is put in the grave and we widows are taken by our *weria*-relatives'[5] wives and washed in a spring and brought and put in the house.'

---

[5] Certain relatives (maternal uncles and male cousins) responsible for burying a person

(426) *Yiena koora=pa yia wua-iwkin naap yiena koora=pa nan ika-i-mik.*
1p.GEN house-LOC 1p.ACC put-2/3p.DS thus 1p.GEN house-LOC there be-Np-1/3p

'They put us in the house and we stay there in our house like that.'

(427) *Koora=pa nan kaik-ap ika-i-mik.*
house-LOC there tie-SS.SEQ be-Np-PR.1/3p

'We stay secluded there in the house.'

(428) *Ik-ok ik-ok moma ik-owa en-em-ik-ok, siiwa kuisow.*
be-SS be-SS taro roast-NMZ eat-SS.SIM-be-SS moon one

'We stay and stay and (only) keep eating roasted taro (until) one month (is gone).'

(429) *Siiwa kuisow nain okaiwi=pa kerer-eya yia maak-i-mik, "Aria*
moon one that1 other.side-LOC appear-2/3s.DS 1p.ACC tell-Np-PR.1/3p alright
aakisa apura nain yak-inok."
now widow that1 bathe-IMP.3s

'When that one month (is finished and) another starts they tell us, "Alright now let the widow bathe."'

(430) *A yak-i-mik, yiena mua weria emeria=ke yook-ap*
INTJ bathe-Np-PR.1/3p 1p.GEN man weria.relative woman-CF follow.us-SS.SEQ
er-iwkin yak-i-mik.
go-2/3p.DS bathe-Np-PR.1/3p

'So we bathe, our *weria*-relatives' wives follow us (there) and we bathe.'

(431) *Er-ap eka damola=pa yaki-ep sosora a-i-mik, maa*
go-SS.SEQ water bad-LOC bathe-SS.SEQ grass.skirt tie-Np-PR.1/3p thing
bala suuw-i-mik, kamukamu, kululuma, sagat.
ornament push-Np-PR.1/3p Job's.tears coloured.bead sagat.shell

'We go and bathe in the bad spring and (then) tie the grass skirt on and put on decorations, Job's tears, coloured beads and sagat shells.'

(432) *Fia yia aw-om-iwkin ofa, ir-ap owowa=pa, yiena koora=pa.*
hair 1p.ACC shave-BEN-2/3p.DS red.dye go-SS.SEQ village-LOC 1p.GEN house-LOC

'When they have shaved our heads we (put on) red dye – having come back – in the village, in our house.'

(433) *Yiena koora=pa op-ap, maa pi-ep, saasaria*
1p.GEN house-LOC hold-SS.SEQ thing stick.in.armband-SS.SEQ plant.sp.
pi-ep owowa uruma ora-i-mik.
stick.in.armband-SS.SEQ village open.space descend-Np-PR.1/3p

'In our house we put on (the red dye), stick things in the armbands, stick *saasaria* plant in the armbands and go down in the open.'

(434) *Or-omkun   mua weria=ke   meta   urupa op-ap*
      descend-1s/p.DS man weria.relative-CF meta.paste cup   hold-ss.SEQ
      keemamuuna, umakuna meta   yia   mik-i-mik.
      knee   neck   meta.paste 1p.ACC stick-Np-PR.1/3p

      'We go down and the *weria*-relatives hold the *meta*-paste cup and stick the *meta* paste on (the back of) our knees and on the neck.'

(435) *Meta   yia   mik-iwkin   mera, waaya, oposia tiira nain yia*
      meta.paste 1p.ACC stick-2/3p.DS fish pig   meat   slice that1 1p.ACC
      aaw-om-iwkin   furun-i-mik.
      get-BEN-2/3p.DS spit-Np-PR.1/3p

      'They₁ stick the *meta* paste on us and when they₂ (=others) get fish and pork, pieces of those meats for us they₁ spit it.'

(436) *Ama urup-owa, ama or-owa   furun-i-mik,   koora ikiw-i-mik.*
      sun ascend-NMZ sun descend-NMZ spit-Np-PR.1/3p house go-Np-PR.1/3p

      'They spit it towards east, they spit it towards west, and we go into the house.'

(437) *Koora ikiw-i-mik   nain mera eka   me enim-i-mik.*
      house go-Np-PR.1/3p that1 fish water not eat-Np-PR.1/3p

      'We who go into the house do not eat fish soup.'

(438) *Mera eka en-owa marew nan   ika-i-mik.*
      fish water eat-NMZ no(ne) there be-Np-PR.1/3p

      'We stay there without eating fish soup.'

(439) *Mera eka en-owa marew ik-ok ik-ok mua weria=ke   ma-i-ya,*
      fish water eat-NMZ no(ne) be-ss be-ss man weria.relative-CF say-Np-PR.3s
      "No   aakisa maa ikina=ko   enim-e."
      2s.UNM now   food smell-NF eat-IMP.2s

      'We stay and stay without eating fish soup and (then) a *weria*-relative says, Now you (can) eat meaty food.'

(440) *Ne maa ikina enim-i-mik,   mera eka   enim-i-mik.*
      ADD food smell eat-Np-PR.1/3p fish water eat-Np-PR.1/3p

      'And we eat meaty food, we eat fish soup.'

(441) *Mera eka   enim-i-mik   nain i   mangala   me enim-i-mik,   waaya*
      fish water eat-Np-PR.1/3p that1 1p.UNM drupa.shell not eat-Np-PR.1/3p pig
      me enim-i-mik,   mua wia   soop-i-mik   nain.
      not eat-Np-PR.1/3p man 3p.ACC bury-Np-PR.1/3p that

      'We eat fish soup but we we do not eat drupa shells, we do not eat pork, we who bury our husbands.'

B.12 Funeral customs

(442) *A   i   sira,   aria   nepa me enim-i-mik,   aara   me enim-i-mik,*
INTJ 1p.UNM custom alright bird not eat-Np-PR.1/3p chicken not eat-Np-PR.1/3p
maroka me enim-i-mik,   sibaur me enim-i-mik.
prawn not eat-Np-PR.1/3p lobster not eat-Np-PR.1/3p

'Oh that is our custom, alright we do not eat bird meat, we do not eat chicken, we do not eat prawns, we do not eat lobsters.'

(443) *Mangala   eka   me enim-i-mik.*
drupa.shell water not eat-Np-PR.1/3p

'We do not eat drupa shell soup.'

(444) *Emi   kekanowa maneka, naap oram ika-i-mik.*
taboo strong   big   thus just be-Np-PR.1/3p

'It is a big taboo, we stay like that just (without many foods).'

(445) *I   ikoka nain enim-i-yen   mua kukusa=ke mia   yia   damol-iwkin*
1p.UNM later that1 eat-Np-FU.1p man spirit-CF body 1p.ACC bad-2/3p.DS
i   eliwa me ika-i-yen.
1p.UNM good not be-Np-FU.1p

'If we later eat that our husbands' spirits will damage our bodies and we will not be well.'

(446) *Mia nigisir-i-yan,   panewowa saarik ika-i-yan.*
body shrink-Np-FU.1p old   like   be-Np-FU.1p

'Our bodies will shrink and we will be like old people.'

(447) *I   sira   naap yiar   ik-ua, i   mua soop-owa sira,   i*
1p.UNM custom thus 1p.DAT 1p.UNM 1p.UNM man bury-NMZ custom 1p.UNM
emeria   sira=ke.
woman custom-CF

'We have a custom like that, the custom of burying our husbands, it is the womens' custom.'

(448) *Aria   i   emeria sira   nan   weeser-e-k.*
alright 1p.UNM woman custom there finish-PA.3s

'Alright (telling about) the women's custom is finished.'

(449) *A   pun naap, mua emeria um-i-mik   wi   koora=pa nan*
INTJ also thus   man woman die-Np-PR.1/3p 3p.UNM house-LOC there
ika-i-mik.
be-Np-PR.1/3p

'Also in the same way, the men's wives die and they stay there in the house.'

(450) *Onak=ke   moma wia   ik-em-ik-om-i-mik,   maa muutumut,*
      3s/p.mother-CF taro   3p.ACC roast-ss.SIM-be-BEN-Np-PR.1/3p food all.kinds
      akia,   iwoka.
      banana yam

      'Their mothers roast taro for them, and all kinds of food, banana, yam.'

(451) *Wia   ik-om-iwkin   en-em-ika-iwkin   en-em-ika-iwkin   siiwa*
      3p.ACC roast-BEN-2/3p.DS eat-ss.SIM-be-2/3p.DS eat-ss.SIM-be-2/3p.DS moon
      kuisow, koora=pa nan ika-i-mik   nain.
      one   house-LOC there be-Np-PR-1/3p that1

      'They₁ roast it for them₂ and they₂ keep eating it (until) a month (is gone), those who stay there in the house.'

(452) *Siiwa kuisow ona   onak=ke   wiawi=ke   ma-i-ya,   "Aakisa*
      moon one   3s.GEN 3s/p.mother-CF 3s/p.father-CF say-Np-PR.3s now
      yo   muuka yak-i-ya."
      1s.UNM son   bathe-Np-PR.3s

      '(After) one month his mother (or) his father says, "Now my son bathes." '

(453) *Mua weria   ekap-ep   koora=pa nan ik-ok muuka*
      man weria.relative come-ss.SEQ house-LOC there be-ss son
      aap-ora-i-mik.
      Bpx-descend-Np-PR.1/3p

      'The *weria*-relatives come and stay (a while) in the house and bring the son down.'

(454) *Muuka p-or-op   p-er-iwkin   yak-i-ya.*
      son   Bpx-descend-ss.SEQ Bpx-go-2/3p.DS bathe-Np-PR.3s

      'They bring the son down and take him (to the spring) and he bathes.'

(455) *Eka=pa   yakuw-ap   p-ir-i-mik.*
      water-LOC wash-ss.SEQ Bpx-come-Np-PR.1/3p

      'They wash him in the water and bring him (to the village).'

(456) *P-ir-ami   sira   naap emeria saarik.*
      Bpx-come-ss.SIM custom thus woman like

      'They bring him and (do) the custom like that, similar to the women('s custom).'

(457) *Mera eka   me ewur   enim-i-ya,   nan ika-i-ya,   eka=iw*
      fish water not quickly eat-Np-PR.3s there be-Np-PR.3s water-INST
      en-em-ika-i-non.
      eat-ss.SIM-be-Np-FU.3s

      'He does not eat fish soup soon, he stays there, he will (only) eat (food cooked) with water.'

B.12 Funeral customs

(458) *Maa eka=iw en-ep en-ep siiwa ara onaria, maa ikina,*
food water-INST est-SS.SEQ eat-SS.SEQ moon section with food smell
mangala wia, waaya wia, aara wia, urema wia, maroka wia, maa
drupa.shell no pig no chicken no bandicoot no prawn no food
muutumut wia.
all.kinds no

'He will keep eating food (cooked) with water until the moon is right, no meaty food, drupa shell, no pork, no chicken, no bandicoot, no prawns; all kinds of food are forbidden.'

(459) *Ikoka ona mua weria=ke wia op-om-iwkin enim-i-non.*
later 3s.GEN man weria.relative-CF 3p.ACC hold-BEN-2/3p.DS eat-Np-FU.3s

'Later when his *weria*-relatives hold them for him (=make a ceremony) he will eat them.'

(460) *A wi mua sira=ke, emeria soop-owa sira, wi mua era=ke.*
INTJ 3p.UNM man custom-CF woman bury-NMZ custom, 3p.UNM man way-CF

'That is the men's custom, the custom of burying one's wife, the way of the men.'

(461) *Opaimika muut nan-e-k.*
talk only there-PA-3s

'There's the talk.'

(462) *Weeser-e-k.*
finish-PA-3s

'It is finished.'

I mua soopowa sira, i yiena kae sira, kome sira, a naap, i wiipa mauwa sira saarik. I mua umiya, mua omep omep omep mua napuma yiar soopimik. Ikiwep eruwa-pa wia wuaimik. Eruwa-pa wia wuaiwkin i emeria apura yiena mua weria emeria nain-ke yia amapikiwep eka-pa yia yakuwap ekapemi koora-pa yia wuaimik. Yiena koora-pa yia wuaiwkin naap yiena koora-pa nan ikaimik. Koora-pa nan kaikap ikaimik.

Ikok ikok moma ikowa enem-ikok, siiwa kuisow. Siiwa kuisow nain okaiwi-pa kerereya yia maakimik, "Aria aakisa apura nain yakinok." A yakimik. Yiena mua weria emeria-ke yookap eriwkin yakimik. Erap eka damola-pa yakiep sosora aimik, maabala suuwimik, kamukamu, kululuma, sagat. Fia yia awomiwkin ofa, irap owowa-pa, yiena koora-pa. Yiena koora-pa opap, maa piep, saasaria piep owowa uruma oraimik. Oromkun mua weria-ke meta urupa opap keema-muuna, umakuna meta yia mikimik. Meta yia mikiwkin mera, waaya, oposia tiira nain yia aawomiwkin furunimik. Ama urupowa, ama orowa furunimik, koora ikiwimik. Koora ikiwimik nain mera eka me enimimik. Mera eka enowa marew nan ikaimik. Mera eka enowa marew ikok ikok mua weria-ke maiya, "No aakisa maa ikina-ko enime." Ne maa ikina enimimik, mera eka enimimik.

Mera eka enimimik nain i mangala me enimimik, waaya me enimimik, mua wia soopimik nain. A i sira, aria nepa me enimimik, aara me enimimik, maroka me enimimik, sibaur me enimimik. Mangala eka me enimimik. Emi kekanowa maneka, naap oram ikaimik. I ikoka nain enimiyen, mua kukusa-ke mia yia damoliwkin i eliwa me ikaiyen. Mia nigisiriyan, panewowa saarik ikaiyan.

I sira naap yiar ikua, i mua soopowa sira, i emeria sira-ke. Aria i emeria sira nan weeserek.

A pun naap, mua emeria umimik wi koora-pa nan ikaimik. Onak-ke moma wia ikemikomimik, maa mutmut, akia, iwoka. Wia ikomiwkin enem-ikaiwkin enem-ikaiwkin siiwa kuisow, koora-pa nan ikaimik nain. Siiwa kuisow ona onak-ke wiawi-ke maiya, "Aakisa yo muuka yakiya."

Mua weria ekapep koora-pa nan ikok muuka aaporaimik. Muuka porop periwkin yakiya. Eka-pa yakuwap pirimik. Pirami sira naap emeria saarik. Mera eka me ewur enimiya, nan ikaiya, eka-iw enem-ikainon. Maa eka-iw enep enep siiwa ara onaria, maa ikina, mangala wia, waaya wia, aara wia, urema wia, maroka wia, maa muutumut wia. Ikoka ona mua weria-ke wia opomiwkin eniminon.

A wi mua sira-ke, emeria soopowa sira, wi mua era-ke. Opaimika muut nanek. Weeserek.

B.13 Tidal wave

by Saror Aduna

(463) *Yo aakisa ifer maneka urup-i-ya nain ma-i-yem.*
1s.UNM now sea big ascend-Np-PR.3s that1 say-Np-PR.1s

'Now I tell about a tidal wave (lit: that when the big sea rises).'

(464) *Yo me baliwep paayar-e-m, oram iperowa=ke nanar-iwkin*
1s.UNM not well understand-PA-1s just middle.aged-CF tell.story-2/3p.DS
miim-a-m.
hear-PA-1s

'I do not understand it well, I have just heard the elders tell stories about it.'

(465) *Kiikir akena menat maneka goron-ep ora-i-ya.*
first very tide big go.down-SS.SEQ descend-Np-PR.3s

'First of all the big tide goes very low down.'

(466) *Goron-ep ora-i-ya nain, mua pepena=ke menat=ke ek-i-ya*
go.down-SS.SEQ descend-Np-PR.3s that1 man ignorant-CF tide-CF go-Np-PR.3s
na-ep menat ora-i-nan.
say/think-SS.SEQ tide descend-Np-FU.2s

'When it goes low down, an ignorant man thinks that the ebb tide is receding and will go down (to catch shellfish).'

B.13 Tidal wave

(467) O   mua amis-ar-owa   nain=ke baurar-i-kuan.
      INTJ man knowledge-INCH that-CF flee-Np-FU.3p
      '(But) the knowledgeable people run away.'

(468) Ae, menat maneka goron-ep   ora-i-ya   nain or-op,
      yes tide   big   go.down-SS.SEQ descend-Np-PR.3s that1 descend-SS.SEQ
      malol.
      deep.sea
      'Yes, the big tide that goes down, goes down (and reaches) the deep sea.'

(469) Malol=pa   neeke   nainiw suuw-urup-i-ya.
      deep.sea-LOC there.CF again push-ascend-Np-PR.3s
      'From the deep sea there it pushes back up again.'

(470) Suuw-urup-ep   urup-ep   owowa erepura=pa nan nainiw
      push-ascend-SS.SEQ ascend-SS.SEQ village side-LOC   there again
      goron-ep   ora-i-ya.
      go.down-SS.SEQ descend-Np-PR.3s
      'It pushes up and rises and from the (upper) side of the village it goes down again.'

(471) Goron-ep   ora-i-ya   nain maa muutitik iiwawun
      go.down-SS.SEQ descend-Np-PR.3s that1 thing all.kinds altogether
      lalat-i-ya.
      wash.away-Np-PR.3s
      'When it goes down it washes away everything.'

(472) Koora=ki   e maa mauwa nain iiwawun   samor-i-ya.
      house-CF.QM or thing what that1 altogether bad-Np-PR.3s
      'It completely destroys houses or whatever.'

(473) Ifera suuw-urup-i-ya   nain, nain pun nomona,   mera, iiwawun   onaiya
      sea   push-ascend-Np-PR.3s that1 that1 also stone/coral fish altogether with
      urup-i-ya.
      ascend-Np-PR.3s
      'When the sea rises, it rises altogether with corals and fish too (i.e. a tidal wave brings up corals and fish with it too).'

(474) Ne mua baurar-ep   ikiw-ep   koka=pa   ika-i-mik.
      ADD man flee-SS.SEQ go-SS.SEQ jungle-LOC be-Np-PR.1/3p
      'And people run away and stay in the jungle.'

(475) *Aakisa fan ifera goron-ep   or-eya   wi   owowa*
now   here sea   go.down.ss.SEQ descend-2/3s.DS 3p.UNM village
ora-i-mik.
descend-Np-PR.1/3p

'Only (lit: just now) when the sea has receded they come down to the village.'

(476) *Owowa or-op   owowa kuuf-i-mik   na owowa iiwawun*
village descend-ss.SEQ village look-Np-PR.1/3p TP village altogether
samor-ar-e-k,   ifera=ke samor-a-k.
bad-INCH-PA-3s sea-CF   bad-PA-3s

'They come down to the village and look at the village – it is completely destroyed; it is the sea that has destroyed it.'

(477) *Ne ifera suuw-i-ya   nain koora pun iiwawun   mu-i-ya.*
ADD sea push-Np-PR.3s that1 house also altogether swallow-Np-PR.3s

'And when the sea pushes up it completely swallows the houses.'

(478) *O   no   mua me baurar-i-nan nain ikoka ifera=ke iiwawun   nefa*
INTJ 2s.UNM man not flee-Np-FU.2s that1 later sea-CF   altogether 2s.ACC
ifakim-i-non.
kill-Np-FU.3s

'You who do not run away will later be completely killed by the sea.'

(479) *Ae, opaimika muut nanek.*
yes talk   only there-PA-3s

'Yes, that is all the talk.'

Yo aakisa ifer maneka urupiya nain maiyem.

Yo me baliwep paayarem, oram iperowa-ke nanariwkin miimam. Kiikir akena menat maneka goronep oraiya. Goronep oraiya nain mua pepena-ke menat-ke ekiya naep menat orainan. O mua amisarowa nain-ke baurarikuan. Ae, menat maneka goronep oraiya nain orop, malol. Malol-pa neeke nainiw suuw-urupiya. Suuw-urupep urupep owowa erepura-pa nan nainiw goronep oraiya. Goronep oraiya nain maa muutitik ii-wawun lalatiya. Koora-ki e maa mauwa nain iiwawun samoriya.

Ifera suuw-urupiya nain nain pun nomona, mera, iiwawun onaiya urupiya. Ne mua baurarep ikiwep koka-pa ikaimik. Aakisa fan ifera goronep oreya wi owowa oraimik. Owowa orop owowa kuufimik na owowa iiwawun samorarek, ifera-ke samorak. Ne ifera suuwiya nain koora pun iiwawun muiya. O no mua me baurarinan nain ikoka ifera-ke iiwawun nefa ifakiminon. Ae, opaimika muut nanek.

References

Ahlman, Erik. 1933. Adverbeista. *Virittäjä* 37. 137–159.
Ameka, Felix K. 2006. Real descriptions: Reflections on native speaker and non-native speaker descriptions of a language. In Felix Ameka, Alan Dench & Nicholas Evans (eds.), *Catching language: The standing challenge of grammar writing*, 69–112. Berlin / New York: Mouton de Gruyter.
Anderson, Stephen. 1985a. Inflectional morphology. In Timothy Shopen (ed.), *Language typology and syntactic description*, vol. 3, 150–201. Cambridge: Cambridge University Press.
Anderson, Stephen. 1985b. Typological distinctions in word formation. In Timothy Shopen (ed.), *Language typology and syntactic description*, vol. 3, 3–56. Cambridge: Cambridge University Press.
Anderson, Stephen & Edward Keenan. 1985. Deixis. In Timothy Shopen (ed.), *Language typology and syntactic description*, vol. 2, 258–308. Cambridge: Cambridge University Press.
Andrews, Avery. 2007a. Relative clauses. In Timothy Shopen (ed.), *Language typology and syntactic description*, vol. 2, 206–236. Cambridge: Cambridge University Press.
Andrews, Avery. 2007b. The major functions of the noun phrase. In Timothy Shopen (ed.), *Language typology and syntactic description*, vol. 1, 132–133. Cambridge: Cambridge University Press.
Bauer, Laurie. 1983. *English word-formation*. Cambridge: Cambridge University Press.
Berghäll (=Järvinen), Liisa. 2006. Negation in Mauwake, a Papuan language. 19. Mickael Suominen, Antti Arppe, Anu Airola nad Orvokki Heinämäki, Matti Miestamo, Urho Määttä, Jussi Niemi, Kari Pitkänen & Kaius Sinnemäki (eds.). Special supplement to SKY Journal of Linguistics, 269–281.
Berlin, Brent & Paul Kay. 1969. *Basic color terms: Their universality and evolution*. Berkeley & Los Angeles: University of California Press.
Bloomfield, Leonard. 1933. *Language*. New York: H. Holt & Co.
Brumm, Geoffrey & Frank Mihalic. 1995. *Sent by the word: 100 years of service by divine word missionaries and sisters servants of the Holy Spirit on mainland New Guinea*. Wewak: Wirui Press.
Bugenhagen, Robert. 1995. *A grammar of Mangap-Mbula: An Austronesian language of Papua New Guinea* (Pacific Linguistics C-101). Canberra: Australian National University.
Bunn, Gordon. 1974. *Golin grammar* (Workpapers in Papua New Guinea Linguistics 5).
Bybee, Joan. 1985. *Morphology: A study of the relation between meaning and form*. Amsterdam: John Benjamins.

References

Capell, Arthur. 1952. Languages of Bogia District, New Guinea. *Oceania* 2(22). 178–207.
Capell, Arthur. 1969. *A survey of New Guinea languages*. Sydney: Sydney University Press.
Chafe, Wallace. 1976. Givenness, contrastiveness, definiteness, subjects, topics, and point of view. In Charles Li (ed.), *Subject and topic*, 25–55. New York: Academic Press.
Comrie, Bernard. 1976. *Aspect*. Cambridge: Cambridge University Press.
Comrie, Bernard. 1981. *Language universals and linguistic typology*. Oxford: Basil Blackwell.
Comrie, Bernard. 1983. Switch-reference in Huichol: A typological study. In John Haiman & Pamela Munro (eds.), *Switch reference and universal grammar* (TSL 2), 17–37. Amsterdam: John Benjamins.
Comrie, Bernard. 1985. *Tense*. Cambridge: Cambridge University Press.
Comrie, Bernard & Kaoru Horie. 1995. Complement clauses versus relative clauses: Some Khmer evidence. In Werner Abraham, Talmy Givón & Sandra A. Thompson (eds.), *Discourse grammar and typology. Papers in honour of John W. M. Verhaar*. Amsterdam / Philadelphia: John Benjamins.
Comrie, Bernard & Sandra A. Thompson. 2007. Lexical nominalization. In Timothy Shopen (ed.), *Language typology and syntactic description*, 2nd edn., vol. 3, 334–381. Cambridge: Cambridge University Press.
Cristofaro, Sonia. 2003. *Subordination*. Oxford: Oxford University Press.
Cristofaro, Sonia. 2006. The organization of reference grammars: A typologist user's point of view. In Felix Ameka, Alan Dench & Nicholas Evans (eds.), *Catching language: The standing challenge of grammar writing*, 137–170. Berlin / New York: Mouton de Gruyter.
Croft, William. 1991. *Syntactic categories and grammatical relations*. Chicago: University of Chicago Press.
Crowley, Terry. 2002. *Serial verbs in Oceanic: A descriptive typology*. New York: Oxford University Press.
Crystal, David. 1967. Word classes in English. *Lingua* 17. 24–56.
Crystal, David. 1997. *A dictionary of linguistics and phonetics*. Fourth. Oxford: Basil Blackwell.
Davies, Hugh. 1999. *Tsunami PNG 1998*. Second and revised edition. Port Moresby: The University of Papua New Guinea.
Davies, John. 1981. *Kobon* (Lingua Descriptive Series 3). Amsterdam: North-Holland Publishing House.
Dik, Simon. 1978. *Functional grammar*. Dordrecht: Foris Publications.
Dixon, R. M. W. 1977. Where have all the adjectives gone? *Studies in language* 1. 19–80.
Dixon, R. M. W. 1997. *The rise and fall of languages*. Cambridge: Cambridge University Press.
Dixon, R. M. W. 2010a. *Basic linguistic theory*. Vol. 1: Methodology. Oxford: Oxford University Press.
Dixon, R. M. W. 2010b. *Basic linguistic theory*. Vol. 2: Grammatical topics. Oxford: Oxford University Press.

Downing, Pamela. 1977. On the creation and use of English compound nouns. *Language* 53. 810–842.

Dryer, Matthew S. 2006a. Descriptive theories, explanatory theories and Basic linguistic theory. In Felix Ameka, Alan Dench & Nicholas Evans (eds.), *Catching language: The standing challenge of grammar writing*, 207–234. Berlin / New York: Mouton de Gruyter.

Dryer, Matthew S. 2006b. Functionalism and the theory-metalanguage confusion. In Grace Wiebe, Gary Libben, Ron Smith & Sam Wang (eds.), *Phonology, morphology, and the empirical imperative: Papers in honour of Bruce Derwing*, 27–59. Taipei: The Crane Publishing Company.

Dryer, Matthew S. 2007a. Clause types. In Timothy Shopen (ed.), *Language typology and syntactic description*, 2nd edn., vol. 1, 224–275. Cambridge: Cambridge University Press.

Dryer, Matthew S. 2007b. Word order. In Timothy Shopen (ed.), *Language typology and syntactic description*, 2nd edn., vol. 1, 61–131. Cambridge: Cambridge University Press.

Duamba, Wenceslaus. 1996. *Foundation of the local church: Evangelization and development*. B. Th. thesis for Holy Spirit Seminary, Bomana, PNG.

Evans, Nicholas & Alan Dench. 2006. Introduction: Catching language. In Felix Ameka, Alan Dench & Nicholas Evans (eds.), *Catching language: The standing challenge of grammar writing*, 1–39. Berlin / New York: Mouton de Gruyter.

Ezard, Bryan. 1977. A basic word list for Papua New Guinea. *Workpapers in Papua New Guinea languages* 21. 45–74.

Farr, Cynthia J. M. 1999. *The interface between syntax and discourse in Korafe, a Papuan language of Papua New Guinea* (Pacific Linguistics C-148).

Farr, Cynthia J. M. & Carl R. Whitehead. 1982. This, that and the other: A study of Korafe demonstratives. *Language and Linguistics in Melanesia* 13. 64–80.

Foley, William A. 1986. *The Papuan languages of New Guinea*. Cambridge: Cambridge University Press.

Foley, William A. & Robert D. Jr. Van Valin. 1984. *Functional syntax and universal grammar*. Cambridge: Cambridge University Press.

Franklin, Karl J. 1971. *A grammar of Kewa, New Guinea* (Pacific Linguistics C-16).

Franklin, Karl J. 1979. Free and bound pronouns in Papuan languages. In R. E. Cooley, M. R. Barnes & J. A. Dunn (eds.), *Papers of the Mid-America Linguistics Conference at Oklahoma*, 355–365. Norman: University of Oklahoma.

Franklin, Karl J. 1983. Some features of interclausal references in Kewa. In John Haiman & Pamela Munro (eds.), *Switch reference and universal grammar* (TSL 2), 39–49. Amsterdam: John Benjamins.

Frawley, William. 1992. *Linguistic semantics*. Hillsdale, NJ: Lawrence Erlbaum.

Givón, Talmy. 1976. Topic, pronoun and grammatical agreement. In Charles Li (ed.), *Subject and topic*, 149–188. New York: Academic Press.

Givón, Talmy. 1979. *On understanding grammar*. New York: Academic Press.

References

Givón, Talmy. 1983. Topic continuity in discourse: The functional domain of switch-reference. In John Haiman & Pamela Munro (eds.), *Switch reference and universal grammar* (TSL 2), 51–82. Amsterdam: John Benjamins.

Givón, Talmy. 1984. *Syntax: A functional-typological introduction.* Vol. 1. Amsterdam / Philadelphia: John Benjamins.

Givón, Talmy. 1990. *Syntax: A functional-typological introduction.* Vol. 2. Amsterdam / Philadelphia: John Benjamins.

Givón, Talmy. 1991. Some substantive issues concerning verb serialization: Grammatical vs. Cognitive packaging. In Claire Lefebvre (ed.), *Serial verbs: Grammatical, comparative and cognitive approaches*, 137–184. Amsterdam: John Benjamins.

Givón, Talmy. 1995. *Functionalism and grammar.* Amsterdam / Philadelphia: John Benjamins.

Goldberg, Adele. 1995. *Constructions: A construction grammar approach to argument structure.* Chicago: The University of Chicago Press.

Goldberg, Adele. 2006. *Constructions at work: The nature of generalization in language.* Oxford: Oxford University Press.

Greenberg, Joseph H. 1954 [1960]. A quantitative approach to the morphological typology of a language. *International journal of American linguistics* 26. 178–194.

Greenberg, Joseph H. 1966 [1963]. Some universals of grammar with particular reference to the order of meaningful elements. In Joseph Greenberg (ed.), *Universals of language*, 73–113. Cambridge, Mass.: M.I.T. Press.

Greenberg, Joseph H. 1971. The Indo-Pacific hypothesis. In T. Sebeok (ed.), *Linguistics in Oceania*, vol. 8 (Current trends in linguistics), 807–876.

Grimes, Barbara. 2000. *Ethnologue.* 14th edn. Dallas: SIL International.

Grimes, J. E. & F. Agard. 1959. Linguistic divergence in Romance. *Language* 35. 598–604.

Haantjens, H. A., E. Reiner, R. G. Robbins & J. C. Saunders. 1976. Land systems. In R. G. Robbins (ed.), *Lands of the Ramu-Madang area, Papua New Guinea* (Land Research Series 37). Melbourne: CSIRO.

Haiman, John. 1978. Conditionals are topics. *Language* 54. 564–589.

Haiman, John. 1979. Review of Wurm, ed, 1975. *Language* (55) (4). 894–903.

Haiman, John. 1980. *Hua, a Papuan language of the eastern highlands of New Guinea* (SLC 5). Amsterdam: John Benjamins.

Haiman, John & Pamela Munro (eds.). 1983. *Switch reference and universal grammar* (TSL 2). Amsterdam: John Benjamins.

Haiman, John & Sandra A. Thompson. 1984. "Subordination" in universal grammar. In *Proceedings of the tenth annual meeting of the Berkeley Linguistics Society*, 510–523. Berkeley: Berkeley Linguistics Society.

Hakulinen, Auli & Fred Karlsson. 1979. *Nykysuomen lauseoppia.* Jyväskylä, Finland: Suomalaisen Kirjallisuuden Seura.

Halliday, M. A. K. 1994. *An introduction to functional grammar.* 2nd edn. London: Edward Arnold.

Halliday, M. A. K. & Ruqaiya Hasan. 1976. *Cohesion in English.* London: Longman.

Hardin, Barbara. 2002. Maia grammar essentials. Unpublished manuscript. SIL archives, Ukarumpa, Papua New Guinea. www.sil.org/resources/archives/49138.

Haspelmath, Martin. 2007. Coordination. In Timothy Shopen (ed.), *Language typology and syntactic description*, 2nd edn., vol. 2, 1–51. Cambridge: Cambridge University Press.

Heine, Bernd. 1997. *Possession: Cognitive sources, forces and grammaticalization*. Cambridge: Cambridge University Press.

Hepner, Mark. 2002. Bargam grammar sketch. Unpublished manuscript. SIL archives, Ukarumpa, Papua New Guinea. www.sil.org/resources/archives/31205.

Hollrung, M. 1888. Das deutsche Schutzgebiet in der Südsee. *Globus* 54. 305–311, 321–325, 337–341.

Höltker, G. 1937. Vorbericht über meine ethnografischen und anthropologischen Forschungen in Bogia-Distrikt (Neu-Guinea). *Anthropos* 32.

Hopper, Paul & Sandra A. Thompson. 1980. Transitivity in grammar and discourse. *Language* 56. 251–259.

Hopper, Paul & Sandra A. Thompson. 1984. The discourse basis for lexical categories in universal grammar. *Language* 60. 703–752.

Hopper, Paul & Sandra A. Thompson. 1985. The iconicity of "noun" and "verb". In John Haiman (ed.), *Iconicity in syntax* (TSL 6), 151–183. Amsterdam: John Benjamins.

James, Dorothy. 1983. Verb serialization in Siane. *Language and linguistics in Melanesia* 14.

Järvinen (=Berghäll), Liisa. 1980. Relative constructions in Mauwake. Unpublished manuscript. SIL archives, Ukarumpa, Papua New Guinea.

Järvinen (=Berghäll), Liisa. 1988a. Focus marking in Mauwake. *Language and Linguistics in Melanesia* 19. 81–96.

Järvinen (=Berghäll), Liisa. 1988b. Mauwake dialect survey. Unpublished manuscript. SIL archives, Ukarumpa, Papua New Guinea.

Järvinen (=Berghäll), Liisa. 1989. A phonological description of Mauwake. Unpublished manuscript. SIL archives, Ukarumpa, Papua New Guinea.

Järvinen (=Berghäll), Liisa. 1990. Mauwake orthography. Unpublished manuscript. SIL archives, Ukarumpa, Papua New Guinea.

Järvinen (=Berghäll), Liisa. 1991. The pronoun system of Mauwake. In Tom Dutton (ed.), *Papers in Papuan linguistics*, vol. 1 (Pacific Linguistics A-73), 57–95.

Järvinen (=Berghäll), Liisa, Poh San Kwan & Saror Aduna. 2001. *Mauwake dictionary*. http://www.sil.org/pacific/png/pubs/49080/Mauwake_dictionary.pdf.

Jespersen, Otto. 1924. *The philosophy of grammar*. London: George Allen & Unwin.

Jespersen, Otto. 1933. *Essentials of English grammar*. London: George Allen & Unwin.

Kadanya, James L. 2006. Writing grammars for the community. *Studies in Language* 30(2). 253–257.

Keenan, Edward. 1985. Relative clauses. In Timothy Shopen (ed.), *Language typology and syntactic description*, vol. 2, 141–170. Cambridge: Cambridge University Press.

Keenan, Edward & Bernard Comrie. 1977. Noun phrase accessibility and universal grammar. *Linguistic Inquiry* 8. 63–99.

References

Kittilä, Seppo. 2002. *Transitivity: Towards a comprehensive typology* (University of Turku publications in general linguistics). Turku, Finland: Åbo Akademis tryckeri.

Kwan, Poh San. 1980. Mauwake (Ulingan) grammar essentials. Unpublished manuscript. SIL archives, Ukarumpa, Papua New Guinea.

Kwan, Poh San. 1983. Transitivity and verb classes in Mauwake. Unpublished manuscript. SIL archives, Ukarumpa, Papua New Guinea.

Kwan, Poh San. 1988. Background study of the Mauwake-speaking people of Madang. Unpublished manuscript. SIL archives, Ukarumpa, Papua New Guinea.

Kwan, Poh San. 1989. The referential meanings of *kema* 'liver' in Mauwake. In Karl Franklin (ed.), *Studies in componential analysis*, vol. 36 (Data papers on Papua New Guinea languages), 47–36.

Kwan, Poh San. 2002. *Topicalization in Mauwake*. Northern Territory University MA thesis.

Lakoff, Robin. 1974. Remarks on *this* and *that*. In M. La Galy, R. Fox & A. Bruck (eds.), *Papers from the tenth regional meeting of the Chicago Linguistic Society*, 345–356. Chicago: Chicago Linguistic Society.

Lang, Ranier. 1976. Review of S. A. Wurm, ed., 1975. *Kivung, Journal of the Linguistic Society of Papua New Guinea* (9) (1). 72–80.

Lean, Glendon A. 1991. *Counting systems in Papua New Guinea. Vol. 15: Madang Province*. 2nd edn. Lae: Department of Mathematics & Statistics, Papua New Guinea University of Technology.

Lees, Robert. 1968. *The grammar of English nominalizations*. The Hague: Mouton.

Lehmann, Christian. 1988. Towards a typology of clause linkage. In John Haiman & Sandra A. Thompson (eds.), *Clause combining in grammar and discourse* (TSL 18), 181–225. Amsterdam / Philadelphia: John Benjamins.

Li, Charles & Sandra A. Thompson. 1976. Subject and topic: A new typology of language. In Charles Li (ed.), *Subject and topic*, 457–489. New York: Academic Press.

Linde, Charlotte. 1979. Focus of attention and the choice of pronouns in discourse. In Talmy Givón (ed.), *Discourse and syntax* (Syntax and semantics 12), 337–354. New York: Academic Press.

Loeweke, Eunice & Jean May. 1982. Grammar of Maiani, Miani and Mala – three languages of the Kaukombaran language family. Unpublished manuscript. SIL archives, Ukarumpa, Papua New Guinea.

Lord, Carol. 1993. *Historical change in serial verb constructions* (TSL 26). Amsterdam: John Benjamins.

Lyons, John. 1968. *Introduction to theoretical linguistics*. Cambridge: Cambridge University Press.

Lyons, John. 1977. *Semantics*. Cambridge: Cambridge University Press.

MacDonald, Lorna. 1990. *A grammar of Tauya*. Berlin: Mouton de Gruyter.

Maddieson, Ian. 1984. *Patterns of sounds*. Cambridge: Cambridge University Press.

Malkiel, Yakov. 1978. Derivational categories. In Joseph H. Greenberg, Charles Ferguson & Edith Moravscik (eds.), *Universals of human language vol. 3: Word structure*, 125–149. Stanford, California: Stanford University Press.

Margetts, Anna. 1999. *Valence and transitivity in Saliba, an Oceanic language of Papua New Guinea.* Nijmegen: Max Planck Institut.

Mathiessen, Christian & Sandra A. Thompson. 1988. The structure of discourse in "subordination". In John Haiman & Sandra A. Thompson (eds.), *Clause combining in grammar and discourse* (TSL 18), 275–329. Amsterdam / Philadelphia: John Benjamins.

McElhanon, Kenneth A. 1973. *Towards a typology of Finisterre-Huon languages, New Guinea* (Pacific Linguistics B-22).

McElhanon, Kenneth A. & C. L. Voorhoeve. 1970. *The trans-New Guinea phylum: Explorations in deep-level genetic relationships* (Pacific Linguistics B-16).

Miestamo, Matti. 2005. *Standard negation: The negation of declarative verbal main clauses in a typological perspective.* Berlin / New York: Mouton de Gruyter.

Moravcsik, Edith. 1978. Reduplicative constructions. In Joseph H. Greenberg, Charles Ferguson & Edith Moravscik (eds.), *Universals of human language vol. 3: Word structure*, 297–334. Stanford, California: Stanford University Press.

Mosel, Ulrike. 2006. Grammaticography. In Felix Ameka, Alan Dench & Nicholas Evans (eds.), *Catching language: The standing challenge of grammar writing*, 41–68. Berlin / New York: Mouton de Gruyter.

Munro, Pamela. 1982. On the transitivity of 'say' verbs. In Paul J. Hopper & Sandra A. Thompson (eds.), *Studies in transitivity* (Syntax and semantics 15). New York: Academic Press.

Murane, Elizabeth. 1974. *Daga grammar from morpheme to discourse.* Glendale, California: The Church Press.

Mushin, Ilana & Lesley Stirling. 2000. *A course on deixis and perspective at Australian Linguistic Institute, University of Melbourne.*

Noonan, Michael. 2006. Grammar writing for a grammar-reading audience. *Studies in Language* 30(2). 351–365.

Noonan, Michael. 2007. Complementation. In Timothy Shopen (ed.), *Language typology and syntactic description*, 2nd edn., vol. 2, 52–150. Cambridge: Cambridge University Press.

Olson, Michael. 1981. *Barai clause junctures: Toward a functional theory of inter-clausal relationships.* Canberra: Australian National University PhD thesis.

Palmer, F. R. 1986. *Mood and modality.* Cambridge: Cambridge University Press.

Pawley, Andrew. 1987. Encoding events in Kalam and English: Different logics for reporting experience. In Russell S. Tomlin (ed.), *Coherence and grounding in discourse* (TSL 11), 329–360. Amsterdam / Philadelphia: John Benjamins.

Pawley, Andrew. 1995. C. L. Voorhoeve and the trans New Guinea phylum hypothesis. In Connie Baak, Mary Bakker & Dick van der Meij (eds.), *Tales from a concave world: Liber amicorum Bert Voorhoeve*, 83–122. Leiden: Projects Division, Department of Languages, Culture of Asia & Oceania, Leiden University.

Pawley, Andrew. 1998. The trans New Guinea phylum hypothesis: A reassessment. In Jelle Miedema, Cecilia Odé & Rien A. C. Dam (eds.), *Perspectives on the Bird's Head of Irian Jaya, Indonesia. Proceedings of the conference, Leiden, 13-17 October 1997.* Projects *division, Department of Languages and Culture of Asia and Oceania, Leiden University*, 655–690.

Pawley, Andrew. 2001. The Proto Trans New Guinea obstruents: Arguments from top-down reconstruction. In Andrew Pawley, Malcolm Ross & Darrell Tryon (eds.), *The boy from Bundaberg: Studies in Melanesian linguistics in honour of Tom Dutton*, 261–300. Canberra: Pacific Linguistics.

Pawley, Andrew. 2005. Preface. In Andrew Pawley, Robert Attenborough, Jack Golson & Robin Hide (eds.), *Papuan pasts: Cultural, linguistic and biological histories of Papuan-speaking peoples*, vi–xvii. Canberra: Pacific Linguistics.

Payne, John R. 1985. Complex phrases and complex sentences. In Timothy Shopen (ed.), *Language typology and syntactic description*, vol. 2, 3–41. Cambridge: Cambridge University Press.

Payne, Thomas. 1997. *Describing morphosyntax: A guide for field linguists*. Cambridge: Cambridge University Press.

Payne, Thomas. 2006. A grammar as a communicative act, or what does a grammatical description really describe? *Studies in Language* 30 (2). 367–383.

Peterson, David. 2007. *Applicative constructions*. Oxford: Oxford University Press.

Quirk, Randolph, Sidney Greenbaum, Geoffrey Leech & Jan Svartvik. 1989 [1985]. *A comprehensive grammar of the English language*. London: Longman.

Radford, Andrew. 1981. *Transformational syntax: A student's guide to Chomsky's extended standard theory*. Cambridge: Cambridge University Press.

Reesink, Ger P. 1983a. On subordination in Usan and other Papuan languages. In Simon Dik (ed.), *Advances in Functional Grammar*, 225–243. Dordrecht: Foris Publications.

Reesink, Ger P. 1983b. Switch reference and topicality hierarchies. *Studies in language* 7. 215–246.

Reesink, Ger P. 1987. *Structures and their function in Usan: A Papuan language of Papua New Guinea* (Studies in Language Companion Series 13). Amsterdam: John Benjamins.

Rice, Keren. 2006a. A typology of good grammars. *Studies in language* 30(2). 385–415.

Rice, Keren. 2006b. Let the language tell its story? In Felix Ameka, Alan Dench & Nicholas Evans (eds.), *Catching language: The standing challenge of grammar writing*, 235–268. Berlin / New York: Mouton de Gruyter.

Roberts, John R. 1987. *Amele*. London: Croom Helm.

Roberts, John R. 1988a. Amele switch reference and the theory of grammar. *Linguistic Inquiry* 19. 45–63.

Roberts, John R. 1988b. Switch reference in Papuan languages. *Australian Journal of Linguistics* 8. 75–117.

Roberts, John R. 1997. Switch-reference in Papua New Guinea: A preliminary survey. In Andrew Pawley (ed.), *Papers in Papuan linguistics No. 3* (Pacific Linguistics A-87), 101–241.

Ross, Malcolm. 1995. The great Papuan pronoun hunt: Recalibrating our sights. In Connie Baak, Mary Bakker & Dick van der Meij (eds.), *Tales from a concave world: Liber amicorum Bert Voorhoeve*, 139–168. Leiden: Projects Division, Department of Languages, Culture of Asia & Oceania, Leiden University.

Ross, Malcolm. 1996. *A preliminary subgrouping of the Madang languages based on pronouns*. Unpublished ms. Research School of Pacific and Asian studies, Australian National University.

Ross, Malcolm. 2005. Pronouns as a preliminary diagnostic for grouping Papuan languages. In Andrew Pawley, Robert Attenborough, Jack Golson & Robin Hide (eds.), *Papuan pasts: Cultural, linguistic and biological histories of Papuan-speaking peoples*, 15–65. Canberra: Pacific Linguistics.

Ross, Malcolm & John Natu Paol. 1978. *A Waskia grammar sketch and vocabulary* (Pacific Linguistics B-56).

Saari, Sinikka. 1985. *Bine-kielen syntaksin pääpiirteet*. University of Helsinki MA thesis.

Sadock, Jerrold & Arnold Zwicky. 1985. Speech act distinctions in syntax. In Timothy Shopen (ed.), *Language typology and syntactic description*, vol. 1, 155–196. Cambridge: Cambridge University Press.

Sapir, Edward. 1921. *Language: An introduction to the study of speech*. New York: Harcourt, Brace & World.

Schachter, Paul. 1985. Parts-of-speech systems. In Timothy Shopen (ed.), *Language typology and syntactic description*, vol. 1, 3–61. Cambridge: Cambridge University Press.

Sebba, Mark. 1987. *The system of serial verbs: An investigation into Sranan and other languages*. Amsterdam: John Benjamins.

Seiler, Hansjakob. 1978. The Cologne project on language universals: Questions, objectives and prospects. In Hansjakob Seiler (ed.), *Language universals. Papers from the conference held at Gummersbach, october 3-8, 1976*. Tübingen: Gunter Narr Verlag.

Shopen, Timothy (ed.). 1985a. *Language typology and syntactic description*. Vol. 1. Cambridge: Cambridge University Press.

Shopen, Timothy (ed.). 1985b. *Language typology and syntactic description*. Vol. 2. Cambridge: Cambridge University Press.

Shopen, Timothy (ed.). 1985c. *Language typology and syntactic description*. Vol. 3. Cambridge: Cambridge University Press.

Shopen, Timothy (ed.). 2007a. *Language typology and syntactic description*. 2nd edn. Vol. 1. Cambridge: Cambridge University Press.

Shopen, Timothy (ed.). 2007b. *Language typology and syntactic description*. 2nd edn. Vol. 2. Cambridge: Cambridge University Press.

Shopen, Timothy (ed.). 2007c. *Language typology and syntactic description*. 2nd edn. Vol. 3. Cambridge: Cambridge University Press.

Simons, Gary. 1977. *Phonostatistic methods* (Workpapers in Papua New Guinea languages 21).

Sommerstein, Alan. 1977. *Modern phonology*. London: Edward Arnold.

Stassen, Leon. 1997. *Intransitive predication*. Oxford: Clarendon Press.

Stassen, Leon. 2008. Comparative constructions. In Martin Haspelmath, Matthew Dryer, David Gil & Bernard Comrie (eds.), *The World Atlas of Language Structures online*, chap. 121. Accessed on 14.6.2009. Munich: Max Planck Digital Library. http://wals.info/feature/121.

References

Talmy, Leonard. 2007. Lexical typologies. In Timothy Shopen (ed.), *Language typology and syntactic description*, 2nd edn., vol. 3, 66–168. Cambridge: Cambridge University Press.

Taylor, John R. 1989. *Linguistic categorization: Prototypes in linguistic theory*. Oxford: Clarendon Press.

Thompson, Sandra A. 1988. A discourse approach to the cross-linguistic category of 'adjective'. In John Hawkins (ed.), *Explaining language universals*, 167–185. Oxford: Blackwell.

Thompson, Sandra A. & Robert Longacre. 1985. Adverbial clauses. In Timothy Shopen (ed.), *Language typology and syntactic description*, vol. 2, 171–234. Cambridge: Cambridge University Press.

Thompson, Sandra A., Robert Longacre & Shin Ja Hwang. 2007. Adverbial clauses. In Timothy Shopen (ed.), *Language typology and syntactic description*, 2nd edn., vol. 2, 237–300. Cambridge: Cambridge University Press.

Tranel, W. 1952. Völkerkundliche und sprachliche Aufzeichnungen aus dem móando-Sprachgebiet in Nordost-Neuguinea. *Anthropos* 47. 447–473.

Van Valin, Robert D. Jr. & Randy J. LaPolla. 1997. *Syntax: Structure, meaning and function*. Cambridge: Cambridge University Press.

Voegelin, C. F. & F. M. Voegelin. 1965. Languages of the world: Indo-Pacific fascicle. *Anthropological linguistics* (7) (9).

Wagner, Herwig & Hermann Reiner (eds.). 1986. *The Lutheran Church in Papua New Guinea: The first hundred years*. Adelaide: Lutheran Publishing House.

Wells, Margaret. 1979. *Siroi grammar* (Pacific Linguistics B-51).

Whitehead, Carl R. 1981. Subject, object and indirect object: Towards a typology of Papuan languages. *Language and linguistics in Melanesia* 13. 32–36.

Whitehead, Carl R. 2004. *A reference grammar of Menya, an Angan language of Papua New Guinea*. University of Manitoba PhD thesis.

Wierzbicka, Anna. 1986. What's in a noun? (or: How do nouns differ in meaning from adjectives?) *Studies in language* 10. 353–389.

Wurm, Stephen A. 1982. *Papuan languages of Oceania*. Tübingen: Gunter Narr Verlag.

Wurm, Stephen A., D. C. Laycock & C. L. Voorhoeve. 1975. General Papuan characteristics. In Stephen A. Wurm (ed.), *New Guinea area languages and language study1: Papuan languages and the New Guinea linguistic scene* (Pacific Linguistics C-38), 935–960.

Ylikoski, Jussi. 2003. Defining non-finites: Action nominals, converbs, and infinitives. *SKY Journal of linguistics* 16. 185–237.

Ylikoski, Jussi. 2009. *Non-finites in North Saami* (Suomalais-Ugrilaisen Seuran toimituksia = Mémoires de la Société Finno-Ougrienne 257). Sastamala: Vammalan Kirjapaino.

Z'Graggen, J. A. 1971. *Classificatory and typological studies in the languages of the Madang District* (Pacific Linguistics C-19).

Z'Graggen, J. A. 1975a. *The languages of the madang district, Papua New Guinea* (Pacific Linguistics B-41).

Z'Graggen, J. A. 1975b. The Madang-Adelbert range subphylum. In Stephen A. Wurm (ed.), *New Guinea area languages and language study1: Papuan languages and the New Guinea linguistic scene* (Pacific Linguistics C-38), 569–612.

Z'Graggen, J. A. 1980. *A comparative word list of the Northern Adelbert Range languages, Madang Province, Papua New Guinea* (Pacific Linguistics D-31).

Name index

Aduna, Saror, 2, 14
Agard, F., 22
Ahlman, Erik, 197
Ameka, Felix K., 3
Anderson, Stephen, 65, 66, 115, 129, 156
Andrews, Avery, 256, 352, 357

Bauer, Laurie, 65
Berghäll (=Järvinen), Liisa, 14, 209, 270, 284
Berlin, Brent, 58, 77
Bloomfield, Leonard, 65, 66
Brumm, Geoffrey, 7, 8
Bugenhagen, Robert, 131, 144
Bunn, Gordon, 117
Bybee, Joan, 133, 281

Capell, Arthur, 13
Chafe, Wallace, 383, 395
Comrie, Bernard, 73, 149, 156, 184, 186, 272, 273, 279, 333, 355, 358, 371
Cristofaro, Sonia, 1–3, 187, 319
Croft, William, 241
Crowley, Terry, 189, 192
Crystal, David, 59, 131, 157, 240, 321, 353, 383

Davies, Hugh, 7
Davies, John, 362
Dench, Alan, 1, 2
Dik, Simon, 383, 387
Dixon, R. M. W., 2, 16, 53, 60, 74, 75, 161, 216, 259, 266, 348, 355, 357, 361, 362, 370, 383, 394
Downing, Pamela, 65, 66
Dryer, Matthew S., 2, 19, 184, 231, 269
Duamba, Wenceslaus, 7

Evans, Nicholas, 1, 2
Ezard, Bryan, 22

Farr, Cynthia J. M., 117, 192, 194, 213, 279, 295, 343, 344, 353, 362, 376
Foley, William A., 14, 18, 25, 32, 50, 54, 88, 96, 117, 142, 149, 151, 152, 173, 183, 186, 189, 190, 194, 224, 251, 255, 281, 333, 349, 366, 369
Franklin, Karl J., 87, 88, 151, 343, 362
Frawley, William, 54, 58, 59, 130

Givón, Talmy, 73, 74, 91, 96, 100, 116, 130, 159, 169, 192, 243, 256, 259, 265, 270, 279, 321, 343, 345, 352, 356, 383, 388, 389, 391
Goldberg, Adele, 259
Greenberg, Joseph H., 13, 133, 184
Grimes, Barbara, 14
Grimes, J. E., 22

Höltker, G., 7
Haantjens, H. A., 5
Haiman, John, 13, 14, 80, 88, 120, 224, 281, 292, 302, 328, 332–334, 343, 352, 376, 383
Hakulinen, Auli, 74, 89, 127, 265, 266
Halliday, M. A. K., 117, 183, 352
Hardin, Barbara, 80, 88, 102, 142, 143, 149, 151, 164, 226, 281, 366
Hasan, Ruqaiya, 117
Haspelmath, Martin, 210, 212, 310, 322, 325
Heine, Bernd, 105, 106, 266–268
Hepner, Mark, 88, 143, 164, 226, 362, 366
Hollrung, M., 7

Name index

Hopper, Paul, 55, 56, 59, 130, 134, 259, 272, 273
Horie, Kaoru, 371
Hwang, Shin Ja, 352, 376

Järvinen (=Berghäll), Liisa, 2, 14, 21, 87, 90, 96, 394, 398
James, Dorothy, 189, 191, 192
Jespersen, Otto, 54, 61, 65, 66, 74

Kadanya, James L., 4
Karlsson, Fred, 74, 89, 127, 265, 266
Kay, Paul, 58, 77
Keenan, Edward, 115, 353, 358
Kittilä, Seppo, 157, 160, 259
Kwan, Poh San, 2, 14, 195

Lakoff, Robin, 295
Lang, Ranier, 14
LaPolla, Randy J., 61, 157, 257, 259, 262
Laycock, D. C., 13, 14
Lean, Glendon A., 82
Lees, Robert, 65
Lehmann, Christian, 352
Li, Charles, 383
Linde, Charlotte, 395
Loeweke, Eunice, 31
Longacre, Robert, 332, 352, 376
Lord, Carol, 189, 190
Lyons, John, 54, 65, 66, 74, 96, 119, 147

MacDonald, Lorna, 14, 302, 376
Maddieson, Ian, 32
Malkiel, Yakov, 133
Margetts, Anna, 192
Mathiessen, Christian, 352
May, Jean, 31
McElhanon, Kenneth A., 14, 88
Miestamo, Matti, 284
Mihalic, Frank, 7, 8
Moravcsik, Edith, 143
Mosel, Ulrike, 1, 4
Munro, Pamela, 333, 334, 343, 362
Murane, Elizabeth, 117

Mushin, Ilana, 297

Noonan, Michael, 2, 271

Olson, Michael, 333

Palmer, F. R., 146, 147
Paol, John Natu, 14, 88, 102, 117, 395
Pawley, Andrew, 6, 14, 18
Payne, John R., 322
Payne, Thomas, 2, 134, 136, 185, 190, 262, 281
Peterson, David, 138

Quirk, Randolph, 65, 66, 127

Radford, Andrew, 259
Reesink, Ger P., 14, 19, 39, 80, 88, 96, 98, 102, 117, 120, 143, 149, 164, 170, 186, 224, 226, 258, 279, 287, 288, 292, 293, 302, 303, 307, 308, 327, 328, 334, 340, 341, 343–346, 348, 352, 353, 366, 369, 370, 376
Reiner, Hermann, 7
Rice, Keren, 2
Roberts, John R., 61, 80, 88, 89, 142, 151, 154, 194, 226, 255, 258, 293, 303, 328, 332–334, 341, 343, 344, 353, 362, 363
Ross, Malcolm, 6, 9, 13–16, 63, 87, 88, 102, 117, 395

Saari, Sinikka, 89, 117
Sadock, Jerrold, 91
Sapir, Edward, 54
Schachter, Paul, 54, 197
Sebba, Mark, 189, 192
Seiler, Hansjakob, 59
Simons, Gary, 22
Sommerstein, Alan, 41
Stassen, Leon, 263, 270, 303
Stirling, Lesley, 297

Talmy, Leonard, 166
Taylor, John R., 58, 59

Name index

Thompson, Sandra A., 55, 56, 59, 73, 74, 130, 134, 241, 259, 272, 273, 279, 332, 352, 376, 383
Tranel, W., 7, 10

Van Valin, Robert D. Jr., 61, 157, 190, 255, 257, 259, 262, 333
Voegelin, C. F., 13
Voegelin, F. M., 13
Voorhoeve, C. L., 13, 14

Wagner, Herwig, 7
Wells, Margaret, 88, 102, 117
Whitehead, Carl R., 117, 194, 258, 279, 295, 353
Wierzbicka, Anna, 58, 59, 74
Wurm, Stephen A., 13, 14, 50, 54, 57, 87, 88, 151, 162, 251, 309, 333

Ylikoski, Jussi, 72, 271, 276

Z'Graggen, J. A., 8, 13, 14, 25, 31, 96
Zwicky, Arnold, 91

Language index

Adelbert Range, 14, 96*
Alam, 5, 9*

Bepour, 14*, 14
Bine, 117
Bunabun, 7, 14

Daga, 117

English, 34, 38, 51, 59, 65, 66, 69*, 97, 99, 100, 104, 107, 113, 128*, 128, 138*, 160*, 160, 161, 168*, 173, 174, 177, 182, 204, 206, 210, 211, 215, 241*, 252, 253*, 259, 262, 310, 315, 370*, 394

Finnish, 65, 174, 197*, 266

German, 7, 10, 65
Golin, 117

Kalam, 18
Kaukombar, 9, 88
Korafe, 117, 194*
Korak-Waskia, 9
Kumil, 5, 14*, 14, 88

Maiani, 7, 9*, 9
Mala, 9*, 9, 50, 138
Manam, 5*, 9, 306
Mandarin Chinese, 65, 241*
Mawak, 9
Meiwok, 22, 23
Miani, 5, 9*, 9, 31, 32
Moere, 14
Muaka, 22–24, 154*
Musar, 14

Papuan, 3, 5, 12, 13*, 13, 16, 17, 18*, 18, 19*, 19, 25, 27, 32, 50*, 54*, 57, 74, 79, 80, 86*, 87, 88, 96*, 116*, 117, 130, 142, 149, 151*, 151, 153*, 173, 179, 180, 183*, 186*, 189, 192, 194, 211*, 213*, 224, 241*, 251, 256*, 258, 274, 279, 281, 282, 284, 287, 294, 296*, 296, 302, 303, 307*, 316*, 328, 333*, 333, 334*, 341*, 341, 343, 344, 345*, 349, 353, 362, 366, 369, 370, 376
Papur, 21–23, 28
Pihom, 14
Proto Croisilles, 87, 88
Proto Madang, 87, 88

Sikor, 22
Siroi, 88, 102*, 117

Tarikapa, 22
Tibor, 9
Tok Pisin, 1, 5, 8, 9, 38, 50, 51, 58, 76, 82, 138*, 138, 178*, 204, 211*, 215*, 226*, 234, 249, 278*, 286, 287, 293, 310, 315, 316*, 331
Trans New Guinea, 9, 13, 14, 16, 19, 50*, 251

Ulingan, 5, 7, 8, 10, 13, 14*, 21–24, 28, 84, 103*, 183, 185, 207, 245, 300, 305, 364
Usan, 14, 74*, 88, 96, 98, 102*, 117, 142, 143, 144*, 149, 151*, 164, 170*, 226*, 258*, 288, 292, 293*, 303*, 308, 340, 344, 348*, 369

Waskia, 14, 88, 102*, 117, 142, 395*

Subject index

action nominal, 271, 367
adjective class, 60, 74, 303*
adjective phrase, 3, 58, 59, 74*, 74, 81, 127, 197, 236, 240, 241, 270
adverb, 3, 94, 120, 124, 129, 134, 136, 142, 155, 178, 197*, 197, 203, 204, 206, 219, 243, 246, 258, 282, 283, 295
adverbial phrase, 3, 192, 197, 203, 207, 231, 243, 248, 258, 265, 270, 385–387, 395
adversative, 120, 211, 224, 322, 325*, 325, 327, 328, 375
adversative coordinator, 327
affixation, 17, 53, 54*, 63, 89
agent, 3, 17, 159, 256, 343, 384
agentive, 164, 166
agglutinative, 17, 130
alienably possessed nouns, 11, 18, 54, 63, 64, 93
allomorphs, 47
allophonic variation, 33, 47
alternative question, 310, 311
alveo-palatal, 28
alveolar, 25, 27, 47
antonymous, 302
article, 21, 119, 209*, 310, 400
aspect, 17, 129, 136*, 142, 150*, 150, 182, 184, 186–188, 192, 272, 318
aspect marking, 153, 351
aspectual distinction, 272
augmented action, 143
auxiliary, 18, 20, 142, 166, 168, 170, 171, 175, 182–186, 188, 189, 191–193, 206, 369

benefactive, 17, 97, 129, 133, 141, 142, 145, 154, 158, 160*, 164, 167, 192, 242, 257
benefactive marking, 350
beneficiary, 3, 95, 97, 115, 130, 133, 140, 141*, 141, 142, 145, 146, 148, 149, 152, 154, 162*, 167, 242, 252, 262, 358, 359
beneficiary form, 96
bilabial, 25, 27, 28, 32
bilingualism, 9
body part, 63, 181, 260, 262

calque, 215*, 331
case, 3, 8, 18, 21, 23, 24, 42, 53–55, 57, 62, 65, 80, 84, 89, 90, 92, 96–98, 101, 103, 108–111, 113, 118, 119, 125, 140, 141, 145, 146, 152, 156, 161, 163, 165, 186, 189, 191, 209, 214–216, 222, 226, 232, 238, 243, 255*, 256, 263, 268, 275, 279, 289, 291, 296*, 301, 305, 324, 331, 333, 339, 342, 351, 354, 355, 359, 363, 373, 383, 400, 401
cataphoric reference, 119
causative, 17, 133, 138, 139, 144*, 157*, 164–166, 170*, 170, 175, 277, 332
clan, 9, 10, 115, 361
clausal constituent, 251, 256, 383
clause, 1, 4, 17, 18, 20, 34, 36, 37, 53, 73, 81, 88, 91, 92, 95, 98, 99, 102, 103, 107–109, 113, 116, 118, 120, 123, 127–130, 133*, 138, 140, 144, 151*, 152, 153*, 153, 155, 156, 158, 164, 168, 188, 192–194, 197, 199, 206–209, 213*, 215, 219, 222, 223, 225–227, 231, 235, 242, 243, 246,

247, 251*, 251, 252, 255, 256*, 256, 257*, 257, 258, 259*, 259, 261, 263, 269–271, 272*, 272–279, 281–284, 287–291, 292*, 293, 296, 299, 300, 302, 307–312, 315–317, 319–321, 323, 324, 326–328, 331–335, 337, 338, 340, 341, 343–346, 348, 353, 355, 356, 360–362, 364, 366, 369–371, 373–376, 380, 383–387, 389, 392–394, 396, 397, 399–402
clause chaining, 186, 192, 210, 319, 328, 333*, 333
clitic, 42, 53, 120, 124, 142, 151*, 206, 207*, 216, 217, 220, 223*, 225, 226*, 226, 238, 239, 243–245, 248, 281, 309, 311, 312, 397–401
closed question, 310
clusters, 41*, 41, 51, 129, 183, 242*
co-referentiality, 343
colour adjective, 77, 172
colour term, 77
comitative, 19, 104*, 104, 114, 216–218, 236, 239, 248, 268, 358, 359, 399
comitative clitic, 85, 114, 216, 217, 249, 359
comparative, 14, 21, 189, 302, 358*
comparison, 21, 31*, 31, 55, 80*, 80, 216, 219, 248, 302, 303*, 303, 304, 358*
complement clause, 120, 180, 293, 309, 352, 361, 365, 366, 370–374
complement-taking verb, 361
completive aspect, 44, 50*, 50, 185, 186
conditional, 17, 36, 146, 224, 334, 352, 376–380, 383
conjunction, 322
connective, 77, 83, 127, 155, 178*, 209, 210, 211*, 211, 212, 213*, 213, 215*, 215, 226, 238, 239, 291, 325–327, 329–332, 379
container, 26, 155
continuity, 143, 153, 188, 211, 343, 346

continuous aspect, 132, 170, 171, 182, 185–188, 193, 277, 318, 339
contrasted element, 225, 290
coordinate, 18, 68, 128*, 192, 193*, 193, 209, 211, 237, 238, 241, 249, 251*, 251, 320, 328, 332–334, 335*, 349, 360, 380, 381
coordinate sentence, 227, 319, 380
coordination, 192, 209, 242, 319, 321–324, 328, 331, 333*
copula, 171, 266*, 269
counterfactual, 17, 120, 132, 133, 146, 149, 281, 366, 377
counterfactual form, 180, 282, 366
counting system, 82
culture, 6, 8, 11, 61

dative, 3, 19, 88, 100, 101, 103–110, 161, 169, 194, 237, 242, 243, 245, 246, 254, 263, 266–268, 283, 299*, 359
dative shift, 164, 256
declarative, 307, 319, 320
declarative sentence, 18, 307
deictic, 21, 90, 116–120, 122–124, 197–199, 201–204, 218, 232, 243, 246–248, 253, 272, 274, 294–296, 297*, 297, 305, 360, 365, 375, 387
deictic centre, 173, 174, 199*, 293, 295, 296, 297*, 297, 364
deictic orientation, 174
deictic shift, 297, 364, 365, 368
deictic system, 117, 123, 293
demonstrative, 61, 81, 89, 98*, 116–120, 127, 133*, 154, 172, 211, 219, 231, 247, 278, 279, 294, 325*, 327, 328, 352, 353, 355, 358, 375
derivation, 53, 54, 122, 123, 131–133, 136*, 152, 192, 350, 351
derivational prefix, 131
descriptive clause, 270
desiderative clause, 367
dialect, 21*, 21, 22*, 22–24, 28, 103*, 112, 154*

Subject index

dimension, 60
diphthong, 39, 40, 42, 43
direct quote, 177, 361–364, 368
directional verb, 161, 173, 174, 337
discourse-pragmatic, 267
disjunction, 212, 242, 310*, 322, 326
distal, 117, 122, 272, 295
distal demonstrative, 118, 119, 215, 237, 294, 327, 381
distal-1 deictic, 21, 117, 355
distal-1 demonstrative, 118, 219, 295, 353, 361, 369, 374, 390
ditransitive, 157, 160*, 260, 261
double causative, 139
dual comitative, 239
dual form, 148

echo question, 312
effect clause, 328
elision, 41, 44, 55, 308
ellipsis, 57, 348
elliptical, 55*, 58, 118, 258, 268, 310, 348
endophoric, 119
enhanced quality, 45
equative clause, 108, 269, 270
exclusive, 19, 88, 118, 149, 383, 400
existential clause, 266
experience verb, 260
experiencer, 17, 181, 195, 260, 345

family, 8–10, 12, 13, 14*, 14, 64, 103, 140, 158, 235, 273, 276, 322, 364, 407
final, 3, 9, 18, 20, 30, 31*, 34, 35, 37, 38, 39*, 41, 43*, 43–48, 50, 53, 55, 56, 73, 89, 92, 94, 109, 131, 132, 134, 143, 151, 155, 156, 180, 181, 183, 186, 192, 203, 208, 226, 227, 251, 270, 292*, 296, 310, 312, 316, 317, 319, 320*, 320–323, 327, 333*, 333, 340, 345, 346, 348, 349, 352, 353, 355, 366, 369, 375, 378, 385, 386, 400
final verb, 34, 35, 147, 152, 155, 156, 171, 189, 193*, 225, 226, 307, 309, 344, 385, 386, 391
finite, 3, 18, 21, 53, 97, 119, 120, 131, 142, 149, 151*, 151–153, 169, 189, 231, 267, 271, 279, 293, 300, 316, 320, 332, 333*, 333, 334, 341, 355, 388*, 388, 390, 391, 397, 398
finite clause, 36, 93, 155, 273, 274, 319, 323, 327, 333, 335, 336, 339, 347, 349, 352, 353, 361, 366, 371
finite verb, 131, 142, 147, 151, 152, 189, 190, 251, 271*, 272, 273, 279, 300, 350, 351, 356, 366, 374
focal, 58, 59, 88, 90, 94, 95, 111, 112, 120, 122, 125, 222, 337
focus, 11, 42, 64, 94*, 120, 122, 125, 153, 178, 179, 185, 194, 222, 224, 225*, 225, 245, 255*, 383, 394, 395, 397, 400–402
focus clitic, 13*, 95, 120, 123, 226, 238, 260, 266, 276, 283, 284, 287, 292, 389, 398–400
focus marker, 94, 98, 123, 125, 224–226, 260, 273, 308, 336, 355*, 355, 395*, 395, 396
focus marking, 122, 224, 226, 269, 274, 355, 389, 394–397, 400, 401
focus of contrast, 395
fractions, 86*, 87
free adverb, 222
frequency, 3, 26, 34, 44, 62, 79*, 109, 115, 116*, 117, 191, 222, 245, 302, 381, 383*
fricative, 27–29, 31, 50
future, 18, 106, 115, 120, 146, 147, 149, 150, 151*, 155, 169, 175, 200, 225, 266, 269, 278, 283, 296, 316, 318, 356, 366, 367, 377–379, 393, 398

geminate vowel, 39, 42, 43, 45, 122
generic verb, 179*, 179, 351
genitive, 3, 19, 21, 55*, 58, 59, 63, 65, 68, 69, 90, 93, 94, 100–103, 107–109, 111, 113, 217, 222, 233–235, 242, 256, 268, 273, 274, 358, 359

Subject index

glottal stop, 25
grammatical word, 53
grammaticalization, 106, 192, 266, 268

habitual, 150*, 150, 171, 182, 185–188, 277, 318, 376, 379
human propensity, 60, 79, 236

illocutionary force, 319, 320
imaginative conditional, 377
imperative, 19, 89, 91, 92, 116*, 116, 120, 132, 133, 146, 147*, 147, 148, 228, 294, 307, 315–317, 319–321, 366–368, 377, 378
imperative clause, 91, 95
impersonal predicate, 344
inceptive meaning, 171
inchoative, 50, 56, 130, 134, 135, 136*, 136, 138, 158, 159*, 173
inchoative verb, 138
inchoative verbaliser, 81
indefinite, 85, 97, 128, 129, 224, 267, 332, 347, 388*, 388–390, 397–399, 401
indirect question, 366, 372
indirect quote, 361, 363, 365, 366
indirect speech, 297, 361, 362, 363*
inducive causative, 166
infinitive, 271
inflection, 18, 54, 55, 119, 131, 133, 134, 189, 190, 242, 257, 266, 281, 315, 333
inflectional affix, 53
inhabitants, 7*, 7, 8, 62, 94, 105
inherently ditransitive, 261
instrumental, 5, 192, 221, 222, 248, 249, 359
instrumental clitic, 221, 246–249
intensifier, 55, 56, 77, 302, 304
intensify, 197*, 205, 316
intensifying function, 80
intensity adverb, 205, 209, 240, 243, 246, 248, 277, 281, 292, 304, 316
interjection, 38, 282, 314, 316

internal connective, 330
internal speech, 179
interrogative, 19, 124, 125, 127, 212, 226*, 307, 319, 320, 331, 335, 357
interrogative marker, 19
interrogative sentence, 128, 307
intonation, 34–38, 128*, 184, 255, 307, 309, 311, 319, 328, 353, 377, 380
intonation contour, 34, 35, 192, 363, 384, 387
intonation pattern, 36, 307, 352
irrealis, 120, 149*, 149, 151*, 225, 281, 366, 398
iterative action, 143
iterativity, 143

kinship system, 11, 12, 64*, 64
kinship term, 11, 63, 240, 392

lateral, 50
limiter, 94, 222, 226
limiter clitic, 207, 222
limiting clitic, 103, 111, 112
loan word, 50, 51
location, 22*, 104, 105, 116, 117, 122, 149, 174, 190*, 219, 243–246, 254, 266, 295, 376, 395, 402
locative, 96, 103, 104*, 104, 105, 116, 117, 120, 121, 123, 124, 126, 129, 161, 164, 174, 197*, 197, 198, 201, 219, 235, 243, 246, 248, 249, 253, 254, 258*, 258, 266, 302, 352, 358–360, 375, 384, 386
locative adverb, 129, 161, 246, 295, 400*
locative adverbial, 103, 161, 169, 237, 253, 254, 258, 350, 360, 374
locative clitic, 161, 176, 198, 219, 220, 244–247, 249
locative phrase, 105, 174, 176, 243–246, 253, 265, 387

main clause, 17, 20, 36, 102, 143, 192, 193, 223, 224, 251, 293, 308, 319–

Subject index

321, 352–357, 359–361, 363, 367–369, 372, 373, 375, 376
manner adverb, 177, 198, 206*, 213, 215, 248, 305
manner adverbs, 20, 117, 122, 197*, 197, 203, 204
manner phrase, 248, 249, 258
material adverb, 197
matrix clause, 364
medial, 3, 18, 20, 23, 30, 36, 41, 43, 89, 92, 93, 128*, 131, 132, 141*, 147, 151*, 151, 152, 155, 156, 168, 169*, 169, 181, 184–187, 189, 190*, 192*, 192, 193, 210, 213, 251, 269, 286, 292, 294, 308, 316, 319, 321–324, 333*, 333–337, 339–341, 344, 345, 347, 349, 366, 371, 374, 377, 378, 385, 391, 400
medial clause, 92, 93, 128, 152, 153, 155, 156, 171, 184, 251, 269, 274, 275, 283, 292, 296, 316, 317, 319–321, 323, 333–337, 339, 340, 343–345, 347–350, 373
medial verb, 44*, 44, 47, 50, 144*, 151, 152, 153*, 153, 156, 169, 180, 186, 190, 193, 214, 274, 292*, 292, 293, 316*, 316, 317*, 317, 321, 333, 338, 339, 346, 350, 351, 378
missionaries, 7*, 7, 8
modal adverb, 206, 281, 311
modality, 146, 272, 281, 283, 369
mode, 281
monosyllabic, 42, 43
mood, 129–131, 146, 147, 152, 281, 316, 321, 335, 377
morpheme breaks, 4, 40
morphophonological alternations, 44
motion verb, 190, 191
myth, 13

negate, 209, 273, 287, 288, 310, 315
negation, 98, 184, 190, 209*, 209, 242, 263, 268, 270, 271, 273, 284, 287–289, 291, 292*, 292, 309, 310, 314, 335, 358, 369, 373, 400
negative interjection, 290, 314
negator, 98, 99, 194, 196, 209, 215*, 215, 240, 254*, 263, 266, 268, 270*, 270, 271, 284–289, 291, 293, 314, 315, 331, 376
negator adverb, 194
nickname, 11
nominalization, 73, 145, 271–276, 279, 352
non-coreferentiality, 107, 108
non-deictic, 115, 197, 199, 201, 203, 247
non-derived, 74, 75, 203
non-reduction type, 355
non-restrictive, 352*, 360, 361
non-scalar, 75
non-verbal predicate, 34, 81, 100, 108, 169, 171, 225, 231, 241, 242, 269, 276, 278, 282, 285, 302, 358, 395, 397, 398, 402
noun, 3, 18–21, 54*, 54, 55*, 55–58, 59*, 59–72, 73*, 73, 74, 76, 79, 80, 86–89, 97, 98*, 100–102, 106*, 109, 119, 126, 127, 129, 130, 134, 136, 160, 172, 197, 198, 201, 207, 216, 217, 219, 222, 223, 231–233, 235–240, 242, 246, 247, 256, 260, 262, 265, 267, 271, 273, 274, 289, 299, 300, 302–304, 353*, 356–358, 361, 370, 375, 387, 398
noun phrase, 3, 19, 55, 57, 62, 67–69, 73, 87, 94, 97, 100, 105, 118, 126, 142, 197, 207, 209, 216–219, 224, 226, 231, 232, 235–249, 256, 257, 267, 270, 272, 275, 279, 287, 289, 298, 299, 336, 346, 353, 354, 356, 357, 384, 388, 392, 395
NP, 231*, 233, 241, 242*, 247, 257*, 259*, 353*
number, 5, 8, 13, 14, 18, 19, 22*, 39*, 41, 46, 47, 49, 51, 53–55, 58, 63, 71, 74, 77, 83, 88, 89, 97, 114, 115, 119, 125–127, 129–132, 134, 143, 147, 149–153, 157, 158, 160, 164,

169, 180, 186, 190, 195*, 211, 216,
218, 236, 239, 243, 256, 258, 260,
272, 294, 298–300, 305, 307, 333,
338, 341, 343, 344, 391, 395
numeral, 54, 81, 82, 84, 86, 89, 98*, 110,
118, 204, 205, 231, 270, 298, 301

object, 3, 17, 21, 45, 55, 62*, 88, 95, 96*,
96, 97*, 97–99, 111, 115, 129, 138,
140, 142, 143, 157–159, 160*, 160–
168, 177–179, 181, 184, 189, 194,
224, 231, 242, 245, 251, 252, 253*,
253, 255, 256, 257*, 257, 258,
259*, 259–263, 265, 266, 274,
275, 277, 287, 289, 300–304, 308,
336, 340, 343, 345, 348, 350, 354–
356, 358*, 358, 359, 361, 366*,
370, 383, 385–387, 389, 390, 392,
395–397, 399
obligation, 9, 151, 276, 283
opposite sex, 11, 12*, 64
OSV, 251*

passive, 18, 336
passive voice, 131, 168
passivization, 164, 256, 383*
past activity, 372
perception verb, 348, 372
permission, 206, 283
person marking, 62, 89, 90, 98, 133, 151,
163, 195, 239, 294, 364, 367
phonology, 1, 16, 25, 38, 50, 131, 149
phonostatistic method, 22
physical property, 60, 79, 236
place name, 62, 94, 232, 235
plosives, 26, 31, 39
plurality, 44, 57, 73, 87, 119, 143, 239, 299–
301
polar question, 36, 309–311, 314, 335
politeness, 92, 345, 401
polysyllabic, 43*, 43, 45
portmanteau, 169, 226
position, 1, 18–20, 30, 34–36, 41–43, 56,
58*, 58, 65, 81, 91, 93, 96, 98,

102, 103, 108, 113, 118, 120*, 123,
124, 127, 130, 133, 137, 141, 145,
147*, 171, 180, 182, 187, 188, 192,
194, 197, 206, 208, 210, 226, 232,
233, 236–238, 241, 243, 247, 251–
254, 255*, 257, 263, 266*, 267,
288, 307, 315, 319, 322, 324, 328,
333*, 337, 352, 355, 356, 376,
381, 383–387, 392, 395, 400, 401
possessee, 266*, 266–268
possession, 63, 68, 74, 93, 100, 106, 107,
268
possessive, 19, 63, 88, 90, 100*, 100, 101,
102*, 102, 103, 105–109, 113, 129,
169, 233–235, 237, 262, 265, 268,
271, 273, 285, 286
possessive clause, 268
possessive construction, 107
possessive phrase, 102, 242
possessor, 63, 64, 100, 101, 103, 106*, 106–
109, 231, 232, 234, 262, 266*,
266–268, 396
possessor raising, 158, 256, 259, 262
post-modifier, 59, 68, 231, 237, 241, 268
postposition, 142, 217, 218, 239, 243, 248,
305, 359
pragmatic connective, 238
pre-modifier, 59, 74
predicate function, 286
predicate-copula, 20
predication, 129, 130, 189, 206, 222, 226,
251, 252, 263, 268, 383, 387
predictive conditional, 377, 380
pretension, 305, 306
pro-drop, 89
progressive, 171, 182, 185–187
prohibition, 284, 315
pronominal object, 158, 274
pronoun, 3, 4, 14, 21, 42, 55*, 58, 62*,
62, 63, 68, 69, 82, 87–91, 93,
94*, 94, 95, 96*, 96–101, 102*,
102, 103, 105–115, 116*, 116, 118,
119, 129, 150, 159, 161, 164, 167,

Subject index

179, 194, 196, 217, 231–237, 239, 240, 242, 243, 245, 246, 252–254, 256, 257, 260, 263, 265–268, 279, 283, 299*, 299, 356, 357, 359–361, 364, 388, 390–392, 394, 401
proper name, 62, 116, 240, 364, 388
proper noun, 61, 360
proposition, 215, 226*, 281, 282, 309, 400
protasis, 17, 327, 329, 376–380, 383
proximate demonstrative, 294, 295, 360
proximity, 117, 119, 173, 295
purpose clause, 277, 367–369

qualifier, 19, 55, 57, 62, 72*, 72, 231, 235
quantification, 3, 142, 298, 300
quantifier, 55*, 81*, 81, 85, 98*, 119, 204, 236, 241, 268, 287–289, 304
quantifier phrase, 81, 127, 241
question clitic, 36, 127, 213, 309, 311, 312, 398
question marker, 36, 83, 94, 127, 213, 216, 226*, 226, 238, 310, 320, 326, 335
question word, 13*, 19, 35, 117, 123, 125–127, 129, 206, 215*, 215, 307–309, 311, 312, 320, 357, 397
quote formula, 362

realis mode, 281
realis-type verb, 120
recipient, 3, 95, 96, 97*, 97, 99, 107, 108, 140, 160, 162*, 163, 164, 252, 253*, 257, 261, 262, 358, 399
reciprocal, 19, 112, 113, 164, 167
recursion, 53, 346
reduplicate, 400
reduplication, 17, 26, 44–46, 57, 67, 73, 80, 83, 142, 143, 201, 299, 300
reference clause, 333, 334, 336, 337, 339–341, 343, 347, 369
reflexive, 19, 82, 94, 112–114, 164, 167
relative clause, 103, 120, 137, 156, 223, 231, 284, 309, 328, 352–356, 361,

375, 381, 387
relative marker, 328, 353, 355, 360, 381
relative proximity, 117
repetition, 143, 191, 346
replacive, 353, 354
restricted use, 58
restrictive pronoun, 94, 103, 113
result clause, 213*, 213, 215
resultative connective, 181
resultative verb, 136, 301
right-dislocation, 337, 378
rites of passage, 11
rituals, 10, 24, 275

same sex, 11
semantic valence, 164, 167
semivowels, 28, 29
sequential action verb, 338
sequentiality, 130, 132, 151*, 185, 338
serial verb, 18, 142, 189, 190*, 191, 192*, 192, 193
similarity, 74, 95, 117, 172, 215, 216, 219, 304–306, 328*, 330, 353, 360, 361
simple sentence, 251*, 251, 319
simultaneity, 130, 132, 151*, 153, 193*, 333
social deixis, 294
SOV, 251*
speaker's location, 117, 293
spirits, 10, 87, 94, 104, 149, 153, 173, 232, 233, 276, 325, 330, 359, 391
spoken language, 93, 289, 400
standard of comparison, 21, 302, 303
stative aspect, 151, 185, 188, 189, 318
stative verb, 168
status system, 149
stress, 29, 34, 35, 37, 41–45, 50, 65–69, 99, 102, 111, 136, 180, 184, 190*, 192, 194, 207*, 216, 228, 234, 255*, 287–289, 311, 343, 402
stress centre, 66–69, 71
stress pattern, 29, 45, 96
subject, 3, 17, 18, 21, 44, 50, 55, 66, 88–95, 97–103, 107–110, 113, 115, 116*,

496

Subject index

116, 118*, 125, 129–132, 138, 140, 147, 148, 151*, 151, 152, 153*, 153, 154, 157, 159, 161, 162, 164, 165, 167, 168, 169*, 169, 171–173, 180, 182–186, 188, 189, 193*, 206, 213, 224, 231, 242, 251–253, 255, 256*, 256, 257*, 257, 260, 263, 266*, 266, 267, 269, 272*, 273–278, 286, 287, 292*, 292–294, 296, 299, 300, 302, 308, 316, 317, 321, 333–338, 340–348, 350, 355, 356, 358, 361, 362, 366–368, 383*, 384, 385, 388, 389, 395*, 395–397, 399
subject disambiguation, 396
subject marking, 154, 155, 217, 218, 256, 257, 293, 342, 344, 345, 390, 391
subject pronoun, 19, 62*, 91, 92, 102, 115, 116*, 116
subordinate clause, 17, 20, 251, 319, 320, 327, 352, 371*, 376
suffix, 32, 44, 47*, 47–50, 55, 72, 81, 95, 97*, 97, 109, 112, 118–120, 123, 129, 131–140, 141*, 141, 142, 145, 146, 148, 149, 152*, 152–154, 157, 158, 160*, 162, 164, 165, 167, 170*, 170, 173, 175, 180, 218, 256, 257, 277, 281, 286, 294, 300, 341, 357, 365, 377
superlative, 302, 304
switch-reference, 151*, 154, 192, 256, 294, 334, 341, 343, 391
syllable, 28, 29, 34, 35, 37, 39*, 39, 40*, 40–42, 43*, 43–48, 50, 65, 67, 111, 122, 125, 137, 175, 207*, 307, 387
syllable type, 43
syntactic subject, 151*, 181, 341, 343, 384
syntactic valence, 164, 167

tail-head linkage, 18, 349, 351, 385, 386
temporal, 18*, 18, 59, 123, 130, 149, 184, 191, 192*, 197*, 197, 199–202, 220, 221, 233, 243, 246, 247, 249, 279, 296, 297*, 297, 323, 324, 333, 334, 339, 340, 344, 352, 356, 358–360, 374, 383, 384, 386, 387, 395
temporal adverb, 205, 246, 278, 364
temporal deixis, 117
temporal phrase, 19, 233, 247, 254, 386
temporal subordinate clause, 120
tense, 17, 18, 20, 32, 35, 44, 47*, 47–49, 115, 120, 122, 129–133, 141*, 145–147, 149–152, 155, 156, 157*, 157, 168–171, 172*, 172, 184, 186–188, 190, 225, 266–269, 272, 281, 296*, 296, 297*, 307, 316, 318, 333, 339, 356, 364, 366, 377–379, 398
tense distinction, 170
tense marking, 133, 155, 157
tense system, 18, 149
tense-mood system, 146
text data, 4, 92, 214, 241*, 381
theme, 17, 37, 91, 93, 98, 99, 110, 111, 118*, 194, 224, 237, 252, 255, 256*, 256, 257, 267, 274, 289, 308, 336, 350, 355, 356, 383–387, 396, 401
time span, 175, 347
tonal language, 34
topic, 19, 90, 98, 99, 116, 119, 120, 151*, 211, 212, 222–224, 252, 256*, 256, 265, 294, 324, 325, 334, 341, 343, 346, 347, 352*, 352, 383*, 383–386, 388–394, 401
topic clitic, 222, 223
topic continuity, 119, 383, 391
topic marker, 92, 94, 223, 224, 226, 325*, 327, 328, 375–377, 379, 393, 394
topicality, 252, 254, 262, 343–346, 356, 383*, 388
topicalized element, 308
transitive clause, 129, 252, 260, 263, 266, 289, 303
transitive verb, 17, 115, 135, 138, 139, 160, 164, 165, 172*, 194, 242, 259
transitivity, 131, 157*, 157, 158, 160, 161,

497

259*, 259, 262

undergoer object, 160, 161, 163*
universal quantifier, 288, 289
universal word order, 16
unmarked pronoun, 19, 82, 94, 98, 100, 102, 109–111, 232, 234, 267, 298, 401
utterance verb, 178, 179, 261, 312, 361–363, 367

velar, 25, 41
velar nasal, 25, 50
verb phrase, 183, 197, 242, 254, 257, 284
verb stems, 18, 41, 48, 133, 184, 190*
verb suffix, 23, 115, 116, 152, 286, 341
verb-final, 17, 189, 251
verbal answer, 314
verbal clause, 263, 272, 273, 278, 289, 319, 356, 361
verbal cluster, 129
verbal group, 182–184, 186, 187, 192, 284
verbal negator, 209, 254, 269–271, 284, 285, 292, 315
verbal suffix, 4, 252, 257, 357, 390, 392, 396
verbal suffixation, 385
verbless clause, 129, 225, 263, 266, 268, 271, 322, 395, 397, 398
visibility, 117
vocative, 91, 116, 154
voicing harmony, 26
vowel elision, 41, 43
vowel length, 33
vowel sequence, 40, 42, 49, 110

word class, 2*, 54*, 54, 133, 183, 205, 309

Subject index